The Oxford Companion to the Economics of Africa

The Oxford Companion to the Economics of Africa

Edited by

Ernest Aryeetey

Shantayanan Devarajan

Ravi Kanbur

Louis Kasekende

OXFORD
UNIVERSITY PRESS

Great Clarendon Street, Oxford OX2 6DP

Oxford University Press is a department of the University of Oxford.
It furthers the University's objective of excellence in research, scholarship,
and education by publishing worldwide in

Oxford New York

Auckland Cape Town Dar es Salaam Hong Kong Karachi
Kuala Lumpur Madrid Melbourne Mexico City Nairobi
New Delhi Shanghai Taipei Toronto

With offices in

Argentina Austria Brazil Chile Czech Republic France Greece
Guatemala Hungary Italy Japan Poland Portugal Singapore
South Korea Switzerland Thailand Turkey Ukraine Vietnam

Oxford is a registered trade mark of Oxford University Press
in the UK and in certain other countries

Published in the United States
by Oxford University Press Inc., New York

© Oxford University Press, 2012

The moral rights of the authors have been asserted
Database right Oxford University Press (maker)

First published 2012

All rights reserved. No part of this publication may be reproduced,
stored in a retrieval system, or transmitted, in any form or by any means,
without the prior permission in writing of Oxford University Press,
or as expressly permitted by law, or under terms agreed with the appropriate
reprographics rights organization. Enquiries concerning reproduction
outside the scope of the above should be sent to the Rights Department,
Oxford University Press, at the address above

You must not circulate this book in any other binding or cover
and you must impose this same condition on any acquirer

British Library Cataloguing in Publication Data
Data available

Library of Congress Cataloging in Publication Data
Library of Congress Control Number: 2011942640

Typeset by SPI Publisher Services, Pondicherry, India
Printed in Great Britain
on acid-free paper by
CPI Group (UK) Ltd, Croydon, CR0 4YY

ISBN 978-0-19-957597-8

10 9 8 7 6 5 4 3 2

■ PREFACE

This compendium of entries, together with an overview, provides thematic and country perspectives by more than 100 leading economic analysts of Africa. The contributors include: the best of young African researchers based in Africa; renowned academics from the top Universities in Africa, Europe and North America; present and past Chief Economists of the African Development Bank; present and past Chief Economists for Africa of the World Bank; present and past Chief Economists of the World Bank; African Central Bank Governors and Finance Ministers; and four Nobel Laureates in Economics. Other than the requirement that the entry be analytical and not polemical, the contributors were given freedom to put forward their particular perspective on a topic. The entries are not therefore surveys of the literature. Further, they cannot by their nature take account of the very recent developments in countries, particularly in the rapidly changing political situation in North Africa. Rather, they constitute a picture of the concerns of modern economics as it is applied to African problems, as seen by the leading economists working on Africa. We hope that this *Companion* will contribute to economic analysis and policy in Africa and thus to African development.

As the proof of this manuscript were being prepared, the editors learnt with great sadness of the untimely death of Gobind Nankani, a contributor to the volume. Gobind was our friend and colleague. His analytical sharpness and wise policy counsel on Ghanaian and African development will always be remembered. We dedicate this volume to his memory.

E.A.
S.D.
R.K.
L.K.

ACKNOWLEDGEMENTS

The Editors would like to thank Sue Snyder of Cornell University for being the administrative anchor of the *Companion* project, and for managing the correspondence with over 100 authors. The *Companion* could not have been produced without her help.

CONTENTS

ENTRIES BY SUBJECT ... xi
    Thematic Perspectives ... xi
    Country Perspectives ... xiii
FIGURES AND TABLES ... xv
ABBREVIATIONS ... xix
DIRECTORY OF CONTRIBUTORS ... xxiii

Overview ... 1

THEMATIC PERSPECTIVES ... 25

African Development Prospects ... 25

Agriculture ... 69

Aid ... 85

Conflict and Reconstruction ... 109

Employment ... 131

Environment ... 145

Globalization ... 159

Governance and Political Economy ... 193

Human and Social Development ... 233

Industry, Investment, and Infrastructure ... 295

Macroeconomics and Finance ... 343

Natural Resources ... 387

COUNTRY PERSPECTIVES ... 423

INDEX ... 635

ENTRIES BY SUBJECT

THEMATIC PERSPECTIVES

African Development Prospects 25

An Overview of African Development Prospects — 26
African Development Prospects and Possibilities — 33
Risk and Vulnerability in Africa — 41
The Sustainability of Africa's Growth Acceleration — 48
Regionalism and African Development — 53
The Development of African Landlocked Countries — 59

Agriculture 69

Why Agriculture Remains the Key to Sub-Saharan African Development — 70
Food Insecurity and Food Aid in Africa — 79

Aid 85

Aid and African Development — 86
Private Aid to Africa — 94
HIPC Debt Relief in Sub-Saharan Africa — 99

Conflict and Reconstruction 109

Conflict and Development — 110
Developing Post-conflict Africa — 115
Post-conflict Recovery in Africa: The Micro Level — 124

Employment 131

Labour and Employment in Africa — 132
The Informal Self-Employed in Africa — 139

Environment 145

Environment and Climate Change — 146
Climate Change and Willingness to Pay for Serving Future Generations — 155

Globalization — 159

The Challenges of Sustaining African Growth in an Interdependent Global Economy	160
Comparative Advantage and African Development	166
The Impact of Asia on Economic Development in Sub-Saharan Africa	174
The Brain Drain in Africa	181
Migration, the Global Financial Crisis, and Poverty Reduction in Africa	187

Governance and Political Economy — 193

Democracy and African Development	194
Institutions and Development in Sub-Saharan Africa	201
Delivering Basic Services in Africa: Institutional Deficiencies and Avenues of Solutions	208
The Political Economy of Growth in Africa	215
Political Economy of Africa's Economic Performance in the Post-Independence Period	224

Human and Social Development — 233

Poverty and Inequality in Sub-Saharan Africa	234
Meeting Africa's Health Challenges	244
Impact of Health on Economic Outcomes	252
HIV/AIDS	258
Education	266
Gender and African Development	274
Accelerating Demographic Transitions in Sub-Saharan Africa	282
Lessons Learned from Field Experiments in Africa	287

Industry, Investment, and Infrastructure — 295

Structural Change in Africa	296
Industry for Africa: Why? How?	304
Africa's Private Sector	312
Foreign Direct Investment in Africa: What Do We Know?	321
Foreign Direct Investment, Growth, and Poverty Reduction in Sub-Saharan Africa	329
Infrastructure	337

Macroeconomics and Finance — 343

Fiscal Policy	344
Exchange Rate Policy	352
Inflation Targeting in Africa	359

African Financial Systems	365
Banks and Credit Markets	374
Microfinance in Africa	380

Natural Resources 387

Managing Natural Resource Booms	388
Natural Resource Exports and African Development	394
Managing Forest Commons in Africa	402
Land Tenure	410
Can Water Undermine Africa's Growth in the 21st Century? Issues and Options	416

COUNTRY PERSPECTIVES 423

Algeria: Development Opportunities and Challenges	424
Algeria, Egypt, Morocco, and Tunisia: Development Prospects for North Africa	430
Angola: China-Led Reconstruction	438
Benin: When Poor Economic Diversification is an Impediment to Poverty Alleviation	441
Botswana: Diamonds, Relative Prices, and Growth Experience	444
Burkina Faso: Economic and Growth Perspectives	448
Burundi: Challenges and Opportunities for Post-conflict Reconstruction	451
Cameroon: A Pragmatic Approach to Policy for Sustainable Growth	457
Chad: Recent Economic Growth	460
Congo, Democratic Republic of (DRC): Unlocking the Political Economy Constraints to Development	463
Congo, Republic of: Entrepreneurship Promotion Policies and Development	466
Côte d'Ivoire: Economic Reversibility	470
Egypt: The Changing Role of the State	475
Equatorial Guinea: Oil and Other Resources, But Slow Growth	479
Eritrea: Economic Performance, Potential, and Constraints	484
Ethiopia: Perspectives Beyond Growth and Poverty	487
Gambia, The: Macroeconomic Management and Development Challenges	491
Ghana: The Development Record and the Washington Consensus	494
Guinea: Poverty, Governance, and Growth	499
Guinea Bissau: Primary Commodity Vulnerability	502
Kenya: A Structural Transformation Paradox and Challenges for the Current Decade	505
Lesotho: Experiences and Challenges from the Textiles Manufacturing Sector	510
Liberia: Debt Relief	514
Libya: Post-war Challenges and Opportunities	519

Madagascar: Poverty and Economic Growth — 524
Malawi: The Psychological and Political Economy of Exchange Rate Policy — 527
Mali: Fragile Economic Dynamics — 530
Mauritania: Sustaining Growth with Equity — 535
Mauritius: A Small Open Economy Fully Integrated into World Markets — 538
Morocco: Positive Reforms — 541
Mozambique: The Promise... — 544
Namibia: History, Politics, and Unequal Growth — 549
Niger: The Importance of National Consensus for Effective Social and Economic Reform — 552
Nigeria: Managing Volatility and Fighting Corruption — 555
Rwanda: Leadership for Economic Growth and Development — 562
Senegal: After Devaluation, Improving Signals — 566
Sierra Leone: Economic Governance, Agriculture, and Rural Development — 570
Somalia: Sustaining an Economy Without Central Authority — 573
South Africa: An Emerging Market in an Emerging Continent — 576
South Africa: Corporate Governance — 584
Sudan: Unable to Accelerate and Sustain Growth — 596
Swaziland: Resilient Amidst Many Challenges — 601
Tanzania: Reflections on Economic Growth — 605
Togo: Diagnosis and Challenges in a Context of Crises — 611
Tunisia: Top Performance in Africa and the Middle East (But Less than Stellar Globally) — 615
Uganda: Turning Sustained Growth into Structural Transformation for Human Development — 621
Zambia: Bringing Back the Shine — 626
Zimbabwe: Returning from the Brink — 630

FIGURES AND TABLES

Overview
Figure 1. Per capita GDP growth by region 3
Figure 2. Africa's share of world income and population 5

THEMATIC PERSPECTIVES

The Development of African Landlocked Countries
Table 1. Trading cost indicators in landlocked countries 60
Table 2. Trade and development indicators 63

Why Agriculture Remains the Key to Sub-Saharan African Development
Figure 1. The structural transformation in Asia and sub-Saharan Africa 71

Food Insecurity and Food Aid in Africa
Figure 1. Child stunting and wasting in Africa, by national income 82

The HIPC Debt Relief in Sub-Saharan Africa
Table 1. Indicators of debt distress before crisis 101
Table 2. Selected macroeconomic indicators for SSA countries 102
Table 3. Debt distress indicators: before and after debt relief 104

Developing Post-conflict Africa
Figure 1. Polity and country policy and institutional assessment 116
Figure 2. GDP per capita growth, Aid/GDP, and real exchange rate undervaluation . . . 119
Figure 3. GDP per capita growth by real exchange rate group 121

Labour and Employment in Africa
Figure 1. Wages and employment 134
Figure 2. Wages and employment in a segmented labour market 135
Figure 3. Non-agricultural employment and unemployment in selected
  African countries 136

Environment and Climate Change
Figure 1. Ecosystem decline: average annual net change in forest area by region,
  1991–2005 147
Table 1. Simulation results for the impacts of climate change on output and welfare
  relative to reference case 151

Delivering Basic Services in Africa

Figure 1. Public expenditure and health system performance: (a) Budgeted resources; (b) Resources received per capita. Source: Gauthier and Wane (2009) — 213

Table 1. Official public spending on education and health in Africa — 210

Table 2. Leakage by sector and country — 211

Table 3. Absence rates by country and sector — 212

Political Economy of Africa's Economic Performance in the Post-Independence Period

Figure 1. The prevalence of authoritarian regimes — 225

Figure 2. Prevalence of control regimes — 227

Figure 3. Regional differences in government policy — 226

Table 1. Countries in the sample — 229

Poverty and Inequality in Sub-Saharan Africa

Figure 1. A hierarchical tree to derive six distinct categories of SSA countries — 237

Table 1. Poverty headcount index and number of poor by region — 235

Table 2. Typology of SSA countries: per capita income, growth, poverty headcount ratios, income/poverty elasticities, and vulnerability index — 238

Meeting Africa's Health Challenges

Figure 1. Life expectancy and GDP per capita, highlighting outliers in 2004 — 245

Table 1. Infant mortality rate and life expectancy in developing countries, 1960–2005 — 245

Education

Table 1. Education statistics for Africa, 1990–2007 — 268

Gender and African Development

Table 1. Gross primary enrolments in selected African countries — 276

Industry for Africa

Table 1. Selected indicators of industrial development, 2005 — 306

Africa's Private Sector

Figure 1. Sector shares of GDP in Africa, 1990 and 2005 — 313

Figure 2. Number of days on which power outages occurred — 314

Figure 3. Distribution of the ratio of net to gross value added, Africa versus China — 315

Figure 4. Distribution of value added by ethnicity — 316

Figure 5. Start-up and current size of indigenous and minority-owned firms — 317

Figure 6. Firms with overdrafts, by ethnicity — 317

Foreign Direct Investment in Africa

Table 1. FDI inflows by region, 1993–2007 — 322

Foreign Direct Investment, Growth, and Poverty Reduction in Sub-Saharan Africa

Figure 1. FDI and aid flows to sub-Saharan Africa, 1980–2007 — 330

Table 1. Difference in wages between foreign-owned and domestically owned
   enterprises in selected African countries ... 332

Fiscal Policy
Table 1. Fiscal aggregates as per cent of GDP, averages 2003–2008 (1997–2002)
   for various SSA country groupings ... 345

African Financial Systems
Figure 1. Institutional investor credit ratings ... 369
Table 1. Financial development and selected determinants, 1995–2007 ... 368

Microfinance in Africa
Table 1. Microfinance data: Africa and other regions, 2007 ... 381

Natural Resource Exports and African Development
Table 1. Composition of exports, 1985 and 2005 ... 395
Table 2. Major manufacturing exports, 2005 ... 395
Table 3. Growth elasticities: African countries, Asian comparators, and norms ... 396

Can Water Undermine Africa's Growth in the 21st Century?
Figure 1. Annual freshwater withdrawals 2002 ... 418

COUNTRY PERSPECTIVES

Algeria, Egypt, Morocco, and Tunisia
Table 1. Growth and poverty in North Africa compared with other developing
   regions, 1985–2005 ... 432

Botswana
Table 1. The real exchange rate, productivity, and growth ... 445

Burundi
Figure 1. Burundi: GDP growth 1962–2007 ... 453
Figure 2. Burundi: agricultural productivity and per capita income ... 454
Table 1. Burundi: social and economic development indicators ... 452

Cameroon
Table 1. Contribution to economic growth by sector ... 458

Equatorial Guinea
Figure 1. Real GDP growth and GDP per capita ... 480
Figure 2. Gross investment ... 481
Figure 3. Private investment and foreign direct investment ... 482

Kenya
Figure 1. Changes in supply and demand, 1990–2000 and 2000–2008 ... 506

Liberia

Figure 1. External debt service and arrears, 1980–2004	515
Figure 2. World Bank CPIA scores, 1980–2009	516

Madagascar

Table 1. Origin of changes in poverty	525
Table 2. Contribution of growth and distributional changes to changes in poverty at national level	525

Mali

Table 1. Dynamics of the Malian economy	532

Rwanda

Figure 1. Real economic growth and agricultural-sector performance	563
Figure 2. Rwanda–EAC trade evolution	563
Figure 3. Rwanda trade with EAC country members	564

Senegal

Figure 1. GDP growth rate, 1980–2008	566

South Africa: An Emerging Market in an Emerging Continent

Table 1. Estimates of poverty and inequality, by race, 1995–2005	578

South Africa: Corporate Governance

Figure 1. Board composition	590
Figure 2. Percentage of companies that perform an annual performance assessment of directors	590
Figure 3. Board size per company	591
Figure 4. Percentage of companies that have an independent board chairman	591
Table 1. Board characteristics and financial variables for JSE companies, 2006	588
Table 2. Descriptive statistics for board activities	590
Table 3. Regression results for the board of directors and financial performance and board	592

Sudan

Figure 1. Inflation and real GDP Growth rates, 1970–2008	597

Swaziland

Table 1. GDP Growth % by sector	601

Uganda

Table 1. Poverty and inequality in Uganda, 2005/6	622
Table 2. Indicators of fundamental country attributes	624

ABBREVIATIONS

ADSP	Agriculture for Development Strategy Papers
AERC/CREA	African Economic Research Consortium/ Consortium pour la Recherche Économique en Afrique
AfDB/BAfD	African Development Bank/Banque Africaine de Développement
AGOA	Africa Growth and Opportunity Act
AWF	African Water Facility
BAU	business as usual
BCEAO	Banque Centrale des États de l'Afrique de l'Ouest
CAADP	Comprehensive African Agriculture Development Program
CDC	Centers for Disease Control and Prevention
CEMAC/ECCAS	Communauté Économique et Monétaire de l'Afrique Centrale/Economic Community of Central African States
CEPR	Centre for Economic Policy Research
CFA	*Coopération financière en Afrique centrale* (financial cooperation in Central Africa): the CFA franc comprises two (effectively interchangeable) currencies used in Africa which are guaranteed by the French treasury: the West African CFA franc and the Central African CFA franc.
CGAP	Consultative Group to Assist the Poor
CGD	Center for Global Development
CGE	computable general equilibrium
CIF	cost, insurance, and freight
CIS	Commonwealth of Independent States
COMESA	Common Market for Eastern and Southern Africa
CPIA	Country Policy and Institutional Assessment
CREDIT	Centre for Research in Economic Development and International Trade (Nottingham)
CSAE	Centre for the Study of African Economies (Oxford)
DAC	Development Assistance Committee, OECD
DFID	Department for International Development (London)
DOE	domestically owned enterprise
DTT	demographic transition theory

EAC	East African Community
EITI	Extractive Industries Transparency Initiative
EPA	economic partnership agreement
EPZ	export processing zone
EVI	Economic Vulnerability Index
FACS	fragile and conflict-affected states (World Bank definition)
FDI	foreign direct investment
FERDI	Fondation pour les Études et Recherches sur le Développement International
FFIT	full-fledged inflation targeting
FOB	free on board
FOCAC	Forum on China–Africa Cooperation
FOE	foreign-owned enterprise
GCC	Gulf Cooperation Council
GDP	gross domestic product
GHG	greenhouse gas
GNI	gross national income
GTAP	Global Trade Analysis Project
HIPC	highly indebted poor country
HPCR	Program on Humanitarian Policy and Conflict Research
IBC	intertemporal budget constraint
IBRD	International Bank for Reconstruction and Development
ICT	information and communication technologies
IDA	International Development Association
IDS	Institute for Development Studies (University of Sussex)
IFAD	UN International Fund for Agricultural Development
IFI	international financial institution
IFPRI	International Food Policy Research Institute
ILRI	International Livestock Research Institute
IMF	International Monetary Fund
IMR	infant mortality rate
IOM	International Organization for Migraton
IPCC	Intergovernmental Panel on Climate Change
IPD	Initiative for Policy Dialogue (Columbia University)
IRWR	internally renewable water resources

IT	inflation targeting
ITL	inflation targeting lite
ITES	information technologies enabled service
IWRM	integrated water resource management
J-PAL	Abdul Latif Jameel Poverty Action Lab
LDC	least developed country
LIC	low-income country
LIT	learning, industrial, and technology (policies etc.)
MDG	Millennium Development Goal
MDRI	Multilateral Debt Relief Initiative
MENA	Middle East and North Africa
MFA	Multi Fibre Arrangement
MFI	micro finance institution
MNC	multinational corporation
NBER	National Bureau of Economic Research
NEPAD	New Partnership for Africa's Development
NIC	newly industrializing country
NIE	newly industrializing economy
NPV	net present value
ODA	overseas development assistance; official development assistance
ODI	Overseas Development Institute
OECD	Organization for Economic Cooperation and Development
PBA	performance-based allocation
PEAP	Poverty Eradication Action Plan
PPP	public–private partnership
	purchasing power parity
PRIO	International Peace Research Institute (Oslo)
PRSP	poverty reduction strategy paper(s)
R&D	research and development
REC	regional economic community
REDD	reducing emissions from deforestation and forest degradation
RER	real exchange rate
RPED	Regional Program on Economic Development (World Bank)
RRA	relative rates of assistance
RTA	regional trade agreement

SACU	South African Customs Union
SADC	Southern African Development Community
SAP	structural adjustment programme
SDR	Special Drawing Right
SMLE	small, medium, large enterprise(s)
SOE	state-owned enterprise
SSA	sub-Saharan Africa
TFP	total factor productivity
UNCTAD	United Nations Conference on Trade and Development
UNDP/PNUD	United Nations Development Programme/Programme des Nations Unis pour le Developpement
UNECA	UN Economic Commission for Africa
UNESCO	United Nations Educational, Cultural and Scientific Organization
UNFCCC	United Nations Framework Convention on Climate Change
UNFPA	United Nations Population Fund
UNIDO	United Nations Industrial Development Organization
UNIFEM	United Nations Development Fund for Women
UNRISD	United Nations Research Institute for Social Development
UNU-WIDER	United Nations University, World Institute for Development Economics Research
WAEMU/UEMOA	West African Economic and Monetary Union/Union économique et monétaire ouest-africaine
WTO	World Trade Organization

DIRECTORY OF CONTRIBUTORS

ALI ISSA ABDI, Horn Economic and Social Policy Institute (HESPI), Addis Ababa
  'Somalia: Sustaining an Economy Without Central Authority'
CHRISTOPHER ADAM, University of Oxford
  'Exchange Rate Policy'
ARUN AGRAWAL, University of Michigan
  'Managing Forest Commons in Africa'
JEHOVANESS AIKAELI, Bank of Tanzania
  'Tanzania: Reflections on Economic Growth'
S. IBI AJAYI, University of Ibadan
  'Foreign Direct Investment in Africa: What Do We Know?'
CHANNING ARNDT, University of Copenhagen
  'Mozambique: The Promise...'
ERNEST ARYEETEY, University of Ghana
  'Overview'
JOHN ASAFU-ADJAYE, University of Queensland
  'Environment and Climate Change'
ELIZABETH ASIEDU, University of Kansas
  'Foreign Direct Investment, Growth and Poverty Reduction in Sub-Saharan Africa'
JEAN-PAUL AZAM, Toulouse School of Economics and Institut Universitaire de France
  'Conflict and Development'
MINA BALIAMOUNE-LUTZ, University of North Florida
  'Morocco: Positive Reforms'
CHRISTOPHER B. BARRETT, Cornell University
  'Food Insecurity and Food Aid in Africa'
BARBARA BARUNGI, African Development Bank
  'Uganda: Turning Sustained Growth into Structural Transformation for Human Development'
ROBERT H. BATES, Harvard University
  'Political Economy of Africa's Economic Performance in the Post-Independence Period'
DAVID BEVAN, University of Oxford
  'Fiscal Policy'
HAROON BHORAT, University of Cape Town
  'South Africa: An Emerging Market in an Emerging Continent'
ARNE BIGSTEN, University of Gothenburg
  'Comparative Advantage and African Development'

CHRISTOPHER BLATTMAN, Yale University
  'Post-conflict Recovery in Africa: The Micro Level'
JEAN CHRISTOPHE BOUNGOU BAZIKA, CERAPE
  'Congo, Republic of: Entrepreneurship Promotion Policies and Development'
SERIGN CHAM, Ministry of Finance, The Gambia
  'Gambia, The: Macroeconomic Management and Development Challenges'
ASHWINI CHHATRE, University of Illinois
  'Managing Forest Commons in Africa'
PAUL COLLIER, University of Oxford
  'An Overview of African Development Prospects'
MASSA COULIBALY, GREAT (Groupe de recherche en économie appliquée et théorique), Université de Bamako
  'Mali: Fragile Economic Dynamics'
VICTOR DAVIES, African Development Bank
  'Sierra Leone: Economic Governance, Agriculture, and Rural Development'
ALAIN DE JANVRY, University of California at Berkeley
  'Why Agriculture Remains the Key to Sub-Saharan African Development'
STEFAN DERCON, University of Oxford
  'Risk and Vulnerability in Africa'
SHANTAYANAN DEVARAJAN, The World Bank
  'Overview'
YAZID DISSOU, University of Ottawa
  'Benin: When Poor Economic Diversification is an Impediment to Poverty Alleviation'
NADJIOUNOUM DJIMTOÏNGAR, Commission de la CEMAC
  'Chad: Recent Economic Growth'
IBRAHIM A. ELBADAWI, The Dubai Economic Council, Dubai (DEC), UAE and Center for Global Development (CGD)
  'Developing Post-conflict Africa'
ADAM B. ELHIRAIKA, UN Economic Commission for Africa
  'Sudan: Unable to Accelerate and Sustain Growth'
AUGUSTIN KWASI FOSU, United Nations University World Institute for Development Economics Research (UNU-WIDER)
  'Ghana: The Development Record and the Washington Consensus'
SÉRAPHIN MAGLOIRE FOUDA, University of Yaoundé II—Cameroon
  'Cameroon: A Pragmatic Approach to Policy for Sustainable Growth'
AHMED GALAL, Economic Research Forum (ERF, Cairo)
  'Algeria, Egypt, Morocco, and Tunisia: Development Prospects for North Africa'
BERNARD GAUTHIER, The World Bank and HEC Montréal
  'Delivering Basic Services in Africa: Institutional Deficiencies and Avenues of Solutions'
ALAN GELB, Center for Global Development (CGD)
  'Natural Resource Exports and African Development'
RACHEL GLENNERSTER, Massachusetts Institute of Technology
  'Lessons Learned from Field Experiments in Africa'

PATRICK GUILLAUMONT, University of Clermont-Ferrand
  'Aid and African Development'
KAMILLA GUMEDE, University of Cape Town
  'Lessons Learned from Field Experiments in Africa'
KWABENA GYIMAH-BREMPONG, University of South Florida
  'Education'
HEBA HANDOUSSA, Egypt Human Development Report
  'Egypt: The Changing Role of the State'
JAMES HEINTZ, University of Massachusetts
  'The Informal Self-Employed in Africa'
ALI HEMAL, Université de Batna
  'Algeria: Development Opportunities and Challenges'
JOHANNES HERDERSCHEE, The World Bank
  'Congo, Democratic Republic of (DRC): Unlocking the Political Economy Constraints to Development'
AMADOU IBRAHIM, The World Bank
  'Niger: On the Importance of National Consensus for Effective Social and Economic Reform'
JENNIFER ISERN, International Finance Corporation
  'Microfinance in Africa'
ABDUL B. KAMARA, African Development Bank
  'Can Water Undermine Africa's Growth in the 21st Century? Issues and Options'
RAVI KANBUR, Cornell University
  'Overview'
LOUIS KASEKENDE, Bank of Uganda
  'Overview'
ABBI KEDIR, University of Leicester
  'Ethiopia: Perspectives Beyond Growth and Poverty'
HOMI KHARAS, The Brookings Institution
  'Private Aid to Africa'
ASMEROM KIDANE, University of Dar es Salaam
  'Eritrea: Economic Performance, Potential, and Constraints'
MWANGI S. KIMENYI, The Brookings Institution
  'Accelerating Demographic Transitions in Sub-Saharan Africa'
JANE KIRINGAI, The World Bank
  'Kenya: A Structural Transformation Paradox and Challenges for the Current Decade'
JACOB KOLSTER, African Development Bank
  'Libya: Post-war Challenges and Opportunities'
STEVEN KYLE, Cornell University
  'Guinea Bissau: Primary Commodity Vulnerability'
ERIN C. LENTZ, Cornell University
  'Food Insecurity and Food Aid in Africa'
BENJAMIN LEO, Center for Global Development (CGD)
  'Liberia: Debt Relief'

JUSTIN YIFU LIN, The World Bank
  'Structural Change in Africa'
WILLIAM LYAKURWA, African Economic Research Consortium (AERC)
  'Tanzania: Reflections on Economic Growth'
DAMIAN ONDO MANE, Economics Advisor to the President, Equatorial Guinea
  'Equatorial Guinea: Oil and Other Investments, but Slow Growth'
ITA MANNATHOKO, International Monetary Fund
  'Botswana: Diamonds, Relative Prices, and Growth Experience'
ADELAIDE R. MATLANYANE, Central Bank of Lesotho
  'Lesotho: Experiences and Challenges from the Textiles Manufacturing Sector'
AHMADOU ALY MBAYE, Faculté des Sciences Economiques et de Gestion, Université Cheikh Anta Diop de Dakar (Senegal)
  'Senegal: After Devaluation, Improving Signals'
ANDREW MCKAY, University of Sussex
  'Infrastructure'
PAULA XIMENE MEJIA, African Development Bank Libya: Post-war Challenges and Opportunities
KUPUKILE MLAMBO, African Development Bank
  'Zimbabwe: Returning from the Brink'
VICTOR MURINDE, University of Birmingham
  'Banks and Credit Markets'
SITUMBEKO MUSOKOTWANE, Ministry of Finance and National Planning, Zambia
  'Zambia: Bringing Back the Shine'
GERMANO MWABU, University of Nairobi
  'HIV/AIDS'
MUSTAPHA K. NABLI, Central Bank of Tunisia
  'Tunisia: Top Performance in Africa and the Middle East (But Less than Stellar Globally)'
VINAYAK NAGARAJ, Ministry of Finance and National Planning, Zambia
  'Zambia: Bringing Back the Shine'
GOBIND NANKANI, International Growth Center, LSE and Oxford University
  'The Political Economy of Growth in Africa'
MTHULI NCUBE, African Development Bank
  'South Africa: Corporate Governance'
LÉONCE NDIKUMANA, University of Massachusetts
  'Burundi: Challenges and Opportunities for Post-conflict Reconstruction'
BENNO NDULU, Central Bank of Tanzania
  'The Challenges of Sustaining African Growth in an Interdependent Global Economy'
NJUGUNA NDUNG'U, Central Bank of Kenya
  'HIPC Debt Relief in Sub-Saharan Africa'
TCHÉTCHÉ N'GUESSAN, African Development Bank
  'Côte d'Ivoire: Economic Reversibility'
PHINDILE NGWENYA, The World Bank
  'Swaziland: Resilient Amidst Many Challenges'

MACHIKO NISSANKE, SOAS, University of London
  'The Impact of Asia on Economic Development in Sub-Saharan Africa'
DOMINIQUE NJINKEU, The World Bank[S1]
  'Regionalism and African Development'
JANVIER D. NKURUNZIZA, United Nations Conference on Trade and Development
  'The Development of African Landlocked Countries'
AKBAR NOMAN, Columbia University
  'African Development Prospects and Possibilities'
KHWIMA NTHARA, The World Bank
  'Malawi: Psychological and Political Economy of Exchange Rate Policy'
KAKO NUBUKPO, West African Economic and Monetary Union (WAEMU) and University of Lomé
  'Togo: Diagnosis and Challenges in a Context of Crises'
YAW NYARKO, New York University
  'The Brain Drain in Africa'
STEPHEN A. O'CONNELL, Swarthmore College
  'Inflation Targeting in Africa'
ABENA D. ODURO, University of Ghana
  'Gender and African Development'
NGOZI OKONJO-IWEALA, Ministry of Finance, Nigeria
  'Nigeria: Managing Volatility and Fighting Corruption'
ELINOR OSTROM, Indiana University
  'Managing Forest Commons in Africa'
JOHN PAGE, The Brookings Institution
  'Industry for Africa: Why? How?'
LAUREN PERSHA, UNC-Chapel Hill
  'Managing Forest Commons in Africa'
PETER QUARTEY, Institute of Statistical Social and Economic Research, University of Ghana
  'Migration, the Global Financial Crisis and Poverty Reduction in Africa'
VIJAYA RAMACHANDRAN, Center for Global Development
  'Africa's Private Sector'
JEAN RAZAFINDRAVONONA, Ministry of Finance and Budget, Madagascar
  'Madagascar: Poverty and Economic Growth'
JAMES A. ROBINSON, Harvard University
  'Institutions and Development in Sub-Saharan Africa'
THOMAS KIGABO RUSUHUZWA, National Bank of Rwanda
  'Rwanda: Leadership for Economic Growth and Development'
ELISABETH SADOULET, University of California at Berkeley
  'Why Agriculture Remains the Key to Sub-Saharan African Development'
DAVID E. SAHN, Cornell University
  'Meeting Africa's Health Challenges' and 'Impact of Health on Economic Outcomes'
ANA SANTANA, University of Stellenbosch
  'Angola: China-Led Reconstruction'

THOMAS SCHELLING, University of Maryland
  'Climate Change and Willingness to Pay for Serving Future Generations'
KHALID SEKKAT, Economic Research Forum (Cairo) and Université Libre de Bruxelles
  'Algeria, Egypt, Morocco and Tunisia: Development Prospects for North Africa'
LEMMA W. SENBET, University of Maryland
  'African Financial Systems'
ROBIN SHERBOURNE, Independent Consultant
  'Namibia: History, Politics, and Unequal Growth'
AMADOU SIDIBÉ, Rural Development Institute, Polytechnic University of Bobo-Dioulasso
  'Burkina Faso: Economic and Growth Perspectives'
MICHAEL SPENCE, New York University
  'The Sustainability of Africa's Growth Acceleration'
WILLIAM STEEL, University of Ghana
  'Microfinance in Africa'
JOSEPH E. STIGLITZ, Columbia University
  'African Development Prospects and Possibilities'
FRANCIS TEAL, Centre for the Study of African Economies, University of Oxford
  'Labour and Employment in Africa'
ERIK THORBECKE, Cornell University
  'Poverty and Inequality in Sub-Saharan Africa'
YAMSSEKRE TIENDRÉBEOGO, Directeur Général de l'Économie et de la Planification, Burkino Faso
  'Burkina Faso: Economic and Growth Perspectives'
CHRISTOPHER UDRY, Yale University
  'Land Tenure'
IMRAAN VALODIA, University of KwaZulu-Natal, Durban
  'The Informal Self-Employed in Africa'
ANTHONY J. VENABLES, University of Oxford
  'Managing Natural Resource Booms'
DÉSIRÉ VENCATACHELLUM, African Development Bank
  'Mauritius: A Small Open Economy Fully Integrated into World Markets'
WALY WANE, The World Bank
  'Delivering Basic Services in Africa: Institutional Deficiencies and Avenues of Solutions'
LEONARD WANTCHEKON, Princeton University
  'Democracy and African Development'
KERFALLA YANSANE, Ministry of Finance, Guinea
  'Guinea: Poverty, Governance, and Growth'
ZEINE OULD ZEIDANE, Former Prime Minister and Governor of the Central Bank of Mauritania
  'Mauritania: Sustaining Growth with Equity'

Overview

Ernest Aryeetey,[1] *Shantayanan Devarajan,*[2]
Ravi Kanbur,[3] *and Louis Kasekende*[4]

1. Introduction

Ex Africa semper aliquid novi. (From Africa always something new)

Pliny's maxim of 2,000 years ago is still valid for African development, whether north or south of the Sahara. For the oil economies of Africa, development has been linked to natural resource exploitation and has cycled with the global price of oil. Peaks in this price have seen the accumulation of great wealth, troughs have brought with them questions of overdependence on a single source of income. For much of Sub-Saharan Africa, post-independence hopes sparkled briefly but were then sorely disappointed and dimmed in the subsequent decades. After three decades of stagnation and decline, however, and the crisis of 2008/9 notwithstanding, Sub-Saharan African countries are now growing at the same rate as all developing countries (save China and India). Seventeen non-oil-exporters sustained better than 4% GDP growth for over a decade before the crisis. However, in many other countries, growth is stalled because of political instability or other internal and external factors. And the legacy of Africa's 'growth tragedy' of the 1980s and 1990s is that Sub-Saharan Africa has the highest poverty rate and lowest human development indicators in the world.

Africa is thus a diverse continent. But is there a pattern to the diversity? Are there commonalities across the countries? And what does economics tell us about the diversity and the commonalities? Following Keynes, we consider economics to be an engine of thought and analysis, rather than a given set of prescriptions. The great diversity of Africa should be reflected in the diversity of analytical findings and prescriptions, just as the commonalities should elicit similarities of perspective in these dimensions. But what is truly common is the application of the economic mode of reasoning to African economies and to the African continent.

[1] Vice Chancellor, University of Ghana.
[2] Chief Economist, Africa Region, The World Bank.
[3] T.H. Lee Professor of World Affairs, Cornell University.
[4] Deputy Governor, Bank of Uganda.

This compendium of entries on the economics of Africa provides thematic and country perspectives by 100 leading economic analysts of Africa. The contributors include: the best of young African researchers based in Africa; renowned academics from the top universities in Africa, Europe and North America; present and past Chief Economists of the African Development Bank; present and past Chief Economists for Africa of the World Bank; present and past Chief Economists of the World Bank; African Central Bank Governors and Finance Ministers; and four recipients of the Nobel Memorial Prize in Economics. Other than the requirement that the entry be analytical and not polemical, the contributors were given freedom to put forward their particular perspective on a topic. The entries are not therefore surveys of the literature. Rather, they constitute a picture of the concerns of modern economics as it is applied to African problems, as seen by the leading economists working on Africa.

It is neither feasible nor desirable to summarize or synthesize the entries in this *Companion*. Rather, we provide in this chapter our own perspective on the economics of Africa, drawing on the entries where relevant, and on the broader literature as necessary.[5] Section 2 begins by setting out the key dimensions of economic diversity and commonality across the continent. From this emerge the major themes tackled in this overview. Section 3 begins the detailed consideration of economic policy by placing Africa in the global context and discussing the opportunities and challenges that the global economy presents to the African economies. Section 4 focuses on macroeconomic policy including monetary and fiscal policy. Section 5 then takes up micro and sectoral issues of poverty and human development. Section 6 turns to a major factor that has been suggested as explaining the diversity of performance—the effectiveness of the state in pursuing a development agenda. Section 7 follows up on a particular manifestation of a failed state that is unfortunately too prevalent in Africa—internal or cross-border conflict. Section 8 looks up from the specifics of current policy making to the long term, in the context of broad environmental and demographic trends. Section 9 concludes.

2. African diversities and commonalities

Africa is home to some of the largest deposits of natural resources in the world—from oil and gas deposits around the Gulf of Guinea and now Sudan and Uganda to precious metals such as gold, diamond, and cobalt in the Democratic Republic of Congo (DRC), Botswana, and South Africa among others. But Africa presents the global community with the biggest challenges. The poverty levels and other development indicators for

---

[5] Partly because of the poverty challenges there, the primary focus of this overview is on sub-Saharan Africa. The Companion itself includes entries on all the North Africa economies. Further, the entries in the volume do not necessarily take into account the latest developments in each country, particularly in the rapidly changing political situation in North Africa.

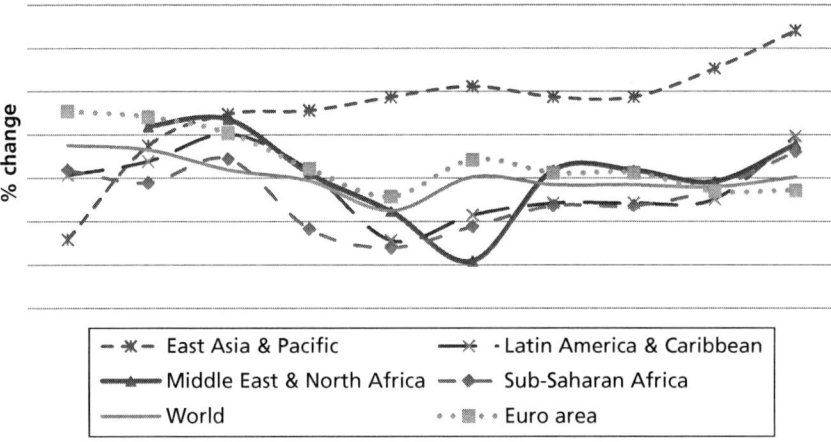

Figure 1. Per capita GDP growth by region (source: World Bank 2009)

Africa, particularly Sub-Saharan Africa, are some of the most unattractive features of the world economy. Apart from the last ten years, Africa was the slowest-growing region, creating a divergence in welfare with all the other regions of the world. The growth performance was in spite of reform efforts embarked on by many countries during the 1980s and the substantial international financial support for most of the post-independence period. According to the World Bank (Figure 1), per capita income growth for sub-Saharan Africa has been below average, except during 2005–9, the period that included the global financial crises, which adversely affected growth in the euro area and other advanced economies while Africa managed to record low but positive growth and enjoy a quick recovery.

Of the world's poorest countries, 33 are in Africa compared to Asia (15) and Latin America and Caribbean (1).[6] Between 2000 and 2008, 48% of African people lived below the poverty line of $1.25 per day. The continent has also stagnated in terms of literacy and life expectancy. The UN Human Development Index indicates that 32 of the 40 countries that rank lowest are in sub-Saharan Africa.

Numerous factors[7] have been identified in explaining the growth performance of Africa (see O'Connell and Ndulu 2000). This overview does not neglect those factors. However, it is necessary to avoid making generalizations about Africa. African economies are very heterogeneous in terms of economic performance, capacity to mobilize

---

[6] The UN classification of countries.

[7] Such factors include external forces, heavy dependence on a small number of internationally low valued primary products, bad policies and economic mismanagement, insecurity and political instability, social conditions, poor policies, lack of openness, and low savings rates.

domestic resources, capacity to absorb aid and ability to attract foreign capital, etc. This means that there are large differences between African countries in respect of their need for aid and the modalities by which aid is best delivered. Emerging economies (such as South Africa and Tunisia) vs Least Developed States (such as Gambia, Burundi, Rwanda, Eritrea); resource-rich (such as Namibia, DRC, Angola) vs resource-poor countries (such as Ethiopia and Eritrea); countries where democracy is taking root (Ghana, Tanzania, and Uganda) and a failed state (such as Somalia) or post-conflict countries (Liberia, Burundi). Any discussion of Africa needs to be properly tailored to Africa's diverse realities and unique characteristics. We start with these and then move to a discussion of the commonalities.

Africa possesses a wide array of climatic and ecological zones due to its varying altitudes, and mountainous ranges. Around the equator, there is a mixture of rain and hot temperatures throughout the year, producing equatorial rainforests, mostly in West Africa. Outside the equatorial zone lies summer and dry savannah grasslands. Further away from the equator, the climate becomes drier (northern Sahel Desert and southern Kalahari Desert). In the far north (Maghreb region) and south (South Africa), temperate climatic characteristics dominate.

Significant diversity exists in terms of population density. A large part of the continent is sparsely populated, with an average of 20 persons per km^2, compared to 148 persons in Asia. There is a vast expanse of empty desert (5 persons per km^2 in Chad) and large areas of sparsely populated savannahs with weak agricultural potential. Cases of relatively high population density include the Great Lakes region of the East African highlands, coastal areas in West Africa, and the Indian Ocean islands. Low levels of population density translate to low levels of urbanization, which in turn raises the costs of providing infrastructure such as road networks, telephone systems, water, sewerage, and financial services.

Africa's major challenge is the underdeveloped and diverse nature of its institutions. Institutional diversity in Africa has been largely attributed to colonial inheritance and geographical differences. The English legal system, for instance, is based on common law, while the governmental system is based on parliamentary democracy. Thus, all the former English colonies virtually have a common law system and a form of parliamentary democracy. By contrast, the French, Portuguese, and Spanish colonies are based on civil law and more autocratic governmental institutions. Well designed institutions stimulate economic progress. However, wholesale redesign of institutional structures based on other, more economically successful countries cannot be appropriate for Africa. It is important to identify beneficial aspects of particular institutions in each African economy and tailor reforms to suit their diverse conditions. Institutional reforms such as property rights and social institutions (especially anti-corruption) tend to be more effective in promoting growth than an overhaul of the whole system.

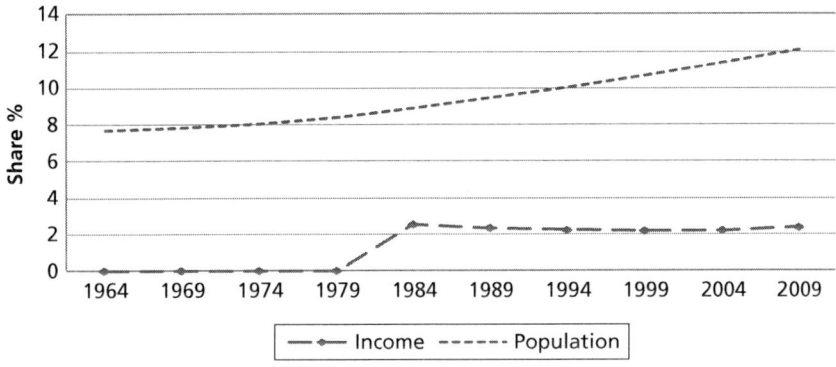

Figure 2. Africa's share of world income and population (source: World Bank 2009)

Turning now to commonalities across the continent, Africa's population is among the fastest-growing in the world. Between 1960 and 2009, Africa's population grew at an average of 2.7% per year (World Bank 2009). Despite this unprecedented growth in population, Africa's share in world income (Figure 2) has been relatively constant, while its share in world population has risen.

Africa has the world's highest youth dependency ratios, a result of the combination of both high fertility rates and declining levels of infant and child mortality rates. High dependency ratios reduce the continent's productive capacity per capita. High youth dependency is also associated with low rates of savings and investment, which in turn lead to slower economic growth.

High levels of product concentration characterize many African economies, especially in the range of exports and sources of revenue. Countries rich in natural resources are the most emblematic, with concentration levels as high as 80% on a single commodity and value addition largely limited. Most of these primary products suffer fluctuations in international prices, and long-term declines in international terms of trade are common across Africa.

With life expectancy at 53.8 years, Africa has the poorest regional health status in the world. The nature of the continent's disease burden is significantly different from other regions: 42.5% of the diseases are caused by infectious and parasitic diseases compared with 28.9% in India and 2.8% in the market economies of Europe, making the continent much more vulnerable to infectious diseases than any other region of the world. Malaria is one of the most lethal health problems faced by the region. Estimates suggest that between 1 and 2 million people in Africa die from malaria each year. In addition, HIV/AIDS is one of the currently most daunting problems of Africa. Of the over 30 million people living with HIV/AIDS in the world, 21 million are in sub-Saharan Africa.

These commonalities and differences are taken up in greater detail in the rest of the overview. We start by placing African development in the context of its engagement with the global economy.

3. Africa in the global economy

In the early post-independence years there were questions among African governments about the appropriateness of participating in global trade and capital transactions. Many saw trade and international capital transactions as being structured to the disadvantage of poorer economies, and tried to stay away from it—hence import-substitution industrialization (Killick 1978). Those were the times when calls for a 'new international economic order' dominated the development debate. Today that debate appears to be largely over, even if questions remain about how best Africa can engage the rest of the world in international exchanges within a fairer environment.

After several years of limited engagement with the international trading system, one of the most conspicuous features of African economies today is the smallness of their shares in global transactions. Their involvement in global trade is the lowest for all regions at 3.5% of world merchandise exports in 2008 compared to 27.7% for Asia. While their involvement with global capital flows expanded significantly before the recent financial crisis, there are several indications that growth in inflows has been slowed down considerably, and lags far behind that of other developing regions. Another major feature of Africa's trading relationships is the paucity of trade among the countries of the region. Only 11.7% of African exports went to other African countries in 2008. This means that many producers do not get the opportunity to experience trading across borders, and what it entails in terms of payments systems, before plunging into larger international markets.

Africa engages with the rest of the world in a few other ways. One of the more significant is through international migration. An aspect of such migration is the brain-drain which sees high proportions of skilled labour migrate to other parts of the world. Migration from Africa grew remarkably in the last decade, depriving many economies of the contributions of such persons. On the other hand, there has been an increase in remittances. The debate about whether remittances make up for the skills and income losses associated with brain-drain will continue for a long time.[8] Also indicative of Africa's current relationship with the global economy is the fairly large size of development assistance it draws from the more developed economies. The significance of aid in

---

[8] For a recent contribution, see Clemens and Petersen (2006).

some countries leads to questions about the sustainability of financing for development projects and programmes.

The question of how best Africa can engage with the rest of the world in international exchanges has been addressed by many studies. One of the more comprehensive studies of Africa and the world trading system from an African perspective was carried out by the African Economic Research Consortium, documenting the paradigm shifts in how Africa has interacted with the rest of the world in the trading of goods and services (Oyejide and Lyakurwa 2005). The issue of how Africa can learn from its Uruguay Round experiences is addressed in that volume, while the age-old market access issues for African exports are also covered. The studies also explain how African agricultural, manufacturing, and mining products might find easier access in international markets within the WTO framework.

Today, many African economies draw inspiration from the experiences of Asian economies. They see how Asian economies have progressively engaged with outward-oriented policies and benefited significantly from them. But they are also mindful of the many risks and challenges that the Asian economies have faced. Many remember the Asian financial crisis of 1997 and wonder if they would have to go through that experience as part of the 'growing up' challenges after opening up markets. The more cynical may see the recent limited adverse impact of the global financial crisis on African economies as 'vindication' of non-integration into the global economy. Overall, however, the view that integration into the global economy can have significant net positive results largely drives policy in most countries.

What will it take for Africa to integrate on a larger scale with the global economy? Aryeetey et al. (2003) have suggested that participating successfully in the global economy requires a strategic approach. They argue that 'integration is multi-dimensional', covering trade, investment, capital flows, and technology. For each of these a different level of openness may be required, depending on the initial conditions of the economy and the specific market of interest. Many countries will have to develop a mix of policies with varied levels of openness. Among the prerequisites often cited for successful integration into the global economy is the need to ensure a stable macroeconomic environment. There have been concerns that an inability to keep inflation and budget deficits at appropriate levels will slow down the integration process. Issues about appropriate and stable exchange rates and real interest rates have often been significant, and need to be addressed in several countries.

The fears associated with trade liberalization are quite well known. African countries have often had an ambivalent position regarding trade liberalization, and this is largely due to the fact that they have fewer options for generating revenues, a point we return to in section 6. There are also major fears about what open markets can do to domestic production of goods and services, leading to possible deindustrialization. There is, however, growing consensus that greater openness may be pursued with better sequencing. To enhance intraregional trade, promoting integration requires significant political commitment as well as huge infrastructural developments. In pursuing greater integration into the global system, it is essential for African economies to strengthen the institutions that make for an outward orientation. These include those that promote transparency in public affairs and support the pursuit of consistency in public policy that will lead to economic growth. The institutional basis of African development will be taken up in Section 6. The next section turns to macroeconomic policies in Africa.

4. **The macroeconomics of Africa**

The policy prescriptions by the economics discipline for Africa have had mixed results, to say the least. Just after the independence of most countries in Africa, the economics discipline prescribed 'big push' and 'state intervention' as means to industrialization and sustainable development. For a large part of the post-independence period, sustainable growth eluded Africa. Strong state intervention was blamed for most economic failings. The pendulum swung to market-based policies to correct for the failings of government. But more recently, especially following the recent experience during the crisis, the need for the role of the state has been emphasized, given that market-based policies have not sufficiently focused on the long-term development challenges of Africa. One can fault most post-independence policy prescriptions for the lack of sufficient focus on country-specific circumstances in the design and implementation of policy. As economists, we are challenged to find appropriate policies that can address the structural constraints to growth in our countries while at the same time harnessing the potential of our economies in terms of natural resources and human capital.[9]

The policy debate aside, the decade leading up to the financial crisis represents a unique period in the economic growth history of Africa. Africa recorded a sustained period of growth while at the same time controlling inflation. The growth experienced was not limited to resource-rich countries, but spread to resource poor countries and fragile states. Analysis of this development reveals that improved macroeconomic framework and political governance in a majority of countries were key drivers for the improved economic performance. Indeed, improved economic policies were a source of resilience to financial crisis and an impetus to observed recovery since 2009. Therefore, at a minimum, African countries must sustain and strengthen policies that have sustained growth in the decade prior to the crisis. However, the sustained growth in the period was not associated with a sufficient drop in poverty across many countries in Africa. Going forward, the balance between growth and equitable distribution on the one

---

[9] We return to this point in section 6 on 'African economies and African states'.

hand and between stimulation of growth and macroeconomic stability on the other will present a challenge to policymakers.

A benign inflation environment, away from an average inflation of about 25% for the decade to 2000, set the bedrock for robust economic growth for both African oil importers and exporters.[10] However, the food and fuel crisis of 2008–9 pushed up inflation rates beyond targets set by central banks. The average inflation rate for 2008 and 2009 was 12.5% and 8.3%, respectively (International Monetary Fund 2010). The subsequent fall in both food and fuel prices, combined with a slack in aggregate demand in the aftermath of the financial crisis, has brought back inflation to about 5% per annum.

The widespread pessimism about African growth prospects prior to 2000 was somewhat dispelled by a fairly broad-based economic upturn that allowed the average income growth rate to exceed the population growth rate, thereby resulting in some gains in per capita income across the continent, especially in sub-Saharan Africa. The growth was quite widespread, benefiting both the low-income and middle-income countries. Indeed, growth in many countries was due to factors outside natural resources including the improved political and economic management. On average, Africa recorded growth rates averaging 5.0% in the ten-year period to 2008, relative to 2.5% in the decade to 1998 (World Bank 2010). However, changes in the sectoral composition of African GDP are somewhat slower than in Asia, especially in the expansion of the manufacturing sector. The export basket continues to reflect products from traditional agriculture and exports of raw material. Unfortunately for Africa, the agricultural sector remains largely conventional due to under-investment by governments, abolition of input and market support systems, and limited financial extension. These constraints must be unlocked if agriculture is to provide additional employment of resources, guarantee food security, and be a basis for export diversification. The high concentration of exports, with an average of 70% of merchandise exports being accounted for by the top three export products, is a source of vulnerability for many economies in Africa, especially in resource-rich economies. Diversification of products and export markets must remain on the development agenda for Africa.

Africa's growth performance stumbled in 2009 largely due to the effects of the crisis. The global economic and financial crisis reduced exports of goods and services from Africa, and also slowed net inflows of remittances and private capital flows. Growth in the middle-income countries and commodity exporters was adversely affected, with some of the countries such as South Africa and Botswana suffering a recession in 2009. The growth in the low-income countries held up better, dropping by only 2%.

---

[10] For the 14 CFA countries that have a fixed exchange rate with the euro, inflation has always been low.

The improved macroeconomic and political environment augurs well for investments to Africa. The continent has become more attractive to foreign capital flows over the decade to 2010, with foreign investments reaching a peak of US$87.6 billion in 2008, compared to US$20.9 billion in 2003 (UN Economic Commission for Africa 2010). However, the volatile nature of these capital flows places private-sector-led growth and Africa's poverty reduction endeavours at great risk.

Continued reliance on Official Development Assistance (ODA) by African economies and the uncertainty over foreign savings places even more emphasis on the need for integrated, sound domestic financial markets across the continent. Also, Africa can reduce external dependency by increasing domestic resource mobilization through bringing the large informal sector into the tax bracket, improved fiscal prudence in the public sector, and better management of revenues from exploitation of natural resources.

The majority of the African continent has received some benefits from more targeted international development initiatives like the Multilateral Debt Relief Initiative (MDRI). External debt levels for Africa as a whole have averaged 40% of GDP in the decade to 2010, compared to above 65% in the preceding decade. Increased international development support, coupled with improved terms of trade, and prudent macroeconomic policies have led to a turnaround in Africa's balance of payments position. The current account improved from an average deficit of 2.4% of GDP in the ten years to 2000 to an average surplus of 1% in the decade to 2010. This, however, is still low compared to an average surplus of close to 5% for the newly industrialized Asian economies over the same period.

Engagement with the global economy and a sound macroeconomic framework are not ends in themselves, but rather the means to achieving poverty reduction and human development. The next section takes up this issue.

5. Poverty and human development

A basic difference between African economies and the more developed regions of the world is the more widespread poverty in the region and low incomes derived from most economic activities. Incomes are generally low as a result of the low productivity associated with most production processes. People involved in low-productivity agriculture and economies have a major challenge in introducing industrial activity. Moving from low-productivity activities to high-productivity ones is extremely difficult in the region for a number of reasons, including institutional challenges and poor market conditions. Structural transformation has also been extremely difficult in the region. In the absence of such transformation, it has been problematic to sustain economic growth for long periods.

The poverty trends in Africa over the last 30 years have been quite revealing. While all other regions of the world saw poverty, captured through the headcount index, going down steadily after 1981, the reverse happened in Africa between 1981 and 1996 (Chen and Ravallion 2008). It was only after 1996 that the headcount index began to decline somewhat, from 56.4 in 1996 to 50.4 in 2005. As many as 384.2 million Africans lived below the poverty line in 2005. Despite the fact that a number of countries have seen significant improvements in poverty in pursuit of the Millennium Development Goals, the numbers of the poor remain a major challenge. Inequality figures may suggest improvements in a number of African countries, as in the paper by Thorbecke in this volume, but there is also strong indication of worsening inequality in other countries, and that is what drives many of the social development and protection programmes found in those countries.

While poverty and inequality will dominate the development discourse in many African countries for a long time, there is little indication that either the governments or their development partners have found the appropriate responses to this challenge. The lack of response is best illustrated by the fact that hardly any policies and programmes facilitate employment-creation on a sustained basis anywhere. Thus, despite several years of economic reforms in most countries, unemployment and underemployment—and especially low productivity in agriculture—remain major obstacles in the fight to reduce poverty. In the absence of jobs, all the other manifestations of poverty, including difficult health and education status, become even more significant and self-reinforcing. The fact that deprivation in Africa has a strong gender dimension means that policies and interventions will have to be gender-specific.

African economies have been waiting for a transformation that will include a new green revolution. The revolution is expected to lead to modernized agriculture that is strongly linked to a new industrial sector through processing and input supply. This has not happened in most countries, despite the fact that governments talk a lot about the need to modernize agriculture and develop value chains. The absence of a new green revolution in Africa and the lack of an appropriate industrial sector have been attributed to a long list of factors, including inadequate financial systems, poor investment climate, land tenure difficulties, poor farmer education, etc. (Djurfeldt, Aryeetey, and Isinika 2010). The challenge facing many African countries is how to step back and begin to prioritize where it will pay best for governments to intervene to solve these problems (Djurfeldt et al. 2010). The role of the state in resource allocation has never been properly determined in Africa—hence the difficult outcomes.

The strong link between health and productivity and incomes is generally accepted. There is evidence that Africa's growth has been affected significantly by poor health (Acemoglu and Johnson 2007). While HIV/AIDS is the problem that draws the most attention in terms of the consequences for mortality and the cost to households and national economies, malaria and several other diseases tend to have greater widespread effect on people and their income-earning capacities. The disease burden in the region is the highest in the world, and this has severe consequences for production processes that are heavily reliant on labour. In many countries the largest challenge facing the authorities is how to increase access to health services, especially in rural areas. Access is more difficult for the poor than for the non-poor. There are significant impediments as a result of poor infrastructure and inadequate human resources. There are regular pressures on governments to increase health spending, as expenditures on health are far less than in other developed regions, both in per capita terms and as a share of income (Poullier et al. 2002).

It is obvious that most African countries cannot fight the healthcare battle alone. This makes development assistance targeting health crucial. Various forms of development assistance have recently been directed at health, especially through Global Health Partnerships. Assessments of their impact have been positive for several diseases, especially in terms of drawing additional resources to those diseases and controlling diseases within countries, particularly through mass vaccinations (Caines et al. 2004). The challenge facing many countries remains how to integrate processes associated with large international health programmes into their own institutional arrangements for the longer-term goal of freeing people from diseases that can easily be controlled.

Several African governments have achieved success in improving access to education, as reflected by improvements in enrolments rates reported in the paper by Gyimah-Brempong, but this varies widely. In rural communities, access generally remains poor. Also, most of the emphasis, beginning from the 1990s, has been on expansion of primary education. There is a growing view that there is a need for more balance among the different levels of education, as they serve different purposes in terms of skills provision.

While access has improved, there is a general perception that the quality of education is low and possibly declining in several countries. The skills required for structural transformation are not being adequately produced by the educational systems. After expanded outlays on education and the still significant challenges in education, the poor delivery of education services is still seen as a reflection of poor institutions and limited accountability. Poor service delivery is not just a resource constraint problem. Governments need to devote greater attention to the efficient management of the systems for generating education outcomes.

Africa has a large population of vulnerable people. They are not able to participate in markets, either as suppliers of labour or as entrepreneurs, because of their health status or lack of functional skills. They may be mainly women and those who depend on them. For these groups of people, a system of social protection is often considered necessary. The last decade has seen several African countries initiating social protection policies and programmes, including cash transfers, food programmes, food for work programmes, and social insurance including micro-insurance, in-kind vouchers, etc. Other related policies may include labour market policies and regulations. They may be effective in encouraging participation in markets or schooling, as they facilitate risk management, increase consumption, and also reduce the irreversible loss in assets. Unfortunately there are hardly any comprehensive evaluations of major social protection programmes, thus making it difficult to assess their impact on people and economies. There are, however, several indications that many of them might become unsustainable, as they place huge burdens on national budgets.

All of the policy prescriptions discussed so far require an effective state for their formulation and implementation. The interaction between economic policy and the African state is taken up in the next section.

6. African economics and the African state

At a speech to the United Nations in 1957, Ghanaian President Kwame Nkrumah argued that, because Ghana's institutions were weak, it needed state-led industrialization to develop. Felix Houphouet-Boigny, who would become his Ivorian counterpart a few years later, disagreed: for precisely the same reason, he said his country would rely on market capitalism. The evolution of Africa's economic performance can be interpreted as oscillating between the two sides of this 'West African Wager'.[11]

Reflecting economics' prevailing paradigm at the time of their independence, most African economies, including Côte d'Ivoire, embarked on ambitious public investment programmes. The rationale was that these countries were replete with market failures—public goods such as bridges, roads, and ports could only be built by collective action. Most countries went further and identified externalities that needed a subsidy to be corrected, the most common being the 'infant industry' argument that resulted in protection to domestic industries from imports. Some countries simply built and ran the firm as a public enterprise: governments produced shoes, batteries, and bread. Finally, to fulfil the redistributive role of government, countries such as Tanzania introduced collective farming.

Three aspects of this phase are worth mentioning. First, the rationale for these interventions was based on standard, neoclassical economic reasoning. There was no sense that the economics of Africa were different from the economics of, say, southern Europe after the Second World War. Second, both sides of the West African Wager were being practised elsewhere—with equally impressive results. The socialist economies of the Soviet Union and Eastern Europe were enjoying rapid economic growth, as were the market economies of the United States, western Europe, and Japan. Third, there was an alignment between the interests of donors, who not only financed the public investments

---

[11] Woronoff (1972).

but also provided technical assistance in building the electric power stations or irrigation canals, and those of recipient governments, who could take credit for correcting market failures.

Starting in the 1970s, this relatively salubrious situation began to deteriorate rapidly. Several African countries lost their democratically elected governments to military strongmen. Nkrumah himself was toppled in a coup d'état, leading some to think that he lost the West African Wager with Houphouet (although, as we show below, it is not clear who won). The advent of non-democratic governments meant that political power lay in the hands of a small elite (usually urban-based citizens) rather than a broad swathe of the population including the rural poor. In turn, this meant that economic policy was geared towards the elite. Countries such as Ghana would run overvalued exchange rates because they kept food and import prices low (which kept the urban elite happy), while discriminating against food producers.

The commodity price shocks of the 1970s, especially the quadrupling of the price of oil, amplified the distortions in African economies to the point where the continent's per capita income started declining. Countries with high tariff barriers found it much harder to adjust to the terms of trade shock because they had limited means of raising foreign exchange to pay for the higher-priced oil; the more open economies of East Asia, for instance, could adjust more smoothly. Even countries that experienced favourable terms of trade shocks—such as Côte d'Ivoire and Kenya—found that governments did a poor job of managing their windfall revenues. When the budget constraint is relaxed, governments spend on unproductive projects or transfer rents to their political clients.

When they were asked to help African countries manage the ensuing balance of payments crises, the international community responded by asking countries to remove some of the government interventions that they themselves had advised them to adopt![12] Not surprisingly, African governments resisted. These reforms threatened the rents of the elites, who were still in power. Since countries had to tighten their belts anyway (to adjust to the transfer of wealth associated with a negative terms of trade shock), the so-called 'structural adjustment' reforms took on a negative connotation. Perhaps more fundamentally, when countries adopted some of these reform measures, the promised results failed to appear. Exchange rate devaluations led to inflation (and sometimes hyperinflation); trade liberalization often resulted in massive current account deficits, banking crises, and eventually a call for import restrictions. Since growth remained anaemic, poverty in Africa continued to rise.

In light of this experience, scholars began to ask if the underlying economics of Africa was different—whether the same policy reforms that worked elsewhere would not work in Africa because of different initial conditions. Exchange rate devaluations did not lead

---

[12] 'The Berg Report' (World Bank 1981).

to increased tradable production, because labour and capital markets were rigid. Inasmuch as governments relied heavily on trade taxes for their revenues, trade liberalization led to massive fiscal deficits which were financed either by foreign borrowing (resulting in a debt crisis) or by domestic borrowing, often resulting in a banking crisis. Finally, some pointed to Africa's ethnic heterogeneity, geographical handicaps (landlockedness, proximity to the tropics, arid land), and weak institutions left by the colonial rulers as contributing to the continent's 'growth tragedy.'

The situation changed significantly from the mid-1990s. Growth started accelerating to an average of 5% a year for about a decade, and the poverty rate, which had been increasing, started declining by one percentage point a year. While there are many reasons for this turnaround, one of them is that African governments began to adopt economic reforms—the same reforms they had rejected in the past. For example, in 1994, the thirteen countries in the CFA zone devalued the CFA franc by 50%. The parity had not been changed since 1947. Although the economies of the 14 countries in the CFA zone had been deteriorating since the fall of commodity prices in the early 1980s and the French franc started appreciating in 1985, governments had been resisting calls for devaluation for about a decade.

These developments raise two questions. Why did these economic reforms work in the late 1990s when they failed in the previous decade? And why did African governments choose to adopt these reforms now, when they had resisted them previously? The answer to the first lies in the fact that the reforms, even if they resembled the 'Washington Consensus', were largely home-grown. The international community had found that structural adjustment conditionality was not working because the political costs of reforms outweighed the monetary benefits. So they switched to providing aid based on the government's own programme. Since the reforms therefore emerged from a domestic political consensus, they were more likely to be sustained, which in turn meant that they would more probably lead to results. It should be noted that, in addition, the populist policies of the past had delivered disappointing results. And the fall of the Soviet Union had (temporarily) discredited the Nkrumah-style socialist model of development.

As to why governments chose to adopt reforms at this stage, recall that the early 1990s saw a dramatic increase in the number of democratically elected governments. African leaders now had to rely on support from a majority of their citizens to stay in power. In particular, since about 70% of the citizens were in rural areas, they had to advocate policies that promoted farmers' interests—including a neutral exchange rate policy. In short, the political climate for pro-poor policies had improved.

In its fifty years of independence, Africa has suffered from market failures and government failures. In the West African Wager, each side ignored one of the two. Today, the people of Africa seem to be striking a better balance—using government to address market failure, but avoiding some of the government failures that might ensue. Such developments bode well for the continent's future. However, the spectre of civil war

7. Conflict and the development of Africa

The previous section discussed government failures, and how they undermined Africa's growth and poverty reduction. Perhaps the biggest failure was several African governments' inability to provide peace, a basic public good. Between 1960 and 1999, 20 African countries have experienced a civil war, with the incidence of war peaking at 8 per year in the 1980s, declining to 7.5 per year in the following decade.[13] In addition to the death and destruction they cause, civil wars have a profound effect on the economy. Investment is one of the biggest casualties: both domestic and foreign investments fall precipitously when war breaks out. Disturbingly, when a civil war ends (or at least a peace treaty is signed), investment does not resume immediately. This 'wait-and-see' attitude of investors perpetuates the slow growth and grinding poverty that civil war brings. It also increases the chances that a civil war will recur.

In a paper titled 'Why are there so many civil wars in Africa?', Elbadawi and Sambanis (2009) go beyond factors such as ethno-linguistic fractionalization—or 'grievance'—and suggest three reasons, two of which were previously identified by Collier and Hoeffler (1998): the presence of natural resources, especially minerals, that are easy to loot and finance rebellions (Angola and Sierra Leone being prominent examples); and low per capita incomes and education levels that make it easy to recruit soldiers (Mozambique and Central African Republic are possible examples). They add, and empirically corroborate, a third—the weakness of democratic institutions that makes it difficult to resolve conflicts peacefully. The vicious cycle of poor governance and weak economic performance that we identified in the previous section may therefore have contributed to the relatively high incidence of civil wars in Africa. This raises the obvious question: Have the improvements in democratic governance since the 1990s helped to lower the incidence of civil war? In addition to the direct effect, improvements in governance would also help reduce the other two factors: unregulated mineral resources and low per-capita income and education levels. Nkurunziza (2008) confirms that there was an average of 3.4 civil wars per year in 2000–7. In the second half of 2007, there were only three ongoing civil wars in Africa—Chad, Sudan, and Somalia.

While these are encouraging statistics, Azam (forthcoming) suggests that there may be more wars waiting to happen. He proposes a model whereby seemingly stable countries such as Côte d'Ivoire erupt into conflict. In these multi-ethnic societies, a strong ruler

---

[13] Nkurunziza (2008).

(like Houphouet-Boigny) is able to maintain a modicum of harmony by transferring small amounts of the country's wealth to every ethnic group, ensuring that no group feels left out. When it appears that the strong ruler's days are numbered, the minority groups feel threatened. Violent conflict ensues, possibly (as in the case of Côte d'Ivoire) lasting a decade. Inasmuch as Africa still has strong rulers, some of whom emerged from a previous civil war, Azam's analysis indicates that we must not be complacent.

We must avoid complacency for another reason. While the incidence of civil wars has declined, Africa's experience with postwar reconstruction has been decidedly mixed. Countries such as Mozambique, Rwanda, and Uganda have emerged from conflict to become dynamic economies. But others, such as Democratic Republic of Congo, Central African Republic, and Chad, are making much slower progress. In fact, these countries seem to be in a low-level equilibrium trap, even after the signing of a peace agreement. Using the World Bank's definition of 'fragile and conflict-affected states' (FACS), we calculate that the probability that a FACS in 2000 will still be a FACS in 2008 is 0.96.

There are a number of reasons for this apparent lack of progress. One is that the international community has, in some cases, withdrawn its peacekeeping operations soon after the first set of elections. As Collier (2009) points out, elections may be the beginning, not the end, of the conflict, especially if the loser has nothing more to lose by taking up arms. But another, perhaps less understood reason is that, if these countries' economies are caught in a low governance–low economic growth trap, the resources made available to fragile states are too little to help them escape the trap. The donor community continues to allocate resources based more or less on the same criteria as for non-conflict countries, namely on the quality of policy and institutions in the country. Not surprisingly, this leads to relatively low amounts going to these post-conflict and fragile countries. It is possible that a new approach to supporting fragile states is needed, one that is akin to a venture capital investment, whereby we take a gamble and pour a lot of money into one fragile state, acknowledging that it is a high-risk but also a high-return proposition. The alternative—dribbling small amounts of resources to these desperately poor countries—may condemn them to remain in poverty.

8. Africa over the long term

The previous sections have looked at various aspects of Africa's history over the last 50 years. What are the key challenges facing Africa over the next 50 years? In this section we highlight the consequences of three major trends—population growth and composition, urbanization, and environmental degradation.

According to the United Nations, Africa's population will grow from around 1 billion in 2009 to around 2 billion in 2050.[14] Within this, North Africa's population will grow from 213 million to 321 million. Population density will grow from 34 to 66 persons per km^2 for Africa as a whole (the numbers are 23–38 for North Africa and 36–72 for sub-Saharan Africa). This compares to a trend from 51 to 67 for the world as a whole. Thus population levels and densities will rise sharply throughout Africa, particularly in sub-Saharan Africa. To be sure, these numbers do not come anywhere near the 231 persons per km^2 projected for south-central Asia (which includes India) for 2050.

These population projections simultaneously alert us to two long-term factors that will influence the development of Africa. First, pressure on land, and particularly agricultural land, will grow as population increases. This will require special attention on the one hand to investment in research and development for raising crop yields after their long period of decline, and on the other hand to environmental degradation as forest cover is denuded at the extensive margin to feed a growing population.[15] The argument that food can be imported takes us to a second argument, especially comparing population density in Africa with that in Asia. Africa's comparative advantage is in land-intensive products, which includes agriculture but also natural resources, and will still be so in 50 years' time. Especially in relation to natural resources, this emphasizes the importance of managing resource rents, and having good governance structures to do so.[16] Finally, one way of altering the comparative advantage would be to change the education and skills of the population, and this suggest a very clear use of resource rents generated by natural resources—to build up the human capital of the population.[17]

Alongside the increase in population will come an increase in urbanization. Africa as a whole will cross the 'tipping point' where more than half the population will be urban, going from 40.0% in 2010 to 61.6% in 2050.[18] (The numbers for sub-Saharan Africa are 37.2% and 60.1%.) As a comparison, the projection for south-central Asia in 2050 is 56.0%. Thus in 2050 Africa will be more urbanized than India (54.2%) and surrounding countries. This fast rate of urbanization is a long-term trend that will define African

---

[14] http://www.un.org/esa/population/publications/ageing/ageing2009.htm.

[15] 'Natural forests and woodlands in Africa have been drastically reduced in size over the last century, but particularly so since independence, as countries have struggled to improve their economies through exploitation of natural resources. Deforestation for commercial timber sales and clearance for agricultural and urban developments are the most intensive pressures, as well as over-harvesting of wood for fuel, medicinal products, and construction materials. Remaining forests have also been degraded as a result of clear felling, fires, selective harvesting, and encroachment' (United Nations Environment Programme 2002: 146).

[16] There is of course a large literature on this. For recent examples of the links between natural resources rents and political economy, see Jensen and Wantchekon (2004) or Collier (2010).

[17] For a discussion of the role of human capital in explaining wages in the presence of international trade, see Wood (2002).

[18] http://esa.un.org/unpd/wup/unup/p2k0data.asp.

development challenges, and raises a number of questions: Is urbanization the result of 'rural push' or 'urban pull'? Is the urban pull itself the result of 'urban bias' in policies that discriminates against rural and agricultural activities?[19] How exactly should governments think about the balance between investing in urban areas to meet the need of a growing urban population, vs investing in rural areas to help the poor there but also, perhaps, to stem the tide of rural to urban migration?

There is considerable controversy around these questions in the literature.[20] The urban bias thesis has strong support, and the realities of African governance, with a focus on the capital city and other big urban agglomerations, tend to support this argument. However, recent work has begun to question the magnitude of this effect. The importance of climatic and geographical factors is increasingly emphasized in empirical findings on the rate and pattern of urbanization in Africa, particularly sub-Saharan Africa. In the words of a recent analysis of urbanization: 'If Africa's rapid urbanization rate is driven by rural distress or migration from near-by land locked countries, allowing conditions in African cities to continue to deteriorate by reducing subsidies is callous at best, and will have little or no effect on urbanization.'[21] Whether one subscribes fully to this thesis or not, we can perhaps accept that there is an inexorable trend of urbanization in Africa, and policymakers will have to get themselves ready for development challenges that are increasingly urban in nature.

At the same time, the 'rural push' side of the urbanization debate highlights another major factor in Africa's long-term development—climate change and its environmental and developmental consequences. Global warming will have diverse consequences in Africa, but there are some common themes.[22] In North Africa, water shortages will be a key challenge of the coming half-century, with attendant consequences for agriculture. Coastal flooding is another major issue, given the concentration of population in these zones. For sub-Saharan Africa, the increased intensity of both drought and floods—greater climate variability—is the major concern. With current agricultural practices, agricultural yields are forecast to decline by 15% between now and 2050. While yields may increase in a very small number of countries, the overall pattern is one of yield decline, going as high as 50% in some cases.[23]

The policy debate on addressing climate change falls under two broad headings—mitigation and adaptation.[24] For the oil-producing economies of Africa, mitigation is a

---

[19] The Urban Bias thesis was popularized by Lipton (1977), and has been remarkably resilient, as evidenced e.g. by its advancement in World Bank (2000: box 6.4, p. 130).
[20] See a review by Corbridge and Jones (2006).
[21] Annez, Buckle, and Kalarickal (2010).
[22] See the broad regional overviews in World Bank (2010).
[23] See World Bank (2010: p. 5, map 1, and p. 6, box 1). For a broad perspective on climate change an Africa, see Low (2005).
[24] For a specific discussion by an African regional Institution, see African Development Bank (2009).

long-term challenge. Cutting through the detailed specifics of different policy proposals, a key plank of mitigation is to make the consumption of fossil fuels more expensive, and to find renewable alternatives to them. Over a 50-year period, this would reduce the incomes of oil-producing economies, and they would need to adapt to this long-term trend through alternative sources of development. Agriculture is the other land-based production activity in which Africa has a comparative advantage, but this itself will be under threat from climate change. So, once again, using current natural resource rents to enhance the human capital of the population seems to be the appropriate long-term strategy.

There is an argument that Africa will bear the consequences of climate change for the next 50 years even if global mitigation efforts are immediately successful. The main policy challenge will therefore be adaptation. The detailed nature of this will depend on the specific circumstances—coastal flooding, drought, excessive rainfall, etc.—but a common feature that emerges from research is the importance of investing in human and social capital to build resilience to shocks.[25] Thus human capital investment is also the right strategy in relation to adaptation to climate change.

9. Conclusion

Africa is a diverse continent, and its development challenges are no less diverse. We reject the 'one size fits all' approaches that have sometimes been applied to African development. We believe that country specificities matter, and that policies that work in one setting may not do so in another setting in Africa. And yet certain key issues and challenges do emerge that are Africa-wide, and that are amenable to, and require, careful economic analysis. These have been detailed in the previous sections. In this conclusion we highlight five major themes that economic analysts and economic policymakers in Africa will have to grapple with in the years and decades to come.

- Managing engagement with the global economy. The debate on whether or not to engage has been settled in favour of engagement. The issues that remain are those of how—how to manage trade liberalization so as to achieve diversification of export and production, how to attract and yet regulate foreign direct investment to create employment, and how to manage the exchange rate to aid diversification.
- Translating the gains of economic growth into poverty reduction and human development. African poverty rose in the periods of low growth, and is falling in those countries that have registered significant growth rates in the past two decades. But inequalities are rising in some places and as a result the impact of growth on poverty reduction may be dissipated. Targeted

---

[25] See Blankespoor et al. (2010).

- policies and interventions to address poverty, human development, and the gender basis of deprivation will remain high on the Africa agenda in the years to come.
- Whether it is macroeconomic policies or policies towards poverty and human development, the central issues concern building effective and responsive institutions of the state which raise revenue and manage its expenditure in the public interest. More generally, African successes and failures have often been explained by the developmental nature of the African state. The future depends on the African state becoming and remaining developmental, with the institutions to back this up.
- For those economies and societies in Africa that are mired in conflict, or just emerging from it, or at risk of descending into it, economic policy has to be at the service of conflict mitigation and conflict management. Even if the major issue is one of political reconciliation, the economic policy framework should help rather than hinder.
- Over the longer term, Africa will bear the consequences of climate change even though it has had no part in causing it. While international support for adaptation to climate change is important and we must argue for it, equally important will be country-specific adaptation measures that protect the poorest while maintaining the growth momentum that has been built up in many countries during the last decade.

There is one final commonality that we wish to highlight. It is the central role that economic analysis, applied rigorously but sensitively, can play in helping African policy-makers assess the many trade-offs among interventions, and to formulate and implement policies for African growth and development. We think that the 100 entries in this *Companion to the Economics of Africa* are a testament to that claim.

REFERENCES

Acemogolu, D., and S. Johnson, 2007. 'Disease and development: the effect of life expectancy on economic growth', *Journal of Political Economy* 115.6.

African Development Bank, 2009. 'Bank group climate risk management and adaptation strategy', http://www.afdb.org/fileadmin/uploads/afdb/Documents/Policy-Documents/Climate%20Risk%20Management%20and%20Adaptation%20Strategy%20_CRMA_%20%282%29.pdf.

Annez, Patricia, Robert Buckley, and Jerry Kalarickal, 2010. 'African urbanization as flight: policy implications of geography', *Urban Forum* 21.3, 221–34.

Aryeetey, E., J. Court, M. Nissanke, and B. Weder, 2003. 'Strengthening Africa's participation in the global economy', Policy Brief, United Nations University, Tokyo.

Azam, Jean-Paul, forthcoming. 'Reflections on Africa's wars,' in Michelle R. Garfinkel and Stergios Skaperdas (eds), *Oxford Handbook of the Economics of Peace and Conflict*.

Blankespoor, Brian, Susmita Dasgupta, Benoit Laplante, and David Wheeler, 2010. 'The economics of adaptation to extreme weather events in developing countries', working paper no.

199, Center for Global Development, http://www.cgdev.org/content/publications/detail/1423545/.

Caines, K., K. Buse, C. Carlson, R. de Loor, N. Druce, C. Grace, M. Pearson, J. Sancho, and R. Sadanandan, 2004. 'Assessing the impact of global health partnerships', mimeo, DFID Health Resource Centre, London.

Chen, S., and M. Ravallion, 2008. 'The developing world is poorer than we thought, but no less successful in the fight against poverty', Policy Research Working Paper No. 4703, The World Bank.

Clemens, Michael, and Gunilla Petersen, 2006. 'New data on African health professionals abroad', Working Paper No. 95, Center for Global Development.

Collier, Paul, 2009. *Wars, Guns and Votes: Democracy in Dangerous Places*. New York: HarperCollins.

—— 2010. *The Plundered Planet*. New York: Oxford University Press.

—— and Anke Hoeffler, 1998. 'On economic causes of civil war,' Oxford Economic Papers 50.4, 563–73.

Corbridge, S., and G. Jones, 2006. *The Continuing Debate About Urban Bias: The Thesis, Its Critics, Its Influence and Implications for Poverty Reduction*. London: DFID.

Djurfeldt, G., Aryeetey, E., and A. Isinika (eds), 2010. *African Smallholders: Food Crops, Markets and Policy*. Wallingford: CABI.

Elbadawi, Ibrahim A., and Nicholas Sambanis, 2009. 'Why are there so many civil wars in Africa? Understanding and preventing violent conflict', *J. Afr. Econ* 9.3, 244–69.

International Monetary Fund, 2010. International Financial Statistics (October).

Jensen, Nathan, and Leonard Wantchekon, 2004. 'Resource wealth and political regimes in Africa', *Comparative Political Studies* 37, 816–41.

Killick, T., 1978. *Development Economics in Action: A Study of Economic Policies in Ghana*. London: Heinemann.

Lipton, Michael, 1977. *Why Poor People Stay Poor: A Study of Urban Bias in World Development*. London: Temple Smith.

Low, Pak Sum (ed.), 2005. *Climate Change and Africa*. Cambridge: Cambridge University Press.

Nkurunziza, Janvier D., 2008. 'Civil war and post-conflict reconstruction in Africa', paper presented at the African Economic Conference.

O'Connell, Stephen A., and Benno J. Ndulu, 2000. 'Africa's growth experience: a focus on the sources of growth'. Mimeo, AERC, Nairobi.

Oyejide, T. A., and W. Lyakurwa (eds), 2005. *Africa and the World Trading System*, vol. 1: *Selected Issues of the Doha Agenda*. Trenton, NJ, and Asmara: Africa World Press.

Poullier, J. P., P. Hernandez, K. Kawabata, and W. Savedoff, 2002. 'Patterns of global health expenditures: results for 191 countries'. EIP Discussion Paper No. 51, WHO, Geneva.

UN Economic Commission for Africa, 2010. *Economic Report on Africa*.

UN Environment Programme, 2002. *Africa Environmental Outlook: Past, Present and Future Prospects*. http://www.unep.org/dewa/Africa/publications/aeo-1/index.htm.

Wood, Adrian, 2002. 'Globalization and wage inequalities: a synthesis of three theories', *Weltwirtschaftliches Archiv* 138.1, 54–82.

World Bank, 1981. *Accelerated Development in Sub-Saharan Africa: An Agenda for Action* ('The Berg Report'). Washington, DC: The World Bank.
—— 2000. *World Development Report 1999/2000: Entering the 21st Century*. Oxford: Oxford University Press.
—— 2009. *World Development Indicators*. World Bank Database.
—— 2010. *World Development Report 2010: Development and Climate Change*. Oxford: Oxford University Press.
Woronoff, Jon, 1972. *West African Wager: Houphouet Versus Nkrumah*. Metuchen, NJ: Scarecrow Press.

Thematic Perspectives
African Development Prospects

An Overview of African Development Prospects

Paul Collier

From the mid-1990s until the onset of the global crisis, most African economies were growing: this contrasted to the stagnation of previous decades. The crisis has punctured this growth but probably not fundamentally derailed it. While capital inflows to the region have been modest, as a result of the reforms made over the past two decades the returns on private investment have risen and are now markedly higher than in other regions (Collier and Warnholz 2009). Quite probably, the conjunction of high returns to investment with modest capital inflows is because capital markets have not yet sufficiently adjusted to the news of improved economic opportunities. While in other regions investors react fast to news, in Africa the cost of information about economic opportunities is unusually high because of the extreme fragmentation of its markets and politics: knowledge about Kenya gives little guide to opportunities in Guinea. Hence, once the crisis recedes, Africa may revert to relatively rapid growth simply as investors catch up with existing opportunities.

However, overlaying this adjustment process will be the fundamentals that shape opportunities. These are developments in the rest of the world, African geography, and the choices made by African governments. This triad will be the focus of this essay.

Global developments

Three monumental developments in the rest of the world are likely to change Africa's opportunities: the growth of China, climate change, and the aftermath of the global crisis. As a result of continued rapid growth putting upward pressure on wages, China will soon cease to be a devastating competitor. However, as Chinese manufacturing companies seek to contain their rising labour costs they will reach the same solution as companies in those economies that are already high-wage, and offshore their production. The only region where labour costs are liable to remain low for several decades and which is also well located for global markets is coastal Africa.

Climate change is forecast to affect Africa more severely than any other region (Collier, Conway, and Venables 2008). Not only will the climate deteriorate more substantially in Africa, but its economies are more exposed to climate change because of the importance of rain-fed agriculture. Whereas African agriculture faces mounting productivity losses due to a drier, hotter, and more shock-prone weather, as the global climate warms huge tracts of Eurasia and North America will become *better* suited to agriculture. Hence, Africa will be losing comparative advantage in its largest economic activity.

As opportunities open in manufacturing and close in agriculture, Africa will face a massive task of facilitating this structural change. Change incurs costs: conceptually, the costs of change are a reasonable definition of what economists mean by investment. Hence, Africa will need much more investment than in the recent past. Unfortunately, these heightened needs are likely to collide with reduced financing for investment. The global crisis is likely to leave an unfortunate legacy of reduced capital inflows to the region. The crisis has radically reduced investor appetite for risk. Even during the global boom of 2003–8 foreign investment into Africa was relatively modest, but at least it was rising rapidly. Although Africa has not been hit by the crisis as hard as most other regions, it has long been perceived as the riskiest region for investment. Hence, although objectively Africa is now relatively less risky than prior to the crisis, since investors now wish to avoid high risks their portfolios are likely to shift to the regions that, despite being hit harder, are still seen as safer than Africa. The likely reduced flow of private capital to Africa will most probably be reinforced by a reduced flow of aid as budgets in the major donor nations face a prolonged period of austerity. Hence, Africa's acute needs for a higher rate of investment are unlikely to be met by its past sources of external finance.

Potentially, new sources of external finance can be accessed. The most substantial will be capital provided in return for the rights to natural assets, with China as the major new partner. Potentially, some of these revenues can be used to benefit countries that are not resource-rich by pooling them into a fund managed by the African Development Bank. There is also the potential to tap into the new Sovereign Wealth Funds of the Middle East and East Asia. President Zoellick of the World Bank has proposed that 1% of these funds be invested in Africa, and even such a modest proportion would amount to major inflows. There is also potential for borrowing on sub-commercial terms, such as through IBRD and SDRs. Unlike IDA, IBRD loans and SDRs do not require OECD governments to increase their public expenditure and so are politically much easier in times of fiscal stringency. For the poorest countries, unable to access capital markets, remittances from emigrants have already become substantial and may become the most important source of external finance. However, even after all these new sources have been taken into account, Africa will also need to finance more from its own resources.

Geographical opportunities

Africa is too large and varied a region to be analysed only as a single entity. At a minimum it is useful to distinguish between those countries where opportunities are dominated by the presence of valuable natural resources; those that, while not so fortunately endowed with resources, at least have a coast; and those that are neither resource-rich nor coastal (Collier and O'Connell 2007).

RESOURCE-RICH ECONOMIES

Africa is widely regarded as a resource-rich region. In fact, the evidence calls this into question. As of 2000, the last date for which global statistics were available, the value of known sub-soil assets beneath the average square kilometre of Africa was only around a fifth that of the average square kilometre of the countries of the OECD (Collier 2010). This massive difference is likely to be due not to differences in geology but to differences in the amount of exploration. Despite appearances, there has been very little exploration in Africa relative to other regions. This has two important implications. One is that the discovery process has evidently gone seriously wrong. Prospecting is an economic activity involving both investment and high risks. Evidently, in Africa the incentives for it have been weaker than those in other regions. The other implication is that were this incentive problem to be successfully addressed, the revenues from natural assets would increase approximately fivefold. Hence, in those countries with potential in resource extraction, this opportunity dwarfs all others.

Revenues from natural resources can potentially be used to finance diversification of the economy. For example, Malaysia used resource revenues to invest in the expansion of light manufactures which now dominate its exports. However, in order to harness natural resources for such diversified development the state unavoidably has a far more important role than if development is to be achieved through other strategies. The successful management of natural resources requires a chain of government decisions that have no parallel in other sectors. The first link in this chain is the discovery process. The lack of discovery in Africa is directly related to the lack of publicly generated geological information and the inability of most governments to credibly commit themselves to agreements. In turn, the commitment problem is due to the extreme concentration of power in the person of the president. However, the problems surrounding development that is based on resource extraction extend well beyond the discovery process. The government must capture the rents from natural resources for society by means of an effective taxation system and then spend these revenues for development. In most of Africa, resource extraction has not been properly taxed. Extraction rights have usually been sold through secret negotiations, exposing the society to problems of both agency and asymmetric information. Companies have routinely bribed government officials to secure favourable tax treatment, and this problem has been compounded by their possession of superior specialist knowledge. Even where revenues have accrued to the government, not enough has been devoted to investment. Dasgupta (2009) reports a measure of comprehensive wealth that includes both natural capital and invested capital. He finds that since 1970 comprehensive wealth per capita in Africa has halved, suggesting that the depletion of natural assets has not adequately been offset by the accumulation of invested assets, whether public or private.

Since government looms so large in the management of natural assets, good governance is critical. Further, since success depends upon an entire chain of distinct economic decisions taken by different actors, it is demanding: it is not enough to have a good minister of finance. Perhaps the most reliable route to success is through building a critical mass of well-informed citizens. Once a society has such a group then there is some chance that decisions can be held to account through formal institutions, and perhaps more importantly, through informal socialization public officials may come to share this common understanding. Two recent global initiatives have tried to build informed opinion in resource-rich societies. The Extractive Industries Transparency Initiative, launched in 2003, already has over thirty governments as signatories, committed to transparency in the reporting of revenues. The Natural Resource Charter, launched in 2009, is a website at www.naturalresourcecharter.org, which complements EITI by setting out the economic decision chain in accessible language. There may also be scope for African governments to strengthen their ability to make commitments by using the WTO. To date, the WTO has largely ignored the distinctive aspects of international transactions in resource extraction, but the plethora of ad hoc international efforts, such as EITI and the Kimberley Process, suggest that there is a need for more systematic attention (Collier and Venables 2009).

COASTAL RESOURCE-SCARCE COUNTRIES

In other developing regions, coastal resource-scarce economies have grown very rapidly through breaking into markets for global manufactures. Coastal countries have an overwhelming advantage over landlocked countries because of their lower transport costs to market, while resource-rich countries are liable to be uncompetitive because their natural resource exports appreciate the exchange rate. Africa's coastal, resource-scarce countries are atypical in not yet having made this breakthrough. African attempts during the 1970s to industrialize behind high trade barriers foundered on account of the small size of domestic markets. Once trade barriers were reduced, these industries proved to be unviable. Much of the historical explanation for the failure of African manufacturing to be competitive in the global market is that the costs of manufacturing business in Africa have been high as a result of inadequate infrastructure, corruption, a lack of appropriate skills and technology, and the regulation of trade and labour markets. Some of these problems have gradually been reduced. However, since the ability to penetrate global markets depends upon efficiency relative to a constantly rising level of competitors, despite absolute improvements in some respects competitiveness has deteriorated. In addition to the relative attractiveness of African and competitor policy environments for manufacturing, two recent trends in the globalization of manufactures have had opposing effects on Africa's opportunities. The favourable development is the change from vertical integration of production to vertical disintegration, known in economics as 'trade in tasks'. For the past three decades production processes have increasingly been split up into distinct stages, or tasks, each of which can be undertaken in the location best suited for it. This makes it easier for African new entrants into global manufacturing, since it is no longer necessary to acquire all at once the wide range of skills required for vertically integrated production. Instead, an African entrant can specialize on the task that comes closest to its current factor endowments and capabilities. The unfavourable development is the importance of cluster scale economies: by clustering together, all firms reduce their costs. This makes it more difficult for new entrants, since a cluster must inevitably start small. To illustrate the combined effect of the two processes, the production of buttons, which is a small task within the chain of making a garment, has become concentrated in a single Chinese city. The city is entirely specialized in button manufacture, and alone accounts for two-thirds of global output. In effect, African industrialization is frustrated by a threshold problem: even if clusters would be competitive once fully formed, the pioneering firms would lose money.

LANDLOCKED RESOURCE-SCARCE ECONOMIES

Africa has a far larger proportion of its population living in landlocked resource-scarce countries than other regions. This reflects the extreme political fragmentation of the region into 54 countries. Globally, such countries have fewer opportunities than the other two categories and have tended historically to grow more slowly, their best opportunity being to grow through trade with their more fortunately endowed neighbours. Good road and rail links to the coast and to neighbours are essential. But these depend not only on investment in physical infrastructure but on political incentives for neighbouring governments to maintain infrastructure well, and not to impede the flow of goods by bureaucratic barriers. The development of air-freight for horticulture has opened new opportunities but requires both the scale for frequent flights and highly efficient logistics. Potentially, the global development of the e-service trade could offer a more substantial lifeline to these economies: Rwanda, which is severely landlocked, is basing its longer-term growth strategy on this opportunity. However, to date the only

African economy that has become competitive in e-services is the tiny island of Cape Verde, which has benefited from the connections of its large diaspora.

Policy choices

The economic policies adopted by African governments have improved substantially since their nadir around the early 1980s. However, beneath this overall improvement there are sharp differences between macroeconomic and microeconomic policies. Macroeconomic policies, such as fiscal deficits, are now largely at or above world standards, which helped to account for the relatively modest impact of the global economic crisis on the region. Microeconomic policies, such as the regulation of business, the provision of infrastructure, and the efficiency of public spending, lag far behind world standards. For example, most African countries score badly on globally comparable indices that measure the costs of doing business and the prevalence of corruption.

This imbalance between macroeconomic and microeconomic policies is explicable in terms both of capacity and of volition. Good macroeconomic policies do not require much government capacity: they can be decided and implemented by a handful of senior politicians and civil servants. They can build a wide consensus of support since, other than in the very short run, bad macroeconomic policies are almost universally damaging. In contrast, good microeconomic policies are very demanding. The delivery of public infrastructure and social services depends upon being able to motivate the public-sector workforce through a complex combination of intrinsic motivation, financial incentives, and penalties. Typically, African public administration now lacks any of these forces for good staff performance. Instead, undemanding jobs in the public sector have become part of the patronage system. Similarly, the regulation of private activity, while necessary, also creates opportunities for extortion well-suited to patronage. The transformation of African polities from autocracies to semi-democracies has increased the scope for patronage politics and so, instead of making the public sector more accountable to ordinary citizens, may even have intensified the problem.

Conclusion

The opportunities discussed above, notably the commercialization of agriculture, the harnessing of natural resources, and breaking into global manufacturing and e-services, can all be frustrated by poor public services and by predatory regulation. Hence, whether Africa succeeds in seizing its opportunities will depend critically upon whether it is able to surmount the political and capacity constraints that to date have condemned its public sectors to being dysfunctional. These challenges amount to the need for radical improvements in governance. It is unfortunate that Africa's endowments and political architecture make its development unusually dependent upon the quality of governance. Harnessing natural resources requires strong state intervention, yet at the same time the large rents involved tend to undermine governance. Similarly, the huge extent of the African landmass requires massive investment in transport infrastructure, yet the extreme political fragmentation considerably complicates the necessary decisions.

REFERENCES

Collier, Paul, 2010. *The Plundered Planet*. New York: Oxford University Press.
—— Gordon Conway, and Tony Venables, 2008. 'Climate change and Africa', *Oxford Review of Economic Policy* 24.2, 337–53.
—— and Stephen A. O'Connell, 2007. 'Opportunities and choices', in Benno J. Ndulu, Stephen A. O'Connell, Robert H. Bates, Paul Collier, and Charles C. Soludo (eds), *The Political Economy of Economic Growth in Africa, 1960–2000*, vol. 1. Cambridge: Cambridge University Press.
—— and Tony Venables, 2009. 'International rules for trade in natural resources'. Geneva: World Trade Organization.
—— and Jean-Louis Warnholz, 2009. 'Now's the time to invest in Africa: breakthrough ideas for 2009', *Harvard Business Review* (February).
Dasgupta, Partha, 2009. 'The place of nature in economic development', in Dani Rodrik and Mark Rosenzweig (eds), *Handbook of Development Economics*, vol. 5. Amsterdam: North-Holland.

African Development Prospects and Possibilities

Akbar Noman and Joseph E. Stiglitz

There are many interwoven dimensions to development, and on some counts Africa's performance has been better than on others. Particularly notable are the improvements in education and health (though the AIDS epidemic has reversed some of the gains). Perhaps, the most disappointing has been the growth record reflected in per capita incomes and poverty: per capita income is roughly the same as in 1970. Hence, Africa's prospects hinge on the answer to the overarching questions: why has the growth performance of Africa been so disappointing? And what are the possibilities and policies for Africa to achieve sustained, rapid growth, and associated structural transformations?[1]

The question is not, of course, as simple as posed above, because of the diversity of African countries and experiences that included the fastest-growing economy in the world during 1960–2000: Botswana; the success story of Mauritius and countries that have experienced fairly good growth (5+ %) over a decade or so, such as Mozambique, Ethiopia, Tanzania, Uganda, and Ghana. These successes, and those elsewhere (notably in East Asia) and the revival of average growth in Africa since the late 1990s (before the 2008 crisis), suggest that there are lessons to be learnt for policy design. A myriad of country-specific factors affect economic performance. In particular, failed/fragile states are not contexts that are amenable to the sort of analysis we undertake. Our concern is with the policy options and prospects for the many African states committed to development.

To put things in perspective, we recall that as Africa emerged from colonialism, Asia was the region in turmoil, with wars, revolutions, and uprisings. A widely held view contrasted Africa's promise with Asia's pitfalls.[2] Also, Africa averaged reasonable growth (5+ %) in the 1960s and 1970s. The ending of this trend in the late 1970s partly reflected adverse exogenous shocks: oil prices, global interest rates, and commodity prices. But they also exposed policy weaknesses: highly overvalued exchange rates, macroeconomic instability, irrational and extreme protection, unproductive or counterproductive rent

---

[1] To address this, the Initiative for Policy Dialogue (IPD) at Columbia University established a task force on Africa. One outcome is Noman et al. (forthcoming).
[2] The pessimism was shared by Nobel laureate Gunnar Myrdal (1968).

seeking, bloated bureaucracies/public sectors, and dysfunctional financial sectors became all too common. Frequently, extensive interventions were undertaken without regard for the capacity to design and implement them effectively.

The response was a set of reforms, often imposed as conditionalities, focused on liberalization and privatization that came to be known by the shorthand term 'Washington Consensus' (WC). To the extent that the Africa version of the WC served to highlight the aforementioned deficiencies and tilt the balance towards the market, it served a useful purpose. But it went too far in the other direction. Neither economic theory nor history provides a case for unfettered markets, even in advanced industrial countries. The results of many of the reforms in Africa were disappointing; for example, when government programmes were cut back, markets often did not arise to fill the gaps; when regulations were stripped back, market performance often did not improve in the ways predicted.

Exogenous vs endogenous growth

Six hypotheses have played a central role in the debate on Africa's performance and prospects. They pertain to (a) geography; (b) terms of trade; (c) the global 'policy' environment e.g. the rules governing trade and aid; (d) inadequate *implementation* of the WC reforms; (e) governance; (f) Africa's failure *because* it followed WC policies.

The first three hypotheses focus on exogenous determinants; the next two focus on aspects of African political economy that, in principle, are under its own control. The final one lays some of the blame for Africa's failure outside the region—on those who imposed WC policies—though ultimately countries are responsible for the policies they adopt. The fourth and sixth agree that policy matters, but differ on what constitutes appropriate policy. Both the advocates of WC and its critics agree that governance matters. But what aspects of governance are critical with what policy implications?

To what extent does geography explain low income as distinct from low growth? Geography may well be an important explanation of why some countries are poorer than others. There are many dimensions to geography, and in Africa much attention has been devoted to being landlocked, notwithstanding the fact there was no significant difference in the growth of landlocked and coastal African countries between 1961–2004. For most countries, transport costs are not so large that they cannot be addressed through appropriate policies and interventions. Their costs may lead to lower incomes. At worst, being landlocked means higher requirement for such investments for any given growth and/or wages, and land rents being lower than they otherwise would be. There is, though, no *a priori* reason that being landlocked should lower growth, especially once the 'adjustments' designed to overcome the barriers are made.[3] Indeed, changes in technology that reduce transport costs will differentially benefit geographically disadvantaged countries, so these might be expected to have faster than average growth. Geography is not destiny. The relevant question is: given their geography, what policies and institutions can best promote growth?

The prices of Africa's exports have been highly variable and correlated. Go and Page (2008: 2–3) address the issue of the extent to which the recent growth spurt can be attributed to terms of trade, arguing that, whilst export prices helped, 'growth acceleration...is due not only to favorable terms of trade and greater aid, but also to better policy...Nonetheless, the sustainability of that growth is fragile, because economic fundamentals, such as savings, investment, productivity, and export diversification remain stagnant.'[4]

The third important external factor for Africa is the quality and quantity of aid. Initiatives like the Paris and Accra declarations and the Commission for Africa contain promising proposals for enhancing aid effectiveness, but implementation remains inadequate. Part of Africa's poor performance is a result of low and stagnating agricultural productivity—with important implications for growth and poverty, since so many of the poor depend on agriculture. This is being addressed by a number of initiatives pertaining to an African green revolution and recognition of the need to reverse underinvestment in agriculture, notably in irrigation. But agriculture's problems are being exacerbated by climate change. An adequate response will require considerable financial and technological assistance.

Africa's prospects also depend on trade negotiations: the current Doha round might adversely affect Africa,[5] while effective enforcement of recent WTO rulings on cotton would bring significant benefits. A successful conclusion to a truly development-oriented round of trade negotiations would be of enormous benefit, but prospects for such an agreement appear dim. A sustained recovery from the current global financial crisis clearly also has an important bearing on Africa's prospects.

POLICY: WASHINGTON CONSENSUS OR NOT?

Underlying the Washington Consensus controversy in Africa is a difference in views about what is critical to economic success. One view sees the essence of development as a transformation of the economy and society (Stiglitz 1998), and emphasizes

---

[3] See Noman et al. (forthcoming).
[4] A more detailed appraisal of this analysis is found in ibid.
[5] Appraisals of the impact of the Doha Round generally show losses for Africa, other than South Africa. See Polaski (2006).

improvements in productivity and how these can best be brought about. The other view focuses on economic efficiency, narrowly defined: ensuring that the economy operates on the production possibilities curve. Those who focus on the first view note that what separates developed and developing countries is not only a gap in resources but a gap in knowledge, and some economic structures are more conducive to reducing that gap (Greenwald and Stiglitz 2006). WC reforms encouraging a focus on activities that reflected static comparative advantages were, from this point of view, counterproductive.

The result was lack of economic diversification and stagnation. The share of manufacturing has been generally declining since 1980 (as has employment in the formal sector). Relatedly, there has been little success in exporting manufactures or in attracting foreign direct investment in non-extractive industries. Much of the growth of the past decade is accounted for by extractive activities in non-renewable resources—metals, minerals, above all oil. Whilst it is difficult to measure learning and technology acquisition directly, these trends suggest there has been little of that.[6]

Africa's economic revival before the 2008 crisis reflects favourable exogenous factors, but also 'better' policies (e.g. avoiding markedly overvalued exchange rates and large macroeconomic imbalances). However, that leaves several relevant policy questions. These revolve around the scope for improving (a) policies, informed by the lessons of success (especially in promoting economic structures conducive to 'developmental transformation' and 'learning'); and (b) governance. We argue that the whilst WC policies may have diminished distortions, they may also have undermined the ability to achieve sustained growth; and that, correspondingly, the governance agenda has not been successful in strengthening governance capacities that enhance long term growth.

Governance and growth: towards an African developmentalist state

Perhaps disappointment with WC policies contributed to a focus on governance as the critical problem. On this view, governance problems make the kinds of policies that led to success in East Asia unlikely to work in Africa. Indeed, they may be counterproductive. The alternative view notes that at the time that East Asia employed its interventions, its governance was far from perfect. More generally, governance itself should be viewed as 'endogenous': it is affected by other variables, including the level of income. Poor countries are more likely to pay low wages to their officials, making them more prone to

---

[6] Total factor productivity could be used in principle, but in practice is fraught with serious data problems and sensitive to the specification of the production function. It is unlikely that reasonably reliable estimates can be made in most African countries (indeed, in any of them).

corruption. And the high level of corruption prevents African governments from intervening effectively in the ways in which highly successful countries have done. The result is a vicious circle—low income leads to poor governance, which sustains low incomes.

One obvious prescription is to limit the role of government—particularly appealing to the WC perspective—in the extreme version of which only a limited set of institutions are important: those necessary for the functioning of markets, i.e. enforcement of contracts and property rights.

Corruption is, of course, bad. Reducing corruption should facilitate and in turn be an outcome of development. But the *elimination* of corruption is neither necessary nor sufficient for development. Moreover, this 'good governance' agenda may not be feasible, especially at an early stage of development. No country has ever implemented the current 'good governance' agenda before embarking on development—neither the now developed countries nor the rapidly 'catching up' countries of Asia. The question is what kinds of 'policies' reduce the scope for corruption, and their incidental effects on development.

There is a conflict between this 'good governance' agenda and what Mushtaq Khan argues should be the agenda from a developmental perspective: what he calls 'growth-enhancing governance'.[7] Successful development requires reforms focused on such governance, and on what Mkandawire calls 'transformative' rather than 'restraining' institutions. Restraining government actions may reduce the scope for corruption, but may also reduce the scope for undertaking growth-enhancing activities.

This alternative approach to governance reform focuses on a small number of measures at each stage directed at improving the governance capabilities required for dealing with the critical market failures holding back growth in a specific context. The pursuit of overly ambitious and complex governance agendas risks making the pursuit of the best an enemy of the good (see Norman et al. forthcoming).

While governance is important, it is not everything, e.g. Sen and te Velde find that 'effective state-business relations...may have a stronger impact on economic growth in Sub-Saharan Africa than the conventional measures of governance'.[8]

And the issue is not rent seeking *per se*—in all societies there is rent seeking. The question is whether it can be put to good use. Nor is being a developmental state or not a binary choice: there is a continuum. The fully-fledged developmental states of Korea and Taiwan did not emerge out of nowhere in a complete form—indeed, Korea in the 1950s was described as a highly dysfunctional and corrupt polity. Countries such as Indonesia, Malaysia, and Thailand did not have as developmental a state as Korea or Taiwan, but

---

[7] See Mushtaq Khan's and Thandika Mkandawire's contributions to the Africa task force in Noman et al. (forthcoming).

[8] Sen and te Velde in Noman et al. (forthcoming).

did succeed with a wide range of interventions. Japan, China and Vietnam—countries with different histories and circumstances—succeeded in different ways, and to varying degrees. This was true also for the 'developmentalism' of South Asia: India, Pakistan, and Bangladesh have achieved considerable successes with interventions, notably including the spread of the 'green revolution'. Latin America also provides many examples, especially Brazil and Chile.

The right questions to focus on are: what sort of state is able to intervene and in what manner? What are the critical requirements of governance and how to go about acquiring them? How can the risks of government failure be mitigated—failures that might make matters worse than market failures? How can countries ensure that they do not repeat the errors of failed statism of the past?

Learning, industrial, and technology policies

Africa is not short of countries that already have (or are able to acquire) the needed governance to undertake a more active role in promoting development. One of the key areas central to the success of the developmental state is learning, industrial, and technology (LIT) policies. The desirability of such policies can be approached from several perspectives.

The theoretical perspective focuses on the reasons that markets, by themselves, are not likely to produce sufficient growth-enhancing investments, such as those associated with learning, knowledge accumulation, and research.[9] Externalities in learning and discovery would support an infant economy/infant industry argument for government intervention (see e.g. Greenwald and Stiglitz 2006). So do capital market imperfections that impede development. But the issues of learning have received scant attention, in marked contrast to those of resource allocation. What we mean by LIT policies are those focused on issues of learning, of infant industries and economies, of promoting exports and the private sector, not only in manufacturing but also in agriculture and in services like information technology or finance.

The orthodoxy has been particularly hostile to LIT policies. Whilst there is much to be said for doing away with irrational, highly distorted structures of protection, LIT polices can be very effective. All countries that have achieved substantial development have used some variant of LIT policies, not just East Asian countries (see e.g. Chang 2002). Indeed,

---

[9] The importance of 'discovery' had been emphasized by Hoff (1997) and by Rodrik and Hausmann (2003). The problem of 'discovery' of entrepreneurs is emphasized by Emran and Stiglitz (2007).

the green revolution in South Asia could be said to be a prime example of LIT policy. In Africa too, there were examples of accomplishments with LIT policies—for example, leather and flower exports in Ethiopia, tea in Kenya, manufactured exports in Mauritius. There have also been many failures, but failure is by no means a unique or even distinctive feature of LIT policies. Poor design, implementation, and 'capture' can trump policy in any area. There have also been, for example, many failed programmes pertaining to stabilization, agriculture, and finance. That does not mean we give up on macroeconomic stability or improvements in agricultural productivity and in finance. The point is to learn lessons of both successes and failures in elaborating policy options, and to examine how the risk:reward ratio can be improved.

Some LIT policies have been criticized because they give rise to rent seeking. But neo-liberal reforms, especially privatizations and concessions, also give rise to rents. The issue is not whether or not there are rents but how those rents are used or what activities they encourage, and the design of institutional arrangements to minimize agency costs. Markets are not 'technology-friendly' (entrepreneurs seldom capture more than a fraction of the marginal contributions), and rents are essential for the acquisition or development of technology. Questions are often raised about the ability of governments to do a better job than the private sector in picking winners; but this way of putting the argument misses the point: the reason for government involvement is because of the externalities and/or other market failures. The diversity of circumstances and LIT policies in East Asia testifies that there is no one-size-fits-all LIT policy: a large part of the East Asian lesson is the pragmatic and flexible method of policy formulation rather than specific measures. In Africa, the potential for LIT policies to get around the 'resource curse'[10] and the associated excessive dependence on commodities can be particularly important. As can their impact on agriculture, which is vital not only for growth but also for making that growth pro-poor.

The past four decades have witnessed a revolution in developmental thinking. Rapid robust growth is possible, even in a region—Asia—in which prospects at the beginning of the period appeared bleak. Before the influence of neo-liberal policies, there had been similar successes in other parts of the world: Brazil had grown at an annual rate of close to 6% for three quarters of a century.

A brief examination of Africa's history shows that both external circumstances and policies matter. Africa has shown in the past that it could experience strong growth. The sort of policy reforms we sketch above, combined with a reasonably favourable external environment, could provide a basis for promising prospects for Africa.

---

[10] There is, of course, far more to ensuring that an endowment of resources become the blessing that they should be. See Humphreys, Sachs, and Stiglitz (2007).

REFERENCES

Chang, Ha-Joon, 2002. *Kicking Away the Ladder: Development Strategy in Historical Perspective*. London: Anthem Press.

Emran, Shahe, and J. E. Stiglitz, 2007. 'Financial liberalization, financial restraint, and entrepreneurial development'; www.josephstiglitz.com.

Go, Delfin, and John Page (eds), 2008. *Africa at a Turning Point?* Washington, DC: World Bank.

Greenwald, Bruce, and J. E. Stiglitz, 2006. 'Helping infant economies grow: foundations of trade policies for developing countries', *American Economic Review* 96.2, 141–6.

Hoff, Karla, 1997. 'Bayesian learning in an infant industry model', *Journal of International Economics* 43, 409–36.

Humphreys, M., J. Sachs, and J. E. Stiglitz (eds), 2007. *Escaping the Resource Curse*. New York: Columbia University Press.

Myrdal, Gunnar, 1968. *Asian Drama*. New York: Twentieth Century Fund.

Noman, Akbar, Kwesi Botchwey, Joseph Stiglitz, and Howard Stein (eds), forthcoming. *Good Growth and Governance in Africa: Rethinking Development Strategies*. Oxford: Oxford University Press.

Polaski, Sandra, 2006. *Winners and Losers: Impact of the Doha Round on Developing Countries*. Washington, DC: Carnegie.

Rodrik, Dani, and Ricardo Hausmann, 2003. 'Economic development as self-discovery', *Journal of Development Economics* 72.2, 603–33.

Stiglitz, J. E., 1998. 'Towards a new paradigm for development: strategies, policies and processes', 9th Raul Prebisch Lecture, UNCTAD. Repr. in Ha-Joon Chang (ed.), *The Rebel Within* (London: Wimbledon Publishing, 2001), ch. 2.

—— forthcoming. 'Development-oriented tax policy', in R. Gordon (ed.), *Tax Policies for Developing Countries*. Oxford: Oxford University Press.

Risk and Vulnerability in Africa

Stefan Dercon

Risk is pervasive in Africa. It affects people's welfare, and it shapes their livelihoods. It affects firms and households in their economic decisions, contributing to the persistence of poverty. Much research on risk and its consequences has been published in the last 15 years, and there are plenty of reviews of this literature, with increasingly more attention to Africa. Examples are Morduch (1995), Townsend (1995), or Dercon (2002).

The nature of risk

Risk can be defined as being external to individuals: examples are climatic, health, or price risk. A first key question is how risky life is in an African context. This is hard to quantify in general. For some types of risks, such as climatic risk, data are increasingly available, from improved local meteorological data as well as from satellite data. For other sources of risks, such as those related to pests, health, animal health, and mortality or crime, data are not systematically available. To measure risks, the most straightforward way is to focus on the realizations of risk, in particular the study of the shocks and events that affect them. Household surveys have increasingly included simple questions related to the events and shocks that have affected households' living standards in the recent past. In most rural settings, weather-related shocks still dominate. In a study from 2004 in rural Ethiopia (Dercon, Hoddinott, and Woldehanna 2005), close to half the respondents reported that drought has affected them in the last five years.

Mortality of adults in the household is also commonly mentioned as a key shock. In the same study, more than 40% reported such an event to have seriously affected the households' living conditions. In areas with more secure rainfall, weather conditions don't necessarily dominate; illness and mortality are the most important shocks. For example, De Weerdt and Dercon (2006) find 30% of households reporting a death in the household with serious consequences in a 10-year period in a coffee and banana growing area of Tanzania, and 48% reporting illness causing similarly serious hardship. In the Ethiopian study, illness and mortality also feature high on the list for the period 1999–2004, with 43% reporting a mortality episode of an adult and 28% reporting illness related problems.

While these are the main types of risks faced, a multitude of other shocks and events are reported, such as those related to input or output prices and market conditions (15% reported this in Ethiopia for a five-year period, and 25% in Tanzania for a ten-year period). Other important risks appear to relate to institutions: crime features highly (23% of households reporting this in Tanzania and 13% in Ethiopia); Ethiopian households also reported further shocks linked to the extractive actions by state institutions, such as arbitrary taxation and forced contributions, or issues related to land redistribution (8%).

The frequency of reported events is strongly suggestive of the types of risks faced by households, not least in rural settings. It shows that households are facing both covariate and idiosyncratic shocks: the former are shocks that are common to all or to a large proportion of a community, while the latter are typically suffered by relatively few people in a community at the same time. In terms of studies of the consequences of risks, most attention has been directed to climatic shocks, the most common covariate shock, as well as the consequences of adult mortality and illness on the household (typically an idiosyncratic shock). Least attention has been paid to the impact of risk related to institutions, partly because these risks may be harder to capture (see Dercon 2008 for a discussion). In any case, it is an important avenue for further work.

The consequences of risk

In economic analysis, although individuals may take risk as given, they do not behave passively. As most risks may affect them considerably, individuals have incentives to actively respond to these risks. They can try to reduce the risks themselves, they can manage their exposure, or they can reduce their impact. These three responses can be referred to as risk reduction, risk management, and risk coping strategies. Examples of risk reduction are preventative measures, such as getting children vaccinated to reduce health risks, or building irrigation canals to reduce drought risks. Risk coping responses take place after a shock has occurred, and examples are selling off livestock to smooth consumption, or relying on informal transfers from neighbours or relatives. Risk management strategies take place before a shock has occurred, and can be seen as part of a continuum starting with risk reduction. The risk itself may not be easily reduced, but a household can change its activities or asset and investment portfolio to change its exposure to risk. Activity or asset diversification—exploiting the benefits from pooling imperfectly correlated risks—is one such response; moving into low-risk activities is another. Examples of diversification can be seen across farming systems in Africa, as farmers tend to grow multiple crops; urban households similarly often engage in multiple activities combining casual wage labour, town garden agriculture, and petty trade. For all these cases, risk may be one of the motivations for such behaviour, although it can easily be modelled as consistent with maximizing profits when input or output markets are imperfect, making its assessment an area for further empirical analysis.

How effective are these risk strategies? The vast majority of academic papers published on risk in poor settings have focused on examining whether in the face of shocks, households manage to keep their consumption or nutrition smooth, focusing largely on coping mechanisms such as depletion of assets, and risk-sharing via informal arrangements. Using nationally representative survey data for 1985–6 for Côte d'Ivoire, Deaton (1997) showed that idiosyncratic shocks dominate when decomposing incomes into idiosyncratic and covariate parts, but that consumption is not affected by these idiosyncratic shocks, suggesting effective coping mechanisms. The same is not necessarily true for covariate shocks. In a study in Nigeria, Udry (1994) found that informal insurance arrangements linked to credit arrangements offered some imperfect risk sharing when faced with shocks. Kazianga and Udry (2006) find imperfect consumption smoothing in Burkina Faso during a period of drought in the early 1980s in Burkina Faso. Analysis of various rounds of the Ethiopian Rural Household Survey (Dercon 2004; 2006; Dercon et al. 2005) showed considerable sensitivity of consumption to rainfall and drought conditions, consistent with imperfect smoothing, although less systematic evidence that illness or mortality shocks affected consumption. Dercon and Krishnan (2000) showed nevertheless that in the southern villages in the same study, female adults were affected by idiosyncratic shocks, consistent with imperfect risk sharing within the household in that area, but no such effects were found in the northern and central highlands of the country. De Weerdt and Dercon (2006) showed imperfect risk sharing related to consumption when faced with health shocks in Kagera, Tanzania. Using a large panel for the same area, World Bank (1999) showed that consumption was kept smooth in the face of prime-age adult mortality shocks, in an area with high HIV-AIDS infection; using a long-term panel from the same data set, Beegle, De Weerdt, and Dercon (2008) showed sensitivity of consumption to adult mortality shocks, but much larger impacts of agricultural shocks.

Households attempt to limit the consequences of shocks on their consumption and nutrition via risk coping strategies, and to some extent they are successful. It would appear that in quite a few settings, idiosyncratic risk may be insured against to some extent by existing coping mechanisms, including informal support networks among neighbours or relatives. However, imperfectly smooth consumption is the outcome: shocks have real consequences. Dercon (2006) offered a simple calculation of how high poverty would have been if all shocks had been effectively 'insured' via safety nets or forms of insurance. He finds that the headcount poverty rate in this sample from rural Ethiopia, based on the consumption data and using the national poverty line, would have been about 33% if the drought shocks had been 'insured', compared to actual measured poverty of 47% in the same sample; if all shocks had been insured, poverty would have stood at 29%.

THE LONG-RUN COST OF RISK

Despite the high implied estimate of the poverty cost of uninsured risks, it is likely to be an underestimate. The reason is that this estimate would not take into account any costs in terms of earnings forgone by households as they spent on risk reduction and management. For example, they may have moved into low-risk activities to reduce their exposure to risk, or invested in lower-return assets if they offered more safety than more risky high-return investments. There is evidence that households in Tanzania and other settings get involved in low-risk crops, such as cassava and sweet potatoes, even though far less income can be earned with these crops compared to the local more risky alternatives, such as cotton or maize (Dercon 1996). Dercon and Christiaensen (2007) found that households in Ethiopia with less protection against downside risk invested less in fertilizer for their cereal production, as this expenditure would be lost if the harvest were to fail, even though on average using fertilizer is a highly profitable activity. The overall result is that we may observe less income risk, but that this would come at the cost of lower income on average. Households may have to choose to be poorer simply to avoid even more disastrous outcomes if they were to engage in more risky activities, despite their higher return. This is not simply because some prefer less risk (risk aversion) but especially because they do not have insurance or other means of protecting themselves if shocks were to occur. The focus on shocks and its poverty costs is misleading for another reason: as not everyone experiences these shocks all the time, a crucial consideration is whether after a disastrous event households manage to recover or whether there are long-term impacts. When shocks occur, households may have to rely on selling assets to smooth their nutrition and consumption, affecting their future earnings potential, and possibly leading to particular downward spirals of impoverishment, often referred to as poverty traps (see Barrett and Swallow 2006). Furthermore, while adults are remarkably resilient to periods of poor nutrition so that they may only suffer limited permanent damage from periods of serious malnutrition, children are known to suffer serious permanent damage to health and cognitive ability when experiencing malnutrition especially in utero or in early childhood (see Strauss and Thomas 2007 for a useful review).

In a study of the 1984–5 famine in Ethiopia, Dercon (2004) found that growth in consumption in 1990s was considerably lower for those who had suffered in the famine compared to those who had not. He also found persistent impacts of other drought shocks well beyond the initial years in which they struck; similar effects were found by Dercon et al. (2005) in relation to the 2001–2 drought. Beegle et al. (2008) found that in

Kagera, Tanzania, agricultural shocks had impacts on consumption even though they had occurred up to ten years earlier. Lybbert et al. (2004) found that livestock dynamics in pastoral areas of Kenya showed the downward spiral: a serious shock could push farmers from relatively high herd sizes to a much lower equilibrium consistent with a poverty trap.

These and other findings reveal important evidence on the long-term impact on children from shocks, especially in crucial periods of early childhood. In the Kagera study, death of an adult in the household had an effect on household consumption of the remaining members, but this was not persistent after its initial impact. Beegle, De Weerdt, and Dercon (2009) found nevertheless that those orphaned by an adult death during childhood experienced long-term consequences in the form of lower educational attainment (by about 20%, or one year) and lower height (by about 2 cm) than those who did not experience such events. Alderman, Hoddinott, and Kinsey (2006) explored the impact of the civil war and drought during the period 1982–4 in Zimbabwe, and the way it affected children of the critical age for nutrition (during their transition to solid foods). They found that at adulthood, these children were shorter by 2.2 cm and their school attainment was 0.7 years lower due to the drought. Dercon and Porter (2009) similarly found that children around 12–36 months during this famine and surviving still suffered long-term consequences, as their height at adulthood was about 2.3 cm lower than comparison groups born earlier or later.

Those faced with high risk, and/or with limited access to risk reduction, management or coping mechanisms, or other means of protecting themselves against risk, can be considered to face high vulnerability to poverty. Vulnerability to poverty can be defined as the extent of the threat of falling into poverty. A number of studies have tried to quantify vulnerability in Africa (Christiaensen and Subbarao 2005 for Kenya, and Calvo and Dercon 2007 for Ethiopia). They show that those facing a threat of poverty are not necessarily the same as those identified as poor by poverty profiles. For example, Calvo and Dercon (2007) show that certain communities with permanent crops such as q'at and coffee were typically not very poor, but had relatively high vulnerability to poverty given the underlying riskiness in circumstances.

The evidence quoted above offers some important pointers to who is most vulnerable, and the types of risk that may require special attention. In those areas in which agriculture is strongly dependent on rainfall and climate in general, those without protection against climatic shocks are highly vulnerable. The evidence also suggests that this may be the case because these shocks are covariate, and therefore harder to protect against using risk coping mechanisms such as savings or informal support; in contrast, there is in most instances relatively little evidence for the high impacts of idiosyncratic shocks, especially in the long term. The key exception appears to be children, especially in early childhood: any shock to nutrition is likely to have permanent impacts.

Policy responses

The standard policy response to shocks, especially when they are covariate such as a drought, is to introduce some form of safety net. This may well be the most appropriate response to reach some of the poorest sections of society, but it is by no means the only response that should be considered. Household risk coping mechanisms mostly tend to rely on savings, informal credit, and informal mutual support arrangements. Strengthening these responses, via careful microfinance interventions, may be more efficient. However, it will require microfinance interventions to move beyond the standard models of credit provision focused on asset formation or entry into particular activities (Armendariz and Morduch 2005). Microsavings and micro-insurance are still relatively rare activities. The evidence of their success or failure in the African context is still rather limited, and definitely an area for further research. Finally, in designing policy responses, it should never be forgotten why the welfare of the poor, especially in rural areas and the informal urban economy, is so precarious. One reason is that current livelihoods are typically based on self-employment, with high dependence on the variability of climate and markets. In richer economies, vulnerability has been partly reduced by the development of social insurance systems. But another contributing factor has been economic growth and the transformation of the economy, so that many of the poor have become absorbed in wage paying, relatively secure occupations. In short, growth and economic transformation may well prove the most important mechanism to reduce the current vulnerability of vast numbers of African households.

REFERENCES

Alderman, H., J. Hoddinott, and W. Kinsey, 2006. 'Long-term consequences of early childhood malnutrition', *Oxford Economic Papers* 58.3, 450–74.
Armendariz de Aghion, B., and J. Morduch, 2005. *The Economics of Microfinance*. Cambridge, Mass.: MIT Press.
Barrett, C. B., and B. M. Swallow, 2006. 'Fractal poverty traps', *World Development* 34, 1–15.
Beegle, K., J. De Weerdt, and S. Dercon, 2008. 'Adult mortality and consumption growth in the age of HIV/AIDS', *Economic Development and Cultural Change* 56, 299–326.
—————— 2009. 'The intergenerational impact of the African orphans crisis: a cohort study from an HIV/AIDS affected area', *International Journal of Epidemiology* 38.2, 561–8.
Calvo, C., and S. Dercon, 2007. 'Vulnerability of poverty', CSAE Working Paper Series WPS 2007-03, Centre for the Study of African Economies, Oxford University.

Christiaensen, L., and K. Subbarao, 2005. 'Towards an understanding of household vulnerability in rural Kenya', *Journal of African Economies* 14.4, 520–58.

Deaton, A., 1997. *The Analysis of Household Surveys: A Microeconometric Approach to Development Policy*. Baltimore: Johns Hopkins University Press/World Bank.

Dercon, S., 1996. 'Risk, crop choice, and savings: evidence from Tanzania', *Economic Development and Cultural Change* 44, 485–513.

—— 2002. 'Income risk, coping strategies and safety nets', *World Bank Research Observer* 17, 141–66.

—— 2004. 'Growth and shocks: evidence from rural Ethiopia', *Journal of Development Economics* (August).

—— 2006. 'Economic reform, growth and the poor: evidence from rural Ethiopia', *Journal of Development Economics* 81.1, 1–24.

—— 2008. 'Fate and fear: risk and its consequences in Africa', *Journal of African Economies* 17 (Supplement 2), 2.97–127.

—— and L. Christiaensen, 2007. 'Consumption risk, technology adoption and poverty traps: evidence from Ethiopia', WPS/2007-06, Oxford: Centre for the Study of African Economies.

—— J. Hoddinott, and T. Woldehanna, 2005. 'Vulnerability and shocks in 15 Ethiopian Villages, 1999–2004', *Journal of African Economies* 14.4, 559–85.

—— and P. Krishnan, 2000. 'In sickness and in health: risk-sharing within households in Ethiopia', *Journal of Political Economy* 108.4, 688–727.

—— and C. Porter, 2009. 'The long-run impact of severe shocks in childhood: evidence from the Ethiopian famine of 1984', mimeo, Oxford University.

De Weerdt, J., and S. Dercon, 2006. 'Risk-sharing networks and insurance against illness', *Journal of Development Economics* 81.2, 337–56.

Kazianga, H., and C. Udry, 2006. 'Consumption smoothing? Livestock, insurance and drought in rural Burkina Faso', *Journal of Development Economics* 79.2, 413–46.

Lybbert, J., C. B. Barrett, S. Desta, and D. L. Coppock, 2004. 'Stochastic wealth dynamics and risk management among a poor population', *Economic Journal* 114, 750–77.

Morduch, J., 1995. 'Income smoothing and consumption smoothing', *Journal of Economic Perspectives* 9, 103–14.

Strauss, J., and D. Thomas, 2007. 'Health over the life course', in T. P. Schultz and J. A. Strauss (eds), *Handbook of Development Economics*, vol. 4. Amsterdam: Elsevier, 3375–3474.

Townsend, R. M., 1995. 'Consumption insurance: an evaluation of risk-bearing systems in low-income economies', *Journal of Economic Perspectives* 9, 83–102.

Udry, C., 1994. 'Risk and insurance in a rural credit market: an empirical investigation of northern Nigeria', *Review of Economic Studies* 61.3, 495–526.

World Bank, 1993. 'Report of a workshop on the economic impact of fatal illness in sub-Saharan Africa', Washington, DC, and the University of Dar es Salaam: World Bank.

—— 1999. *Tanzania: Social Sector Review*. Washington, DC: World Bank.

The Sustainability of Africa's Growth Acceleration

Michael Spence

In 2008, the Commission on Growth and Development published its report, *The Growth Report: Strategies for Sustained Growth and Inclusive Development*. That report identified a number of ingredients in all the known recipes for sustained high growth in the postwar period. They included:

- openness to the global economy to access its knowledge and technology in order to increase potential output quickly;
- use of global demand to remove constraints on growth, specialization, and the exploitation of comparative advantage;
- high levels of public investment to raise the returns to and elevate private investment (domestic and foreign);
- substantial domestic financing of investment via high savings;
- commitment of public resources to infrastructure and education with an emphasis on effectiveness and outputs;
- long time horizon and governance consistent with the pursuit of long-term growth in opportunities for all citizens;
- a focus on inclusiveness with attention to equity and to protecting people in transitions in an economy that is evolving structurally;
- use of and non-interference in market incentives and dynamics market process of entry and exit, to allow the structural change and productivity growth to occur;
- effective management of natural resource wealth in countries in which this is an important asset.

A large number of African countries in the past decade have been moving steadily toward alignment with this general configuration, facing and effectively addressing challenges and deficits on both the economic and political sides of the ledger. The evidence of progress is a rising level of growth on the continent over the past decade and a reasonably resilient response to the externally generated crisis in the global economy and financial systems.

There always remain challenges in all developing countries, and this applies to those in Africa as well. In many ways, success creates the next round of challenges and the binding constraints shift. Education remains an major issue that affects growth and inclusiveness. Trained teachers are in short supply, and as a result there are issues with the output of cognitive skills. Public investment levels still fall below the *Growth Report* guideline of 5–7% of GDP, and there are issues with the effective management and targeting of infrastructure investment, some of which requires regional coordination. Effective management of the complex, multi-step process of turning natural resource wealth into the basis for sustained growth, economic diversification, and structural change is still not at the level needed. But on all fronts there is progress.

External assistance to many African countries should focus on these key challenges. The most important is keeping the global economy open in a difficult lower growth environment (with high unemployment in advanced countries) where the incentives for protectionist measures are elevated. Second, other countries further along the income spectrum, advanced and developing, could make a major contribution in the area of education with large-scale teacher-training programmes. Third, the major development banks should be well capitalized, and should focus substantial effort and resources on providing financing and technical assistance in the area of infrastructure.

Many African countries are small. The goal of fairly rapidly creating expertise in a wide range of aspects of economic management (macro, public investment, natural resource management) may be unrealistically ambitious. Alternatives in which the expertise is developed in trusted multinational institutions and shared may be more effective, and exploring that option in a number of areas should be a priority. This effort could and should be led and supported by the major African economies that have the capacity to build the requisite multi-dimensional expertise, and by the African Development Bank.

Large countries have huge advantages in growth and development. The potential domestic market is large, and hence the potential dependence on external markets somewhat less. Large countries benefit from significant scale economies in governance institutions. Talent pools are larger (just because of the numbers), and that gets reflected in the speed of buildup of effective management on the public and private sector side. Retaining talent is easier and the net human capital flows are less adverse. Perhaps most importantly, external investors including MNCs are attracted in part by supply chain opportunities but also by the large potential future domestic market and the desire to benefit from an early start.

Africa's population numbers over a billion people, in 53 countries (including northern Africa). To develop effectively, African countries need to follow the European model and begin a long journey toward market and economic integration.

The 2008–9 crisis was a setback for every country in the world. Africa, like most of the developing countries, has rebounded very well. In the developing world, balance sheet damage in the household, financial, and public sectors was much less than in the industrialized countries. Restoring and sustaining growth will face both headwinds and tailwinds.

In the latter category is the remarkable restoration of growth in the major emerging economies. The restoration of growth in Asia and Latin America is a major positive. I have argued elsewhere that this growth is probably sustainable even in an environment of slow recovery and extended depressed growth in the advanced economies. In addition, major parts of China are entering the middle income transition which involves a structural shift in the economy away from the labour-intensive process manufacturing industries in the export sector. This will not happen overnight, but as it does, the space created for countries at earlier stages of development will be enormous, because of China's size and share in these industries.

External investment levels are rising, and interest in the investment opportunities in much of Africa is growing in parallel. The major emerging economies, China prominently but also India and some of the Middle Eastern countries, are becoming large investors in Africa. Some of this investment is motivated by a desire to secure access to natural resources to meet a rising level of emerging market demand. Their investment model increasingly involves bundling access to natural resources with things like infrastructure construction. Also bundled into the packages are normal private sector incentives and some public participation in the form either of direct aid or of risk sharing or risk mitigation. This is a new and somewhat experimental model of investment and development assistance.

It makes the industrialized countries and the IFIs uncomfortable. The traditional Western view is based on a sharp division of roles between the public and private sectors in the advanced economies. In the Western model, private-sector entities with profit objectives bid competitively for extraction rights. In the new model, the sharp division between private-sector incentives on the one hand and domestic and international state objectives on the other is not there.

African countries will be urged to stay with the industrialized countries' approach. I would advise them to reject this advice. To be sure, making contracts that are in the long-term interests of the country is important. Competition among bidders is an important tool in achieving that objective. But the new bidders may present more persuasive cases in part because they are trying to align the interests of the various parties (state and private sector) with fewer constraints imposed by the model.

One might argue that such an approach precludes competitive bidding. That is probably not right. There is nothing to prevent Western governments and development banks from participating in the bidding process in partnership with private-sector entities, bundling aid and technical competence and support with the resource rights. They will be reluctant to do that, but if the alternative proposals meet compelling needs in Africa countries, that may force the issue.

Getting this right in a pragmatic way will have a potentially major impact on the pace of development in Africa.

Inclusiveness is a deeply embedded and critically important aspect of successful growth strategies. While it has many dimensions, in pragmatic terms inclusiveness is most centrally about the rapid creation of productive employment to which all working-age people and families have access. African countries continue to face major obstacles in this dimension, in part the legacy of a colonial past. The most commonly cited factors that affect inclusive access to employment are on the supply side: literacy, education, experience. These are important. But there are others.

In many countries the labour market structure laws and the political economy create and sustain a dual labour market structure, the effect of which is to block access to global market supply chains for many citizens. To deliver on inclusiveness, these structures have to be modified to remove that blockage. Unions and their political allies will resist this for understandable reasons. The supply of potential competition on the labour supply side is large, and will be perceived as a threat as long as the labour supply–demand balance tips toward excess supply. But it is a battle worth fighting, because these structures impede the flow of surplus labour in traditional sectors like agriculture, into the export sector. It was the Nobel laureate Sir Arthur Lewis who understood and explained the large growth potential of drawing surplus labour into the modern and globally connected part of the economy. With barriers to mobility, including man-made ones, this growth engine stops working. The alternative to addressing these mobility issues effectively is a dual economy with rising social tensions, which will have their own destructive effect.

The answers to these structural challenges in labour markets probably do not lie in the direction of a direct challenge to the incomes and institutions in the formal labour market sector. Rather, what is needed is access to employment with MNCs and hence to global supply chains, outside the formal labour market structures. This means that MNCs would not be required to operate only in the formal sector as presently configured. An alternative is subsidizing wages so as to reduce the threat of downward pressure on formal sector wages. That has the cost of slowing the rate of growth of the export sector, but may be needed in a transition.

To summarize briefly, African countries are increasingly aligned in terms of governance, policy, and strategy with guidelines that characterize the known cases of sustained high growth. Engagement with the global economy and the high-speed learning process that goes with it is expanding but is not fully developed across sectors. Governance is improving in intention, leadership, and effectiveness. There are opportunities and challenges in the management of natural resource wealth. A Natural Resource Charter is in development to provide guidelines for the management of resource wealth in support of a sustainable pattern of growth. One hopes that it will have an impact.

Public-sector investment needs to increase in magnitude and efficiency to support the resumption of the growth acceleration in the post-crisis world. Trade with major emerging markets will be a key driver of growth in the next decade, and deserves to be a priority.

Finally, the continent needs to make further progress in exploiting its overall size to overcome the challenges of smallness at the national level. In doing this, it will benefit from further integration of markets, supporting infrastructure, and sharing of expertise in policy formation and implementation.

From today's vantage point, there is every reason to be optimistic that the remaining challenges will be met, and that the growth acceleration that has been under way for a decade will indeed be the beginning of a sustained period of breakout growth and poverty reduction.

Regionalism and African Development

Dominique Njinkeu

1. Introduction

Countries that have grown strongly for sustained periods have done so while properly connected to the global economy through international trade. The most successful countries also consistently diversified exports with respect both to their destination and to their composition. Such diversification protected them against negative external shocks. African export is dominated by natural resources or primary commodities that are sold in the same limited number of markets where they enjoy preferential access. As a result, African countries have failed to consistently expand their trade and generate the level of per capita economic growth that would lead to overall welfare improvement.

The mindset of African trade officials has slowly been shifting towards more appreciation of the benefits of open trade regimes. Success stories are increasing reported and praised (see World Bank 2010). With the onset of the economic crisis, collectively the G20 committed itself to pursuing liberal trade policies by not raising new barriers to investment or to trade in goods and services. It also agreed to refrain from including in its stimulus packages new export restrictions, or WTO inconsistent measures. Although overall it has have kept these commitments, from mid-2008 new trade restrictions were selectively introduced on a range of products (see Gregory et al. 2010). The unfortunate side effect for African industrialization has been an increase in calls for active trade policymaking, including because some of these WTO consistent policies are not available to African policymakers. The current crisis could shift the debate on the continent, reversing several years of improved policymaking; this would be unfortunate. This note argues that African countries should stay the course by pursuing and deepening their reform programmes in such a manner as to secure their smooth integration in the multilateral trading system. This could be done by pursuing an open regionalism agenda combined with a properly designed and delivered aid-for-trade programme to support African industrialization. The process would bring together governments, the donor community, and private sectors working as partners in development.

2. Looking at the global economy through regional lenses

There is a consensus among African trade officials and observers that intraregional trade should be liberalized. Implementation of common policies in the subregional context increases market size, reduces transactions costs, and increases economic efficiency. The subregional setting provides opportunities for mobilizing the human and financial resources necessary to undertake investments that can have a lasting effect on trade expansion and economic development. A dynamic subregional market would provide a learning base for trade at the international level.

African regional integration, initiated shortly after independence to sustain an import-substitution trade, has been hampered by the spaghetti bowl of institutions with overlapping and at times contradictory mandates. Numerous decisions have been taken but hardly implemented. Fortunately, the situation is improving, stimulated by trade reform undertaken at the national level; the new wave of regionalism is driven by the search to enhance market opportunities instead of protecting an infant industry. For example, the three main regional economic communities (REC) in Eastern and Southern Africa, SADC, EAC, and COMESA, have put in motion a rationalization process aiming at creating a dynamic market with free movement of goods, people, and services. A similar consolidation trend is taking place in other subregions, and coordinated at the pan-African level by the African Union. Properly undertaken, this wave of REC consolidation can be a building block toward integration of the African continent in the world trading system.

Due attention should be paid to how this process unfolds. A guiding principle is to aim at levelling the playing field. Regional integration would provide an overall supportive policy framework that helps to increase policy transparency and stability and to enhance policy credibility. Regionalism could nurture a market-friendly environment that fosters implementation of decisions and minimizes policy reversals. Open regionalism can also facilitate conditions conducive to the transfer of technology. These will help stimulate investment and increase productivity and competitiveness. An important element will be the extent to which the regional trade agreement (RTA) is credible, and promotes rather than undermines trade and development. Credibility comes essentially if decisions are implemented. Policy lock-in will be obtained if built on broad-based consensus with all partners, including through appropriate partnership arrangements with non-African countries or regions. The ongoing economic partnership agreements (EPAs) could provide the framework for moving in that direction, especially by fostering the condition for implementing regional integration programmes that have been on the books for many years and could not be implemented.

A key concern in the EPA negotiations has been the fact that some liberalization commitments would lead the least developed countries (LDCs) to liberalize beyond their

WTO obligations, or some countries to reverse aspects of their regional integration process. This situation is due to the presence in the same negotiations of configurations of developing and least developed countries that are treated differently at the WTO. In the short term it is necessary to build on the achievements of RECs and treat all members equally—which itself requires actions at the WTO with respect to reciprocity of liberalization. Although preferential access could provide benefits in the short run, prolonged reliance on preferences could be counterproductive. At the same time, abrupt termination of preferential treatment could cause serious adjustment difficulties. Preferences have been useful where the beneficiary had designed a phased-out strategy and a smooth integration into the multilateral trading system. Overall, in view of the efficiency gains that can be obtained through competition, non-reciprocal trading arrangement is not necessarily in the long-term interest of African countries; some form of carefully negotiated non-reciprocal arrangement is necessary. A way forward is to see any non-reciprocal preference scheme as an intermediary step toward reciprocal arrangement. Reciprocity should be a goal that should be progressively pursued.

In sum, African countries require support to pursue their trade reform in the regional context, where regionalism is a building block in the process of multilateral liberalization in the WTO context. In the short term, the obligations of members of African RECs need to be aligned with those that pertain to the least privileged among them, the LDCs. All members of these African RECs should be treated equally at the WTO (see Njinkeu 2004). In return, African countries should commit to completing the rationalization of REC as well as to accelerating liberalization at the subregional level.

3. Aid-for-trade to support a competitiveness agenda

Numerous case studies have shown that having the policy environment right is only part of the equation. This should be combined with a carefully designed and delivered aid-for-trade programme with a primary focus on improving production and trade capacity. The above consensus on trade policy and regional integration may not lead to trade expansion and economic development without the simultaneous introduction of specific actions that enhance the ability to increase the number of products exported and to move to dynamic niche markets. Africa cannot do this without becoming competitive, which is achieved through measures that overall improve the business environment and reduce transactions to all players. Brenton et al. (2009) argue that borders in Africa are stronger than in other parts of the world, and thus limit beneficial interaction and the pooling of resources. Consequently, growth spillovers, which were major drivers of development in other parts of the world, are virtually absent in Africa.

Aid-for-trade can help in three areas: (1) helping to improve the overall policy environment, (2) trade facilitation, and (3) harnessing the untapped opportunity of trade in services.

With respect to the first area, policy reforms and actions that can lead to significant improvement of the business environment and attract investment are of a public good nature: the associated outputs are non-excludable and non-rival in consumption—hence the need for a collective action solution at a regional level. Weak capacity of existing regional integration agencies and pro-reform civil society groups, and the diffuse nature of the benefits of existing integration mechanisms for the private sector, are a significant impediment. Aid-for trade should be deployed for work on the political economy of regional cooperation and coordination, with a view to increasing the incentives for implementation. Actions that benefit the pro-reform agents and allow champions to emerge should be prioritized (Hoekman and Njinkeu 2007).

Aid-for-trade should give more prominence to service trades. Intervention could aim to expand the range of exports on current markets, develop new export products, or start exporting existing service activities to new markets. Since services are an essential input in the production of agricultural and industrial goods, competitive, cheaper, and more available services would have a spillover effect on the overall economy.

African policymakers are still very apprehensive about the service trade agenda because of the sophisticated nature of the process of identifying priorities and distinguishing between behind-the-border and at-the-border policy measures. The complexity comes from the fact that each service sector needs to be understood from the perspective of the exporters or importers, according to market access and natural treatment, and for each of the four modes of supply. This is further compounded by the need to involve officials in trade ministries, those in charge of economic development and regional integration, officials with responsibility for services (such as transport or telecommunication), regulators, and the providers and users of services.

The challenge is to provide an approach that will enable the necessary consultation. One way is to focus on areas where winners can emerge. One such area is the range of information technologies enabled services (ITES)—services delivered via the internet or any other medium that can enable exchange of data through cross-border supply (Mode 1). They present tremendous opportunities, as the basic infrastructural requirements are IT networks. A value-chain approach (UNDP 2006) can be used. At the lowest level of the spectrum, where many Africa countries are situated, are low-skilled, labour-intensive back-office functions such as data entry, digitization, and conversion activities, and basic clerical services. The next layer would include teleworking services, which involve rule-based processing and simple voice and online customer relations services. This category includes call centre services, email processing, data processing, billing and payments, account opening, and screening of credit card applications. The third layer encompasses activities that involve problem-solving and decision-making, such as developing solutions for improving processes or streamlining systems. The fourth layer involves complex multimedia support services such as those teleworking services that require direct interaction with customers and more elaborated transactions with the client. Examples include web support, telemarketing, technical back office processing, e-customer relationship management, website design, software development for entire business processes, and hardware support services. The most sophisticated layer requires domain expertise and specialized skills such as in research and engineering, financial analysis, risk management, equity research services, and consulting and advisory services.

Aid-for-trade in the service trade area could help on several fronts: the prohibitive fixed cost of entering capital-intensive sectors; lack of access to financing for export or business development; difficulties encountered in establishing credibility with international suppliers; lack of access to reliable and inexpensive infrastructure; and lack of access to a range of formal and informal networks and institutional facilities necessary for trade (see Sauve 2008).

The third area for the aid-for-trade intervention is trade facilitation, especially measures that foster adequate regulation of services in transportation and other logistical services. Aid-for-trade could focus on measures that foster a strong and effective competitive regime that help enhance the availability and reliability of services. The agenda could also encompass solutions to market failures, with the aim of ensuring secured and competitive access to market information.

4. Conclusions

African countries need a broad scheme that is part of a positive agenda for promoting development. The main features of such a scheme would include improved market access and increased financial and technical assistance, in return for these countries consenting to a credible open regional and South–South liberalization agenda. It should also include special trade remedies for those low-income countries that cannot effectively resort to traditional remedy instruments.

African regional economic communities should be allowed to undertake WTO commitments that would not reduce the policy space available to LDCs—which would require that African developing countries have their multilateral liberalization commitments aligned to those of their LDC counterpart. Infant industry policies could be allowed in return for countries engaging in open regionalism with a timetable for introducing reciprocity. Such a timetable could be coupled with a progressive phasing out linked to an agreed competitiveness agenda. Such improvement would be engineered by a properly funded and implemented aid-for-trade programme focusing on appropriate supportive institutional framework, adequate infrastructure, supportive macroeconomic policies, and proper integration in dynamic production networks. A pre-announced phasing-out calendar, for example, could motivate firms to catch up in terms of productivity and competitiveness.

A positive approach to regional integration can leverage regional cooperation and reform to play a key role in implementing such a framework for competitiveness and diversification, and allows for the scaling up of capacities to attain the productivity necessary to compete.

REFERENCES

Brenton, P., T. Farole, B. Hoekman, and C. Staritz, 2009. 'Export diversification, regional integration, and inclusive growth in southern Africa'. World Bank (July).

Gregory, R., C. Henn, B. McDonald, and M. Saito, 2010. 'Trade and the crisis: protect or recover'. IMF (April).

Hoekman, B., and D. Njinkeu, 2011. 'Aid for trade and export competitiveness: new opportunities for Africa', in A. Oyejide and O. Ajakaiye (eds), *Trade Infrastructure and Economic Development*. London: Routledge.

Njinkeu, D., 2004. 'Uniform treatment of Africa in the WTO', *World Trade Review* 3, 433–40.

Sauve, P., 2008. 'Services-related projects in aid-for-trade', in D. Njinkeu and H. Cameron (eds), *Aid for Trade and Development*. Cambridge: Cambridge University Press.

UNDP, 2006. 'Selling services across frontiers', *Asia Pacific Human Development Report*, ch. 5.

World Bank, 2010. 'Yes Africa can: stories from a dynamic continent'. www.worldbank.org/countries/Africa

The Development of African Landlocked Countries

Janvier D. Nkurunziza

1. Introduction

Africa has 15 landlocked countries: Botswana, Burkina Faso, Burundi, the Central African Republic (CAR), Chad, Ethiopia, Lesotho, Malawi, Mali, Niger, Rwanda, Swaziland, Uganda, Zambia, and Zimbabwe. Measured in population size, Africa is the region with the largest proportion of its population living in landlocked countries. Data for 2007 covering 180 developed and developing countries show that about 30% of Africans south of the Sahara live in landlocked countries, compared to only 3% of the population in Asia and 4% elsewhere (UNCTAD 2009a).[1] This suggests that the problems associated with landlocked countries primarily concern Africa.

Why does being landlocked matter for Africa's economic development when it does not seem to matter elsewhere? Why is Burundi suffering from being landlocked when Switzerland, a European landlocked country, is not? The objective of this essay is to highlight some major constraints facing the development of African landlocked countries. Section 2 discusses the reasons why being landlocked in Africa matters for economic development. Section 3 analyses the effect of landlocked and transit countries' policies on the development of landlocked countries. Section 4 concludes by proposing some policy directions.

2. The development of Africa's landlocked countries

2.1. WHAT IS THE PROBLEM?

Landlocked African countries face three major interrelated constraints. First, they cannot rely on their poor neighbours who produce similar primary commodities as

---

[1] 'Elsewhere' includes Europe, the Americas, and Oceania. In the Americas, only Paraguay and Bolivia are landlocked and they have relatively small populations. Europe has 15 landlocked countries, the same number as in Africa, but they are all very small. The total European population living in landlocked countries is less than Ethiopia's.

viable economic partners. The fact that landlocked Switzerland has strong economic ties with its rich neighbours (France, Germany, Italy, Austria, and Liechtenstein), who have diversified economies, makes the country less sensitive to its geographical location away from the coast.

In Africa, Chad provides a contrasting picture. Not only is the country too far from the coast (Table 1) but it is also surrounded by some of the poorest countries in the world. An exporter in Chad pays $5,367 to move a 20-ft container from the capital city, N'Djamena, to the closest port of Douala, before it is shipped to international markets (World Bank 2009). This is the highest export cost in the world.[2] Comparable costs for Lesotho and Malawi, two landlocked countries which are closer to the coast and located in the relatively developed Southern Africa region, are $1,549 and $1,671, respectively.

The second constraint relates to the fact that being landlocked reduces the development benefits of trade, a factor which is amplified by Africa's remoteness from its major markets. One key reason why trading costs are generally high in Africa is that African countries' main trading partners are far away in Europe and North America. Only 9% of

Table 1. Trading cost indicators in landlocked countries (median 2007 values)

Country	Distance to coast (km)	Export cost (US$)	Export cost per km (US$)	Exports to regional market[a] (%)	Main export[b]
Botswana	905	2,508	2.77	13.36	Diamonds
Burkina Faso	1,154	2,132	1.85	31.37	Cotton, livestock
Burundi	1,254	2,147	1.71	12.29	Coffee
Central African Republic	1,518	5,121	3.37	10.61	Cotton, coffee
Chad	1,669	5,367	3.22	0.01	Cotton, cattle
Ethiopia	781	2,087	2.67	9.31	Coffee
Lesotho	575	1,549	2.69	18.38	Textiles & garments
Malawi	803	1,671	2.08	28.11	Tobacco
Mali	1,225	2,012	1.64	9.79	Cotton
Niger	1,057	3,545	3.35	30.24	Uranium
Rwanda	1,867	3,275	1.75	29.63	Coffee
Swaziland	193	2,184	11.32	81.52	Sugar
Uganda	1,187	3,090	2.60	29.22	Coffee
Zambia	1,975	2,664	1.35	30.66	Copper
Zimbabwe	464	2,678	5.77	53.18	Mineral products

[a] Exports to regional market are exports to the main regional integration group of the country.
[b] Oil exports are not included.
Source: Distance to coast (Faye et al, 2004); Export cost (World Bank, 2009); Export to regional market (UNCTAD, 2009b); Main export (several sources).

---

[2] Swaziland has the highest cost per km, probably due to the very short distance separating it from the sea.

Africa's officially recorded exports are destined for other African countries, whereas 71% of European exports go to European countries (UNCTAD 2009b). Hence, African landlocked countries are doubly isolated, due to Africa's geographical isolation from major markets in Europe, America, and Asia, and, additionally, to these countries' location far from the coast. Relative to coastal countries, African landlocked countries need 18 more days to ship a container from the factory to the port. This difference is due to additional delays in securing the required documentation and inland transit (Freund and Rocha 2009). It is as if being landlocked added 1,260 km to the distance separating landlocked countries from their markets.[3]

Great distance between Africa and its markets makes African producers far detached from their consumers. Adding to this the poor quality of supply routes explains the high level of uncertainty over supplies and deliveries prevailing in African landlocked countries. Firms in Zimbabwe and Burundi, for example, are forced to build larger than optimal stocks of imported raw material, in anticipation of supply disruptions. This is a necessary strategy but a costly one, because it ties up financial resources that could be used more productively (Fafchamps, Gunning, and Oostendorp 2000; Nkurunziza and Ngaruko 2008).

The third constraint facing African landlocked countries is their total dependence on their own and transit countries' very weak infrastructure (Limao and Venables 2001). This is particularly the case with land transport infrastructure, which is the key transport mode used in Africa given the bulky nature of its agricultural and mineral primary commodity exports which dominate its external trade (Table 1).[4] Dependence on transit countries' poor infrastructure is less binding in countries which trade substantially with their neighbours because short distances reduce transport costs. For example, despite the fact that Swaziland has the highest export cost per kilometre, the distance covered is shorter, since 80% of the country's trade is with neighbouring countries, particularly South Africa.

Why do landlocked countries fail to make a strategic choice to trade more with their neighbours in order to reduce trading costs? There are at least three reasons. First, landlocked countries' trade infrastructure is still affected by the colonial legacy, being oriented to Europe and not to other African countries. Second, very few export opportunities exist in other African countries, given the similarities of the products traded. Coffee, cotton, and minerals, the main exports of landlocked countries, are not particularly attractive to African consumers. Third, even if opportunities were available, severe internal barriers, including domestic transport infrastructure,

---

[3] Each additional day corresponds to a country distancing itself from its trade partners by an average of 70 km (Djankov, Freund, and Pham 2009).

[4] Botswana is an exception. Diamonds, the country's main primary commodity export, are not bulky, so they are exported by air, which eliminates dependence on transit countries.

constrain trade with neighbouring economies. This is probably the main reason why African landlocked countries are the only group which does not enjoy a positive neighbourhood effect. Outside Africa, landlocked countries grow by 0.7 of a percentage point when a neighbour's growth increases by 1 percentage point (Collier and O'Connell 2008).

2.2. LOCATION COMPETITIVENESS OF LANDLOCKED COUNTRIES

Economic geography teaches us that a country's competitiveness is determined by the physical and institutional environment in which firms and other economic agents operate. The physical environment is defined by the availability of resources, capabilities, and markets. Institutions provide the incentive structure governing production and exchange (Dunning and Zhang 2008). The main factors that attract investment are market size, low cost of production, and market access (Krugman 1991). Most landlocked African countries have failed to attract foreign investors because they fare poorly on all these factors. Out of 15 countries, only Ethiopia and, to some extent, Uganda, have relatively large domestic markets measured in population size (83 million and 31 million, respectively). Measured in income, 14 out of all 15 landlocked African countries are very poor, with GDP per capita below $1,000 per year.[5] Africa's landlocked countries are also characterized by uncompetitive production, due mainly to the high cost of imported inputs (Table 2).[6] With respect to market access, only Lesotho has been relatively successful in attracting investors into its textile and garments industry thanks to the country's preferential market access under trade schemes such as the Africa Growth and Opportunity Act (AGOA).

The combination of high trading costs and low investment in landlocked countries seriously limits their economic development.[7] All indicators in Table 2 show that landlocked countries in Africa fare worse than non-landlocked countries. Their export and import costs are much higher, almost twice the costs in non-landlocked countries both in sub-Saharan Africa and elsewhere. As a result, African landlocked countries import and export less than other countries. There is also a very large difference in income levels between landlocked and non-landlocked African countries. The latter group of countries has nominal GDP per capita which is 120% higher than in landlocked countries.

---

[5] Botswana is the only country with a relatively high income per capita, which stands at $5,739 (UNCTAD 2009a).

[6] Import costs are higher than export costs for all but one country, the Central African Republic (ibid.).

[7] It should be clear that being landlocked in Africa is just a contributing factor in poor economic performance; there are other reasons why these economies are not developed.

Table 2. Trade and development indicators (median values)

Indicator	Sub-Saharan Africa		Others
	Landlocked	Non-landlocked	
Export to GDP ratio	18.75	26.41	29.22
Import to GDP ratio	31.77	36.71	41.06
Export cost in US$	2508.00	1302.00	1050.00
Import cost in US$	3335.00	1529.00	1175.00
Export time in days	45	26	18
Import time in days	54	30	20
Nominal GDP per capita	402.68	891.40	4959.95
Poverty headcount	62.15	44.54	–
Gini coefficient	0.48	0.45	–
Human development index	0.41	0.52	–

Notes: The first 4 variables are median current values for 2007. 'Others' include all but SSA countries. Poverty figures represent the proportion of the population living on less than $1.25 a day per person in 2005. The data covers the period 2000–2006.
Source: Based on UNCTAD (2009a); World Bank (2008; 2009); UNDP (2009).

Not all economic problems plaguing landlocked countries should be attributed to geography. African landlocked countries are not just passive victims of destiny. Even if geography is important, other factors help to explain the poor development indicators of landlocked countries summarized in Table 2. The discussion of these factors is the objective of section 3.

3. The effect of policy choices on landlocked countries' development

It is difficult to argue that the difference in development outcomes between landlocked and non-landlocked countries, namely the high level of poverty and inequality and low level of human development (Table 2), is just due to the long distance between landlocked countries and their economic partners. These outcomes are in large part the result of policy choices made by landlocked countries and their transit countries. Indeed, the negative effect of geographical isolation on development can be reduced or amplified by the types of policy choices made.

3.1. TRANSIT COUNTRIES' POLICIES AFFECT DEVELOPMENT OUTCOMES IN LANDLOCKED COUNTRIES

To some extent, landlocked countries are at the mercy of their neighbours. Faye et al. (2004) review the main risks and uncertainties facing landlocked countries as a result of their dependence on transit countries. In addition to the dependence on neighbours' infrastructure discussed above, landlocked countries also depend on maintaining good political relations with their neighbours. Transit countries can use their status as a political tool to constrain landlocked countries to behave in a way that preserves transit countries' interests. For example, in July 1996, Burundi's transit countries—Kenya, Rwanda, Tanzania, and Uganda—imposed a total economic embargo on the country following a coup d'état. Because Burundi is landlocked, this decision totally isolated it from the outside world.[8] Some analysts have argued that the embargo, which lasted about three years, precipitated the collapse of Burundi's economy; it has yet to recover.

Landlocked countries are also vulnerable to their neighbours' political instability. Extreme political instability paralyses the administrative and economic activities which are necessary to facilitate landlocked countries' trade. For example, the violence that followed disputed presidential elections in Kenya in December 2007 affected rail and road traffic, disrupting supply lines serving Uganda, Rwanda, and Burundi. Just a few days after the conflict erupted, these countries were feeling the consequences because they are highly dependent on Kenya's transport infrastructure linking them to the port of Mombasa. Malawi also experienced a similar effect during Mozambique's war for independence in the late 1970s. Malawi lost its access to the shortest route to the sea, which crossed Mozambique. It was estimated that the cost associated with the diversion of trade through longer routes amounted to 1.5 percentage points of GDP growth per year during the 1970s (Chipeta and Mkandawire 2008).

Transit countries' administrative practices are another factor that constrains landlocked countries' trade. An importer or exporter from a landlocked country needs to comply with his country's bureaucratic procedures but also with transit countries' requirements. Delays in customs clearance, cargo inspections, road inspections, and other controls impose a high cost on African landlocked countries. Such administrative hurdles account for about 75% of shipping delays, poor road and port infrastructure accounting for the remaining 25% (Djankov, Freund, and Pham 2009). This partly explains the large differences in import and export costs as well as import and export times between landlocked African and coastal countries (Table 2).

---

[8] Embargoes have also been imposed on coastal countries but the effect is smaller, as these countries can relatively easily flout these sanctions using sea supply lines which remain in their control.

3.2. LANDLOCKED COUNTRIES' OWN POLICY CHOICES ARE PARTLY TO BLAME

Simplifying trade procedures governing exports and imports can substantially cut trading costs and time, particularly non-transport costs. Non-transport export costs include fees relating to pre-shipment activities, inland handling, port handling and storage, and customs and technical control. Reducing the number of procedures and the fees attached to them would help to cut down export costs. With respect to time costs, it has been estimated that if Uganda could reduce the number of days it takes to have goods moved from factory to ship from its current 58 days to the sample's average of 27 days, the country would increase its exports by 31% (Djankov et al. 2009). Hence, adopting the right trade policies and fostering trade efficiency can increase trade flows and hence their development benefits.

Landlocked African countries can counterbalance the negative effect of their geographical isolation by adopting good economic policies. Is there evidence that these countries have substantially better trade and other economic policies than non-landlocked countries in order to compensate for the negative effect of their location? A comparative analysis of institutional quality in both groups of countries helps to answer this question.

The quality of institutions is measured using an indicator that varies from 1 (lowest score) to 6 (highest score).[9] The median score of African landlocked countries on the quality of trade policy, the most relevant indicator, was 3.5 in 2006 compared with 4.0 for non-landlocked countries. This result suggests that part of the problems discussed here could be due to poor trade policies pursued by landlocked countries. Other economic policies do not seem to show a difference in favour of coastal countries. The score for economic management is 3.7 compared to 3.25 for coastal countries. On public sector management, the scores are 3.3 and 2.9, respectively. Both groups score 3.0 on the quality of public administration. On transparency, accountability and corruption in the public sector, landlocked countries score 3 against 2.5 for non-landlocked countries (World Bank 2008).

These statistics show that with the exception of trade policy, landlocked countries do not seem to have worse economic policies than coastal countries. If anything, landlocked countries seem to do slightly better than coastal countries on most indicators. However, with an overall score oscillating around 3.0, which is half the best score, landlocked countries do not seem to have used economic policies to alleviate the burden of their geographical location.

What about political institutions? Could the poor economic and social performance of landlocked countries be due to bad political institutions? Even though the experience of

---

[9] Refer to World Bank (2008) for a full description of these indicators.

some Asian countries has shown that good politics is not always a prerequisite for good economic performance, there is evidence that good political institutions are important for economic performance in Africa (Fosu 2002; Nkurunziza and Bates 2002). In poor political environments, even the best economic policies cannot deliver sustained prosperity. The quality of political institutions can be assessed using information in the Polity IV database which captures key qualities of executive recruitment, constraints on executive authority, and political competition. Aggregate country scores show a country's level of political openness and competition, which are key qualities of a good political system.

On a scale from −10 (hereditary monarchy) to 10 (consolidated democracy), the landlocked countries' median score is 0.5 compared to a median score of 5.0 for non-landlocked countries.[10] Out of 12 landlocked countries in the sample, half have zero or negative scores (Burkina Faso, Central African Republic, Rwanda, Swaziland, Uganda, and Zimbabwe). In comparison, 11 out of 28 coastal countries have negative scores. Hence, the large difference in median scores between the two groups of countries is not just the result of some outlier; it seems to reflect some fundamental difference in political systems. Although it is not clear why landlocked countries have much poorer political institutions than coastal countries, there is suggestive evidence of a positive correlation between the quality of political institutions and economic policy choices. For example, the complexity of trade procedures in landlocked countries provides opportunities for expansive controls which, in a poor political environment, could be used by the ruling elites to create and appropriate rents. In Burundi, external trade policy was used as a source of economic rents through exchange rate policies, the allocation of import licences, price controls, and the protection of state and private-sector monopolies (Nkurunziza and Ngaruko 2008). In Malawi, trucking cartels and restrictions on the operation of foreign vehicles partly explain the country's relatively high transport costs (Chipeta and Mkandawire 2008).

Landlocked countries such as Burundi, Central African Republic, Chad, Rwanda, and Uganda have experienced extreme political instability which, in most cases, resulted from a long tradition of poor political institutions. These episodes of extreme political instability have had long-term negative effects on development. It is also in relation to these political institutions that the three development indicators shown in Table 2 should be interpreted: poverty, inequality, and overall human development have an important political dimension (Ndulu et al. 2008).

---

[10] Accessed on 30 July 2009 at: http://www.systemicpeace.org/polity/polity06.htm#ssaf. The list comprises 40 African countries, including 12 landlocked countries.

4. Conclusion

Africa has by far the largest share of the population living in landlocked countries—the worst possible location in terms of economic opportunities. These countries have the highest trading costs in the world, and their small sizes and low income levels have limited flows of foreign investment. These factors have had important negative effects on the development of Africa's landlocked countries. The adoption of 'good' policies could have reduced the negative impact of geographical location on development. However, this option does not seem to have been well utilized. In fact, the plight of landlocked countries has been further complicated by poor political institutions that have led to economic choices based on the interests of the ruling elites while penalizing the majority of the population. It is not clear why these countries particularly adopted poor trade policies. One possible explanation is that, more than in coastal countries, trade in landlocked countries offers potentially important rents which are captured by the ruling elites through restrictive policies.

Landlocked countries could reduce their location constraint by vigorously pursuing regional integration. This process can not only open up landlocked countries' access to the sea but also give them the opportunity to influence transit countries' policies in their favour. Most importantly, however, landlocked countries should reform their own trade and other economic sectors to reduce the cost of trading. For example, these countries should reorient their economies towards the production and trading of less bulky goods and services to minimize transport costs. Moreover, the development of landlocked countries will most probably require better political systems that reduce inequalities and promote overall human development.

REFERENCES

Chipeta, C., and M. Mkandawire, 2008. 'Man-made opportunities and growth', in Ndulu et al. (2008: 143–65).

Collier, P., and S. O'Connell, 2008. 'Opportunities and choices', in B. Ndulu, S. O'Connell, R. H. Bates, P. Collier, and C. Soludo (eds), *The Political Economy of Economic Growth in Africa, 1960–2000*, vol. 1. Cambridge: Cambridge University Press, 76–136.

Djankov, S., C. Freund, and C. Pham, 2009. 'Trading on time'. MS, World Bank.

Dunning, J. H., and F. Zhang, 2008. 'Foreign direct investment and the locational competitiveness of countries', *Transnational Corporations* 17.3, 1–30.

Fafchamps, M., J. W. Gunning, and R. Oostendorp, 2000. 'Inventories and risk in African manufacturing', *Economic Journal* 110.466, 861–93.

Fosu, A. K., 2002. 'Political instability and economic growth: implications of coup events in Sub-Saharan Africa', *American Journal of Economics and Sociology* 61.1, 329–48.

Freund, C., and N. Rocha, 2009. 'What constrains Africa's exports?' World Bank Policy Research Working Paper No. 5184.

Krugman, P. R., 1991. *Geography and Trade*. Cambridge, Mass.: MIT Press.

Limao, N., and A. J. Venables, 2001. 'Infrastructure, geographical disadvantage and transport costs', *World Bank Economic Review* 15.3, 451–79.

Ndulu, B., S. O'Connell, J.-P. Azam, R. H. Bates, A. K. Fosu, J. W. Gunning, and D. Njinkeu (eds), 2008. *The Political Economy of Economic Growth in Africa, 1960–2000*, vol. 2. Cambridge: Cambridge University Press.

Nkurunziza, J. D., and R. Bates, 2002. 'Political institutions and economic growth in Africa'. Center for International Development working paper, Harvard University.

—— and F. Ngaruko, 2008. 'Why has Burundi grown so slowly? The political economy of redistribution', in Ndulu et al. (2008: 51–85).

UNCTAD, 2009a. *Handbook of Statistics*. Available online at: http://www.unctad.org.

—— 2009b. *Economic Development in Africa Report: Strengthening Regional Integration for Africa's Development*. New York and Geneva.

UNDP, 2009. *Human Development Indices*. New York.

World Bank, 2008. *World Development Indicators 2008*. Available online at: http://www.worldbank.org.

—— 2009. Doing Business 2009 database. Available online at: http://www.doingbusiness.org.

Thematic Perspectives
Agriculture

Why Agriculture Remains the Key to Sub-Saharan African Development

Alain de Janvry and Elisabeth Sadoulet

Agriculture for development

Since 2004 the growth of sub-Saharan Africa has accelerated mainly due to increased demand and favourable prices for its abundant mining products, creating expectations that primary exports can offer a new road to prosperity. Large land sale and rental deals have created the expectation that large farms could boost the growth of agriculture and help deliver development to rural Africa (Collier 2008). Rapid migration to the cities has created the expectation that economies of scale in urban-based manufacturing activities can finally be captured (World Bank 2008). And approaches to food security through trade policy instruments and social safety nets, as used to respond to the 2006–8 food crisis, have created the expectation that famines can be overcome.

We argue here that these are all misleading signals. In spite of the desire to move on to growth based on large-scale farms, modern industry (as in China), and modern services (as in India), agricultural growth remains quintessential to the development of sub-Saharan Africa. Structural transformation of the economy, whereby labour is extracted from agriculture to contribute to GDP per capita growth, as successfully done in Asia, has not worked in Africa (Figure 1). Labour has been transferred, but per capita GDP growth has not followed. This continued role of agriculture may be easy to accept for policymakers, as it only tells them that the phase of successful agricultural growth cannot be skipped and that it is a precondition to moving toward large-scale farming and urban-based modern industry and services as the future engines of growth. However, the situation is not that straightforward. There are four warnings related to successfully using agriculture for development, and as a step to the next phase.

The first is that the unique conditions of sub-Saharan Africa agriculture require a *specifically African productivity revolution* that needs to be designed, experimented with, supported, and implemented. Much can be learned from experiences in the rest of the world and from localized success stories in Africa in doing this, but a blueprint Green Revolution for Africa simply does not exist. It has to be imagined. The second is that the

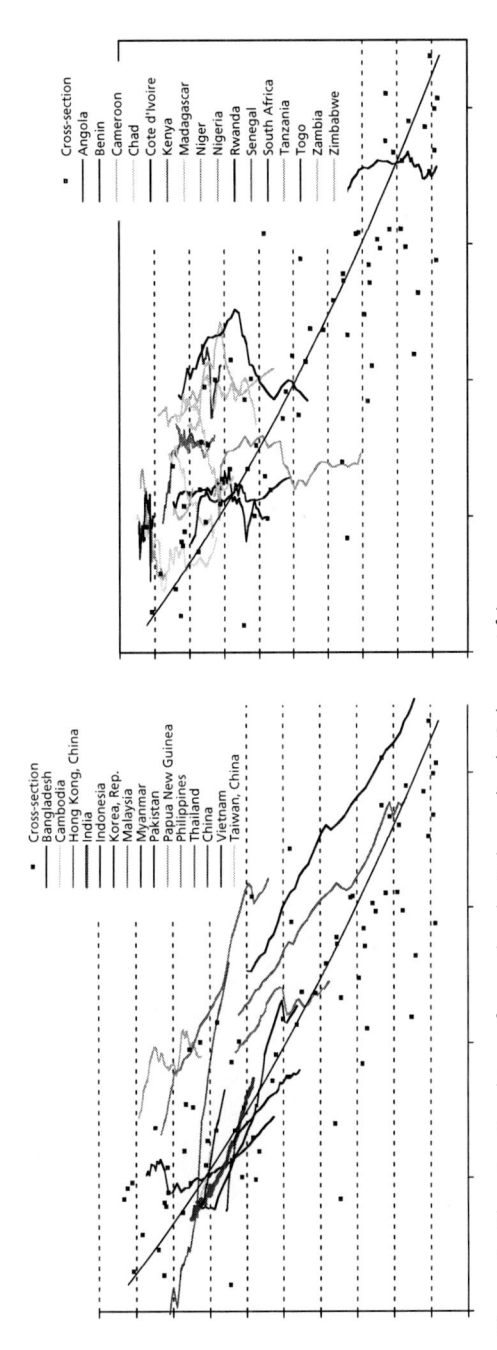

Figure 1. The structural transformation in Asia and sub-Saharan Africa

very process through which agricultural growth is achieved will determine its success in delivering development. Hence, not any type of agricultural growth will do: it has to be largely smallholder-based. Because there are trade-offs in the development outcomes produced by agricultural growth, participatory priority setting is a key aspect of using agriculture for development. Priority setting in the PRSP (Poverty Reduction Strategy Papers) process must consequently be extended to an ADSP (Agriculture for Development Strategy Papers) process.

The third is that achieving food security in countries that have large rural populations and weak fiscal and administrative capacities requires looking beyond trade and social policy instruments, and giving special attention to *subsistence farming* and the resilience of smallholder farming systems. Hence, food security requires investing in the capacity of smallholders to produce food for their own consumption and to generate income in markets. The fourth is that agriculture will not deliver development without a *strong state for agriculture* that can prioritize, regulate, compensate for market failures, and partner with the private sector and producer organizations. Yet current ministries of agriculture have been diminished by structural adjustment, and have not been adapted to the new contexts for agriculture and their new tasks in achieving development. Major innovations are needed on this front as well if success in expanded expenditures on agriculture, following commitments made by the G8 and renewed emphasis on agriculture by the World Bank and other donors such as the Gates and Rockefeller Foundations, is to follow, as opposed to a repeat of past failures—a serious risk.

The dimensions of development

Aggregate income growth is the fundamental instrument for development, but development goes beyond growth. In using agriculture for development, we would thus expect agriculture to contribute not only to GDP growth but also to improvements in the multiple dimensions of human welfare (World Bank 2007). At a minimum, they include poverty reduction, decreased vulnerability and provision of food security, reduction of disparities between sectors and individuals, saving on resources that can be made available for use in other economic sectors of the economy and by future generations, and provision of environmental services. In using agriculture for development, the challenge is thus to depend on one instrument, agricultural growth, to achieve a multiplicity of development outcomes. This means that the process through which growth is achieved has to be designed to deliver development outcomes for which markets fail. Clearly, there may be win-wins in these outcomes, but the rule is the existence of trade-offs, implying that tough choices have to be made in prioritizing desired outcomes, based on adequate information and participation. This says that a condition to effectively use agriculture for development—as opposed to simply achieving agricultural growth—is acquiring the capacity to make the social choices that will result in outcomes that are recognized by stakeholders as development.

Agriculture remains essential for economic development in sub-Saharan Africa

Historically, few countries with large rural populations have been able to industrialize without a previous successful productivity revolution in agriculture. Sub-Saharan Africa countries belong to this category. There are several reasons for this to be the case. The first is that agricultural growth is directly effective for aggregate growth simply because agriculture is such a large sector of the economy, accounting on average for 30% of GDP when South Africa and a few mining countries are excluded. The second is that agriculture has comparative advantage, often by default due to the institutional demands of modern industry and services while the investment climate for these sectors is still precarious. The third is that, with domestic supply strongly influencing domestic food price and hence nominal wages, competitiveness of all sectors in the economy depends on the performance of domestic agriculture in securing low-priced food. And agriculture can indeed grow successfully. Several African countries have highly dynamic sectors in their agricultures, frequently associated with exports such as green beans (Senegal, Kenya), cut flowers (Ethiopia), tropical fruits (South Africa), speciality coffee (Rwanda), and high-quality cocoa (Ghana). But there are also success stories in food crops, such as new rice varieties in West Africa, cassava in East Africa, and dairying in Kenya. Scaling up these success stories offers potential for aggregate growth. Agriculture can in turn offer a road to industrialization through the emergence of agro-processing linked to value addition in the dynamic production sectors.

Agriculture growth can be especially effective for poverty and disparity reduction, both directly in production and indirectly through the rural non-farm economy and linkages with other sectors. This has been extensively documented in the *2008 World Development Report* (World Bank 2007). Strong empirical support exists on the poverty reduction value of agricultural growth based on cross-country data. In Ghana, increased productivity in cocoa production has been a major driver of successful poverty reduction since 1995.

Food security also importantly depends on domestic agricultural production. This is for two reasons. One is that high transactions costs on markets and limited import capacity imply that domestic prices are importantly determined by domestic production capacity. Many countries such as Ethiopia and Mali are currently experiencing food price inflation that is basically due to imbalance between domestic consumption and production capacity. The other is the very large importance of subsistence farming on which the majority of the poor depend for their food security.

Agricultural growth can be redesigned to save on resources such as water and land that can be freed for other sectors of the economy, urban-based in particular. It can also be a major source of environmental services if market failures are removed, in particular through schemes of payments for environmental services. For Africa, with abundant forests and lands that can be cultivated with minimum tillage methods, sale of carbon maintenance/capture services and biodiversity conservation can become important sources of revenue as markets are being put into place.

The conclusion is thus that few sub-Saharan Africa countries can afford to neglect their agricultures if they want to achieve development. The question is how this can be successfully achieved. We identify four essential but demanding conditions for this to happen.

Need for an endogenous productivity revolution in agriculture

Rainfed agriculture, which accounts for 88% of sub-Saharan Africa's cultivated area, is characterized by a high degree of heterogeneity of conditions (highly varied agro-ecological environments, multiplicity of crops and farming systems, and differential exposures to risks). Managing this heterogeneity requires decentralization and participation in order to design and implement local solutions. Heterogeneity also originates in highly varied social systems with a great diversity of institutional arrangements. Multiple constraints require a multisectoral approach. Key issues to be addressed include exhausted soils, insufficient infrastructure (roads, water), low levels of education and health, a private sector limited by an uninviting investment climate, incipient producer organizations, and weak governance for agriculture. Small countries and large economies of scale in such investments as R&D and infrastructure invite regional cooperation.

The challenges of a productivity revolution in smallholder farming in sub-Saharan Africa are daunting, yet need to be confronted, and there are good signs that success can be achieved. There are basically six aspects to this challenge.

The first is innovation. Productivity growth must succeed where it has failed before, and success must be rapid to avoid major human disasters. Old recipes will consequently not work. Innovations have to be part of the solution.

The second is specificity. The approach must be specific to the conditions of sub-Saharan Africa, characterized by a great degree of heterogeneity and weak broader supporting conditions in terms of markets, institutions, and public goods, thus requiring participatory multi-pronged approaches that can be designed as integrated territorial approaches, as explored for example in the Millennium Development Villages. Territorial approaches can be effective in helping coordinate agriculture with a broad array of rural non-farm activities that can offer expanding income opportunities to the local population.

The third is environmental sustainability. The programme must deal with the challenges of sustainability and environmental friendliness that were not concerns in the original Green Revolution in Asia. The classical seed–fertilizer–water package will consequently not suffice. It needs to be complemented by environmentally sustainable approaches such as agro-ecology and conservation agriculture.

The fourth factor is scope. It must go beyond cereals to include high-value activities—including fruits and vegetables, livestock, fish, and forest products—and provide opportunities to link to integrated value chains for high-value products in catering to non-traditional exports and supermarkets.

The fifth is new challenges. It must address brand new challenges such as climate change (particularly vulnerability to climate shocks and risk management) and the forces of globalization (particularly volatile prices and the rapidly changing demands of value chains).

The sixth is the role of the state, which must be redefined in support of agriculture for development. This includes the issues of land property rights that are still incomplete for security of access in many parts of the continent, use of 'smart' subsidies to induce productivity change and to cope with price shocks, public-private partnerships in the delivery of public goods and productive investments, redesigned functions for ministries of agriculture, and an active role for civil society in participating in public affairs.

Addressing these challenges thus requires new approaches adapted to contexts. Research, design, experimentation, and evaluation are key elements in achieving an endogenous productivity revolution in African agriculture. Believing that we know what is to be done, and all that remains is to do it, would be a serious mistake.

Need for smallholder-based agriculture growth

In using agriculture for development, the process through which growth in agriculture is obtained is as important as the outcome, in particular to achieve poverty reduction, gender equality, and environmental sustainability. We should recall that 70% of the poor in sub-Saharan Africa are rural households, and that agriculture is the source of income and food security for most of them. Contrary to middle-income countries like Brazil and Mexico, rural poverty will not be reduced by massive income transfers. Smallholder farming must for this reason be the dominant approach, in spite of some advantages associated with large-scale farming and the contracting out of land to international agribusiness that has recently been advocated by some development economists and pursued by several governments. The process through which growth is achieved is thus essential for poverty reduction, and this involves anchoring agricultural growth in access to modern inputs and productivity gains in smallholder farming and the associated off-farm activities.

Large farms can be an option where there is much under-used land. However, they have to be seen in terms of how they contribute to development, not only to agricultural growth. Large farms can have advantages of access to technology and international markets. However, in the African context, they should be looked at with caution if they are to deliver development. Property rights over land are generally poorly established, with the risk that carving out large farms where they did not exist before will result in the uncompensated displacement of current users. Labour markets, which could help create opportunities for the rural labour force, are typically poorly developed. Contracts over land use are typically incomplete in terms of environmental protection. History tells us that large-scale farming has most often failed in Africa, and that there are almost always institutional alternatives to large-scale corporate farming through contractual arrangements with organized smallholders. And large farm operations are notably volatile, with the potential of leaving irreversibly transformed rural communities if the large employer moves out. However, large farms can be used if they effectively complement small farms and create opportunities for the latter that they would not otherwise have, and there are examples of successful integration between the two types of farms.

Even if difficult to achieve, given current conditions, there is little alternative to a smallholder-centred agriculture system in pursuing growth in Africa. Making smallholder farmers competitive in a globalized context is thus one of the current challenges of using agriculture for development in Africa.

Need for food security based on subsistence and smallholder farming

The current food situation in sub-Saharan Africa is one of rising volatility of production and prices, but weakness of traditional food security instruments such as trade tariffs and taxes, price subsidies, and social safety nets. Hence the need is for an approach to food security that puts agricultural production and who produces food at the centre of a strategy. In Africa today, most rural households participate in agricultural activities (97% in Malawi, 90% in Nigeria, 89% in Ghana) and self-employment in agriculture is the main source of income (74% in Ethiopia, 67% in Malawi, 65% in Zambia, and 55% in Ghana and Nigeria). A majority of smallholders are net buyers of food. As a consequence, production for home consumption is a key determinant of food security. Yields in subsistence farming are typically very low, as modern seeds and inputs are barely used. There is consequently a huge opportunity to reduce malnutrition and hunger, and to provide protection against food price fluctuations, by raising land productivity among smallholders, first and foremost to produce for home consumption, and second to generate a marketable surplus, providing autonomous incomes to purchase additional foods. Yet attention to the farming systems used in subsistence agriculture and their resilience to weather shocks has been badly neglected. In the short run at least, more attention needs to be given to subsistence farming as a major opportunity for productivity gains, poverty reduction, and food security.

Need for redesigned governance for agriculture

A lesson learned from the last 25 years of neglect and misuse of agriculture is that agricultural growth, and using the process of growth for development, cannot be achieved without a strong and proactive state. There are too many market failures in achieving development through agricultural growth for agriculture to be simply left to private-sector support. The state has functions in delivering public goods, regulating private-sector activity, internalizing externalities, and most importantly partnering with the private sector in triggering growth for development. Current forms of governance for agriculture have been diminished by the sequels of structural adjustment, and have not been adapted to what the state needs to do to spend on agriculture and expect development to be the outcome. Lessons must be learned from the past about failures and successes in using agriculture for development. Experimentation with redesigns of ministerial and cabinet-level arrangements in guiding and coordinating agriculture with other sectors must be conducted. Business as usual with diminished ministries of agriculture will not do. A reform of the state apparatus in support of using agriculture for development is thus a major condition for success—again a difficult task.

Conclusion

Like it or not, agriculture remains a cornerstone for economic development in most sub-Saharan Africa countries. The process through which agricultural growth is achieved is key if this growth is to deliver sustainable development. Productivity growth in smallholder agriculture and value chains are essential for this purpose. Designing, experimenting with, evaluating, and scaling up new approaches is needed. This can be done, but it is not easy, and difficulties must not be underestimated. The key for success is consequently to be found not only in major increases in resource commitments—as promised at the July 2009 meeting of the G8—but also in the development of badly missing expertise in using agriculture for development, experimentation with new approaches that allow more efficient use of resources, and sustained commitments by governments and donors so that difficult approaches have a chance to mature and succeed.

REFERENCES

Collier, Paul, 2008. 'The Politics of Hunger', *Foreign Affairs* (November/December).
World Bank, 2007. *Agriculture for Development: World Development Report 2008*. Washington, DC.
—— 2008. *Reshaping Economic Geography: World Development Report 2009*. Washington, DC.

Food Insecurity and Food Aid in Africa

Christopher B. Barrett and Erin C. Lentz

Concepts and Terms

The prevailing definition of food security, agreed upon at the 1996 World Food Summit, is 'a situation that exists when all people, at all times, have physical, social and economic access to sufficient, safe and nutritious food that meets their dietary needs and food preferences for an active and healthy life'. Food insecurity exists when that condition does not hold.

Food security is commonly conceptualized as resting on three pillars: availability, access, and utilization. These concepts are inherently hierarchical, with availability necessary but not sufficient to ensure access, which is in turn necessary but not sufficient for effective utilization. Availability reflects the supply side. Access reflects food demand, as mediated by cash availability, prices, and intra-household resource allocation. Utilization reflects whether individuals and households make good use of the food to which they have access, commonly focused on the intake of essential micronutrients such as iodine, iron or zinc, and vitamins A and D. Some consider stability to be a fourth dimension of food insecurity, capturing individuals' susceptibility to food insecurity due to interruptions in access, availability or utilization.

The temporal aspect of stability links to the oft-made distinction between chronic and transitory food insecurity. Chronic food insecurity reflects a long-term lack of access to adequate food, and is typically associated with structural problems of availability, access, or utilization, especially poor access due to chronic poverty. Most food insecurity is chronic (Barrett 2002). Transitory food insecurity, by contrast, is associated with sudden and temporary disruptions. The most serious episodes of transitory food insecurity are commonly labelled 'famine', typically caused by simultaneous or sequential availability, access, and humanitarian response failures.

Food insecurity in Africa

By UN (2009) figures, 29% of Africa's sub-Saharan population was undernourished in 2008, a slight decrease from 32% in 1990–92. Meanwhile, the proportion of undernourished North Africans remains near 3% (UN 2009). But these figures offer only a snapshot of those suffering from insufficient macronutrient intake at any given moment. They neglect both those suffering micronutrient deficiencies and those at risk of being food-insecure. While no rigorous, widely accepted estimates of this greater population exist, it almost surely doubles the proportion suffering food insecurity (Barrett 2002).

Such highly aggregated estimates mask considerable heterogeneity within Africa. Food insecurity has substantially worsened in some countries—especially those suffering sustained political violence, such as DR Congo and Zimbabwe—while others, such as Cameroon, Ghana, and Nigeria, have achieved significant progress. Some post-conflict countries, such as Angola and Mozambique, have experienced rapid declines in undernourishment, but overall levels remain high. In east and southern Africa, undernutrition rates have fallen even while, due to population growth, the number of people suffering undernutrition has increased (FAO 2008).

Threats to food security

Food insecurity usually has multiple causes that coexist at the individual, household, community, and national levels. A solid understanding of the 'covariate' causes of food insecurity common to a broad subpopulation (due e.g. to prices, extreme climate events or civil unrest) is essential to generalized interventions (e.g. food aid) and to long-term, aggregate improvement in food security at the level of communities, countries, and regions. Meanwhile, an understanding of the individual-level ('idiosyncratic') causes of food insecurity is essential to successful targeting of interventions to specific food insecure persons.

COVARIATE THREATS TO FOOD SECURITY

Most people in any country—even highly agrarian ones—are net food buyers, dependent on markets for food. While higher food prices induce increased local food production, they also threaten the food security of low-income consumers. Because a large share of smallholder food producers are net food buyers due to limited landholdings and low productivity, food insecure agrarian populations commonly benefit in the short run from lower food prices (Barrett 2002; 2008). Price spikes can be catastrophic for poor populations, who commonly spend half or more of their total income on food and rarely have adequate assets to draw on during periods of crisis.

The food price spike that began in late 2006 returned attention to food availability questions. African countries missed out on Green Revolution-style agricultural productivity increases. Indeed, because domestic food production dwarfs cross-border commercial food trade or international food aid shipments, low domestic agricultural productivity remains the primary determinant of chronic food insecurity in Africa. Improving small farmers' access to improved technologies and productive assets stimulates both greater production and greater marketed supply, and thus improved domestic agricultural productivity and marketing is widely seen as central to improving food security in Africa. And because a small minority of large landowners produce the overwhelming majority of food surpluses marketed in sub-Saharan Africa, even productivity growth only among non-poor farmers can improve food security, by increasing food supply and thereby lowering domestic prices, and by stimulating demand for unskilled farm labour (Minten and Barrett 2008).

Compared to other regions, sub-Saharan Africa is particularly vulnerable to hunger induced by natural hazards, such as slow-onset drought (IFRCRC 2009). And the number and impact of African disasters seem to be growing. Over the past two decades, the number of food emergencies in Africa has tripled, while 68% more Africans perished in disaster-related deaths during 1999–2008 than the previous decade (IFRCRC 2009). More frequent extreme climate events due to anthropogenic climate change threaten more frequent, severe, local food supply disruptions.

Conflict displaces huge numbers of people, and was a primary cause in nearly half of Africa's 20th-century famines (Devereux and Maxwell 2001). IFRCRC (2009) reports that in 2008 in Africa there were 15.3 million refugees or internally displaced persons. Conflict not only destroys lives and livelihoods, it disrupts markets, production cycles, and humanitarian operations. The resulting misery and desperation too often begets a vicious circle.

IDIOSYNCRATIC THREATS TO FOOD SECURITY

Some individuals are food-insecure for idiosyncratic reasons, even in communities that are food-secure in aggregate. A critical factor driving individual and household-level food insecurity is poverty. Throughout Africa, land holdings are becoming more concentrated; most variation in per capita farm sizes occurs within rather than between villages (Jayne et al. 2003). Rates of child wasting and, especially, stunting fall rapidly with increases in gross national income, as reflected in Figure 1, reflecting the strong, bidirectional relation between poverty and food insecurity. Yet, the benefits of growth can be distributed unevenly across households, with many facing food insecurity even

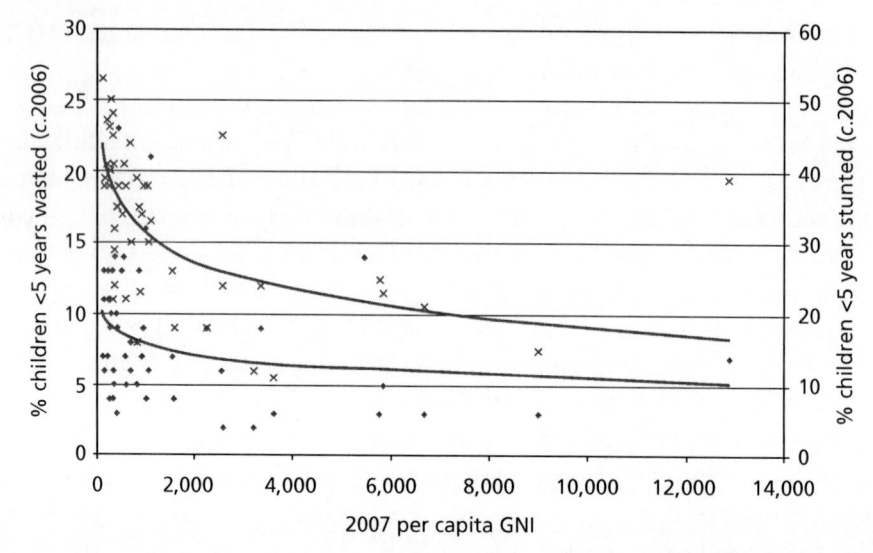

Figure 1. Child stunting and wasting in Africa, by national income. Lines represent logarithmic regressions of stunting on income and of wasting on income, respectively.
(Source: UNICEF 2008.)

during periods of rapid economic growth (Ahmed et al. 2007). Households that face social exclusion, or have less political voice and power, are typically more vulnerable to suffering food insecurity (Chambers 1989).

Disparities in wealth, unequal benefits of growth, and individual influence are not the only reason for within-country variation in food security. Because most asset and income shocks appear idiosyncratic and most African households have limited access to risk management mechanisms such as insurance and credit, risk often translates into food insecurity. Fear of jeopardizing future livelihoods often causes people to choose temporary food insecurity over the sale of productive assets. And within households, the most vulnerable members of shock-affected populations—children and women, in particular—typically suffer disproportionately from food consumption shortfalls during episodes of acute food insecurity, often suffering even when other household members manage to cushion themselves against shocks (Hoddinott 2006). These transitory phenomena can have permanent consequences. Short-term deprivation, especially among very young children in formative stages of cognitive and physiological development, often leads to permanent impairment of performance and earning potential, transmitting food insecurity intergenerationally. Even among adults, severe short-term food insecurity can ensnare individuals and households in nutritional poverty traps (Dasgupta 1997).

Food aid in Africa

Food aid—the international, concessional transfer of food or cash for the express purchase of food—has been the global community's traditional response to food insecurity in low-income, food-deficit countries. When shortages emerge, high-income agricultural exporters donate from their surpluses, although these volumes have declined steadily as OECD government-held surpluses have largely vanished over the past 20 years. Food aid nonetheless remains a dominant form of development assistance to Africa. For example, more than half of US economic assistance to Burkina Faso, Cape Verde, Ethiopia, and Niger in 1999–2005 arrived as food aid (Simmons 2009).

Food aid is widely criticized. First, food aid is budgeted in monetary, not physical units. Therefore, food aid volumes vary inversely with food prices and transportation costs, falling precisely as need peaks. Second, food aid deliveries take months, often arriving too late to respond effectively to emergencies. Third, because most food aid is 'tied'—i.e. shipped from the donor country, in violation of OECD agreements limiting aid tying—it is significantly more expensive, on average, than food procured in or near the destination. Fourth, by expanding aggregate marketed supply, food aid—especially that monetized through markets by government or NGO recipients—can depress and destabilize prices, creating disincentives for local producers on whom aggregate food security most fundamentally depends, although the evidence on food aid's effects on prices and production is quite mixed (Abdulai, Barrett, and Hoddinott 2005; Barrett and Maxwell 2005).

Food aid nonetheless remains essential in response to emergencies marked by food availability shortfalls and poorly functioning local food markets—conditions that obtain with some frequency in Africa. Over the past decade, donor countries have been reforming food aid practices so as to improve their utility in responding to covariate shocks that give rise to widespread food insecurity (Barrett et al. 2009). Local and regional purchases and cash transfers are becoming much more common in Africa, early warning systems continue to improve, and a wider range of more nutritionally appropriate foods are in use, including micronutrient-enriched therapeutic foods for children suffering severe undernutrition.

So long as food insecurity in Africa remains widespread and commonly triggered by covariate shocks, international transfers, including food aid, will remain necessary. But food aid is merely one instrument in the broader pursuit of food security; and its continued reform is desirable in order not to disrupt fragile food marketing systems or depress recipient country producer incentives. Moreover, food aid is of considerably less importance than are improvements to African agricultural productivity and market functioning, and increased incomes and enhanced safety nets to provide increased security against severe shocks. Such advances will turn fundamentally on technological advances, and on institutional and policy improvements, well beyond the domain of food aid.

REFERENCES

Abdulai, A., C. Barrett, and J. Hoddinott, 2005. 'Does food aid really have disincentive effects? New evidence from sub-Saharan Africa', *World Development* 33.10, 1689–1704.

Ahmed, A., R. Vargas Hill, L. Smith, D. Wiesmann, and T. Frankenberger, 2007. *The World's Most Deprived: Characteristics and Causes of Extreme Poverty and Hunger*. Washington, DC: IFPRI.

Barrett, C., 2002. 'Food security and food assistance programs', in B. L. Gardner and G. Rausser (eds), *Handbook of Agricultural Economics*, vol. 2b. Amsterdam: Elsevier.

—— 2008. 'Smallholder market participation: concepts and evidence from eastern and southern Africa', *Food Policy* 33.4, 299–317.

—— R. Bell, E. Lentz, and D. Maxwell, 2009. 'Market information and food insecurity response analysis', *Food Security* 1, 151–68.

—— and D. G. Maxwell, 2005. *Food Aid After Fifty Years: Recasting Its Role*. New York: Routledge.

Chambers, R., 1989. 'Vulnerability, coping and policy', *IDS Bulletin* 20, 1–7.

Dasgupta, P., 1997. 'Nutritional status, the capacity for work, and poverty traps', *Journal of Econometrics* 77.1, 5–37.

Devereux, S., and S. Maxwell (eds), 2001. *Food Security in Sub-Saharan Africa*. London: Practical Action.

Food and Agriculture Organization, 2008. *The State of Food Insecurity in the World 2008*. Rome: FAO.

Hoddinott, J., 2006. 'Shocks and their consequences across and within households in rural Zimbabwe', *Journal of Development Studies* 42, 301–21.

International Federation of Red Cross and Red Crescent Societies, 2009. *World Disasters Report: Focus on Early Warning, Early Action*. Geneva: International Federation.

Jayne, T., T. Yamano, M. T. Weber, et al., 2003. 'Smallholder income and land distribution in Africa: implications for poverty reduction strategies', *Food Policy* 28.3, 253–75.

Minten, B., and C. B. Barrett, 2008. 'Agricultural technology, productivity and poverty in Madagascar', *World Development* 36.5, 797–822.

Simmons, E., 2009. 'Monetization of food aid: reconsidering US policy and practice'. Washington, DC: Partnership to Cut Hunger and Poverty in Africa (June).

UN, 2009. *The Millennium Development Goals Report, 2009*. New York: UN.

UNICEF, 2008. *The State of the World's Children 2009*. New York: UNICEF.

Thematic Perspectives
Aid

Aid and African Development

Patrick Guillaumont

For half a century, aid to sub-Saharan Africa has been debated. And it has been so from very opposite points of view. However, either coming from the right or from the left, arguments used against aid are often similar: it would be inefficient, financing more or less directly 'white elephants' and new oligarchies. In spite of the criticisms, there has been a seemingly official consensus in favour of aid to Africa, not without an actual political debate. During these 50 years, African governments have not ceased to complain about the low level of aid and the gap between this level and the targets adopted by the international community. At the same time northern governments have repeated their commitment to these targets, in particular for Africa, while very often moving in the opposite direction.[1]

This chapter addresses five main issues that might explain the source of the opposing views. First, are there specific needs for external assistance to Africa? The answer is yes. Second, are the usual criticisms of aid effectiveness in Africa robust? The answer is no. Third, do the effects of aid on economic growth and poverty reduction depend only or mainly on policy and governance factors? Again, the answer is no: other relevant factors matter, especially the structural economic vulnerability of recipient countries, which is particularly high in Africa. Fourth, should this vulnerability be taken into account in the geographical allocation of aid resources, besides other more usual criteria such as those related to policy and governance? My answer is yes. Fifth, is the present practice of conditionality of budget support consistent with the needed African policy ownership? The answer is probably no. Policy and governance, the importance of which cannot be denied, are more relevant factors to be considered for the choice of aid channels and modalities than for aid conditionality and geographical aid allocation.

---

[1] During the last decade, while prominent authors opposed one to the other in popular books on the needs for aid (Sachs, 2005, Easterly 2006), the North promises of Monterrey UN Conference in 2002 and G8 Gleneagles meeting in 2005 came up against the consequences of the world economic crisis.

The special context of aid to Africa

Nobody would object to the fact that African development is the responsibility of Africa and needs appropriate African policies. Nor is it debated that external assistance to African development should be designed as transitory. Nevertheless, views are likely to diverge about what policies are appropriate and about the length of the transition period leading to the end of aid. Three main factors are to be considered here: demographic trends, climate change, and peace.

Africa faces the most rapid population growth in the world, which is an exceptional challenge. It requires massive investments, and special support from foreign resources, considering that private capital flows to Africa are far less than to elsewhere. At the same time, the increasing population density is increasing the returns on the needed infrastructure investments. Moreover, with economic growth and the extension of girls' schooling, this is likely to slow down the demographic expansion.

Climate change is another long-term challenge for Africa. The demographic change, along with economic growth, will increasingly make Africa a major source of pollution, calling for the continent's increased participation in the international mitigation effort. Even more important, the vulnerability of Africa to climate change is expected to be particularly high, calling for international support for the domestic efforts of adaptation, inseparable from development programmes and development aid. Since Africa is the region least responsible for climate change, international support to Africa for both mitigation and adaptation is clearly legitimate.

Finally, a third factor that will make the transition towards the end of aid long and difficult is the recurrence of conflicts. The incidence of conflicts, although declining, is still high (and higher in Africa than elsewhere), and the threat of new conflicts is real. Aid has a crucial role to play in post-conflict situations, and a no less important role in the prevention of conflicts.

Misplaced global criticism of aid ineffectiveness for growth in Africa

The main criticism of aid to Africa is as follows. During the last forty years Africa is the one area in the world that has received the largest amount of aid (as a percentage of GDP and per capita). It is also the area where growth rates have been the lowest. This view generally gives rise to two immediate answers, complementary, but not sufficient.

The first is that there is a lot of evidence of aid projects being effective. Recent impact analysis has made more robust the knowledge of what works effectively, in particular for health projects. However, from these impact analyses it is not possible to draw lessons concerning the macroeconomic effects of aid without confronting the traditional issue of fungibility: these projects might have been achieved with domestic resources, the aid support simply freeing resources for marginal expenditures. The positive impact associated with aid projects should then be located in the technology transfer they facilitate.

The second answer is related to the counterfactual. What would have been the long-term growth in Africa in the absence of aid? We need here a model adequately specified to include the relevant control variables, and addressing the issue of possible endogeneity of aid. Actually, building and testing growth regression models has been a popular exercise for economists during the last twelve years, but very few have limited their sample to consider only Africa.[2]

The debate about these models has concerned the robustness of estimations. The influential paper by Burnside and Dollar (2000) arguing that aid is effective only when policy is good (the test variable being a variable multiplying aid by an indicator of policy) has been found to be not robust in many other studies. The main technical difficulties are linked to the need to capture the heterogeneity of the sample both by introducing the relevant variables on which aid effectiveness depends (through multiplicative variables) and by taking into account the fact that it also depends on the level of aid itself. In addition to these topics, widely debated in the literature, two more important issues should be underlined.

The first one is the concept of 'overseas development assistance' (ODA) used to measure 'aid', a 40-year old concept and a very debatable one indeed. Not only does its meaning and content change with the level of interest rates, but, more importantly, the measured flow does not correspond to what is really brought to a country in a given period of time (including items such as expenditures for refugees and foreign students).

The second issue is the lack of a dynamic perspective in the usual aid–growth econometrics. Simply stated, since aid is intended to end in development, the success of aid involves the vanishing of the relationship between aid and growth. It is sometimes argued that emerging economies (such as South Korea, Thailand, or Tunisia) have been growing fast without a significant amount of aid. Although this is true in recent times, it has not been so in the past. On the contrary, these countries received large aid inflows at the beginning of their development process. It is also true that at the beginning of these success stories, the level of education was not as low as in most African countries. Clearly the time dimension of the relationship between aid and growth has not been properly tackled.

---

[2] An exception is found in Gomanee et al. (2005).

Aid as a factor dampening the impact of shocks to Africa

Among the various factors affecting aid effectiveness, vulnerability is of particular relevance for Africa. Most African countries are highly vulnerable to exogenous shocks, either external or natural. While their vulnerability may appear in some cases to be amplified by weak policy resilience, it is firstly a structural vulnerability, resulting both from the size of the shocks they face and from their exposure to the shocks, as evidenced by the Economic Vulnerability Index (EVI) used by the UN for the identification of the least developed countries. Economic vulnerability to shocks not only has long-term negative consequences on economic growth; it is also an important factor for the risk of civil conflict noted above.

What is the role of aid in this respect? Aid volatility, while often mentioned, is not a problem as such; aid unpredictability, which is more difficult to measure, may be the problem. Relying on *ex post* measures, the concern has shifted from aid volatility to whether aid is procyclical or countercyclical, with regard to another flow supposed to be independent of aid. More relevant is whether aid is stabilizing or destabilizing, the stabilizing character being measured by the difference between the instability of the reference flow and the instability of the aggregate of this flow and aid. Even if procyclical, aid can be stabilizing when its instability is lower than that of the flow to which it is compared. With reference to the exports of goods and services (more exogenous than the fiscal revenue to which aid is sometimes compared), aid to Africa appears to have been more often stabilizing than destabilizing. An overall test of this stabilizing impact is also given by the negative effect of the aid to GDP ratio on the volatility of income in a cross-country regression, where exogenous factors of instability are taken into account.[3]

The shock-dampening effect of aid to Africa has important implications for its contribution to growth. It is a corollary of the agreed idea that income instability lowers long-term income growth. Moreover, as evidenced in various papers relying on cross-country regressions, the contribution of aid to growth is significantly and positively conditioned by the instability of exports: aid dampens the negative influence of exogenous shocks, such as export instability, on growth (tested through a multiplicative variable, aid × export instability). Moreover, it seems that vulnerability not only enhances the marginal effect of aid on growth but also slows its decrease when aid increases, in other words it expands the absorptive capacity of aid.

Additional support to these macroeconomic tests is given by an analysis of the factors determining the rate of success of World Bank projects: vulnerable countries (i.e. facing high export instability), like African countries, appear to be less subject to decreasing

---

[3] These issues are analysed in Chauvet and Guillaumont (2009).

returns when the level of aid increases. It is another token of a high absorptive capacity in Africa.

The shock-dampening effect of aid has implications beyond economic growth. First, there seems to be increasing evidence that a more stable growth is more pro-poor: income instability has lasting consequences on the extent of poverty, due to irreversible effects of negative shocks. Thus, if aid has a dampening effect, it not only supports a sustained growth, but can also contribute to make this growth more pro-poor. Second, by dampening economic shocks, aid can contribute to lowering the risk of civil wars.

Can this dampening effect be reinforced? A natural response is in setting up schemes to compensate for the (negative) shocks.[4] To be effective, insurance aid should be highly concessional and automatic, and designed so that moral hazard is avoided. Although they are needed and likely to be improved, compensatory schemes are not at present an adequate way of addressing the structural vulnerability of African economies.

Aid allocation criteria among African countries to be revised

Since the debated paper by Burnside and Dollar, there has been a strong tendency to argue that aid should be allocated among developing (African) countries according to the quality of their policy, institutions, and governance. The selectivity of aid is assessed essentially with regard to this criterion.[5] And the multilateral development banks, including the African Development Bank (AfDB), use a so-called 'performance-based allocation' (PBA) model, that relies on a formula where the assessment of the policy and governance (through the clusters of the Country Policy and Institutional Assessment, CPIA) has an overwhelming impact on the allocation of aid among eligible countries. Until recently the growing scepticism about the robustness of the relationship between aid effectiveness and policy, as well as some discontent about the subjective assessment of 'performance', had not weakened the donors' support for the model; but the reliance on a policy and governance criterion had become justified less by the search for effectiveness than by an incentive impact, itself uncertain. Moreover, in the process of facing the impossible task of applying the PBA to the most fragile states, where policy and governance indicators are rather low but needs are high, exceptions and special windows have emerged. Actually the present PBA seems to meet none of the main

---

[4] The schemes implemented (compensatory finance facility, then exogenous shocks facility of the IMF, Stabex of the Lomé Conventions, replaced by 'Flex' of Cotonou Convention) show the difficulties in mobilizing resources quickly and adequately in case of shocks.

[5] Exception in Amprou, Guillaumont, and Guillaumont Jeanneney (2007).

principles that should govern aid allocation, namely effectiveness, equity, and transparency.

Aware of the limitations of the present PBA,[6] the AfDB has commissioned a report to examine how the formula could be improved in the specific case of Africa. The report refers to the three principles quoted above. It suggests the addition of measures of structural economic vulnerability and of (low-level) human capital as criteria, first because they are structural handicaps to growth to be compensated in order to make opportunities less unequal among countries. The vulnerability criterion is also legitimated by two additional reasons: it meets the principle of effectiveness, because vulnerability enhances the marginal effectiveness of aid, and it allows aid to fragile states to be allocated in an integrated framework, making the whole allocation more transparent, and the treatment of fragility preventive as well as curative. The report also makes proposals to augment the support given to regional integration and the incentive to use this support, which is another way of addressing the vulnerability issue.

Finally, the inclusion of these two structural criteria alongside the policy and governance criterion would reduce the weight of the latter, often considered as too strong and reflecting too uniform a view of what is the best policy and governance. Indeed, this criterion hardly fits the principles of ownership and alignment (as regards the recipient policy choices) that is at the heart of the Paris Declaration (2005),[7] which was followed by the Accra Agenda for Action (2008).

African ownership, conditionality reform, and the optimal share of budget support

One of the most acute criticisms of aid to Africa concerns its impact on independence and ownership. This complex issue arouses passionate debate. Many studies have tried to identify crowding-out effects of aid on variables such as domestic savings and fiscal revenue, with mixed results. The uncertainty of results comes from the heterogeneity of the flows to be compared, the treatment of aid endogeneity and the time frame of the studies. For instance, aid may weaken the tax effort in the short term, but if it allows the country to achieve more public investments or to tax private enterprises less heavily, it may favour long-term growth leading to increased fiscal revenues.

---

[6] Previously analysed by Kanbur (2005).

[7] 'The Paris Declaration, endorsed on 2 March 2005, is an international agreement by which over 100 ministers, heads of agencies, and other senior officials "committed their countries and organisations to continue to increase efforts towards harmonisation, alignment, and managing aid for results with a set of monitorable actions and indicators"' (OECD website).

Whatever the quantitative estimations of the crowding out effects of aid, governments of countries which are highly dependent on aid used to be more accountable to external donors than to their citizens. It is all the more debatable now that the African countries are becoming more democratic. And aid may weaken the democracy itself. Donors often consider that the lack of ownership of policies by African governments comes from a lack of capacities, and that the right response is in capacity building. While it is right to pursue capacity building, even if much has been built in the last decades, this is not a sufficient answer.

To overcome the institutional limits to absorptive capacity, aid itself should be reformed. This is particularly so in the case of budget support, now a major part of total aid to Africa. Previously, budget support seemed less intrusive than project aid; but opinions have changed with the adjustment period where the conditionality of budget support showed its challenges. Of course, conditionality has shifted, becoming less detailed, less dogmatic, and more coordinated between donors. However, it essentially remains a conditionality related to policy instruments or measures, leaving limited room for ownership.

For the above reason it has been recommended that the traditional, albeit amended, conditionality based on the adoption of policy reforms should be replaced with conditionality based on outcomes or performance—performance being measured in terms of ultimate objectives, such as the progress obtained in reduction of child mortality or knowledge acquisition by children.[8] This allows for better ownership of reforms, since policy instruments are chosen by the country; it avoids arbitrary judgement of multiple heterogeneous policy measures; it allows for a support modulated according to the outcomes; and by eliminating the scope of discordant policy advices, it facilitates coordination between donors

The principle of this proposal is consistent with the international rhetoric on alignment, harmonization, and ownership. However its implementation remains limited. A pioneering initiative of the European Commission has gone only half-way, as the retained conditions refer to intermediate indicators still related to policy instruments. Transferring the full responsibility for policy choices runs up against the habits of partners, in particular of aid donor administrations or agencies. Transfer also requires a capacity to assess performances (outcomes), after taking into account the result of exogenous shocks.

It remains the case that reform cannot be undertaken everywhere in Africa. It is difficult to apply an outcome-based conditionality in failing states. In that case, it might be better, at least temporarily, to avoid budget support and to deliver aid by other channels, bypassing the failed state. As is already clear for aid allocation, bad governance

---

[8] As argued by Collier, Guillaumont, Guillaumont Jeanneney, and Gunning (1999), and Adam, Chambas, Guillaumont, Guillaumont Jeanneney, and Gunning (2004).

should not lead to the punishment of citizens already suffering from it: aid modalities should be adapted to make aid deliverable by other means.

A simple conclusion emerges. The big push needed to move African countries definitively out of the poverty trap may effectively be supported by an aid increase if aid modalities are simultaneously improved. Absorptive capacity depends on the modalities of aid.

REFERENCES

Adam, Christopher, Gérard Chambas, Patrick Guillaumont, Sylviane Guillaumont Jeanneney, and Jan Willem Gunning, 2004. 'Performance-based conditionality: a European perspective', *World Development* 32.6, 1059–70.

Amprou, Jacky, Patrick Guillaumont, and Sylviane Guillaumont Jeanneney, 2007. 'Aid selectivity according to augmented criteria', *World Economy* 30.5, 733–63.

Burnside, Craig, and David Dollar, 2000. 'Aid, policies and growth', *American Economic Review* 90.4, 847–68.

Chauvet L., and P. Guillaumont, 2009. 'Aid, volatility and growth again: when aid volatility matters and when it does not', *Review of Development Economics* 13.3, 452–63.

Collier, P., P. Guillaumont, S. Guillaumont Jeanneney, and J.W. Gunning, 1999. 'Reforming Stabex', *World Economy* 22.5, 669–82.

Easterly, William, 2006. *The White Man's Burden: Why the West's Efforts to Aid the Rest Have Done So Much Ill and So Little Good*. Oxford/New York: Oxford University Press/Penguin.

Gomanee, K., O. Morrissey, P. Mosley, and A. Verschoor, 2005. 'Aid, government expenditure and aggregate welfare', *World Development* 33, 355–71.

Guillaumont, P., 2009. 'Aid effectiveness for poverty reduction: macroeconomic overview and emerging issues', FERDI Working Paper 5, Clermont Ferrand.

—— and S. Guillaumont Jeanneney, 2010. 'Big push versus absorptive capacity: how to reconcile the two approaches', in G. Mavrotas (ed.), *Foreign Aid for Development: Issues, Challenges, and the New Agenda*. Oxford: Oxford University Press, 297–322.

—— —— and D. Vencatachellum, 2009. 'Accounting for vulnerability of African countries in performance based allocation', Working Paper 103 (October), African Development Bank.

Kanbur, Ravi, 2005. 'Reforming the formula: a modest proposal for introducing development outcomes in IDA allocation procedures', *Revue d'Économie du Développement*, 79–99.

Sachs, Jeffrey, 2005. *The End of Poverty: Economic Possibilities for Our Time*. Harmondsworth: Penguin.

Private Aid to Africa

Homi Kharas

Can private aid to Africa succeed where official aid has failed? That is the tantalizing promise now being made to Africa. Foreign aid from private sources is rapidly changing the landscape of international development assistance. In 2008, international giving from US-based foundations, NGOs, churches, corporations, and other private actors totalled $37.3 billion (over $10 billion more than US official development assistance in 2008) and globally private aid probably amounts to between $55–65 billion per year.[1] Although statistics on the regional distribution of this aid are poor, somewhere between one-quarter to two-fifths of private aid may go to sub-Saharan Africa, implying that private aid to Africa might be in the range of $14–30 billion annually.[2]

Despite the financial crisis, private aid has been resilient and growing rapidly. According to InterAction, an umbrella group of 172 of the largest US foundations and charities raising over $6 billion annually from private sources, the private NGO sector has evolved from a community dependent on official resources for 70% of its activities 10 years ago to one that is now 70% funded directly from private member contributions. Long time series statistics on the value of private international aid do not exist, because the first reliable measures only date from 2006, but other data suggest that private aid has in fact grown rapidly over the last twenty years. For example, the sheer number of private foundations in the United States has grown from 40,100 in 1995 to 71,000 in 2005 (with more than 650 making grants for international affairs).[3] Meanwhile, the number of international NGOs quadrupled from 6,000 to 26,000 in the 1990s, and could have reached some 40,000 organizations today.[4]

This rapid growth in private aid stands in contrast to the more gradual increase in official aid to Africa. According to the OECD, Africa is likely to receive only $11 billion of the $25 billion increase promised by donors at Gleneagles in 2005.[5] In nominal US dollar terms, net official aid from DAC donors fell in 2009 compared to 2008. Although the $44 billion in official development assistance to Africa in 2008 from all donors—

---

[1] Center for Global Prosperity (2010).
[2] Koch et al (2008).
[3] Lawrence et al. (2007); Renz and Atienza (2006).
[4] Keohane and Nye (2000).
[5] 2010 aid forecast by the OECD DAC: http://www.oecd.org/document/11/0,3343,en_2649_34487_44981579_1_1_1_1,00.html

bilateral and multilateral—still dwarfs private aid,[6] much of that is an accounting entry for unpaid and unpayable debts or for expatriate technical assistance of questionable development value. Some estimates suggest that Africa receives only about $20 billion in aid for development projects and programmes, and up to half of this may be diverted from its intended purposes before reaching the final beneficiary.[7]

But the public/private aid divide is about more than the shift in dollars. At its heart there is a debate about how best to give aid. Official donors are increasingly moving towards providing money directly to poor country governments in the form of budget support, based on the realization that if aid is not 'owned' by recipients, then it is unlikely to have a sustainable development impact. At just the same time, private donors are looking to provide goods, services, and new business models in a very hands-on, engaged contribution to development.

The promise of private aid is that it is large, growing rapidly and, in the eyes of some, potentially more effective as it bypasses the public sector that in many African countries is perceived as corrupt or incompetent. Private aid spans traditional service delivery areas, such as health, education, and smallholder agriculture, as well as new forms of 'social investment' that sit at the intersection of the non-profit and for-profit private sectors.

Is private aid making a difference? In some of the basic service delivery areas, an argument can be made that the answer is yes. The list of aid programmes that have been shown to be effective through a rigorous academic study, as constructed by Banerjee and He,[8] would be familiar to most NGOs: education vouchers and adult literacy; deworming and vitamin/nutritional supplements; vaccinations and HIV/AIDS prevention; anti-mosquito bed netting; fertilizers and clean water supply. From a micro point of view, these programmes have demonstrably high rates of return. Because NGOs operate with local staff and partners, they can also avoid high expatriate salaries and have lower overhead costs. All this, coupled with the NGO approach of providing services rather than money for development, suggests that NGO programmes might suffer from less leakage than official aid.

At almost the other end of the development spectrum, private aid is more and more linked with private businesses in hybrid models that have attracted a new set of supporters—those who believe in development as a business rather than as charity. These 'social entrepreneurs' promote flexible pilot start-ups that can be taken to scale

---

[6] OECD DAC Statistics at http://stats.oecd.org/Index.aspx?DatasetCode=ODA_RECIP. Note that aid from some non-DAC donors, most importantly China, is not included in this figure.
[7] Kharas and Hermias (2008).
[8] Banerjee and He (2008).

once a new business model is developed with an understanding of the economics of the 'base of the pyramid.'[9] The business models are heavily influenced by the opportunities afforded by new technologies, such as mobile phones, and other management breakthroughs in distribution or marketing that reduce the transaction costs of reaching the poor enough to create new industries where none existed before.[10]

In the corporate and foundation worlds of rich countries, much of the wealth being ploughed back into developing countries is IT-related. Names like Google.org, the Omidyar Network, the Bill and Melinda Gates Foundation, and Cisco Networking Academy are now recognized as major development partners. These foundations reflect the history of their own growth by focusing on the ability of innovation, technology, and modern management methods (including empirical randomized trials) to address problems of extreme poverty. Staff from the organizations are closely involved with project design and implementation, in the same way as 'angel investors' provide knowhow along with financial resources in start-up companies.

But the promise of private aid in Africa remains just that—a promise, not a reality. A multi-country effort by the Monitor group, a private consultancy, to identify suitable bottom-of-the-pyramid firms in Africa found that the pipeline of businesses that had the potential to be scaled up was thin. There were many encouraging examples, but not sufficient quantity to change the development trajectory of a country. Some private aid groups, like the New York-based Acumen Fund, are actively looking for development partners in Africa but with only moderate success. The online microfinance lending outfit, Kiva.org, feels it is more limited by inadequate demand (for zero interest loans) than by inadequate supply of funds.

In fact, for all its promise, there is very little evidence for or against the idea that private aid is cost-effective. All the evaluations of good development practice come from official development projects. While there are plenty of anecdotes about the positive impact of many private aid interventions, these organizations tend not to conduct evaluations with the same degree of independence and academic rigour as is expected of public aid.[11] The few academic studies of private aid tend to find mixed results—difficulty in linking private aid to changes in economy-wide aggregates, like infant mortality or female illiteracy; herding behaviour in country selectivity, in the same way as official aid; some 'faddishness' in aid allocations. Country characteristics like good governance or poverty appear to affect online private aid-givers less than official aid.[12]

---

[9] Prahalad (2009).
[10] *The Economist* (2010).
[11] For example, Kiva.org has its field partners post 'business journals' identifying how the loan is being used and the effect on business owners, but these serve as devices to make a personal connection between the recipient and donor rather than as a formal evaluation.
[12] See Masud and Yontcheva (2005); Dreher, Mölders, and Nunnenkamp (2007); Koch et al. (2008); Major et al. (2006); Desai and Kharas (2010).

NGOs have also had their fair share of corrupt and sometimes criminal activity, with corporate officers siphoning off funds for personal gain.[13] Many local NGOs have come into being precisely because of government inadequacies and failures—in these cases, private aid can be in opposition to what government is trying to do, risking loss of sustainability and ownership. This does not matter when NGOs are operating on a small scale, as they tend to do. But as the number of NGOs grows, it can contribute to the growing fragmentation of projects and lack of coordination in progressing towards common, national goals.

In fact, private aid is simply different from official aid, neither observably better or worse. Individuals, NGOs and foundations allocate aid differently from official donors. Private aid supports people—children, women, the poor, small entrepreneurs. It operates at a micro level. In contrast, official aid supports governments and countries. It operates at a macroeconomic level. Both are needed for development to occur.

The combination of significant funding through private aid poses new challenges for aid policy, planning, and coordination. The institutional mechanisms for making policy only incorporate official aid donors. For example, databases on the amount of aid flowing into a country and into specific sectors within the country typically only include official aid. Official donors sometimes collaborate to prepare joint country assistance strategies, but private donors have not, as yet, participated in these exercises in Africa. Lessons from evaluations of projects done by private aid agencies are not systematically included into official aid projects.

That is slowly changing. New forms of collaboration at a sectoral level are being developed within countries. In several African countries, technical sectoral working groups are developing needs assessments, sharing information and debating policy involving not just public and private aid donors but also local civil society as well as government ministries and local communities. These groups are most active in health and education, but also extend to water, sanitation, and other public services.

Through these sectoral working groups, private aid is better coordinated with national programmes and indeed helps shape such programmes. Perhaps most importantly, the presence of private aid has helped to rebalance development policy toward more bottom-up approaches where the voices of poor people, local civil society, and communities are heard and their active participation in project implementation is sought. Private aid flows primarily through local civil society organizations, and as it expands, the voice of these groups grows commensurately.

Private aid does not flow through government budgets (nor, in most cases, does official aid) but it can affect national strategies. Private aid tends to be more innovative, people-centred, long-term, and grounded in local adaptation.[14] In several cases,

---

[13] Fremont-Smith and Kosaras (2003).
[14] Worthington and Pipa (2010).

governments have taken to scale pilot programmes initiated with support from private aid. Private aid has helped build capabilities in local civil society and communities that help ensure that policy decisions and local service delivery take into account the real needs of poor people.

REFERENCES

Banerjee, Abhijit, and Ruimin He, 2008. 'Making aid work', in William Easterly (ed.), *Reinventing Foreign Aid*. Cambridge, Mass.: MIT Press.

Center for Global Prosperity, 2010. *The Index of Global Philanthropy and Remittances*. Washington, DC: Hudson Institute.

Desai, Raj, and Homi Kharas, 2010. 'Democratizing foreign aid', *Journal of International Law and Politics* 42.4.

Dreher, Axel, Florian Mölders, and Peter Nunnenkamp, 2007. 'Are NGOs the better donors?', Kiel Institute for the World Economy, Working Paper 1383.

Economist, The, 2010. 'Here be dragons: the emerging world is teeming with new business models', *The Economist* print edition V.395 No. 8678.

Fremont-Smith, Marion R., and Andras Kosaras, 2003. 'Wrongdoing by officers and directors of charities: a survey of press reports 1995–2002', Hauser Center Working Paper No. 20: http://www.ksghauser.harvard.edu/publications/working_papers/workingpaperlist.htm.

Keohane, Robert, and Joseph S. Nye, 2000. 'Introduction', in Joseph S. Nye and John Donohue (eds), *Governance in a Globalizing World*. Washington, DC: Brookings Institution.

Kharas, Homi, and Joshua Hermias, 2008. 'The new realities of aid', Washington, DC: Brookings Institution: http://www.brookings.edu/~/media/Files/Centers/wc/new_realities_of_aid.ashx.

Koch, Dirk-Jan et al., 2008. 'Keeping a low profile: what determines the allocation of aid by nongovernmental organizations', Kiel Institute for the World Economy, Working Paper 1406.

Lawrence, Steven, et al., 2007. *Foundation Growth and Giving Estimates*. New York: Foundation Center.

Major, Solomon, et al., 2006. 'The allocation of private development aid: empowering recipients or advancing donor interests', American Political Science Association conference paper: http://www.allacademic.com/meta/p150437_index.html.

Masud, Nadia, and Boriana Yontcheva, 2005. 'Does foreign aid reduce poverty? Empirical evidence from nongovernmental and bilateral aid', IMF Working Paper WP/05/100.

Prahalad, C. K., 2009. *The Fortune at the Bottom of the Pyramid: Eradicating Poverty Through Profits*. Upper Saddle River, NJ: FT Press.

Renz, Loren, and Jose Atienza, 2006. *International Grantmaking Update*. New York: Foundation Center.

Worthington, Sam, and Tony Pipa, 2010. 'International NGOs and foundations: essential partners in creating an effective architecture for aid': http://www.brookings.edu/~/media/Files/rc/papers/2010/09_development_aid/09_development_aid.pdf.

HIPC Debt Relief in Sub-Saharan Africa

Njuguna Ndung'u

1. Introduction

The main question in the 1990s was whether African countries would repay their huge external debt, given the state of their economies and the macroeconomic problems that were plaguing them. Several initiatives have been developed since then. This chapter analyses the impact of debt relief on growth, and whether the debt scenario of the most highly indebted poor countries (HIPCs) in sub-Saharan Africa has improved since the grim outlook of the 1990s.

The external debt problem had major implications in Africa, the most important at the time being lack of fiscal space—reduced fiscal adjustment and a weakened ability to build capacity that could facilitate growth and external debt re-payments. For example, to support future payment ability, export supply capacity had to be improved. But this required a set of incentives, which could not be maintained in the presence of macro imbalances. Thus external debt overhang problems became a force and a major risk in Africa, preventing appropriate adjustment and reforms in the 1990s. The empirical and analytical studies in the 1990s were unanimous that the magnitude of external debt problem in Africa was shackling its growth and investment (see e.g. Elbadawi, Ndulu, and Ndung'u 1997; Ndung'u 2003; Clements, Bhattacharya, and Nguyen 2003). The debt burden significantly threatened Africa's hope of future economic growth recovery. Drastic actions were needed to help these countries out of the conundrum.

Those persuasive arguments led to bilateral and multilateral initiatives to either cancel or restructure Africa's external debt. The HIPC Initiative was launched in 1996 to reduce external debt of the HIPCs to manageable levels, and also to create an appropriate signalling mechanism for macroeconomic stability and low country risk. The Multilateral Debt Relief Initiative (MDRI) was launched in 2005 to make available additional resources to the HIPCs to help them achieve UN Millennium Development Goals (MDGs).

The chapter highlights the evolution and magnitude of the external debt problem in Section 2. It traces the debt relief initiatives in Section 3, while Sections 4 and 5 evaluate their success and challenges, respectively. It ends with a summary and conclusion in Section 6.

2. The evolution and magnitude of the problem

The external debt in sub-Saharan Africa (SSA) countries was considered a crisis in the 1990s. Of the 33 countries classified as HIPCs, 26 were in SSA. Debt servicing took an average of about 21% of total exports in 1988, before falling to 15% in 1995. It consumed over 20% of government revenue. The per capita growth for the African region was negative in 1990s. Given these pervasive debt indicators, it was clear that this crisis required feasible solutions.

2.1. CONTRIBUTORY FACTORS

But how did these debt levels come about? The main factors include the following:

- Lack of sustained adjustment policies, particularly in the face of exogenous shocks (terms of trade shocks), gave rise to sizeable financing needs and weakened the capacity to service debt. For example, the commodity export booms in the 1980s and 1990s induced higher government spending that later led to excessive borrowing.
- Lack of prudent debt management policies combined with worsening terms of borrowing, particularly lending on commercial terms and reduced grant element in the official debt commitments.
- Increased debt scheduling: formal rescheduling increased from an average of 5 per year in 1975–80 to 148 per year in 1980–90. The amount of debts rescheduled increased from US $558 million in 1980 to US$5 billion in 1983 and US$10 billion in 1990 (Thisen 1994).
- A combination of changes of interest rate regime from fixed to variable international interest rates on US-denominated external debt and a stronger US dollar tremendously increased the cost of servicing loans.
- The implementation of structural adjustment programmes in the 1980s without appropriate sequencing also contributed to the debt crisis (see Elbadawi et al. 1997).

2.2. MAGNITUDE OF THE EXTERNAL DEBT PROBLEM BEFORE DEBT RELIEF

Indicators of debt distress of HIPCs before debt relief are summarized in Table 1. The table compares countries in four different categories, HIPC 1, HIPC 2, HIPC 3, and non-HIPC. Total debt service as a ratio of gross national income (TDS/GNI) ranged between an average of 4% and 5% with post-completion-point HIPCs (HIPC 1 countries[1]) having a higher ratio. As a ratio of exports of goods and services (TDS/XGS), which indicates ability and capacity to pay, this averaged 24% in 1990–94 but declined to 20% between 1995–9 for HIPC 1 countries. For non-HIPCs, it declined from an average of 11.6% to 9% in 1990–94 and 1995–9, respectively. In other words, in HIPCs, 20 cents was spent to service external debt for every dollar of exports in the 1990s, while in non-HIPCs 9 cents was servicing the debt for each dollar earned. Debt overhang is very evident from the stock of external debt as a ratio of gross national income (EDT/GNI) and exports of goods and services (EDT/XGS). For HIPCs, the external debt was on average more than their GNI. For post-completion-point countries, external debt was 120% of GNI in 1990–94. In terms of EDT/XGS, the HIPCs had external debt stock more than five times their exports, while the ratio in non-HPICs was about 100%.

Table 1. Indicators of debt distress before crisis

	TDS/GNI (%)		TDS/XGS (%)		EDT/GNI (%)		EDT/XGS (%)	
	1990–94	1995–99	1990–94	1995–99	1990–94	1995–99	1990–94	1995–99
HIPC 1	5.02	5.12	23.59	19.82	120.35	118.64	715.20	692.93
HIPC 2	4.24	3.06	19.15	21.66	152.22	246.99	1192.4	1256.2
HIPC 3	4.87	4.04	16.21	9.36	134.46	91.89	277.64	262.72
Non-HIPC	5.15	5.00	11.56	8.90	73.22	63.33	132.12	109.91

TDS: Total Debt Service; EDT: External Debt Stock; GNI: Gross National Income; XGS: exports of goods and services.
HIPC 1: Post-completion-point HIPC countries: Benin, Burkina Faso, Cameroon, Ethiopia, Ghana, Gambia, Madagascar, Malawi, Mali, Mauritania, Mozambique, Niger, Rwanda, Sao Tome, Senegal, Sierra Leone, Tanzania, Uganda, and Zambia.
HIPC 2: Interim countries at decision point: Burundi, Central African Republic, Chad, Congo Democratic, Congo Republic, Guinea, Guinea Bissau, and Liberia.
HIPC 3: Pre-decision-point HIPC countries: Côte d'Ivoire, Comoros, Eritrea, Somalia, Sudan, and Togo.
Non-HIPC countries: Botswana, Cape Verde, Equatorial Guinea, Gabon, Kenya, Lesotho, Mauritius, Namibia, Nigeria, Seychelles, South Africa, Swaziland, and Zimbabwe.
Source: World Bank World Development Indicators database 2009.

---

[1] HIPC 1 countries include Benin, Burkina Faso, Cameroon, Ethiopia, Ghana, Gambia, Madagascar, Malawi, Mali, Mauritania, Mozambique, Niger, Rwanda, Sao Tome, Senegal, Sierra Leone, Tanzania, Uganda, and Zambia.

Table 2. Selected macroeconomic indicators for SSA countries

	GDP growth (%)		Inflation (%)		Foreign Direct Investment as % of GDP		Exports of goods and services as % of GDP	
	1990–94	1995–99	1990–94	1995–99	1990–94	1995–99	1990–94	1995–99
HIPC 1	1.36	4.32	23.79	13.42	0.97	1.74	20.12	21.80
HIPC 2	0.25	1.79	24.22	15.13	1.14	4.19	18.53	21.93
HIPC 3	3.18	4.50	6.18	5.45	0.50	3.87	22.81	27.21
Non HIPC	3.72	3.90	13.65	10.82	2.60	12.77	40.60	48.72

Source: World Bank World Development Indicators database 2009.

Table 2 summarizes macroeconomic indicators for the same group of countries. In 1990–94, the GDP growth rate for HIPCs was on average lower than that for the non-HIPCs. However, it increased for HIPCs in 1995–9, especially for HIPC 1 countries, which recovered from an average growth of 1.36% to 4.32%. A similar pattern is observed for inflation: the inflation in HIPC 1 and HIPC 2 countries[2] was relatively high (at an average of 24%) in 1990–94 before declining to 14% in 1995–9. On average, foreign direct investment (FDI) as a percent of GDP was higher for non-HIPCs (2.6%) than HIPCs (0.87%) in 1990–94. This increased marginally for HIPCs (to 3.3%) and substantially for non-HIPCs (to 12.8%) in 1995–9. Similarly, exports of goods and services as a percentage of GDP for non-HIPCs was double that for HIPCs, at 40.6% and 48.7% in 1990–94 and 1995–9, respectively, versus 20.5% and 23.6% for the same periods.

These countries were heavily indebted, and this prevented any form of fiscal adjustment. Their macro indicators and capacity to service debt was being threatened by macro imbalance and low growth trajectory. Solutions were required; Section 3 turns to the HIPC Initiative as a solution.

3. Debt relief initiatives for African countries

The HIPC Initiative was one of the most comprehensive proposals put forward as a solution to debt distress problems for SSA countries. There was consensus that external debt relief could liberate resources that could be directed towards activities that would support sustainable growth and development. Improvement in the quality of public expenditures would support institutional capacity, enhance the delivery of social services and support poverty reduction. Three years after the launch of the HIPC Initiative, its

---

[2] HIPC 2 countries include Burundi, Central African Republic, Chad, Congo Democratic, Congo Republic, Guinea, Guinea Bissau, and Liberia.

results were evident, forcing an upgrade to Enhanced HIPC Initiative that allowed the IMF and the World Bank to provide faster, deeper, and broader debt relief, and strengthened the links with poverty reduction and social policies.

For HIPC eligibility, the first step (decision point) was to fulfil the following conditions: eligibility to borrow from the World Bank's International Development Agency (IDA) and IMF's Poverty Reduction and Growth Facility; debt burden beyond the prescribed threshold; an established track record of reform and a poverty reduction strategy in place.

At the completion point, the country would qualify to receive full and irrevocable debt reduction agreed upon at the decision point, if it satisfactorily implemented the reforms agreed upon. Countries that remained committed to sound poverty reduction policies throughout the period between decision point and completion point would qualify for assistance during the interim relief period.

As at the end of June 2009, 40 countries were eligible or potentially eligible for HIPC Initiative assistance, of which 33 were SSA countries. Of these, 21 were receiving full debt relief after reaching their completion points, while 8 were at the interim stage.

In addition to the HIPC Initiative, MDRI was meant to accelerate progress towards achieving the MDGs and has been implemented since 2006. The MDRI was to provide 100% cancellation of eligible debt stock owed to multilateral financial institutions for countries that reach the completion point. The overall assistance committed to the 33 post-decision point HIPCs amounted to US$117 billion (in nominal terms), including US$49 billion under the MDRI.

4. What are the successes of debt relief so far?

Debt relief has had a direct impact on the levels of external debt in recipient countries. Table 3 shows that post-completion (HIPC 1) countries' total debt service as a ratio of GNI (TDS/GNI) has declined by half from an average of 5.1% in 1995–9 to 2.1% in 2006–7. Not only had total debt service declined in these countries, it had declined more than in non-HIPCs, where TDS/GNI fell from an average of 5.0% to 3.6%. This provides a strong conclusion that even though the burden of debt declined in Africa, it declined more for debt relief recipients. The same is observed when total debt service is measured as a ratio of exports (TDS/XGS). It declined by half, from an average of 19.8% to 9.2% for HIPC 1 countries and from an average of 8.9% to 5.4% in 1995–9 and 2006–7 for non-HIPCs, respectively. Again the decline in the share was more pronounced in HIPCs, where it declined by about 10%, compared to 3.5% in non-HIPCs.

Table 3 further shows that external debt stock as a ratio of GNI (EDT/GNI) declined from an average of 118.64% in 1995–9 to 43.14% in 2006–7. As a ratio of exports of

Table 3. Debt distress indicators: before and after debt relief

	TDS/GNI			TDS/XGS			EDT/GNI			EDT/XGS		
	1995–99	2000–2005	2006–7	1995–99	2000–2005	2006–7	1995–99	2000–2005	2006–7	1995–99	2000–2005	2006–7
HIPC 1	5.12	3.07	2.05	19.82	12.71	9.21	118.64	110.50	43.14	692.93	510.2	176.85
HIPC 2	3.06	3.56	4.00	21.66	19.46	23.06	246.99	211.59	152.67	1256.2	827.5	508.14
HIPC 3	4.04	2.50	1.75	9.36	5.93	3.03	91.89	94.63	72.25	262.72	240.8	143.21
Non HIPC	5.00	3.97	3.57	8.90	7.55	5.37	63.33	49.69	40.95	109.91	84.54	54.46

	INT/XGS			XGS/GDP			TR/GDP			Reserves (months import cover)		
	1995–99	2000–2005	2006–7	1995–99	2000–2005	2006–7	1995–99	2000–2005	2006–7	1995–99	2000–2005	2006–7
HIPC 1	7.13	4.32	2.19	21.80	23.34	26.94	12.32	13.37	14.60	3.02	4.14	4.59
HIPC 2	7.69	5.46	3.88	21.93	28.65	32.93	8.87	6.36	–	2.66	2.61	2.38
HIPC 3	4.12	2.63	0.57	27.21	26.25	27.52	17.19	14.59	15.39	2.58	2.09	2.84
Non HIPC	3.44	2.26	1.88	48.72	54.58	54.15	24.37	25.29	27.92	3.79	4.57	5.54

	FDI			GDP growth			Inflation		
	1995–99	2000–2005	2006–7	1995–99	2000–2005	2006–7	1995–99	2000–2005	2006–7
HIPC 1	1.74	3.84	4.21	4.32	5.33	6.34	13.42	8.99	8.52
HIPC 2	4.19	7.09	10.32	1.79	3.73	3.93	15.13	8.30	8.80
HIPC 3	3.87	1.85	1.30	4.50	0.89	1.29	5.45	7.34	4.06
Non HIPC	12.77	3.22	3.5	3.90	2.88	5.58	10.82	23.70	8.00

Source: World Bank (2009).

goods and services (EDT/XGS), it declined substantially from an average of 693% in 1995–9 to 176.85% in 2006–7. These were more pronounced declines compared to non-HIPCs, where the ratios declined from an average of 63.3% to 41% and 109% to 54.5%, respectively.

The above picture is also supported by the substantial declines in interest payments on external debt. In general, the results show that the debt burdens for HIPCs have been reduced markedly when compared to non-HIPCs, thanks to the debt relief initiatives. These results support assertions by Espejo and Unigovskaya (2008) that debt service by these countries has declined by about 3 percentage points of GDP between 1999 and 2006 and their poverty-reducing expenditures increased by about the same magnitude. On average, spending on health, education, and other social services is more than five times the amount of debt service payments.

Has debt relief delivered its promise? First, the sharp decline in external debt in countries that have reached post-completion point is directly attributed to the debt relief efforts (see Table 3). In general, these countries have stronger GDP and export growth and their debt sustainability outlook has improved substantially, with 21 out of 34 countries classified at a low or moderate risk of debt distress at the end of 2007 (see also Le Manchec 2008).

Second, most post-completion-point countries are in a better debt situation than other HIPCs and non-HIPCs (IDA/IMF 2008). For example at the end of 2007, their net present value (NPV) of the debt-to-export ratio averaged 63%, compared with an average of 200% for pre-completion-point HIPCs. The distribution of risk ratings is also better for HIPC 1 countries than for non-HIPCs.

Third, as a result of debt relief, most HIPCs have strengthened macroeconomic fundamentals and lowered their domestic debt levels. This has increased their attractiveness to a wide range of investors, brought new opportunities to meet Africa's large investment needs, and supported the development of domestic financial markets (see Le Manchec 2008). For example, the domestic securities market is now booming and foreign participation has increased significantly. Countries like Ghana and Gabon have issued sovereign bonds, while others like Tanzania had similar ambitions which were only halted by the recent global financial crisis. This is because their risk profile has changed after dislodging the external debt burden and international ratings have substantially improved. In addition, a larger group of bilateral lenders are now active in Africa, with creditors outside the traditional OECD-based donor community initiating or expanding their operations in the continent. The confidence of African countries in their improved macroeconomic environment is also seen in the courage of more SSA economies subjecting themselves to international credit rating.

Fourth, the fiscal space created by debt relief efforts is supporting poverty-reducing expenditures. The debt service ratios have declined substantially owing to a combination of low debt levels and increased export earnings.

Finally, a combination of these factors and macro stability have boosted economic prospects for Africa, with faster growth in the 5–6% range, low inflation in recent years, increased inflow of FDI, domestic investment, and fiscal adjustment.

5. What are the challenges?

Despite the achievements described above, a number of risks and challenges remain.

First, while the multilateral and bilateral creditors have signed up for the HIPC Initiative, participation of commercial creditors remains low. Additionally, resources freed are far less than those required for achieving the MDGs. Secondly, although the debt burden of many HIPCs has been substantially reduced, maintaining long-term debt sustainability beyond the completion point still remains a challenge. According to IDA/IMF (2008), only about 40% of these countries have a low risk of debt distress. Thirdly, most of the HIPCs are still susceptible to shocks, particularly those affecting exports. Debt sustainability analysis by the World Bank and the IMF showed that the net present value (NPV) of external debt to exports ratio was below its relevant threshold in 2007 in post-completion-point countries. These countries' vulnerability to shocks is deepened by their overdependence on commodity exports.

Fourth, their debt sustainability is highly sensitive to the terms of new financing (IDA/IMF 2008). In a scenario that assumes less favourable terms for new borrowing, results show that about 60% of post-completion-point HIPCs would have the NPV of external debt-to-exports ratio beyond its threshold, compared to 30% for non-HIPCs. Fifth, some of the HIPCs are post-conflict countries buffeted by shocks that are purely exogenous to the HIPC Initiative. For some, therefore, progress has been slow and recovery has been fragile. Post-conflict recovery remains a challenge, and these countries require a different package to enhance their HIPC participation. Sixth, the post-HIPC countries stand a high risk of accumulating unsustainable debt unless they strengthen their capacity in public debt and resources management and appropriate fiscal space. While Africa's eligibility for non-concessional lending is a big improvement for its image, such lending poses additional risks for debt sustainability and should thus be accessed with caution.

Lastly, debt relief was supposed to dislodge the debt overhang problem and enable HIPCs to get back on their feet again. It was hoped that this would provide space for reform to solve the structural weaknesses in their economies. However, this is still a challenge. Institutional reforms are difficult unless driven by political reforms. In short, to mitigate debt-related vulnerabilities and spur growth, structural reforms are needed to enable these countries to increase domestic revenue mobilization, diversify their production and export bases, and strengthen public institutions.

6. Summary and conclusions

The HIPC debt relief efforts have been successful in reducing the debt burden of post-completion HIPCs, as reflected by the marked improvement in debt indicators of these countries relative to non-HIPCs. Economic growth and foundations for growth are strong for recipient countries—macroeconomic environment has improved and investment base widened, thanks to reforms associated with the HIPC Initiative. However, long-term debt sustainability still poses a challenge. Concerns still remain whether the debt relief initiatives have solved the causes of the initial debt problem once and for all. A number of high and significant risks still need to be tackled.

First, these economies are still vulnerable to external shocks, particularly those affecting exports, and are highly sensitive to the terms of new financing. Secondly, even though the external debt situation has improved, structural reforms are needed to enable these countries to increase domestic revenue mobilization, diversify their production and export bases, rationalize public expenditure, and strengthen public institutions. Unless trade reforms are undertaken to expand exports growth and exports as a share of GDP, coupled with financial reforms to encourage domestic and foreign direct investment, and unless fiscal reforms are undertaken, the current progress made could be checked. Third, SSA post-conflict countries still require a specific focus. There is a need to develop post-conflict reconstruction support in HIPCs.

Overall, debt relief in SSA is likely to have a larger impact if situated as part of broader reforms and incentives that include access to world markets, institutional reforms, political stability, and increased efficiency of investment and production. Policy reforms can help mitigate debt-related vulnerabilities. The regulatory and institutional framework of these countries' financial systems must be strengthened in the face of rising private inflows to allow a close monitoring of exchange, liquidity, and rollover risks. Public investment selection and debt management capabilities must also be enhanced to ensure the efficient use of foreign and domestic resources. These efforts will prevent SSA from sinking again into external debt crisis.

REFERENCES

Clements, B. J., R. Bhattacharya, and T. Nguyen, 2003. 'External debt, public investment, and growth in low-income countries', IMF Working Paper 03/249.

Elbadawi, I., B. Ndulu, and N. S. Ndung'u, 1997. 'Debt overhang and economic growth in sub-Saharan Africa', in Z. Iqbal and R. Kanbur (eds), *External Finance for Low-Income Countries*. Washington, DC: International Monetary Fund, ch. 5.

Espejo, A., and A. Unigovskaya, 2008. 'Debt relief bringing benefits to Africa', *IMF Survey Magazine* (25 February).

IDA/IMF, 2008. 'Heavily Indebted Poor Countries Initiative and Multilateral Debt Relief Initiative Status of Implementation': http://www.imf.org/external/np/pp/eng/2008/091208.

Le Manchec, Marie-Hélène, 2008. 'Africa's improved debt outlook sparks investor interest', *IMF Survey Magazine* (25 February).

Ndung'u, N. S., 2003. 'External debt and its impact on fiscal policy, investment and growth in sub-Saharan Africa', in F. Carlucci and F. Marzano (eds), *Poverty, Growth and Welfare in the World Economy in the 21st Century*. Bern: Peter Lang.

Thisen, L., 1994. 'The projection of Africa's external debt by the year 2000', UNCTAD Discussion Paper 82 (March).

World Bank, 2009. *World Development Indicators Database*.

Thematic Perspectives
Conflict and Reconstruction

Conflict and Development

Jean-Paul Azam

Civil wars and other forms of violent conflict are obviously disasters that prevent economic development and the lifting of millions of people out of poverty all over the world, and in Africa in particular. What is less obvious is that peace is not a natural state of affairs. Conflict prevention requires the conscious investment of resources. Peace is a public good that is produced using two costly inputs: redistribution and deterrence. The next section briefly sketches the theory of war and peace, which has evolved from the two papers by Azam (1995) and Fearon (1995). Since peace is a costly public good that requires an effective government to be produced, the subsequent section discusses the kind of political equilibrium that will prevail depending on the relative importance of deterrence and redistribution in producing the peace—or a descent into civil war. The empirical literature took some time to reconcile this theoretical framework with the observed fact that civil wars occur predominantly in resource-rich developing countries. Hence, the final section briefly presents the debates that followed the empirical findings of Fearon (2005), which brought out the special role of oil exports in fuelling civil wars in otherwise poor countries. It concludes on the potential role of foreign aid in supporting peace and development.

A sketch of the theory of war and peace

Any conflict of interests entails an implicit threat of violence. This negative externality can be abated by using either a transfer payment (partial concession) or a counter-threat (deterrence). The standard framework of the principal-agent model can be adapted to analyse this kind of problem. Faced with a potential rebel group, the incumbent government, or the winning side in a post-conflict situation, is in a position to combine these two instruments for buying the peace, if it wishes to establish a lasting peace. Its decision process can be decomposed into two stages.

First, the dominant player—called 'the ruler' for short below—must evaluate the cost of peace, by determining the cheapest combination of redistribution and deterrence that can buy the peace. In order to do so, the ruler must take into account the potential rebel group's 'participation constraint': to choose peace, the latter must get in the case of peace at least as much, in expected value, as it could expect to gain by waging a civil war.

Otherwise, the rebels would be better off by choosing war. This participation constraint presents a trade-off to the ruler, as the higher the effort made at deterrence, the lower the required transfer. The ruler will then choose a cost-minimizing policy mix, taking due account of the relative cost and efficiency of the two instruments. The relative importance of redistribution and deterrence in the chosen policy mix entails some important consequences for the type of political regime that will be established (Azam 2006), and this is discussed below.

Second, once this cost of peace is determined, the ruler will choose between war and peace by comparing the cost of peace to the cost of war. The latter is made up of two components. There is first a resource cost of war: soldiers will have to be paid, weapons and ammunition procured, and a lot of productive resources reallocated to military use, thus reducing output. In addition, there is the expected cost of losing the war. In this case, the vanquished will lose a lot of assets, with some probability, and a lot of lives may be lost by his group in the worst case.

The theory of war and peace thus captures the social cost of peace, i.e. some resources have to be invested in redistribution and deterrence, rather than in fuelling growth and development. But it is a cost worth paying because, were these costs saved, a much worse outcome would follow, i.e., the outbreak of a civil war.

The political economy of war and peace

The history of post-independence Africa provides a long list of praetorian regimes, where a military junta imposes a rule of fear that keeps the peace by repressing any kind of potential opposition. The framework presented above provides an explanation for such behaviour: these governments are facing a much lower relative cost of deterrence and a much higher efficiency at it, compared to redistribution. In Africa, the main cost of deterrence is that of running a large army, which is largely determined by the opportunity cost of labour. Soldiers coming from poor ethnic groups will generally be cheaper than soldiers coming from richer and more productive groups. Hence, *ceteris paribus*, this framework suggests that a praetorian regime is more likely to prevail when the group in power comes from a poorer part of the country than when the opposite is true. The case of Nigeria immediately comes to mind, as the Hausa and their Fulani allies have run most military governments in this country, while President Obasanjo, a Yoruba, was twice involved in the return to civilian rule, in 1979 and 1999. Military rule prevailed when the government mainly represented the interests of the poorer Sahelian groups, while civilian rule was supported by a representative of the richer southern groups.

Moreover, one can also argue that people from poorer regions are more effective fighters than people from more privileged areas. In the case of West Africa, several arguments can be advanced to support this assertion. The poorest places there belong to the Sahelian zone, where some well-structured political organizations have prevailed since time immemorial. In particular, a caste system is in operation in the former Mali Empire, where free men and descendants of slaves are used to obeying orders coming from upper-caste people, and in particular from members of the traditional warrior caste. The opposite is true of people from the forest zone, where the rich crops like coffee and cocoa, as well as some extractive commodities like bauxite, oil, and phosphates, are found. Here, the traditional political order is much looser, bordering on basic anarchy, for example, in the case of the ethnic groups from the so-called Mano River area, the coastal area between Casamance in the north and south-western Côte d'Ivoire in the south-east. Some have also argued that herdsmen, who used to be kept out of the forest zone by the tsetse fly, are more used to spilling blood than the forest people. This would make them more determined and efficient in fighting other human beings.

These remarks lead us to expect that civilian rule should prevail when the ruling group comes from a richer and more productive area. As the opportunity cost of labour is higher for these people, we would expect them to rely more on redistribution than on deterrence. A clear example fitting this prediction is given by Côte d'Ivoire under Houphouët-Boigny. The latter was keeping a very small army, with fewer than 5,000 soldiers until 1990, using the motto: 'No soldiers, no coup.' Moreover, he was taxing quite heavily the farmers of his own ethnic group, the relatively rich Akan cocoa and coffee growers, through a price stabilization fund. The proceeds from this implicit tax were not used for stabilization purposes, but rather for funding a massive flow of redistribution in favour of the other groups, and especially the much poorer Sahelian ones.

A large component of Houphouët-Boigny's redistribution strategy was devoted to subsidizing education, making sure that children from all ethnic groups were benefiting from it. In particular, there was a time, when world prices of cocoa and coffee were very high, that scholarships for tertiary education were higher than the salaries of most of the civil servants. Moreover, he was massively investing in infrastructure in the northern and western parts of the country, building roads and extending the electricity network. This system also funded to a large extent the new harbour of San Pedro in the homeland of the Bété, in south-western Côte d'Ivoire. Less than ten years after his death, after his successors had dismantled this system, a brutal civil war erupted. Restoring a system of credible and lasting redistribution is more difficult than recruiting a repressive army within one's own ethnic group.

Institutional constraints on redistribution

Using redistribution to buy peace requires a stronger institutional framework than does imposing repression. Think of it as a social contract: 'If you don't get armed to challenge my position, then I will give you some agreed grant.' This raises at least two issues. The first one is credible commitment, which has been much discussed in the literature since Azam (1995) and Fearon (1995). There are no third parties to enforce such a promise, so that the ruler is in a position to renege once the potential rebels have given up the means to launch a rebellion, as they lose their power to make credible threats. What is needed is a way for the ruler to tie his own hands. In mature democracies, this has been achieved by developing 'checks and balances', i.e. institutions that make it costly for the ruler to renege. Such institutions are usually lacking in poor countries, where personal rule is the most prevalent form of government. In the case of Houphouët-Boigny described above, the key to his success was that he had built up over time a reputation of keeping his promises. However, this commitment device died with him, and did not enable his successor to keep the country at peace. When the probability of delivering the promised amounts is low, then the ruler must promise more to reach the same expected value, and this might in turn strain credulity by hitting the budget constraint.

The second issue is that of corruption, which is so pervasive in some cases that the ruler can only get a small fraction of the money to the targeted people. In other words, both the lack of credible commitment and the lack of control over corruption—two prominent features of the weak institutional environments of many African countries—act like transaction costs that increase the cost of redistribution. When compared to the cost of war, this kind of additional costs might be high enough to tip the balance in favour of war.

Both types of problems prevail in most African resource-rich countries, and especially among oil-exporting countries. Fearon (2005) has shown econometrically that oil production is a significant determinant of the incidence of civil war, and that oil-producing countries have an especially bad reputation regarding their credible commitment capacity. Among African oil-producing countries, only Gabon and Cameroon have managed to avoid the outbreak of civil war (Ghazvinian 2007). It seems that a well-controlled, centralized corruption system is the key to buying the peace at an affordable price in such cases.

It follows, therefore, that to reduce the risk of conflict and foster development, the donor community should focus its interventions on strengthening African governments' ability to pursue a cost-effective redistribution policy, by helping them to build checks and balances and to control disorderly corruption.

■ REFERENCES

Azam, Jean-Paul, 1995. 'How to pay for the peace? A theoretical framework with references to African countries', *Public Choice* 83.1/2, 173–84.
—— 2006. 'The paradox of power reconsidered: a theory of political regimes in Africa', *Journal of African Economies* 15.1, 26–58.

Fearon, James D., 1995. 'Ethnic war as a commitment problem', paper presented at the Annual Meeting of the American Political Science Association (New York, 1994). MS, Stanford, Calif.
—— 2005. 'Primary commodity exports and civil war', *Journal of Conflict Resolution* 49.4, 483–507.
Ghazvinian, John, 2007. *Untapped: The Scramble for Africa's Oil*. San Diego, Calif.: Harcourt.

Developing Post-conflict Africa

Ibrahim A. Elbadawi

1. Introduction[1]

A highly influential multi-agency report on the prospects of Africa's development in the new century identifies the task of overcoming the conflict-poverty trap as the most serious challenge facing Sub-Saharan Africa today.[2] Overcoming this trap requires the simultaneous achievement of multiple transitions: from warfare to peacekeeping; from large armies to public agencies of law and order; and, most importantly, from autocracies and unstable factional polity to inclusive and stable democracies. However, these transitions are all the more difficult because a typical post-conflict country is likely to be socially polarized, landlocked, and surrounded by non-democratic or unstable countries. Moreover, many of these countries are also dependent on natural resource rents, and thus also likely to suffer from the resource curse, especially with regard to its corrosive effects on political and economic institutions.

Some scholars argue that the design and effective implementation of peace-building and post-conflict reconstruction agenda requires more emphasis on economic policy (what I call the 'policy-plus' school). Others, however, mostly political scientists and civil society activists, argue that the post-conflict agenda should focus more on better designing the emerging political institutions in post-conflict (the 'politics-plus' school).

Subscribing to both perspectives, this chapter makes two concrete proposals. First, I argue that the politics-plus agenda needs a stronger commitment to democracy as the only viable institution for sustainable peace in multi-identity post-conflict African societies. Second, with regard to the policy-plus agenda, I propose the Chinese development model of real currency undervaluation as a credible strategy for sustaining growth in post-conflict Africa. Finally, I argue that democratization and real currency undervaluation are not actually the odd couples they might seem.

---

[1] The views expressed in this chapter do not necessarily represent the official positions of the Dubai Economic Council or the Center for Global Development. I am grateful to Dani Rodrik for sharing his real exchange rate undervaluation index with me. The author would also like to acknowledge the research support by Zamira Simkins. I would also like to thank, without implications, Alan Gelb and Abdel Hameed Elias for helpful comments to an earlier draft.

[2] World Bank (2000), which is jointly prepared and sponsored by the World Bank and four other development institutions: the African Development Bank, the Economic Commission for Africa, the African Economic Research Consortium, and the Global Coalition for Africa.

2. The politics-plus agenda: democracy matters

Democratization is a standard component of the policy and academic discourse on post-conflict situations.[3] However, building stable democratic institutions in the ethnically divided post-conflict societies has been slow and difficult. For example, the median country in post-conflict Africa scored a disappointing −2 in the Polity scale (−10: extreme autocracy to +10: mature democracy), even ten years after the end of conflicts (Fig. 1).[4] To succeed, post-conflict democracy requires existing state structures and the acceptance of the common state by most, if not all, components of the society. However, the latter cannot be achieved without the presence of some measure of democracy to

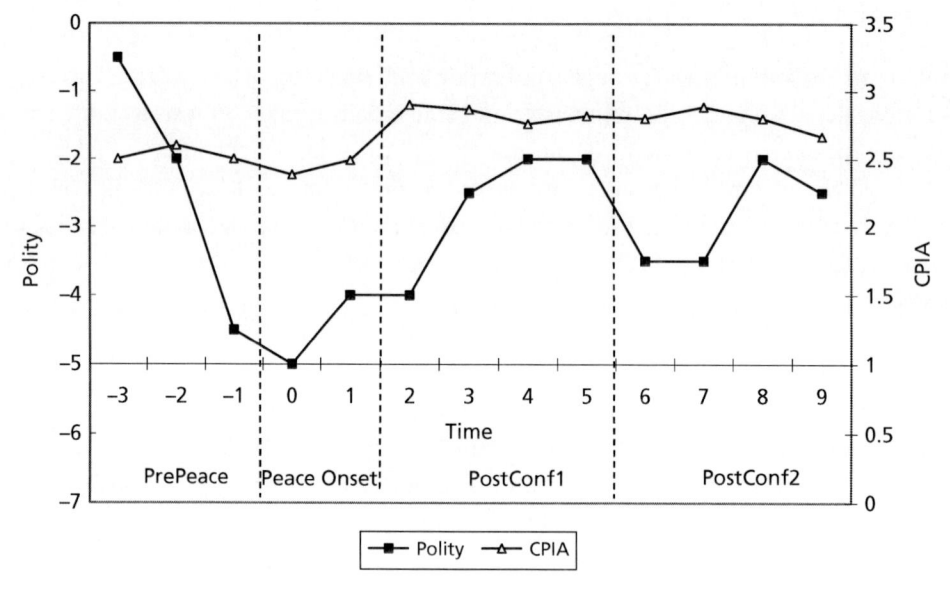

Figure 1. Polity and country policy and institutional assessment (African countries, median values)

1. Source: Based on data from 19 post-conflict African countries (World Bank data base).
2. The Polity IV Index (http://www.cidcm.umd.edu/inscr/polity/) is based on two concepts: 'institutionalized democracy' (DEM) and 'institutionalized autocracy' (AUT). The DEM score is coded according to four measures of regime characteristics: competitiveness of executive recruitment; openness of executive recruitment; constraints on the chief executive; and competitiveness of political participation. These measures, along with regulation of participation, contribute to the AUT score. The Polity score (POL) is computed by subtracting the AUT score from the DEM score, resulting in a score from −10 (strongly autocratic) to 10 (strongly democratic).
3. The Country Policy and Institutional Assessment index is produced by the World Bank. The index ranges from 1 to 6 and is an average of four components covering economic management, structural policies, policies for social inclusion/equity, and public sector management and institutions.

---

[3] See e.g. Doyle and Sambanis (2000; 2006) and Sambanis (2008).
[4] See the notes to Figure 1 for citation and full definition.

permit a meaningful bargaining process between ethnically defined social groups. It has been argued, therefore, that post-conflict democratization seems to be impeded by a vicious circle.

To tackle this challenge, the literature suggests three options (Gromes 2009). One approach assigns top priority to pursuing only nation-building during an interim period in order to subsequently constitute a common democratic state. The second approach calls for emphasizing the primacy of establishing democratic state institutions and thereby paving the way for a viable process of nation-building. And finally the third way argues that both democratization and nation-building are required for achieving sustainable peace in post-conflict. According to this view, there exist influential exogenous factors that could be exploited to allow overcoming the democracy-nation-building trap. For example, the case of post-conflict democratization in Bosnia Herzegovina was cited as an example, where the European democratic neighbourhood and the promise of the EU membership, in addition to the robust and broadly mandated peacekeeping operation, provided the exogenous influences needed to break the trap.

It appears that the 'nation-building first' approach has substantially defined the operational peace-building processes in Africa. The demise of the Soviet Union in the early 1990s marked the end of decisive victories in civil wars and the dominance of negotiated peace settlements and peace agreements brokered by international and regional actors.[5] Naturally, if they had to share power, both sides to the conflict have a common interest in excluding other stakeholders not involved in the conflict. Moreover, external actors tend to acquiesce or, at best, only half-heartedly press for a more broad-based peace process. Perhaps the 2005 Comprehensive Peace Agreement (CPA) that ended the Sudanese civil war was the most concrete example of this approach. However, as the experience with the CPA suggests, confining power-sharing to the military groups could very well create unpleasant realities that might be difficult to overcome moving forward. First, excluded groups might ignite new conflicts as the old ones were being resolved, as happened in the Darfur region of Sudan. Second, the parties to the interim power-sharing government might collude to pre-empt the democratic agenda of the peace agreement now that they are in control. Third, given the usually wide ethnic and political distance between the former parties to the conflict, the power-sharing arrangements might very well collapse, possibly leading to post-conflict relapse or non-cooperative sessions. It is widely believed that the second outcome has in fact happened in the recent Sudanese elections, and that the third is a distinct possibility.[6]

---

[5] A rare exception in recent years is the decisive victory of the government of Sri Lanka over the Tamil rebels in 2009, which put an end to one of the longest and most bloody civil wars in Asia.

[6] See e.g. the report of the Carter Center on the Sudanese elections of 2010 (www.emory.edu/CARTER_CENTER). Despite high hopes that the Sudanese April 2010 elections would turn the country into a genuinely decentralized federal multi-party democracy—hence enhancing the chances for the country to remain united and to amicably resolve the Darfur crisis—the two ruling parties (the National Congress Party

At a broad conceptual level, perhaps the preference by diplomats and other actors in the peace-building community for the 'nation-building first' approach—or at least its acceptance by them as a *de facto* option—also reflects the influence of the dominant strand of the modern civil war literature—mostly associated with the work of Professor Paul Collier and his research collaborators.[7] According to this literature, economic growth is by far the dominant factor in reducing post-conflict risks, while democracy is at best an unstable influence. It can be inferred, therefore, that aside from direct security measures, the only other viable response to post-conflict risks should be to directly address the problems of slow growth; and that political legitimacy, desirable as it may be for its own intrinsic value, has no role in this process.

However, despite the creativity and rigour of the empirical work of Collier and his associates, it has failed to account for the potentially varied impacts on post-conflict risks of different types of democratic institutions. Instead, another strand of the literature that takes a more nuanced approach finds that regime types that are most vulnerable to conflict—from violent demonstrations to coups and civil wars—are factional democracies, while non-factional democracies are no more risky than autocracies (Bodea and Elbadawi 2007). More importantly, in a formal empirical model covering 118 post-conflict societies during 1985–2002, Binningsbø (2005) finds consociational democracy—especially the proportional representation and territorial autonomy features of this type of democracy—to be positively associated with lasting peace in ethnically polarized post-conflict societies. Of the 29 post-conflict societies with no consociational features, 48% reverted to war, while this proportion is much lower for the post-conflict societies with one (38%), two (40%), and three (0%) consociational features.

Another important contribution arguing for democracy as a risk-mitigating factor focuses on the regional dimensions of civil wars. For example, Raleigh (2007) estimates the risk of civil war in a model that accounts for the standard of democracy in a country's neighbourhood and finds that for countries surrounded by stable, developed democracies the risk of conflict, regardless of income, never increases past 4%. On the other hand, she finds that low-income countries in an autocratic or anocratic neighbourhood will experience exceptionally high risk.

---

in the north and the Sudanese People Liberation Movement in the south) apparently abused their incumbency to pre-empt any serious challenge from the opposition. The Sudanese post-conflict elections are therefore not likely to consolidate nation-building nor to achieve democratization. Instead, and with the acquiescence of the African and international communities, it was turned into a sideshow and an event in the CPA schedule leading to the real decision in early 2011, when the Southern Sudanese voted on self-determination. As widely anticipated, they opted for partitioning of the country and the creation of the new southern Sudanese state, which was formally inaugurated on 9 July.

[7] See e.g. Collier and Goderis (2007), Collier and Rohner (2008), and Collier, Hoeffler, and Söderbom (2008).

These findings, therefore, suggest that a more nuanced diagnosis should investigate approaches to promote consociational but non-factional democracy, because it cannot be riskier than full autocracy, especially when a country is located in democratic regional neighbourhoods, or when such democratic discourse can be positively influenced by other global or regional external actors, most notably the nascent democracy camp within the Continent.

3. The policy-plus agenda: real currency undervaluation

The median post-conflict country rebounds from negative per capita growth rate of about −1% in the year before peace onset to more than 2% in the second year; despite the high volatility across countries, the average median growth hovered around 2.5% up to the sixth year before decelerating to around 0.1% thereafter (Fig. 2). Moreover, this rather high median growth spell in the immediate aftermath of conflicts does not seem to have been

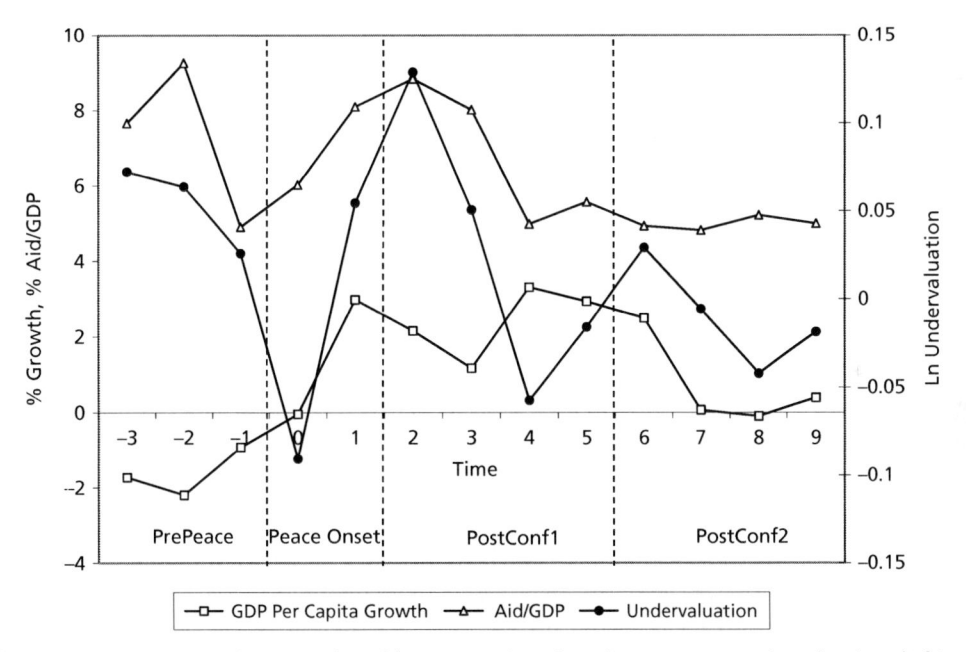

Figure 2. GDP per capita growth, Aid/GDP, and real exchange rate undervaluation (African countries, median values, in percentages)

1. Source: Based on data from 19 post-conflict African countries (World Bank database).
2. The real exchange rate (real currency) undervaluation index is due to Dani Rodrik (2008), which is based on Penn World Tables data on price levels in individual countries. This index 'is essentially a real exchange rate adjusted for the Balassa-Samuelson effect. It captures the relative price of tradables to non-tradables, adjusting for the fact that richer countries have higher relative prices of non-tradables (due to higher productivity in tradables).'

associated with improved institutions. If anything, while the median African post-conflict country remained autocratic, though at much higher levels than during conflicts; the economic governance institutions were almost as poor as during the war (see Fig. 1 above).

The key issue, therefore, is why growth tends to eventually decelerate at the beginning of the second phase of the post-conflict recovery (starting in year six). First, aid donors might have withdrawn prematurely, as can be seen from the declining trend of the median aid per GDP starting with the fourth year following war termination. However, this is not likely to be a compelling argument because in all likelihood aid effectiveness might have started to hit the point of diminishing returns, especially given the limited progress in the quality of economic governance. The key factor behind the growth deceleration in post-conflict, therefore, may not be limited aid but rather the lack of progress in building the required institutional capacity for sustaining aid effectiveness and growth.

The new policy-plus agenda has focused on the quality of institutions for managing aid, especially with regard to infrastructure and the delivery of social services. Moreover, and due to the high share of oil and other mineral exporting countries among post-conflict countries, the literature has also focused on management of commodity booms and institutions for ensuring the fairness and transparency of granting minerals and oil concessions (e.g. Collier 2009). It is of course, a no-brainer to stress that this agenda is absolutely critical and should be diligently pursued. However, these policies need time to take hold. Moreover, the aid boom that is premised on these reforms is likely to lead to real exchange rate (RER, or real currency) overvaluation,[8] which can inflict substantial damage in short order (Elbadawi, Kaltani, and Schmidt-Hebbel 2008).

Instead, it is real currency undervaluation that is found to be robustly associated with high and sustained growth (Rodrik 2008). These findings from the literature appear to perfectly cohere with the African post-conflict experiences. While the deceleration of growth during the second phase of post-conflict was clearly associated with real currency overvaluation (Figure 2), those post-conflict countries that were able to engineer RER undervaluation have consistently grown more than those with overvalued economies (Fig. 3).

Countries that have managed to engineer a currency undervaluation (China being the most notable example) appear to have resolved some deep institutional constraints (Rodrik 2008). This is because, though 'weak institutions' penalize the entire economy, the impact is likely to be more severe in dynamic activities such as agricultural and

---

[8] Simply put, a country will experience a real currency overvaluation (undervaluation) when it produces a given basket of goods and services that can be traded across international borders at a higher (lower) cost than what would be consistent with its sustainable economic fundamentals—such as the external terms of trade, the level of sophistication of its economy, or the stock of wealth generated by or endowed with the economy. Moreover, real exchange rate (real currency) undervaluation (overvaluation) is consistent with higher price of tradables relative to non-traded domestic goods and services.

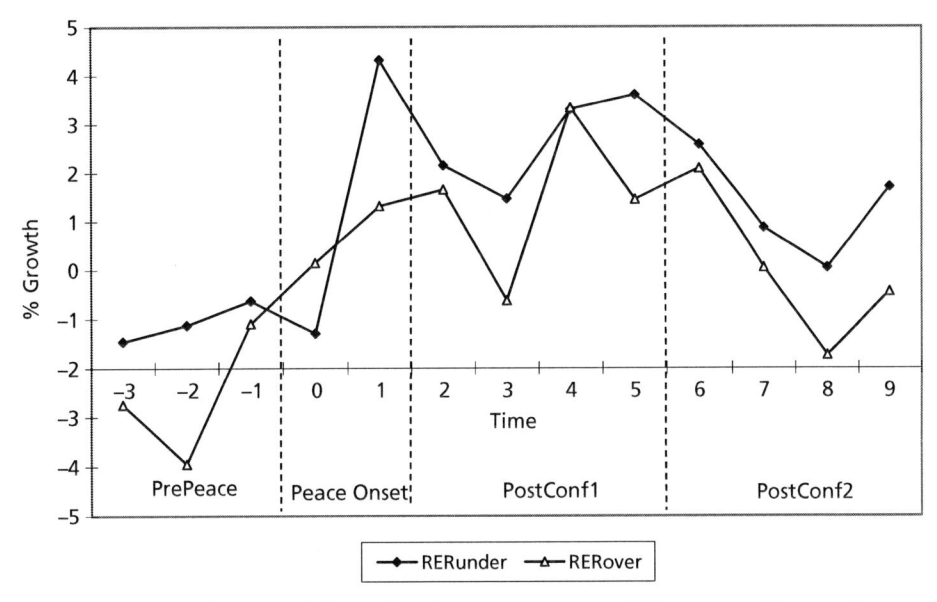

Figure 3. GDP per capita growth by real exchange rate group (African countries, median values, in percentages)

Source: Based on data from 19 post-conflict African countries (World Bank database).

industrial exportables in low-income countries. They are also more complex because they entail relatively more complementary transaction-intensive activities (e.g. transport, finance).

Therefore, by raising the relative price and, hence, profitability in the most dynamic set of activities in the economy, real currency undervaluation acts as an economy-wide industrial policy favouring these activities. Moreover, being an economy-wide instrument, undervaluation, unlike traditional industrial policy, does not require the kind of institutional rigour that would be necessary for the success of industrial policy.

4. Conclusions

I have offered two concrete proposals for dealing with the challenge of post-conflict development in Africa. First, post-conflict consociational democratization is unavoidable for sustainable peace in ethnically polarized Africa. A first step should be to avoid confining the interim power-sharing arrangements only to the military parties to the conflict.

The second proposal calls for the adoption of a real currency undervaluation as a cornerstone of the post-conflict growth strategy because it provides an economy-wide subsidy to tradable sectors, which are the most dynamic in post-conflict economies, yet also likely to be the most impacted by institutional weakness.

Finally, one might question the compatibility between democratic polity and a policy of maintaining low real value of a national currency. I would, however, argue that in post-conflict societies where rural communities tend to be the largest as well as the most affected, an economic strategy that would positively favour them would not only make good development policy but should also be consistent with democratic political contests. For the foreseeable future, real currency undervaluation is not only developmental and democratic but also a boon to peace in post-conflict Africa.

REFERENCES

Binningsbø, Helga Malmin, 2005. 'Consociational democracy and postconflict peace: will power-sharing institutions increase the probability of lasting peace after civil war?', mimeo, International Peace Research Institute (PRIO), Oslo.

Bodea, Cristina, and Ibrahim Elbadawi, 2007. 'Riots, coups and civil war: revisiting the greed and grievance debate', Post-Conflict Transition-Policy Research Working Paper 4397, Development Economic Research Group, World Bank, Washington, DC.

Collier, Paul, 2009. 'Post-conflict recovery: how should policies be distinctive?', *Journal of African Economies* 18 (Supplement 1), 99–131.

—— and Benedikt Goderis, 2007. 'Commodity prices and the resource curse: resolving a conundrum', mimeo, Department of Economics, University of Oxford.

—— Anke Hoeffler, and Måns Söderbom, 2008. 'Post-conflict risks', *Journal of Peace Research*, 461–78.

—— and Dominic Rohner, 2008. 'Conflict, democracy and development', *Journal of the European Economic Association*.

Doyle, Michael W., and Nicholas Sambanis, 2000. 'International peacebuilding: a theoretical and quantitative analysis', *American Political Science Review* 94.4, 779–801.

—— —— 2006. *Making War and Building Peace: United Nations Peace Operations*. Princeton, NJ: Princeton University Press.

Elbadawi, Ibrahim, 2008. 'Postconflict transitions: an overview', *World Bank Economic Review* 22.1, 1–7.

—— Linda Kaltani, and Klaus Schmidt-Hebbel, 2008. 'Foreign aid, the real exchange rate, and economic growth in the aftermath of civil wars', *World Bank Economic Review* 22.1, 113–40.

Gromes, Thorsten, 2009. 'The vicious circle of state-building and nation-building during the democratization of ethnically divided post-civil war societies', mimeo, Peace Research Institute, Frankfurt a.M.

Raleigh, Clionadh, 2007. 'Civil war risk in democratic and non-democratic neighborhoods', Post-Conflict Transition-Policy Research Working Paper 4260, Development Economic Research Group, World Bank, Washington, DC.

Rodrik, Dani, 1999. 'Where did all the growth go? External shocks, social conflict, and growth collapses', *Journal of Economic Growth* 4.4, 385–412.

—— 2008. 'The real exchange rate and economic growth', *Brookings Papers on Economic Activity* 2: 365–412.

Sambanis, Nicholas, 2008. 'Short- and long-term effects of United Nations peace operations', *World Bank Economic Review* 22.1.

World Bank, 2000. *Can Africa Claim the 21st Century?* Washington, DC: World Bank.

Post-conflict Recovery in Africa
The Micro Level

Christopher Blattman

Development in Africa is inseparable from warfare. In the mid-1990s alone, a third of sub-Saharan African countries had an active civil war; many lasted a decade or more. Mass violence has afflicted nearly every African nation since independence. These conflicts are epic events in each nation's history, destroying life, skills, wealth, and infrastructure, and potentially damaging a society's social bonds and institutions.

We have only a rough understanding of the macroeconomic consequences of internal war worldwide: output falls dramatically then recovers slowly but steadily over time.[1] One of the greatest barriers to understanding macro-level impacts and recovery is the dearth of micro foundations. The majority of unanswered questions are empirical: what factors of production fall and by how much? How fast does each recover? What is the distribution of gains and losses? What role is there for public policy and programmes?

We are especially far from a satisfactory body of micro-empirical evidence. Until about ten years ago, most of our micro-knowledge came from public health: epidemiologists measured mortality, morbidity, and disease; psychologists measured the incidence and determinants of post-traumatic stress disorder (PTSD). In the 1990s a handful of labour economists studied the labour market impacts of military service, but limited their attention to American and European veterans. In the past decade, however, economists and political scientists have attacked these questions with increasing vigour and rigour.[2] Most of the new evidence comes from Africa, partly because Africa has had more war, and partly (one speculates) because African states have been less able to deter meddling researchers from data collection.

Two events drove this surge of micro investigation. First, for development economists, wars became impossible to ignore. As the 20th century closed, conflict afflicted more and more countries. By some accounts, conflict represented the central impediment to African development. Second, as wars ended in the early years of the new century, governments and researchers could safely collect micro data. In a few especially valuable

---

[1] Surveys of the macro literature include Blattman and Miguel (2010), Collier and Hoeffler (2007), and Humphreys (2003).

[2] Surveys include Blattman and Miguel (2010) and Justino (2007; 2008); New papers are commonly published at http://www.hicn.org.

instances, enterprising researchers followed up representative samples of prewar national household surveys to create a pre- and postwar panel.[3] Combined with data on the location and severity of war violence, these panels could be used to create differences-in-differences estimates of the micro-level impacts of war. In most war-torn nations, unfortunately, prewar data were destroyed or (more often) never existed in the first place. Thus another approach has been to collect cross-sectional data after war, using plausibly exogenous variation in violence to assess the lasting effects.[4] Nearly all our micro evidence on war comes from one of these two (largely reduced-form) empirical strategies. Structural modelling and estimation of war impacts remains unfortunately rare.[5]

This piecemeal and opportunistic approach means the existing evidence is fragmentary and incomplete. How to organize the evidence in a meaningful way and chart a path forward? Growth theory offers a useful frame. Growth accounting is usually employed at the macro level, decomposing growth into its contributing factors: labour, human capital, physical capital, and that elusive residual, 'technology'. Viewed through this lens, the gaps in our knowledge become clear.

Most of the new micro evidence on war measures the effects of war on capital, human and physical, and the consequent impacts on labour market performance and poverty. Human and physical capital are more straightforward to measure at the micro level than more ethereal factors like technology change or social networks, especially with the data and empirical strategies just described. As with macro-level accounting, however, our understanding of the all-important residual factors—social organization, innovation, culture, and so forth—remains weak.

Let us take these factors one by one. First, consider physical capital. When livestock are killed, houses burned, or resources plundered, the nation's capital stock depletes. The damage depends largely on the nature and extent of the war. In a nation like Ethiopia—where the civil war was limited to a small peripheral region, and where the centre was captured quickly—fewer farms, businesses, and infrastructure were destroyed. Not so in Liberia, where a series of wars consumed the nation, and warlords and ostensible peacekeepers looted every asset imaginable.

Neoclassical growth theory tells us that nations should return to steady-state incomes and growth paths after such capital shocks. Evidence from Japan, Germany, and Vietnam suggest that, within one to two decades, a nation's capital stock returns to prewar levels. Yet we have little micro-level evidence on the speed of recovery in Africa.

---

[3] e.g. Akresh, Bundervoet, and Verwimp (2009).
[4] e.g. Miguel and Roland (2005), Bellows and Miguel (2006), Shemyakina (2006), Humphreys and Weinstein (2007), and Blattman and Annan (2010).
[5] Brück (2001) is one exception.

To the extent that African businesses and households are more credit-constrained, recovery may be slower than in the more developed states.

More important may be the political and institutional environment after war. In neoclassical models, capital returns to the prewar equilibrium path so long as the factors that determine that equilibrium remain unchanged. If a nation emerges from war more politically stable, or better governed, than before, then capital will not only rebound but could exceed its previous levels and growth in the new investment climate. Good examples from Africa include Uganda after 1986, or Rwanda after 1994, where rebel forces achieved decisive victories, established new eras of political stability, and embraced market reforms. On the other hand, weak regimes supported by foreign powers, or warring factions held in an unsteady equilibrium solely through peacekeeping forces and power-sharing agreements, could diminish the investment climate and lower equilibrium capital per worker.

The micro-empirical literature on human capital is richer than that of physical capital. When warfare kills or maims the adult population, it destroys a labour force and a vast stock of human capital. Mortality studies suggest that internal wars kill many more people through indirect rather than direct means—that is, through sickness and hunger rather than battle deaths or murders. Mortality levels are often hotly disputed, largely due to disagreements over the appropriate counterfactual mortality rate, but the unbalanced effect on civilian death is widely recognized.

More seldom measured is the human capital lost. In principle, if life is lost faster than capital is destroyed, capital per worker (and incomes) could rise as a result of war. This argument has been applied, with some controversy, to the AIDS crisis in Africa. While plausible, it is hard to find clear examples of war presenting this unintended gift. One reason could be that, when life is lost, so is human capital. Moreover, the destruction of families takes a toll on related factors, such as social networks and social capital; extended families are the principal mechanism of insurance in rural Africa, and the death of workers and the disruption of social networks and support is likely to have adverse effects on recovery. Hence the numerator of the capital-per-worker ratio may fall as fast as (or faster than) the denominator. Here we have little economic evidence, however, save a number of public health, psychological, and 'child protection' studies that suggest the loss of a primary caregiver is a strong correlate of lower lifetime health.

Among survivors, a large body of evidence suggests that war, like disasters, interrupts schooling, either because populations are displaced, education systems collapse, or (especially in the case of combatants) youth are pulled out of school. These educational effects are typically lowest among women, older adolescents, and the poor, all of whom in the absence of war are less likely to have attended school—perhaps a sadder statement on their opportunities in peacetime than war.

Education appears to recover more slowly than physical capital for a number of reasons. A labour force killed or maimed will need to wait a generation to fully recover its size and skill level. For those who saw schooling interrupted, skills may be reacquired, but the pace of education has obvious physical and logistical limits, and so is difficult to accelerate. Moreover, those deterred from school often do not return, meaning that the rate of recovery for a whole cohort may be zero. Where schooling is fee-based, any wealth loss from war further reduces the probability of return to schooling. Finally, war may have destroyed school infrastructure, or teachers may not want to serve in poor and war-torn areas. As a consequence of these factors, rates of return to school, and the speed of recovery, appear to be tied to the length of war, the scale of destruction in the school system, opportunities for (and cost of) remedial or vocational education, and postwar returns to schooling.

War harms physical health as well. Injuries may disable youth in their working prime. A growing body of evidence suggests even longer-term impacts through child stunting. War and displacement reduce child nutrition, which in turn is linked to lower lifetime physical and cognitive functioning, and with it lower productivity. It is difficult to make general statements about war's impact on health, as the depth of the shock depends on the context, especially the intensity and nature of the conflict. Serious injuries are persistent, however, and so whatever the depth of the shock, the rate of convergence to pre-war health could be slower than that of physical capital. These rates of recovery should be accelerated by the quality of health care services during and after war, including the availability of food relief. Rapid recovery of health systems could mean rapid recovery of health-related human capital, since people start from a low base. As a consequence, such services are among the first and highest priority provided by emergency aid.

Mental health gets less attention in the economics literature than education and physical health, but deserves special consideration in any discussion of war. War trauma is closely linked with painful and sometimes debilitating emotional distress, such as PTSD. While epidemiological studies commonly find high rates of PTSD among war-affected populations—especially veterans and the direct victims of violence—debilitating emotional distress appears to be the exception rather than the norm. Victims and perpetrators display surprising resilience, especially when they return to supportive families and friends after war. Moderate to serious symptoms of distress (including depression, anxiety, or hallucinations) arise in large numbers of victims and perpetrators, but typically it is a minority of those exposed to violence.[6]

Moreover, however painful these effects (and however important to treat for humanitarian reasons), symptoms of emotional distress do not necessarily impede education or work, except among those with the most severe symptoms. Magnitudes vary with degree of exposure and context (and difficulty of cross-cultural measurement), but it seems

---

[6] See Masten (2001) or Annan and Patel (2009) for reviews.

likely that education and physical health are more important determinants of post-conflict economic recovery than mental health.

This is not to say that education and physical health deserve more attention from policymakers after war. Post-conflict interventions ought to aim where their marginal impact is greatest. The size of war's impact, and the consequent growth effects, are just one variable in this decision. We also need to consider the effectiveness of the policy tools at hand; depression and PTSD are among the most straightforwardly treated disorders, and so aid programmes may be particularly effective here. Also, the existing skills and institutions for dealing with psychological disorder are extremely poor in Africa, as there is an almost total absence of trained professionals and programmes. Hence the marginal impact of mental health programmes could be very high.

In truth, we do not know. The point is not that mental health deserves attention, but that when considering post-conflict policy priorities, the effectiveness of available programmes and the existing stock of interventions ought to guide decisions as much as the growth effects of a particular factor.

A growing number of post-conflict programme evaluations will help answer such questions and link research to concrete policy. Dozens of experimental and observational evaluations are under way in locations as diverse as Nepal, Sri Lanka, Afghanistan, Liberia, and Sudan. They range from ex-combatant reintegration to peace radio programming to job creation. This is a promising new avenue that over the next three to five years could challenge or confirm the cautious conclusions above.

Together, this loss of factors—physical capital, education, and physical and mental health—imply that households become poorer and are less able to generate income. The same reduced-form studies that demonstrate factor losses also find increases in household poverty after war.

The aggregate effect on national income and growth depends on the proportion of the population affected. Unfortunately the data and empirical strategies employed make it difficult to identify partial from general equilibrium effects. We thus have little evidence on whether war's impacts are increasing or constant in scale. There are strong theoretical reasons to fear that the adverse impacts are increasing in scale, not least because of the damage to the social fabric. In principle, the experimental projects discussed above could attempt to isolate the general and partial equilibrium effects, especially when large, nationwide reconstruction programmes are studied. Such a finding requires a specific and careful design, and no attempts appear to be under way.

Another major gap in our knowledge is the effect of conflict on institutions and innovation at the micro level. Theories of growth—neoclassical and endogenous—identify technology, institutions, and social organization as the fundamental determinants of development. As noted above, the steady state to which a post-conflict society returns is largely a function of these elusive factors. Any micro-level impacts to these factors could contribute to a long-term decline in both income and growth rates.

It is tempting to assume that war always and everywhere diminishes social and institutional strength. There are clear instances of war doing just this: polarizing ethnic tensions in Sudan or Nigeria, or prompting looting and capital flight in 1990s Sierra Leone and Liberia. Nevertheless, war can sometimes have the opposite effect. At the macro level, Latin America's and (especially) Europe's state stability and strength are commonly attributed to centuries of internal and external warfare. Political scientists have drawn modern parallels to African states like Uganda and Rwanda, whose institutions appear to have emerged stronger from conflict.

At the micro level, there is also evidence that war and violence can have unexpectedly positive social and political effects. In a widening number of studies from around the world, experiences of war violence are highly correlated with greater levels of social capital and higher levels of peaceful political engagement. One possibility is that individuals are activated by violence and injustice rather than destroyed by it; war establishes a taste for peace and good governance.[7]

These findings even extend to ex-combatants themselves. While some veterans are socially excluded, aggressive, or face difficulty gaining social acceptance, survey and qualitative evidence suggests that ex-combatants are widely accepted and function at par with (or more successfully than) others in their community. While the 'tastes' explanation may apply, other explanations are that ex-combatants may have gained valuable leadership and organizational experience or (perhaps more likely) that they wish to signal their reintegration into society by engaging productively and peacefully in their communities.

The effects of war and violence on trust, cooperation, social organization, and politics is one of the most interesting and important frontiers of research. We lack theories of behaviour that explain the emerging stylized facts, and so the further study of war could challenge (and improve) basic theories of economic and political behaviour.

Overall the trend in the study of warfare has been towards more and better data, more rigour and structure in methods, more integration of quantitative work with case and qualitative work, and more links to formal theory. The field will only benefit if these trends continue. The multitude of post-conflict field experiments under way is also exciting. One worry is that these experiments, conducted on select samples with limited replication, and implemented where the opportunity arises rather than theory demands, will have limited external validity and speak to the less important questions. The big questions and unknowns remain the speed of relative recovery of human and physical capital in alternative social and institutional environments, and the institutional and social conditions (micro and macro) that give rise to recovery and continued growth.

---

[7] See Blattman (2009) for one example and a review of evidence.

REFERENCES

Akresh, Richard, Tom Bundervoet, and Philip Verwimp, 2009. 'Health and civil war in Burundi', *Journal of Human Resources* 44.2, 536–63.

Annan, Jeannie, and Ana Cutter Patel, 2009. 'Critical issues and lessons in social reintegration: balancing justice, psychological well being, and community reconciliation', paper presented at International DDR Congress (CIDDR), Cartagena, Colombia.

Bellows, John, and Edward Miguel, 2006. 'War and institutions: new evidence from Sierra Leone', *American Economic Association, Papers and Proceedings* 96.2, 394–9.

Blattman, Christopher, 2009. 'From violence to voting: war and political participation in Uganda', *American Political Science Review* 103.2.

Blattman, Christopher and Jeannie Annan, 2010. 'The consequences of child soldiering', *Review of Economics and Statistics* 92.4, 882–98.

—— and Edward Miguel, 2010. 'Civil war', *Journal of Economic Literature* 48.1, 3–57.

Bruck, T., 2001. 'Coping with peace: post-war household strategies in northern Mozambique', D. Phil. thesis, Oxford University.

Collier, Paul, and Anke Hoeffler, 2007. 'Civil war', in K. Hartley and T. Sandler (eds), *Handbook of Defense Economics*. Amsterdam: Elsevier North-Holland.

Humphreys, Macartan, 2003. 'Economics and violent conflict', Cambridge, Mass.: Program on Humanitarian Policy and Conflict Research.

—— and Jeremy M. Weinstein, 2007. 'Demobilization and reintegration', *Journal of Conflict Resolution* 51.4, 531–67.

Justino, Patricia, 2007. 'On the links between violent conflict and household poverty: how much do we really know?', MICROCON Research Working Paper 1.

—— 2008. 'Poverty and violent conflict: a micro-level perspective on the causes and duration of warfare', working paper, Harvard University/IDS at the University of Sussex.

Masten, A. S., 2001. 'Ordinary magic: resilience processes in development', *American Psychologist* 56.3, 227–38.

Miguel, Edward, and Gerard Roland, forthcoming. 'The long run impact of bombing Vietnam', *Journal of Development Economics*.

Shemyakina, Olga, forthcoming. 'The Effect of Armed Conflict on Accumulation of Schooling: Results from Tajikistan', *Journal of Development Economics*.

Thematic Perspectives
Employment

Labour and Employment in Africa

Francis Teal

Understanding how labour markets operate in any country is central to understanding how incomes are generated. Africa is no exception. The focus in poverty analysis on measures of consumption at the household level, while essential for their purposes, has tended to shift attention away from understanding the links between labour markets, employment, and incomes. As it is income that determines consumption, understanding how income and employment link is essential to understanding both the causes of poverty and the source of its alleviation.

This contribution will address the question as to what determines incomes by examining the factors that determine the price of labour and returns to employment.

The price of labour

In thinking about labour markets in any economy, the notion of *the* price for labour needs to be treated with great caution. The earnings function, due originally to Mincer (1974), is the standard tool for asking what factors influence the price of labour. The characteristics of labour can usefully be divided between those that capture dimensions of human capital—work experience, education, and training—and those that reflect the sector or enterprise type in which employment takes place—its location, sector, and size. All of these factors have been shown to be highly correlated with the earnings both of those in wage employment and of those in self-employment. However, only a rather limited amount of the diversity of earnings can be explained by the observable human capital characteristics of the individuals. How the role of the other factors—size and sector, for example—are to be interpreted is of central importance if we wish to understand how labour is priced (Mortensen 2005).

Employment

As Sen (1975) pointed out in his classic study, it is far from clear what it means to be employed in countries where formal labour contracts are the exception rather than the rule. Sen argues that employment can best be understood by thinking about its various dimensions, which include an income, output, and a recognition aspect. They are not mutually exclusive, and income may be in kind rather than as a monetary reward. In virtually all countries in sub-Saharan Africa, with the exception of South Africa, formal employment contracts for labour services are the exception not the rule. So in understanding the determinants of employment we need to understand how output and income are linked when employment is not governed by labour contracts and the implications of a shift to a market structure where they are. Doing so will provide us with insights into why unemployment appears to be South Africa's central economic problem and to be practically absent from other countries in Africa.

Labour incomes

Most poor people in Africa work in small-scale enterprises, and the income that accrues to their labour depends on the value of the assets. The enterprise may be a farm, it may be a family run business, it may be in trade, it may be some combination of all these, but the common factor across all of them is that the scale is small. Scale will be linked to incomes through two factors. First, small scale implies low levels of assets, so incomes will be low unless the value of the assets is high. Second, human capital can be complementary to physical capital, and in many cases physical capital requires a substantially larger scale of operation than occurs in rural and self-employed business in Africa. Incomes to labour in Africa have been, and remain, very much a function of the scale of the enterprise (Falco et al. 2010).

However, the importance of scale is wider than the link from incomes to assets in small-scale enterprises. For wage employees, incomes rise with the scale of the enterprise in part due to the fact that larger enterprises employ more skilled labour and in part because there is a size effect on wages (Söderbom and Teal 2004; Söderbom, Teal, and Wambugu 2005). The relative importance of the human capital component of wages and the role of firm characteristics are central empirical issues in understanding why wages differ as much as they do and why wages can be so much higher than non-wage sources of income in poor countries.

Numerous reasons have been advanced as to why size and wages are related (Oi and Idson 1999). One possibility is that certain sectors or firms have more desirable characteristics than others, in which case wages will reflect an element of compensating differentials. Another model suggests that workers may be harder to monitor in some firms or occupations, in which case the wages may be part of the inducement mechanism to work harder. This and other versions of the efficiency wage argument all suggest reasons why firms will choose to pay more than the reservation wage of the workers (e.g. Stiglitz 1974). In contrast to models which focus on why firms will wish to offer higher wages are theories which predict that more profitable firms will pay more as workers capture some of the rents from higher profits (Teal 1996).

The determinants of employment

What factors determine employment? It is useful to begin with the simplest model of the demand and supply for a given type of labour (Fig. 1). We can see that the two factors which determine how employment grows are the speed with which the demand curve for labour shifts to the right and the elasticity of the supply of labour. The shape of the labour supply curve has been the focus of the 'surplus' labour model which has been very influential in thinking about development issues. The Lewis (1954) model in its simplest form postulates that income growth occurs by employment expanding in a high-wage modern sector the speed of whose growth is driven by the rate of investment in that sector. In the simplest form of the surplus labour model, output does not fall as labour shifts from the traditional (read rural) to the modern (read urban) sector. Sen (1975) provides an overview of the conditions that are required for this to occur.

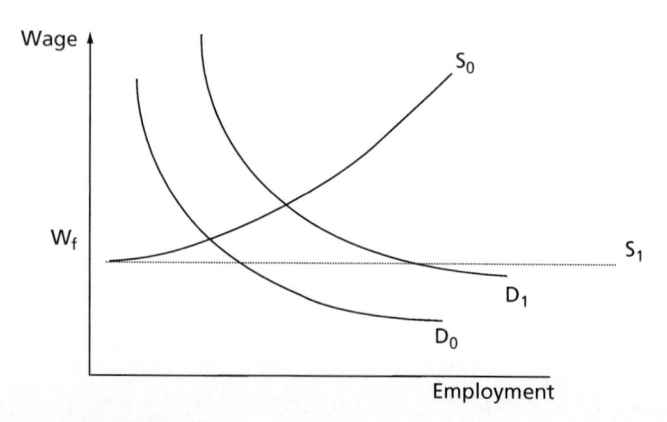

Figure 1. Wages and employment

The Harris–Todaro model and the Fields extension

Figure 2 sets out a version of a model of labour markets which makes it explicit that sectors are linked. On the left-hand axis are the wages available in the urban sector, on the right-hand axis incomes to labour in the rural sector. In the original Harris–Todaro (1970) model, individuals based their choice of whether to work in the urban or the rural sector by comparing the expected wage in the urban sector (w^f) with the actual return to labour in the rural sector (w_a). In the extension of this model due to Fields (1975) there is a 'murky' urban sector, more usually termed the 'informal sector', where access is free and wages low. Figure 2 shows that there are four possible employment outcomes: working in the urban formal or informal sectors, rural employment, or open unemployment. The key insight of Harris and Todaro is that unemployment may act as a device which equilibrates wages in the two sectors so that the expected wage of working in the urban sector equals the expected wage in the rural sector. The former is equal to the actual wage (w^f) multiplied by the probability of getting a job, which is in turn the number of jobs E^f relative to the number of urban job seekers L^u.

$$E(w^f) = w^f \frac{E^f}{L^u} = w_a \qquad (1)$$

Fields' (1975) extension of this model was to show that the introduction of the informal sector is to generate wages in the informal sector, which bring the predictions of the model much closer to the data. Such labour markets where wages differ across sectors for similarly skilled labour are often termed 'segmented'.

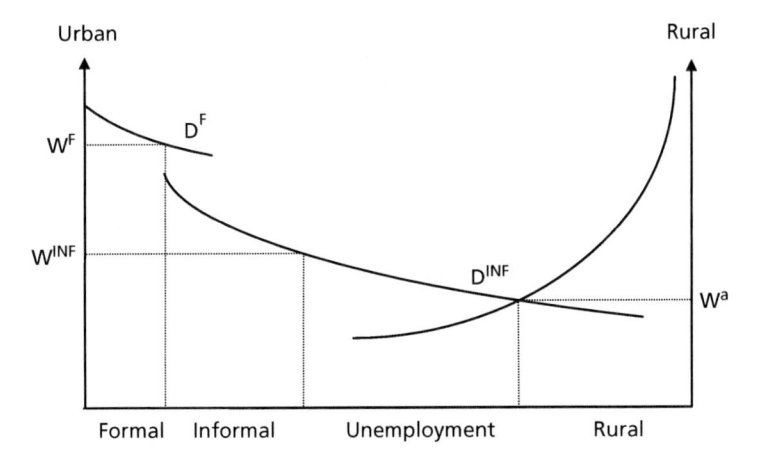

Figure 2. Wages and employment in a segmented labour market

Is there segmentation in urban labour markets?

The facts about labour markets in Africa are not widely disputed. What is in dispute is the explanation for those facts. Kingdon, Sandefur, and Teal (2006) identify three common empirical findings across urban labour markets in Africa over the last decade, illustrated in Figure 3. First, the level of wage employment has increased in absolute terms, but has failed to keep pace with a growing labour force. Second, the share of the informal sector in total employment has grown rapidly. Third, African economies with high unemployment rates have relatively small informal sectors.

Figure 3 illustrates the great disparity in unemployment rates and the size of the informal economy across urban sectors within SSA. Ghana, Tanzania, and Uganda display extraordinarily low unemployment rates, while Ethiopia and South Africa have among the highest unemployment rates in the world. In terms of the size of the informal sector, the pattern is essentially the mirror image. Underlying these different employment structures across the countries are substantial differences in earnings across sectors. Do they reflect high formal-sector wages and labour market segmentation?

Early tests of the segmented market thesis sought to show that wages for similar types of labour differed across sectors. However, this test is problematic for many reasons. Differences in earnings across individuals, even with the same observable characteristics, do not necessarily imply segmentation. Heckman's (2001) Nobel lecture stressed that any analysis of micro data must allow for the role of unobserved heterogeneity and the Roy (1951) model of occupational sorting pointed out that treating any sector effect as

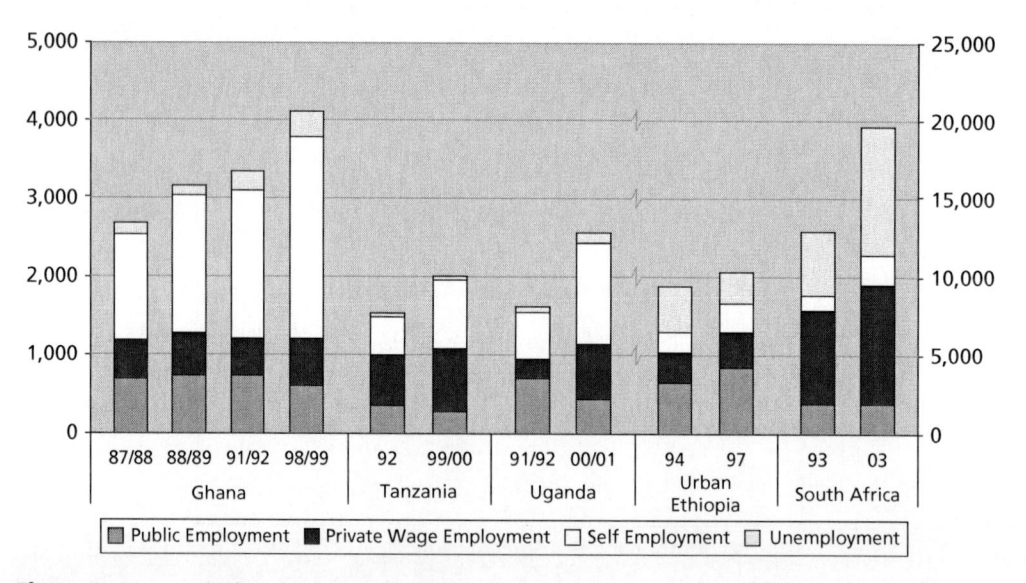

Figure 3. Non-agricultural employment and unemployment in selected African countries

causal missed the point that the occupation was chosen. Magnac (1991) provides a discussion and one of the first tests. The fact that formal workers earn more than informal ones does not imply that an informal worker who switched to formal employment would earn more. An alternative view to the Harris and Todaro explanation for what we observe is due to Lucas (2004), who developed a model in which the 'unemployed' were learning about the application of their skills to urban job opportunities. Another line of research focused on the implications of the Harris–Todaro model that unemployment and wages should be positively related. The extensive work on the wage curve pioneered by Blanchflower and Oswald (1995) showed that wages and unemployment were generally *inversely* related, a result which has been found for Africa (Hoddinott 1996; Kingdom and Knight 2006).

African labour markets are dominated by enterprises of small scale. The underlying issue in analysing these markets is whether this reflects some form of market failure—segmentation between the formal and informal or rationed access to wage employment—or a market clearing response to employment opportunities dominated by low skills. We need to know the answer to how these labour markets work in order to understand which policies will be most effective at raising the price of unskilled labour.

REFERENCES

Blanchflower, D., and A. Oswald, 1995. *The Wage Curve*. Cambridge, Mass.: MIT Press.

Falco, P., A. Kerr, N. Rankin, J. Sandefur, and F. Teal, 2010. 'The returns to formality and informality in urban Africa', CSAE working paper, 2010-03: http://www.csae.ox.ac.uk/workingpapers/pdfs/2010-03text.pdf.

Fields, G. S., 1975. 'Rural–urban migration, urban unemployment and under-development, and job-search security in LDCs', *Journal of Development Economics* 2, 165–87.

Harris, J. R., and M. P. Todaro, 1970. 'Migration, unemployment and development: a two-sector analysis', *American Economic Review* 60, 126–42.

Heckman, J. J., 2001. 'Micro data, heterogeneity, and the evaluation of public policy: Nobel lecture', *Journal of Political Economy* 109.4, 673–748.

Hoddinott, J., 1996. 'Wages and unemployment in an urban African labor market', *Economic Journal* 106: 1610–26.

Kingdon, G., and J. Knight, 2006. 'How flexible are wages in response to local unemployment in South Africa?', *Industrial and Labor Relations Review* 59.3.

—— J. Sandefur, and F. Teal, 2006. 'Labour market flexibility, wages and incomes in sub-Saharan Africa in the 1990s', *African Development Review* 18.3, 392–427.

Lewis, W. A., 1954. 'Economic development with unlimited supplies of labour', *Manchester School* 22, 139–91.

Lucas, R. E., 2004. 'Life earnings and rural–urban migration', *Journal of Political Economy* 112. 1, pt 2.

Magnac, T., 1991. 'Segmented or competitive labor markets', *Econometrica* 59, 165–87.

Mincer, J., 1974. *Schooling, Experience and Earnings*. New York: National Bureau of Economic Research.

Mortensen, D. T., 2005. *Wage Dispersion: Why Are Similar Workers Paid Differently?* Cambridge, Mass.: MIT Press.

Oi, W.Y., and T. L. Idson, 1999. 'Firm size and wages', in O. C. Ashenfelter and D. Card (eds), *Handbook of Labor Economics*, vol. 3b. New York: Elsevier.

Roy, A. D., 1951. 'Some thoughts on the distribution of earnings', *Oxford Economic Papers* (new series) 3, 135–46.

Sen, A. K., 1975. *Employment, Technology and Development*. Oxford: Oxford University Press.

Söderbom, M., and F. Teal, 2004. 'Size and efficiency in African manufacturing firms: evidence from firm-level panel data', *Journal of Development Economics* 73: 369–94.

—— —— and A. Wambugu, 2005. 'Unobserved heterogeneity and the relation between earnings and firm size: evidence from two developing countries', *Economic Letters* 87, 153–9.

Stiglitz, J., 1974. 'Alternative theories of wage determination and unemployment in LDCs: the labor turnover model', *Quarterly Journal of Economics* 88.2, 194–227.

Teal, F., 1996. 'The size and sources of economic rents in a developing country manufacturing labor market', *Economic Journal* 106, 963–76.

The Informal Self-Employed in Africa

James Heintz and Imraan Valodia

Self-employment in small-scale enterprises and farms dominates the employment picture in most African countries. The majority of these enterprises operate in the informal sector—i.e. their productive activities are not governed, or are governed to a limited extent by formal laws, regulations, and social protections. Their attachment to formal institutions is weak—not only government institutions, but also private sector entities, such as commercial banks. However, the informal self-employed are not shut off from the formal economy. Interactions are commonplace, but are frequently characterized by structural inequalities, such as those that exist between a street trader and larger intermediaries which supply the goods sold.

This chapter focuses on issues relevant to self-employment in informal enterprises with an emphasis on non-agricultural activities. The chapter reviews the extent and nature of informal self-employment in Africa and suggests policies that may improve the productivity and earnings of these workers.

The extent and nature of informal self-employment in Africa

Given the prevalence of informal self-employment, it is not surprising that the term 'informal sector' was first used to describe employment in sub-Saharan Africa—specifically, in Ghana (Hart 1973) and Kenya (ILO 1972). Detailed information on informal employment has improved since these early studies. Nevertheless, the limited availability of representative data prevents us from generalizing to the whole of sub-Saharan Africa. Therefore, we draw on illustrative examples of informal self-employment in this overview.

Estimates based on recent survey data for Ghana and Kenya illustrate the continued importance of informal self-employment. In Ghana, self-employment in informal enterprises accounted for 38% of men's non-agricultural employment and 77% of women's non-agricultural employment.[1] If we include agricultural employment, informal self-employment accounted for 73% of men's total employment and 89% of women's. Similarly, in Kenya, where wage employment is more prevalent, these categories of employment accounted for 27% of men's non-agricultural employment and 47% of women's.[2] For women in sub-Saharan Africa, who are often under-represented in wage employment, particularly outside of the public sector, informal self-employment provides a critical source of paid employment (Chen et al. 2005).

Own-account workers, unpaid contributing family workers, and self-employed individuals in very small-scale enterprises typically earn less and face higher risks of income and consumption poverty than other non-agricultural workers (UNECA 2005; Heintz 2008; Chen et al. 2005). On average, however, earnings tend to be higher and poverty risks lower for these workers compared to individuals in agricultural employment. Therefore, movement into non-agricultural informal activities represents an intermediate step in the transition out of agriculture, particularly in the context of widespread informality. The earnings differential also helps explain rural-to-urban migration, in which individuals leave agriculture to work informally in cities.[3] Inadequate policies to support rural and agricultural informal enterprises, relative to urban self-employment, would contribute to this dynamic.

A large proportion of the informal self-employed, outside of agriculture, work in the service sector, with many working as traders. For example, in Kenya, over 80% of all informal household enterprises are engaged in the provision of services, with 64% in retail trade. Less than 10% work in manufacturing. These informal enterprises are typically very small: over half have no paid employees and 95% have two employees or fewer.[4] Similar patterns are apparent in other African countries. Estimates for Madagascar show that 87% of non-agricultural household enterprises are engaged in service provision and about a fifth are engaged in trading. Of these enterprises, 92% have no paid employees.[5]

---

[1] Authors' calculations based on the 1998/9 Ghana Living Standards Survey. Informal enterprises defined as unregistered enterprises.

[2] Authors' calculations based on 2005/6 Kenya Integrated Household Budget Survey (KIHBS). Informal enterprises defined as unregistered enterprises.

[3] In an early paper, Fields (1975) discusses these dynamics expanding the earlier analysis of Harris and Todaro (1970).

[4] Authors' calculations based on 2005/6 Kenya Integrated Household Budget Survey (KIHBS).

[5] Authors' calculations based on data from the Enquête Auprès des Ménages, 2005. Informal enterprises are those who do not possess a *numéro statistique*—i.e. are unregistered.

Improving the productivity and earnings of the informal self-employed

The fact that many of the informal self-employed work in service activities has important implications for productivity and earnings. Productivity in services is distinct from productivity in manufacturing and industrial activities. Productivity in services, and by extension earnings in service activities, is strongly influenced by the level of demand. For example, a street trader's productivity will be largely determined by the quantity of goods she sells within a given time period. In manufacturing, productivity is often thought of as a supply-side factor, linked to the development of technology. In services, the boundary between the supply side and demand side is blurred in the determination of productivity.

Information on barriers to entry into informal activities is occasionally available, and such survey data provides insights into the primary constraints individuals in these forms of employment face. For example, the most common barriers to entry identified by Malagasy respondents who operated informal household enterprises were lack of access to capital or credit (45%) and lack of access to markets (12%).[6]

The linkages that exist between informal and formal economic activities in African countries are not fully understood. However, these relationships are of critical importance. For example, the ease with which workers move between formal and informal forms of employment has implications for our understanding of labour market segmentation, the persistence of poverty, and livelihood strategies more generally. Labour mobility represents only one aspect of the relationship between formal and informal activities. Given limited access to capital and markets, one pathway for informal workers to increase their incomes is through improved integration with the formal economy. Thus, linkages between informal enterprises and those in the formal sector with regard to markets, contracts, and bargaining dynamics have a direct impact on the livelihoods of the informal self-employed.

Most African countries do not have data which allow us to explore how individuals move between formal and informal employment over time. One exception is South Africa. Valodia et al. (2006) use the panel component of South Africa's labour force survey to examine mobility between formal and informal employment. They find that a surprisingly large number of workers move between the formal and informal sectors. This suggests that workers in low-income occupations adopt creative strategies to cope with low incomes and high levels of insecurity in their

---

[6] Other barriers identified by the survey included lack of technical know-how, lack of specialized equipment, and lack of business skills. About 17% of informal household enterprises reported no barriers to entry.

employment, which involves regularly seeking out opportunities in both formal and informal sectors.

A study of market relationships in South Africa by Skinner (2005) provides indicators of forward and backward linkages in the informal economy, drawing on a detailed survey of informal enterprises in the greater Durban area of South Africa. The most frequently cited source of materials for informal enterprises is medium to large firms, with six in every ten owners identifying these firms as suppliers. This indicates strong backward linkages with the formal economy. The second most cited source was small enterprises or traders, with over five in every ten respondents identifying this as a source. Some informal activities are more strongly linked into the formal economy than others. Clothing traders, retail activities operated out of one's own residence ('spaza shops'), informal bars ('shebeens'), and crèches tended to source their goods from medium and larger suppliers.

In this same study, the overwhelming majority of respondents—98% of those interviewed—sold their goods and services to private individuals or households. The forward linkages with formal and other informal enterprises are not strong. The reliance on domestic demand observed in South Africa is common elsewhere. This is not surprising, since services account for most urban informal employment. A similar dependence on domestic demand in local markets has been documented for Ghana (Barwa 1995). Survey evidence reveals that over 99% of all household enterprises in Kenya sell in domestic markets.[7] Given the reliance of the informal self-employed on domestic markets, barriers to market access and insufficient local demand limit the ability of these individuals to realize income from their productive activities.

There are a number of interventions which increase access to domestic markets. Infrastructure improvements and other forms of public investment are critical. Better roads increase access to population centres where demand is more concentrated, and reduce transportation costs through efficiency gains. When small-scale producers can access markets themselves, their reliance on intermediaries is reduced and their terms of trade improve. For example, Durban's municipal government established buy-back centres to purchase recyclable materials from self-employed waste collectors. By consolidating the purchase and sale of recyclables, self-employed individuals were able to increase access to markets, raise productivity, and improve their earnings (Chen et al. 2005). Procurement policies could also be used to provide more equitable access to government demand for certain informal activities (e.g. furniture production).

Another factor which limits the earnings and productivity of the informal self-employed is the lack of private assets. Private savings is the single most important source of start-up finance used to establish small-scale enterprises. According to survey data in

---

[7] Authors' calculation based on survey data from the KIHBS.

Kenya, 83% of enterprises got their start-up capital from their own savings (62%) or from relatives (21%). In Madagascar, 84% financed their initial investments from these same sources. Credit from financial institutions—formal, informal, and micro lending—is a relatively unimportant source of capital for these enterprises.

The dominance of own-savings as a source of finance raises an important conundrum. Savings provides the resources for making productivity-improving investments, but poor households, which rely on earnings from informal activities, have very low levels of savings to begin with.

Financial intermediation is the means through which savings can be pooled and resources allocated to relax capital constraints. However, limited access to credit is a severe problem for the informal self-employed. For small-scale borrowers, transactions costs and market imperfections raise the cost of credit from commercial banks and often result in credit rationing. Because many African banks have traditionally extended credit to the public sector or to finance trade, they may be inefficient in managing loans to small enterprises. Many do not have the institutional arrangements in place to assess creditworthiness outside their traditional clientele. The lack of information causes banks to ration credit to informal enterprises, even though research suggests that default rates among these borrowers are often low (Steele et al. 1997).

Improving access to credit for the informal self-employed requires institutional change. Commercial banks must develop the capacity to administer small-scale loans. Credit registries, which explicitly include small-scale borrowers, could facilitate this process. Informal financial institutions, such as collective savings and credit arrangements, often fill the gap left by formal banks. Building stronger links between government policy, commercial banks, and informal finance would increase access to basic financial services. Finally, microfinance institutions, often run by non-government organizations, have been used to extend credit to informal enterprises.

As this overview has emphasized, any serious analysis of employment in African countries must recognize the critical importance of informal self-employment. Policies that aim to reduce poverty and improve human development must take into account the constraints, institutional relationships, and resource endowments which define the economic environment with which the informal self-employed must contend.

REFERENCES

Barwa, S. D., 1995. 'Structural adjustment programmes and the urban informal sector in Ghana', Issues in Development Discussion Paper 3, ILO, Geneva.

Chen, M., J. Vanek, F. Lund, J. Heintz, R. Jhabvala, and C. Bonner, 2005. *Progress of the World's Women 2005: Women, Work, and Poverty.* New York: UNIFEM.

Fields, Gary, 1975. 'Rural–urban migration, urban unemployment and underemployment, and job-search activity in LDCs', *Journal of Development Economics* 2.2, 165–87.

Harris, John R., and Michael P. Todaro, 1970. 'Migration, unemployment, and development: a two-sector analysis', *American Economic Review* 60.1, 126–42.

Hart, Keith, 1973. 'Informal income opportunities and urban employment in Ghana', *Journal of Modern African Studies* 11.1, 61–89.

Heintz, James, 2008. 'Employment, informality and poverty: an empirical overview of six countries with a focus on gender and race', background paper prepared for the Flagship Report on Poverty, UNRISD, Geneva.

International Labour Organization, 1972. *Employment, Incomes, and Equity: A Strategy for Increasing Productive Employment in Kenya*. Geneva: ILO.

Skinner, Caroline, 2005. 'Constraints to growth and employment in Durban: evidence from the informal economy', Research Report 65, School of Development Studies, University of Kwa-Zulu-Natal.

Steele, William, Ernest Aryeetey, Hemamala Hettige, and Machiko Nissanke, 1997. 'Informal financial markets under liberalization in four African countries', *World Development* 25.5, 817–30.

UN Economic Commission for Africa, 2005. *Economic Report on Africa 2005: Meeting the Challenge of Unemployment and Poverty*. Addis Ababa: UNECA.

Valodia, Imraan, Lekani Lebani, Caroline Skinner, and Richard Devey, 2006. 'Low-waged and informal employment in South Africa', *Transformation* 60, 90–126.

Thematic Perspectives
Environment

Environment and Climate Change

John Asafu-Adjaye

1. Introduction

After decades of poor or negative growth, African economies have now recorded consistently high growth rates since the year 2000. The average gross domestic product (GDP) growth rate for the period 2000–2008 was about 5%, which is more than double the average growth rate of 2.1% recorded for the decade of 1980–90 (World Bank 2009). With the exception of China and India, Africa's growth rate has exceeded that of developing countries, most of which have struggled, especially in the last few years due to the global financial crisis. This impressive performance can be attributed in part to improved commodity prices and implementation of economic reforms in a number of countries. However, the spurt in economic growth has been insufficient to reverse years of economic degradation.

Although Africa accounts for 15% of the world's population (Population Reference Bureau 2008), it constitutes about 28% of the world's poverty (World Bank 2009). Africa accounts for only 1% of global GDP, 2% of global trade and 3% of foreign direct investment (UNCTAD 2004). Poverty indicators in this continent are the highest in the world. Nearly all of the countries with a low Human Development Index are African countries, and only eight of the bottom half of countries ranked in the Human Poverty Index are non-African (UNDP 2008). There are now serious concerns that countries in this region will have problems achieving their Millennium Development Goals (MDGs).

Africa's problems are likely to be compounded by climate change. This is because it is likely to be the continent most vulnerable to climate change given that it relies mainly on agriculture, which is the most climate-sensitive of all the productive sectors. In light of these concerns, this chapter examines the potential impacts of climate change on African economies and addresses the policy implications.

2. State of the environment: biodiversity loss and pollution

Due to population growth and increase in economic activities, the world's stock of renewable natural resources is decreasing at an alarming rate. The 2005 Millennium Ecosystem Assessment found that 15 out of 24 ecosystem services it assessed were in global decline (Millennium Ecosystem Assessment 2005).[1] Tropical rainforests, although constituting only 7% of the Earth's land surface, nevertheless contain more than half the species in the entire world biota (Wilson 1988). Africa occupies about one-fifth of the earth's land surface and contains about one-fifth of all known species of plants, mammals, and birds in the world, as well as one-sixth of amphibians and reptiles (Siegfried 1989).

Figure 1 shows changes in forest area for selected parts of the world for the period 1991–2005. As is widely known, the rate of loss of forest area is highest in Latin America, with an annual average loss of about 43,000 km², followed by sub-Saharan Africa (SSA) where 29,000 km² of forest area is lost on average per year. In contrast, forest area in the

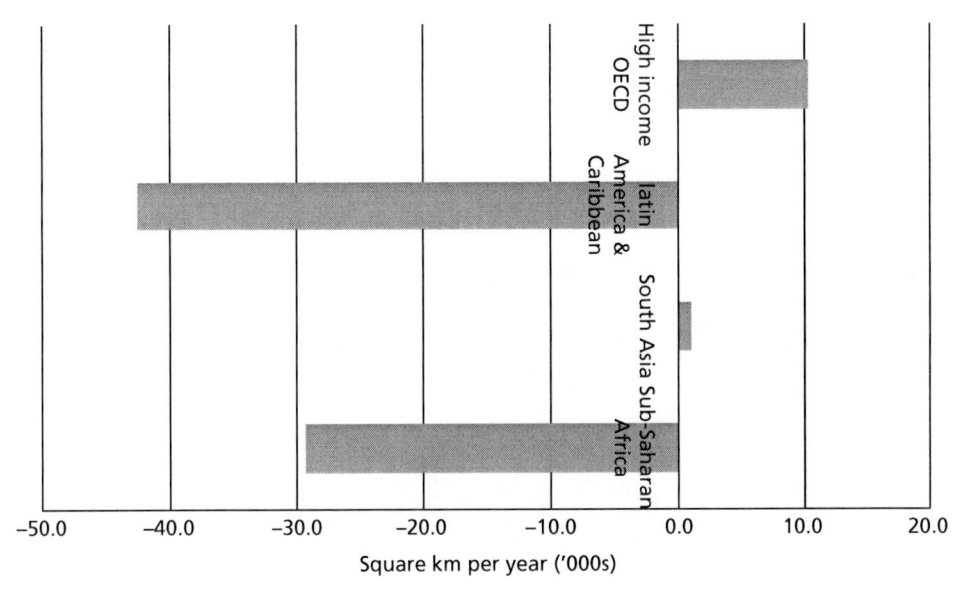

Figure 1. Ecosystem decline: average annual net change in forest area by region, 1991–2005 (based on World Bank 2009)

---

[1] Ecosystem services assessed included plant pollination, provision of fresh water, woodfuels, wild foods, and fish.

high-income OECD countries has increased by just over 10,000 km² per year on average in this period.

One major contributor to the deterioration of the environment globally has been the escalation in greenhouse gases (GHGs) since pre-industrial times. For example, between 1750 and 2005, carbon dioxide (CO_2) emissions grew from 280 parts per million (ppm) to 379 ppm, while methane grew from 715 to 1774 ppm (Intergovernmental Panel on Climate Change (IPCC) 2007). In 2004, developed countries held a 20% share in world population but accounted for 46% of global GHG emissions. In sharp contrast, Africa accounted for only 8% of global GHG emissions, while South Asia accounted for 13%. However, about two-thirds of the flow of new GHG emissions into the atmosphere is currently produced by developing countries, and without new policies this share is set to rise further to 2050 (IPCC 2007).

There is now an overwhelming body of scientific evidence linking the rising temperatures to increased atmospheric concentrations of CO_2 and other GHGs. Estimates of possible temperature rise by the end of the century range between 1.1 and 4.5°C, and sea levels are likely to rise by 28–43 cm (IPCC 2007). For the African continent as a whole, the estimates project median temperature increases of between 3°C and 4°C, which is one and a half times greater than the global mean response. Section 3 briefly describes the climate change impacts on Africa, with specific reference to biological and water resources.

3. Impacts of climate change

3.1. AGRICULTURAL PRODUCTION

The agricultural sector is dominant in most African economies, contributing roughly a third of GDP on average, and for some countries 50% or more of GDP (World Bank 2009). A number of studies using a variety of climate models and emissions scenarios have concluded that climate change will have an overall negative impact on African agriculture. While agricultural production in a few parts of Africa (e.g. East Africa) may actually be enhanced due to increased rainfall and temperature, as well as an increased growing season (see e.g. Thornton et al. 2006), these gains are likely to be offset by the projected losses in central, western, and southern Africa. Cline (2007) has conducted a comprehensive analysis of the impacts of climate change on global agriculture through until the 2080s using a series of agricultural impact models. For African countries that rely on dry-land agriculture, weighted average crop losses under a 'business as usual' (BAU) scenario without carbon fertilization range from 84% (Senegal) to 2% (Uganda), with a mean decline of 27.8% for the sample. An issue of major concern is the high number of severe effects for dryland agriculture. Four countries in his sample have declines of 100%, while another three experience declines of about 50% or more.

3.2. BIODIVERSITY AND WATER RESOURCES

It is estimated that by the 2080s, the proportion of arid and semi-arid lands in Africa is likely to increase by 5–8% (IPCC 2001). These changes will lead to loss of flora and fauna and hence reduce Africa's biodiversity, posing adverse implications for Africa's food and water security. Climate change could also affect marine and coastal ecosystems, impacting on endangered species such as turtles and migratory birds. Sea-level rise from climate change could lead to increased colonization of coastal lagoons by mangroves (Rocha et al. 2005), while warming would lead to the disappearance of low-lying coral and loss of marine biodiversity (Payet and Obura 2004). These changes will negatively impact on commercial and subsistence fisheries, as well as tourism. Current pressures on water resources in the region are affected by both anthropogenic and climatic factors. Using various climate models and scenarios, Arnell (2004) projects that the number of people living in water-stressed areas in Africa is estimated to be in the range of 35 to 403 million by 2055 in the absence of climate change. With climate change, the population at risk of increased water stress in Africa is projected to reach 350–600 million people by 2055. In most parts of Africa, infrastructure to store and serve water is mostly overstretched in capacity, and may be inadequate to deal with extreme events such as floods.

4. Economic impacts of climate change with specific reference to agriculture

A number of global impact studies (e.g. IPCC and the Stern Review, 2006) have estimated the economic impacts of climate change on various regions of the world. However, these models tend to be highly aggregated and therefore do not sufficiently capture regional and local specific impacts. In this section, we present quantitative estimates of how climate change will affect economic growth in African countries relative to other regions of the world.

4.1. MODELLING APPROACH AND ASSUMPTIONS

We employ a computable general equilibrium (CGE) model to investigate the economic impacts of climate change, with specific reference to the expected losses in agricultural production. The model used here is the Global Trade Analysis Project (GTAP) model, a multiregional static CGE model which captures world economic activity in 57 different industries of 87 regions of the world (Hertel 1997). In this simulation, we have aggregated the database into 16 regions: EU, Japan, US, China, India, 10 SSA regions, and the rest of the world. The reference case for the simulation is a scenario in which it is assumed that there are no climate change impacts on future economic growth. This situation is then compared to a BAU climate change scenario without carbon fertilization. The assumed losses in agricultural productivity were taken from Cline (2007) and further details on the assumptions are provided in Asafu-Adjaye (2008).

4.2 SIMULATION RESULTS

The simulation results are presented in Table 1. As can be seen, global warming leads to a decline in agricultural production worldwide. However, the decline in Africa will be much higher relative to the rest of the world on the basis of the climate predictions. The agricultural productivity losses in Africa range from 11% (Uganda) to 39% (rest of SSA). By comparison, output declines by about 2% for EU, US, and Japan, and by 11% for the rest of the world (Cline 2007). The fall in agricultural output has greater adverse impacts on African countries because their economies are agriculture-based. The simulation results in Table 1 indicate that GDP declines by as much as 49% for Zambia, 35% for South Africa, and 34% for Zimbabwe. By contrast, GDP increases by 4% for the EU, 6% for the US, and 5% for Japan.

The terms of trade decline for SSA countries but increase for the three advanced countries. This results in a decline in household disposable incomes, as farmers receive less for their produce. The net effect of global warming is thus a decline in welfare in all regions across the world, reflecting a decline in both agricultural and non-agricultural activities. The results in Table 1 also indicate that falling agricultural production will put upward pressure on inflation. This can be seen from the rise in agricultural import prices and the GDP deflator, which implies that poverty will increase as a result of climate change.

5. Policy responses and challenges

The key policy responses to climate change are adaptation and mitigation. However, adaptation by itself does not prevent climate change, and is indeed part of the cost of climate change. Therefore, an effective response to deal with the negative impacts of climate change must consider both adaptation and mitigation strategies.

Table 1. Simulation results for the impacts of climate change on output and welfare relative to reference case

Country/region	GDP	Household disposable income	Welfare impacts (US$ million)	Agric import prices	GDP deflator
EU	4.4	3.6	−320.140	8.4	0.1
US	6.2	5.6	−366,321	12.5	0.2
Japan	4.9	3.9	−165572	9.7	0.1
China	−24.5	−29.2	−1,601	10.1	1.5
India	−29.0	−35.2	−553	11.6	7.3
Botswana	−26.5	−30.8	−1,363	15.4	0.2
Malawi	−13.0	−15.9	−719	15.6	3.9
Madagascar	−34.6	−41.8	−38,925	9.5	4.4
Mozambique	−19.9	−22.4	−2,260	14.0	2.5
South Africa	−12.1	−14.1	−863	13.8	0.7
Tanzania	−48.6	−56.5	−1,767	12.3	6.4
Uganda	−34.4	−41.8	−4,929	10.9	6.3
Zambia	−40.5	−48.0	−60,783	14.6	4.3
Zimbabwe	−10.5	−13.2	−1,403,443	14.4	1.6
Rest of SSA	−4.4	−3.6	−320.140	11.5	2.7
Rest of the world	−6.2	−5.6	−366,321	10.4	0.4

Unless otherwise indicated, all the figures are in percentage changes.
Source: Asafu-Adjaye (2008).

5.1. ADAPTATION

Effective adaptation to climate change will require planned responses at the farm, regional, and national levels. In the short to medium term, farmers can adapt to climate change and variability by means of appropriate crop selection and changing the timing of planting. However, such measures may only be effective for adapting to temperature changes in the region of 1–2°C, and will be ineffective at higher temperatures. Measures such as introduction of new varieties, diversification of production systems and livelihoods, and a shift to intensive agriculture will be required at higher temperatures. Farmers' adaptive capacity can be considerably enhanced by providing them with timely adaptation and climate information. Other measures that could assist in building adaptive capacity include providing extension services, access to capital, weather insurance, and safety nets. In most parts of Africa, there is need for major investments to shift from dryland to irrigated agriculture. Adaptive capacity can also be enhanced by improving governance at the local, state, and national levels, and by strengthening appropriate local institutions such as community credit and savings groups and other forms of social capital. Factors that limit individuals' and communities' abilities to adapt to climate change include financial constraints, low educational levels, and poor institutions.

5.2. MITIGATION

Although the advanced countries have a greater responsibility to undertake mitigation because they are primarily responsible for the past accumulation of GHGs, developing countries also have a responsibility to mitigate because they will become major GHG emitters by the 2050s. One area where Africa is fast becoming a major GHG emitter is land-use change, in particular deforestation. Africa now accounts for 20% of world emissions in this area. There is a need for African countries to mainstream climate mitigation and adaptation strategies into their national, subnational, and sectoral planning processes.[2] Implementation of these plans must be incorporated into the national budget process, which requires the active participation of a core ministry such as finance or economic planning. Traditional planning processes in most African countries have adopted a top-down approach. There is a need to switch to a bottom-up approach involving local communities and other stakeholders. Such an approach is more likely to meet the needs of the people and to create a sense of ownership, and is therefore more likely to yield positive outcomes.

6. Summary and conclusions

Climate change poses a serious threat to economic development in the world in general and Africa in particular. Considering just the effects of changes in agricultural productivity, our modelling results indicate that climate change will increase GDP for the EU, Japan, and the US but will decrease GDP by significant amounts in Africa. The agricultural productivity losses in Africa will also lead to a decline in the terms of trade, a reduction in disposable incomes, a reduction in welfare, and an increase in poverty. African countries therefore have no choice but to undertake adaptation, the only near-term means to offset the negative impacts of climate change. However, the costs of adapting to climate change will be high, and most African countries do not have the financial and human resources to undertake these measures. There is therefore a responsibility for the developed countries, which have emitted the greatest share of GHGs already locked into the climate system, to provide assistance. Given that

---

[2] The key constraints to mainstreaming climate change include lack of adequate budgetary resources and lack of technical capacity.

developing countries in general, and Africa in particular, have now become major emitters of GHGs from deforestation and land degradation, there is an urgent need for them to adopt policies that encourage sustainable use of their forest resources.

REFERENCES

Arnell, N. W., 2004. 'Climate change and global water resources: SRES emissions and socio-economic scenarios', *Global Environmental Change* 14, 31–52.

Asafu-Adjaye, J., 2008. 'Climate change, trade and competitiveness in Sub-Saharan Africa', paper presented at the African Economic Research Consortium (AERC) Senior Policy Seminar X on Climate Change and Economic Development in Sub-Saharan Africa, Addis Ababa, 7–9 April.

Cline, W., 2007. *Global Warming and Agriculture: Impact Estimates by Country*. Washington, DC: Center for Global Development and Peterson Institute for International Economics. Accessed 13 December 2007 at: www.cgdev.org/content/publications/detail/14090#Chpt.

Hertel, T. W. (ed.), 1997. *Global Trade Analysis Project: Modeling and Applications*. Cambridge: Cambridge University Press.

Intergovernmental Panel on Climate Change, 2001. *Climate Change 2001: Impacts, Adaptation and Vulnerability. Contribution of Working Group II to the Third Assessment Report of the Intergovernmental Panel on Climate Change*, eds. P. Desanka and C. Magadaza. Cambridge: Cambridge University Press.

—— 2007. 'Summary for policymakers', in B. Metz, O. R. Davidson, P. R. Bosch, R. Dave, and L. A. Meyer (eds), *Climate Change 2007: Mitigation Contribution of Working Group III to the Fourth Assessment Report of the Intergovernmental Panel on Climate Change*. Cambridge: Cambridge University Press.

Millennium Ecosystem Assessment, 2005. *Ecosystems and Human Well-Being: Biodiversity Synthesis*. Washington, DC: World Resources Institute. Accessed 20 May 2009 at: http://www.millenniumassessment.org/documents/document.354.aspx.pdf.

Payet, R., and D. Obura, 2004. 'The negative impacts of human activities in the Eastern African region: an international waters perspective', *Ambio* 33, 24–33.

Population Reference Bureau, 2008. *2008 World Population Highlights*. Accessed 18 December 2008 at: http://www.prb.org/pdf08/63.3highlights.pdf.

Rocha, L. A., D. R. Robertson, C. R. Rocha, J. L. Van Tassell, M. T. Craig, and B. W. Bowens, 2005. 'Recent invasion of the tropical Atlantic by an Indo-Pacific coral reef fish', *Molecular Ecology* 14, 3921–8.

Siegfried, W. R., 1989. 'Preservation of species in southern African nature reserves', in B. J. Huntley (ed.), *Biotic Diversity in Southern Africa: Concepts and Conservation*. Cape Town: Oxford University Press, 186–201.

Stern, N., 2006. *The Economics of Climate Change: The Stern Review*. Cambridge: Cambridge University Press.

Thomas, C. D., A. Cameron, R. E. Green, M. Bakkenes, L. J. Beaumont, Y. C. Collingham, B. F. N. Erasmus, M. F.M de Siqueira, et al., 2004, 'Extinction from climate change', *Nature* 427, 145–8.

Thornton, P. K., P. G. Jones, T. M. Owiyo, R. L. Kruska, M. Herero, P. Kristjanson, A. Notenbaert, N. Bekele, et al., 2006. 'Mapping climate vulnerability and poverty in Africa'. Report to the Department for International Development, ILRI, Nairobi.

UNCTAD, 2004. 'Economic development in Africa: trade performance and commodity dependence', Publication UNCTAD/GDS/AFRIC A/2003/1, 84.

UNDP, 2008. Human Development Report: *Fighting Climate Change: Solidarity in a Divided World*. New York: UNDP.

Wilson, E. O., 1988, 'The current state of biodiversity', in E. O. Wilson (ed.), *Biodiversity*. Washington, DC: National Academy Press.

World Bank, 2009. *World Development Indicators*, online version. Washington, DC: World Bank.

Climate Change and Willingness to Pay for Serving Future Generations

Thomas Schelling

There is a special relation between this topic, future generations, and Africa. Most of the resources likely to be devoted to mitigating climate change will come from the advanced nations of north America and western Europe, Japan, Australia, and a few others. Most of the benefits of mitigation, in the form of reduced damage to productivity and health, will accrue to the peoples of less-developed nations after the middle of the current century. The beneficiaries will thus be 'distant' from the investors in both time and space.

It is not evident that the citizens of the advanced nations appreciate that their concerns with climate change—focused on health, comfort, storm damage, and wildlife—are of an entirely different magnitude from the prospective impacts on the lesser developed, who depend so much on agricultural productivity and other outdoor activities. The difference is sometimes reflected in estimates of reduced Gross World Product from climate change, which reflect the superimposition of climate change on rising levels of productivity. Many more than a billion people live on much less than the equivalent of two dollars per day. If they were to lose half their income from climate change—not likely, we hope, but not out of the question—the result would be catastrophic, but the world's gross product would lose less than $365 billion, less than 1%. The poorest have so little to lose that their losses almost disappear in the aggregate.

Many estimates of the impact of climate change are susceptible to 'discounting', as if they were investments in future consumption. A quite common approach to discounting the benefits, in reduced damage to consumption, of some generations in the future is to make the discount rate a summation of two variables. One is 'pure time preference'—the tendency for present consumption to be preferred to delayed, sometimes considered a little irrational—and the other is the reduced marginal value of consumption in the future due to higher levels of consumption. Both of these arguments for discounting are flawed.

The first, pure time preference is almost entirely a phenomenon of an individual's preference regarding his or her own consumption, not the preferences one has for another's consumption. No matter how impatient I am for immediate pleasure, I am not likely to be impatient for someone else's enjoyment. In fact, people often arrange in their wills for heirs to be unable to dissipate their inheritance through impatience. Whether I'd like a benefit to accrue to someone whom I'll never know who doesn't yet exist fifty years from now, or another a hundred years from now, doesn't seem to involve impatience or 'pure time preference.'

The second argument in that discount formula recognizes that in all probability future generations will be wealthier than today's, and will gain less enjoyment per dollar of reduced losses than we sacrifice per dollar in transferring benefits forward in time. The argument is that we invest today in their future consumption because the amount of damage to their consumption that we forestall is much greater than the reduction in our own—more than offsetting the reduced 'marginal' value.

But that argument homogenizes the population: by assuming that all the world's peoples will have higher incomes in the future, it fails to acknowledge that the living standards of today's poor, in today's poor nations, will still, in the second half of this century, be substantially below the living standards of today's populations in the nations that can afford to invest in climate mitigation, or invest in adaptation in the countries most affected by climate change.

There is another dimension to the issue of willingness to invest in future generations. It is whether, even with such climate change as is probably inevitable, those future generations in the poor nations will be better off than their present-day ancestors. Will they, while appreciating whatever the wealthy of today will have done to avert disaster for them—or whatever the wealthy of today will have done to make their own descendants better off and in the process improve the lives of distant peoples—regret that so little was done to lift their ancestors out of poverty, disease, and malnutrition?

It is unlikely that citizens of the nations most able to invest in transforming their energy economies realize that they may, in doing so, be doing more for the poor in poor countries than for their own descendants. It is perhaps equally unlikely that they are greatly interested in the impact of climate change on the people of the African continent. Fortunately, this may not matter as long as they can be mobilized to save the climate for their own successors. It is important, however, that the wealthy nations not demand that the poor nations jeopardize their continued development by participating in global efforts to slow climate change: their best defence against climate change will be their own continued development.

Special efforts may be needed in decades to come to combat some of the health effects of climate change. These will be of two kinds. One may be the increasing virulence of many of the vector-borne diseases together with their geographical spread. Another may be the reduced availability of food: very many people in Africa depend on local production of food. And water may become less available. Essentially, these are today's problems in most of Africa that will be aggravated by climate change.

Special efforts may also be needed to help farmers, perhaps especially subsistence farmers, to adapt their choice of crops and methods of cultivation. In advanced nations there are scientific resources available to farmers to help them adapt; most African nations have no such scientific infrastructure.

A particular problem for much of the world's agriculture is likely to be significant changes in the availability of water for irrigation. This problem will not be peculiar to the developing world, and will differ depending on whether water for irrigation comes from winter snows in the Himalayas, Andes, Alps, Rockies, etc., or from rainfall. Substantial investments in infrastructure may be required to store and transport water for irrigation. Such investments would be beyond the resources of most African nations.

A likely consequence of these considerations is that the advanced nations will have to become more cognizant of the vulnerability of developing nations, especially those that have not managed to develop institutions, including government, that can cope with potential disaster. The issue may not be concern for *future* generations so much as for *distant* generations—distant in space, culture, heritage, and language, as well as in time.

Thematic Perspectives
Globalization

The Challenges of Sustaining African Growth in an Interdependent Global Economy[1]

Benno Ndulu

1. Introduction

The first half century of African growth since independence has been not only slow but also very erratic. Compared to the rest of the emerging and developing world, sub-Saharan African (SSA) incomes per head have on average grown at one fifth of the pace in these other regions. Only in a handful out of the 40 African economies for which there is complete and comparable data for the whole period has growth been rapid and persistent. As a result of the slow and erratic growth, by 2004—more than 50 years after most countries achieved independence—incomes per capita in 9 countries either stagnated or declined relative to the levels in 1960;[2] 6 of the 13 African middle-income countries have experienced a more than twofold increase of their income per capita;[3] and the rest—18 out of the 40—have seen very marginal progress, ranging between 0.1 to a doubling of income per capita over the entire period. In contrast, the average per capita income of the most rapidly growing region, Southeast Asia, increased almost tenfold over the same period (Ndulu, Lopamudra, et al. 2007).

Analysis of the long-term growth performance of the region (Collins and Bosworth 1996; 2003; Ndulu and O'Connell 2003; Ndulu, Lopamudra, et al. 2007; Ndulu, O'Connell, et al. 2008) points to three major factors behind this comparatively poor African growth record. First, although lower levels of investment have been a frequently cited factor behind slower African growth, *slower productivity growth* more sharply distinguishes the region from the rest of the developing world. Investment in African

---

[1] I acknowledge very helpful support by Dr Pantaleo Kessy in finalizing this paper.
[2] Only 3 among these suffered prolonged civil strife: Sierra Leone, Democratic Republic of Congo, and Angola. Since 2004 Angola has left the group as peace has returned and oil riches have come back on stream.
[3] The ratio of income per capita in 2004 relative to 1960 exceeded 2 in Gabon, Republic of Congo, Mauritius, Cape Verde, Botswana, and Lesotho.

economies on average yielded between one third and half of the growth in other regions for the same level of resources committed. Secondly, *geographical isolation of a large number of landlocked economies and higher fragmentation of the region* accounted for a third of the growth difference with other regions. *Delayed demographic transition* is the third distinct feature in Africa that has proved to be a relatively bigger drag on growth. Empirical studies of the sources of growth differences estimate that up to two thirds of the difference in growth is due to differences in the burden (fiscal, savings, and human capital formation) from higher age dependency and more rapid growth in the labour force unmatched by growth in employment opportunities.

However, the last decade and a half have seen a major turnaround in growth performance in the region. This has been partly associated with significant improvements in the growth environment in the region resulting from macroeconomic reforms, the reduction in the number of conflict situations, and improvements in governance. These measures enabled effective exploitation of the significant improvements in the terms of trade for the region driven by a combination of sharp increase in the primary commodities and relative decline in the price of manufactures as the emerging economies have added both to the global demand for these commodities and to the hugely increased supply of cheaper manufactures. As a consequence, 15 out of 44 countries grew at more than 5.3% on average over the last decade and nearly half of them (21 countries) grew at over 5% in the last 5 years. It is noteworthy that productivity growth has led the way in the recovery of growth since mid-1990s (Berthélemy and Söderling 2001; Ndulu, Lopamudra, et al. 2007) to complement improved levels of investment and revenue generation.

This growth turnaround has been accompanied by significant changes in the macroeconomic environment, a modest build-up of resilience to shocks, and a significant change in the composition of investment and development finance. Recent pressures from oil and food prices aside, average inflation in 2007 was still in single digits in two thirds of SSA countries. It is remarkable that inflation spirals of 1973 and 1979 oil price shocks were avoided in the recent major oil price shock (2007–8) and global food shortages (2008). More than two thirds of SSA countries have seen investment rates rise to exceed 20% of GDP. Notwithstanding its recent recovery from the 1990 decline, the significance of official grants in development financing in SSA as a whole has declined. It stands at less than 1% of GDP (just less than 3% excluding SA and Nigeria). National saving has risen, revenue effort (revenue to GDP ratio) has increased, and foreign direct investment has sharply risen from $11b in 2000 to $53b in 2007. There has been also a significant build-up of international reserves in most countries from the boom in commodity exports as self-insurance against shocks.

The big question now for analysts and policymakers is whether the region can sustain this recent success and build on it. Can African economies avoid the episodic growth performance of the past despite the pressures from external shocks? This question is particularly pertinent in light of the ongoing global financial crisis and great dependence of African economies on the global economy. The fallout from the crisis may set back the steady progress made in the last decade. It will endanger sustainability of growth (a possible repeat of second oil shock recession of the 1980s and 1990s); undermine macro stability achieved in the last decade; erode progress in social wellbeing—education, health—as countries face large fiscal gaps; endanger the deterioration in the stock of infrastructure due to shortfalls in financing; push achievement of Millennium Development Goals further away; and pose a threat to social and political stability if safety nets against vulnerabilities—jobs and food—are not provided.

2. The new reality of the global interdependence and vulnerability to shocks

The ongoing global financial and economic crisis has reopened a significant front of development discourse for the region that dominated discussions in the 1960s and 1970s. This is the question of the region's resilience to shocks originating in crises in systemically important economies and financial powerhouses. In this context, the region has not only to deal with the growth fundamentals that have held back its progress for the past decades but also to weather the storms originating from outside its borders. This challenge has to be faced in the context of a vastly enhanced global interdependence.

The global economy has experienced a mammoth transformation since the 1980s. Economies have become significantly more interdependent—production systems have globalized into a giant factory with different stages of processes locating across the globe; trade has grown much faster than production; and international financial resource flows (capital and private remittances) now dwarf domestic savings and ODA. Relatedly, key economic and financial players are not constrained by borders, significantly weakening the role of nation-states. In many cases multinational entities have dwarfed their host governments in terms of size and financial clout based on their global financial capacity. In the absence of an effective global governance system, these multinational entities have become ungovernable and unregulated. Global interdependence has also meant that contagion has become a powerful tool for transmission of a crisis from one country to another. Because the sufferers of such consequences are often victims of contagion, it is in the global interest to see an emergence of an effective governance system that can exercise even-handedness in regulating the behaviour of key players irrespective of their size and clout. These systems are currently either absent or ineffective.

African economies have significantly benefited from this interdependence. As pointed out earlier, a significant factor in scaling up recent growth has been the rapid expansion in the demand for primary commodities. In particular, metals and oil have over a five-year period before the crisis enjoyed high market prices resulting from strong global demand, especially originating from China and India. These emerging giants have also been a key source of cheaper imported manufactures, including investment goods. More broadly, empirical studies have shown very strong statistical relationship between African and trading partners' growth, underscoring the importance of staying engaged and creating conditions for enhanced exploitation of opportunities offered by the global system.

African vulnerabilities to the international economic system depend on several factors:

- the extent of exposure of domestic production to external demand and in turn dependence on primary commodities and natural resources—the region's comparative advantage;
- the degree of dependence on foreign savings for financing investment (FDI and ODA);
- the extent of dependence on imports for domestic production—primary and manufactured products;
- weaknesses from acting individually as small countries and markets, when the rest of the world is forming defensive blocs through integration.

The challenge is how to minimize the risks of being part of the interdependent global economy and build greater resilience to shocks. The terms of engagement with the global economy can be strategically changed over time. There are several measures—centred on the development strategies chosen and those requiring international action based on the improved effectiveness of the global governance and regulatory systems/institutions—that can help the region change those terms.

The literature is replete with suggestions for how African economies can work towards diversifying their economies to avoid depending on a few primary commodities with the attendant high risk from volatility in world market prices. Adding value to these commodities and diversification into manufactures has been proposed, particularly for coastal economies with location advantages in terms of access to markets. These countries can pursue manufactured export-led growth akin to the main Asian model. This requires significant investment in training, technology, and infrastructure, but African countries may also be able to take advantage of the rising wages in East Asia to compete more effectively in the export markets of labour-intensive manufactures. Other countries, particularly in the landlocked resource-poor countries such as Rwanda, can pursue in earnest trade in services exploiting information technology. Yet others may be able to follow the emerging Latin American model of modern agriculture—adding value through agro-processing—or move toward natural resource-based, export-oriented agro-industrialization such as in Malaysia and Indonesia (Ndulu, Lopamudra, et al. 2007: 155).

Another area in which the resilience of African economies may be strengthened against global shocks is better integration of production and consumption processes—

so that the trade becomes an extension from what African countries produce and consume rather than the current situation, where countries typically produce what they do not consume and consume what they do not produce. This would help to strengthen the scope for using domestic demand measures to help bridge global demand gaps when they occur, as China has been able to do successfully recently under its stimulus package.

Africa can learn from Asia in the pursuit of its collective initiatives for self-insurance against shocks. Learning from the 1997 Asian financial crisis, Asian countries have pursued a two-pronged approach towards self-insurance: building up national reserves for the time of need and establishing of a regional reserve pool, which can be accessed expeditiously and more flexibly than if countries were to seek such support from the international financial institutions. This approach has been further buttressed by currency swap arrangements within the region to fill foreign-exchange gaps, particularly for trade. African countries have also built up their reserves, which have been instrumental in cushioning against the shocks and exchange pressures from the crisis. But the region has yet to pursue the pooling of reserves or enable greater use of national or regional currencies for the growing cross-border trade within the region. At sub-regional level this is in place in the CFA franc zone, and steps are being taken to develop greater regional economic integration elsewhere on the continent, most notably in the East African Community.

Finally, countries in the region should work towards reducing dependence on aid and enhancing reliance on domestic savings mobilization, as well as diversifying sources of foreign savings through greater use of the global capital markets. In pursuing this strategy, African countries can exploit recently achieved higher creditworthiness resulting from debt relief and faster growth of GDP and exports.

3. Conclusion

Unlike their Asian counterparts, African countries have been characterized by slow and episodic growth. However, in the past decade and a half many countries in the region appear to have turned the corner and moved to a path of faster and steadier economic growth. This is partly due to macroeconomic stability, the peace dividend, and the improved political climate, together with a favourable external environment—particularly the rapid expansion in the demand for primary commodities. The big challenge for African policymakers now is how to sustain the recent growth performance despite the external shocks that continue to assail their economies. This will require decisive measures to minimize risks of being part of the interdependent global economy, in addition to dealing with economic fundamentals that held back the region's economic progress in the 1970 and 1980s.

REFERENCES

Berthélemy, Jean-Claude, and Ludvig Söderling, 2001. 'The role of capital accumulation, adjustment and structural change for economic take-off: empirical evidence from African growth episodes', *World Development* 29.2, 32–43.

Collins, Susan, and Barry P. Bosworth, 1996. 'Economic growth in East Asia: accumulation versus assimilation', *Brookings Papers on Economic Activity* 2, 135–203.

—— —— 2003. 'The empirics of growth: an update', *Brookings Papers on Economic Activity* 2, 113–206.

Ndulu, B. J., C. Lopamudra, L. Lebohang, R. Vijaya, and W. Jerome, 2007. *Challenges of African Growth: Opportunities, Constraints, and Strategic Directions*. Washington, DC: World Bank.

—— and Stephen O'Connell, 2003. 'Revised Collins/Bosworth growth accounting decomposition', Explaining African Economic Growth Project, AERC, Nairobi.

—— —— Robert H. Bates, Paul Collier, Chukwama C. Soludo, et al. (eds), 2008. *The Political Economy of Economic Growth in Africa, 1960–2000*. Cambridge: Cambridge University Press.

Comparative Advantage and African Development

Arne Bigsten

Sub-Saharan Africa (hereafter referred to as Africa) grew very slowly from the 1970s to the turn of the century. There was growth acceleration in the new millennium but little progress in terms of economic diversification. Manufacturing production and export growth was modest. This is a concern, since economic growth in LDCs has generally been associated with export growth, particularly modern sector export growth. Patillo, Gupta, and Carey (2005) show that trade has been closely associated with growth accelerations also in Africa. Bigsten et al. (2004) find that there is a positive effect of exporting on the productivity in exporting manufacturing firms in Africa, which one does not find in more advanced economies. An economic take-off in Africa will not happen without diversification and export growth.

The notion in economics is that countries export goods in which they have a comparative advantage. To understand comparative advantage is therefore essential for our understanding of the growth process in Africa.

What is comparative advantage?

Ricardo assumed that comparative advantage is due to relative technological or productivity differences across countries. He showed that countries gain from exporting commodities in which they are relatively most productive. Most current analysis in international trade is based on the Heckscher–Ohlin model, where comparative advantage depends on relative factor abundance. A country which has an abundance of labour relative to capital will export goods that use this factor intensively.

Apart from these classical determinants of comparative advantage, other explanations have emerged. Institutional quality or the business climate can be the source of comparative advantage. Eifert, Gelb, and Ramachandran (2005: 7) define the business environment as 'the nexus of policies, institutions, physical infrastructure, human resources, and geographical features that influence the efficiency with which different firms and industries operate'. These factors influence the cost of production of firms and have an effect via market structure and competition. The impact of these factors is mostly felt in tradables such as manufacturing, which rely heavily on logistics, regulation, and infrastructure. A poor business environment hinders firms from supplying goods for export competitively, even if they have good control of factory-level costs.

Levchenko (2007) analyses the relationship between institutional comparative advantage (focusing on contracting institutions) and the pattern of trade. For Africa to be able to shift its production structure in the direction of this type of good, it needs to create a better business climate or to provide public goods that make it possible for producers relying on the business climate to supply goods effectively. The manufacturing sector is highly dependent on a good environment. Krugman (1980) has shown that the pattern of trade may also be influenced by the presence of economies of scale. These can be internal to a firm or due to agglomeration economies, which mean that the joint location of firms enhances their productivity.

Economic development has always been associated with structural change. Typically it has meant that traditional low-productivity agriculture has become relatively less important, while the more advanced industrial sector has expanded. How the economic structure changes during the growth process is influenced by changes in comparative advantage, which can be due to changes in factor endowments or technology or the other determinants of comparative advantage.

Models of economic development generally assume that there is a process of capital deepening shifting the pattern of specialization towards more capital-intensive goods (Leamer 1987). The classical factor behind changes in comparative advantages is technological progress. Findlay (1970) shows that comparative advantage in the long run depends on the propensity to save and the growth rate of the labour force. A high savings rate relative to labour growth will shift production towards capital-intensive goods.

New trade models tend to be characterized by increasing returns to scale, product innovation, and a product cycle where the south imitates the north. These models are more appropriate to explain the new patterns of trade, where the south exports manufacturing goods as well. Dynamic comparative advantage can be created through learning, network effects, and spillovers (Krugman 1991). Puga and Venables (1999) show that economic development can proceed in waves, as poor countries one by one benefit from relative price changes that trigger industrial relocation. Grossman and Helpman (1991) describe how new innovative products are developed and produced in the north and exported to the south. Eventually the south develops the capacity to imitate, and production shifts to this region. An increase in north–south knowledge diffusion enables the south to diversify production.

Africa's pattern of trade

African economies have liberalized over recent decades, implying that policy distortions will mean less and comparative advantage more for the pattern of trade. Still, because of the resource boom (improving Africa's terms of trade by 52% between 2000 and 2008: Oyejide 2009), export concentration has actually increased since 1995 (UNCTAD 2008). What does the literature say about Africa's comparative advantage?

Bigsten and Durevall (2008) measure changes in relative factor endowments in Kenya 1964–2000. With growing labour and slowly growing capital there is a shift out of agriculture into the non-agricultural sectors, but since capital has become increasingly scarce since 1980, labour has shifted into labour-intensive informal production instead of capital-intensive formal manufacturing. Kenya has seen some expansion of manufacturing exports, but the most buoyant sector has been advanced agricultural production, such as horticulture and flowers. So the factor accumulation pattern in Kenya did not change the pattern of comparative advantage in favour of manufacturing. This is a typical pattern of development in Africa, and helps explain the poor performance of manufacturing exports.

Wood and his co-authors pursue a factor abundance explanation. Wood (1994) argues that capital is highly mobile internationally, which means that it cannot be the basis of comparative advantage. Instead it is due to factors that are specific to the country, such as labour or skills and natural resources.

Wood and Berge (1997) and Wood and Mayer (2001) have analysed the determinants of export composition, and show that an abundance of skills and natural resources are important determinants of the export pattern. They argue that since Africa has an abundance of natural resources and is short of skilled labour, it will tend to be locked into the export of primary commodities and find it hard to break into the manufacturing exports markets. Owens and Wood (1997) argue that African economies do not have the skills required to be competitive in the processing of its raw materials. Wood believes that the trade pattern of Africa will resemble that of Latin America rather than that of Asia. Mauritius is one of the few African economies that have been successful in manufacturing exports, but the resource endowment there is more akin to that of Asia than that of mainland Africa.

The new literature on trade focuses on learning, network effects, and inter-industry spillovers. The importance of these externalities is generally supported by the path dependence of growth in specific industries and the high degree of specialization in narrow industrial subsectors (Burgess and Venables 2004). There are also many examples in Africa of industrial clustering being associated with successful development such as Kenya's horticulture industry and garments in Mauritius. The paucity of such developments is related to the low quality of African governments, which have created a high cost transactions environment (Collier 2000).

Global production (particularly in manufacturing) is becoming increasingly fragmented. This means that comparative advantage now may reside in a narrowly defined task. This may benefit African countries, since it should be easier to create comparative advantage through learning and economies of scale in the production of a limited item. It is important to have a dense network of firms, both within the same sector and in other input–output related sectors. Since there often are few firms in each sector, they can dominate and reduce competition, which in turn reduces the dynamic competition effects.

Even if some African locations were to provide an investment climate that is as good as in Asia, they would still suffer from the fact that Asia had a head start. This means that Asian firms can benefit from already existing knowledge clusters as well as availability of specialized inputs and experienced labour. African locations thus face an entry threshold.

Venables (2009) emphasizes that transaction costs matter for trade. Asian countries have been able to integrate with the global production networks and thus to benefit from globalization. Africa has on the whole not managed to meet the necessary conditions for this, since transaction costs remain high and deliveries are unreliable (Venables and Limau 1994). Since Africa does not provide an investment climate comparable to that of Asia, investments in manufacturing have essentially bypassed Africa.

African manufacturing firms generally have rather low productivity (Söderbom and Teal, 2003). Eifert et al. (2005) find that total factor productivity for African manufacturing firms is below that of Chinese manufacturers. They furthermore show that indirect costs are higher in poorly performing African economies and that, with adjustments for the differences in indirect costs, African firms are even further behind the Chinese ones.

Another factor holding back an African breakthrough in manufacturing is that Africa's price level compared to other regions is high. Eifert et al. (2005) estimate Balassa's income price curve and find that poor performers in Africa tend to lie above it, which indicates that prices are higher than one would expect from their income levels. This means that these countries have high costs of producing non-traded inputs to production, which makes it harder to become internationally competitive. Sala-i-Martín and Artadi (2003) find that capital costs in Africa are one third higher than the world level. Rodrik (2008) shows that overvalued exchange rates have seriously hindered exports and thus also economic growth.

Policy discussion

It seems reasonable to argue that one should nurture upcoming industries. The old 'infant industry' argument says that new industries need protection early on while learning the business; later, when their productivity has improved, the protection can be removed. This was the argument underlying the industrialization strategy of import substitution that was pursued in Africa from the 1960s. The crucial question is whether the new firms set up behind tariff walls will increase their productivity. The experience in Africa has been poor, possibly due to the lack of competitive pressure on firms to become efficient. The Asian experience is better, but there the firms were not allowed indefinite high protection, and were forced to show export results to get access to subsidies and protection. Rodrik (1998) also notes that import restrictions function as export restrictions, and that import tariffs thus reduce manufactured exports. Since experiences in Africa with tariff protection are poor, other routes to nurture new and upcoming firms should be sought.

A key question is how the government should design its policies to bring about a structural transformation that is efficiency-enhancing and that generates new comparative advantages. There may be potential comparative advantages that cannot be exploited because the infrastructure environment is so poor that firms cannot get their products to the market in time or at sufficiently low cost to be competitive. Economic policy should therefore begin by removing such obstacles.

Policymakers might pursue industrial policies to create comparative advantages. If the interventions affect costs and prices in all sectors equally, there will not be any change in the pattern of comparative advantages. But if they are geared to support some sectors, the pattern of comparative advantages can shift. For example, improved infrastructure in certain dimensions may be more important for manufacturing than for agriculture; by investing in such infrastructure, therefore, one can improve the chances for manufacturers to export.

Hausmann, Rodrik, and Sabel (2008) argue for efficient search and discovery processes for new lines of comparative advantage. Benchmarking, monitoring, and experimentation are essential ingredients in the policy they propose. They distinguish between two types of policies. One is small-scale industrial policy, which relates to removing obstacles for some existing activities. The other is large-scale industrial policy, which is about identifying either strategic priorities or bets on new sectors that could be essential for long-term growth.

Hausmann and Rodrik (2003) argue that the lumpiness of modern sector growth is very troublesome for small economies. They must be able to pass a certain threshold to be able to exploit economies of scale and become competitive in modern sector production. So far, Africa has not been an attractive location for producers because of the threshold effects. Numerous studies of the manufacturing sector show that successful firms are large (Bigsten and Söderbom 2006). So what can policymakers do to support the emergence of larger firms? They can try to create a good business environment, and they can also help build business confidence by being committed to institutional development. They may also seek to concentrate resources in certain locations such as export-processing zones. This will make it possible to provide cheaper complementary inputs and utilities. It will also help create agglomeration advantages in production. They can also try to create a policy supporting technological acquisition.

Hausmann and Rodrik (2006) suggest that producers should be subsidized rather than protected from international competition, but this is hard to do effectively in Africa. For example, it is hard to withdraw an intervention even if it does not work well. Therefore Collier and Venables (2007) argue for trade preferences on the part of developed countries, instead of direct interventions against the specific domestic distortions. The advantages of such preferences are threefold. First, they are immune to internal political economy manipulations. Second, since they support export, they only benefit exporters. To benefit, firms must become internationally competitive. Third, the policies do not have any fiscal cost. The problem with the current set of trade preferences is that they have rules of origin that are at variance with the new types of trade in tasks (including only a small part of value added in a location). The schemes should instead make it possible for countries to participate in modern international production networks. The African Growth and Opportunity Act has offered generous access to African exporters, and the impact on apparel exports in several African countries has been very positive.

The current global financial crisis has reduced African trade revenues and capital inflows and thus economic growth. Still, the negative effect is somewhat muted, since African producers are not fully integrated with OECD producers, and since they increasingly trade with the more stable Asia. Nevertheless, economic recovery requires export expansion and capital inflows. To facilitate resource inflows, recipient countries in Africa should continue with institutional reforms to make the economies more attractive to investors.

REFERENCES

Bigsten, A., et al., 2004. 'Do African manufacturing firms learn from exporting?', *Journal of Development Studies* 40.3, 115–71.
—— and D. Durevall, 2008. 'Factor proportions, openness and factor prices in Kenya, 1965–2000', *Journal of Development Studies* 44.2, 289–310.
—— and M. Söderbom, 2006. 'What have we learned from a decade of manufacturing enterprise surveys in Africa?', *World Bank Research Observer* 21.2, 241–65.

Burgess, R., and A. Venables, 2004. 'Towards a microeconomics of growth', World Bank Policy Research Working Paper 3257, Washington, DC.

Collier, P., 2000. 'Africa's comparative advantage', in H. Jalilian, M. Tribe, and J. Weiss (eds), *Industrial Development and Policy in Africa*. Cheltenham: Edward Elgar.

—— and A. Venables, 2007. 'Rethinking trade preferences: how Africa can diversify its exports', *World Economy* 30.8, 1326–45.

Eifert, B., A. Gelb, and V. Ramachandran, 2005. 'Business environment and comparative advantage in Africa: evidence from the investment climate data', Working Paper 56, Centre for Global Development, Washington, DC.

Findlay, R., 1970. 'Factor proportions and comparative advantage in the long run', *Journal of Political Economy* 78.1, 27–34.

Grossman, G., and E. Helpman, 1991. *Innovation and Growth in the Global Economy*. Cambridge, Mass.: MIT Press.

Hausmann, R., and D. Rodrik, 2003. 'Economic development as self-discovery', *Journal of Development Economics* 72.2, 603–33.

—— —— 2006. 'Doomed to choose: industrial policy as predicament', mimeo, Harvard University.

—— —— and C. P. Sabel, 2008. 'Reconfiguring industrial policy: a framework with an application to South Africa', Working Paper 168, Center for International Development, Harvard University.

Krugman, P., 1980. 'Scale economies, product differentiation, and the pattern of trade', *American Economic Review* 89.5, 950–59.

—— 1991. 'Increasing returns and economic geography', *Journal of Political Economy* 99.3, 483–99.

Leamer, E., 1987. 'Paths of development in the three-factor n-goods General Equilibrium Model', *Journal of Political Economy* 95.5, 961–99.

Levchenko, A. A., 2007. 'Institutional quality and international trade', *Review of Economic Studies* 74: 791–819.

Owens, T., and A. Wood, 1997. 'Export-oriented industrialization through primary processing', *World Development* 25.9, 1453–70.

Oyejide, T. A., 2009. 'Global financial crisis: impact on Africa's trade and policy options', paper for an AERC Senior Policy Seminar, Lusaka.

Patillo, C., S. Gupta, and K. Carey, 2005. 'Sustaining growth accelerations and pro-poor growth in Africa', IMF Working Paper 195, Washington, DC.

Puga, D., and A. Venables, 1999. 'Agglomeration and economic development: import substitution versus trade liberalisation', *Economic Journal* 109, 292–331.

Rodrik, D., 1998. 'Trade policy and economic performance in sub-Saharan Africa', Working Paper 6562, NBER, Cambridge, Mass.

—— 2008. 'The real exchange rate and economic growth', *Brookings Papers on Economic Activity* (Fall).

Sala-i-Martín, X., and E. Artadi, 2003. 'The tragedy of the 20th century: growth in Africa', Columbia University Discussion paper 0203-17.

Söderbom, M., and F. Teal, 2003. 'Are manufactured exports the key to economic success in Africa?', *Journal of African Economies* 12.1, 1–29.

UNCTAD, 2008. 'Export performance and trade liberalization: some patterns and policy perspectives'. Geneva.

Venables, A., 2009. 'Rethinking economic growth in a globalizing world: an economic geography law', *African Economic Review* 21.2, 331–51.

—— and N. Limau, 1994. 'Infrastructure, geographical disadvantage and transport costs'. Washington, DC: World Bank.

Wood, A., 1994. *North–South Trade, Employment and Inequality: Changing Fortunes in a Skill-Driven World*. Oxford: Clarendon Press.

—— and K. Berge, 1997. 'Exporting manufactures: human resources, natural resources, and trade policy', *Journal of Development Studies* 34, 35–59.

—— and J. Mayer, 2001. 'Africa's export structure in a comparative perspective', *Cambridge Journal of Economics* 25, 369–94.

The Impact of Asia on Economic Development in Sub-Saharan Africa

Machiko Nissanke

Over the last two decades, the emergence of large Asian economies such as China and India as rising economic powers has been shaping a new world economic order. Though in terms of per capita income they remain low-income developing countries, China and India entered a period of accelerated growth path in the 1990s following the earlier experiences of other newly industrializing countries (NICs) in Asia. Accounting for 37% of the world population in 2005, combined with the demographical characteristic of a high proportion of the population in economically active working age in contrast to an aging society in the mature economies in the West, the two Asian giants are poised to be new engines of growth for the world economy (Nayyer 2008). Hence, it is not surprising to observe the ever-intensifying interaction between the Asian and the African economies and the growing influence that the Asian economies have been exerting on the African economies. The nature of economic relationships between the two regions has been evolving rapidly.

Indeed, the influence of the 'Asian Drivers' on African economies has become truly pronounced, with visible effects manifesting in almost all the spheres of daily economic life in the African continent. In a number of important ways they are certainly making a lasting impact on the future course of the economic development of Africa. This chapter describes the newly emerging economic relationships between the two developing regions, and discusses the implications of these forces for the future growth and development prospects of the African economies. Focusing on the two manifestations of dynamic changes, I first discuss how the Asian economies have acted both as a competitor and as a facilitator for the growth of African economies in international trade. I then examine how Asia has increasingly engaged with Africa as a critical partner for economic development, proclaiming a new form of 'South–South' economic cooperation. Though a number of Asian emerging economies, including China, India, South Korea, and Malaysia, have expanded their economic relationships with Africa, the discussion will centre on China's strategic re-engagement with Africa through a provider of aid in package deals with investment and trade expansion.

The effects of the Asian economies as competitor and facilitator in international trade and their implications for the future course of African development

One of most conspicuous economic effects of the rise of the Asian economies on Africa is felt by fragile domestic industries and service sectors. Competitively priced manufactured goods and services from the Asian economies, in particular from China, have increasingly driven out, and in some cases almost wiped out the domestic industries producing low-skill labour-intensive goods such as clothing and textiles. Generally, it is not only in home markets, where sweeping trade liberalization has been effected, but also more globally in third export markets, that goods produced in other developing countries are deemed to have lost their comparative advantage and competitive edge to goods and services from the Asian economies such as China and India—the countries with large reserves of unskilled surplus labour in rural areas. Numerous studies examine whether the decisive opening of China and India to world trade would block the road to industrialization of other developing countries, by preventing the vital process of 'learning-by-doing' from taking place, starting with labour-intensive manufacturing.[1]

Kaplinsky and Morris (2008) note that both existing and potential manufacturing exporters in SSA are particularly adversely affected by the advance of the Asian Drivers due to the endogenously existing supply constraints in responding to global market opportunities as well as exogenous dynamics in the global economy. Manufacturing activities in SSA are heavily concentrated in low-skill-intensive and low-value-added activities, a sector in which China's inroad to world markets was first felt strongly. Home markets in many SSA countries were flooded by cheap imported clothing from China, benefiting the consumers. However, clothing and textile exporting countries such as Lesotho, Madagascar, Kenya, and Swaziland, which enjoyed an advantage from the US preferential provision under the African Growth and Opportunities act (AGOA), lost out to China, when the quota-based preferential regime under the Multi Fibre Arrangement (MFA) expired in January 2005. Consequently, these countries suffered heavily from the sudden loss in formal employment as well as in export revenues.

Other manufactured exports such as wood-based products and footwear have also faced a similar decline in the face of competition from China, Vietnam, and other Asian suppliers. Former exporters of furniture in West and Central Africa are reported to have switched to exporting raw logs and sawn timber instead, whilst small and medium-size

---

[1] See e.g. various chapters in Winters and Yusof (2007) and Kaplinsky and Messner (2008) for general discussion on the effects of China and India on the World Economy and the developing world respectively. Wood and Mayer (2009) present estimates of the one-off effect of China's entry to trade, causing an increase of the world average relative factor endowments of labour relative to other production factors.

producers of footwear in Ethiopia had experienced a sharp decline as domestic consumers switched to imported shoes from China (Kaplinsky and Morris 2008). India has not yet presented itself as a threat to other developing countries in manufacturing trade, but it has emerged as an important supply source of services globally, as witnessed in the growth of offshore services in many fields.

Indeed, competition from China and India has now extended globally from low-skill-intensive manufactured industries to all other sectors, including those producing more skill- and knowledge-intensive goods and services, particularly technology and communication (ICT) industries. For example, the share of high-technology products in China's exports rose from 13% in 1995 to 33% in 2005. This has narrowed considerably the option of developing over the almost entire range of manufactured production and exports for other developing countries.

This may not pose a severe long-term developmental issue for other countries if China and India can move their comparative advantage fast and in an orderly manner along the skill and technology ladder, as observed in the recycling of comparative advantages in the Asia-Pacific region. In the latter region, a gradual shift of comparative advantages concurrently with successive flows of export-oriented FDI and relocation of production sites has taken place first from Japan to the first-tier NIEs and then to countries in Southeast Asia and China, as postulated in the 'flying geese' hypothesis that is applied to the evolution of regional dynamism in Asia (Nissanke and Thorbecke 2010).

However, given the sheer extent of surplus labour in rural areas, China and India would retain their comparative advantages in low-skill-intensive sectors for some time to come while gaining new capabilities in medium- to high-tech sectors. Hence, the recycling of comparative advantages from the Asian giants is not likely to take place in a smooth succession globally among developing nations, thus providing an easy kick-start for industrialization of small low-income countries. In this respect, competitive forces emanating from Asian producers would cast a shadow over the prospect of African industrialization if the present trend were to continue.

At the same time, the Asian Drivers have provided a growing market for primary commodity exports from African countries (Kaplinsky 2010). Ever-increasing demand for natural resources and energy from the Asian Drivers that have followed a high material- and energy-intensive growth path so far is one of the major factors behind the recent commodity boom and the sustained economic growth of a number of resource-rich economies in Africa during 2002–8. Further, China and India have increased their imports from Africa not only in terms of mineral resources such as oil and metals and other minerals but also in terms of agricultural products. For example, as its per capita income has increased, China has become a net food importer in 2003, importing many agricultural products, including grains, soybeans, and vegetable oils as well as raw materials such as cotton and rubber. China's increased demand for agricultural products are also behind the steep rise in prices of foods and other agricultural materials in the world markets in 2007–8. For example, according to Goldstein et al. (2006), China's contribution to growth of global demand for cotton exceeded 100% in 2006. Though Africa suffers from food deficits itself, China is a growing market for Africa's export crops such as cotton, coffee, and cocoa. On the whole, China has become the main bilateral trading partner for several resource-rich African countries (Goldstein et. al. 2006).

Given the competitive and complementary trade effects combined, the Asian Drivers' integration into the world economy has shifted the terms of trade in world economy in two directions: First, the recent 'super-commodity price cycle' over the medium term has produced a tilting of the relative prices in favour of primary commodities against manufactured goods after the long-term declining trend in the former in the 1980s and 1990s. Second, the relative price of labour intensive manufactured goods to other technology-intensive manufactured goods has been markedly falling as a result of export push of those goods by Asian NICs and China. These combined relative price changes have produced a structural shift in the terms of trade in favour of primary commodities (Kaplinsky 2010).

Finally, though Africa has diversified trading partners beyond the traditional destinations in Europe, Africa's trade structure with the Asian Drivers remains fundamentally similar to that with the rest of the world. Africa's exports to China are overwhelmingly oil and other primary commodities, while Africa's exports to India are slightly more diversified, but still mainly composed of resource-based products. Clearly, for securing sustainable development, it is imperative for African economies to undergo structural transformation by diversifying trade and production structures from those moulded in the colonial era. It is yet to be seen whether China and India can make a real difference to Africa's development by bringing about fundamental changes to the structure of their bilateral trade with Africa beyond those based on primary commodities and resources.

Asian Drivers' engagement with Africa as South–South economic cooperation[2]

Economic relationships between African countries and a number of large emerging economies such as China, India, Malaysia, South Korea, Russia, and Brazil have increased markedly in the new millennium. In particular, the Chinese government has intensified its efforts to forge a new partnership with Africa as part of the 'Going Global' strategy adopted in late 1990s, marked by the inauguration in 2000 of the high-level Forum on China–Africa Cooperation (FOCAC). The strategy was formulated in light of

---

[2] See Nissanke and Soderberg (2011) for detailed analysis of China's strategic engagement with Africa and its impact on African development, with a full reference list.

its own domestic conditions, which include both foreign policy considerations and economic factors.[3]

Chinese officials emphasize that China's engagement with Africa is built on the genuine concept of partnership based on 'political equality, mutual trust, economic win-win cooperation and cultural exchanges'.[4] China offers aid in package with trade and investment within the framework of South–South cooperation, with no conditionality attached to economic and governance reforms.[5] Though the actual amount of aid provided by China to Africa is still small compared to aid volume from the traditional donors, i.e. the members of the OECD Development Assistance Committee (DAC), it has been steadily increasing over the short span of time. Doubling every three years, aid from China is expected to reach US $10 billion by 2012, while China has also offered debt cancellation to 32 African countries so far. Moreover, it is the form of China's engagement in Africa that has attracted wide-ranging comments, often expressed in anxieties and concerns both in Africa and worldwide.

Focused initially heavily on infrastructure development that is widely recognized as one of the main bottlenecks for African development, Chinese aid is given in terms of preferential loans with the use of Chinese contractors, materials, and workers under the 'resources for infrastructure' format, known as 'the Angola mode'. Provided in tied form, infrastructure project aid executed under this mode is closely intertwined with direct investment in resource extraction and associated trade deals. Chinese firms (usually state-owned companies) who win contracts either in infrastructure projects or in resource extraction under a single package deal get access to funds on preferential terms from the Export-Import Bank of China with sovereign official credit guarantee. Therefore, financial risks are underwritten for Chinese companies, and aid-funded projects can be used as a launching pad for Chinese firms to enter African markets and later bid for more commercial projects, once they accumulate enough experience.

At the same time, this practice deprives local workers of opportunities to participate, interact and learn, and hence there is a danger that local workers and firms are sidelined in the process. So far, Chinese aid-funded projects have not yet created much-needed job opportunities for local workers, wider spillover effects, or technology–knowledge transfer. Though without detailed information it is hard to ascertain actual or potential distributional outcomes from these deals, the 'mutual benefit' promised in the

---

[3] Economic conditions behind China's 'Going Global' strategy include: its thirst for natural resources; increasingly competitive and saturated domestic markets for construction industries and other sectors; the desire to increase FDI with accumulated reserves, to allow state-owned enterprises (SOEs) to acquire international experiences; and the need to find outlets for rural migrant workers abroad.

[4] Official communiqué released at the summit meeting of the Forum on China–Africa Cooperation (FOCAC) in November 2006.

[5] India has also expanded aid to Africa in conjunction with increasing outward FDI and trade flows. However, its aid is provided overwhelmingly in the form of technical assistance.

cooperation agreements may be in reality skewed in favour of Chinese firms and contractors. Under the aid-investment modality in operation, local firms appear to have benefited little from subcontracting arrangements, the use of local materials and resources, or other backward and forward linkages. Further, some evidence suggests that because of strong pressures and incentives for the Chinese firms to make short-term returns quickly, the long-term developmental aspiration and interests of African stakeholders, including environmental and social sustainability of aid-funded operations, may get overlooked. Indeed, non-transparency surrounding the deals the Chinese government strikes with many African leaders has often left local stakeholders alienated from the process, and created tensions among those affected on ground.

However, the Chinese–African economic relationships have been evolving constantly, with China adjusting to fresh challenges encountered, and the Chinese government has been responding to some legitimate concerns and shortcomings of their operations and modalities that have given rise to friction and backlashes in Africa. Indeed, a greater degree of flexibility and diversity has been very much evident in Chinese approaches, as China's African strategy is both adaptive and instrumental. China's cooperation has by now extended well beyond resource sectors and economic infrastructure projects, expanding fast into the agricultural sector—another key bottleneck Africa faces in attaining a substantive poverty reduction among the rural poor.[6] China has also consolidated its cooperation in areas covering information technology, manufacturing, and fishing, as well as soft infrastructure building such as health and education. Indeed, while big state-owned enterprises have dominated in large infrastructure projects and resource-extraction sectors, it is Chinese private companies who have become active across other sectors with official financial and other supports. Today, China's engagement with Africa has become truly diversified, involving numerous heterogeneous private operators, evolving from the 'state-centric' form of cooperation to operations centred on private businesses, backed by blessing from the state.

Concluding remarks

In this millennium, Asian emerging market economies have markedly increased their engagement with Africa in search of investment and business opportunities. This is a real sea change, and one that Africa has longed for, as the continent needs real investment, not hand-outs, from the rest of the world. The fast and dynamically evolving interface

---

[6] Yet, in this area too, Chinese farmers' rapid advancement in developing commercial farming in Africa, dubbed as 'land grab', has caused backlashes in Africa.

between Asia and Africa presents new challenges and potential opportunities across all channels of economic relationships. Further, the development experiences of the Asian economies, which are at variance with the development model contained in the Washington and post-Washington Consensus, provide some useful lessons for formulating a strategy for Africa's future in the light of conditions prevailing in the continent.[7] Indeed, it is up to Africans to take a strategic position towards new opportunities so that Asia's desire to engage with Africa will truly work for African development and stakeholders.

REFERENCES

Goldstein, A., N. Pinaud, H. Reisen, and X. Chen, 2006. 'The rise of China and India: what's in it for Africa?', Paris: OECD.

Kaplinsky, R., 2010. 'Asian Drivers, commodity prices and the terms of trade', in M. Nissanke and G. Mavrotas (eds), *Commodities, Governance and Economic Development under Globalization*. Basingstoke: Palgrave/Macmillan, ch. 6.

—— and D. Messner, 2008. 'The impact of Asian Drivers on the developing countries', *World Development* 36.2, 197–209.

—— and M. Morris, 2008. 'Do the Asian Drivers undermine export-oriented industrialization in SSA?', *World Development* 36.2, 254–73.

Nayyar, D., 2008. 'China, India, Brazil and South Africa in the world economy: engines of growth?', UNU/WIDER Discussion Paper 2008/05, Helsinki.

Nissanke, M., and E. Aryeetey, 2003. *Comparative Development Experiences of Sub-Saharan Africa and East Asia: An Institutional Approach*, Aldershot: Ashgate.

—— and M. Söderberg, 2011. 'The changing landscape in aid relationships in Africa: can China's engagements make a difference to prospects of African development?', Discussion Paper 2011/2 (January), Swedish Institute of International Affairs, Stockholm.

—— and E. Thorbecke, 2010. 'Comparative analysis of the globalization–poverty nexus in Asia, Latin America and Africa', in M. Nissanke and E. Thorbecke (eds), *The Poor under Globalization in Asia, Latin America and Africa*, Oxford: Oxford University Press, ch. 1.

Winters, L., and S. Yusof (eds), 2007. *Dancing with Giants, China and India and the Global Economy*, Washington, DC: World Bank and Institute of Policy Studies.

Wood, A., and J. Mayer, 2009. 'Has China de-industrialised other developing countries?', Working Paper 175, Queen Elizabeth House, Oxford University.

---

[7] See Nissanke and Aryeetey (2003) for a detailed discussion on comparative development experiences of the two regions from an institutional perspective.

The Brain Drain in Africa

Yaw Nyarko

Introduction

Increased attention has recently been paid to the phenomenon of the brain drain of skilled (and often unskilled) Africans from their home countries to countries in the West. In part this is because of the relatively large percentages of skilled Africans going abroad. It is also due to the increased focus on the economic development of Africa in general, and the concern that many countries in Africa may be lagging behind economically and stuck in a poverty trap. Further, human capital, educated workers, and technology are perceived to be instrumental for economic development and competitiveness in today's world, so the drain of skilled professionals is of concern (see e.g. Benhabib and Spiegel 2005).

Although in the popular press and in some political circles the migration of skilled Africans is presented as an unmitigated minus for Africa, there are a large number of important caveats to this which present a very different picture.

Historical context

When reviewing the economics of the brain drain and skilled migration, it is first important to note that this is neither a new phenomenon nor a recent literature. The term 'brain drain' was, I believe, first used in the context of the loss of skills from the UK to the USA in the late 1950s and early 1960s. Given the often loud and xenophobic reactions of the right wing in Europe to African immigration there, it is amusing to recall that the mother of all migrations was probably the movement of early man up the East African Rift Valley which ultimately resulted in the settlement of man in Europe. Further, from the 1500s onwards it was Europe which experienced the mass emigrations which successfully settled many parts of the New World and Africa.

The data

Although the data on the brain drain remains incomplete, an important development in academic literature has been the recent data sets produced by Carrington and Detragiache (1998), Docquier and Marfouk (2005), and others. These data use various extensions to the Barro and Lee (1993) school attainment figures to determine the number of skilled individuals in the source countries. The authors then use census and other similar data sets in the US, western European, and other OECD nations to compute the numbers of foreign-born residents of different skill levels residing in those countries.

The 2000 data of Docquier and Marfouk (2005) indicates that many African nations have very high skilled emigration rates (i.e. the fraction of nationals with tertiary degrees who were born in the country but live outside it). Further, the brain drain today is almost exclusively an African phenomenon. Many of the small countries, like Cape Verde, as well as some bigger countries like Ghana and Kenya, have high skilled emigration rates, as just defined, ranging from 67% to 45%. In contrast, for example, the high skilled emigration rates of China and India are around 3% and 4%.

A look at the data in a little more detail, however, shows some nuances and caveats. As was pointed out in Easterly and Nyarko (2009), census data in the UK distinguishes between white and black immigrants. In many African countries, a substantial proportion of those emigrating are non-blacks. For example, in South Africa only 3% of the emigrants to the UK are black, while in Tanzania the figure is 13%. Presumably there are other more complicated racial and political issues in those countries explaining the emigration; in particular, the emigration is not that of the standard stereotype of the black African skilled professional trained at local expense and going to seek greener economic pastures abroad.

A more important revelation from the data is the exceptionally small number of skilled people in different countries. For example, the Docquier and Marfouk (2005) data put that the total number of tertiary educated Ghanaians in 2000 (at home and abroad) at 150,000. This is for a country whose population is currently in excess of 20 million, and was close to that level in 2000. Many universities in the US have close to a quarter that number, with many single universities having almost that number. This is an incredibly low stock of tertiary educated Ghanaians. The brain drain accounts for a significant portion of this; but the data signal an inadequate output of skills more than anything else.

The picture from the data on skilled (i.e. tertiary educated) nationals is mirrored with healthcare works and particularly doctors (see Bhargava and Docquier 2007; Clemens and Pettersson 2008). Healthcare workers are a group that has received a disproportionate amount of attention particularly in the media, but also in the academic literature.

Again, a large number of doctors are abroad, resulting in a high patient to doctor ratio in the home country. However, even if all those doctors return and there is nothing done about the total supply of doctors, the patient–doctor ratio will improve but will still be exceptionally bad relative to international standards. In a few years the 2010 censuses will be out; it is not yet clear how different the picture will be from that obtained from the 2000 data.

Remittances

One important aspect of the emigration of Africans is the level of remittances sent back to the source countries. Many statistics seem to indicate that this level is extremely high. For some countries the remittances represent major fractions of foreign exchange receipts of the country. A big issue here, of course, is the quality of the data. It is often hard to obtain data on remittances, since these are often given in cash and are also outside the formal banking system. The main sources of the data are official balance of payments statistics (World Bank, World Development Indicators), national central banks, and also a number of surveys (e.g. the United Nations International Fund for Agricultural Development, IFAD). Many surveys and estimates indicate that the level of remittances is very high for many African nations—indeed, so high that it often dwarfs foreign development aid.

One interesting question in the literature is whether it is the skilled or unskilled who send larger remittances home, with some arguing that it may be the unskilled (see Faini 2007).

Return of the skilled, and brain circulation

The data on the brain drain really represent snapshots, or moments in time, of stocks of human capital residing abroad versus in the home country. They do not measure return flows or circulation. It is also clear that the returned migrants have big impacts on their countries. Both Nnamdi Azikiwe, Nigeria's first President, and Kwame Nkrumah, Ghana's first President, studied in the US, and hence at some time were counted in the snapshot of the brain drain, but returned to be instrumental in their respective country's independence movements. An early study of the more recent return of skilled personnel is that by Pires, Kassimir, and Berhane (1999), which investigated the return of African PhDs from 1986 to 1996. Their data seem to suggest that for many countries the return probability is significant. For example, they suggest that, of the Africans obtaining their PhDs in US institutions, almost two thirds return to their country of origin. Their data show within-country differences, though: return rates of around 80% in for Uganda and Tanzania, versus 34% for Ghana and Nigeria.

Much more data work is needed to provide a better and fuller picture of return and brain circulation. Casual observation seems to indicate that the recent dynamism in many African countries owes much to recent returnees who come with new skills and new ideas (Ghana's top non-governmental, non-secular university, Ashesi University, and its top indigenous investment bank, Databank, are examples of these). There is also a lot of research looking into the role of diaspora and migrant networks abroad as channels of transfer of technology, especially internet and communication technologies, into the home countries.

NPV computations

Easterly and Nyarko (2009) take the data one step further and perform calculations which compute the costs and benefits of the higher education, taking explicit account of migrations out of the local economy due to the Brain Drain. The computation takes into account the remittances, returned migrants with better skills, and the costs of tertiary education. These calculations seem to suggest a positive return to tertiary education. In particular, since those who leave return remittances and/or return with skills, there could be a net positive on the costs and benefits of tertiary education even in the face of large brain drain probabilities.

There is also the recent phenomenon of unemployment among the skilled labour force. This might make one pause when arguing that the brain drain is an unmitigated problem in Africa, as those who are educated do not always seem to be adequately employed.

Incentives

Many authors have also pointed out that there is an incentive effect related to the potential migration of skilled workers. When there is the possibility of leaving the local economy and presumably making significantly more money abroad, there is more investment in education (either the time and work effort of individuals, or the money or foregone earnings used when embarking on tertiary education). It is possible that this incentive effect is so strong that even after some have migrated, the number of skilled left behind exceeds that which would have existed if the brain drain and its incentive effects were absent (see e.g. Stark 2004).

This is not unlike what is now the African 'foot drain', where top African soccer players migrate to play in European teams. Many more Africans are investing in soccer education and training, and it is possible that this has resulted in many more top soccer players than would have been the case if there was, for example, a ban on African soccer players playing abroad.

This short chapter has focused on source country issues. In the West, there is currently some competition for talent in the US and EU. The European Union is currently debating the concept of a 'Blue Card' to compete with the US's Green Card in attracting skilled migrants from abroad.

Conclusion

Many African countries face high percentages of skill emigration. Stocks of skilled nationals (at home and abroad) are exceptionally low. However, skilled migration is a means of skills acquisition and human capital development, provides remittances, and is a powerful incentive for human capital investments at home. A major concern in the current financial crisis is that the pipeline for Africans studying abroad will be closed; paradoxically, this could potentially have bad consequences for increasing the stock of human capital in Africa.

■ REFERENCES

Barro, Robert J., and Lee Jong-Wha, 1993. 'International comparisons of educational attainment', *Journal of Monetary Economics* 32.3, 63–94.

Benhabib, J., and M. Spiegel, 2005. 'Human capital and technology diffusion', in Philippe Aghion and Steven Durlauf (eds), *Handbook of Economic Growth*. Amsterdam: North-Holland.

Bhargava, A., and F. Docquier, 2007. 'A new panel data set on physicians' emigration rates (1991–2004)', World Bank.

Carrington, W. J., and E. Detragiache, 1998. 'How big is the brain drain?', IMF Research Department Working Paper WP/98/102.

Clemens, M., and G. Pettersson, 2008. 'New data on African health professionals abroad', *Human Resources for Health* 6.1.

Docquier, F., and A. Marfouk, 2005. 'International migration by educational attainment: release 1.1', World Bank.

Easterly, W., and Y. Nyarko, 2009. 'Is the brain drain good for Africa?', in J. Bhagwati and G. Hansen (eds), *Skilled Immigration Today: Prospects, Problems, and Policies*. Oxford: Oxford University Press.

Faini, R., 2007. 'Remittances and the brain drain: do more skilled migrants remit more?', *World Bank Economic Review*.

Pires, M., Kassimir, R., and M. Berhane, 1999. *Investing in Return: Rates of Return of African Ph.D.'s Trained in North America*. New York: Social Science Research Council.

Stark, O., 2004. 'Rethinking the brain drain', *World Development* 32.1, 15–22.

Migration, the Global Financial Crisis, and Poverty Reduction in Africa

Peter Quartey

1. Introduction

Migration can be described as a double-edged sword since it provides great opportunities for growth and poverty reduction but is also associated with enormous challenges, which often slow its impact on development. For instance, international migration encourages remittance flows to developing countries including Africa but also leads to the outflow of skilled personnel with its socio-economic consequences. The reasons for such labour migration from Africa are numerous but prominent among them are: poor working conditions in these countries coupled with huge wage disparities between the migrants' home country and the destination country. Colonial ties, language, culture as well as networks significantly explain migration patterns in Africa (Page and Plaza 2006). In the case of migration within West Africa, Adepoju (2005) notes that migration has been initially due to internecine warfare, trade, colonialization of new lands, slavery and evangelism. However, economic factors as well as some of the factors mentioned above explain recent migratory trends in West Africa.

Despite the challenges brought about by such movements, migration brings with it significant benefits to the migrants' household, community and country of origin as well as the destination country. Although these benefits often help in reducing poverty, a major setback to migration and poverty reduction has been the effect of the global financial crisis on migrant households and their families. This paper examines how migration contributes to poverty reduction in recent times and how this has been affected by the global financial crisis. It also suggests ways to maximize the gains from migration to ensure sustained poverty reduction.

2. Migration and poverty reduction nexus

2.1. THEORETICAL LINKAGES

International migration has prompted growing interest as the number of migrants globally has increased, and the economic, social and political implications of migration for developing and developed countries assert themselves. However, while migration is often analyzed in terms of the 'push-pull model', which looks at the (negative) push factors which drive people to leave their countries and the (positive) pull factors which attract them to their new destinations, discussions on the consequences of migration always tended to focus on the negative impacts on the sending (source) country alone. However, migration creates both opportunities and risks for the sending and receiving countries, thus it is imperative that a holistic approach be given to discussions on the socio-economic impacts of migration (Katseli, Lucas, and Xenogiani 2006).

The movement of people, particularly labour from one country to another creates for the two countries both negative and positive socio-economic effects. For the receiving countries, the positive benefits from immigration are the infusion of 'cheap labour' into their economies and the cross-fertilization of cultures. In terms of cost, the increasing flow of foreign immigrants often leads to a distortion of the labour markets and social tensions such as crime, unemployment, public welfare burden and other security concerns. The social fabric of a source country could be polluted with norms, customs, culture and values acquired by returned migrants from abroad and can hurt the social capital. Also, at the community and family levels, regardless of the skill level of migrants, their departure can lead to family disorganization, reduced labour force and loss of decision makers in the community. Interestingly most of these migrant, largely, no longer go back to stay in their communities when they return.

2.2. REMITTANCES AND POVERTY REDUCTION

The most notable positive economic effect, short-term though, of migration is found in remittances. This refers to monetary and other cash transfers sent from migrants to their families and communities in the country of origin. Migration affects poverty through remittances spent on consumption, education, health, housing, and investments to mention but a few. According to the 2009 Human Development Report, such movements increase the HDI of a country by at least 10% and sometimes thrice the HDI figure in the case of Uganda. Remittance flows globally currently exceed USD$100 billion which is higher than the value of official development assistance (ODA). Remittances to SSA amounted to US$ 19 billion in 2007 and accounted for 2.2% of GDP (UNDP HDR, 2009). Sander (2003) also reported that remittances have proved to be the most stable flow compared to ODA and to private capital flows (also see Maimbo 2003; Quartey 2006; 2009a; 2009b; 2009c).

Remittances have been noted to play critical roles in countries' development. However, an issue that remains unresolved is whether remittance flows to these African countries will be sustainable and therefore can continue to serve as a vital source of future income for households. The global financial crisis and other unforeseen global conditions can affect the degree to which remittances can continue to play this key role in national development. Another key challenge for many African migrants is the tightening of immigration rules and the admission of many lesser developed European countries into the EU. This implies that African migrants are less favoured in jobs they used to dominate which has effect on remittances.

2.3. INTERNAL MIGRATION

Migration within and between different regions in Africa has therefore reflected the general global pattern in which a set of push factors such as deteriorating economy, political instability, droughts, and wars, are largely responsible for the exit of people from the sending countries/areas, and other pull factors such as relative economic prosperity, peace, and stability are responsible for the attraction of migrants to the receiving areas (Adepoju 1998; Adedokun 2003). As a result, the movements were unstructured and occurred in groups; the migrants were demographically undifferentiated.

The dominant trend in internal migration in more recent times has been the movement from rural to urban areas. Contact with Western Europe facilitated the emergence of new towns and other urban centres that served as colonial administrative centres or as economic or industrial centres. Many capital cities of West African countries developed as artificial ports built on vacant or sparsely populated sites. The new towns developed certain characteristics that contrasted sharply with the traditional culture. An improved physical environment such as sanitary facilities, roads, street lighting, and health services combined with other rudiments of urbanism provide the background to the rural-to-urban migration that was a hallmark of the colonial period.

Regional economic disparities were not the only factors that prompted internal migration, particularly in the colonial times and thereafter. The transformation of agriculture during this period that resulted from the creation of large plantations by the colonizers in certain regions of the continent was a major factor. Also colonial fiscal measures, particularly the introduction of the head tax payable in cash gave rise to migration. It was impossible for most rural families to raise the necessary sums from the village, and this necessitated the migration of one or more members of a household to the city. In other instances, villagers fled the tax by migrating to neighbouring territories.

Intra-and inter-country migrations remain a prominent feature of African life. The persistence is partly the outcome of the fact that migrants have always considered the various sub-regions as single economic units within which trade in goods and services flowed. But more important, intra-regional migration has been sustained by the persistence and intensification of widespread poverty, the deteriorating economic situation, and the consequences of the various macroeconomic adjustment measures. In addition, conflicts and environmental degradation, desertification, and cyclical famines have further aggravated the pressure for migration from poorer to relatively prosperous regions of the continent. On the other hand, the violent conflicts that have plagued the political landscape of many African countries has accounted for the increase in the number of African refugees. Many have chosen to remain as migrants in the countries of their sanctuary even after conflicts have ceased in their homelands.

2.3. The global financial crisis, migration, and poverty reduction

The financial and economic crisis has had serious repercussions on both developing and developed countries but the magnitude varies. The IMF estimates that about 30% of low income countries could be considered as highly vulnerable to the consequence of the crisis. About 50% of the highly vulnerable are in sub-Saharan Africa (SSA) with Ghana being no exception. Ghana and Zambia are classified as highly vulnerable followed by Benin, Nigeria, Kenya and Uganda. The crisis is likely to affect remittances, return migration and economic development and therefore the need for a comprehensive response from government.

The financial and economic crisis has led to loss of jobs/income by migrants and this has affected remittances to African countries. According to the World Bank (2009), remittances will fall by 4.4% in 2009. The financial and economic crisis has also led to reduced demand (and price) for some African exports besides the decline in Aid inflows and Foreign Direct Investment (FDI). All these have led to reduced foreign exchange receipts and excess demand for foreign exchange which has led to depreciation in the local currency. The exchange rate movements (depreciation) have also put pressure on prices (inflationary pressures) and this has had implications on economic growth and poverty reduction.

The crisis is also expected to affect return migration which can result in economic and social instability in migrants' home countries. However, no evidence of significant return migration has been reported so far in many of these African countries.

4. Conclusions and policy lessons

Several studies point to the developmental impact of migration, particularly its impact on livelihood of migrant households, communities, home and host country. On the other hand, migration is associated with challenges which if not minimized can worsen poverty and other social outcomes. However, the recent global financial crisis has made the challenge even more pronounced. This paper has discussed the migration poverty nexus and how this has been affected by the global financial crisis in Africa.

A major observation is that whereas remittances have continued to flow to Africa, issues about its future sustainability remain unresolved. Also, the global financial crisis that initially hit the industrialized countries has had 'ripple effect' on Africa. The crisis has affected remittance flow since migrants have lost jobs or overtime wages as a result of the economic downturn. The crisis has also affected other economic indicators such as FDI, exports, inflation and the exchange rate which have consequently affected poverty negatively thereby reducing the expected impact of migration on poverty.

On the basis of the above, the paper suggests that in order to minimize the cost of migration, a comprehensive policy on how to meaningfully engage the diaspora to harness resources should be developed. Secondly, a scheme should be developed whereby skilled personnel who intend to migrate refund the cost of training while more of such skills are trained to fill in the vacancies often created as a result of out-migration. Also, return migration should be promoted through short term visas and temporary permits for skilled diaspora to work in their countries of origin. A secure legal status at destination with work and residence permits, recognition of dual citizenship by countries concerned are measures needed for circulation to take place. In the case of irregular migration, managing the return, repatriation and resettlement of refugees and internally displaced persons is an integral component of migration management.

■ REFERENCES

Adedokun, Olaide A., 2003. *The Rights of Migrant Workers and Members of their Families: Nigeria.* UNESCO, SHS/2003/MC/7.

Adepoju, Aderanti, 1998. 'Linkage between internal and international migration: the African situation', *International Social Science Journal* 50.15, 387–95.

—— 2005. 'Patterns of migration in West Africa', in Takyiwaa Manuh (ed.), *At Home in the World? International Migration and Development in Contemporary Ghana and West Africa.* Accra: Sub-Saharan Publishers.

Katseli, L. T., R. E. B. Lucas, and T. Xenogiani, 2006. 'Effects of migration on sending countries: what do we know?', OECD Development Centre Working Paper 250.

Maimbo, S., 2003. 'The money exchange dealers of Kabul: a study of the Hawala system in Afghanistan', Washington, DC: World Bank.

Page, J., and S. Plaza, 2006. 'Migration, remittances and development: a review of global evidence', *Journal of African Economies* 15 (Supplement 2), 245–336.

Quartey, P., 2006. 'The impact of migrant remittances on household welfare in Ghana', AERC Working Paper 158, Nairobi.

—— 2009a. 'The impact of rich countries' policies on poverty in developing countries: the case of migrant nurses from Ghana to the UK', *Ghana Social Science Journal*.

—— 2009b. 'International migration in Ghana: national profile for strategic development', report prepared for the EU/IOM Migration Profile Project. Geneva: IOM.

—— 2009c. 'Providers of remittance service in sub-Saharan Africa: Ghana country case study', World Bank.

Sander, C., 2003. 'Migrant remittances to developing countries: a scoping study. Overview and introduction to issues for pro-poor financial services'. London: DFID.

World Bank, 2009. *Global Economic Prospects 2009; Commodities at the Crossroads*, Washington, D.C.

Thematic Perspectives
Governance and Political Economy

Democracy and African Development

Leonard Wantchekon

Democracy is defined as a set of representative institutions that strive to uphold liberal values. It is increasingly perceived, for better or worse, that democracy offers a solution to major social and economic problems. Warring factions in Mozambique, anti-corruption activists in Guinea, and educational reformers in Benin share a belief that democratic reforms will be the ultimate institutional remedy to their respective struggles with civil war, corruption, and poor education. This is in sharp contrast with the scholarly view in political science that economic development requires some form of autocratic government (Huntington 1968). According to Olson (1982), even in countries where citizens have long enjoyed freedom of organization without the stain of upheaval or invasion, there will eventually emerge a growth-repressing restraint on social movements (Olson 1982: 77).

There are reasons to believe in the instrumental value of democracy. The guarantee of political freedoms and multi-party elections enables voters to hold governments more accountable not only in terms of delivering public services but also in assuring the security of property rights (Przeworski and Limongi 1997; Besley and Prat 2006). Early empirical support for the instrumental approach to democracy was provided by Sen (1999: 10): 'freedoms are not only the primary ends of development, but they are also among its primary means.'

Yet research on democratic institutions and economic growth has reported mixed findings. Benabou (1996) highlights the inconsistency of empirical findings when investigating the effect of democracy on growth. Meanwhile, Alesina and Perotti (1997) reject the hypothesis that democratic institutions can diminish the prospects for growth. Following this work, literature in political economy has shifted away from comparing the prospects for development under democracies and dictatorships towards investigating the specific features of democracy that are likely to promote economic growth. I will focus on two such aspects of democracy that are relevant to development: electoral accountability and conflict resolution.[1]

---

[1] I would like to thank Jenny G. Rodriguez and Omar G. Ponce for research assistance.

Accountability

Democratic theorists contend that elections offer citizens an opportunity to influence the way governments behave. Through voting, a population can either threaten to remove a representative or can reward her with a renewed reputation for competency and an additional term in office (Campbell et al. 1960; Fenno 1978; Fiorina 1981). Elections, however, do not guarantee accountability. On one hand, democratic accountability may entail overlooking minority interests (Maskin and Tirole 2004). This behaviour may be normatively undesirable. On the other hand, the accountability mechanism may fail for several reasons. Voters may lack the information they need to form accurate judgements about candidates. Alternatively, citizens may have conflicting preferences and may be unable to coordinate to hold the ruler accountable (Manin, Przeworski, and Stokes 1999). Clientelism and identity politics may also encourage voters to support a corrupt politician because she happens to be one of their own.

The evidence suggests that accountability mechanisms work particularly well in the presence of strong political participation by citizens during and between elections. Political participation provides incentives for government policies to be responsive to citizens' preferences. For instance, if the segment of voters with low incomes increases, the government should implement more policies that favour the lower-income groups. In theory, a more democratic system is more likely to produce policy outcomes that coincide with citizens' preferences than a less democratic system. A number of studies drawing cross-national data from surveys have found a positive relationship between political participation and measures of economic development, such as education and income (Powell 1980; Verba, Nie, and Kim 1978; Verba and Nie 1972). Stasavage (2005) suggests that the shift to multi-party competition in African countries may have prompted African governments to spend more on education. Others argue that Olson's conjecture of elite capture of democracies is more likely to occur in scenarios of low political participation. For example, Li, Squire, and Zou (1998) find that elite capture is more likely to occur in countries where participation is low and where democratic institutions are weak.

Recent studies suggest that democracy allocates resources more efficiently than autocracies. This is attributed to the accountability of public officials and to transparency in both government spending and policymaking. According to Alesina and Perotti, the less understanding the electorate has about the budgetary processes, the greater is the ability of politicians to act strategically and use fiscal deficits and overspending to achieve opportunistic goals (1996: 16). From this perspective, democratic institutions are expected to attract investment and to stimulate growth by improving budgetary transparency. Similarly, democracies outperform autocracies when it comes to the provision of public services. For example, democratic regimes tend to spend more on education and health than do autocracies (Brown and Hunter 1999; Kaufman and Segura-Ubiergo 2001).[2] Ferraz and Finan (2008) find that, in Brazil, corrupt local politicians are less likely to be re-elected in places where there is better access to information.

In short, democratic accountability promotes development through its effective use of government responsiveness and public service delivery. Evidence compiled by the Mo Ibrahim Foundation from 2001 to 2009 confirms this condition: more democratic countries in Africa are better governed. With the exception of Tunisia under Ben Ali, there is no country among the fifteen best-governed countries that is not fairly democratic. In addition, all fifteen worst-governed countries are autocratic (Mo Ibrahim Foundation 2009).

Conflict resolution

According to Przeworski et al. (1995), democracy is more than a set of representative institutions. It also an institutionalized procedure through which political conflicts are resolved. Building on this approach, Wantchekon (2004) develops a theory of post-conflict democracy which holds that democracy can work as an arbitration mechanism that allows self-interested warring factions—in a situation of endless and costly conflict—to maximize their own economic welfare. In post-civil war countries such as Liberia or Mozambique, democratic institutions secure the protection of ordinary citizens against illegal expropriation at the hands of warring factions. These institutions can also facilitate peaceful power sharing between the factions. This occurs because warring factions need to convince each other and the citizens that they are ready to take turns in ruling the country. They also need to convince citizens that they are serious about eliminating political banditry. As result, they simultaneously set up law enforcement institutions—such as an effective police force and a criminal justice system—and political institutions—such as a depoliticized judiciary and electoral commission. Without these institutions, the promise of securing the citizens' ownership of their property or of receiving political rights from the warring factions will not be realized, and the choice of democracy will not be validated (Wantchekon 2004: 22). The rise of democratic institutions in Mozambique, Liberia, and Namibia has been associated with a sharp decline in political violence and a significant improvement in personal safety (Mo Ibrahim Foundation 2009).

However, once established in unstable environments, these institutions may still fail to foster growth. On the one hand, democracy may hinder growth if there are pressures for

---

[2] However, according to the World Development Report (2004), the correlation between health and education spending and health and education outcomes is very weak.

immediate consumption that reduce investment (Keefer 2005). Plumper and Martin (2003) find a U-shaped relationship between the level of democracy and government spending. At higher levels of political competition, countries may experience a lower level of economic growth. In these situations, democratic mechanisms (i.e. the pursuit of political support through the provision of benefits) may become overly distributive (see also Persson and Tabellini 2003). On the other hand, democratic governments maintain a framework for private (economic) activity of contractors who are also capable of providing law and order. Independent enforcement of the rule of law thus promotes growth under democratic institutions, even if these are not directly provided by the government. Leblang (1996) shows that those economies that protect property rights grow more rapidly than those that do not. Similarly, among developing countries, those regimes that offer high levels of political and civil liberties to their citizens achieve significantly higher GDP growth rates than those countries under autocratic governments (Nelson and Singh 1998). Finally, Baum and Lake (2003) show that even if democracy has no effect on growth, it is correlated with higher life expectancy and higher levels of secondary education in countries that are not poor. Thus, it is unclear whether the result holds in the context of Africa.

Concluding remarks

Democracy increasingly appears to be a prerequisite for growth and development in Africa. This view is confirmed by a recent study showing that, by and large, growth and poverty reduction strategies have been most effective in countries where democratic reforms have been successful (Mattes 2009). For example, political freedoms between 1999 and 2008 are inversely correlated with levels of poverty in Ghana, Madagascar, Senegal, Zambia, and Zimbabwe during the same period. Despite its imperfection, democracy is the best political system ever tried on the continent since independence.

■ REFERENCES

Alesina, Alberto, and Roberto Perrotti, 1996. 'Budget deficits and budget institutions', IMF Working Paper 96/52.
—— 1997. 'The politics of growth: a survey', in V. Bergström (ed.), *Government and Growth*. Oxford: Clarendon Press, 11–49.
—— and Dani Rodrik, 1994. 'Distributive politics and economic growth', *Quarterly Journal of Economics* 109.2, 465–90.
Barro, Robert, 1997. *Determinants of Economic Growth*. Cambridge, Mass.: MIT Press.

Baum, Matthew, and David A. Lake, 2003. 'The political economy of growth: democracy and human capital', *Journal of Political Science* 47.2, 333–47.

Benabou, Roland, 1996. 'Inequality and growth', in B. Bernanke and J. Rotemberg (eds), *NBER Macroeconomics Annual*. Cambridge, Mass.: MIT Press.

Besley, Timothy, and Robin Burgess, 2002. 'The political economy of government responsiveness: theory and evidence from India', *Quarterly Journal of Economics* 117.4, 1415–51.

—— and Andrea Prat, 2006. 'Handcuffs for the grabbing hand? Media capture and government accountability', *American Economic Review* 96.3, 720–36.

Blair, Harry, 2000. 'Participation and accountability at the periphery: democratic local governance in six countries', *World Development* 28.1, 21–39.

Brown, David, and Wendy Hunter, 1999. 'Democracy and social spending in Latin America', *American Political Science Review* 93.4, 779–90.

Campbell, Angus, Philip E. Converse, Warren E. Miller, and Donald E. Stokes, 1960. *The American Voter*. New York: Wiley.

Cheibub, Jose Antonio, and Adam Przeworski, 1999. 'Democracy, elections, and accountability for economic outcomes', in Przeworski et al. (1999: 222–51).

Cleary, Matthew R., 2007. 'Electoral competition, participation, and government responsiveness in Mexico', *American Journal of Political Science* 51.2, 283–99.

Curvale, Carolina, and Adam Przeworski, 2006. 'Does politics explain the economic gap between the United States and Latin America?', in proceedings of conference on 'Explaining the Gap between Latin America and the United States', Buenos Aires, November. Fondo de Cultura Economica.

Fearon, James, 2000. 'Why use elections to allocate power?', working paper, Stanford University.

Fenno, Richard F., 1978. *Home Style: House Members in Their Districts*. Boston: Little, Brown.

Ferraz, Claudio, and Federico Finan, 2008. 'Exposing corrupt politicians: the effects of Brazil's publicly-released audits on electoral outcomes', *Quarterly Journal of Economics* 123.2, 703–45.

Fiorina, Morris P., 1981. *Retrospective Voting in American National Elections*. New Haven, Conn.: Yale University Press.

Friedman, M., 1962. *Capitalism and Freedom*. Chicago: Chicago University Press.

Granato, J., R. Inglehart, and D. Leblang, 1996. 'Cultural values, stable democracy, and economic development: theory, hypothesis, and some empirical tests', *American Journal of Political Science* 40.3, 607–31.

Huntington, Samuel, 1968. *Political Order in Changing Societies*. New Haven, Conn.: Yale University Press.

Kaufman, Robert R., and Alex Segura-Ubiergo, 2001. 'Globalization, domestic politics, and social spending in Latin America', *World Politics* 53.4, 553–87.

Keefer, Philip, 2005. 'Democratization and clientelism: why are young democracies badly governed?', World Bank working paper.

La Porta, Rafael, Florencio Lopez-de-Silanes, Andrei Shleifer, and Robert W. Vishny, 1997. 'Trust in large organizations,', *American Economic Review* 87, 333–8.

Leblang, David A., 1996. 'Property rights, democracy and economic growth', *Political Research Quarterly* 49.1, 5–26.

Li, H., L. Squire, and H. Zou, 1998. 'Explaining international and intertemporal variations in income inequality', *Economic Journal* 108, 26–43.

Manin, Bernard, Adam Przeworski, and Susan Stokes (eds), 1999. *Democracy, Accountability, and Representation*. Cambridge: Cambridge University Press.

Maskin, Eric, and Jean Tirole, 2004. 'The politician and the judge: accountability in government', *American Economic Review* 94.4, 1034–54.

Mattes, Robert, 2009. 'Poverty reduction, economic growth and democratization in sub-Saharan Africa', Afrobarometer Briefing Paper 68.

Mo Ibrahim Foundation, 2009. Report on Ibrahim Index on Governance: http://www.moibrahimfoundation.org/en/section/the-ibrahim-index.

Nelson, Michael A., and Ram D. Singh, 1998. 'Democracy, economic freedom, fiscal policy, and growth in LDCs: a fresh look', *Economic Development and Cultural Change* 46.4, 677–96.

Olson, M., 1982. *The Rise and Decline of Nations*. New Haven, Conn.: Yale University Press.

Persson, Torsten, and Guido Tabellini, 2003. *The Economic Effects of Constitutions*. Cambridge, Mass.: MIT Press.

—— —— 2009. 'Democratic capital: the nexus of political and economic change', *American Economic Journal: Macroeconomics* 1.2, 88–126.

Plumper, Thomas, and Christian Martin, 2003. 'Democracy, government spending, and economic growth: a political-economic explanation', *Public Choice* 117: 27–50.

Powell, G. B., Jr., 1980. 'Voting turnout in thirty democracies: partisan, legal, and socio-economic Influences', In R. Rose (ed.), *Electoral Participation: A Comparative Analysis*. Beverly Hills, Calif.: Sage.

Przeworski, Adam, et al., 1995. *Sustainable Democracy*. Cambridge: Cambridge University Press.

Przeworski A., M. Alvarez, J. A. Cheibub, and F. Limongi, 2000. *Democracy and Development: Political Institutions and Well Being in the World 1950–1999*. New York: Cambridge University Press.

—— and F. Limongi, 1997. 'Modernization: theories and facts', *World Politics* 49.2, 155–83.

—— S. Stokes, and Bernard Manin (eds), 1999. *Democracy, Accountability and Representation*. New York: Cambridge University Press.

Reinikka, Ritva, and Jakob Svensson, 2004. 'The power of information: evidence from a newspaper campaign to reduce capture', World Bank Policy Research Working Paper 3239.

Sen, Amartya, 1999. *Democracy as Freedom*. Oxford University Press.

Stasavage, David, 2005. 'Democracy and education spending in Africa', *American Journal of Political Science* 49, 343–58.

Svensson, Jakob, 1999. 'Aid, growth and democracy', *Economics and Politics* 11.3, 275–97.

Uk, Heo, and Alexander C. Tan, 2001. 'Democracy and economic growth: a causal analysis', *Comparative Politics* 33.4, 463–73.

Verba, Sydney, and Norman Nie, 1972. *Participation in America: Political Democracy and Social Equality*. New York: Harper and Row.

—— —— and J.-O. Kim, 1978. *Participation and Political Equality: A Seven Nation Comparison*. Cambridge: Cambridge University Press.

Wantchekon, Leonard, 2004. 'The paradox of "warlord" democracy: a theoretical investigation', *American Political Science Review* 98.1, 17–33.

World Development Report, 2004. *Making Services Work For Poor People*. Washington, DC: World Bank.

Institutions and Development in Sub-Saharan Africa

James A. Robinson[1]

The dominant explanation of comparative development, thought of simply in terms of per capita income, attributes variation in performance to differences in economic institutions, construed sufficiently broadly to include economic policies. Some countries have economic institutions that create an incentive environment which stimulates development, others do not. According to this perspective, the main reasons that African nations are poor today is that their citizens live with economic incentives that do not encourage them to save and invest, or to adopt or create better technologies. Property rights are insecure and very inefficiently organized, markets do not function well, states are weak, and political systems do not provide public goods. There is a great deal of evidence consistent with these claims both at the macro (Acemoglu, Johnson, and Robinson 2001; 2002) and the micro (Goldstein and Udry 2008) level.

This finding raises the question of why Africa has such poor economic institutions. These institutions are the outcome of a political process, so we can restate the puzzle in terms of why it is that the political processes of African societies generate such poor economic institutions.

For the independence period, these political processes have been well described by political scientists, who describe them, following Max Weber, as 'patrimonial'. In the words of Bratton and van der Walle (1997: 62)

> the right to rule in...patrimonial regimes is ascribed to a person rather than to an office, despite the official existence of a written constitution. One individual...often a president for life, dominates the state apparatus and stands above its laws. Relationships of loyalty and dependence pervade a formal political and administrative system, and officials occupy bureaucratic positions less to perform public service...than to acquire personal wealth and status. Although state functionaries receive an official salary, they also enjoy access to various forms of illicit rents, prebends, and petty corruption, which constitute...an entitlement of office. The chief executive and his inner circle undermine the effectiveness of the nominally modern state administration by using it for systematic patronage and clientelist practices in order to maintain political order.

---

[1] I greatly benefited from discussions with Jan Vansina on the topic of this chapter.

Starting with Bates (1981), a series of works showed that the patrimonial nature of politics in Africa fundamentally shaped economic institutions in a way which reproduced poverty. Institutions were designed to distort markets to create rents, dedicated to redistributing resources and consolidating political power rather than promoting development. The juxtaposition of these created a terrible incentive environment and, after independence, generalized economic decline. The one glaring counterexample, Botswana, fitted in well with these ideas, since its rapid development was underpinned by the absence of patrimonialism (Acemoglu, Johnson, and Robinson 2003).

In this chapter I wish to focus on the issue of why the political equilibrium of Africa looks like this. Why is African politics so patrimonial?

Patrimonialism is a very natural way to organize and control power, and seems to have characterized most polities historically. Following Weber, many social scientists use this as a paradigm to describe how European states functioned at the start of the early modern period (see Adams 2005 for a powerful statement of this view, and Aylmer 1961 for an application to the early Stuarts in England), and the concepts have been widely used (e.g. in Southeast Asia; see Bakker 1988; Reid 1993).

In the European case, patrimonialism disappeared as a consequence of attempts to build centralized bureaucratic states. In the British case, though elements of the state, for instance the navy, were gradually modernized in the 17th century, it was the political transition brought by the Glorious Revolution of 1688 that led to the massive reorganization of the state (Brewer 1988; Pincus 2009). State modernization and the definitive move away from patrimonial rule came with the end of absolutism and the rise of parliament. This moved the British state towards one with an interest and capability to provide public goods, organize property rights and the tax system efficiently, and create institutions, such as the Bank of England, whose goal was to stimulate 'manufactures'. It is not a coincidence that these processes were followed by the Industrial Revolution.

The processes of state formation and institutional change which led to the demise of patrimonial rule in Britain did not take place historically in Africa. There are parts of Africa, such as northern Ethiopia during the height of Aksum in 400 AD, or in the Sahel during the medieval period, where states developed which were probably as complex as, and quite similar to, their contemporaries anywhere in the world. Nevertheless, it is clear that Aksum, Ghana, Songhay, Mali, or Great Zimbabwe were the exception, not the rule. It is not just that Africa was late in developing centralized states; also, as the research in Vansina (1990) and the essays in McIntosh (1999) make clear, Africa experienced very many different paths of political development. In central Africa, for instance, the same original polities diverged into polities some of which, like the Kongo, were complex and highly centralized, while others, such as the Tio, were complex but not centralized at all. In general, African political development seems to have been heavily influenced by the presence of many cross-cutting cleavages, such as cults, secret societies, or age groups and the persistence of egalitarian features manifested in practices such as witchcraft.

These features impeded the centralization of power, and they could also lead to very different ways in which to take advantage of the benefits typically associated with central states, for instance the provision of law and conflict resolution. A fascinating example is that of the Igbo of Nigeria (see Northrup 1978). Instead of a central state, the Igbo used the oracle of Ibini Okpabe at Aru Chukwu to resolve disputes and coordinate their actions, for instance war-making.

The unique dynamics of state formation in Africa meant that patrimonial rule persisted and states did not develop which were capable of or interested in organizing economic institutions in a way which would promote development in Africa.[2] Though we know little about incomes historically, we do know that Africa lagged behind the rest of the world in terms of technology. The wheel was not used south of the Sahara, and outside of Ethiopia African societies did not innovate such basic technologies as writing or the plough (Austen and Headrick 1983). This is so even though these technologies were widely known about after 1500 (Law 1980). Though we lack satisfactory answers to these puzzles about technology adoption, some hints can be drawn about why Kongolese farmers might have been reluctant to adopt better technology. The Kongo was governed by a king in São Salvador and an elite whose wealth was based on slave plantations and the extraction of taxes from the rest of the country. Central to the economy was slaving. This was practised by the elite both to supply their own plantations and also to supply Europeans at the coast. Taxes were arbitrary; one was even collected every time the king's beret fell off (Thornton 1983: 24). Instead of investing to increase their productivity and trying to access the market with their products, the Kongolese moved their villages away from the roads in order to reduce the incidence of plunder and escape the reach of slave-traders (Thornton 1983: 41). It is clear from existing historical accounts that property and human rights were highly insecure in the Kongo, thus completely undermining the incentive of anyone to adopt better technologies (except firearms). The problems of technology adoption in the Kongo of the 16th and 17th centuries therefore seem rather similar to those which faced the citizens of the Congo during the reign of King Leopold and the Belgian colonial state, and indeed the citizens of Zaire during the long reign of Joseph Mobutu in the 20th century.[3]

The organization of the Kongo state was exceptional, as my previous discussion made clear, but my sense is that the economic incentives people faced were similar elsewhere, albeit under very different sets of political institutions. A fascinating example is provided by the comparison between the Bushong and Lele in the modern Democratic

---

[2] It will be clear that I disagree with those, like Hopkins (1973), who argue that economic institutions were efficient historically in Africa and that technologies such as the wheel or plough were not 'appropriate' to the continent.

[3] Ewald (1988) demonstrates how the patrimonial politics of the Taqali Kingdom in the Sudan even precluded the widespread adoption of writing by the rulers, who wished to preserve the ambiguity and discretion presented by oral communication.

Republic of the Congo. As Douglas (1962: 211) put it: 'the Lele are poor, while the Bushong are rich... Everything that the Lele have or can do, the Bushong have more and can do better.'

Some of the reasons for this relative poverty were obvious to Douglas. For example, the Lele used inferior technology, they did not use nets for hunting, and Douglas noted 'the absence of nets is consistent with a general Lele tendency not to invest time and labor in long-term equipment' except firearms (p. 216). Douglas argued that the Lele were trapped in an inefficient social equilibrium. There was no process of political centralization; 'Those who have anything to do with the Lele must have noticed the absence of anyone who could give orders with a reasonable hope of being obeyed... This lack of authority goes a long way to explaining their poverty' (p. 1). Society was based on a self-reproducing system of dominance of young men by old men. 'Old men monopolized economic activities and resources to extract rents', while young men were diverted into raiding and abducting, 'such insecurity [being] obviously inimical to trade' (p. 227).

Like the kingdom of the Kongo, the economic institutions of the Lele could not create development.[4] Indeed, Vansina (1978) showed that it was a nascent process of state formation and bureaucratization which changed economic institutions amongst the Bushong, making them more prosperous.

The differential dynamics of state formation and institutions in Africa and Europe in the early modern period were influenced not just by the unique nature of African societies. They are also explained by differences in the shocks which hit these different continents, and in the way societies reacted to these shocks—something which depended on their initial institutions. Not only did the relative technological backwardness of Africa in 1500 mean that Africans missed out on directly participating in the economic opportunities created by the discovery of the Americas, but the *form* of their institutions meant that they got indirectly involved through exporting slaves. This created a very perverse institutional dynamic which further precluded many societies in West and Central Africa from taking advantage of all the innovations in economic institutions and technology then taking place. As we saw in the Kongo, the focus of the state on slaving created terrible economic incentives for citizens; and while slaving led to the rise of a few states, like Oyo or Asante, its effect on average was probably to destroy political centralization. In addition, the Atlantic slave trade intensified domestic slavery in Africa, which persisted well into the 20th century with obvious adverse effects on economic incentives (see Lovejoy 2000 for an overview of the perverse institutional effects of the slave trade on Africa).

---

[4] As with the Kongo, one can dispute how representative this evidence is, but see Colson (1959) for a similar analysis of the Plateau Tonga of Zambia.

These dysfunctional dynamics were then further reinforced by colonialism. This overturned nascent economic modernization in the 19th century in parts of southern Africa, and created what development economists of the 1950s christened 'dual economies' (see Palmer and Parsons 1977; Bundy 1979). Colonialism also cut off any possibility of endogenous institutional reform, and even when it didn't block African economic advance it didn't assist it. As Hill (1963) showed in Ghana, African capitalism developed without the assistance of the British colonial state, which not only refused to build roads to help the cocoa farmers to export but created a marketing board which would eventually almost wipe them out. This meant that even outside of the areas, like the Congo, where there was a great deal of plundering, or Madagascar, Namibia, and Tanzania, where there was mass disruption and murder, there was little chance for Africa to change its institutional path.

Even worse, the structures of colonial rule, from the dual economies to the 'gatekeeper' states (Cooper 2002), through indirect rule (Mamdani 1996), to the ad hoc construction of independent polities (Englebert 2000), left Africa with a more complex institutional legacy in the 1960s than it had had at the start of the colonial period. The political incentives these structures created led to the intensification of patrimonialism, which reproduced the historical patterns of insecure and inefficient property rights and despotic but weak states with little ability or interest in providing public goods. Only Botswana escaped this general pattern, and it fits very well into the model. What is distinct about the country is the process of institutional modernization in the 19th century and the fact that postcolonial leaders were able to continue this project (Schapera 1970). This was because the country escaped the worst effects of colonialism, and at independence had a coherence that most others did not.

The African path of institutions strongly resembles that which Brenner (1976) suggested for eastern Europe in the wake of the Black Death. The Black Death interacted with initially strong patrimonial political institutions to create an intensification of serfdom, rather than the reverse, which is what happened in western Europe, where political institutions were better. Later, Acemoglu, Johnson, and Robinson (2005) pointed out something similar in the case of Atlantic trade expansion after 1492. Where initial political institutions were relatively better, as in Britain, they subsequently improved. But where institutions were worse, as in Spain, they deteriorated. In this way, what might initially have been relatively small differences in institutions are magnified over time. Those that were initially a little better become much better over time because of the way they interact with shocks, while those which may have been only a little worse to start with get substantially worse. Normally there can be feedbacks in this process that limit what can happen. But Africa was more isolated from these and experienced much more pernicious institutional dynamics, especially with respect to slavery and its legacies and subsequently colonization. Africa is poor today because it has experienced a long vicious circle of the development of political and economic institutions.

REFERENCES

Acemoglu, Daron, Simon Johnson, and James A. Robinson, 2001. 'The colonial origins of comparative development: an empirical investigation', *American Economic Review* 91, 1369–1401.

––– ––– ––– 2002. 'Reversal of fortune: geography and institutions in the making of the modern world income distribution', *Quarterly Journal of Economics* 118, 1231–94.

––– ––– ––– 2003. 'An African success: Botswana', in Dani Rodrik (ed.), *In Search of Prosperity: Analytic Narratives on Economic Growth.* Princeton, NJ: Princeton University Press.

––– ––– ––– 2005. 'The rise of Europe: Atlantic trade, institutional change, and economic growth', *American Economic Review* 95, 546–79.

Adams, Julia, 2005. *The Familial State: Ruling Families and Merchant Capitalism in Early Modern Europe.* Ithaca, NY: Cornell University Press.

Austen, Ralph A., and Daniel Headrick, 1983. 'The role of technology in the African past', *African Studies Review* 26, 163–84.

Aylmer, G. E., 1961. *The King's Servants: The Civil Service of Charles I, 1625–1642.* New York: Columbia University Press.

Bakker, J. I. Hans, 1988. *Patrimonialism, Involution, and the Agrarian Question in Java: A Weberian Analysis of Class Relations and Servile Labour.* London: Unwin Hyman.

Bates, Robert H., 1981. *Markets and States in Tropical Africa.* Berkeley: University of Caifornia Press.

Bratton, Michael, and Nicolas van de Walle, 1997. *Democratic Experiments in Africa: Regime Transitions in Comparative Perspective.* New York: Cambridge University Press.

Brenner, Robert, 1976. 'Agrarian class structure and economic development in preindustrial Europe', *Past and Present* 70, 30–75.

Brewer, John, 1988. *The Sinews of Power: War, Money and the English State, 1688–1773.* Cambridge, Mass.: Harvard University Press.

Bundy, Colin, 1979. *The Rise and Fall of the South African Peasantry.* Berkeley: University of California Press.

Colson, Elizabeth, 1959. 'The Plateau Tonga of northern Rhodesia', in Elizabeth Colson and Max Gluckman (eds), *Seven Tribes of Central Africa.* Manchester: Manchester University Press.

Cooper, Frederick, 2002. *Africa since 1940: The Past of the Present.* New York: Cambridge University Press.

Douglas, Mary, 1962. 'Lele economy compared to the Bushong', in Paul Bohannan and George Dalton (eds), *Markets in Africa.* Evanston, Ill.: Northwestern University Press.

––– 1963. *The Lele of Kasai.* New York: Oxford University Press.

Englebert, Pierre, 2000. *State Legitimacy and Development in Africa.* Boulder, Colo.: Lynne Rienner.

Ewald, Janet, 1988. 'Writing and authority: explorations in and from the kingdom of Taqali', *Comparative Studies in Society and History* 30, 199–224.

Goldstein, Markus, and Christopher Udry, 2008. 'The profits of power: land rights and agricultural investment in Ghana', *Journal of Political Economy* 116, 981–1022.

Hill, Polly, 1963. *The Migrant Cocoa Farmers of Southern Ghana: A Study in Rural Capitalism.* New York: Cambridge University Press.

Hopkins, Anthony G., 1973. *An Economic History of West Africa.* New York: Addison Wesley Longman.

Law, Robin C., 1980. 'Wheeled transportation in pre-colonial West Africa', *Africa* 50, 249–62.

Lovejoy, Paul E., 2000. *Transformations in Slavery: A History of Slavery in Africa*, 2nd edn. New York: Cambridge University Press.

Mamdani, Mahmood, 1996. *Citizen and Subject: Contemporary Africa and the Legacy of Late Colonialism.* Princeton, NJ: Princeton University Press.

McIntosh, Susan Keech (ed.), 1999. *Beyond Chiefdoms: Pathways to Complexity in Africa.* New York: Cambridge University Press.

Palmer, Robin, and Q. Neil Parsons (eds), 1977. *The Roots of Rural Poverty in Central and Southern Africa.* London: Heinemann.

Northrup, David, 1978. *Trade without Rulers: Pre-Colonial Economic Development in Southeast Nigeria.* Oxford: Clarendon Press.

Pincus, Steven C. A., 2009. *1688: The First Modern Revolution.* New Haven, Conn.: Yale University Press.

Reid, Anthony, 1993. *Southeast Asia in the Age of Commerce, 1450–1680*, vol. 2: *Expansion and Crisis.* New Haven, Conn.: Yale University Press.

Schapera, Isaac, 1970. *Tribal Innovators: Tswana Chiefs and Social Change, 1795–1940.* London: Athlone Press.

Thornton, John, 1983. *The Kingdom of Kongo.* Madison: University of Wisconsin Press.

Vansina, Jan, 1978. *The Children of Woot: A History of the Kuba Peoples.* Madison: University of Wisconsin Press.

—— 1990. *Paths in the Rainforests.* London: James Currey.

Delivering Basic Services in Africa
Institutional Deficiencies and Avenues of Solutions

Bernard Gauthier and Waly Wane

1. Introduction

Despite its proven importance for social welfare, public service delivery—in say education, health, and water and sanitation—is often severely deficient in developing countries, especially in sub-Saharan Africa (SSA).

Inadequate service delivery is reflected in the poor showing of social outcomes. Most health and education indicators are very low, and given the rate of progress, many SSA countries will not meet the 2015 Millennium Development Goals (MDG) targets. For instance, with an average under-5 mortality rate at 158 per 1,000, the region accounts for more than half of the 10 million children around the world who will die each year before their 5th birthday. Furthermore, almost one third of the primary school-age population in the region does not attend school, representing almost half of the unschooled children worldwide while accounting for only one fifth of primary school-age children. Mathematics and reading scores for those attending school are also low. Close to 40% of the adult population remains illiterate, of whom 62% are women. Also, about 44% of the population currently does not have access to safe drinking water, and about 37% have no access to sanitation facility.

In recent years, governments, donors and NGOs have committed increasing financial resources to improving basic service delivery. However, in countries with weak institutions it has been shown that budget allocations barely explain the quality and quantity of services (Filmer and Pritchett 1999; World Bank 2003). Two major reasons are generally put forward to rationalize this situation. First, official public funds committed officially may not necessarily reach front-line providers for reasons related to capture, corruption and leakage of funds (Reinikka and Svensson 2004). Second, even if public resources reach front-line providers, their effective use to produce services of acceptable quality is not guaranteed.

This chapter reviews institutional deficiencies that impact service delivery performance and explores avenues of solutions.

2. Institutional arrangements of service delivery

In SSA countries, services such as education, health, water, and sanitation are provided by a mixture of public, private (for-profit and not-for-profit) providers. In the last two decades, the not-for-profit sector has steadily grown by serving areas neglected by public providers and not attractive for profit-driven providers, especially rural and remote regions. Private for-profit providers generally offer education and health services to urban populations. However, the public sector is still the major player in service delivery in most countries. In addition to formal-sector providers, many informal providers also offer traditional services, especially in the health and water sectors.

2.1 INSTITUTIONAL ARRANGEMENTS

Service delivery outcomes are the results of a complex web of principal–agent relationships involving citizens, providers, and government. Because information is asymmetric and imperfect, citizens—the ultimate principal—whose objectives may differ from the agents' (government and providers) have a weak capacity to exercise control in this delegation game. These institutional arrangements give rise to various governance and accountability problems which are at the root of the poor outcomes.

The difficulty of control inherent to principal–agent settings is reinforced in public service delivery mainly due to four aspects in which public and private provision markedly differ (Besley and Ghatak 2003):

- Measurability and attributability: service providers' objectives are often fuzzy and barely amenable to measurement. For instance, the overall objective of a school is to provide 'quality' education, which is very difficult to define. In such contexts, it is hard to identify good performance measures on which to condition the reward or penalty of agents.
- Multi-tasking: service providers perform a multiplicity of tasks which renders evaluation of results even more difficult.
- Multi-principals: service delivery is also characterized by the presence of multiple principals (e.g. in the education sector, parents, employers, school boards, ministry of education officials, and politicians), who might have different preferences concerning the outcome of the various tasks carried out by the agents (e.g. teachers), rendering incentive schemes difficult to design.

- Functional interdependence: moral hazard problems are reinforced due to functional interdependence between multiple agents engaged in a joint production process. Various basic elements have to be provided upstream in the service delivery supply chain (i.e. financing, infrastructure, human resources, material and equipment, governance structure, and incentives) in order for quality services to be accessible and produced downstream at the front line.

We now review some of the deficiencies related to the institutional environment.

3. Deficiencies in service delivery

Public spending in health and education in Africa varies greatly among countries, representing between 2% to 22 % of GDP, much below the levels observed in OECD countries, which are about 13% (Table 1). Spending per capita varies even more widely, from as low as US$6 in Burundi to US$750 in Botswana.

Official public spending figures could be deceptive for assessing countries' actual commitment to social sectors in weak institutional environment, as funding may not translate into increased available resources and improved services given leakage and inadequate incentives. Leakage, which is broadly defined as the share of resources earmarked to specific beneficiaries which fail to reach them, was found to be important in developing countries, including Africa (Table 2).

Greater leakage has been associated with greater discretionary power granted to particular administrative units, especially combined with weak supervision and poor incentives (Reinikka and Svensson, 2004). In Chad for instance, where no fixed

Table 1. Official public spending on education and health in Africa

	Education (% of GDP)	Health (% of GDP)	Sum ($US per capita)
Botswana	9.74	4.45	751.77
Burundi	5.10	0.97	6.43
Chad	1.91	1.47	19.00
Ghana	5.44	2.11	36.52
Guinea	1.63	0.67	6.57
Kenya	7.31	2.10	49.39
Mozambique	5.02	2.73	25.96
Senegal	5.43	1.71	50.95
Uganda*	5.24	2.23	18.30
Zambia	1.99	2.74	29.44
SSA average	4.68	2.93	119.97
OECD Average	5.44	7.07	4 582.19

Source: World Bank WDI on line. Data are for year 2005 except (*) 2004.

Table 2. Leakage by sector and country (%)

Country	Education	Health
Chad, 2004	–	99
Ghana, 1998	49	80
Kenya, 2004	–	38
Tanzania, 1998	57	41
Uganda, 1991–95	87	–
Zambia, 2001	10 (rule-based) 76 (discretionary)	–

Source: Gauthier and Reinikka (2008).

allocation rules apply for most resource allocation, only 1% of non-wage recurrent resources allocated to regional health administration arrived at the facility level. This represented less than US$ 0.02 per capita of (non wages) annual budget available for primary healthcare in 2003 (Gauthier and Wane 2009).

With inadequate levels of public resources at the front line, health and school facilities in SSA often lack the basic infrastructure (electricity, water, and sanitation), and also often face important constraints of basic material and equipment. For instance, the SACMEQ II survey found that over half of grade 6 students in several SSA countries did not have a single book. Given that front-line providers are often left to their own devices to finance their activities, they rely more heavily on user fees, which could thus be very substantial. In addition to official fees, users of services in SSA also face important informal payments which increase accessibility problems, especially for the poor.

Other weaknesses in the broader institutional architecture are associated with inadequate staff incentives which translate into shortage of skilled staff and high absenteeism, especially in poorer and rural areas.

Improving outcomes would require more than an adequate level of qualified personnel; it would also require such personnel to be present to deliver services. However, large multi-country studies show that a high level of absenteeism is prevalent in SSA and other developing countries due to poor accountability and weak staff incentives (Table 3).

4. Avenues of solutions

Improving effectiveness of public spending in service delivery could have important benefits. In Chad, it was shown that reduction of leakage could have led to important improvement in utilization rates of health facilities. Indeed, the negative relationship between official public resources and health output (Fig. 1a) is reversed when leakage is taken into account as effective public resources (i.e. those that reach the regions) have a strong positive impact on health output (Fig. 1b). In Chad, if all public resources

Table 3. Absence rates by country and sector (%)

Country	Primary schools	Health centers
Bangladesh	16	35
Chad	–	21
India	25	40
Indonesia	19	40
Peru	11	25
Uganda	27	37
Zambia	17	–

Source: Chaudhury et al. (2006); World Bank (2003).

officially budgeted for regional delegations in 2003 had reached the front-line providers, the number of patients seeking primary healthcare would have more than doubled during the year. Public expenditures could therefore contribute to the improvement of the population's health, provided they reach the population.

The main solutions examined to improve service delivery performance have focused on reducing information asymmetry and strengthening the accountability relationships which are at the root of institutional deficiencies within service delivery systems.

In order to enhance transparency and accountability within the public administrative apparatus, reforms have focused on improving internal controls, in particular incentives for better accounting and reporting systems. Furthermore, mechanisms have been explored to improve service providers' incentive systems. For instance, Duflo, Hanna, and Ryan (2008) tested whether incentives linked to teacher presence in class could reduce absenteeism, and whether they promote teaching and student learning.

In addition, there is a growing belief that local participation by citizens in service delivery and better information can help achieve better outcomes, especially using a mechanism that enables clients to monitor and directly discipline service providers (World Bank 2003). The availability of information could be improved through the use of new micro-level surveys, notably through public expenditure tracking surveys, quantitative service delivery surveys, and staff absenteeism surveys. These have allowed examination of the performance of service providers, and the obtaining of information on service delivery constraints and inefficiencies. For instance, they have been used to identify leakage in Uganda and measure the effect of an information campaign which sought to provide clients with a stronger bargaining power, leading ultimately to a significant reduction in leakage (Reinikka and Svensson 2004).

Furthermore, citizen report cards (CRCs) have been used to promote citizen awareness and participation. CRCs are tools that are used to collect (periodic) information from users about their experiences of service quality that is disseminated back to the citizens/users. A randomized evaluation of a CRC intervention in the health sector in

Public Expenditure and Health System Performance
Budgeted and Received Resources at the Regional Level

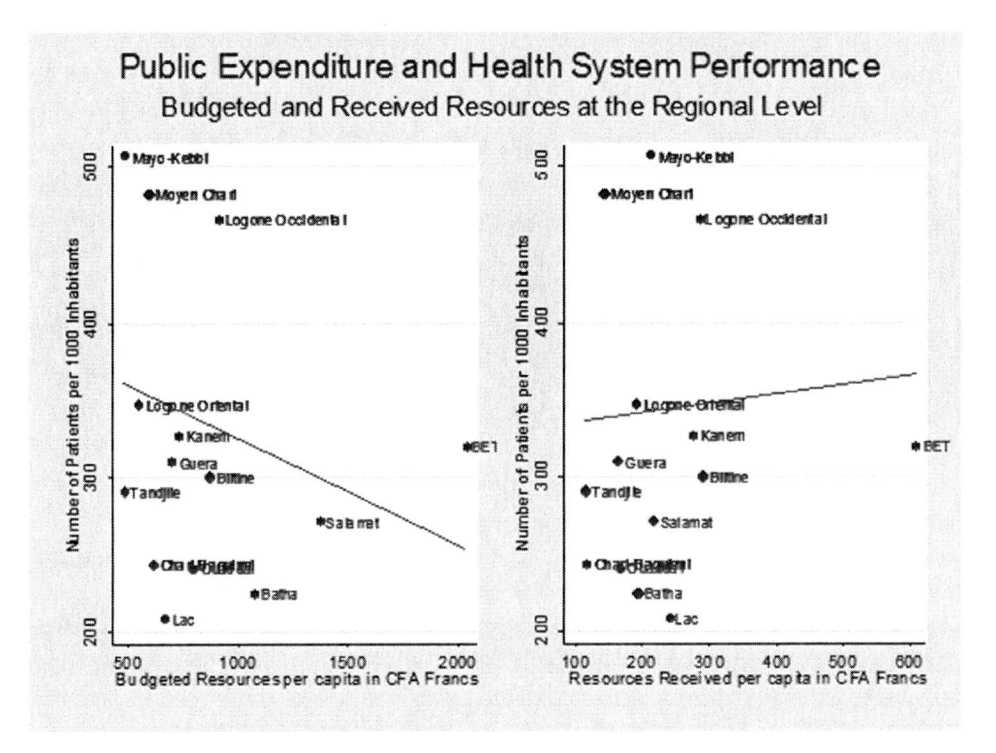

Figure 1. Public expenditure and health system performance (a) Budgeted resources per capita (b) Resources received per capita. Source: Gauthier and Wane (2009).

Uganda in 2003–4 has shown that it has led to significant improvement in the quality and quantity of primary health care provision and resulted in improved health outcomes (Björkman and Svensson 2009).

Ultimately, improving monitoring and benchmarking the quality and performance of services over time and across countries could prove essential to ensuring better effectiveness of public resources, better services, and improved population outcomes (Bold et al. 2011).

REFERENCES

Besley, Timothy, and Maitreesh Ghatak, 2003. 'Incentives, choice and accountability in the provision of public services', *Oxford Review of Economic Policy* 19.2, 235–49.

Björkman, Martina, and Jakob Svensson, 2009. 'Power to the people: evidence from a randomized field experiment on community-based monitoring in Uganda', *Quarterly Journal of Economics* 124.2.

Bold, Tessa, Bernard Gauthier, Ottar Maestad, Jakob Svensson, and Waly Wane, 2011. 'Service Delivery Indicators: Pilot in Education and Health Care in Africa', AERC and The World Bank (February).

Chaudhury, Nazmul, Jeffrey Hammer, Michael Kremer, Karthik Muralidharan, and Halsey Rogers, 2006. 'Missing in action: teacher and health worker absence in developing countries', *Journal of Economic Perspectives* 20.1, 91–116.

Duflo, Esther, Rema Hanna, and Stephen Ryan, 2008. 'Monitoring works: getting teachers to come to school', *CEPR discussion papers 6682*, London (February).

Filmer, Deon, and Lant H. Pritchett, 1999. 'The impact of public spending on health: does money matter?', *Social Science and Medicine* 58: 247–58.

Gauthier, Bernard, and Ritva Reinikka, 2008. 'Methodological approaches to the study of institutions and service delivery: a review of PETS, QSDS and CRCS in Africa', AERC Framework paper.

—— and Waly Wane, 2009. 'Leakage of public resources in the health sector: an empirical investigation of Chad', *Journal of African Economies* 18, 52–83.

Reinikka, Ritva, and Jakob Svensson, 2004. 'Local capture: evidence from a central government transfer program in Uganda', *Quarterly Journal of Economics* 119.2, 1–28.

SACMEQ II: Southern and Eastern Africa Consortium for Monitoring Educational Quality II, 2000–2002. http://www.sacmeq.org/index.htm.

World Bank, 2003. *World Development Report 2004: Making Services Work for Poor People*. Washington, DC and Oxford: World Bank and Oxford University Press.

The Political Economy of Growth in Africa

Gobind Nankani

Economic growth remains Africa's biggest challenge. Over 50% of Africa's population lives below the poverty line, a ratio higher than for any other region in the world. The single most important reason for this has been the relatively low rate of economic growth for most of the last 50 years. The recent upsurge in growth in Africa, since the mid-1990s and especially between 2002 and 2008, is now in retreat as the global economy seeks to rebalance itself. Why has growth been so elusive in Africa, especially compared to Asia?

Drawing on the recent literature on growth—which has increasingly highlighted both its elusive nature and the strong role of political economy factors—and on the experience of policy reforms in African countries, I suggest below that:

1. Growth has been stymied by political economy factors. Variances in the growth record of countries, including those in Africa, are significantly influenced by the alignment, or lack thereof, between the needed reforms and the institutional inheritance, as constrained by the success of leadership in creatively overcoming institutional constraints.

2. Future growth in African countries will depend on how well leaders are able to align institutional innovation with reforms. An emerging pattern suggests that countries fall into two main groups: (a) growing economies drawing on liberal capitalist approaches; (b) growing economies relying on partially liberal capitalist approaches. This would still leave a residual group of conflict-prone and broadly stagnating economies in which leaders are unable to align institutions with reforms. Debates about these two alternatives are likely to persist. More creative approaches to micro-level institutional innovation may offer another approach.

Growth and political economy

The recent literature on growth has emphasized that high and sustained growth is difficult but possible. The Commission on Growth and Development (2008), led by Nobel laureate Michael Spence, identifies thirteen countries that have shown strong and persistent growth in the last 50 years. Together with Rodrik (2003) and the World Bank (2005), the Commission's report has drawn attention to the importance of country-specific factors that underlie successful growth experiences. There is no 'one size that fits all', even though a few common features do characterize all successful growth experiences: macroeconomic stability, openness to the global economy, high domestic savings, and market-friendly policies combined with a non-zero but well-calibrated role of the state. A final common feature stressed especially by Spence is the role of leadership: 'a capable, credible and committed government'—i.e. leadership that continually aligns policies and institutions to changing circumstances and opportunities, while being credible and enjoying broad support. This emphasis on leadership in growth successes also reinforces the argument of Acemoglu and Robinson (2010) that growth is difficult because reforms are stymied by existing institutions. Institutions demonstrate high inertia, because they reflect the existing balance of power. While institutions do change, it is difficult to predict when and how they do, and reversals are not uncommon.

Growth and political economy in Africa

The experience of growth, or its lack, in Africa has also been related to political economy factors. Ndulu et al. (2007) have put out an authoritative book on the political economy of growth in Africa, which essentially explains Africa's poor growth record through 2000 as due largely to the anti-growth policy syndromes that were spawned by political factors. In particular, the attempt to secure political power and to retain it led many African governments to opt for narrower anti-growth policies. As Bates (1981) argues, poor institutions meant that patronage politics, or neo-patrimonialism, was the dominant political framework for decision-making, even where the overt forms of democratic institutions were in place. More recent attempts to understand the 'drivers of change' in countries like Ghana (Booth et al. 2005) have also concluded that neo-patrimonialism continues to get in the way of reforms in key areas such as public-sector reform and budgeting for results.

The cross-country evidence on political forms (democratic and non-democratic) shows no clear correlation between these and growth. Within this broad characterization, there are many underlying perspectives. For example, Collier (2010) has argued that superficially democratic institutions, under certain conditions, permit elites to loot a country's resources, and diminish its growth possibilities. Many external observers as well as civil-society organizations within African countries attribute the tragedy of

African non-growth to poor governance. The anti-aid stances of Easterly (2006), Dambisa (2009), and others are aimed at deflecting the locus of economic decision making towards non-governmental actors and the private sector, and away from the state and governments.

But where there has been growth in Africa, what does the evidence suggest? Botswana is the one African country among the thirteen successful growth cases in the Spence study. Acemoglu, Johnson, and Robinson (2003) interpret Botswana's success as due to the alignment of inherited institutions and elite interests, thus making possible the use of Botswana's diamond resources for growth-oriented national development rather than for private uses, as has been the case in many other resource-rich countries.

More anecdotal evidence from recent experiences also reinforces the view that political economy factors and institutions play a key role in shaping policies in favour of growth. Post-conflict countries such as Mozambique and Rwanda have exhibited strong growth for close to fifteen years each, a period long enough to not be entirely due to the low base from which they resumed growth. Political economy factors were clearly at play here, as was the ability to adopt pro-growth policies because the earlier conflict had significantly flattened the landscape of potential gainers and losers from the new reforms and policies.

Growth reforms, political economy, and leadership

What reforms are needed for growth, and how do political economy and leadership factors come into play in facilitating or thwarting such reforms? In particular, how do the common success factors identified by the Spence study—macroeconomic stability, openness to the global economy, market-friendly policies, and high domestic savings—fare in African political economies, and what does it take for leaders to put and hold these in place? And how do leadership and political economy factors interact with the country-specific factors that seem to explain the growth successes of the last few decades?

Macroeconomic stability, openness to the global economy, and market-friendly policies have all improved across Africa since the 1990s. Inflation levels have dropped, trade volumes have risen, and the state has withdrawn from many sectors of the economy. Citizens have understood the high costs of inflation especially for the poor, have enjoyed the favourable prices of Chinese manufactures, and have seen innovation in privately run telecommunications services. Despite this progress, deepening reforms in these three areas remains a challenge in many African countries. And there is little evidence of the astute use of country-specific characteristics to spur sustained growth, except in the cases of Botswana and Mauritius.

On the macroeconomic front, fiscal deficits tend to be pro-cyclical, particularly because of the pressure of public-sector wage bills. The difficulties in undertaking public-sector wage and employment reforms remain high. Urban-based public employees, health and education employees providing key services, and party-related employment pressures, together combine to counter governments' efforts at containing the share of public wages in total expenditures. Mobilizing support from groups that would gain from greater restraint on public sector wages—especially the rural population and the private sector—is difficult, and the nuisance value of strikes in urban areas and key public service sectors is very high. Political power relations—rather than economic considerations—thus drive public-sector wage policies.

With respect to openness to the global economy, the availability of cheap imports has led to increased demands for protectionism, especially in textiles and some agricultural products such as poultry and rice. While political pressures from these groups are more easily handled by governments than those from public employees, there is no consensus on what a coherent trade and industrial strategy might be. As a result, less attention is paid to investment climate issues and to fostering new entrepreneurs and innovations than would be expected. Again, the policy agenda is dominated by existing powerful groups, rather than potential future producers, and governments have developed few institutional mechanisms for supporting the latter.

The use of discretionary state activities to complement market-friendly approaches in the interests of higher growth remains fraught with dangers in many African countries. Hard lessons were learnt in the import-substitution phase in the aftermath of independence. Today, there are new risks relating to subsidies for products such as petroleum, electricity, water, and fertilizers, and for services such as health. In some of these cases, temporary and budgeted subsidies can be justified. But political factors often make these difficult to remove once introduced. Indeed many African governments give in to pre-election populist pressures to amplify subsidies or introduce new unfunded social programmes. The constructive role of the state in promoting new ventures, as in the growth of the salmon industry in Chile (Chandra 2006) or of efficient Special Economic Zones in China, is yet to be significantly manifested in African countries. The very few examples in Africa, such as in Botswana (diamond processing) and Ethiopia (horticulture), are the exceptions that prove the rule.

Turning to country-specific attributes of growth, an interesting example is that of China. Deng Xiaoping is reported to have described the Chinese approach as 'crossing the river by feeling the stones'. In systematically experimenting widely, abandoning failed attempts, and scaling up successes, the Chinese have demonstrated the usefulness of a learning approach to new initiatives in development. The unparalleled ability of the Chinese Communist Party to implement its plans, and to undertake mid-course corrections, has certainly been a contributory factor to its success. Rodrik and Hausmann (2003) have sought to capture the experimental country-specific approach by describing development as a 'journey of self-discovery'. There are a few examples of innovative activities in African countries, such as the introduction of horticulture in countries such as Kenya and Ethiopia and, more recently, of information technology-based services in countries such as Senegal and Ghana. The introduction of the outgrower-based production system in agriculture is another interesting innovation. But so far, these attempts have not benefited from a scaling-up effect, such as was witnessed, for example, with garment exports from Bangladesh or wines from Chile. Interviews with entrepreneurs in horticulture and IT-based services suggest that their biggest obstacles come from the short supply of important public goods such as simplified procedures, certification of standards, and complementary infrastructure. The ability of new entrepreneurs to shape government policy is hampered by their lack of organization and resources compared to the more established private sector.

Confronting pressures related to public sector wages and employment, protectionism, and populist social programmes, and seeking out new entrepreneurs, require both leadership and institutions. In each case, a short-term sacrifice or cost needs to be traded against a future growth benefit. Patronage politics plays precisely to such short-term pressures, unless the leadership commands credibility and institutions are in place to reinforce this credibility.

The growth successes of the East Asian economies have been explained by many competing hypotheses. Some claim that their success demonstrates the power of following a market-driven export-led strategy; others have stressed that state-led reforms played the critical role, and that this was facilitated by, at least for a period, non-democratic forms of governing; still others have placed the emphasis on leadership and its ability to develop a vision and rally society around that vision, trading off short-term sacrifices in favour of longer-term growth. Campos and Root (1996), in particular, argue that leaders in East Asian countries worked hard to encourage new alliances with and between entrepreneurs, as well as assuring their citizens that they would share in the gains from growth by investing in their education, in land reform, rural infrastructure, small and medium enterprises, public housing, and allocations of corporate equity, depending on the country. This activist stance with respect to crafting new growth-oriented micro-level institutions and credible mechanisms for promising inclusion, a leadership role *par excellence*, is strikingly absent in many African countries. The emphasis has been on various macro-institutional initiatives and on patronage instruments aimed largely at reinforcing the political economy status quo. Weak inherited institutions have often meant that leaders end up being more reactive than activist.

The future of growth in Africa

African growth remains the biggest development challenge of our generation. The global recession has once again raised doubts about the sustainability of the high growth trajectory of the last decade or so. Collier's classification of African countries as coastal, resource-rich, or landlocked is useful here. Some countries, especially the non-resource-rich landlocked ones and those that are mired in internal conflicts, are likely to grow slowly, if at all. (There are exceptions here too: Burkina Faso, landlocked and with few resources, has been one of the success stories in Africa.) For the others, whether resource-rich or coastal or both, there are opportunities to grow, arising in part from their readier access to global markets. For all countries, however, deepening growth-related reforms will be essential. Patronage politics, weak institutions, and leadership's responses to these will be an important determinant of progress on growth.

East Asian leaders made good use of crises in fostering reforms. In addition to crises, other triggers can also be used to usher in a new wave of reforms: for example, new resource discoveries, and possibly regionally binding agreements. But the degree of freedom available to leaders is limited by their inheritance of weak institutions. As one looks across the range of political-economic arrangements in Africa today, leaving aside very weak states in conflict, one is struck by the coexistence of two prototypes—liberal capitalism and partially liberal capitalism, reminiscent of the contrast between the two fast growers in Asia today, India and China.[1]

The liberal capitalist group includes countries such as Ghana, Senegal, Kenya, and Zambia. In these countries, liberal democratic processes and institutions are embedded in an economy largely oriented towards the private sector, with an overlay of strong patronage politics. In the partially liberal capitalist group, in which one might include countries such as Burkina Faso, Ethiopia, Tanzania, Uganda, Rwanda, and Mozambique, partial adherence to liberal democratic processes and institutions with some strong departures from the latter (e.g. absence of term limits, or single-party states, or *de facto* single party states) are combined with a much weaker overlay of patronage politics. In effect, some institutional constraints are imposed on the liberal democratic approach, in order to offset some of the pressures that would otherwise lead to strong patronage politics.

A superficial comparison of recent growth rates in these two groups of countries, as in the comparison between India and China, suggests an interesting hypothesis: that both groups grow, but the partially liberal group has higher growth rates. This is a hypothesis that remains to be tested. And the real test is not spurts of growth, of which African

---

[1] I owe this parallel with the political economy paths of India and China to Devesh Kapur, in a private communication.

countries have had many, but sustained levels of high growth. But it does raise the question, as in matters of growth, whether the political economy dimensions of growth do not also warrant a combination of a few common attributes including most importantly accountability, and a complement of country-specific institutional approaches aimed ultimately at attaining a liberal democratic capitalist system. If growth policies need to be country-specific, might not the configuration of political institutions also need to be less rigidly defined, as long as there is accountability and progress towards a liberal democratic capitalist system?

It is important here to assess the views of African citizens on their political preferences. Afrobarometer surveys periodically report on the political preferences of Africans across the continent. Three findings stand out: first, most Africans (over two thirds) have a strong preference for democracy; second, an even larger share (about four fifths) are against authoritarian forms of government. This suggests that partially liberal capitalist approaches are decidedly opposed by most Africans.

The same surveys suggest, thirdly, that the preference for democracy declines at the margin when economic performance deteriorates, and revives as economic performance improves or following a change of government. Thus, the strong political preference for democracy, at least at the margin, appears to also exhibit some trade-off with economic performance. Should this trade-off prove to be significant and enduring, then it would suggest that the two forms of capitalism will persist, and will increasingly be debated in African countries.

Conclusion

This reflection on the political economy of growth in Africa does not leave us with any easy answers. The strong preference of Africans for liberal democracy is underlined by Afrobarometer's surveys. And there are many examples of non-liberal or partially liberal governments in Africa, such as Equatorial Guinea and Gabon, which have had low (non-resource) growth, increasing poverty, and rising inequality. The presumption has to be in favour of a liberal democratic capitalist approach, within which the critical need is for leaders to be accountable to their peoples in multi-faceted ways, and not just once every few years through the ballot box.

At the same time, it may also be true that, unless liberal democratic leaders find ways of enhancing growth through institutional innovation as in East Asia, focusing strongly on micro-level institutions as emphasized by Campos for East Asia, there may be pressures in the direction of partially liberal approaches in the search for improved economic performance. China's growth success to date, relative to that of India, provides a graphic example on the global stage of the contrasts between the economic performance of a partially liberal capitalist and a liberal capitalist approach, and will be carefully watched as African citizens and their governments grope for different institutional approaches to improving their wellbeing.

African countries have, over the last two decades, developed two broad approaches while in some cases superficially keeping the institutional forms of liberal democracy. These two approaches are likely to persist and to fuel the search for ever better ways of handling the political economy of growth in Africa. The choice of approach notwithstanding, the scope for micro-level institutional innovation has barely been explored in African countries. There is no easy substitute for effective leadership: the experience of successful growth tells us that leaders, as individuals, matter a great deal.

■ REFERENCES

Acemoglu, D., and J. Robinson, 2010. 'The role of institutions in growth and development', in D. Brady and M. Spence (eds), *Leadership and Growth*. Washington, DC: World Bank, 135–64.

—— S. Johnson, and J. Robinson, 2003. 'An African success: Botswana', in Rodrik (2003).

Adam, C., and S. Dercon, 2009. 'Introduction: the political economy of development', *Oxford Review of Economic Policy* 25.2.

Afrobarometer. www. Afrobarometer.org.

Bates, R., 1981. *Markets and States in Tropical Africa: The Political Basis of Agricultural Policies*. Berkeley: University of California Press.

Booth, D., et al., 2005. 'What are the drivers of change in Ghana?', Policy Briefs on Drivers of Change in Ghana 1, ODI, London.

Brady, D., and M. Spence, 2009. 'Leadership and politics: a perspective from the commission on growth and development', *Oxford Review of Economic Policy* 25.2.

Campos, José Edgardo L., and Hilton L. Root, 1996. *The Key to the Asian Miracle: Making Shared Growth Credible*. Washington, DC: Brookings Institution Press.

Chandra, V. (ed.), 2006. *Technology, Adaptation and Exports: How Some Developing Countries Got it Right*. Washington, DC: World Bank.

Collier, P., 2008. *The Bottom Billion*. New York: Oxford University Press.

—— 2010. *Wars, Guns and Votes*. London: HarperCollins.

Commission on Growth and Development, 2008. *The Growth Report: Strategies for Sustained Growth and Inclusive Development*. Washington, DC: World Bank.

Dambisa, M., 2009. *Dead Aid: Why Aid Is Not Working and How There Is Another Way for Africa*. London: Allen Lane.

Easterly, W. R., 2006. *The White Man's Burden: Why the West's Efforts to Aid the Rest Have Done So Much Ill and So Little Good*. London: Penguin.

Ndulu, B. J., S. A. O'Connell, R. H. Bates, P. Collier, and C. C. Soludo (eds), 2007. *The Political Economy of Economic Growth in Africa, 1960–2000*, vol. 1. Cambridge: Cambridge University Press.

Rodrik, D. (ed.), 2003. *In Search of Prosperity: Analytical Narratives on Economic Growth.* Princeton, NJ: Princeton University Press.
—— and R. Hausmann, 2003. 'Economic development as self discovery', *Journal of Development Economics* 72.
World Bank, 2005. *Economic Growth in the 1990s: Learning from a Decade of Reform.* Washington, DC: World Bank.

Political Economy of Africa's Economic Performance in the Post-Independence Period

Robert H. Bates

Upon achieving self-government in the 1960s,[1] many states in Africa adopted authoritarian political regimes.[2] By the 1990s, many had allowed political opposition to organize and to compete in open elections. Focusing on Africa's political institutions, this chapter stresses their impact on policy choice and political stability and the impact of both on the performance of Africa's economies.

Authoritarianism

In most instances, even before becoming independent, colonial states were self-governing: while the metropolitan government presided over international relations, a prime minister, chosen in local elections, was charged with responsibility for domestic affairs. In an effort to extricate themselves from the continent, colonial governments preferred that local citizens chose their own governments; the elections were therefore competitive and contested by rival political parties. As noted by Collier (1982), however, even in the brief interval between securing self-government and achieving independence, the number of opposition parties rapidly declined. In some countries, opposition parties were suppressed; in others, they merged with the ruling party. In the mid-1960s, coups became more common. And by the end of the first decade of independence, over 60% of the states of Africa were governed by authoritarian political regimes (Fig. 1).

In their analysis of Africa's economic performance 1960–2000, Ndulu et al. (2008) stress the impact of government policies and, in particular, of their adoption of 'anti-growth' policy regimes. The most common of these were 'control regimes.' Governments

---

[1] Conventionally, 1960 is taken as marking the end of colonial rule. Some countries—Liberia, Sudan, South Africa, and Guinea—gained independence earlier; some in southern Africa, a decade later.
[2] For present purposes, a country is considered authoritarian if ruled by a military regime or by a civilian regime in which opposition parties are banned from contesting national elections.

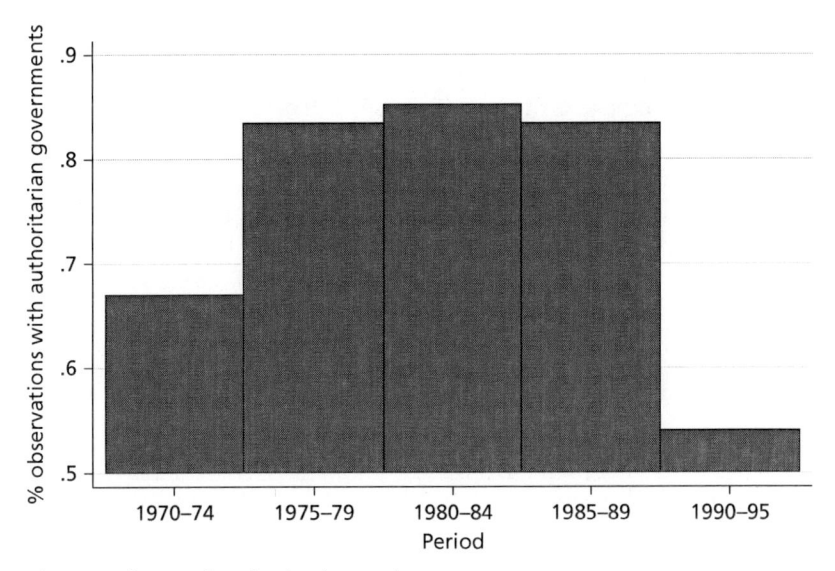

Figure 1. The prevalance of authoritarian regimes

that impose control regimes, Ndulu et al. write, seek to allocate resources politically rather than through the market. They dictate the interest and exchange rates and, by regulating markets for commodities and factors of production, the prices faced by consumers and firms. Because the success of such measures depends upon the separation of domestic from foreign markets, governments that implement control regimes often ration foreign exchange, license exports and imports, and erect tariff barriers. Governments that adopt control regimes tend also to favour public ownership of commercial and financial institutions as well as manufacturing firms (Bates 2008a). By the 1970s, the majority of African governments had adopted such policies (Fig. 2).

Ndulu (2008) argues that the adoption of these policies was motivated in part by the 'climate of opinion' at the time, a climate influenced by socialist models of development and the widespread belief that governments could secure the growth of industry and higher rates of economic growth than could markets. The choice of policies proved costly, however: Collier and O'Connell (2008) and Ndulu (2008) find that the movement from growth-oriented policies ('syndrome free', in their language) to control regimes lowered the expected annual rate of economic growth in Africa by roughly 1.6 percentage points in the post-independence period.

By the mid-1970s, the failure of such policies was evident. One reason was the high level of taxation that such policies inflicted upon agriculture, Africa's largest industry (World Bank 1995). As confirmed by recent World Bank studies of agricultural pricing policies, throughout the second half of the 20th century, Africa's governments imposed the most adverse economic policies of those in any region of the developing world.

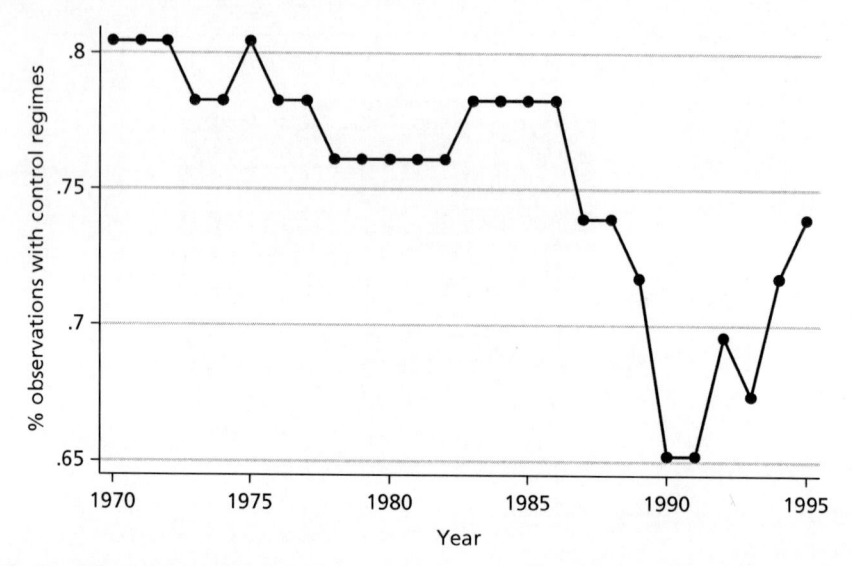

Figure 2. Prevalence of control regimes

Indicative is Figure 3, which records the relative rates of assistance (RRA) to agriculture as opposed to industry. The index is based upon the degree to which government policies generate domestic prices that depart from world prices in the two sectors. Any index above 0 suggests a bias in favour of agriculture; those below 0, a bias in favour of industry. Overvaluation of the exchange rate, taxes on exports, the protection of manufactures from competition—such measures served to shift relative prices against farmers, thus weakening incentives for them to expend effort or to invest capital in farming.

While Ndulu's argument (2008) helps to account for the initial choice of control regimes, the question remains: in the face of clear evidence that such policies were not working, why did governments continue to impose them?

An answer lies in the nature of African political institutions. One reason was the relationship between political structures and policy choices. There appears to have been an 'elective affinity' between authoritarian politics and the choice of control regimes. The source of this relationship lies in the underlying politics: the struggle among organized interests to use political power to redistribute income.

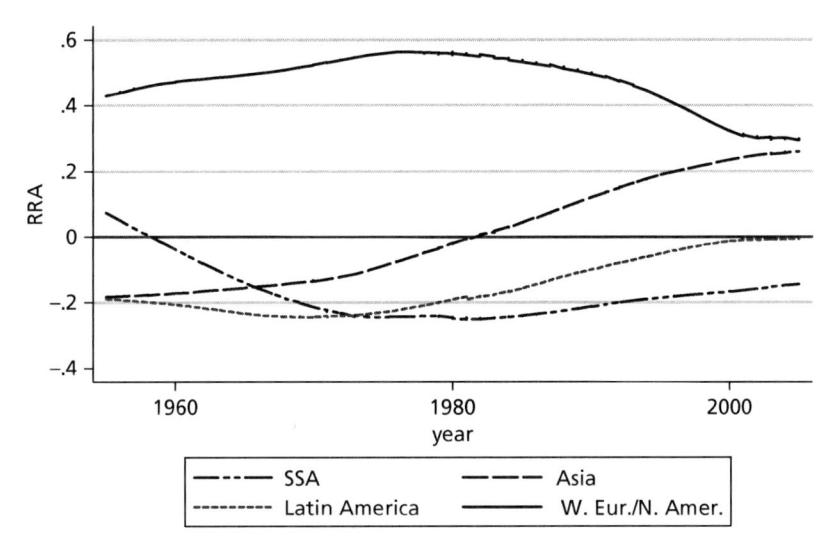

Figure 3. Regional differences in government policy
Source: (Bates and Block 2010)

Interest group politics

While not overt, political competition pervades even authoritarian regimes. Rather than open competition between political parties, however, competition takes the form of rivalry between organized interests.

Given Africa's poverty and the composition of its economies, the political struggles naturally focused on the extraction of resources from agriculture. And in this rivalry, the difference in the costs and benefits of political mobilization favoured urban and industrial interests over those from farming.

Africa's economies are poor. Given Engels' law, Africa's consumers therefore demand low food prices. As with other poor economies, Africa's are largely agrarian; a small percentage of its people and economic activity lodge in town. Given that the rural population was broadly spread and the urban population concentrated, the costs of organizing were higher for rural than for urban dwellers. As in other developing economies, the government policies promoted high levels of industrial concentration in industry (Little, Scitovsky, and Scott 1970; Lal 1983). Given that farms are small relative to the market and firms are not, the private incentives to organize politically were therefore higher in towns. The nature of the preferences and the incentives to organize thus favoured the mobilization of urban and industrial over rural and agricultural interests. The result was the creation of a narrow but organized political base that checked attempts to alter government policies that favoured the urban sector (Bates 1981).

Political change

While Africa's authoritarian regimes thus generated a political base prepared to defend the political and economic bias in favour of industry, economic realities did what political incentives could not: they penetrated and eroded the authoritarian political settlement. The policies were not sustainable. If only because exports were highly taxed, Africa's economies generated less foreign exchange than they consumed; to make good the difference, they had to borrow; and by the early 1980s, Africa's creditors began to probe the causes of Africa's economic decline. In doing so, they confronted the question: why would governments knowingly choose policies that inflicted economic harm? The reason, they concluded, was that the interests of Africa's governments stood apart from those of the people they governed. To align the interests of the governments with those of society, they sought not just policy change but also political reform. They therefore sought to render governments accountable. While calling for political accountability, those abroad were echoing the demands of an increasing number of Africa's own citizens. Given that governments depended on taxes on trade, the recession of the 1980s led to a decline in demand for Africa's exports and thus in government revenues. The resultant decay of the public services fuelled political discontent. And when governments could not pay their employees, or debased the currency in order to do so, public employees and those they served began to defect from the ranks of the government's core constituency. They began to demand the reform of political institutions, such that they could openly oppose—and politically displace—those in power.

For decades, bilateral donors and international agencies had criticized the policies of Africa's governments. But under the pressure of the Western governments that provided their capital, these agencies had repeatedly renewed their lines of credit. With the end of the Cold War, however, Western governments no longer felt the need to bid for the support of Africa's authoritarian regimes. To secure further aid, Africa's governments needed to reform, legalizing opposition parties and reintroducing electoral competition.

The consequences

As indicated in Figure 1, in the 1990s, Africa's political institutions changed: whereas in the 1970s and 1980s, 85% of the governments had suppressed open political competition, in the 1990s, 50% were chosen in elections in which opposition parties had openly campaigned. As indicated in Figure 3, in the 1990s, governments altered their policy choices (for the sample, see Table 1). Control regimes gave way to 'syndrome free' policies, i.e. policies that sought to achieve economic growth and to accommodate to the forces of the market (Ndulu et al. 2008). A major reason for the change in policy was the change in political institutions. In countries where the vast majority of the citizens lived in the countryside, when campaigning for votes, those competing for power would face strong political incentives to endorse policies that favoured, rather than harmed, the interests of farmers.

As indicated by Bates (2008b), one of the unintended by-products was increased political violence. Initially, authoritarians, believing themselves popular, surrendered to pressures for reform. As evidence mounted that few would survive the transition to a competitive political regime, others bridled at making the transition. This was particularly the case when their prior brutality gave them reason to fear subsequent reprisals, should they lose power. The threat of the loss of office thus induced higher levels of political repression, leading in many cases to open conflict and the breakdown of political order.

Table 1. Countries in the sample

1. Angola	24. Madagascar
2. Benin	25. Malawi
3. Botswana	26. Mali
4. Burkina Faso	27. Mauritania
5. Burundi	28. Mauritius
6. Cameroon	29. Mozambique
7. Cape Verde	30. Namibia
8. Central Africa Republic	31. Niger
9. Chad	32. Nigeria
10. Comoros	33. Rwanda
11. Congo, Republic	34. Sao Tome and Principe
12. Cote d'Ivoire	35. Senegal
13. Djibouti	36. Seychelles
14. Equatorial Guinea	37. Sierra Leone
15. Ethiopia	38. Somalia
16. Gabon	39. Sudan
17. The Gambia	40. Swaziland
18. Ghana	41. Tanzania
19. Guinea	42. Togo
20. Guinea-Bissau	43. Uganda
21. Kenya	44. Dem. Rep. of Congo
22. Lesotho	45. Zambia
23. Liberia	46. Zimbabwe

Note: South Africa omitted because of its distinctive political history and economic structure.

Research by Collier and O'Connell (2008) identifies political conflict as the most pernicious of the anti-growth syndromes; by their calculations, its onset generates a two percentage point decline in the rate of economic growth. The turmoil that accompanied the shift in political institutions was thus costly, further lowering the rate of Africa's economic growth.

Conclusion

Looming behind this discussion is the possibility that political structures and policy choices are jointly determined by other variables, such as ethnic diversity (as in Easterly and Levine 1997), regional inequality (as in Azam 2008), or resource abundance (as in Collier and Gunning 1999). In his research, Bates (2008b) finds little relationship between ethnic diversity and the choice of institutions; while he finds some evidence to suggest that military coups are launched by elites from poorer regions, he finds no evidence of a relationship between the value of natural resources and the type of political regime.

In the last decade, Africa has prospered, with the rate of growth of real GDP averaging over 4% per annum. While the contribution of policy reform has yet to be identified, it is clear that factors outside of Africa, and in particular the growth of the Asian economies, account for a major portion of this economic revival. Research by Bates (2008b) and Remmer (2009) suggests that economic prosperity generates a bias in favour of incumbents. It stabilizes authoritarian regimes and increases support for those in office in democratic systems. In response, in times of prosperity, incumbents became popular and therefore vulnerable to the temptation to prolong their time in office. In keeping with this pattern in recent years, ten heads of state have attempted to remove constitutional limitations on succession to office, seven successfully. This trend—plus the efforts of incumbents to rig elections in Malawi, Kenya, and Nigeria—provides troubling signs of a possible return to authoritarian forms of politics.

REFERENCES

Azam, J.-P., 2008. 'The political geography of redistribution', in Ndulu et al. (2008).
Bank, W., 1981. *Accelerated Development in Sub-Saharan Africa: An Agenda for Action.* Washington, DC: World Bank.
Bates, R. H., 1981. *Markets and States in Tropical Africa.* Berkeley: University of California Press.
—— 2008a. 'Domestic interests and control regimes', in Ndulu et al. (2008).
—— 2008b. *When Things Fell Apart: State Failure in Late Century Africa.* New York: Cambridge University Press.

—— and S. A. Block, 2010. 'Agricultural Distortions', in Kym Anderson, ed. *The Political Economy of Agricultural Development*. New York: Cambridge University Press.

Collier, P., and J. W. Gunning, 1999. 'Why has Africa grown slowly?', *Journal of Economic Perspectives* 13.3, 3–22.

—— and S. A. O'Connell, 2008. 'Opportunities and choices', in Ndulu et al. (2008).

Collier, R., 1982. *Regimes in Tropical Africa*. Berkeley: University of California Press.

Easterly, W., and R. Levine, 1997. 'Africa's growth tragedy: policies and ethnic divisions', *Quarterly Journal of Economics* 112.4, 1203–50.

Lal, D., 1983. *The Poverty of 'Development Economics'*. London: Institute of Economic Affairs.

Little, I. M. D., T. Scitovsky, and M. Scott, 1970. *Industry and Trade in Some Developing Countries*. Oxford: Oxford University Press.

Ndulu, B. J., 2008. 'The evolution of global development paradigms and their influence on African economic growth', in Ndulu et al. (2008).

Ndulu, B. J., S. A. O'Connell, R. H. Bates, P. Collier, and C. C. Saludo (eds), 2008. *The Political Economy of Economic Growth in Africa, 1960–2000*. New York: Cambridge University Press.

Remmer, K., 2009. 'The political consequences of economic crisis: lessons from Latin America'. Department of Political Science, Duke University.

World Bank, 1995. *A Continent in Transition*. Washington, DC: World Bank, Africa Division.

Thematic Perspectives
Human and Social Development

Poverty and Inequality in Sub-Saharan Africa

Erik Thorbecke

Sub-Saharan Africa (SSA) is the only region in the developing world, with the exception of Eastern Europe and Central Asia, where the proportion of the poor has not declined between 1981 and 2005 and where the absolute number of poor actually increased significantly. It is also a region that includes many countries characterized by extremely high income inequality. Before scrutinizing poverty and inequality trends, it is essential to confront the data problem. The World Bank's 'PovCalNet' data set used here is based on official statistics provided by the statistical offices of the member countries. Even though it is the most comprehensive and internally consistent data set available on poverty and inequality, at the country level, it is particularly incomplete in its coverage of SSA and the World Bank apparently undertakes only a minimum of quality control.

With these qualifications in mind, Table 1 summarizes the poverty trends between 1981 and 2005 for the main regions in terms of the headcount ratio based on the $1.25 international poverty line. It can be seen that the proportion of poor in the developing world, as a whole, was halved from 52 to 25.7% during this period. While all other regions—except for Eastern Europe—succeeded in reducing the proportion of poor, there was no progress in SSA, where half the population remained below the poverty line in 2005—the same level as in 1981. Table 1 (bottom panel) shows that the declining overall poverty incidence trend in the third world from 1.9 billion to 1.4 billion was not shared by SSA, where the total number of poor almost doubled from 202 million to 384 million throughout the same time-span.

Historically, income inequality in SSA has been among the highest in the world. However there is some evidence that income inequality has declined somewhat between the mid-1990s and the mid-2000s. Out of the 27 SSA countries in Table 2 for which comparative data were available, 12 reported a drop, 6 indicated a rise, and 9 reported no change in their Gini coefficients.[1] The combination of initial endemic poverty, high inequality, and low growth has been lethal to the achievement of poverty reduction—increasingly accepted as the primary objective of socioeconomic development.

---

[1] A change of less than 5% in the base year (mid-1990s) Gini coefficients is assumed to represent no change in inequality.

Table 1. Poverty headcount index and number of poor by region, using International Poverty Line of $1.25 a day

Headcount index

Region	1981	1984	1987	1990	1993	1996	1999	2002	2005
East Asia and Pacific	78.8	67.0	54.4	56.0	51.2	37.1	35.5	29.6	17.9
of which China	84.0	69.4	54.0	60.2	53.7	36.4	35.6	28.4	15.9
Eastern Europe and Central Asia	1.6	1.2	1.0	1.5	3.8	4.5	5.4	5.6	5.0
Latin America and Caribbean	12.3	13.9	12.4	10.7	10.8	11.5	11.6	10.1	8.2
Middle East and North Africa	8.6	6.8	6.9	5.4	5.2	5.3	5.8	4.7	4.6
South Asia	59.4	55.6	54.1	51.1	46.1	46.9	44.1	43.8	40.3
of which India	50.8	55.5	53.6	51.3	49.4	46.6	44.8	43.0	41.6
Sub-Saharan Africa	50.8	54.7	53.4	54.9	54.8	57.5	56.4	52.7	50.4
Total	52.0	47.1	41.8	41.6	38.9	34.8	33.7	31.0	25.7

Source: Chen and Ravallion (2008).

Number of poor by region (millions)

Region	1981	1984	1987	1990	1993	1996	1999	2002	2005
East Asia and Pacific	1,087.6	968.8	826.2	893.4	851.7	642.2	635.7	543.9	336.9
of which China	835.1	719.9	585.7	683.2	632.7	442.8	446.7	363.2	207.7
Eastern Europe and Central Asia	6.6	5.0	4.3	7.0	17.8	21.1	25.7	26.7	23.9
Latin America and Caribbean	44.9	54.3	51.4	46.7	49.7	56.0	58.8	53.7	45.1
Middle East and North Africa	14.9	12.9	14.3	12.2	12.7	13.7	16.0	13.5	14.0
South Asia	548.3	542.3	568.2	572.3	549.5	593.1	588.9	616.1	595.5
of which India	420.5	416.0	428.0	435.5	444.3	441.8	447.2	460.5	455.8
Sub-Saharan Africa	202.0	237.1	252.8	283.7	305.9	347.8	370.0	373.2	384.2
Total	1,904.3	1,825.8	1,717.7	1,815.5	1,787.2	1,673.8	1,695.1	1,627.0	1,399.6

Source: Chen and Ravallion (2008).

Bourguignon (2004) argues cogently that 'the real challenge to establishing a development strategy for reducing poverty lies in the interactions between distribution and growth, and not in the relationship between poverty and growth on one hand and poverty and inequality, on the other, which are essentially arithmetic'. It is therefore essential to spell out explicitly those interactions and identify the mechanisms through which they operate.

Two conflicting theoretical strands underlie the causal chain from income and wealth inequality to growth: first, the traditional (classical) approach and secondly, the 'new' political economy of development theories. Whilst the former emphasizes the growth-enhancing effects of income inequality and wealth inequality through the saving-enhancing effects as well as the existence of investment indivisibilities and incentive effects,[2] the latter links greater inequality to reduced growth through various channels such as the diffusion of political and social instability leading to greater uncertainty and lower investment; unproductive rent-seeking activities, high transaction costs, and increased insecurity of property rights.[3]

Fosu (2009) showed rather conclusively that the impact of income growth on poverty reduction is a decreasing function of initial inequality for all three FGT poverty measures. In addition, the income-growth elasticity in the SSA region is only one third of that in the rest of the developing world, so that accelerating growth would bring forth a much smaller reduction in poverty than would be the case in non-SSA. In many African countries, high levels of initial income inequality dampen the impact of growth on poverty reduction. The main policy implication of these findings is that to achieve poverty reduction in most SSA nations would require significantly larger declines in inequality or accelerations in growth than elsewhere in the world.

Ndulu et al. (2008) identified a number of anti-growth syndromes which contributed in large measure to the poor growth performance. These syndromes fall into four main groupings of government behaviour:

1. regulatory, based on reliance on controls and nationalization;
2. ethno-regional redistribution (including looting);
3. intertemporal redistribution that transfer resources from future to present; and
4. state breakdown (inability to maintain internal security).

Econometric evidence suggests that out of the 3.5% gap in per capita annual GDP growth during the period from 1960 to 2000 between the African economies and those of other developing countries, 1 percentage point could be accounted for by the constraints inherent in being a landlocked resource-scarce or resource-rich economy (by world standards Africa is unusually landlocked and resource-rich) and 2 percentage points by the presence of anti-growth syndromes.

To the extent that initial conditions differ significantly within Africa, a typology distinguishing SSA countries according to their development patterns and the ways growth, inequality, and poverty interact can contribute to a better understanding of the anatomy of growth in different parts of SSA and to the design of future development strategies appropriate to each prototype category. Among the most important features that affect the anatomy of development within and among SSA countries and regions are geographical location, resource endowment (particularly in terms of mineral and oil resources), level of development, land distribution and quality (soil fertility and, more generally, extent of how favourable or unfavourable agricultural conditions are), speed and form of structural transformation, prevailing wealth and income distribution,

---

[2] See Kaldor (1956) and Aghion, Cardi, and Garcia-Penalosa (1999).
[3] See Thorbecke and Charumilind (2002).

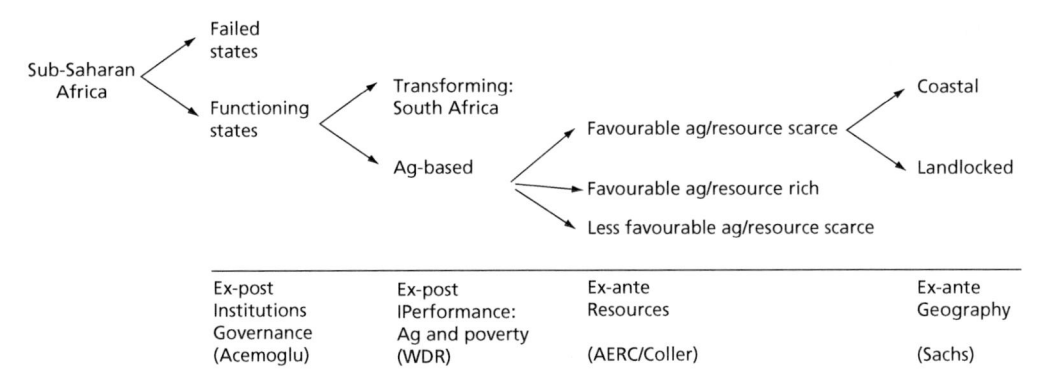

Figure 1. A hierarchical tree to derive six distinct categories of SSA countries (source: Thorbecke 2009)

historical growth pattern, extent of ethno-linguistic fragmentation and quality of governance and institutions.

Thorbecke (2009) in an attempt to capture the different anatomies of growth derived a growth-inequality–poverty typology of SSA countries.[4] The classification relies on a hierarchical tree based on the use of four criteria; first, the *ex post* quality of institutions that allows a breakdown between failed states and functioning states (Acemoglu, Johnson, and Robinson 2004); secondly, the *ex post* structure of production and the importance of agriculture in overall growth and poverty reduction (World Bank 2008); thirdly, the role of resources and whether a country is resource scarce or resource-rich (Ndulu et al. 2007; 2008); and, finally, at the lowest level of aggregation, the role of geography and whether a country is coastal or landlocked (Gallup and Sachs 1998). Figure 1 illustrates the above taxonomic process. Six relatively distinct categories of SSA countries were identified following these criteria: Table 2 gives the list of countries in these six groups and provides information on current GDP per capita, past and recent GDP per capita growth performance, poverty and inequality trends, the income growth/poverty elasticity, and a vulnerability index.[5]

The key characteristics of each group, including its political economy history as reflected by the prevalence of different combinations of anti-growth syndromes, are discussed briefly next, to help identify the major components of the specific development strategy best suited to the underlying conditions prevailing in each category of countries.

---

[4] The discussion that follows draws on Thorbecke (2009).
[5] The vulnerability index measures the extent to which countries have a capacity to protect themselves against price increases on the international market and to organize policy response to protect their poor. For details see Kamgnia (2009). Developing countries are classified in three categories representing, respectively 'High Vulnerability', 'Average Vulnerability', and 'Low Vulnerability'.

Table 2. Typology of SSA countries: per capita income, growth, poverty headcount ratios, income/poverty elasticities, and vulnerability index

Region	$ppp 2000	GDP (%) 61–00	GDP (%) 2000–06	HC ratio mid-90s	HC ratio 2000s	Gini mid-90s	Gini 2000s	Survey years 1st	Survey years Last	I/P elast.	Vuln. index
1. South African region											
South Africa	1,836	0.9	2.9	21	26	57	58	1995	2000	.93	Low
Namibia	3,230	0.6	3.4	49		74		1993		.64	Low
Lesotho	868			48	43	63	53	1995	2002	.83	Avg
Swaziland	566			79	63	61	51	1994	2000	1.05	Low
Botswana	(8,700)	6.3			(32)		(63)			.87	Avg
2. Failed states											
Somalia	(600)										
Sudan	(1,900)										
Zimbabwe	(500)									1.06	Avg
Chad	495				62		40		2002		High
DR Congo	556				59		44		2005		
Côte d'Ivoire	870	0.6	–1.5	21	23	37	48	1995	2002	1.09	Avg
CAR	(700)									.87	High
Equ. Guinea	444			37	70	40	43	1994	2003		
3. Coastal resource-poor: more favourable agriculture											
Benin	633	0.6	0.7		47		39		2003	1.26	
Ghana	520	–0,2	3.2	39	30	41	43	1998	2005	1.23	Avg
Kenya	580	1,2	1.5	29	20	42	48	1994	2005	1.19	Avg
Gambia	492			67	34	50	47	1998	2003		
Togo	350	0.9	–0.4		39		34		2006		High
Guinea Bissau	581			52	49	48	36	1993	2002		
Tanzania	270	1.8	3.9	73	89	34	35	1991	2000	1.33	
Mozambique	439	–0.4	6.2	81	75	44	47	1996	2002	1.11	High
Senegal	802	–0.2	2.1	54	34	41	39	1994	2005	1.22	High
4. Landlocked resource-poor: more favourable agriculture											
Burkina Faso	562	1.3	2.6	71	57	51	40	1994	2003	1.25	Avg
Ethiopia	616	0.4	3.7	61	39	40	30	1995	2005	1.41	Avg
Malawi	409	1.4	1.1	83	74	50	39	1997	2004	1.26	High
Uganda	632	1.4	2.2	64	52	37	43	1996	2005	1.14	Avg
5. Resource-rich: more favourable agriculture											
Cameroon	927	0.7	1.7	51	33	47	46	1996	2001	1.16	
Sierra Leone	614	–1.4	8.6	63	53	63	43	1989	2003	.84	Avg
Angola	755	–1.2	8.3		53		59		2000		
Rep Congo	648	1.3	1.5		54		47		2005		
Zambia	517	–1.3	3.2	62	64	50	51	1996	2004	1.05	High
Nigeria	474	0.3	3.4	69	64	47	43	1996	2004	1.21	High

6. Less favourable agriculture											
Comoros	1133				46		64		2004		
Burundi	348	0.2	–0,6	86	81	42	33	1998	2006	1.20	
Niger	498	–1.7	0.3	78	66	42	44	1994	2005	1.13	
Mali	590	–0.3	2.7?	86	51	51	39	1994	2006	1.24	Avg
Rwanda	405	–0.3	2.7?	63	77	29	47	1984	2000	1.12	High
Madagascar	538	1.2	1.5	73	68	46	47	1993	2005	1.11	High
Mauritania	1,060	1.3	2.1	23	21	37	39	1995	2000	1.26	
Gabon	1,802				5		41		2005		
Cape Verde	1,474				21		51		2001	1.05	Avg

Columns: 1, 4, 5, 6, 7, 8, 9: World Bank. PovCalNet Data Base except Col. 1 in parenthesis: country estimates.
Column 2: Ndulu et al. (2008).
Column 3: World Bank, World Development Tables.
Column 10: income/poverty elasticities: Fosu (2009).
Column 11: vulnerability index (for definition see text): Kamgnia (2009).
Source: Adapted from Thorbecke (2009).

Failed states

A common characteristic of these countries is that they are plagued by a large degree of fragmentation and fractionalization along a combination of ethnic, religious, geographical, and political lines. These failed states suffer from a high dosage of most of the anti-growth syndromes described earlier, and epitomize more particularly the effects of state breakdown accelerated by ethnoregional and intertemporal redistribution. It is not at all clear what can be done to provide the impetus to change the status quo from within those societies. Probably the most effective potential action will have to be external pressure applied by the African Union and the world community for reform—including moral suasion, sanctions, and other actions exerted by the ex-colonial powers that may still have some influence over their previous colonies. Until a threshold of political and economic stability is achieved, it would be fruitless to suggest suitable strategies except the restoration of stability and law and order.

The South African region

The determining criteria for the second category of countries in our typology (i.e. South Africa and neighbouring countries—Namibia, Swaziland, Botswana, and Lesotho) are geographical and institutional. These economies together form the South African Customs Union (SACU). Their major socioeconomic characteristics are relatively high (by SSA standards) per capita incomes, extremely high income inequality, low income/poverty elasticities, and low vulnerability indices (see Table 2). The growth and development performance of the three adjacent economies depends largely on the performance of the South African economy. The massive relative size of the latter dwarfs that of these countries and can act as a powerful magnet and growth pole within SACU —further enhanced by the complementary nature of the resource endowments of South Africa compared to the three bordering countries. The fact that Lesotho and Swaziland were free of anti-growth syndromes throughout the post-independence period augurs well and suggests that the neighbouring effect can act as the necessary growth engine. Clearly a successful development strategy for this South African group will require a major effort to reduce inequality on at least two grounds—first, because it would be likely to accelerate future growth (high inequality acts as brake on growth) and secondly, because a growth pattern that results in high inequality and poverty incidence cannot be equated with development.

The case for including Botswana in this group is debatable. Botswana has been one of the fastest-growing countries in the world in the last forty years. Good governance and a consistent macroeconomic policy prevented it from falling prey to the anti-growth syndromes. Even though Botswana is less competitive than South Africa and faces higher transaction costs of transportation and utilities, a case can be made that through careful strategic coordination within SACU the region can move successfully towards industrialization.

Coastal countries, resource-scarce with more favourable agricultural potential

The next group consists of the coastal countries endowed with more favourable agricultural potential—including on the west coast, Senegal, Ghana, Benin, The Gambia, Togo, and Guinea Bissau; and on the east coast, Kenya, Tanzania, and Mozambique.[6] These are low-income countries with per capita income in the mid-2000s ranging between $340 and $750. This group displays less poverty, on average, than other categories. The headcount ratio is less than 50% except in Mozambique and Tanzania. The range of inequality (Gini coefficient) is also relatively low by African standards—0.34 to 0.48, which translates into relatively high income/poverty elasticities and vulnerability indices (see Table 2). Coastal resource-poor economies were most strongly exposed to the regulatory regime which can be explained by three driving forces: ideology, the rent-generating nature of controls, and the prevailing regional wealth inequality (Ndulu et al. 2008). Under the impetus of structural adjustment and the forces of globalization, this group of countries managed to succeed in the transition from

---

[6] Côte d'Ivoire could be added to this list once it regains a threshold of political stability.

socialist and Marxist regimes to more liberalized regimes. These coastal economies would benefit much from reducing trade barriers and transaction costs in order to embark on export-competing strategies. A major investment in infrastructure (network of roads and improved harbour facilities) appears to be a precondition. There are at least three potential export options open to them: traditional agricultural exports, non-traditional agricultural exports, and non-agricultural labour-intensive manufactures.

Since most of these economies are characterized by a dual agriculture, successful development strategies require concentrating on both subsectors—avoiding giving too high a priority to export crops.

Landlocked countries, resource-scarce with more favourable agricultural potential

Landlocked economies are the poorest in terms of per capita income, on average, of all the groups, and suffer from a high incidence of poverty but relatively low inequality (Gini ranging between 0.30 and 0.43. Here again, low inequality means that growth has a relatively greater impact on poverty reduction (manifested through high income/poverty elasticities. Ndulu et al. (2008) found a high correlation between landlockedness and poor governance—particularly ethnoregional redistribution. These countries have the most to gain from reducing transaction costs (particularly transportation costs) through infrastructure investment and regional integration with their coastal neighbours. They are at a strong comparative disadvantage when it comes to competing in international trade.

It has been estimated that landlocked economies face transport costs that on average are 50% higher than the typical coastal country. It appears that these landlocked economies would embrace regional integration schemes with their coastal neighbours. In most of these economies an increase in agricultural output will need to come from land intensification (higher yields) rather than through land expansion or extensification (cultivating new land areas) as in the past.

Resource-rich countries with more favourable agricultural potential

The dismal growth performance of the resource-rich countries until the turn of the century is a good illustration of the resource curse (over a 40 years period, per capita GDP fell at an annual rate of more than 1% in Sierra Leone, Angola, and Zambia, as Table 2 shows). This group displays high poverty and inequality. Of all SSA country categories, resource-rich economies experienced the highest exposure to the intertemporal redistribution syndrome. Resource rents are an attractive source of revenue for non-representative regimes, absolving them of the need to provide effective public services in return for tax revenue (Collier and Gunning 2008). Nigeria and the Democratic Republic of Congo are the most typical examples of how easy access to resources bred autocratic regimes with a devastating impact on socioeconomic development. The exploitation of mineral resources relies on a capital-intensive technology, and occurs typically within an enclave with relatively very few backward or forward linkages to the rest of the economy. This means that, structurally speaking, growth driven by this sector, with no government intervention, will provide very little poverty alleviation in the rural areas. The two key desirable components of a development strategy in this group are, first, to establish a governance structure that funnels resource earnings into other sectors and, secondly, to follow a strict macroeconomic policy to avoid the Dutch Disease. In the same way that an intersectoral transfer from agriculture to the rest of the economy (in the form of an agricultural surplus) can contribute to the growth of the industrial sector, a transfer from the resource sector to agriculture and other sectors can have a major impact on development and poverty reduction.

Countries with less favourable agricultural potential

The final category in the present typology consists of the economies facing less favourable agricultural potential. This is a miscellaneous group consisting of four very poor landlocked and resource-poor countries (Burundi, Niger, Mali, and Rwanda); three coastal, resource-poor states (Comoros, Madagascar, and Cape Verde); and two coastal, resource-rich countries (Mauritania and Gabon). The first sub-group is facing the worst initial development characteristics and the third sub-group the best, their initial conditions being both coastal and resource–rich. It is somewhat of a stretch to group these countries together based exclusively on the lack of agricultural potential. The only possible rationale is that agriculture, while still by far the most important sector, will face greater obstacles operating as the main growth engine in this group. Yet at the early stage of development these countries find themselves in, they have no choice but to attempt to accelerate agricultural growth by whatever means available. Potential pay-off for investment in agricultural research could be one such means, particularly if it were undertaken regionally—possibly as part of a regional integration process—and its benefits spread across borders.

REFERENCES

Acemoglu, D., S. Johnson, and J. A. Robinson, 2004. 'Institutions as the fundamental cause of long term growth', CEPR Discussion Paper 4458, London.

Aghion, P., and P. Bolton, 1997. 'A theory of trickle-down growth and development', *Review of Economic Studies* 64.2, 151–72.

Aghion P., E. Cardi, and C. Garcia-Penalosa, 1999. 'Inequality and economic growth: the perspective of the new growth theories', *Journal of Economic Literature* 37, 1615–60.

Bourguignon, F., 2004. 'The poverty–growth–inequality triangle', paper presented at the Indian Council for Research on International Economic Relations.

Collier, P. and J. W. Gunning, 2008. 'Sacrificing the future: intertemporal strategies and their implications for growth', in Ndulu et al. (2008: ch. 5).

Fosu, A. K., 2009. 'Inequality and the impact of growth on poverty: comparative evidence for sub-Saharan Africa', *Journal of Development Studies* 45.5, 726–45.

Gallup, J. L., and J. Sachs, 1998. 'Geography and economic growth', paper prepared for the Annual Bank Conference on Development Economics, Washington, DC.

Kaldor, N., 1956. 'Alternative theories of distribution', *Review of Economic Studies* 23.2, 83–100.

Kamgnia, B., 2009. 'Global food price shocks: causes, consequences and policy options in Africa', paper presented at the AERC Plenary Session, Mombasa, June.

Ndulu, B., S. O'Connell, J. P. Azam, R. Bates, A. K. Fosu, J. W. Gunning, and D. Njinkeu (eds), 2007. *The Political Economy of Economic Growth in Africa, 1960–2000*, vol. 1. Cambridge: Cambridge University Press.

—— —— —— —— —— —— —— (eds), 2008. *The Political Economy of Economic Growth in Africa, 1960–2000*, vol. 2. Cambridge: Cambridge University Press.

Thorbecke, E., 2009. 'The anatomy of growth and development in sub-Saharan Africa', paper prepared for the African Economic Research Consortium Collaborative Project on Growth and Poverty.

—— and C. Charumilind, 2002. 'Economic inequality and its socioeconomic impact', *World Development* 30.9, 1477–95.

World Bank, 2008. World Development Report: *Agriculture and Development*. Washington, DC.

Meeting Africa's Health Challenges

David E. Sahn

Africa's health challenge in the global context

Available statistics present a uniformly discouraging picture of health status in Africa, especially when compared to other regions. During the 1960s, Africa's infant mortality rate (IMR) of 154 deaths per 1,000 live births was similar to that of the Middle East and South Asia (Table 1). East Asia, too, had a high IMR of 133. Over the next few decades, the rate of improvement in Africa was markedly slower than other regions, especially East Asia, where dramatic drops in IMR were noted. Similarly disappointing is the fact that Africa's low life expectancy in the 1960s, in the 40–50-year range, remains virtually unchanged while other regions have shown sustained improvements.

Other indicators of health status paint a similarly bleak picture. Women are at heightened risk because of their reproductive roles. Given the high fertility rates, the astounding implication is that over a woman's lifetime, the risk of maternal death in sub-Saharan Africa is 1 in 16, compared with 1 in 2,800 in the developed world, and 1 in 46 in the region with the next highest risk, south-central Asia (Meyerhoefer and Sahn 2008).

Figure 1 provides part of the answer why health status in Africa continues to lag so far behind the rest of the world. The curve plots the relationship between GDP per capita and life expectancy (Strauss and Thomas 2008). First, it illustrates the strength of this exponential relationship, especially at lower levels of income. Second, an asymptote is quickly reached at an income of around $1,500, where life expectancy tends to range between 70 and 80 years. Third, virtually all the countries with low GDP and low life expectancy are in Africa. By implication, improved incomes in Africa will yield large returns in terms of health.

Fourth, the curve has shifted upward over time. A country in 1930 would need an income level approximately 2.6 times higher than in 1960 to achieve the same life expectancy among people living to 40 years of age; and 84% of the increase in life expectancy between 1930 and 1960 was due to factors other than levels of income (Preston 1975).

The dramatic upward shift in the Preston curve is in part due to improvements in health technology and efficiencies in the delivery of health services, as well as to related

Table 1. Infant mortality rate[a] (number of deaths before age 1 per 1,000 live births) and life expectancy[b] in developing countries, 1960–2005

Region	1960		1970		1980		1990		2001		2005	
	IMR	LE[c]	IMR	LE	IMR	LE[c]	IMR	LE	IMR	LE	IMR	LE
Sub-Saharan Africa	154	40	145	44	120	48	112	50	107	48	101	46
Middle East/North Africa	154	46	128	52	91	57	59	63	47	67	43	69
Latin America and the Caribbean	105	54	86	60	61	62	43	68	28	70	26	72
South Asia	146	46	130	48	115	60	89	58	70	62	63	64
East Asia	133	46	84	58	55	60	43	66	33	69	26	71
East Europe/Former Soviet Union	76		68	66	55		44	68	30	69	29	67

[a] Source: UNICEF (2007) http://www.childinfo.org/areas/childmortality/infantdata.php
[b] UNICEF (State of World Children Reports 1998–2007)
[c] http://earthtrends.wri.org/text/population-health/variable-379.html (their source is UNICEF and WHO; data tally with 90, 00, 05, 0)

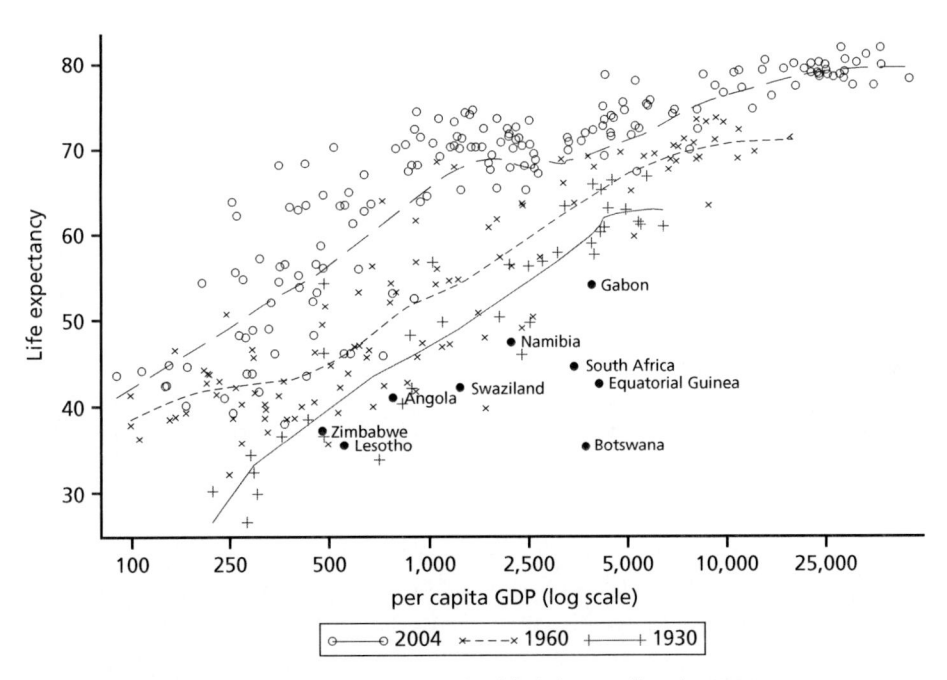

Figure 1. Life expectancy and GDP per capita, highlighting outliers in 2004

Source: Reprinted from Strauss, J. and Thomas, D. (2008) in Schultz, T. P. and Strauss, J. (eds), Handbook of Development Economics, Volume 4, Amsterdam: North-Holland. With permission from Elsevier.

factors such as improved nutrition. This relates to the final point of considerable interest in the figure: that the greater the vertical distance below the regression line, the lower the health achievement relative to the level of income. Furthermore, African countries tend to have a lifespan that is lower than that expected, largely attributable to HIV/AIDS. In South Africa and other countries, such as Equatorial Guinea, high income inequality also likely contributes to this finding.

Modelling behaviour: production and demand for health

Beyond the association between health and income, a range of other inputs affect health status. More specifically, the health production function includes a range of both health inputs and behaviours. The former may include, for example, nutrients and health care services. Behaviours cover a wide range of possibilities, including high-risk practices such as smoking and engaging in unprotected sexual intercourse. The important point is that these inputs are a matter of choice, or at least determined by decisions of the individual. They are also a function of individual characteristics, such as gender and age, as well as available technology and environmental conditions. Finally, unobservables also affect health outcomes, such as genetics.

A large share of the research conducted by health economists has been focused on understanding the health production function and accounting for unobserved heterogeneity in order to isolate the impact of socioeconomic status and other policy variables on health outcomes. In practice, the majority of literature on production of health outcomes in Africa has been from econometric estimates based on household survey data. These studies generally employ reduced-form estimates, or other quasi-experimental designs, and have established the critical importance of incomes, health infrastructure, prices, and education in determining health outcomes.[1] In addition, the importance of intra-household decision-making processes has been highlighted in a growing literature that finds that greater bargaining power and income control among women generally contributes to better health outcomes for children and for pregnant and lactating women.

Recently, a great deal of attention has been placed on evaluating the impact of intervention programmes on health outcomes in Africa that follow two categories. The first are quasi-experimental and instrumental variable studies. These are illustrated by Mwabu (2009), who shows the large impact of tetanus vaccinations in Kenya on birthweight; Thirumurthy, Zivin, and Goldstein (2008), who contributes to the growing literature regarding the effectiveness of anti-retroviral therapy for treating HIV/AIDS;

---

[1] See, e.g. Haddad et al. (2003).

and Linnemayr and Alderman (2008), who find an impact of an integrated package of health inputs on the anthropometric status of children in three regions in rural Senegal.

The second category of studies are randomized control studies which, while fewer in number, are considered by many to be the gold standard for proving causation, despite problems of external validity and being limited in terms of the questions that can be asked. There are important lessons for Africa from health experiments that have been undertaken recently. Examples include the study by Miguel and Kremer (2004) of a deworming programme in schools in Kenya which shows the treatment group had substantially better health outcomes; the work of Björkman and Svensson (2009) that shows the positive impact on infant mortality in Uganda of interventions designed to improve health institutions; and evaluation by Cohen and Dupas (2007) showing the effectiveness in Africa of distribution of bed nets as a strategy to control malaria.

Finally, inputs into the health production function at a given time affect not just contemporaneous health outcomes, but those across the entire lifecycle (Strauss and Thomas 2008). One particularly interesting area of work in emerging literature shows the importance to health and economic impact of health early in life, even *in utero*, over the life course (Barker 1994). This finding focuses attention on the importance of improving the health of mothers and their newborns through the provision of reproductive health services. Failure to do so will not only increase maternal morbidity and mortality and prenatal death, but will also be associated with higher prevalence of chronic diseases like diabetes and heart disease.

Demand for health services

While research continues on how health production functions and determinants can assist in identifying causes of health status and potential responses in terms of the provision of health care, there remains the important issue of health-seeking demand behaviour of consumers. Sahn, Younger, and Genicot (2003) find that consumers in Tanzania are highly responsive to the price of health care; this responsiveness is greater for individuals at the lower end of the income distribution. They also find a high degree of substitution between public and private care in response to changes in price. These results complement earlier research from Africa, including evidence from Ghana (Waddington and Enyimayew 1990), Kenya (Mwabu 1989), and Swaziland (Yoder 1989). Another important story from Tanzania and other studies is the importance of quality and availability of doctors/nurses, drugs, and the clinic environment, on demand.

Recent experimental work on user fees such as Miguel and Kremer's (2007) Kenya study of deworming drugs also indicates that user fees dramatically reduce utilization. Hoffmann, Barrett, and Just (2009) show that mosquito nets distributed to targeted households unlikely or unable to purchase the nets will generally not be resold, even in an artificially frictionless market. The implication is that there is little 'external leakage' to the non-poor, and that the free distribution will not interfere with the commercial market for net distribution. A high price elasticity of demand for water purification tablets was also found by Ashraf, Berry, and Shapiro (2007). The implications of this pattern of high price elasticities of demand for a range of health-related services are that there is potential for underuse of services among the poor, that low-cost treatments can be promoted by low-cost incentives, and that local knowledge and beliefs need to be addressed to overcome this seemingly adverse behaviour (Kremer and Holla 2009).

Inequalities in health

The previous discussion highlights Africa's health crisis, but overlooks the fact that health outcomes within African states are highly unequal. This in part reflects institutional failures that tend to give disproportionate voice to the rich, who for example have a greater interest in government subsidies for tertiary care that provide free and otherwise potentially costly catastrophic care. There are three important motivations for focusing on health inequality: social justice; health inequalities may contribute to public institutions that are inefficient and unequal in terms of protecting and promoting the needs of those in greatest need; and psychosocial effects of relative deprivation may represent a risk factor for poor health.

Evidence suggests that across countries in Africa, health indicators vary dramatically. Within countries, there are also dramatic differences in health outcomes by gender, location, and incomes. Generally, across the main dimensions of health, households in the lowest quintile of income distribution have health indicators twice as bad as those in the upper quintile of income distribution (Gwatkin et al. 2007).

A similar story is found in the case of access to, and utilization of, various types of health services such as pre-natal care and vaccinations (Gwatkin et al. 2007). Sahn and Younger (2000) find that hospitals are the least progressive service in the health sector; while primary care tends to be far more progressive than hospital-based care and is also more progressive than the existing unequal distribution of income, the rich benefit disproportionately even in the case of basic health services.

Sahn and Younger (2009) also find evidence of large intra-household inequality in health outcomes in two African countries. However, they are unable to disentangle whether this is due to differences in endowment (e.g. genetics) or to issues such as intra-household inequalities in bargaining and decision-making authority.

While continued attention to health inequality is warranted, other dimensions of social arrangements such as the overall allocation of resources to health should take precedence. More specifically, greater health inequality could be achieved, on the one hand, by reducing spending on certain high-cost treatments with limited effectiveness, measured in terms of reducing age-weighted disability-adjusted life years lost. If the savings are allocated to health spending on highly efficacious preventative measures and basic services that raise the mean level of health, redistribution would be a policy worthy of pursuit. On the other hand, if the savings are instead allocated to wasteful spending in other sectors, or even to deficit reduction, so that the overall commitment of government to the healthfulness of the population is diminished, achieving greater health equality is a less worthy pursuit.

Conclusions

Africa's health challenges are daunting. Even as Africa continues to be mired in a battle against malnutrition and infectious and communicable diseases, such as malaria, tuberculosis, and HIV/AIDS, the face of premature mortality continues to evolve. Africa is in the early stages of the epidemiological transition whereby non-communicable chronic diseases are increasingly important in terms of demand for and cost of health care, as well as the cause of death. As rapid urbanization occurs, and as the nature both of food systems and of personal behaviours change, Africa now confronts the burden of dealing with non-communicable lifestyle-related disease alongside communicable diseases. Estimates of the World Health Organization (2008) indicate that in 2005, nearly 2.5 million people died of chronic disease, and this figure will rise to 28 million by 2015.

The implications for the changing nature of morbidity and early death are enormous, both in economic costs and in terms of demands for the provision of preventative and curative care. Thus, while the challenge remains of employing low-cost technologies (e.g. bed nets, condoms, oral rehydration) to control infectious, parasitic, and communicable disease, this is compounded by the emergence of degenerative, lifestyle-related disease and disabilities that are associated with even higher costs in terms of treatment and control.

■ REFERENCES

Ashraf, N., J. Berry, and J. M. Shapiro, 2007. 'Can higher prices stimulate product use? Evidence from a field experiment in Zambia', NBER Working Paper 13247, Washington, DC.

Barker, D. J. P., 1994. *Mothers, Babies and Disease in Later Life*. London: British Medical Journal Books.

Björkman, Martina, and Jakob Svensson, 2009. 'Power to the people: evidence from a randomized experiment on community-based monitoring in Uganda', *Quarterly Journal of Economics* 124.2, 735–69.

Cohen, Jessica and Pascaline Dupas, 2007. 'Free distribution or cost-sharing? Evidence from a randomized malaria prevention experiment', Brookings Global Economy and Development Working Paper 11, Washington, DC.

Gwatkin, Davidson R., Shea Rutstein, Kiersten Johnson, Eldaw Suliman, Adam Wagstaff, and Agbessi Amouzou, 2007. *Socio-Economic Differences in Health, Nutrition, and Population*. Washington, DC: World Bank.

Haddad, Lawrence, Harold Alderman, Simon Appleton, Lina Song, and Yishehac Yohannes, 2003. 'Reducing child malnutrition: how far does income growth take us?', *World Bank Economic Review* 17.1, 107–32.

Hoffmann, Vivian, Christopher B. Barrett, and David R. Just, 2009. 'Do free goods stick to poor households? Experimental evidence on insecticide treated bednets', *World Development* 37.3, 607–17.

Kremer, Michael, and Alaka Holla, 2009. 'Pricing and access: lessons from randomized evaluation in education and health', in W. Easterly and J. Cohen (eds), *What Works in Development? Thinking Big and Thinking Small*. Washington, DC: Brookings Institution Press.

Linnemayr, Sebastian, and Harold Alderman, 2008. 'Almost random: evaluating a large-scale randomized nutrition program in the presence of crossover', Policy Research Working Paper 4784, World Bank, Washington, DC.

Meyerhoefer, C., and David E. Sahn, 2008. 'The relationship between poverty and maternal morbidity and mortality in sub-Saharan Africa', Cornell Food and Nutrition Policy Program Working Paper 213, Cornell University, Ithaca, NY.

Miguel, E., and M. Kremer, 2004. 'Worms: identifying impacts on education and health in the presence of treatment externalities', *Econometrica* 72.1, 159–217.

—— —— 2007. 'The illusion of sustainability', *Quarterly Journal of Economics* 112.3, 1007–65.

Mwabu, G. M., 1989. 'Referral systems and health care seeking behaviour of patients: an economic analysis', *World Development* 17.1, 85–91.

—— 2009. 'The production of child health in Kenya: a structural model of birth weight', *Journal of African Economies* 18.2, 212–60.

Preston, S. H., 1975. 'The changing relation between mortality and level of economic development', *Population Studies* 29.2, 231–48.

Sahn, David E., and Stephen D. Younger, 2000. 'Expenditure incidence in Africa: microeconomic evidence', *Fiscal Studies* 21.3, 329–47.

—— —— 2009. 'Measuring intra-household inequality: explorations using the Body Mass Index', *Health Economics* 18.S1, S13–S36 (UNU-WIDER Special Issue on Health and Development).

—— —— and Garance Genicot, 2003. 'Demand for health care services in rural Tanzania', *Oxford Bulletin of Economics and Statistics* 65.2, 241–60.

Strauss, J., and D. Thomas, 2008. 'Health over the lifecourse', in T. P. Schultz and J. Strauss (eds), *Handbook of Development Economics*, vol. 4. Amsterdam: Elsevier/North-Holland, ch. 54.

Thirumurthy, Harsha, Joshua Graff Zivin, and Markus Goldstein, 2008. 'The economic impact of AIDS treatment labor supply in western Kenya', *Journal of Human Resources* 43.3, 511–52.

Waddington, C. J., and K. A. Enyimayew, 1990. 'A price to pay: the impact of user charges in the Volta region of Ghana', *International Journal of Health Planning and Management* 5.4, 287–312.

World Health Organization, 2008. *2008–2013 Action Plan for the Global Strategy for the Prevention and Control of Noncommunicable Diseases*. Geneva: WHO.

Yoder, R., 1989. 'Are people willing and able to pay for health services?', *Social Science and Medicine* 29.1, 35–42.

Impact of Health on Economic Outcomes

David E. Sahn

Conceptual and theoretical relationships

Health plays an important role in explaining productivity, incomes, and poverty. This applies both to effects of health on the ability to perform a wide range of productive work in the short term and to the impact of health, especially during youth and reproductive age, on the entire life course and that of future generations. This relationship has been recognized as far back as Adam Smith's *The Wealth of Nations*, in 1776 (Smith 1960). A largely theoretical body of literature on the efficiency wage hypothesis formulated by, among others, Leibenstein (1957) and Bliss and Stern (1978) revitalized interest in this theme among economists.

There are several reasons why the relationship between health and economic outcomes is of particular interest in the African context. First, health problems are most acute in Africa. Second, for a given level of poor health, the productivity consequences will be worse in areas where hard physical labour is the critical input. This characterizes rural Africa, where there is virtually no formal wage labour market and most work is directly reliant on strength and stamina.

Third, own production and self-provisioning is of great importance in most African economies. Under such circumstances, reduced levels of output (from temporary ailments and disease, for example) can contribute to large consumption shortfalls—an outcome less likely to occur in more market-oriented economies where wage employment is rare. The propensity for health shocks to have serious repercussions is increased in environments characterized by credit and insurance market failures. Under such circumstances, shocks will simultaneously exacerbate economic inefficiencies such as underinvestment in health and reduce agricultural and microenterprise capital, as limited household savings are redirected to health care costs. Absence of labour-saving technologies and institutions that provide services such as child care also worsen the impact of health-related or other exogenous shocks that heighten time constraints in the production of health, home production (e.g. care of children), and income.

The link between health and productivity is of special importance for African women, who both assume a predominant role in the production of food crops and suffer widely from various forms of gender-related discrimination. Another aspect of African women's special vulnerabilities is related to reproductive health, including the arduous demands of childbearing, which they share with women throughout the developing world. Additionally, they suffer the acute burden associated with social norms and behaviours that have resulted in women bearing the brunt of the ravages of HIV/AIDS in Africa. Women, particularly of reproductive age, also face unique health risks associated with sexual violence. Even as women are more likely to be afflicted by health and nutrition shocks, the impact goes beyond their productive role in the labour market, impacting their joint production role as caregivers for their children.

Regardless of gender, health assaults that lower productivity of workers can directly lead to a downward spiral where reduced output leads to poverty, and subsequently, to a worsening of health and nutritional outcomes for their children. This, in turn, contributes to lower productivity across generations as sick children become less productive adults. Similarly, poor parental health and nutrition can contribute to children leaving school to substitute for sick parents, further exacerbating this downward cycle of poor health contributing to economic stagnation.

Disease and early mortality among children have adverse long-term effects as mediated through reduced incentives for parents to invest in their education, as manifested both in delayed entry into school and in repetition and early exits. Cognitive functioning and ability to learn is also diminished, reducing the quality of human capital and subsequent earnings when the child enters the labour market. Parents' expectations of a short lifespan, both for themselves and their children, will also reduce savings, and thus investment in physical and human capital.

Empirical evidence

Not only are these arguments persuasive at the conceptual level, but there is considerable empirical evidence that health matters for economic growth and productivity. The work of Acemoglu and Johnson (2007) provides a history of how the hostile health and disease environment in Africa dissuaded colonialists from investing in social and economic institutions that would have fostered economic prosperity. Instead of building schools, creating water and sanitation infrastructure, and establishing systems of governance and administration that would promote property rights, the Europeans focused their efforts on extractive industries, with the consequent deleterious long-term effects on economic growth and sustainability.

Numerous other recent efforts to link health to economic outcomes have relied on the examination of cross-country associations among health, economic growth, and poverty. For example, Barro (1997) estimates that an increase in life expectancy of 10% will lead to an increased economic growth of 0.4% per year. His work is broadly consistent with the results of others showing that health-induced increases in productivity play an important role in determining world distribution of income (Gallup, Sachs, and Mellinger 1999). In combination, however, such cross-country studies need to be approached with caution. Specifications are often ad hoc, data often unreliable, and most important, unobservable variables may jointly affect health status and income, generally contributing to an upward bias in the coefficient of the impact of health on economic outcomes (Weil 2007).

Another strand of literature on the impact of health examines the impact of the 'demographic dividend' on economic outcomes. The logic is simple: improvements in health services and availability of modern technology will bring about a decline in mortality; and after a considerable lag, this will lead to a fall in fertility as parents adjust to the higher probabilities of their children's survival into adulthood. For a short period of time, there will be an increase in the dependency ratio, as there is a bulge in the working age population relative to the rest of the population. This demographic transition contributes to a large economic dividend (Lee 2003). Bloom et al. (2007) note the importance of institutional reform and transparent political and economic environment in order for Africa to follow Asia's lead in benefiting from this demographic change.

Another important area of work has been focused on macroeconomic implications of various diseases such as tuberculosis, malaria, and HIV/AIDS. For example, estimates are that economic costs of tuberculosis to the poor are around US$12 billion (WHO 2001). Much attention has also been given to the macroeconomic impacts of HIV/AIDS. Early work, such as that by Bloom and Mahal (1997), observed little impact on economic growth. This optimism was consistent with a Solow-type growth framework where the impact of disease on growth was mitigated by a drop in labour supply relative to capital, which in turn increased productivity of labour. Young (2005) even conjectures a positive impact of HIV/AIDS on growth through a process of the epidemic contributing to reduced fertility and a decline in the dependency ratio, subsequently leading to increases in per capita consumption as well as savings. The assumption is that this will not only lead to increased investment but also provide resources for health and related support for those suffering from AIDS.

Other estimates of the impact of AIDS are far more sobering. For example, Arndt and Lewis (2000), using a simulation model, conclude that GDP will be reduced by 17%, and per capita incomes by 8%, between 1997 and 2010, as a result of the AIDS epidemic in South Africa. Bell, Devarajan, and Gersbach (2006), capturing the effects on human capital formation mentioned earlier, find possibly devastating long-run effects of HIV/AIDS if the epidemic in southern Africa continues unchecked.

The actual impact of these communicable diseases on economic growth will depend on the economic structure of each country, whether land or labour are greater constraints to growth, and the existence of economic and social infrastructure. Likewise, the extent to which pharmaceuticals are available will have an enormous impact on such estimates. And while economic costs associated with such diseases in terms of lost productivity are large, so too are costs of treatment. This is illustrated by estimates from Over (2009), who shows that US-funded AIDS treatment could grow to $12 billion annually by 2016. While highly effective, the projected costs of anti-retroviral therapy represent more than half of the United States' spending on overseas development assistance in 2006. However, it is not just infectious diseases that will have high costs to households, government, and donors. A recent study on the emerging epidemic of chronic disease in Africa suggests that in 2000, there were over 7 million cases of diabetes in Africa, and that direct treatment costs exceeded US$1,000 per person, implying staggering costs associated with treating diabetes and other non-infectious lifestyle diseases as they increase dramatically in years ahead.

There is also considerable micro evidence from Africa linking health status to worker productivity, labour supply, and educational outcomes. For example, a substantial impact of nutrition on agricultural output and wages was found by Strauss (1996) in Sierra Leone. Glick and Sahn (1997) have shown the importance of nutrition in urban areas, where wage workers and the self-employed in Conakry, Guinea (Glick and Sahn 1998) see a substantial economic return to health status. Schultz and Tansel's (1993) study on workers in Ghana and Côte d'Ivoire indicates that wage returns to height and body mass index (BMI) in Ghana were also quite large, with a centimetre increase being associated with an 8–10% increase in wages. These findings ignore likely additional labour productivity effects operating through occupation choice (Fogel 1986).

These studies relied on econometric models, generally using instrument variables, or alternatively taking certain outcomes such as adult height as exogenous. However, issues of identification and causation remain, thus motivating a greater interest in experimental studies. Much of the biomedical and recent economics literature relies on randomized control trials to examine the impact of health on economic outcomes. For example, Wolgemuth et al. (1982) report on a study showing that road workers in Kenya witness small productivity gains as a result of energy supplementation. Several other studies, particularly on the impact of iron, iodine, and micronutrients, have illustrated the importance of nutrition on physical work performance and cognition (Pollitt 1993; Thomas, Lavy, and Strauss 1996).

Beyond the issue of worker productivity and labour market outcomes, the impact of health on schooling and cognition has also been widely studied. Among recent work in this area, both the design and results of the experiment conducted by Miguel and Kremer (2004) in Kenya are noteworthy. They report that treatment of helminthic infections (caused by worms) in schools contribute to a reduction in absentee rates by one quarter, although they do not find an improvement in test score outcomes. While such experimental evidence is rare, econometric studies are much more widely available. Glewwe and Jacoby (1995) use instrumental variables and fixed effects estimator to find that stunted growth among young children will lead to delayed enrolment, but not eventual attainment. A study from Zimbabwe employing a quasi-experimental method (Alderman, Hoddinott, and Kinsey 2006) also indicates a large impact of heights on school attainment.

Conclusions

Both empirical and theoretical literature suggest there are large productivity increases and economic gains from improved health. These are mediated by schooling (age of entry, duration, and attendance), cognition, strength, and stamina, as well as increased savings associated with reduced expenditures on health and greater incentives to invest in children who are expected to live longer and be more economically productive over their life course.

Information asymmetries, as well as market failures, such as for credit and insurance, will likely contribute to underinvestment in health-related human capital and, therefore, to large associated economic costs. While government policies to address these market failures may jointly improve health and economic outcomes, there are likely to be large externalities associated with improving health that further justify government investments in the health sector. These include reducing the spread of infectious diseases, which are the cause of most early deaths in Africa. Thus, in Africa, there is a clear and compelling case for investment in health, given that social rates exceed private rates of return.

REFERENCES

Acemoglu, Daron, and Simon Johnson, 2007. 'Disease and development: the effect of life expectancy on economic growth', *Journal of Political Economy* 115.6, 925–85.

Alderman, Harold, John Hoddinott, and Bill Kinsey, 2006. 'Long term consequences of early childhood malnutrition', *Oxford Economic Papers* 58.3, 450–74.

Arndt, C., and J. D. Lewis, 2000. 'The macro implications of HIV/AIDS in South Africa: a preliminary assessment', *South African Journal of Economics* 68.5, 380–84.

Barro, R., 1997. *Determinants of Economic Growth: A Cross-Country Empirical Study*. Cambridge, Mass.: MIT Press.

Bell, C., S. Devarajan, and H. Gersbach, 2006. 'The long-run economic costs of AIDS: theory and an application to South Africa', *World Bank Economic Review* 20.1, 55–89.

Bliss, Christopher, and Nicholas Stern, 1978. 'Productivity, wages and nutrition, Part I: The theory', *Journal of Development Economics* 5.4, 331–62.

Bloom, David E., David Canning, Richard K. Mansfield, and Michael Moore, 2007. 'Demographic change, social security systems, and savings', *Journal of Monetary Economics* 54.1, 92–114.

—— and Ajay S. Mahal, 1997. 'Does the AIDS epidemic threaten economic growth?', *Journal of Econometrics* 77.1, 105–24.

Fogel, Robert W., 1986. 'Nutrition and the decline in mortality since 1700: some additional preliminary findings', NBER Working Papers 1802, Washington, DC.

Gallup, John Luke, Jeffrey D. Sachs, and Andrew D. Mellinger, 1999. 'Geography and economic development', *International Regional Science Review* 22.2, 179–232.

Glewwe, Paul, and Hanan Jacoby, 1995. 'An economic analysis of delayed primary school enrollment in a low income country: the role of early childhood nutrition', *Review of Economics and Statistics* 77.1, 156–69.

Glick, Peter, and David E. Sahn, 1997. 'Gender and education impacts on employment and earnings in West Africa: evidence from Guinea', *Economic Development and Cultural Change* 45.4, 793–823.

—— —— 1998. 'Health and productivity in a heterogeneous urban labour market', *Applied Economics* 30.2, 203–16.

Lee, Ronald D., 2003. 'The demographic transition: three centuries of fundamental change', *Journal of Economic Perspectives* 17.4, 167–90.

Leibenstein, H. A., 1957. *Economic Backwardness and Economic Growth*. New York: Wiley.

Miguel, E., and M. Kremer, 2004. 'Worms: identifying impacts on education and health in the presence of treatment externalities', *Econometrica* 72.1, 159–217.

Over, Mead, 2009. 'Prevention failure: the ballooning entitlement burden of U.S. global AIDS treatment spending and what to do about it', Working Paper 144, Center for Global Development, Washington, DC.

Pollitt, E., 1993. 'Iron deficiency and cognitive function', *Annual Review of Nutrition* 13, 521–37.

Schultz, T. P., and A. Tansel, 1993. 'Measurement of returns to adult health: morbidity effects on wage rates in Côte d'Ivoire and Ghana', Paper 95, Living Standards Measurement, World Bank, Washington, DC.

Smith, Adam, 1960. *The Wealth of Nations*. New York: Modern Library.

Strauss, J., 1996. 'Does better nutrition raise farm productivity?', *Journal of Political Economy* 94.2, 297–320.

Thomas, Duncan, Victor Lavy, and John Strauss, 1996. 'Public policy and anthropometric outcomes in Côte d'Ivoire', *Journal of Public Economics* 61.2, 155–92.

Weil, David N., 2007. 'Accounting for the effect of health on economic growth', *Quarterly Journal of Economics* 122.3, 1265–1306.

Wolgemuth, J. C., M. C. Latham, A. Hall, A. Chesher, and D. W. Crompton, 1982. 'Worker productivity and the nutritional status of Kenyan road construction laborers', *American Journal of Clinical Nutrition* 36.1, 68–78.

World Health Organization, 2001. *Macroeconomics and Health: Investing in Health for Economic Development*. Report of the Commission on Macroeconomics and Health, Geneva: WHO.

Young, Alwyn, 2005. 'In sorrow to bring forth children: fertility amidst the plague of HIV', *Journal of Economic Growth* 12.4, 283–327.

HIV/AIDS

Germano Mwabu

1. Background

Since its emergence, first as a disease in 1981 and later in the 1990s as a social and economic problem, HIV/AIDS has attracted the attention of policymakers, researchers, philanthropists, and ordinary citizens. However, HIV/AIDS is more prevalent in sub-Saharan Africa (SSA) than in any other world region (UNAIDS 2007). About 23 million people are living with HIV/AIDS in SSA, representing nearly two thirds of such individuals worldwide (Avert.org 2010). Over the past several years, some 1.4 million people died from AIDS in Africa and a further 2 million became infected. Since the beginning of the epidemic in the early 1980s, more than 14 million African children have lost one or both of the parents to the disease.

Unless prevention, treatment, and care efforts are scaled up soon, AIDS death toll in Africa is likely to rise significantly over the next decade, with devastating effects on economies and communities. Even though HIV infection rate seems to have peaked in the 1990s, African policy makers face five main challenges from HIV/AIDS over the next decade:

(a) providing antiretroviral therapies (ARTs) at health institutions and supporting home-based care for a rising number of people living with HIV/AIDS;
(b) stemming the toll from new HIV infections through prevention, counselling, testing, and treatment interventions;
(c) mitigating economic and social impacts of accumulated numbers of AIDS deaths and orphans;
(d) devising sustainable mechanisms of financing ARTs and distributing them equitably to HIV/AIDS patients;
(e) prevention of mother-to-child transmission of HIV infections.

Each of the five challenges is a major concern of health policymakers in virtually every African country, except in West and North Africa, where HIV infection rates are relatively low. However, even in these countries prevention efforts are needed.

Points (a)–(d) are closely related. In many African countries, access to health facilities through which ARTs are provided is difficult, partly due to prohibitive transport costs, and partly because information about the therapies is not broadly available. As result, many AIDS patients remain untreated even when drugs are available. Similarly, persons at high risk of infection cannot be reached with protection interventions.

Moreover, sustainability of treatment and prevention interventions is uncertain, as the interventions are currently financed using external funds which cannot be guaranteed over the long term. Domestic sourcing of public funds to finance AIDS prevention and treatment is a major challenge because economies in the region have limited taxable capacities. However, through regional cooperation entities such as the trading blocs and continental-level organizations, such as the African Union, the African Development Bank, and Economic Commission for Africa, substantial funds can be raised from within Africa for countries in the region that are hardest hit by AIDS epidemic.

Because of widespread poverty on the continent, African governments in a number of countries have instituted periodic cash transfers to households with AIDS orphans. Challenges in these transfers include identification of needy households and adequate financing of the transfers. Although cash transfers have been shown to be effective in fighting poverty and in improving health status of mothers and children in Latin America (Schultz 2004), their effectiveness in Africa remains largely unknown. In particular, design of the transfers in a way that can allow rigorous evaluation of their effectiveness remains problematic in Africa.

Regarding point (e) above, a large number of children might be at the risk of infection every year through the mother-to-child transmission (MTCT) of the virus. MTCT typically occurs during pregnancy, childbirth, or breastfeeding. 'Without interventions, there is a 20–45% chance that an HIV-positive mother will pass infection on to her child' (Avert.org 2010). Relevant MTCT interventions, especially the treatment of expectant mothers, can play a vital role in the control HIV/AIDS among children.

In the ensuing section, a conceptual model for assessing welfare impacts of interventions against HIV/AIDS is presented. The model can also be used to design and implement such interventions. The main value of the model is to indicate to policymakers the kinds of data that need to be collected in order to assess impacts of AIDS-related interventions on health, education, labour supply, household income, and national development.

2. Framework of analysis

A household welfare determination model can be used to assess the socioeconomic impacts of interventions against HIV/AIDS. The framework is a slight modification of a model originally proposed by Rosenzweig and Schultz (1982). The modification is in adopting broad definitions for the variables specified in the original model. In the model presented here, the concept of health capital (Grossman 1972) is replaced with a broader notion of human capital.

In the model, the determinants of household welfare are outputs produced by activities undertaken by households. A welfare-enhancing activity is presumed to yield beneficial goods, some of which are purchased from the market whereas others are self-produced. In particular, the household is assumed to benefit from human capital neutral-commodities (X) from human capital related-goods (Y) and from human capital (H). The term 'human capital' is used to include a broad range of human skills, cognitive abilities, physical fitness, and nutritional and biological endowments that are part and parcel of human beings (Schultz 1961).

Examples of X-goods include furniture and clothing, while examples of Y-goods are health services and behaviours that promote health, such as exercise and personal hygiene. The household or its members can acquire all the X-goods from the market. Moreover, some of the Y-goods such as healthcare services and nutrients can also be acquired from the marketplace. However, the household must self-produce some of the Y-goods, e.g. exercise and health-improving behaviours, such as the avoidance of smoking and drinking by pregnant mothers.

2.1 THE MODEL

The household is assumed to produce health (H) of its members using market goods and non-market inputs such as own time. In the context of this study, the key inputs into health production include purchased interventions (the market components of Y) and its non-market elements, such as the various behavioural changes that reduce the risk of HIV infections (Frolich and Vazquez-Alvarez 2009; Centers for Disease Control 2008).

Under the above circumstances, the amount of health that the household can produce for its members depends on its resource endowment, including the time that the members can devote to health maintenance activities. The amount of health produced depends on health inputs that the household can acquire using its budget. Moreover, the quantity of health inputs (and thus the amount of health produced) depends on prices of health inputs. In particular, for a fixed budget, the higher the input prices, the smaller the quantity of inputs that the household can acquire and the lower the amount of health that will be produced. The amount of health produced includes a portion that is outside the control of the household, which is an outcome of genetic material, environmental conditions, and cultural background.

The prices of health-improving goods (i.e. health inputs such medical services, nutrition, exercises, voluntary counselling and testing) and the prices of health-neutral goods such as furniture play critical roles in health production. More broadly, these prices affect the human capital through the household budget. In technical terms, prices influence the demand for quantities of the factors that the household uses to produce health or human capital. In particular, prices are important determinants of the demand for interventions against HIV/AIDS. Unless these interventions are taken up by households (e.g. voluntary counselling and testing, treatments for opportunistic diseases, and antiretroviral therapies), they will have no impact on households' human capital.

Moreover, the relationship between health capital and the demand for health inputs is the link between healthcare consumption (e.g. use of ARTs and counselling services) and the human capital accumulation by households. This relationship facilitates an evaluation of the welfare impacts of interventions against HIV/AIDS in terms of improvements in human capital at the household level.

2.2. WELFARE EVALUATION

The effects of ARVs and other interventions on human capital, and the impacts of human capital on labour supply, household income, labour productivity, and national development, can be measured using the above model. The measurement is accomplished by relating (statistically or experimentally) labour market outcomes such as labour supply, wages, and intrahousehold time allocation to changes in human capital following ARV treatments. In the measurement exercise, account should be taken of the fact that interventions such as the ARVs are endogenous to human capital outcomes. Generally speaking, ARVs are said to be endogenous to human capital in the sense that ARVs are affected by factors that also directly influence human capital, so that the causal effect of ARVs on human capital is difficult to discern. Similarly, it should be recognized that human capital is endogenous to labour market outcomes such as wages, labour supply, and labour force participation. Statistical and/or experimental methods can be used to deal with the endogeneity problem (Thirumurthy, Zivin, and Goldstein 2008). Human capital here may include nutrition and status, school attendance, and cognitive skills. The next section reviews the literature for evidence on determinants of demand for interventions against HIV/AIDS. Evidence on socioeconomic effects of human capital conditional on the interventions against HIV/AIDS is also of interest in that review.

3. Evidence from the literature

3.1 DETERMINANTS OF DEMAND FOR HIV/AIDS TREATMENT AND PREVENTION

There are few econometric studies of demand for AIDS treatment such as ARVs or of HIV prevention interventions such as condom use or voluntary testing and counselling. In a study in India, Over et al. (2006) report that user fees or the financial cost of treatment is the single most important determinant of access to ARVs in India. Despite the fact that India manufactures its own ARVs, financial cost is still a major barrier to ARVs consumption in India. Thus, it is reasonable to assume that financial costs are a barrier to ARV usage in Africa, a region that imports these medicines. There is thus a need to subsidize ARVs in Africa to make them broadly available to the poor. Over et al. (2006) show that household wealth substantially affects demand for all components of ARV therapies, including voluntary counselling and testing.

Studies in Kenya (Frolich and Vazquez-Alvarez 2009) and in Madagascar (Glick, Randriamamonjy, and Sahn 2009) show that education, assets, and public health information campaigns, particularly via the radio, are key determinants of knowledge that households possess about the measures they can take to protect themselves against HIV infection. However, while the health impacts of ARV therapies are clear (Frolich and Vazquez-Alvarez 2009), the health effects associated with knowledge are mixed (Glick et al. 2009).

3.2. THE IMPACTS OF ARVS AND HIV/AIDS KNOWLEDGE ON HEALTH STATUS

Substantial improvements in health status have been reported in several countries for patients under ARV therapies. There is clear evidence that ARVs have prolonged lives in Africa and elsewhere (see e.g. Palella et al. 1998; Thirumurthy et al. 2006; 2008; Over et al. 2006). However, the effects of the knowledge on the measures available to reduce the risks of HIV infection are not clear-cut. The effect of such knowledge has been shown to reduce the probability of HIV-positive status among young women in Kenya, using the Demography and Health Survey data for 2003 (Frolich and Vazquez-Alvarez 2009). However, no effects were found for older population groups or for men. Factors such as attitudes towards sex or social norms may undermine effective application of the knowledge that people have in the prevention of HIV infection.

3.3. EFFECTS OF BEHAVIOURAL CHANGE AND CULTURAL PRACTICES ON HIV STATUS

Behavioural change, such as widespread adoption of condom use, and cultural practices, such as male circumcision and polygamy, are some of the non-market inputs that enter a health production function in an environment of high risks of HIV infection. There exists a large and controversial literature linking male circumcision to reduced risk of HIV infection (Howe 2005; CDC 2008). However, this literature shows that the causal relationship from male circumcision to HIV transmission in Africa (and in other parts of the world) has not been conclusively established.

3.4. EFFECTS OF BETTER HEALTH CONDITIONAL ON ARV TREATMENT

A large macroeconomic literature shows that HIV/AIDS reduces economic growth (see e.g. Kambou, Devarajan, and Over 1992; Cuddington 1993; McDonald and Roberts 2006). HIV/AIDS reduces growth by accelerating depreciation of health human capital, shortening life expectancy, decreasing saving, and weakening the motive to invest, particularly in education human capital (see UNAIDS 2007). The world regions with the highest poverty rates also have the highest rates of HIV infection. This finding suggests a positive correlation between effective treatment of HIV/AIDS and economic growth in Africa. The causal link from HIV/AIDS to economic growth in Africa remains controversial.

Research in western Kenya (Thirumurthy et al. 2006; 2008) has shown that better health after ARVs treatment is associated with improved nutrition for children and increased school attendance. The studies showed increased labour supply for adult household members and reduced labour supplies for women and children after ARV therapies. There is further evidence of differences in reallocation of time across market and non-market activities among treated and untreated AIDS patients. These differences have welfare implications for current and future generations in treated and untreated households (Thirumurthy et al. 2008). Evidence from South Africa suggests that ARV treatment is associated with considerable reduction in work absenteeism and with increases in labour productivity (Habyarimana, Mbakile, and Pop-Eleches 2007).

The foregoing findings indicate that assessment of cost-effectiveness of ARV therapies should be based on considerations beyond their immediate effects on health or other dimensions of human capital. The possibility that the scaling up of these therapies could lead to HIV resistance against the first-line drugs should be considered.

4. Conclusion

Policies to fight HIV/AIDS must be based on a good understanding of the mechanisms through which the virus causing AIDS infects people. There are five main channels through which HIV is transmitted from one person to another: (a) unprotected sex with an infected partner, (b) the sharing of infected injection equipment, (c) childbirth and breastfeeding (mother-to-child transmission), (d) transfusion of contaminated blood and blood products, and (e) health facilities that do not take precautions to protect their patients and staff against HIV (World Bank 2005). In Africa, HIV infection seems to be mainly through unprotected sex and via MTCT. Thus, prevention efforts in Africa should focus on these two areas.

The positive correlation between HIV/AIDS and poverty suggests the need for a global response to the AIDS crisis in Africa. In the short run, the affected countries cannot afford to implement large-scale HIV/AIDS prevention and treatment programmes, given the high rates of poverty on the continent (Ali and Thorbecke 2000). However, over the long run, African governments must find collective mechanisms to finance such programmes to ensure their sustainability.

REFERENCES

Ali, A. G., and Erik Thorbecke, 2000. 'The state and path of poverty in sub-Saharan Africa', *Journal of African Economies* 9.1, 9–40.

Avert.org, 2010. 'HIV and AIDS in Africa', www.avert.org/aids-hiv-africa.htm (accessed on 7 March 2010).

Centers for Disease Control and Prevention, 2008. 'Male circumcision and the risk for HIV transmission and other health conditions: implications for the United States', CDC HIV/AIDS Science Facts, http://www.cdc.gov/hiv, accessed 11 September 2009.

Cuddington, J. T., 1993. 'Modeling the macroeconomic effects of AIDS with an application to Tanzania', *World Bank Economic Review* 7.2, 173–89.

D'Adda, Giovanna, M. Goldstein, J. Zivin, M. Nangami, and H. Thirumurthy, 2009. 'ARV treatment and time allocation to household tasks: evidence from Kenya', *African Development Review* 21.1, 180–208.

Frolich, M., and R. Vazquez-Alvarez, 2009. 'HIV/AIDS knowledge and behavior: have information campaigns reduced HIV infection? The case of Kenya', *African Development Review* 21.1, 86–146.

Glick, Peter, J. Randriamamonjy, and D. E. Sahn, 2009. 'Determinants of HIV knowledge and condom use among women in Madagascar: an analysis using matched household and community data', *African Development Review* 21.1, 147–79.

Grossman, Michael, 1972. 'On the concept of health capital and the demand for health', *Journal of Political Economy* 80, 223–55.

Habyarimana, James, Bekezela Mbakile, and Christian Pop-Eleches, 2007. 'HIV/AIDS, ARV treatment and worker absenteeism: evidence from a large African firm', Public Policy Institute, Georgetown University.

Howe, Robert S., 2005. 'HIV infection and circumcision: cutting through the hyperbole', *Journal of the Royal Society for the Promotion of Health* 125.6, 259–65.

Kambou, G., S. Devarajan, and M. Over, 1992. 'The economic impact of AIDS in an African country: simulations with a general equilibrium model for Cameroon', *Journal of African Economies* 1.1, 109–30.

McDonald, S., and J. Roberts, 2006. 'AIDS and economic growth: a human capital approach', *Journal of Development Economics* 80.1, 228–50.

Over, M., E. Marseille, K. Sudhakar, et al., 2006. 'Antiretroviral therapy and HIV prevention in India: modeling costs and consequences of policy options', *Sexually Transmitted Diseases* 33.10, S145–S152.

Palella, Frank, Kathleen M. Delaney, et al., 1998. 'Declining morbidity and mortality among patients with advanced Human Immunodeficiency Virus infection', *New England Journal of Medicine* 338.13, 853–60.

Rosenzweig, M. R., and T. Paul Schultz, 1982. 'The behavior of mothers as inputs to child health: the determinants of birth weight, gestation, and the rate of fetal growth', in V. R. Fuchs (ed.), *Economic Aspects of Health*. Chicago: University of Chicago Press, 53–92.

Schultz, T. Paul, 2004. 'School subsidies for the poor: evaluating the Mexican Progresa poverty program', *Journal of Development Economics* 74.1, 199–250.

Schultz, T. W., 1961. 'Investments in human capital', *American Economic Review* 51.1, 1–17.

Thirumurthy, Harsha, Joshua G. Zivin, and Markus Goldstein, 2006. 'AIDS treatment and intrahousehold resource allocations: children's nutrition and schooling in Kenya', discussion paper, Center for Global Development, Washington, DC.

—————— 2008. 'The economic impact of AIDS treatment: labor supply in western Kenya', *Journal of Human Resources* 43.3, 511–52.

UNAIDS, 2007. AIDS Epidemic Update, Joint United Nations Programme on HIV/AIDS. New York: United Nations.

World Bank, 2005. *Committing to Results: Improving the Effectiveness of HIV/AIDS Assistance*. Washington, DC: World Bank.

Education

Kwabena Gyimah-Brempong

> If you plan for a year, plant a seed. If for ten years, plant a tree. If for a hundred years, teach the people. When you sow a seed once, you will reap a single harvest. When you teach the people, you will reap a hundred harvests.
>
> (Guan Zhong, Chinese philosopher, 7th century BC)

1. Introduction

Education is a fundamental element of expanded human capabilities at the heart of human development (Sen 1999).[1] Education can be pursued either in a formal setting or in an informal setting, and the process can be structured or unstructured. Although the discussion in this chapter refers to the broader concept of education, it will focus on formal education when we attempt to quantify the stock of education. Education is at once a desirable outcome that enhances the quality of life (Millennium Development Goal 2) and a development input (human capital) as the quote from Zhong suggests.[2] The relationship between education and development is bidirectional: education affects development and development affects education.[3]

Education affects economic development through income growth (Artadi and Sala-i-Martín 2003; Gyimah-Brempong, Paddison, and Mitiku 2006; Mankiw, Romer, and Weil 1992; Barro 1999). Indirectly, education affects development through technical change (Lucas 1993), improved health (Gyimah-Brempong and Wilson 2004; Jamison, Jamison, and Hanushek 2007), improved governance (Spilimbergo 2009), and social cohesion (Gradstein and Justman 2002). It is not only the stock, but the *quality* of education and *who* gets educated that matter for development. Increased education is necessary for improved health but improved health (longer life expectancy) leads to more investment in education.

---

[1] Although education is mostly discussed within the context of *economic growth*, I focus on the relation between education and *development*.

[2] See e.g. Gyimah-Brempong and Wilson (2004), Spilimbergo (2009).

[3] Health programmes rely on skills learned in school; health sector relies on education to train health personnel; productivity increases from education increase returns to health investment, and therefore produces more investment in health.

The rest of the chapter is organized as follows. Section 2 describes the stock and investments in education in Africa; section 3 discusses education production in Africa, while section 4 discusses the effects of education on human development in Africa. Section 5 concludes the chapter.

2. **Educational attainment in Africa**

Educational attainment can be measured in several ways, including the average years of education of the adult population, the proportion of the adult population that has attained a certain level of education (e.g. graduated from high school), or adult literacy rates. These are measures of formal education. As shown in Table 1, the stock and quality of education in Africa is low compared to other regions of the developing world. Average literacy rates of the adult population lags behind those of other parts of the developing world. An alternative way to look at education is the rate at which a region (country) is adding to its stock of education human capital as measured by enrolment rates. Table 1 suggests that while Africa's enrolment rate is catching up with those of other parts of the developing world at the primary school level, it compares unfavourably with other parts of the world at the secondary and tertiary levels.

Two dimensions of how education contributes to human development in a society are the gender composition of the educated and what subjects are studied. Education in the sciences and engineering focusing on practical problem solving is more likely to increase the quality of life than one that focuses on the fine arts or religion. Because women raise children, and are the pivots of families and social cohesion, female education in the current period will have a positive impact on the education of future generations.[4] This implies that educating girls is likely to have longer-lasting impact on human development than educating boys. Table 1 indicates that, compared to other parts of the world, African education produces far fewer scientists and engineers and educates far fewer women, as the gender ratio at every level of education is significantly less than unity. These characteristics of education in Africa have long-run consequences for human development in Africa.

Although Africa lags behind the world, it has made tremendous progress in educational attainment over the last half century. Between 1991 and 2006, primary school enrolment ratio rose from 78% to 90% of the world average, suggesting that enrolment ratio rose faster in Africa than the world average. A broader measure of education, adult

---

[4] The adage, 'when you educate a man you educate and individual, when you educate a woman you educate a nation' is relevant here.

Table 1. Education statistics for Africa, 1990–2007

A. Adult literacy rates			
	Africa	S. Korea	China
	66.10	98.42	90.91
B. Enrolment rates			
	Primary		Secondary
	Africa S. Korea		Africa S. Korea
	77.49 97.06		34.26 91.89
C. Gender ratios: female/male			
	Primary	Secondary	Tertiary
	86.78	73.22	57.65
D. Pupil–teacher ratios			
Primary			
	Africa	S. Korea	China
	41.55	29.64	19.20
Secondary			
	Africa	S. Korea	China
	25.30	18.95	17.91
E. Per pupil expenditure on education			
Ratio of per pupil expenditure in primary education to per capita GDP			
	Africa	S. Korea	China
	14.72	17.99	16.68
Ratio of expenditure per student in primary/tertiary education			
	0.0489	0.6770	0.1280
F. % tertiary enrolment in STEM			
	Africa	S. Korea	China
	0.2000	0.412	0.401

Source: Calculated from UNESCO, *Global Educational Digest*, various years, Montreal, UNESCO Institute for Statistics.

literacy rate, increased from 32% to 63% between 1970 and 2007.[5] In addition to increased quantity of education in Africa over the last half century, the gender gap is also fast closing at the primary school level. What is not improving rapidly is the *quality* of education on the continent. Although it is hard to measure the quality of education, Africa does poorly, compared to other parts of the world, in international achievement tests in mathematics and English (Hanushek and Luque: 2003).

3. Education production in Africa

African countries are aware of the need to increase the quantity and quality of the stock of education in order to quicken the pace of human development. To do so requires an

---

[5] Calculated from UNESCO (various years), *Global Educational Digest*: Montreal, UNESCO Institute for Statistics.

understanding of efficiency in education production in Africa. In addition to increasing the quantity and quality of inputs to the education sector, it may be necessary to improve efficiency in the education production process as well as making the curricula relevant to the needs of Africa. Although there are few empirical studies of the production of education in Africa, the studies conducted suggest that there are large-scale inefficiencies in educational production in Africa. These include low quantity and quality of education inputs, inefficiency in the utilization of education resources, and irrelevance of the curricula for Africa's development.

Table 1 shows that the quantity and quality of education resources in Africa are generally low. On average, per pupil expenditure/per capita GDP ratio in Africa at the primary school level is about 15%. The comparable figures for South Korea and China are 18% and 17% respectively. The relatively low per capita GPD in Africa suggests that in absolute terms, per pupil expenditure in Africa is much lower than in other parts of the world. An alternative way to look at the resource gap is to compare the pupil–teacher ratio in Africa to those of other parts of the world since this may reflect the quality of teacher attention students get. The pupil–teacher ratio in primary school is 42, while that in secondary school is 25. For South Korea, the comparable figures are 30 and 19, while the figures for China are 20 and 18 respectively. Other resources, such as physical infrastructure, books, and laboratories, are low in quantity and quality as well. A large influence on education is the home environment. The high illiteracy rates in Africa imply that parents cannot help their children with home work or provide reading materials, resources that improve the learning experience.

Education resources could be better allocated to increase educational outcomes in Africa. At the system level, too much of education resources are spent on tertiary education while not enough is spent on primary education. Table 1 shows that Africa spends about 20 times per tertiary student that it spends on a primary school student. This compares to 1.48 for South Korea and 7.8 for China. Given low levels of education funding in Africa, this structure of allocation allows little funding for quality primary education, yet a high-quality primary education is necessary for any good performance at the secondary and tertiary levels. This pattern of allocation decreases the quality, if not the quantity of education generally.

At the school (university) level, non-optimal input ratios lead to inefficiency in education production. A disproportionately large share of school resources is spent on teachers, while little else goes to provide complementary inputs. Researchers find that lack of physical facilities, books, laboratories, and qualified teachers contribute to inefficiency at all levels of education production in Africa (Gyimah-Brempong and Appiah 2008; Michaelowa 2001; Glewe 1999). In addition, there is evidence that high rates of teacher absenteeism negatively affect educational outcomes in Africa (Kremer and Holla 2009; Michaelowa 2001). Reinikka and Svensson (2004) finds that only 10% of money allocated to rural schools in Uganda is spent on the schools, with the rest pocketed by officials in the educational hierarchy.

Besides direct school inputs, lack of other complementary inputs, such as health services, decreases school input effectiveness in education production. Miguel and Kremer (2004) find that de-worming primary school children in Kenya dramatically increases school attendance and test scores; similarly, the school feeding programme in Ghana has increased school attendance and student performance.

4. Education and development in Africa

How has education affected human development in Africa? Although this broader question has not been analysed for Africa generally, one can look at the impact of education on some aspects of human development—such as income growth, employment, health, and governance—to illustrate the effects of education on African development. I adopt this approach in this sub-section.[6]

While there may be disagreement on the size; there is a consensus that education has significant and positive effects on economic growth in Africa. Artadi and Sala-i-Martín (2003) argue that had Africa maintained the same level of primary school enrolment rates as those of OECD countries, per capita income would have grown at 2.39% per annum instead of 0.9% between 1970 and 2005. Other studies (Gyimah-Brempong et al. 2006; Appiah and McMahon 2002) conclude that education increases income growth rate in Africa. These studies also find that education positively affects human development through improved health, better institutions, conflict prevention, and nation-building generally.

The rapid growth of education human capital in postcolonial Africa has not translated into rapid development for a number of reasons. For education to have a major impact on development, the quality and type of education should be relevant to the needs of countries, the pedagogy geared towards problem solving and genuine scientific inquiry, and—most important—educated people should be effectively employed. Virtually all education systems in Africa are relics of the colonial system—designed to produce public servants to administer colonies but not to develop nations. However, Africa needs graduates who can invent, design, build, and produce things in addition to those who can run bureaucracies to further development. Yet postcolonial African educational systems continue to follow the colonial education system, with its emphasis on reading and numeracy, and little critical thinking. This leads to a mismatch between the supply of skills and labour needs of African countries—a mismatch that leaves college graduates

---

[6] In addition to the *size*, there is also a disagreement on whether the level of education is important for economic growth in Africa. See Gyimah-Brempong et al. (2006) for a summary of the issue.

unemployed, while Africa imports engineers, scientists, and doctors. Partly as a result of this mismatch, an increasing number of educated Africans are emigrating to OECD countries, even if it is to drive taxi cabs in New York City, Washington, DC, or London.

One reason education may not have contributed its maximum to development in Africa is that educated people are not productively employed. A large proportion of human capital developed in Africa is lost to rent-seeking activities rather than employed in directly productive activities (Berthélemy, Pissarides, and Varoudakis 2000; Al-Samarrai and Bennell 2007), lost by emigration to the developed world (Rogers: 2008), or not employed in the sectors for which they trained (Al-Samarrai and Bennell 2007). Al-Samarrai and Bennell find that, on average, about 2% of university graduates, 14% of senior secondary school graduates, and 12.5% of junior secondary school graduates in Malawi, Tanzania, Uganda and Zimbabwe are unemployed.[7] A factor contributing to the emigration of educated Africans is the mismatch mentioned above. Another contributing factor to this mismatch is wrong incentive structures in labour markets in African countries. Often graduates with critical skills are compensated at the same rate as those with less scarce skills. This has two perverse effects: first, there are no incentives for students to acquire the scarce skills which may be more in demand; second, those who acquire those skills have incentives to seek better opportunities in OECD countries. For example, Clemens (2007) estimates that 28% of physicians trained in sub-Saharan Africa were practising in nine developed countries in 2000, while Africa faces severe shortages of physicians. The rate of emigration ranged from 9% for Niger to 71% for Guinea.

5. Policies and conclusion

The discussion above suggests that if Africa is to benefit from increased education, it must pursue policies to: (i) improve efficiency in the production of education, (ii) find ways to employ educated Africans effectively, and (iii) reduce emigration of its highly skilled labour force. While policies may differ across countries, improving efficiency in education production would involve increased resources to education, reallocating resources within the education sector (from tertiary to primary and from personnel to books and equipment (to change input ratios)), as well as better monitoring of teachers and holding school authorities accountable. Providing complementary services, such as health services and the highly successful school feeding programs, in school could improve the quality of education in Africa. In addition, any reform of education will

---

[7] Anecdotal evidence points to increasing unemployment of graduates, especially in West Africa, where university graduates have to resort to informal-sector activities for employment. For example, the government of Ghana, the main formal sector employer, has imposed a two-year moratorium on graduate employment.

involve changes in curriculum to reflect the needs of African development with an emphasis on science, technology, engineering, and business. Pedagogy should also involve problem-solving approaches to learning rather than the 'book-centred' learning that has characterized education in Africa. This may involve partnering with businesses through internships and other forms of applied research.

Any strategy to realign education with the needs of Africa will only be possible if it is combined with labour market reforms, especially those in which wages reflect the scarcity value of skills. Similarly, reducing the emigration of skilled labour to the developed world may require African countries to pay competitive wages for these skills. Finally, African countries may have to find ways to attract the services of skills in their diasporas, just as India, Israel, South Korea, and China have done.

REFERENCES

Al-Samarrai, S., and P. Bennell, 2007. 'Where has all the education gone in sub-Saharan Africa? Employment and outcomes among secondary school and university leavers', *Journal of Development Studies* 43.7, 1270–1300.

Appiah, E. N., and W. McMahon, 2002. 'The social outcomes of education and feedbacks on growth in Africa', *Journal of Development Studies* 38.4, 27–68.

Artadi, E. V., and X. Sala-i-Martín, 2003. 'The economic tragedy of the XXth century: growth in Africa', NBER Working Paper No. 9865, Cambridge, Mass.

Barro, R. J., 1999. 'Human capital and growth in cross-country regressions', *Swedish Economic Policy Review* 6.2, 23–77.

Berthélemy, J., C. Pissarides, and A. Varoudakis, 2000. 'Human capital and growth: the cost of rent seeking activities', in M. S. Oosterbann, T. R. van Steveninck, and N. van der Windt (eds), *Economic Growth and Its Determinants*. Dordrecht: Kluwer.

Clemens, M., 2007. 'Do visas kill? Health effects of African health professional emigration', Center for Global Development Working Paper 114, Washington, DC.

Glewe, P., 1999. *The Economics of School Quality Investments in Developing Countries: An Empirical Study of Ghana*. New York: St. Martin's Press.

Gradstein, M., and M. Justman, 2002. 'Education, social cohesion and growth', *American Economic Review* 92.4. 1192–1204.

Gyimah-Brempong, K., and E. Appiah, 2008. 'Technical efficiency in Ghanaian secondary schools', in E. Aryeetey and R. Kanbur (eds), *The Economy of Ghana: Analytical Perspectives on Stability, Growth and Poverty*. Oxford: James Currey.

—— O. Paddison, and W. Mitiku, 2006. 'Higher education and economic growth in Africa', *Journal of Development Studies* 42.3, 509–29.

—— and M. Wilson, 2004. 'Health, human capital and economic growth in sub-Saharan Africa and OECD Countries', *Quarterly Review of Economics and Finance* 44.2, 296–320.

Jamison, E. A., T. J. Jamison, and E. A. Hanushek, 2007. 'The effects of education quality on income growth and mortality decline', *Economics of Education Review* 26, 772–89.

Kremer, M., and A. Holla, 2009. 'Improving education in the developing world: what have we learned from randomized evaluation?', *Annual Review of Economics* 1, 1–33.

Lucas, R., 1993. 'Making a miracle', *Econometrica* 61.2, 251–72.

Mankiw, N. G., D. Romer, and D. N. Weil, 1992. 'A contribution to the empirics of economic growth', *Quarterly Journal of Economics* 107.2, 407–37.

Michaelowa, K., 2001. 'Primary education quality in francophone sub-Saharan Africa: determinants of learning achievement and efficiency considerations', *World Development* 29.10, 1699–1716.

Miguel, E., and M. Kremer, 2004. 'Worms: identifying impacts on education and health in the presence of treatment externalities', *Econometrica* 72.1, 159–217.

Reinikka, R., and J. Svensson, 2004. 'Local capture: evidence from a central government transfer program in Uganda', *Quarterly Journal of Economics* 119.2, 679–705.

Rogers, M., 2008. 'Directly unproductive schooling: how country characteristics affect the impact of schooling on growth', *European Economic Review* 52.2, 356–85.

Sen, A., 1999. *Development as Freedom*. New York: Knopf.

Spilimbergo, A., 2009. 'Democracy and foreign education', *American Economic Review* 99.1, 528–43.

Gender and African Development

Abena D. Oduro

Introduction

The UN Office of the Special Advisor on Gender Issues and Advancement of Women defines gender as the 'social attributes and opportunities with being male and female and the relationships between women and men, and girls and boys, as well as the relationship between women and those between men'.[1] This definition of gender is broader and more explicit than that provided by the World Bank. Gender as defined by the World Bank (2000: 2) is the 'socially constructed roles and the socially learned behaviours associated with females and males'. The definition of the UN is explicit in including within the concept of gender relationships between women and relationships between men. Relationships between women and between men will, for example, be influenced by age, ethnicity, religion, marital status, position in the family, whether or not the individual has children, and income. These are important dimensions that are at the same time separate from gender and integral defining components of gender. For example, amongst some ethnic groups single women have greater opportunity to earn income and have greater control over their incomes than do married women (Endeley 2001). An example of the influencing role of age is when the younger woman must defer to the older woman who is herself limited by the social norms regulating her relationship with men. Cornwall, Harrison, and Whitehead (2007: 15) found that 'it was, in many women's accounts, other *women* who caused them most grief'. Mayoux (2001: 440) observes that 'the "social capital" of some women may operate to the serious disadvantage of others'.

Incorporating relations between the sexes within the concept of gender raises the issue of the heterogeneity amongst women and amongst men. Invariably, discussions on gender and presentations on sex-disaggregated data tend to present women and men as two separate and homogeneous groups. However, the heterogeneity within these groups is marked (Oduro 2008). This heterogeneity amongst women can be illustrated by the findings of a case study of three farming communities in southern Ghana. Takane (2002) classified control over land and security of tenure by married women under five

---

[1] http://www.un.org/womenwatch/osagi/pdf/factsheet.

headings. A married woman may have full control over the land she farms and the income from the products, and therefore be completely independent of her husband. This is probably because she probably obtained land as a gift from her father. A second group of women have usufruct rights to land and control over the product. These are women who may have tenancy arrangements. The third category of women comprises those who have usufruct rights to their husband's land for cocoa farming and have control over the income generated from the farm. The fourth category have usufruct rights over land but can only farm food crops; and the final category have usufruct rights but are not in control of the disposal and income of the crops grown on the farm. Women who fall into the first two categories have the most independence and control over the use of their labour and any investments they may have made on the farm. The third category has a less secure tenure because the rights to the land and its output are determined by the relationship with the husband. However, that the husband has agreed to the planting of cocoa—a tree crop—is a signal that he might hand over the land to the wife in the future. It was found that 36% of the married women surveyed could be classified under the first two headings. Forty-four per cent of married women were classified in the fifth category, where rights to land and the output were the most restricted. Cornwall (2007: 77), in a paper that reviews the gender agenda in the last thirty years, 'calls for seeing "women" and "men" as plural categories constructed by social practice'.

Relationships between men and women affect relationships between women, and vice versa. For example, in the context of polygamy, which is widespread across the continent, women spouses in a polygamous marriage can 'compete' amongst themselves for the male spouse's attention. He, on the other hand, can take advantage of this and renege on his responsibilities.

Underlying gender relations are inequitable power relations. This can be quite explicit in communities where women and children are at worst considered to be the assets of men (Endeley 2001; Nkiema, Haddad, and Potvin 2008) or at best their dependants. In such circumstances the sphere of decision-making for women is narrow. The inequitable power balance is not confined to relationships between women and men, but also exists in relationships between women and between men. Thus, in the previous example of the young woman who has to defer to the older woman, the young woman in this situation is severely constrained in the choices and options facing her.

The process of development involves the structural transformation of economies and societies. It also encompasses the UNDP definition of human development, i.e. the process of enlarging people's choices. Gender relations can infringe in a very fundamental way on the human rights of the individual, limit their choices, and slow down the process of development.

How gender can impact development and growth

Gender impacts development and growth through two major channels. The first is through the direct impact of gender on the physical, human, and social capital accumulation process. Girls are less likely to attend school compared to boys. In several African countries the gross primary enrolment rate of girls is lower than that of boys (Table 1). It is interesting to note, however, that in some countries such as Gambia, Malawi, Uganda, and South Africa the reverse is the case.[2]

National averages mask wide variations within countries. In Ghana, for example, in 32 out of the 110 administrative districts in 2003, the net primary enrolment rate amongst girls was higher than that of boys. In 34 districts the net enrolment rate in junior (lower) secondary was higher amongst girls. These gender gaps in education reduce the total human capital stock of an economy.

Table 1. Gross primary enrolments in selected African countries

Country	Girls		Boys		Gender Parity Index	
	2000	2007	2000	2007	2000	2007
Algeria	103	106	112	113	0.97	0.99
Burkina Faso	36	60	51	71	0.60	0.72
Ethiopia	41	85	63	97	0.48	0.65
Gambia	81	89	92	84	0.91	1.10
Ghana	77	97	83	98	0.79	0.85
Kenya	96	112	98	113	0.86	0.87
Malawi	134	119	139	114	1.13	1.22
Mozambique	64	103	85	119	0.62	0.71
Niger	27	46	39	61	0.59	0.64
Namibia	106	109	106	110	0.97	0.96
Rwanda	94	149	97	146	0.63	0.66
Senegal	62	84	72	84	0.74	0.86
Sudan	45	61	53	71	0.74	0.75
South Africa	106	101	111	104	1.05	1.07
Swaziland	97	109	102	118	0.89	0.86
Togo	91	90	102	118	1.01	0.86
Uganda	122	117	129	116	1.04	1.11
Tanzania	68	111	69	113	0.61	0.61
Zambia	77	117	83	121	0.66	0.69

Source: UNESCO.

---

[2] The lower enrolment rate amongst boys may be because of economic conditions that require the services of boys—e.g. boys in herding communities may have to look after the livestock.

Gender relations as articulated through inheritance norms, marital regimes, and norms that govern access to resources and assets can slow down the physical capital accumulation process. The physical accumulation process will also be reduced when women's productivity and income-earning capacity is reduced by norms that restrict women's access to inputs.

Investments in human, physical, and social capital are determinants of economic growth and development. Thus by constraining the accumulation of these assets, gender can hamper African growth and development.

The second channel through which gender can affect growth and development is through the resulting gendered distribution of human, physical, and social capital. There appears to be consensus on the negative effect of income inequality on growth and poverty reduction (Persson and Tabellini 1994; Lundberg and Squire 2003). There is a growing body of work on the relationship between gender inequality and growth and development. Recent studies present mixed findings on the relationship between gender inequality in education and growth. In a cross-section study of 109 countries covering the period 1960–90, Klassen (2002) finds that the difference between African and East Asian growth rates can be explained partly by differences in gender inequality in education. However, a later study that updates the data to 2000 but reduces the number of countries finds that in the 1990s the poor growth performance of Africa could be attributed largely to factors other than gender inequality in education (Klassen and Lamanna 2009).

Agricultural productivity of women in Africa tends to be below the potential largely because they do not have the same access to fertilizer and other inputs as men (Udry 1996; Goldstein and Udry 2002). Gender inequality in access to inputs, credit, and extension services, for example, can slow down the adoption of new technologies and the pace of growth. Thus agricultural transformation can be undermined by gender-biased access to necessary inputs. In some parts of Africa, women in farming households must provide unpaid labour services on their spouse's farms. The male spouse is not obliged to reciprocate. This arrangement creates an incentive for women to reduce effort on male farms. In Kenya, for example, the increase in yields that is expected after weeding was found to be less on farms in male-headed households compared to yields after weeding on farms in female-headed households. Women are more time-constrained compared to men. The woman in the farming households must provide labour services on her husband's farm and on her own farm, and in addition she must provide unpaid services in the home. Under these circumstances the woman farmer will be less likely to adopt new technologies that are labour-intensive and time-consuming.

Data on the gender distribution of physical and financial assets is limited. Most available data from large household quantitative surveys is at the level of the household. This is not adequate to investigate the asset accumulation process of men and women and to understand how the distribution in the ownership of these assets between women and men affects growth, development, and welfare.

Gender does matter for African development. The attainment of the Millennium Development Goals will be compromised if gender inequalities persist. For example, gender inequalities that reduce growth of agricultural output can undermine progress towards reducing hunger. Universal primary education will not be achieved if there is continued gender inequality in access to education.

Reducing the gender gaps

If gender gaps are to be reduced if not closed altogether, policies and actions must be taken to address preferences and the power inequalities that are the immediate cause of gender inequality. Preferences and power inequalities are determined and defined by norms and practices. Power inequalities must be addressed if any progress is to be made in closing the gender gap. For example, educating girls is expected to have a snowball effect because educated women are more likely to send all their children to school. However, the daughter of a married educated woman will not be sent to school if the decision to do so is not within the control of the mother. The critical importance of dealing with power inequalities can be illustrated further by the experience with the provision of micro credit to empower women. The objective of women's empowerment will not be achieved if micro credit is provided to women who do not have control over their incomes (Endeley 2001). Micro credit programmes must be supported by programmes that work towards reducing male control and domination in those communities and societies where women's independence to earn and control their income does not exist.

The change in the balance of power between the sexes and in preferences that are required if the gender gap is to be closed will be resisted by the group(s) that expects to lose from the change in the status quo. This means that some dimensions of gender inequality will take a much longer time to address than others. Policies and legislation can change incentives and therefore preferences, but they may not be enough to change attitudes and mindsets. Policies and legislations may take a long time to be set up or enacted because of resistance from vested interests. Even when policy frameworks are set up and laws are enacted, implementation may be difficult because of lack of commitment to do so. Policy and legislation will not always be effective in reducing the gender gap. This is because attitudes and world views will have to change as well.

Advocacy that emphasizes the benefits of reduced gender inequality for both men and women is an important component of any strategy to reduce gender inequality. Democratizing the policymaking and planning process is another means to improve the capacity of policy and legislation to bring about effective change. By 'democratization of the policymaking process' we mean opening up the process to a broader constituency. Some of the initial parameters that were to inform the process of preparing and implementing poverty reduction strategy papers (PRSP) were participation and consultation. Civil society was to be actively involved in their preparation. There was also scope for civil society organizations to be involved in monitoring the implementation of the PRSPs. The active involvement of civil society organizations with a focus on gender equality in this process was an opportunity for gender mainstreaming of policies in several African countries. Unfortunately the experience of the preparation of PRSPs in Africa was one of limited participation and consultation. Sometimes the timing of the consultations was not appropriate for any meaningful impact to be made. The monitoring framework did not have indicators that were gender-sensitive, thus making it difficult to monitor the implementation of the PRSP strategy even when there was some semblance of gender mainstreaming in the document (Oduro 2008).

Education should be a priority area of policy focus. It is an important catalyst for change, and can influence attitudes and thought processes. Second, there is a high probability that educated men and women will invest in the education of their children. Gross primary enrolment rates for both boys and girls is rising (Table 1). The gender parity index—measured as the ratio of the gross enrolment rate of girls to the gross enrolment rate of boys—is rising, indicative of a decline in the gender gap at that level of education. Transition rates to secondary and tertiary education for girls still lag behind that of boys. Policies must be introduced that will change the preference of parents as regards educating girls. This will include reducing the distances that children must travel to get to school and reducing the opportunity costs of sending girls to school (Glick 2008). These measures may be adequate to encourage parents to send girls to school, but may not be enough to ensure that they stay in school as long as boys. If parents are to invest as much in the education of girls as they do for boys, measures must be introduced that will increase the private rate of return to education for girls (Glick 2008). This will require the introduction of wage policies that prohibit practices that introduce wage differentials between the sexes that cannot be explained by differences in the skills, level of education, and experience of men and women. In many communities, the investment by parents in education of their daughters is less than it is for boys because of the expectation that girls will marry and will spend less time in the labour market and therefore will be less likely to take care of their parents in the future. However, a universal pension policy could break the link between investment in a child's education and the future return expected by parents in terms of remittances from the child. This is because parents will not have to depend on their children for support in their old age, and will therefore be more willing to invest in the education of children irrespective of the sex of the child.

Most African women are self-employed working on farms and/or running micro and small-scale businesses. Access to finance is important for the effective day-to-day management of the business and also to smooth consumption over time. Women need access to independent sources of finance, i.e. they must have access to financial resources that will not perpetuate a dependent and possibly exploitative relationship. In addition, they need opportunities to save that are secure. Improved access of women to micro finance can be enhanced through an improved geographical coverage of banks, savings, and loans organizations and other semi-formal financial institutions. Second, the financial institutions must introduce innovative financial packages characterized by flexibility, i.e. flexibility in terms of size of loans they will administer and the savings deposits they will receive, flexibility in the maturity of the loan and the savings period, flexibility of repayment plans, and flexibility in the use that can be made of the loan. The micro finance institutions in Asia, such as the Grameen Bank, have changed their lending and savings practices to incorporate flexibility in these various dimensions. There is a lot that micro finance institutions in Africa could learn from that experience and adapt to the conditions in Africa.

Conclusion

Can the increase in the primary enrolment rate of girls (see Table 1) be attributed to whatever growth and development that has occurred in African countries in the last decade or so? What role will development play in reducing gender gaps and inequality? Development that increases incomes and reduces the opportunity cost of sending all children to school is not enough to remove, for example, gender inequality in education. Gender inequalities—gender wage inequalities and biases in the distribution of unpaid domestic work—persist in the industrialized countries. In Africa, the gender biases are more evident and are more pernicious to the wellbeing of individuals. The virtuous cycle of development in Africa and reduction in gender inequality will not materialize if Africa's development process does not involve the transformation of power relations between the sexes within households, families, and society at large.

■ REFERENCES

Cornwall, A., 2007. 'Revisiting the "gender agenda"', *IDS Bulletin* 38.2, 69–78.
—— E. Harrison, and A. Whitehead, 2007. 'Gender myths and feminist fables: the struggle for interpretive power in gender and development', *Development and Change* 38.1, 1–20.
Endeley, J. B., 2001. 'Conceptualising women's empowerment in societies in Cameroon: how does money fit in?', *Gender and Development* 9, 34–41.
Glick, P., 2008. 'What policies will reduce gender schooling gaps in developing countries? Evidence and interpretation', *World Development* 36.9, 1623–46.

Goldstein, M., and C. Udry, 2002. *Gender, Land Rights and Agriculture in Ghana.* London: LSE.

Klassen, S., 2002. 'Low schooling for girls, slower growth for all? Cross-country evidence on the effect of gender inequality in education on economic development', *World Bank Economic Review* 16.3, 345–73.

—— and F. Lamanna, 2009. 'The impact of gender inequality in education and employment on economic growth: new evidence for a panel of countries', *Feminist Economics* 15.3, 91–132.

Lundberg, M., and L. Squire, 2003. 'The simultaneous evolution of growth and inequality', *Economic Journal* 113, 326–44.

Mayoux, L., 2001. 'Tackling the down side: social capital, women's empowerment and microfinance in Cameroon', *Development and Change* 32: 421–50.

Nikiema, B., S. Haddad, and L. Potvin, 2008. 'Women bargaining to seek healthcare: norms, domestic practices, and implications in rural Burkina Faso', *World Development* 36, 608–24.

Oduro, A. D., 2008. 'Achieving gender equity in Ghana: how useful is the Ghana poverty reduction strategy?', in J. Amoako-Tuffour and B. Armah (eds), *Poverty Reduction Strategies in Action: Perspectives and Lessons from Ghana.* Lanham, Md.: Rowman & Littlefield.

Persson, T., and G. Tabellini, 1994. 'Is inequality harmful for growth?', *American Economic Review* 84.3, 600–20.

Takane, T., 2002. *The Cocoa Farmers of Southern Ghana. Incentives, Institutions and Change in Rural West Africa.* Chiba: Institute of Developing Economies—Japan External Trade Organization.

Udry, C., 1996. 'Gender, agricultural production and the theory of the household', *Journal of Political Economy* 104, 551–69.

World Bank, 2000. *Engendering Development.* New York/Washington, DC: Oxford University Press/World Bank.

Accelerating Demographic Transitions in Sub-Saharan Africa

Mwangi S. Kimenyi

Introduction

A demographic transition is a societal shift from high mortality and fertility rates to longer lives and smaller families. The onset of a demographic transition is marked by a sharp decline in fertility. Historically, demographic transitions take 50–150 years from start to completion, but modern transitions in developing countries have been much shorter. Demographic transitions have occurred in every region of the world except for most of sub-Saharan Africa (SSA), where fertility rates have declined only slightly. Thus, Africa has not benefited from the socioeconomic dividends of demographic transitions. Accelerating demographic transitions in African countries has a direct bearing on the long-term economic growth prospects of those countries, and is therefore an issue of policy concern. This chapter discusses the causes of demographic transitions, the failure of demographic transitions in SSA, and the policy implications.[1]

Europe was the first region to undergo a demographic transition, and most of the continent was near the replacement level of 2.1 births per woman in 1955 (Caldwell 2001). By 1980, every region of the world except SSA had seen at least the preliminary decline in fertility of 10%. Fertility declined only slightly in SSA, from 6.59 in 1955–60 to 5.90 in 1990–95 (Caldwell 2001). Southeastern Asia, which had similar socioeconomic status to SSA in 1960, experienced a reduction in fertility from 6.07 to 3.05 over the same period (UN Population Division 2009). Even the small decline in fertility in SSA overstates the change, as South Africa's fertility transition accounts for most of the decline. Of the 49 least developed countries (LDCs) identified by the United Nations, 31 are in SSA. Fertility in these 31 countries fell from 6.6 in 1970 to 6.5 in 1995, and then to 5.8 in 2005. In the other 18 LDCs, fertility declined from 6.4 in 1970 to 4.1 in 1995, and then to 3.3 in 2005 (UN Population Division 2009). Regardless of the comparison group, SSA lags behind its peers in the pace of demographic transition.

---

[1] Nicholas Krafft and Stephanie Lipinski provided helpful research assistance.

Demographic transition theory

Demographic transition theory (DTT) seeks to explain the aforementioned discrepancy in fertility declines, and suggests that modernization generally triggers a demographic transition (Kirk 1996). However, because a pure cross-country socioeconomic comparison does not adequately explain the lag in SSA, a number of societal factors must be considered. John Caldwell, a prominent demographer, proposes a multifaceted explanation of fertility decline involving four key societal factors: socioeconomic growth, cultural frictions, availability of contraceptives, and government will.

The role of socioeconomic growth in fertility decline is itself multifaceted. Richard Easterlin has attempted to build an economic model involving factors of demand, supply, and costs, which all affect the level of fertility. Demand factors reflect the idea that development causes parents to want fewer children because they pose an additional cost from expenses such as education and offer less benefit because child household labour is less prevalent. Supply factors mainly include the cultural aspects of fertility, such as the society's sexual structure. Costs primarily reflect the monetary and time costs of birth control (Kirk 1996). Caldwell's wealth flows theory says that in premodern societies, wealth flows from child to parent, but in modern societies, parents increasingly direct wealth toward their children, reducing the number of children they choose to have. This theory corroborates Easterlin's model, as it also observes that education expenses increase the costs of child rearing and reduce the availability of children's labour to supplement household income (Kirk 1996).

Declines in mortality rates, which are often correlated with socioeconomic growth, are also discussed as a trigger for demographic transitions, although the direction of causality between low mortality rates and low fertility rates is not clear and several studies have obtained mixed results (Kirk 1996). Kirk argues that a causal channel could involve the psychological effects of perceiving more control and less fatalism, which may lead to active family planning. He acknowledges that mortality reductions may initially put strains on resources, but that in general, fertility declines that follow will outweigh this concern.

Caldwell has also advanced the cultural aspects of fertility, arguing in his wealth flows theory that fertility declines are associated with Westernization, the copying of Western ideals into other regions (Kirk 1996). He also notes that Africa's tribal society was particularly suited for high fertility because of views about family size and ancestry, which has caused resistance towards fertility reduction policies (Caldwell, Orubuloye, and Caldwell 1992). Kimenyi, Shughart, and Tollison (1988) also suggest that competition among heterogeneous groups can add to the pressure to increase group size. These cultural differences have persisted to the present, and the African sexual systems are still vastly different from those in Asian countries that experienced fertility declines, as evidenced by the high incidence of premarital sex in many African societies (Caldwell et al. 1992).

The primary channel through which culture affects fertility is the propensity to use contraceptives. Because of these cultural frictions, government prioritization of national planning is particularly important for provision of contraceptives and other family planning resources. In the 31 LDCs in SSA, only 27% of the need for contraceptives is met, compared to 39% in other LDCs, and only 12% of married women or those in a union use modern contraceptives (UN Population Division 2009). In the 17 SSA LDCs with contraceptive use below 10%, only 5 publicly considered their fertility too high in 1985; by 1995, only 8 had policies to lower fertility; and by 2005, 4 countries still considered their fertility satisfactory or too low (UN Population Division 2009). Universal government commitment to family planning is critically important, and generally results in significant increases of both access to and acculturation of contraceptives.

Demographic transitions in sub-Saharan Africa

In light of the theory discussed above, Caldwell (2006) highlights socioeconomic development and government policy as the key missing ingredients for SSA in the last forty years. In 1992, Caldwell et al. laid out a template for what an African fertility transition could look like. They note that Botswana, Kenya, and Zimbabwe, the only SSA countries which had recently experienced the 10% onset of a demographic transition, all had regionally low infant mortality rates, high contraception prevalence, and high education levels, especially among girls (Caldwell et al. 1992). They also note that extrapolating from the socioeconomic characteristics of the three transitioning countries, only a handful more appeared poised for transition by 2000. A follow-up conference paper (Caldwell and Caldwell 2002) observed that these countries had indeed experienced declines of varying degrees, although to levels that are still high by international standards. Thus, the authors again stressed the importance of socioeconomic development, along with continued government efforts to overcome cultural frictions and spread the transition throughout SSA.

Government coordination is also important for broad demographic transitions and has increased in the last two decades, starting with the Dakor–Ngor Declaration, which was adopted in 1993 as the result of a 1992 conference. The declaration affirmed the commitment of African governments to address population issues, and came in advance of a 1994 meeting, the International Conference on Population and Development. This conference set forth a twenty-year plan of action, the results of which have been reviewed at five-year intervals. The Economic Commission for Africa Communication Team (2004) highlighted the fact that 96% of countries now incorporated population into their development plans, up from 25% in 1994. While government will has certainly increased, tangible results are mixed. SSA LDCs have seen reductions in their fertility rates in the last decade for the first time since fertility became part of the global agenda. While the 2005 rate of 5.8 children per woman is still too high, that number is more a reflection of the high starting point. The low prevalence of contraceptives also provides a striking opportunity for SSA to improve.

There are some encouraging cases of countries setting and realizing aggressive goals for fertility declines. One example is Cape Verde, a country that was an LDC until 2007 and in 1989 had fertility of 6 children per woman. By 2003, fertility had decreased to 2.9 children per woman, and contraceptive use had increased to 57%, with 17% unmet need among married women (UN Population Division 2009). UNPD attributes this change to the government's acknowledgement that fertility was too high, and its subsequent and continuous commitment to providing family planning services. Botswana, whose transition was mentioned above, had a population plan as part of a broader government strategy, which extended social services including service delivery investments, universal free education, and an integrated healthcare system that included family planning (UN Economic Commission for Africa 2001).

Economic and policy implications

These country-specific cases are encouraging, particularly because successful fertility transitions may enable SSA countries to develop socioeconomically. There is encouraging evidence on the consequences of transition. Bloom and Williamson (1998) studied East Asian economic growth and concluded that having a decreasing dependent population, supported by an increasing working population, accounted for as much as one third to one-half of economic growth in the region from 1965 to 1990. This 'demographic dividend' has the potential to produce high levels of economic growth as it did in East Asia. The budgetary implications of family planning policies are also encouraging, because for every dollar spent on family planning, two to six dollars can be saved in interventions aimed at achieving other development goals (UN Population Division 2009). For example, fertility control can help achieve universal education simply by reducing the number of children of school age (UN Population Division 2009). Stemming population growth may also ameliorate the economic costs of environmental and agricultural problems caused by climate change, which may further strain African economies (World Population Program 2008).

Realizing demographic dividends is one of the keys to socioeconomic development in SSA. The lack of fertility declines in SSA the last fifty years stands in stark contrast to the demographic changes in other parts of the world. The relationship between fertility and development is difficult to disentangle because continued population growth is both a cause and effect of socioeconomic stagnation. Regardless, it has been demonstrated that active government policy which encourages family planning can help end this vicious cycle, and may result in demographic dividends, especially if combined with policies to reduce infant mortality and increase female access to education and the labour force. Recent commitments to these policies from SSA governments are encouraging, but sustained effort must be made to ensure that governments fully enact them. Otherwise, rapidly growing populations may continue to contribute to underdevelopment in SSA.

REFERENCES

Bloom, D. E., and J. G. Williamson, 1998. 'Demographic transitions and economic miracles in emerging Asia', *World Bank Economic Review* 12(3), 419–55.

Caldwell, J. C., 2001. 'The globalization of fertility behavior', *Population and Development Review* 27, Supplement, 94.

—— 2006. *Demographic Transition Theory*. Amsterdam: Springer, 257.

—— and P. Caldwell, 2002. 'The fertility transition in sub-Saharan Africa', in Department of Social Development, Pretoria, South Africa, *Fertility and the Current South African Issues of Poverty, HIV/AIDS and Youth*; viewed 28 September 2009 at: http://www.sarpn.org.za/documents/d0000082/P79_Caldwell.pdf.

—— I. O. Orubuloye, and P. Caldwell, 1992. 'Fertility decline in Africa: a new type of transition?', *Population and Development Review* 18.2, 211–42.

Economic Commission for Africa Communication Team, 2004. 'African countries increasingly aware on population', ECA Press Release 14/2004, 1.

Kimenyi, M. S., W. F. Shughart, and R. D. Tollison, 1988. 'An interest-group theory of population growth', *Population Economics* 1.2, 131–9.

Kirk, D., 1996. 'Demographic transition theory', *Population Studies* 50.3, 361–87.

UN Population Division, 2009. UN Population Division Policy Brief 2009/1. New York: UN Department of Economic and Social Affairs, 1–8.

UN Economic Commission for Africa, 2001. *The State of Demographic Transition in Africa*. New York: United Nations, 35.

World Population Program, 2008. '2007 Update of Probabilistic World Population Projections', International Institute for Applied Systems Analysis, viewed 28 September 2009 at: http://www.iiasa.ac.at/Research/POP/proj07/index.html?sb=5.

Lessons Learned from Field Experiments in Africa

Rachel Glennerster and Kamilla Gumede

When international gatherings discuss Africa, there is usually a combination of boosterism (inspiring examples and promises that if we just devote more money we can achieve great things) and hand wringing (so little has been achieved, influxes of money seem to make little lasting difference). But no one with any moral conscience would suggest that we, whether we are citizens of Africa or anywhere else, should give up seeking to reduce poverty in Africa. Nor would anyone suggest that all past efforts have been effective, that every possible policy option currently being touted will be equally effective, or that there will be unlimited funds available, from tax revenues or aid, to tackle the continent's problems. So the relevant question is: how can we spend limited funds to best effect?

Despite decades of policy reforms and thousands of different programs launched, there is relatively little rigorous evidence to answer this question. Why do we know so little? The answer is twofold. First, without careful methods it is not always possible to tell how well a program is working; second, in the past we have not availed ourselves of the opportunity to rigorously evaluate these programs and policies at their rollout. But that is beginning to change, in Africa and around the world. Fifteen years ago researchers started working with a small NGO in western Kenya, introducing an element of random variation in how they rolled out their programs. These first randomized evaluations demonstrated that it was possible to combine the most rigorous research methods with the practical constraints faced by organizations implementing projects in poor communities and, in the process, help answer key questions about how best to reduce poverty.

In this chapter we briefly explain why it can be difficult to know what impact a program is having without rigorous impact evaluation, and then go on to discuss some of the important policy lessons for Africa and elsewhere that have emerged from the many randomized evaluations conducted in the last fifteen years.

The attribution problem

In assessing whether a program works, we need to assess it against its specific objectives. The goal of a program that provides free school uniforms, for example, may be to help poor households overcome financial barriers associated with the cost of a uniform, and to enable them to send their children to school. If the program targets uniforms to teenage girls, it might have the further benefit of keeping girls in school and thereby reducing teen pregnancies and potentially the spread of HIV/AIDS (Duflo et al. 2006). To determine whether the program is working, we must determine whether it was successful in changing the outcomes it was intended to affect.

One can, of course, observe the outcome of interest—school attendance records, teen pregnancies, HIV prevalence, and so on—simply by following participants after they leave the program. But this does not necessarily tell us whether the changes in outcomes seen over time were due to the program or to other factors that would have occurred even without the program. Additionally, if program participants are self-selected into the program, then they may have characteristics that distinguish them from non-participants. For example, women who sign up for microcredit programs may be more motivated or entrepreneurial than those who do not sign up, thus their observed change in outcome from participating in the program is likely to differ from those who did not choose to partake—an effect known as 'selection bias'. The true impact of a program is the difference between the observed outcomes of participants (e.g. their school dropout rates and HIV prevalence after a year) and what those outcomes would have been in the absence of the program. Of course, what would have happened to participants in the absence of the program is forever hidden from view. To identify the impact of a program, researchers therefore have to attempt to estimate what the outcome would have been in the absence of the program—otherwise known as the 'counterfactual'. The extent to which researchers are able to reliably construct a counterfactual is the litmus test of any impact evaluation.

Random assignment offers a simple way to create a counterfactual. If assignment to the program or to the comparison group is completely random, then selection into one group or the other is by definition unrelated to any characteristics of the individual and therefore probably also to the individual's subsequent outcomes. Thus, any systematic differences in outcomes at the end of the program between the two groups can confidently be attributed to the program intervention.

Suppose, as in the above example, that we wish to evaluate the *causal* effect of school uniforms on additional school attendance and HIV risks. If we were to simply compare girls who have school uniforms with girls who don't, we are likely to obtain a misleading estimate of the impact of giving out uniforms. First, girls who don't have a uniform are more likely to come from poorer families than girls who have uniforms. As such, these girls tend to be disadvantaged in other ways (beyond the uniforms) that may affect their education status and HIV risk. Moreover, girls only obtain uniforms when they know they are going to school. Why does this matter? Because if the observed correlations can be explained by characteristics of study participants, then giving out free uniforms may not actually lead to more girls attending school or have any effect on their HIV status. A randomized field trial, however, that assigns uniforms to some students and not to others will be able to isolate the causal effect of uniforms on school attendance and HIV risk over time.

Although this simple example illustrates the fundamental elements of a field experiment, the range of possible variations on this basic theme is enormous. The ability to blend randomized evaluations into everyday operations of development practitioners around the world has transformed randomized evaluations from a rare and extremely expensive operation to a more flexible, and therefore more commonly used, approach to evaluation. Because randomized impact studies test the effectiveness of real-world programmes, the evidence is solution-oriented and helps inform policies on how to overcome barriers to development, rather than just identifying them. This is important, as the most cost-effective way to improving well being and development is not always to tackle the biggest barrier. Cost-effectiveness comparisons that identify the most effective way of addressing a specific policy objective within a limited budget are therefore particularly useful.

From research to policy effectiveness

Research of any kind is seldom the determining factor in shaping public policy. Field experiments are no exception to that rule. Nevertheless, in part because of such experiments' intuitive appeal and credibility, policymakers are increasingly paying attention to the results of this research. There are important examples of programs that were found to be effective through randomized evaluations being scaled up by African governments and NGOs.

In the space of less than two decades cash transfer programs have become the cornerstone of poverty reduction and social protection policies in a large and growing number of countries. Originally piloted amongst poor rural villages in Mexico (as PROGRESA, now called Oportunidades), cash transfer programs are being rolled out across the world and increasingly in Africa. Most of the research findings have come from Latin America, with one recent, important exception. A randomized control trial in Malawi found that even very small cash transfers ($5 per month) can boost education for girls, and that the effect was just as big when the transfers were unconditional as when they were conditional on school attendance (Baird, McIntosh, and Ozler 2009). The momentum for their expansion across so many countries and within the pioneering countries, and their continued support, was aided largely by the careful efforts made to rigorously pilot and carefully document the program's positive social impact on poor families.

Another notable example is the massive scale-up of school-based deworming campaigns. These campaigns now exist in 26 countries (20 in Africa), and over 5 million children in Africa have benefited since 2009, when Edward Miguel of the University of California at Berkeley and Michael Kremer from Harvard University tested the impact of a deworming program in western Kenya. The NGO running the program only had the capacity to roll it out in 25 schools a year, so they randomized schools into three equal groups which were phased into treatment over three years. Over those three years the researchers compared outcomes for children in schools that had received the program with those that had not yet received the program. They found that deworming lead to a 25% reduction in school absenteeism. Subsequent studies in very different contexts have also found similar results, and at a cost of only $3.27 per additional year of school participation, deworming is one of the most cost-effective ways of increasing education of any rigorously tested program.

A third area where policy change is reflecting the findings from field experiments is the pricing of health goods. In many countries, user fees are promoted for reasons such as better targeting of products to people who need them the most and reduced wastage in health programs. Several experiments in different countries, most of them in Africa, have found very little support for these views (Kremer and Miguel 2007; Cohen and Dupas 2010; Hoffman 2009; Ashraf, Berry, and Shapiro 2007). In every study where this was tested, charging even very small fees dramatically reduced the take-up of highly cost-effective health prevention products like bednets, to protect against malaria, or dilute chlorine (water guard) to prevent diarrhoea. In no case did the act of paying for a product encourage people to use it, nor target a product to those who need it. The families of children with high worm loads were no more likely to pay for deworming treatment than the families of children with low worm loads (Kremer and Miguel 2007). Pregnant women who chose to purchase bednets in Kenya were no more anaemic than those who received nets free of charge (Cohen and Dupas 2010). Families with children under 5, who are particularly vulnerable to the negative effects of diarrhoea, were no more likely to buy chlorine to add to their water than other households (Ashraf et al. 2007). In the past few years, many agencies have reconsidered their policies on charge for health services, opting instead to distribute bednets and other health products free of charge. The elimination of user fees is now strongly supported by a number of influential organizations including the British Department for International Development (DFID), Save the Children UK, the United Nations Millennium Project, and the Commission for Africa. In 2009, the British government cited the study by Cohen and Dupas in calling for the abolition of user fees for health products and services in poor countries. Many countries, including Burundi, Nepal, Malawi, Zambia, Sierra Leone, Ghana, and Liberia, are responding to this call, taking major steps towards the provision of free services.[1]

Lastly, the challenge of delivering quality education is an increasing area of concern across the developing world now that so much progress has been made in getting children into primary school. Pratham, a large NGO in India, has successfully developed programs to help children who are falling behind the standard curricula in India to learn to read. J-PAL (Abdul Latif Jameel Poverty Action Lab) researchers evaluated a remedial education program designed by Pratham and found it to be highly successful in enabling children who were falling behind to catch up on basic literacy and numeracy at an exceedingly low cost of $2.25 per child. Other versions of the program designed to work in rural areas were also found to be very successful. The program used less trained but highly accountable teachers trained in a very specific pedagogy and focused specifically on basic skills with the objective of helping children catch up to their peers. Another evaluation in Kenya also found that more accountable teachers could outperform regular government teachers. It also found that splitting classes by knowledge level so that teachers could teach at a level more tailored to the children had big returns. Pratham has since expanded its program to reach 33 million children in India. In Africa, the government of Ghana is currently adapting the lessons from India and Kenya to their own environment and experimentally testing the winning Pratham concept to improve literacy rates in Ghana. If the pilot is successful, the program will be rolled out across basic education schools in Ghana.

In addition to those discussed above, the following are policy areas in which experimental field studies are starting to shape policy discourse in Africa and help decision makers base policy on evidence:

1. Access to and quality of education. Randomized evaluations in Africa began in the sector of education. The initial focus was on various school inputs for learning, like textbooks and school buildings. Later trials have tested community monitoring, incentives for teachers or pupils, and technology and curriculum innovations. Ongoing studies are assessing returns to post-primary education and vocational training programs.

2. Access to safe drinking water. Piped water that delivers uncontaminated, chlorinated water to households is highly effective in reducing diarrhoea, but often prohibitively expensive. Randomized evaluations across Africa are testing alternative ways of making clean, safe water available to poor households outside cities. Kremer, Zwane, and Ahuja (2010) summarize the findings.

3. Agriculture and technology adoption. Whether in the form of new crops, improved breeds of animals, or changes in agricultural practices, technology has the potential to sharply improve

---

[1] www.povertyactionlab.org/scaleups.

the welfare of small farmers. An increasing number of evaluations are looking at how to improve the take-up of these new technologies.

4. HIV prevention. Many millions of dollars are channelled into HIV prevention campaigns every year, and randomized evaluations are helping to sort effective HIV prevention campaigns from those that don't work.

5. Community participation and empowerment programmes. Randomized evaluations have also been used to test the effectiveness of community participation programmes in improving the quality of public projects, services, and community-focused social cohesion programs.

6. Access to financial services and asset formation. Many ongoing randomized evaluations in Africa today are testing programs to make financial services affordable and accessible to poor households, as well as financial literacy programs that aim to make poor people better consumers of financial services.

Conclusion

As we build more and more evidence about what works across Africa in reducing poverty, we are increasingly finding similar patterns in what works in different contexts. But while the results of completed randomized evaluations already provide many useful lessons about how to design more effective programs, there are still many important policy questions in Africa for which there is little rigorous evidence. There is a tremendous opportunity to use the introduction of new programs across the continent to learn more and develop smarter and more effective strategies for addressing the needs of the poor.

REFERENCES

Ashraf, Nava, James Berry, and Jesse M. Shapiro, 2007. 'Can higher prices stimulate product use? Evidence from a field experiment in Zambia', NBER Working Paper 13247, Cambridge, Mass.

Baird, Sarah, Craig McIntosh, and Berk Ozler, 2009. 'Designing cost-effective cash transfer programs to boost schooling among young women in sub-Saharan Africa', World Bank Policy Research Working Paper 5090, Washington, DC.

Björkman, Martina, and Jakob Svensson, 2009. 'Power to the people: evidence from a randomized experiment on community-based monitoring in Uganda', *Quarterly Journal of Economics* 124.2, 735–69.

Cohen, Jessica, and Pascaline Dupas, 2010. 'Free distribution or cost sharing? Evidence from a randomized malaria prevention experiment', *Quarterly Journal of Economics* 125, 1–45.

Duflo, Esther, Pascaline Dupas, Michael Kremer, and Samuel Sinei, 2006. 'Education and HIV/AIDS prevention: evidence from a randomized evaluation in western Kenya', available at: www.povertyactionlab.org.

Dupas, Pascaline, 2009. 'What matters (and what does not) in households' decisions to invest in malaria prevention?', *American Economic Review* 99.2.

—— 2011. 'Do teenagers respond to HIV risk information? Evidence from a field experiment in Kenya', *American Economic Journal: Applied Economics* 3.1, 1–34.

Evans, David, Michael Kremer, and Muthoni Ngatia, 2008. 'The impact of distributing school uniforms on children's education in Kenya', mimeo, Harvard University.

Hoffman, Vivian, 2009. 'Psychology, gender, and the intrahousehold allocation of free and purchased mosquito nets', *American Economic Review* 99.2.

J-PAL, 2009. 'Showing up is the first step', policy bulletin, available on: www.povertyactionlab.org

Kremer, Michael, and Alaka Holla, 2008. 'Pricing and access: lessons from randomized evaluations in education and health', mimeo, Harvard University.

—— —— 2009. 'Improving education in the developing world: what have we learned from randomized evaluations?', in Kenneth J. Arrow and Timothy F. Bresnahan (eds), *Annual Review of Economics*, vol. 1.

—— and Edward Miguel, 2004. 'Worms: identifying impacts on education and health in the presence of treatment externalities', *Econometrica* 72.1, 159–217.

—— —— 2007. 'The illusion of sustainability', *Quarterly Journal of Economics* 112.3, 1007–65.

—— —— Sendhil Mullainathan, Clair Null, and Alix Peterson Zwane, 2009. 'Making water safe: price, persuasion, peers, promoters, or product design?', mimeo, University of California, Berkeley.

—— Alix Peterson Zwane, and Amrita Ahuja, 2010. 'Providing safe water: evidence from randomized evaluations', available on: http://www.economics.harvard.edu/faculty/kremer

Thornton, Rebecca, 2008. 'The demand for and impact of learning HIV status', *American Economic Review* 98.5, 1829–63.

World Bank, 2009. *Conditional Cash Transfers*. Washington, DC: World Bank.

Thematic Perspectives
Industry, Investment, and Infrastructure

Structural Change in Africa

Justin Yifu Lin

Some theoretical considerations

Sustained economic growth is essentially about structural transformation and technological upgrading. The shift of resources out of traditional agriculture and other low-productivity primary activities, and the expansion of 'modern' sectors (including non-traditional agriculture), have been at the core of the sustained productivity gains that characterize economic development. Indeed, there is ample consensus that rising productivity accounts for the bulk of long-term growth.

Industrialization is an essential component of structural transformation. It has long been recognized as one of the main engines of economic growth, especially in the early stages of development.[1] Its essential characteristics include: (i) an increase in the proportion of the national income derived from manufacturing activities and from secondary industry in general, except perhaps for cyclical interruptions; (ii) a rising trend in the proportion of working population engaged in manufacturing; and (iii) an associated increase in the income per head of the population (Bagchi 1990). Few countries have been economically successful without industrializing. Only in circumstances such as extraordinary abundance of natural resources or land have countries been able to do so (UNIDO 2009).

Moreover, globalization provides an almost infinite potential for industrialization in many low-income countries. Whereas economic growth based on exploitation of natural resources or agricultural land eventually faces the constraint of shortages of quantity, a development strategy based on producing manufactured goods for the global market benefits from economies of scale due to increasingly lower unit costs of production. Several decades ago, low-income countries faced the constraints of their limited market size, high transportation costs, and trade barriers, and could not take advantage of the opportunities offered by manufacturing. With globalization, virtually any country can identify products for which it has overt or latent comparative advantage and scale it up almost without limit, thereby creating its own niche in the world market.

---

[1] Earlier analyses of the process, dating back to the 1950s and 1960s (Datta 1952; Kuznets 1966), found that manufacturing in particular tends to play a larger role in total output in richer countries—a pattern corroborated by the UNIDO report (2009)—and that higher incomes are associated with a substantially bigger role of transport and machinery sectors.

Despite its importance, mainstream development economics has paid only limited attention to industrialization and its role in structural transformation in recent decades. This may be explained primarily by the failure of industrial policies in developing countries, and the theoretical argument that the state cannot do better than the private sector in identifying the new industries. The pervasive failures of government interventions across the world—mainly in Latin America, Africa, South Asia, and in the countries of the former Warsaw Pact—have led to the dominant view that policies aiming at 'picking winners' are bound to create unsustainable and socially costly distortions. Despite the apparent success of some countries that have actively pursued industrial policies—mainly in East Asia—the dominant view in the economic literature is a sceptical one. In their critical review of various rationales for industrial policy, Pack and Saggi (2006) note sarcastically that the required knowledge needed for civil servants to successfully design and implement government intervention would make them omniscient. In fact, much of the literature on industrial policy did not make an important distinction among country strategies: those that are inconsistent with the comparative advantage of the economy or attempt to protect old industries that have lost comparative advantage generally fail, whereas policies to facilitate the development of new industries that are consistent with the comparative advantages of the economy often succeed (Lin and Monga 2010).

In addition to the widespread scepticism about industrial policies, establishing the empirical regularities of the changing patterns of industrial structure and technological upgrading across the world is not a straightforward exercise. Industrialization has been a key feature of successful developing economies lifting themselves out of poverty but the recent trend in the most advanced economies has been towards de-industrialization, that is, a decline of employment in manufacturing as a share of total employment that mirrors a decline in the share of manufacturing value added in GDP. This has been observed not only in the United States and Europe but also in the newly industrialized East Asian economies (Korea, Singapore, Hong Kong, China, Taiwan, China). By contrast, the share of employment accounted for by the services sector has increased steadily both in high-income and low-income brackets.

These trends, whether similar or contrasting, reflect fundamentally different patterns of change: de-industrialization in advanced and successful economies might suggest at first glance that domestic expenditure on manufactured goods has declined while expenditures on services have increased. Empirical analyses and country studies, however, reveals that this is actually not the case. Measured in real terms, the share of domestic expenditure on manufactured goods has been broadly stable over decades.[2]

---

[2] According to Rowthorn and Ramaswamy (1997), expenditure on services in current price terms has increased in the advanced economies. But this growth can be accounted for by the fact that labour productivity has grown more slowly in services than in manufacturing, pushing up the relative price of services and making manufacturing relatively cheaper.

Consequently, de-industrialization is simply the reflection of higher productivity in manufacturing than in services, with the patterns of trade specialization among the advanced economies explaining why the trend is faster in some countries. It is therefore the feature of successful economic development. By contrast, the decline in manufacturing share of total value-added in some low-income countries in recent decades reflects the failure of long-term growth strategies.

A second aspect of structural transformation is technological upgrading and innovation, which are essential ingredients for long-run productivity growth. In low-income countries where budgets for research and development are scarce and industries located far away from the technological frontier, technological upgrading and innovation typically take the form of adaptation and adoption of known technologies rather than introduction of new ones. There has been little economic research on the scope and determinants of these activities. Yet they often involve externalities that, if unaddressed, may lead to low rates of technological upgrading. For instance, the appropriate level and type of innovative activity in all likelihood varies across the development process. Mainstream innovation diagnostics take the implicit view that more is necessarily better. This is not plausible, because the scarcity of resources and the low level of development of the private sector in poor countries would surely make it inefficient for them to undertake an innovation effort on the same scale as in rich countries. Observed patterns of technological adoption, education, and R&D strategies indicate that appropriate innovation strategies depend on endowment structure and stages of development.

Economic diversification is another aspect of structural transformation. Not only does it protect countries from vulnerability to shocks, it also reflects the pace at which low-income economies reallocate their resources to take advantage of emerging opportunities. While high-income countries tend to exhibit substantial convergence in productivity levels across sectors, the situation is generally the opposite in low-income countries. Therefore, structural change—defined as the shift of resources and labour from low- to high-productivity industries—is both a cause and consequence of sustained economic growth (Chenery 1986). Empirical research suggests that growth rates tend to be lower in economies that fail to engage in that process, and that technological progress is faster in relatively sophisticated sectors (Hulten and Isaksson 2007).

Structural transformation in Africa has been limited

African economies exhibit signs of limited structural transformation that explain why progress has remained slow since independence. In 1965, agricultural value-added represented 22% of SSA's GDP, services 47%, and industry 31% (of which manufacturing contributed 17.5%). In 2007, it was estimated that agricultural value-added still contributed a healthy 15% of GDP, while services contributed 52% and industry 33% (of which manufacturing represented less than 15%).[3] In terms of employment, things have not changed much in nearly half a century: African economies were overwhelmingly rural in 1960, with agriculture accounting for 85% of the labour force. While the rural share of the population has fallen steadily over the past four decades, in 2000 it was still, at 63%, slightly above the 1960 average for non-SSA developing countries. Against the background of high population growth, such little change meant that rural population density increased substantially, putting pressure on arable land per capita. It also meant that urban population grew very rapidly and exacerbated economic, social, and political tensions.

The failure to develop and upgrade their industrial structure and to diversify is a particularly disturbing stylized fact of African economies. Unlike other developing regions of the world—especially Asia—SSA has only gained limited benefits from de-industrialization in high-income countries. The transition towards a service-dominated economic structure in the United States, the European Union, Japan, and elsewhere, often stimulated by innovation and technological upgrading, has involved by implication a retreat of their industrial sector (Debande 2006). Globalization and the quest for competitiveness and profitability have led many firms to relocate labour-intensive manufacturing production away from advanced economies to middle- and low-income countries. Yet few African countries have attracted substantial and transformative levels of foreign capital.

The decline in the agricultural share of the labour force is one of the stylized facts of economic development. In a closed-economy context, such structural change can be sustained only if labour productivity in agriculture increases rapidly enough to feed a growing urban population. In an open economy, food can be imported, but agricultural productivity remains a key determinant of overall living standards and an essential source of foreign exchange for imported capital goods (Ndulu et al. 2008). But there is little evidence that the modest observed shift out of agriculture was driven by advances in rural labour productivity. In the forty-year period 1960–2000, agricultural value-added per worker rose at a trend rate of one 0.5% per year in SSA, less than a third of the prevailing rate within other developing regions.[4] Empirical studies using growth accounting techniques generally conclude that the growth in real GDP per worker in SSA has been driven by the contributions of physical and human capital accumulation per worker, and that total factor productivity (the so-called growth residual) has often

---

[3] World Development Indicators database, World Bank.
[4] Cereal yields did only slightly better, rising at 0.7% per year as compared with 2.4% outside SSA (Ndulu et al. 2008). They also note that relative food prices show little evidence of a systemic food crisis, but the answer may lie in rising food imports: the ratio of net imports of food to GDP rose by 1.4 percentage points a decade in SSA, 8 times faster than outside SSA.

been nil or negative (Hall and Jones 1999; Ndulu et al. 2008). Not surprisingly, the process of industrial upgrading has remained very slow in many African economies.

Economic diversification has also been limited, as evidenced by the high degree of vulnerability of SSA countries to shocks and volatility of annual growth rates, much higher than in other developing regions. Many of these small economies rely primarily on exports. Yet exports have remained concentrated in a narrow band of primary commodities of volatile prices (Monga 2006), and in many cases have become more concentrated over time via the exploitation of mineral resources (Gersovitz and Paxson 1990; Berthélemy and Soderling 2001).

Fostering structural change through market reforms and government strategy

Despite its grim long-run performance and the potentially heavy economic and human cost of the recent global crisis, there is renewed optimism about Africa's economic prospects: the continent has embarked since the mid-1990s on a new and higher growth trajectory. Recent empirical work by leading economists even suggests that Africa may be on the verge of an economic takeoff. For example, Young (2010) sees an 'African growth miracle' in his analysis of measures of real consumption based upon the ownership of durable goods, the quality of housing, the health and mortality of children, the education of youth, and the allocation of female time in the household, which indicate that Sub-Saharan living standards have, for the past two decades, been growing in excess of 3% per annum, i.e. more than three times the rate indicated in international data sets. Using a new methodology to estimate income distributions, poverty rates, and inequality and welfare indices for African countries for the period 1970–2006, Pinkovskiy and Sala-i-Martín (2010) conclude that African poverty is falling rapidly, and that the growth spurt that began in 1995 seems to have decreased African income inequality instead of increasing it.

SSA's improved performance has been made possible largely by improved political and macroeconomic stability, a strengthened political commitment to private-sector growth, and increased investment in infrastructure and education (Okonjo-Iweala 2010). High prices for oil, minerals, and other commodities have substantially contributed to GDP growth, but new research by the McKinsey Global institute show that resources accounted only for about a third of the improvement in performance. The rest resulted from internal structural changes that have spurred the broader domestic economy (Leke et al. 2010). Most economies in the region have indeed been implementing macroeconomic, institutional, and sectoral reforms to improve the business climate and reduce transaction costs. For instance, as of 2010, twenty-eight SSA countries have adopted the

Extractive Industries Transparency Initiative with the aim of improving transparency and governance through the verification and publication of company payments for and government revenue from oil, gas, and mining. In industries such as telecommunications, the continent has made great strides. It has become the fastest-growing region in the global cellular market, going from less than 2 million mobile phones in 1998 to more than 400 million in a decade. Beyond telecommunications, other industries such as banking, retailing, or construction are booming and private investment inflows are surging—though from a low level.

While the region's collective GDP still roughly equals that of a single emerging economy such as Brazil (about $1.6 trillion in 2008), its recent economic progress cannot be underestimated. Since 1990, SSA has almost tripled its level of exports and diversified its trade partners.[5] Clearly, natural resources will continue to be the main source of export revenue for the region as global demand also grows. But with continued reforms and increasing levels of foreign direct investment going to industries with overt or latent comparative advantage, African economies are likely to become more diversified in the future, as the global demand for non-traditional exports is also growing. The key question now is to find a way to sustain that momentum and foster structural transformation in SSA.

Africa's transformation offers both opportunities and challenges to economists and policymakers, who must better understand the roles of the market and the state and how they interact to strengthen the private sector in the process of economic development. This poses several important questions. How to ensure that the ongoing economic transitions work smoothly? How to design and implement successful development approaches to facilitate the smooth diversification and upgrading from one industrial structure to another? Given the existing distortions due to excessive or insufficient interventions by governments, how can African countries move to a first-best, distortion-free world (Lin 2011)?

Given the importance and complexity of the task and the fact that structural change is a multi-faceted concept, it may be conceptually useful to aim at better understanding the dynamics of industrial structure, technological upgrading and macroeconomic performance. Lin and Monga (2011) suggest a framework for growth identification and facilitation, which policymakers can use as an operational guide to strategic macro and micro decisions. Further research on industrial structure could be carried out on the operationalization of this important agenda in specific country contexts.

---

[5] Okonjo-Iweala (2010) notes that the combined share of SSA's share of exports to the European Union and the United States fell to 49%, from 73% in 1990. During this time, its exports to China alone increased to over $13 billion, from $64 million.

REFERENCES

Bagchi, A. K., 1990. 'Industrialization', in *The New Palgrave: Economic Development*. New York: Norton & Co. 160–73.

Berthélemy, J.-C., and L. Soderling, 2001. 'The role of capital accumulation, adjustment and structural change for economic take-off: empirical evidence from African growth episodes', *World Development* 29.2, 323–43.

Chenery, H., 1986. 'Growth and transformation', in H. Chenery, S. Robinson, and M. Syrquin (eds), *Industrialization and Growth: A Comparative Study*. Oxford and Washington, DC: Oxford University Press for the World Bank, 13–36.

Datta, B., 1952. *Economics of Industrialization*. Calcutta: World Press.

Debande, O., 2006. 'De-industrialization', *European Investment Bank Papers* 11.1, 65–82.

Gersovitz, M., and C. Paxson, 1990. *The Economies of Africa and the Prices of Their Exports*. Princeton, NJ: Princeton University, Department of Economics, International Finance Section.

Hall, Robert J., and R. Jones, 1999. 'Why do some countries produce so much more output than others?', *Quarterly Journal of Economics* 114.1, 83–116.

Hulten, C., and A. Isaksson, 2007. 'Why development levels differ: the sources of differential economic growth in a panel of high and low income countries', NBER working paper 13469, Cambridge, Mass.

Kuznets, S., 1966. *Modern Economic Growth: Rate, Structure and Spread*. New Haven, Conn.: Yale University Press.

—— 1971. 'Modern economic growth: findings and reflections', Nobel Lecture, Oslo, December 11.

Leke, A., S. Lund, C. Roxburgh, and A. van Wamelen, 2010. 'What is driving Africa's growth?,' *McKinsey Quarterly* (June).

Lin, J. Y., 2011. 'New structural economics: a framework for rethinking development', *World Bank Research Observer*, 26; 193–221, World Bank.

—— and C. Monga, 2011. 'Growth identification and facilitation: the role of the state in the dynamics of structural change', *Development Policy Review* 29(3), 264–90, World Bank.

Monga, C., 2006. 'Commodities, Mercedes-Benz, and adjustment: an episode in West African history', in E. K. Akyeampong (ed.), *Themes in West Africa's History*. Oxford: James Currey, 227–64.

Ndulu, B., S. O'Connell, R. Bates, P. Collier, and C. Soludo, 2008. *The Political Economy of Economic Growth in Africa, 1960–2000*, Vol. 1. New York: Cambridge University Press.

Okonjo-Iweala, N., 2010. 'Fulfilling the promise of sub-Saharan Africa', *McKinsey Quarterly* (June).

Pack, H., and K. Saggi, 2006. 'Is there a case for industrial policy? A critical survey', *World Bank Research Observer* 21.2, 267–97.

Pinkovskiy, M., and X. Sala-i-Martín, 2010. 'African poverty is falling...much faster than you think!': http://www.columbia.edu/~xs23/papers/pdfs/Africa_Paper_VX3.2.pdf.

Rowthorn, R., and R. Ramaswamy, 1997. 'Deindustrialization: causes and implications', IMF Working Paper WP/97/42 (April), IMF.

UNIDO, 2009. *Industrial Development Report 2009: Breaking In and Moving Up: New Industrial Challenges for the Bottom Billion and the Middle-Income Countries.* New York: United Nations.

Young, A., 2010. 'The African growth miracle': http://mfi.uchicago.edu/programs/fy10_events/papers/feb_26/AfricanGrowthMiracle.pdf.

Industry for Africa
Why? How?

John Page

> Industry rather than agriculture is the means by which rapid improvement in
> Africa's living standards is possible.   (Kwame Nkrumah, 1965)

After four decades, industry is making its way back onto Africa's economic agenda.[1] The continent's post-independence leaders experimented with state-led, import-substituting industrialization, but the industries they created were frequently uncompetitive and unsustainable, and efforts to spur industrial development through public policy largely vanished with the economic collapses and adjustment programmes of the 1980s and 1990s. From 1990 to 2007, during the massive expansion of manufacturing production and exports by developing economies, Africa remained on the sidelines (UNIDO 2009). Now—driven by concerns over the durability of Africa's recent growth and new academic thinking—questions of why and how to industrialize Africa are again beginning to emerge.

Why industrialize?

There are two substantial risks inherent in Africa's continued marginalization from global industrial production and trade. First, because industrial development drives structural change—the main source of long-run growth—lack of industry limits Africa's growth prospects. Second, because geographical concentrations of industry—agglomerations—confer powerful benefits to firms located in them, economies that already have industry are the most likely to attract more.

---

[1] In this chapter I will use the term 'industry and industrialization' to encompass high productivity activities including manufacturing, tradable services, and agro-processing.

WHAT AFRICA MAKES MATTERS: DIVERSITY, SOPHISTICATION, AND STRUCTURAL CHANGE

It is possible for economies to grow based on abundant land or natural resources, but more often structural change—the shift of resources from low-productivity to higher-productivity sectors—is the key driver of economic growth.[2] While Africa has enjoyed a growth recovery since the mid-1990s, it has been driven by the expansion of primary commodity exports and avoiding the growth collapses of the past. Little structural change has taken place, and even before the global economic crisis of 2008–9, growth had become increasingly fragile (Arbache and Page 2008; 2009).

Two recent empirical findings highlight the risks posed by Africa's lack of structural change. The first is that countries with more diversified production (Imbs and Wacziarg 2003) and export (Carrere, Strauss-Kahn, and Cadot 2007) structures have higher incomes per capita. The second is that countries that produce and export more sophisticated products—those that are primarily manufactured by countries at higher income levels—tend to grow faster (Hausman, Hwang, and Rodrik 2007; UNIDO 2009).

The link between diversity, sophistication, and growth most likely runs through productivity change. Generally, industrial diversification occurs at lower levels of per capita income than export diversification (UNIDO 2009), suggesting that more diverse economies are better able to take advantage of export opportunities. As the manufacturing base broadens, economies build industrial competence and begin to export new products, raising productivity by 'learning through exporting'.[3] A wide range of industrial activities may also boost productivity growth through 'churning'—the entry or expansion of more productive firms and the exit of less productive ones.

WHERE AFRICA MAKES IT MATTERS: AGGLOMERATION ECONOMIES

Manufacturing and service industries tend to locate in cities or clusters (Fujita, Krugman, and Venables 1999). Proximity to input suppliers and customers allows firms to realize economies of scale and to resolve coordination problems. Information spillovers, such as the sharing of technological, management, or marketing knowledge, are enhanced when firms in the same industry are located near one another. Workers with specialized skills are attracted to areas where employers use such skills intensively,

---

[2] Cases of successful resource-based development are relatively rare (Collier and Goderis 2007).
[3] The learning by exporting hypothesis is subject to criticism that more productive firms may self-select to export. UNIDO (2009) concludes that the balance of the evidence supports the conclusion that in low-income countries, while self-selection may occur, firms also learn from exporting.

and firms are attracted to areas in which there are a large number of workers (or managers) with skills relevant to their industry.

Agglomeration significantly increases firm-level productivity in high- and middle-income economies (Glaeser et al. 1992; Henderson 1997). More limited evidence suggests that agglomerations also benefit firms in low-income countries, where information spillovers and labour market externalities may be especially important (McCormick 1999; Bigsten, Gebreeyesus, and Söderbom 2008; UNIDO 2009). Because agglomerations raise firm-level productivity, starting a new industrial location is a form of collective action problem: no single firm has the incentive to locate in a new area in the absence of others. Thus, countries which lack significant concentrations of industry will find it difficult both to compete globally and to attract new industry.

Africa's 'de-industrialization'

Manufacturing moved out of Africa in the 1980s and 1990s (UNIDO 2009). The region's share of global manufacturing production (excluding South Africa) fell from 0.4% in 1980 to 0.3% in 2005, and its share of world manufactured exports from 0.3 to 0.2% (UNIDO 2009). Table 1 compares selected indicators of industrial development for Africa and all developing countries in 2005. The share of manufacturing in GDP is about one third of the average for developing countries, and in contrast with developing countries as a whole, it is declining. Per capita (p.c.) manufactured output and exports are less than 20% and 10% of the developing country average, respectively. The region has low levels of manufactured exports in total exports and of medium- and high-technology goods in manufactured exports. These measures have changed little since the 1990s (UNIDO 2009).

The decline in Africa's manufacturing base has been accompanied by a decline in the diversity of the region's manufacturing sectors and a fall in the sophistication of the products produced (Page 2009). The manufacturing sector produced a narrower range of

Table 1. Selected indicators of industrial development, 2005

	Mfg exports p.c. 2005 (US$)	Growth p.c. mfg exports 2000–2005 (%)	Share mfg exports in total (%)	Share medium– high tech. in total mfg exports (%)	Mfg value added p.c. 2005 (US$)	Share of mfg in GDP 2005 (%)	Change in mfg share of GDP 2000–2005
Africa average	39.0	1.65	54.9	13.3	63.6	07.6	–
Developing countries	487.2	10.05	75.8	57.3	372.9	21.7	+

Source: UNIDO database; author's calculations.

less sophisticated products in the 1990s than in the 1980s in sixteen of the eighteen African economies for which production data exist.[4] The fall in manufacturing sophistication was especially sharp in some of the region's early industrializers—Ghana, Kenya, Tanzania, and Zambia.

This narrowing of the production base in manufacturing toward less sophisticated activities resulted from the closure of non-competitive, import substitution industries—many of them state-owned—following the trade liberalizations and privatizations of the adjustment period. These reforms were partially successful: because those manufacturing activities that remained following trade liberalization were more competitive internationally, Africa modestly increased its revealed comparative advantage in exports of low-sophistication products between 1975 and 2000 (Page 2009).

But, the structural adjustment in industry was incomplete. Liberalized international trade benefited the consumers of industrial products and weeded out obviously non-competitive firms, but Africa's industry failed to grow, even in the product lines that remained competitive following the economic reforms. There was little subsequent expansion of manufactured exports or output, and in contrast with rapidly growing low-income countries, neither product nor export sophistication increased in Africa. Private investment remained low, direct foreign investment was largely concentrated in mining and minerals, and despite some notable successes—cut flowers in East Africa, back office services in West Africa, garments in Madagascar and Lesotho—exports remained highly concentrated in traditional activities.

How to industrialize

What policies are appropriate, if Africa is to re-industrialize? Two types of public action will be needed: improvements to the investment climate and helping firms learn to compete.

IMPROVING THE INVESTMENT CLIMATE

Reacting to the unsuccessful—and sometimes disastrous—results of Africa's early experiment with industrialization, the consensus view since the mid-1990s—especially from the international donor community—is that the origins of Africa's poor industrial performance can be traced to deficiencies in the 'investment climate'—the physical, institutional, and regulatory environment within which private investors make their decisions. In short,

---

[4] Sophistication is defined (following Hausmann, Hwang, and Rodrik 2007) as the weighted average per capita income level of the production and export product basket of each country, where the income level of products is defined by the per capita income of countries that intensively produce them (see UNIDO 2009).

Africa lags in industrial development because it is a high-cost, high-risk place in which to do business (Commission on Growth and Development 2008).

The policy agenda for the investment climate has centred on regulatory and labour market reforms designed to lower the cost of doing business by reducing the role of government.[5] These policy and institutional changes are perhaps necessary, but they are not sufficient.[6] A more active role for government is needed in three key areas:

- *Infrastructure.* Africa continues to lag behind other regions badly in terms of the quality and coverage of its basic infrastructure. It is at least 20 percentage points behind the average for low-income countries on almost all major infrastructure measures.[7] In addition, the quality of service is low, supplies are unreliable, and disruptions are frequent and unpredictable. Three closely related initiatives are needed to close the infrastructure gap: first, changing public expenditure priorities to increase the share of the budget devoted to infrastructure investments; second, improving the quality of investment and service delivery—including by encouraging private investment and operation; third, reaching new understandings with development partners concerning the need to support infrastructure.

- *Skills.* Lack of skills limits Africa's industrial potential. Recent research indicates a strong empirical link between export sophistication and the percentage of the labour force that has completed post-primary schooling (World Bank 2007). There is also evidence to suggest that enterprises managed by university graduates in Africa have a higher propensity to export (Wood and Jordan 2000; Clarke 2005), and that among firms owned by indigenous entrepreneurs those with university-educated owners tend to show higher growth rates (Ramachandran and Shah 2007). But, while East Asia increased its secondary and tertiary enrolment rates by 21 and 12 percentage points between 1990 and 2002, Africa raised its secondary and tertiary rates by only 7 and 1 percentage points from a much lower base. Creating new skills in Africa will require major increases in expenditure and improvements in service delivery in post-primary education, including curriculum reform. New agreements with international donors to support a broader definition of human capital formation than that embodied in the current primary education Millennium Development Goal will also be needed.

- *Regional integration.* Regional integration matters a great deal for industrialization in Africa. In part this is because Africa's landlocked countries depend on their neighbours for access to markets. In larger part, however, it matters because Africa is made up of small countries, and small countries have small cities. Big cities generate powerful agglomeration economies. A firm operating in a city of 10,000,000 people has unit costs around 40% lower than if it operated in a city of only 100,000 people (UNIDO 2009). To overcome this problem, a form of regional integration that permits the free movement of goods, capital, and people across borders—allowing the formation of regional cities—will be needed.

---

[5] See e.g. the Doing Business surveys of the World Bank or the World Competitiveness Report of the World Economic Forum.

[6] The relationship between 'doing business' reforms and investment, industrial development, and growth has not been well established empirically. A number of rapid industrializers—notably in Southeast Asia and Central America—score as badly on the 'doing business' surveys as many African economies.

[7] The largest gaps are for rural roads (29 percentage points) and electricity (21 percentage points).

LEARNING TO COMPETE

Investment climate reforms focus explicitly on the environment *external* to the firm. Recent research shows that what takes place *within* the firm also matters for growth. Differences in productivity levels between firms are substantially larger in low-income countries than in high-income countries, and narrowing the gaps in total factor productivity across firms can translate into higher aggregate productivity and higher income levels: growth takes place when firms learn to compete.[8]

The debate about what, if anything, governments can do to raise firm-level competitiveness is at the centre of the decades-long controversy over industrial policy.[9] What is often overlooked in the debate between 'picking winners' and 'levelling the playing field' is that governments make industrial policy every day via the public expenditure programme, institutional and regulatory changes, and international economic policy.[10] These choices favour some enterprises or sectors at the expense of others, but in Africa they often lack a coherent strategic focus.

Although careful studies of firm performance in Africa are severely limited, the available evidence suggests that the early steps in learning to compete should be focused on three strategic objectives:

- *Creating an export push*. There is solid evidence that productivity increases in African firms that export (Söderbom and Teal 2003; Bigsten et al. 2004; Mengiste and Patillo 2004)—perhaps by as much as 9% per year (Bigsten et al. 2004)—and that these productivity gains spill over to other firms (Bigsten, Gebreeyesus, and Söderbom 2008). The public policy implications of such learning by exporting are straightforward but powerful: an 'export push' strategy, involving a concerted set of investments, combined with policy and institutional reforms to promote manufactured exports can boost competitiveness. Few African governments, however, have made such an export push a strategic focus of public policy. While trade reforms have reduced anti-export bias, 'beyond the border' reforms affecting such areas as trade logistics, standards and certification, and export promotion are notably lacking.

- *Supporting industrial clusters*. Africa has few industrial clusters, and solving the collective action problem of starting new industry is therefore a priority. One spatial policy instrument that has worked effectively in Asia is the export processing zone (EPZ). An EPZ provides a clear focus for government investments and institutional reforms designed to encourage the location of firms in a specific area. It is also subject to an efficiency test: firms located in the cluster must be able

---

[8] Hsieh and Klenow (2009), for example, show that these gaps are larger in China and India than in the United States, and that they have the potential to explain between a quarter and a third of the differences in aggregate productivity between the United States and China and India in the manufacturing sector.

[9] The Commission on Growth (2008) concludes that proponents of selective industrial policies have failed to establish their general efficacy, but that some policy interventions have yielded positive results in individual country or institutional settings.

[10] Rodrik (2007) makes a similar point.

to export. Africa has few functioning EPZs (Madani 1999); most lack the minimum level of physical, human, and institutional capital needed to attract a critical mass of firms.

- *Attracting trade in tasks*. In some manufacturing activities the production process can be decomposed into a series of distinct steps, or tasks (Grossman and Rossi-Hansberg 2006). As transport and coordination costs have fallen, different tasks have located in different countries, and low-income countries—including some in Africa—have gained a foothold in end stage assembly of consumer products. End stage tasks are highly mobile, and African economies can benefit from this mobility through concerted programmes of investment promotion, provision of infrastructure, and improvements in the investment climate. A logical place to begin is in an export processing zone.

Conclusions

This chapter began by asking why and how Africa should industrialize. The answer to 'why' is relatively simple: for the vast majority of the region's economies lack of industry acts as a powerful constraint to growth. The answer to 'how' is more complex. Undoubtedly, improvements to the investment climate are still needed. But Africa's enterprises must also learn to compete. Here, the role of public policy is more controversial, and Africa's past experiments have been largely unsuccessful. Nevertheless, strategies to create an export push, support industrial clusters, and attract task-based production—perhaps brought together initially through effective use of EPZs—offer an opportunity for a new start on industrialization.

■ REFERENCES

Arbache, J. S., and J. Page, 2008. 'Patterns of long term growth in sub-Saharan Africa', in D. Go and J. Page (eds), *Africa at a Turning Point? Growth, Aid and External Shocks*. Washington, DC: World Bank.

———— 2009. 'How fragile is Africa's recent growth?', *Journal of African Economies* 19.1, 1–24.

Bigsten, Arne, et al., 2004. 'Do African exporters learn from exporting?', *Journal of Development Studies* 40.3, 115–41.

——Mulu Gebreeyesus, and Måns Söderbom, 2008. 'Agglomeration effects in Ethiopian manufacturing', Department of Economics, University of Gothenburg.

Carrere, Celine, Vanessa Strauss-Kahn, and Olivier Cadot, 2007. 'Export diversification: what's behind the hump?', CEPR Discussion Paper 6590, London.

Clarke, George R. G., 2005. 'Beyond tariffs and quotas: why don't African manufacturers export more?', Policy Research Working Paper 4317, World Bank.

Collier, Paul, and B. Goderis, 2007. 'Prospects for commodity exporters: hunky dory or Humpty Dumpty?', *World Economics* 8, 1–18.

Commission on Growth and Development, 2008. *The Growth Report: Strategies for Sustained Growth and Inclusive Development.* Washington, DC: World Bank.

Fujita, M., P. Krugman, and A. J. Venables, 1999. *The Spatial Economy: Cities, Regions and International Trade.* Cambridge, Mass.: MIT Press.

Glaeser, E. L., H. D. Kallal, A. Scheinkman, and A. Shleifer, 1992. 'Growth in cities', *Journal of Political Economy* 100: 1126–52.

Grossman, G., and E. Rossi-Hansberg, 2006. 'The rise of offshoring: it's not wine for cloth anymore', in *The New Economic Geography: Effects and Policy Implications.* Conference Volume, Federal Reserve Bank of Kansas City.

Hausmann, R., J. Hwang, and D. Rodrik, 2007. 'What you export matters', *Journal of Economic Growth* 12.1, 1–25.

Henderson, J. V., 1997. 'Externalities and industrial development', *Journal of Urban Economics* 42.3, 449–70.

Hsieh, Chang-Tai, and Peter Klenow, 2009. 'Misallocation and manufacturing TFP in China and India', *Quarterly Journal of Economics* 124.4, 1403–48.

Imbs, Jean, and R. Wacziarg, 2003. 'Stages of diversification', *American Economic Review* 93.1, 63–86.

Madani, Dorsati, 1999. 'A review of the role and impact of export processing zones', Washington, DC: World Bank.

McCormick, D., 1999. 'African enterprise clusters and industrialization: theory and reality', *World Development* 27.9, 1531–51.

Mengiste, T., and Cathy Patillo, 2004. 'Export orientation and productivity in sub-Saharan Africa', *IMF Staff Papers* 51.2, 327–53.

Page, John, 2009. 'Should Africa industrialize?', paper presented at the UNU-WIDER/UNU-MERIT/UNIDO workshop 'Pathways to Industrialization in the 21st Century', 22–3 October, UNU-MERIT.

Ramachandran, Vijaya, and Manju Shah, 2007. 'Why are there so few black-owned firms in Africa? Preliminary results from enterprise survey data', Center for Global Development Working Paper 104, Washington, DC.

Rodrik, D., 2007. 'Normalizing industrial policy', Commission on Growth and Development Working Paper 3, Washington, DC.

Söderbom, Mans, and Francis Teal, 2003. 'Are manufacturing exports the key to economic success in Africa?', *Journal of African Economies* 12.1, 1–29.

UNIDO, 2009. *Industrial Development Report, 2009 Breaking in and Moving Up: New Industrial Challenges for the Bottom Billion and the Middle Income Countries.* Geneva: UNIDO.

Wood, Adrian, and Kate Jordan, 2000. 'Why does Zimbabwe export manufactures and Uganda not?', *Journal of Development Studies* 37.2, 91–116.

World Bank, 2007. 'Expanding the possible in sub-Saharan Africa: how tertiary institutions can increase growth and competitiveness', Washington, DC: World Bank.

Africa's Private Sector

Vijaya Ramachandran

Introduction

The performance of Africa's economies has improved recently, but there is still a huge lag in terms of long-term growth, structural change, and industrial development. Why is business performance lagging in Africa? And is Africa different from the rest of the developing world? Africa is distinctive in several ways—in particular, economies are both very small and very sparse, and their manufacturing sectors are modest. These structural factors have several implications for industrial structure and performance, through factors such as the cost of providing infrastructure and the potential for competition. Unlike the rapidly growing Asian economies, whose rising incomes have been associated with structural shifts from agriculture to industry, even the better-performing low-income African economies have tended to move from agriculture toward the tertiary sector, with relatively slow growth in industry and sluggish industrial employment growth (Fig. 1). In addition, total investment has often grown less than might be expected given the substantial gains in foreign direct investment, suggesting that domestic processes of accumulation and investment are still weak. Moreover, due to low incomes in Africa, the gap with other regions continues to widen in absolute terms even if there is a slow convergence in percentage terms. This is very different from the picture in China and other countries in Asia, where rapid growth and penetration of world markets with manufactured exports are driving the economic and social transformation of those countries.

In a typical low-income African country, most private activity is in agriculture, small-scale services and industry, and finance. A small component of the private sector consists of large-scale, more sophisticated firms, in some cases expatriate or minority, sometimes with close ties to government. The mining sector is dominated by very large firms, as are other resource extraction industries. Overall, the private sector in Africa has low capitalization and relatively low skills, but due to the dichotomy between resource and non-resource related activity, there is also a fairly large spread in terms of capital and skill level. In many countries, much of the formal sector consists of government, while many firms operate in semi-formal or informal environments. The transformation of the private sector to modern firms, especially in manufacturing (including resource processing), has been slow (as Fig. 1 suggests). In this essay, I will cover both internal

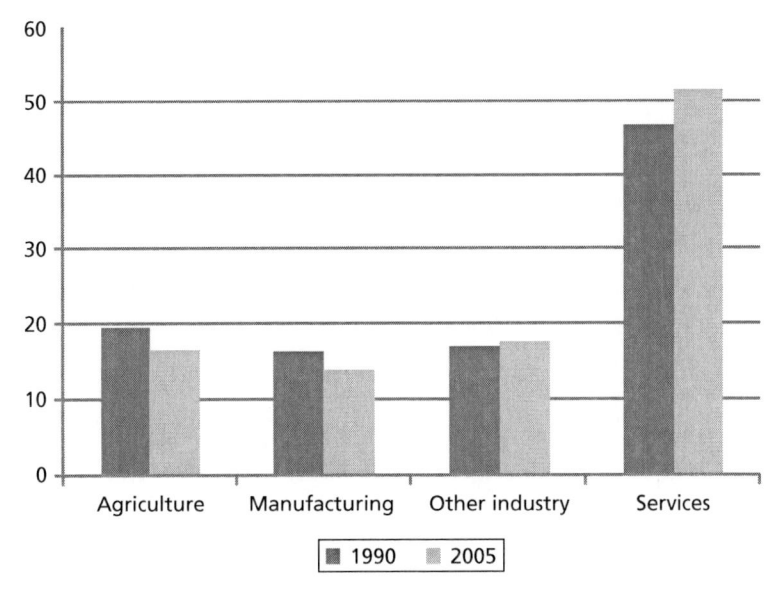

Figure 1. Sector shares of GDP in Africa, 1990 and 2005 (% of GDP) (source: World Development Indicators)

points like capabilities and external ones such as costs imposed by the business environment.

The cost of doing business in Africa

Perhaps the most important determinant of performance is the business environment in which firms operate. Does it encourage firms to learn, to invest and grow, and to compete on a global scale? Or does it involve high costs and risks that create disincentives for an entrepreneur who might wish to establish a business, invest in it, or increase its productivity? Is the business environment competitive enough to spur innovation and expansion, or does it impede change? Data from the World Bank's Enterprise Surveys and other sources show that many African countries bear a heavy burden of indirect costs and losses that make their overall profitability lower than might be expected on the basis of their factory-floor productivity (Eifert, Gelb and Ramachandran 2008). Despite low productivity and serious skill deficiencies, unit labour costs may not be the binding constraint on firms in Africa. Many of Africa's firms are quite productive, and the question often is how to bring down indirect costs and losses to enable higher value-added production and generate profits to feed into investment, fund growing, and higher pay for the workforce.

The observed lags in the development of the private sector in Africa are based on the interaction of several factors (Söderbom and Teal 2003). These include the small size of markets and overall economic sparseness, which together discourage competition and innovation, reduce the entry of new firms, and increase demands on infrastructure. With increasing economic activity, the lack of a reliable source of power has emerged as a particularly serious constraint on private sector activity. More than half of all private-sector firms rank the lack of a reliable supply of power as their worst constraint. Firms that are able to compensate for lack of electricity by using generators are able to survive better than firms that do not have a generator, but self-generation is extremely costly, about triple the price of power from a grid. Moreover, the low density of economic activity lowers the return to investing in infrastructure.

Figure 3 illustrates the impact of the high-cost business environment on firm productivity. Defining net value added as gross value added minus the costs of indirect inputs such as electricity and transportation, it shows the difference in the distributions of productivity across firms within China, Kenya, Tanzania, and Zambia. The China distribution is heavily skewed to the right, with most of the mass of firms between 0.75 and 0.95. The African distributions have a great deal of mass on the left, in the 0.30–0.60 range, suggesting that many African firms see their ability to produce value beyond the cost of their direct and indirect inputs heavily constrained by the magnitude of cost of the latter. That is true in Zambia in particular, where the distribution is centred around 0.40.

Another issue to consider is whether the private sector's performance can be attributed to overvaluation of exchange rates in Africa and/or the undervaluation of the Chinese exchange rate. African countries do tend to have higher price levels than those predicted by the Balassa–Samuelson rule, which holds that lower relative price

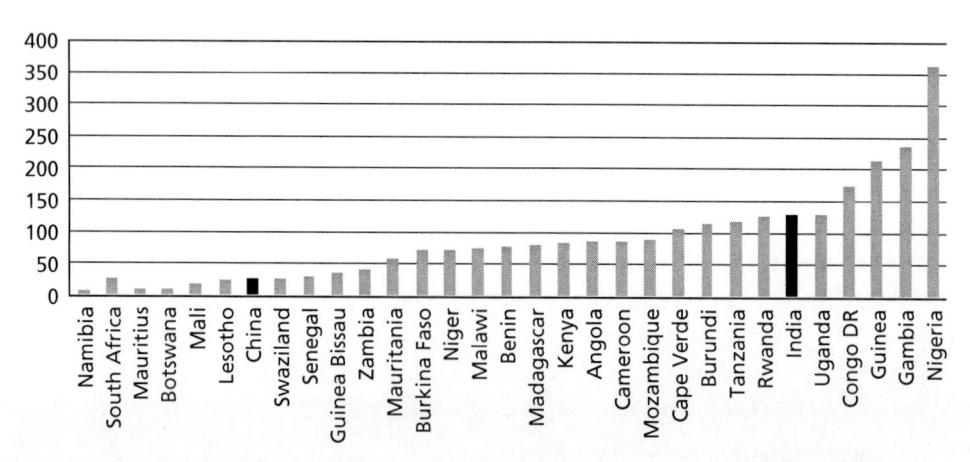

Figure 2. Number of days on which power outages occurred (source: Enterprise Surveys)

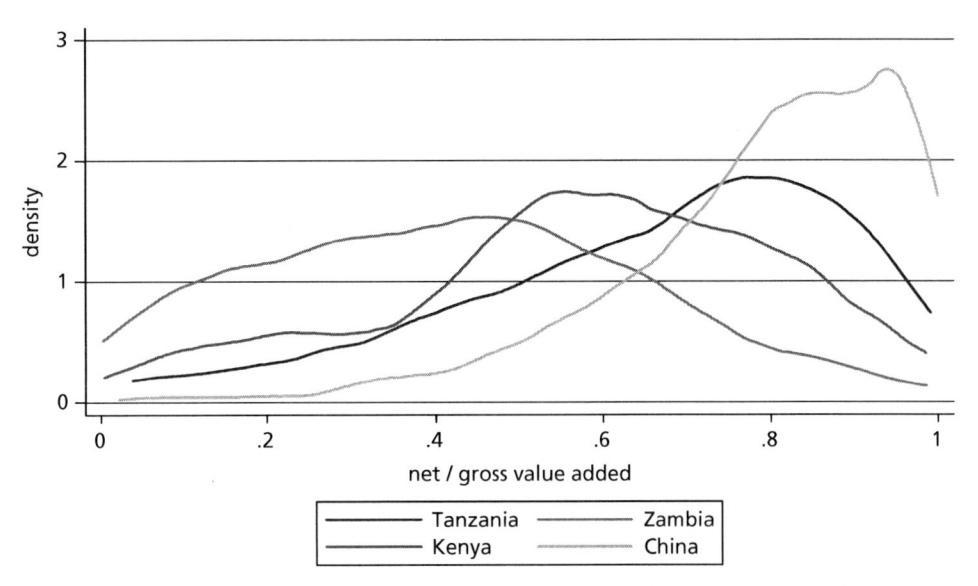

Figure 3. Distribution of the ratio of net to gross value added, Africa versus China (kernel density estimation)

Source: Reprinted from Eifert, Benn, Alan Gelb and Vijaya Ramachandran, "The Cost of Doing Business in Africa: Evidence from Enterprise Survey Data," World Development, Vol. 36, No. 9, pp. 1531–1546, 2008. With permission from Elsevier.

levels for non-tradables in poorer countries should translate into lower overall price levels. Several rounds of purchasing power parity (PPP) data indicate that prices in Africa's low-income countries were higher in absolute terms than prices in China and South Asia, and about 30% above the level predicted by per capita income; in comparison, prices in Asia were 13–20% below predictions. But when African firms were asked about the prices that they paid for raw materials, they indicated that the prices they paid were *two to three times* what firms in China paid (Eifert et al. 2008). This cannot be due entirely to exchange rate valuation. Furthermore there is considerable variation in costs across sectors and firms—the imbalances must be driven by other factors. Finally, exchange rate overvaluation should affect the cost of domestic inputs relative to imported inputs rather than the total cost of inputs. But we observe very high costs for imported inputs (including capital) and often low quality as well—neither of which seems to be explained very well by exchange rate overvaluation. Costly and variable logistical services are probably to blame.

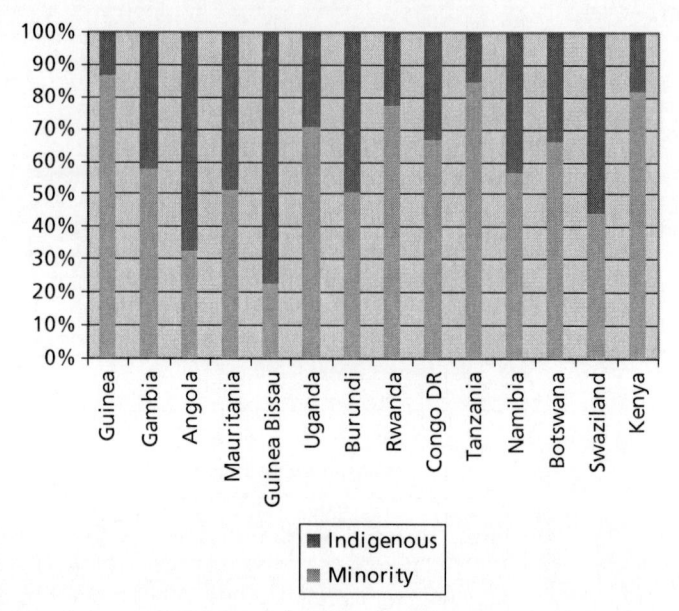

Figure 4. Distribution of value added by ethnicity (%) (source: Enterprise Surveys)

Indigenous entrepreneurship in Africa

The vast majority of firms in Africa are in fact indigenous-owned, but a relatively small share of minority-owned firms controls the vast majority of value added in the sample of countries across Africa described for a sample of countries in Figure 4.[1] The data show that minority-owned firms control the vast majority of industrial value added in surveys conducted in a number of African countries. In Guinea, Tanzania, and Kenya, they control more than 80% of value added.

Figure 5, which gives the start-up and current size of indigenous and minority-owned firms, shows that indigenous firms enter the market at significantly smaller sizes than minority-owned businesses. While the average firm size at start-up of minority-owned firms in Tanzania was about sixty employees, the number was just under twenty for indigenous businesses. For most countries, minority firms start at a size that is two to three times greater than that of indigenous businesses.

Indigenous firms also suffer from less access to credit. They are less likely to have bank accounts, overdraft protection, and loans. It is an open question whether access to the banking sector correlated with financial depth or whether banks are simply sorting firms

---

[1] 'Indigenous-owned' refers to firms that are owned by black Africans or have majority of black African shareholders. 'Minority-owned' refers to firms that are owned by African nationals of Asian, Middle Eastern, or Caucasian descent.

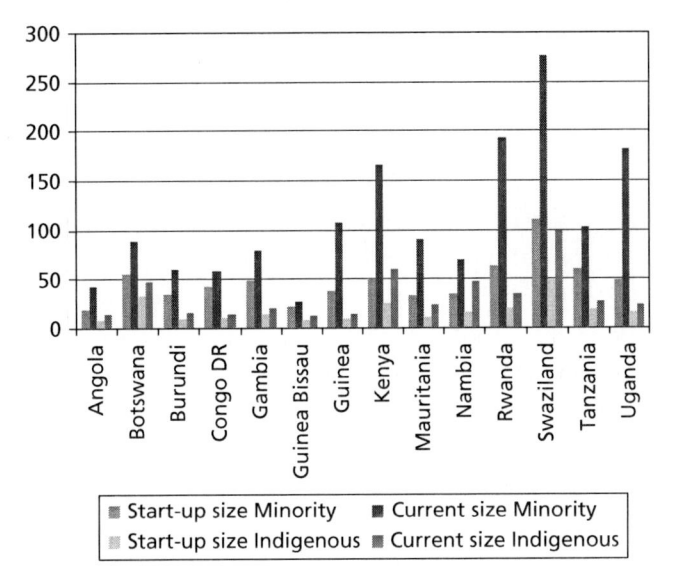

Figure 5. Start-up and current size of indigenous and minority-owned firms (no. of employees) (source: Enterprise Surveys)

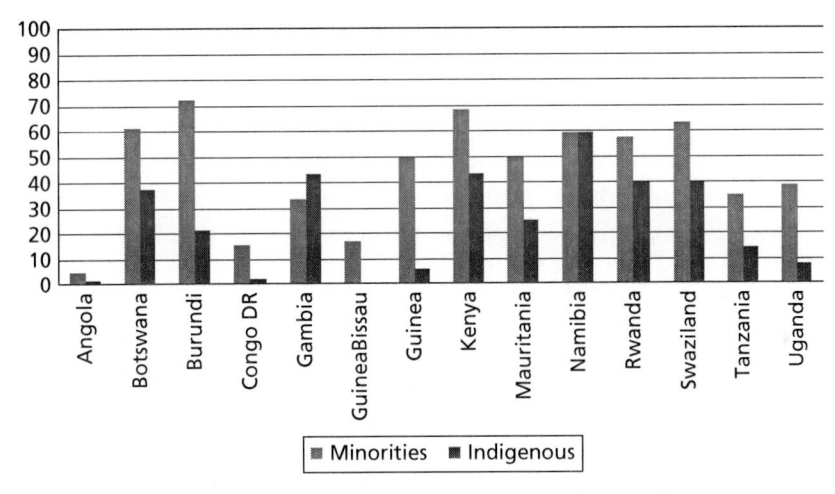

Figure 6. Firms with overdrafts, by ethnicity (source: Enterprise Surveys)

according to their creditworthiness (Fig. 6).[2] Certainly, there are differences in the share of firms with audited accounts when disaggregated by ethnicity. Indigenous firms are less likely than minority-owned firms to own their business premises; consequently, they

---

[2] Access to loans follows a pattern similar to that for overdrafts, but the differences across ethnicity are not pronounced. In fact, in countries such as Botswana, Swaziland, and Namibia, more indigenous firms than minority firms use loans. It may well be that indigenous firms simply choose to use a different type of financing.

have less collateral with which to obtain financing. These firms are less likely to be creditworthy, and perhaps have less access to finance for this reason. The data do show, however, that education is important for indigenous firm owners—those with a university degree are likely to start larger businesses and grow them faster than those who did not go to university.

One explanation for these results lies in the role of networks (Biggs and Shah 2006). Usually within ethnic minority communities, networks help firms overcome the limitations of financial markets. At the same time, they effectively exclude outsiders from areas of business. Networks operate in many other regions, including fast-growing Asian countries, where they may have similarly positive effects in enabling their members to compensate for dysfunctional market institutions. But their overall impact is likely to be different in Asia and Africa, because of differences in economic density, market size, and the abundance of land (Platteau and Hayami 1998). In Asia, their adverse effect in stifling competition is likely to be small because of the competitive pressure that results from having many firms that belong to many networks. However, in Africa's very small economies, the adverse effect of a few dominant networks or firms is likely to be far greater. Firms in sparse economies are likely to give more weight to the costs and risks of encouraging entry through reforms than are firms in dense economies.

Small, sparse industrial sectors dominated by a few, often ethnically segmented, firms with high market share are therefore likely to see less dynamic competition. The greater access of larger, networked firms to technology, credit, and business expertise creates rents that, even if shared with government, would be dissipated by more open entry. That can reduce the incentive to push hard for better regulation and business services. The segmented nature of many African business communities can complicate the process of developing effective means of communication between the business and government sectors to improve the business environment. At the same time, the prominent role of minority and expatriate firms increases the public's reservations over the market economy model, including large privatizations. The danger is a low-level equilibrium with high costs, limited pressure for reform from the business community and the public, and limited response from government.

Overall, the interaction of a high-cost, low-density business environment, and the dominance of a few firms—often larger, minority-owned businesses—may underlie the absence of a broad-based, productive private sector in many African countries.

Solutions to broaden the private sector

The implementation of solutions to these problems remains a serious challenge. Despite decades of donor advice and some significant reforms, it is still relatively difficult to find policymakers who really trust markets to deliver results; given the choice, governments often prefer a regulatory or administrative solution (Emery 2003). Governments are sometimes concerned that liberalizations or reforms will benefit already entrenched business groups. In other cases, they may be concerned that reforms are potentially threatening to the position of the relatively few large businesses, which often have large market shares and longstanding relationships with government.

Some Africa scholars argue that it is convenient to have a private sector that is dominated by ethnic minorities, who do not pose a significant threat to political power and often provide a steady stream of rents. The minority Asian community in East Africa, which has thrived even in difficult times, often coexists with a small, wealthy, indigenous private sector; both are closely aligned with the president or his associates (Tangri 1999). The survival of this group depends on its political connections and rent-sharing arrangements with the government. The government in turn relies on it for extra-budgetary revenues. Other scholars reinforce this perspective, arguing that the political elite in Africa have found mechanisms by which to preserve rent-seeking arrangements with the help of a small private sector enclave (van de Walle 2001). When faced with donor country-driven reforms, governments have often reacted by accomplishing partial reform, thereby satisfying the rich countries while preserving rent-seeking arrangements (van de Walle 2001). As a result, there has not been much change in the structure or competitiveness of the private sector. Indeed, reforms often have increased the level of uncertainty for the business community more than anything else.

How can governments be convinced that a broad-based, relatively unfettered private sector is both possible and in their interest? Some governments have tried drastic measures to curb the rights of minority entrepreneurs, but these have not resulted in viable opportunities for indigenous entrepreneurs. Others fear the emergence of a private sector that will be unmanageable, but experience from around the world suggests that a more competitive private sector will not immediately translate into a threat to whoever is in office. Available evidence shows that, for the most part, reforms to promote private-sector development have led, at least in the early stages, to a proliferation of small and medium firms in countries such as Taiwan and Malaysia. These firms are hardly a challenge to political incumbents, and indeed are probably less likely to lead to political problems than systems which foster the rise of a small, wealthy class of tycoons.

In addition, there is no central authority to make critically needed regional investments—no equivalent of a federal government or a pan-African highway administration or power authority, with a mandate to fill the gaps in regional investments, especially in the area of infrastructure. Internal markets remain small and segmented, exporters face high costs of transportation, and key bottlenecks to growth are yet to be alleviated. For a broad-based private sector to emerge, key reforms must include:

- open borders, which encourage conglomeration, increase the scale of markets, and the density of economic activity;
- improvements in infrastructure, especially power and logistics (especially roads), and further planning of these to reinforce conglomeration and scale economies;
- introduction of service guarantees to improve the responsiveness of governments to businesses' service needs;
- efforts to broaden the base of the private sector, strengthening business services, private–public dialogue, and support of home-grown efforts such as the Investment Climate Facility for Africa.

There is no single binding constraint and no 'silver bullet' to eliminate it, but the research and data that are becoming available on Africa's firms and business climate can help increase the possibility of accelerating regulatory and institutional reforms to complement improvements in infrastructure and macroeconomic management. We must continue to identify specific approaches to private-sector development that we believe will make a difference for growth in the African private sector. Although the better information on the quality of regulation and business services now becoming available can be a powerful tool for accelerating reforms, this information needs to be integrated more systematically with reforms in other key areas of the business environment, such as infrastructure investment, and into a structured dialogue between governments and private-sector groups.

REFERENCES

Biggs, Tyler, and Manju Kedia Shah, 2006. 'African small and medium enterprises, networks, and manufacturing performance', World Bank Policy Research Working Paper 3855.

Eifert, Benn, Alan Gelb, and Vijaya Ramachandran, 2008. 'The cost of doing business in Africa: evidence from enterprise survey data', *World Development* 36.9, 1531–46.

Emery, James, 2003. 'Governance and private investment in Africa', in Nicolas van de Walle, Nicole Ball, and Vijaya Ramachandran (eds), *Beyond Structural Adjustment: The Institutional Context of African Development*. New York: Palgrave Macmillan.

Platteau, Jean-Philippe, and Yujiro Hayami, 1998. 'Resource endowments and agricultural development: Africa versus Asia', in Yujiro Hayami and Masahiko Aoki (eds), *The Institutional Foundations of East Asian Economic Development*. Basingstoke: Macmillan, 357–410.

Söderbom, Måns, and Francis Teal, 2003. 'Are manufactured exports the key to economic success in Africa?', *Journal of African Economies* 12.1, 1–29.

Tangri, Roger, 1999. *The Politics of Patronage in Africa*. Trenton, NJ: Africa World Press.

Van de Walle, Nicolas, 2001. *African Economies and the Politics of Permanent Crisis, 1979–1999*. Cambridge: Cambridge University Press.

World Bank Enterprise Surveys. 2001–present: www.enterprisesurveys.org.

Foreign Direct Investment in Africa: What Do We Know?

S. Ibi Ajayi

Introduction

With the exception of a few countries, the vast majority of the fast-growing economies of the world relied heavily on foreign direct investment (FDI) to jump-start and sustain their rapid economic transformation. As a result of FDI's potential role in accelerating growth and economic transformation, many developing countries in general, and Africa in particular, seek such investments to accelerate their development efforts. A number of African countries have been putting in place various measures which they hope will attract FDI. They have introduced different incentive structures (sometimes called 'sweeteners') to ensure that resources are directed to areas and sectors which can deal with issues such as employment generation and poverty elimination. It is not clear, however, whether FDI is actually being attracted into industries and sectors that have the greatest multiplier effect in promoting sustained growth and indirectly alleviating poverty. It is also not often realized that in order for a country to fully benefit from the spillover effects of FDI, there must be a minimum threshold of absorptive capacity. Right policies therefore do matter in order to benefit from this aspect of globalization.[1] The broad objective of this chapter is to document what we do know about foreign direct investment in Africa.

Trends in FDI in Africa

In the period 1993–8, Africa attracted $7.1 billion of FDI inflows, and its share of FDI to developing countries was 5.1%. The inflows rose steadily until they reached $20 billion in 2001, but declined thereafter. In 2004 FDI inflows started an upward trend again,

---

[1] For details of the various policy changes that are required see Ajayi (2000).

Table 1. FDI inflows by region, 1993–2007 (billions of US$)

Region	1993–8 (annual average)	1999	2000	2001	2002	2003	2004	2005	2006	2007
Developing economies	138.9	232.5	252.2	217.8	155.5	166.3	233.2	316.4	413.0	499.7
Africa	7.1	11.9	9.6	20	13	18	18.1	29.5	45.8	53.0
Latin America and the Caribbean	47.9	108.6	97.5	89.1	50.5	46.9	67.5	76.4	93.0	126.3
Asia and Oceania	83.9	112	146	108.7	92	101.4	147.6	210.6	274.3	320.5
Asia	83.4	111.6	145.7	108.6	92	101.3	147.5	210.0	209.1	202.1
West Asia	3.5	1.9	3.8	7.1	5.7	6.5	9.8	42.6	64.0	71.5
East Asia	51.6	77.3	116.2	78.7	67.3	72.1	105	116.2	131.9	156.7
China	38.5	40.3	40.7	46.9	52.7	53.5	60.6	72.4	72.7	83.5
South Asia	2.9	3.1	3.1	4.1	4.5	5.3	7	12.1	25.8	30.6
Southeast Asia	25.3	29.3	22.6	18.8	14.5	17.4	25.7	39.1	51.2	60.5
Oceania	0.4	0.4	0.3	0.1	0	0.1	0.1	0.55	1.4	1.1
Southeast Europe and the CIS	6.6	10.5	9.1	11.8	12.8	24.1	34.9	30.0	57.2	85.9
Southeast Europe	1.6	3.7	3.6	4.5	3.8	8.4	10.8	4.8	10.0	11.9
CIS	5	6.8	5.5	7.3	9	15.7	24.1	26.1	47.2	74.0
World	401.7	1,092.1	1,396.5	825.9	716.1	632.6	648.1	958.7	1,411.0	1,833.3

Source: UNCTAD (2005b; 2009).

reaching $53 billion in 2007.[2] This upsurge was brought about by rising corporate profits and high commodity prices, especially that of petroleum. The upsurge notwithstanding, the region's share in global FDI continued to be low, at just 3%. Table 1 presents relevant statistics on FDI inflows by regions.

Africa continues to attract FDI only into sectors where competitive advantages outweigh the continent's negative factors. These include minerals, timber, coffee, and oil (Mills and Oppenheimer 2002). Contrary to common perception, however, the concentration of FDI in Africa is not only in mineral resources. Even in the oil-exporting countries, services and manufacturing are becoming key sectors for FDI.[3] In 1992, for example, 30% of FDI stock in Nigeria was in the primary sector, 50% in manufacturing, and 20% in services. Similarly in 1995, 48% of FDI inflows into Egypt were in services, 47% in manufacturing, and only about 4% in the primary sector. Over time, Mauritius has been attracting FDI into the manufacturing sector, mainly textiles and electronics. Morocco's FDI receipts have risen fivefold in the past decade, most of it in manufacturing and services. Telecommunications has assumed great importance, with the privatization of telephone companies in many countries and the emergence of the global system of communication.

---

[2] The 10 main beneficiaries of FDI in Africa are Nigeria, Egypt, Morocco, Libya, South Africa, Sudan, Tunisia, Madagascar, Equatorial Guinea, and Algeria.

[3] For more details see 'Fact Sheet on Foreign Direct Investment: Focus on the New Africa': http://www.fdi.net/unctad/fdiafrica_frame.htm.

The leading sources of FDI into Africa are the USA, the UK, France, and Germany. Germany's FDI has increasingly been going into the manufacturing sector, while more than 60% of the British FDI stock is in the manufacturing and service sector. FDI from the United States has been going into manufacturing, mainly in food and metal products, primary and fabricated metals. The US share of FDI stock in Africa in the primary sector dropped from 79% in 1986 to 53% in 1996 (Ikiara 2003). There are of course country differences based on historical linkages, mainly political and diplomatic relationship. In recent times, there has been increasing FDI from developing countries, mainly China, India, and other Asian countries. There have been flows from South Africa to other parts of Africa.

What do we know about the determinants of FDI?

In a survey of the evidence on the various determinants of FDI in Africa, Ajayi (2004) identifies the following:[4]

- size of the market and growth;
- costs and skill of the labour force;
- availability of good infrastructure;
- country risk;
- openness of the economy;
- institutional environment;
- availability of natural resources;
- concentration of other investors (agglomeration effects);
- return on investment;
- enforceability of contracts and transparency of the judicial system;
- macroeconomic stability;
- availability of 'sweetener' policies.

The empirical results on the determinants of foreign direct investment show two strands of results which are important to Africa. First, they show that governments in the region can play a major role in promoting FDI through appropriate policy framework, and that FDI to Africa is not solely driven by natural resources endowment but is also influenced by other factors (see Asiedu 2006).

The second strand of results arises from the International Monetary Fund/African Economic Research Consortium (IMF/AERC) special workshop on 'The Determinants of Foreign Direct Investment in Africa'.[5] It was clear that different policies have been

---

[4] The list is by no means exhaustive.
[5] The workshop took place in Nairobi in December 2004; the dissemination workshop took place in Accra in September 2006.

adopted by different countries, and that the responses to the policies have been different. It was found out, first, that there is no unanimously accepted single factor determining the flow of FDI. Second, while the list of factors determining investment is fairly long, not all determinants are equally important to every investor in every location at all times. Third, some determinants are more important at a given time than another time. The weights attached to the various factors influencing investment flows vary between investors. Fourth, macroeconomic and political stability are necessary but not sufficient for FDI inflows. Fifth, a critical minimum level of factors is important for the flows of FDI, and policies do matter in each of the countries. Sixth, for countries to derive positive effects of FDI inflows, they must be in the driver's seat in terms of putting in place appropriate development strategy.[6]

The FDI–growth linkage

How does FDI affect growth? While the positive FDI–growth linkage is not unambiguously accepted, macroeconomic studies nevertheless support a positive role for FDI, especially in particular environments. Existing literature identifies three main channels through which FDI can bring about economic growth. The first is through the release from the constraint of domestic savings brought about by foreign capital inflows. Second, FDI is the main conduit through which technological transfer takes place. Third, FDI leads to increases in exports as a result of increased capacity and competitiveness in domestic production. Empirical analysis of the positive relationship is often said to depend on one other factor, 'absorptive capacity', and includes the level of human capital development, type of trade regimes, and degree of openness of the economy.

The macroeconomic empirical literature finds weak support for an exogenous positive effect of FDI on economic growth. For 72 developing countries between 1960 and 1978, Jackman (1982) finds that FDI had no significant impact on growth once cognizance is taken of the country's size. Rothgeb (1984) finds that FDI was negatively linked to growth for the set of eighteen developing countries as a whole, while for the set of Latin American countries, FDI positively affected growth. Most recent evidence has established a robust link between FDI and growth. In the aggregate cross-country studies, de Mello (1996) finds evidence that FDI gives rise to growth in five Latin American economies. Williams and Williams (1999) find that for the Eastern Caribbean central bank unified currency area, FDI appears to crowd in gross investment and has a positive impact on growth. Borensztein, Gregorie, and Lee (1998) find that FDI is an important

---

[6] Papers presented at the conference by Ajayi, Asante, Khan, Obwona, Ogunkola, Mwega, Siphambe, and Akinboade are listed in the References section.

vehicle for the transfer of technology, contributing more to growth than domestic investment. Country- and industry-level studies find positive impacts of FDI on economic growth. Obwona (1999) found a positive relationship between FDI and growth for Uganda.

From the literature, it is clear that a country's ability to take advantage of the positive effects of FDI might be limited by local conditions such as the development of the local financial markets, or the educational level of the country. This is called 'absorptive capacity'. Borensztein et al. (1998) and Xu (2000) show that FDI brings technology, which translates into higher growth only when the host country has a minimum threshold of stock of human capital. The research by Alfaro et al. (2006) shows:

- An increase in FDI leads to higher growth rates in financially developed countries as opposed to the rates observed in financially undeveloped countries.
- The best connections are between final and intermediate industry sectors, not necessarily between domestic and foreign final goods producers.
- Human capital plays a critical role in achieving growth benefits from FDI.

Thus the jury is still out concerning whether FDI directly causes economic growth without preconditions.

FDI is also not without its negative impacts. While I have explored the positive aspects of FDI, this does not mean that it cannot lead to undesirable outcomes. In most cases, as I shall show, these negative trends are not unavoidable. Indeed, they are the results of distortions and inefficiencies in the domestic economy, which can be avoided through appropriate policies and sound regulatory framework (Sun 2002). The three negative effects that are mentioned in the literature are: the crowding-out effect of FDI, the balance of payments problems of FDI, and the enclaves economy created by FDI.

The various findings (in particular, the mixed results) with respect to the FDI–growth linkage have significant policy implications for Africa.[7] First, the fact that the FDI–growth linkage is not automatic implies that policies must be designed by various countries to ensure that FDI is directed to areas and sectors where it will have the greatest impact. Second, whether there is a positive FDI–growth linkage depends on the country and sectors of the economy. In other words, there is need for specific country and sector study in order to meaningfully assess the FDI–growth linkage. Third, the issue of absorptive capacity mentioned in terms of human capital development, and financial development are important. It can therefore be rightly said that whether FDI contributes to development depends on the macroeconomic policies and structural conditions in host countries.

---

[7] UNCTAD (2005: 64) takes the position that there is little evidence to suggest that FDI in Africa (or elsewhere in the developing world) plays a leading role in the growth process.

What then are the policies that can create a friendly environment for FDI inflows in Africa?

African countries have in the last decade made considerable efforts to improve their investment climate. Many governments have liberalized, and some are still liberalizing, their FDI regimes, as they associate FDI with positive effects on economic development and poverty reduction. The significant upsurge that is expected in FDI inflows as a result of the improvements in economic performance and the liberalization of policies is, however, yet to occur.

In a previous section I discussed various factors that can inhibit FDI flows. From available surveys and cross-country studies, the following are the most promising high-return policies to improve the investment climate and attract FDI inflows.

(i) Reduction of obstacles to FDI by removing excessive regulations and putting in place policies which are favourable to FDI.

(ii) Protecting and enforcing property rights: the legal framework—especially the ability to enforce property rights, contracts, and impartial avenues for conflict resolution—is a key element of an enabling environment for private sector development.

(iii) Reduction in the level of corruption (or better: zero tolerance for corruption) and an improvement in the quality of the bureaucracy.

(iv) Improvement in the quality and availability of infrastructure: in many African countries some infrastructure components, like water and electricity, are erratic. If investors have to provide their own electricity and water, these are additional costs.

(v) Need for political stability: countries that are mired in conflicts, wars and turbulence as demonstrated by assassinations, coups, and revolutions are unlikely to attract FDI.

REFERENCES

Ajayi, S. Ibi, 2000. 'What Africa needs to do to benefit from globalization', *Finance and Development* 38.4.

——2003. 'Globalization and Africa', *Journal of African Economies* 12, 120–50.

——2004. 'Issues of globalization in Africa: the opportunities and the challenges', *Ibadan Journal of the Social Sciences* 2.1.

——2007a. 'FDI and its role in promoting the private sector', paper presented at the Annual Meeting of the Islamic Development Bank Group, 28 May, Dakar.

——2007b. 'The determinants of foreign direct investment in Africa: a survey of the evidence', in S. Ibi Ajayi (ed.), *Foreign Direct Investment in Sub-Saharan Africa: Determinants, Origins, Targets, Impact and Potential*. Nairobi: African Economic Research Consortium.

——2009. 'Foreign direct investment and economic development in Africa', in *Accelerating Africa's Development Five years into the 21st Century*. Tunis: African Development Bank.

Akinboade, O., 2004. 'Foreign direct investment in South Africa', paper presented at the IMF/AERC special workshop on the determinants of FDI in Africa, 2–3 December, Nairobi.

Alfaro, Laura, et al., 2006. 'How does foreign direct investment promote economic growth? Exploring the effects of financial markets on linkages', NBER Working Paper 12522, Cambridge, Mass.

Asante, Y., 2004. 'Foreign direct investment flows to Ghana', paper presented at the IMF/AERC Special Workshop on the Determinants of FDI in Africa, 2–3 December, Nairobi.

Asiedu, E., 2006. 'Foreign direct investment in Africa: the role of natural resources, market size, government policy, institutions and political instability', *World Economy* 29.1, 63–77.

Borensztein, Eduardo, Jose de Gregorie, and Jong-Wha Lee, 1998. 'How does foreign direct investment affect economic growth?', *Journal of International Economics* 45, 115–35.

de Mello, Luiz R., Jr, 1996. 'Foreign direct investment, international knowledge transfers and endogenous growth: time series evidence', mimeo, Department of Economics, University of Kent.

Ikiara, M. M., 2003. 'Foreign direct investment (FDI), technology transfer, and poverty alleviation: Africa's hopes and dilemma', ATPS Special Paper Series No. 16, Nairobi: African Technology Policy Studies.

Jackman, R. W., 1982. 'Dependence on foreign investment and economic growth in the third world', *World Politics* 34.2, 175–96.

Khan, S., 2004. 'An analysis of foreign direct investment flows to Cameroon', paper presented at the IMF/AERC special workshop on the determinants of FDI in Africa, 2–3 December, Nairobi.

Mills, G., and J. Oppenheimer, 2002. 'Making Africa succeed', paper presented to the World Economic Forum.

Mwenga, F., 2004. 'Foreign direct investment in Kenya', paper presented at the IMF/AERC special workshop on the determinants of FDI in Africa, 2–3 December, Nairobi.

Obwona, Marios, 1999. 'Foreign direct investments growth linkage and institutional constraints in sub-Saharan Africa: a case of Uganda', *African Review of Money, Finance and Banking*: supplementary issue of savings and development, 99–126.

——2004. 'Foreign direct investment flows in sub-Saharan Africa: Uganda country case study', paper presented at the IMF/AERC special workshop on the determinants of FDI in Africa, 2–3 December, Nairobi.

——and Benon Mutambi, 2004. 'Foreign direct investment in Africa: trends, determinants and linkages with growth and poverty', paper presented at the policy seminar on growth and poverty reduction, Kampala.

Ogunkola, E., and A. Jerome, 2004. 'Foreign direct investment in Nigeria: magnitude, direction and prospects', paper presented at the IMF/AERC special workshop on the determinants of FDI in Africa, 2–3 December, Nairobi.

Rothgeb, J., 1984. 'The effects of foreign investment on overall and sectoral growth in third world states', *Journal of Peace Research* 21.1.

Siphambe, H., 2004. 'Foreign direct investment in Africa: Botswana case study', paper presented at the IMF/AERC special workshop on the determinants of FDI in Africa, 2–3 December, Nairobi.

Sun, X., 2002. 'How to promote FDI? The regulatory and institutional environment for attracting FDI': http://unpan1.un.org/intradoc/groups/public/documents/un/unpan006349.pdf.

UNCTAD, 2003. *World Investment Report*. Geneva.

——2005. World Investment Report: http://www.unctad.org/Templates/WebFlyer.asp?intItemID =3489&lang=1.

Williams, O., and S. Williams, 1999. 'The impact of foreign direct investment flows to the Eastern Caribbean Central Bank Unified Currency Area', *Savings and Development* 23.2, 131–46.

Xu, Bin, 2000. 'Multinational enterprises, technology diffusion, and host country productivity growth', *Journal of Development Economics* 62.2, 477–93.

Foreign Direct Investment, Growth, and Poverty Reduction in Sub-Saharan Africa

Elizabeth Asiedu

We [the United Nations General Assembly] resolve to halve, by the year 2015, the proportion of the world's people whose income is less than one dollar a day. We also resolve to take special measures to address the challenges of poverty eradication and sustainable development in Africa, including debt cancellation, improved market access, enhanced Official Development Assistance and increased flows of Foreign Direct Investment...

(United Nations Millennium Declaration, 8 September 2000)

1. Introduction

The above quotation suggests that an increase in foreign direct investment (FDI) and foreign aid to Africa could help the continent achieve its Millennium Development Goal (MDG) of reducing poverty rates by half in 2015. The importance of FDI and foreign aid in eradicating poverty is also echoed in the New Partnership for Africa's Development (NEPAD) declaration, which stipulates that in order for Africa to achieve the MDG, the continent needs to fill an annual resource gap of $64 billion, which is about 12% of GDP. Since income levels and domestic savings in the region are low, this resource gap needs to be filled by foreign capital. Now, there are three main forms of foreign capital:

(i) foreign aid;
(ii) foreign indirect investment (which includes portfolio investments, bond finance and bank lending) and
(iii) foreign direct investment.

Foreign indirect investment is unavailable to most African countries, because most of the countries in the region cannot raise funds from international capital markets. As a consequence, a bulk of the external resources needed for poverty alleviation has to come from FDI and foreign aid. Indeed, since the adoption of the Millennium

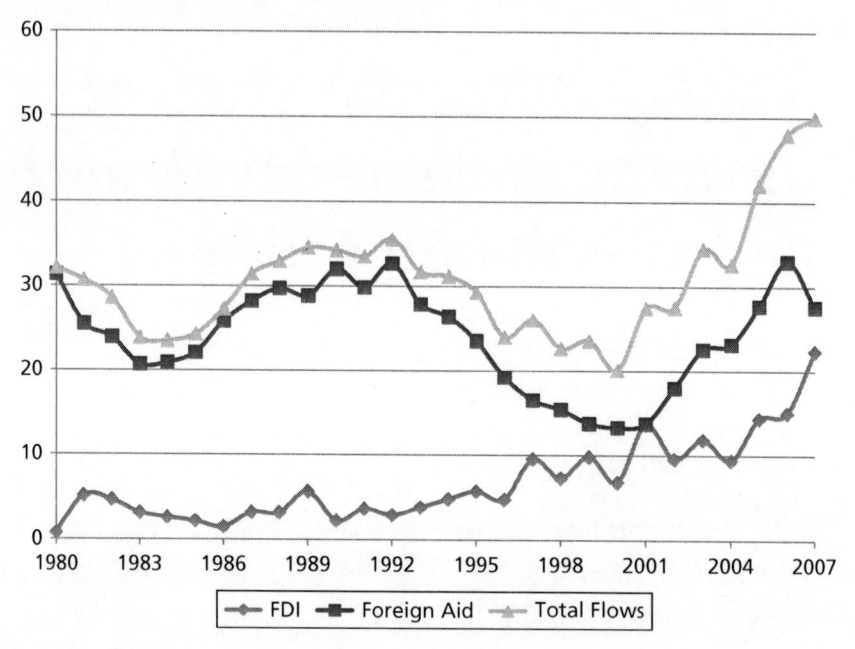

Figure 1. FDI and aid flows to sub-Saharan Africa, 1980–2007 (constant US$, billions)

Declaration in 2000, official development assistance (ODA) and official aid to sub-Saharan Africa (SSA) has increased substantially. In addition, FDI to the region has also been increasing since 1990 (Fig. 1). Over the periods 1996–2001 to 2002–7, the annual average ODA and official aid to SSA increased from about $14.5 billion to about $27.7 billion constant dollars, an increase of about 91%. During the same period, annual net FDI to SSA increased by about 83 %, from $8 billion to $15 billion (World Bank 2009). Thus, as shown in Figure 1, the resource gap has declined steadily, from $44 billion in 2000 to about $14 billion in 2007.

Two issues naturally come to bear. First, in order to reach the target set by NEPAD, foreign aid and FDI need to increase by about $14 billion. The second and probably more important point is whether the increase in aid and/or FDI will necessarily lead to poverty reduction and enhance growth in SSA. This chapter discusses the effectiveness of using FDI as a tool for poverty reduction and growth enhancement in SSA (see Easterly 2009 for discussion of the effect of foreign aid). It argues that one of the key mechanisms by which FDI may impact on growth and poverty is through employment creation by multinational enterprises (MNEs). However, FDI in SSA is largely concentrated in natural resources, and foreign investments in natural resources do not generate employment in host countries (Asiedu 2004). Furthermore, an increase in natural resource FDI can have an adverse impact on the economies of host countries. As a consequence, even if SSA is successful in filling the resource gap with FDI, the increase in FDI may not necessarily lead to poverty reduction and growth, and may have negative consequences.

2. Multinational employment, poverty reduction, and economic growth

The importance of FDI in reducing poverty and promoting growth is well articulated in UNCTAD (2002: 5):

Foreign direct investment contributes toward financing sustained economic growth over the long term. It is especially important for its potential to transfer knowledge and technology, create jobs, boost overall productivity, enhance competitiveness and entrepreneurship, and ultimately eradicate poverty through economic growth and development.

Below, I describe four ways by which MNE employment can promote growth and reduce poverty, and provide empirical evidence of the impact of MNE employment on wages, employment and productivity in selected African countries. The discussion draws heavily on Asiedu (2004).

2.1. MNE EMPLOYMENT HAS BOTH A DIRECT AND AN INDIRECT IMPACT ON DOMESTIC EMPLOYMENT

FDI often generates new employment (direct employment) and creates jobs indirectly through forward and backward linkages with domestic firms. Estimates for a number of developing countries indicate that FDI has a multiplier effect on domestic employment. For example, Iyanda (1999) finds that about two to four jobs are created for each worker employed by foreign affiliates in Namibia.

2.2. MNE EMPLOYMENT BOOSTS WAGES IN HOST COUNTRIES

A number of studies have shown that MNEs pay higher wages than domestic firms, even after controlling for firm and worker characteristics (see Lipsey 2004 for a survey). Furthermore, the presence of multinationals generates wage spillovers: wages tend to be higher in industries and in provinces that have a greater foreign presence. Table 1 summarizes the results of three empirical studies that examine differences in wages between foreign-owned enterprises and domestic-owned firms in selected African countries. The results show that foreign firms pay higher wages, with a wage premium ranging from 10% in Côte d'Ivoire to about 130% in Morocco.

Table 1. Difference in wages between foreign-owned and domestically owned enterprises in selected African countries

Study	Country	Results
Harrison (1996)	Morocco & Côte d'Ivoire	Foreign-owned firms pay higher wages in 3 out of 12 industries in Côte d'Ivoire and 12 out of 18 industries in Morocco. Wage premium ranges from 10% to 90% in Côte d'Ivoire and 30% to 130% in Morocco.
Mazumdar and Mazaheri (2000)	Cameroon, Côte d'Ivoire, Ghana, Kenya, Tanzania, Zambia & Zimbabwe	100% foreign-owned firms pay higher wages than other firms in Cameroon (25%), Côte d'Ivoire (29%), Ghana (24%), Kenya (22%), Zambia (28%) and Zimbabwe (38%). No significant difference in wages for Tanzania.
Velde te & Morrissey (2001)	Cameroon, Ghana, Kenya, Zambia & Zimbabwe	Foreign-owned firms pay higher wages in Cameroon (8%), Ghana (22%), Kenya (17%), Zambia (23%) and Zimbabwe (13%).

2.3. MNE EMPLOYMENT FOSTERS TECHNOLOGICAL TRANSFERS

One of the most common and least expensive ways by which foreign technology gets diffused in host countries is through labour turnover, as domestic employees move from foreign firms to domestic firms.

2.4. MNE EMPLOYMENT ENHANCES THE PRODUCTIVITY OF THE LABOUR FORCE IN THE HOST COUNTRY

Several studies have shown that workers in foreign-owned enterprises (FOEs) are more productive than workers in domestic-owned enterprises (DOEs). For example, Harrison (1996) analysed differences in labour productivity between FOEs and locally owned firms in Morocco. In eight out of twelve industries, output per worker was higher in FOEs than in DOEs, with a difference in productivity ranging from 50% in electronics to about 130% in non-metallic minerals. Ramachandran and Shah (1998) also report that added value per worker is 59% higher for wholly foreign-owned enterprises than for local firms in Kenya, 178% higher for FOEs in Zimbabwe and 1,422% higher for FOEs in Ghana.

3. Implications of recent FDI flows to SSA[1]

As shown in Figure 1, FDI to SSA has increased substantially since 2000. Furthermore, according to UNCTAD (2007), most of the investments are in the extractive industry. The surge in extractive-industry FDI can be largely explained by the following factors.

---

[1] The data cited in this section are from UNCTAD (2007).

First, there has been an increase in the global demand for minerals (including metallic, non-metallic minerals, and energy minerals) and this trend is expected to continue in the next five to ten years. For example, from 2001 to 2006, world energy consumption increased by about 17%, and it is expected to increase by 16% by 2015. Second, the increase in the demand for minerals has led to a commodity price boom, which in turn has fuelled a rise in profits in the extractive industry, and subsequently led to an increase in global investments in the exploration and production of minerals in developing countries.[2] Another point is that the demand in mineral consumption is being met by increasing production in developing countries, in particular SSA. For example, from 1995 to 2005, oil production in SSA by MNEs increased by 51%, and by about 133% and 195% in Angola and Swaziland, respectively. This compares with an increase of about 43% for all developing countries. Also, between 2000 and 2006, US FDI in extractive industries in SSA increased by about 112%. This contrasts with an increase of 4% for Latin America and the Caribbean, 30% for the Middle East and North Africa, a decline of 14% for South and East Asia, and an increase of 35% for all developing countries. Indeed, the increase in investments in mineral prospecting in SSA seems to have paid off. For example, recently, oil and gas discoveries have been made in sixteen African countries: Uganda, Ghana, Congo-Brazzaville, Angola, Gabon, Guinea Bissau, Guinea, Sierra Leone, Algeria, Egypt, Cameroon, Nigeria, Tanzania, Zambia, Namibia, and São Tome and Principe.

The increase in the production and exploration of minerals in Africa has several implications for the economies of host countries in the region. On the one hand, the increase in FDI to SSA is beneficial in that it serves as a source of foreign exchange, boosts government revenue, and also helps fill the resource gap (i.e. provides the capital needed for poverty alleviation). On the other hand, FDI in extractive industries poses several challenges to host countries. For example, an increase in production of minerals may have adverse environmental and social effects. In addition, mineral extraction is primarily an export-oriented activity, and therefore countries where FDI is concentrated in minerals and oil tend to be natural resource-exporting countries. Thus, continued investment in SSA implies that there will be an increase in the number of natural resource-exporting countries in the region and also an increase in the natural resource-intensiveness of exports from SSA. This may be problematic for several reasons. First, it exposes more countries in the region to the classic 'Dutch disease' (see e.g. Sachs and Warner 1995). Second, several studies have shown that natural resource-exporting countries tend to exhibit the following characteristics:

(i) their exports are less diversified, and this makes the country's economy more vulnerable to external shocks, which in turn leads to macroeconomic instability;

---

[2] The price of oil increased from about $19 per barrel in 2002 to about $130 in 2008.

(ii) they invest less in physical and human capital;
(iii) they tend to have weak institutions; and
(iv) they tend to curtail civil and political liberties (see Asiedu and Lien 2011).

Finally, we note that extractive industry FDI does not facilitate the transfer of technology and knowledge, and has limited effects on employment in host countries. As a consequence, two of the most important potential benefits of FDI are not realized. The fact that FDI to SSA does not generate employment in host countries is particularly problematic because, for many countries in the region, unemployment is prevalent and wages are low. Furthermore, as discussed in section 2, employment by multinational enterprises (MNEs) can promote growth and reduce poverty in host countries.

4. Conclusion

Our discussion so far suggests that the challenge facing countries in SSA goes beyond attracting more FDI. Specifically, countries in the region should not just focus on attracting more FDI, but should also be aggressive in attracting FDI in non-extractive industries. According to a recent survey, the most important location criterion for MNEs in manufacturing and services is market size (UNCTAD 2009).[3] This suggests that regional economic cooperation may facilitate FDI to SSA. The reason is that countries in the region are small, in terms of population and income. For example, 15 out of the 48 countries in SSA have a population of less than 2 million, and about half of the countries have a population of less than 6 million. With regards to income, about half the countries have a GDP of less than $3 billion. Indeed, the total GDP of SSA in 2007 was $847 billion, which is equal to 80% of the GDP of Mexico and 65% of the GDP of Brazil (World Bank 2009). Thus, due to the small size of African countries (both in terms of income and population), a large number of countries will have to be included in the regional bloc in order to achieve a critical market size that will be large enough to be attractive to foreign investors. The caveat is that policy coordination becomes difficult as the number of countries in the regional bloc increases. Indeed, the difficulty of coordinating and enforcing policies across many countries may be too costly in terms of time and resources—such that regionalism may be an infeasible option. Finally, we note that an increase in FDI, even in manufacturing, does not necessarily translate into higher economic growth. Indeed, the empirical relationship between FDI and growth is unclear (see Carkovic and Levine 2005). Some studies find a positive effect; others do not find a significant effect; and some conclude that FDI enhances growth only under certain

---

[3] For the survey report, see http://www.unctad.org/en/docs/diaeia20098_en.pdf.

conditions: when the host country's education exceeds a certain threshold; when the country has achieved a certain level of income; and when the host country has a well-developed financial sector. Note that many countries in SSA are unlikely to pass the 'threshold' test. These studies seem to suggest that for countries in SSA, reaping the benefits that accrue from FDI, if any, may be more difficult than attracting FDI. However, there is room for optimism. The policies that promote FDI to Africa (good infrastructure, openness to trade, good institutions, educated labour force) also have a direct impact on long-term economic growth. As a consequence, African countries cannot go wrong implementing such policies.

REFERENCES

Asiedu, Elizabeth, 2004. 'The determinants of employment of affiliates of U.S. multinational enterprises in Africa', *Development Policy Review* 22.4, 371–9.

——and Donald Lien, 2011. 'Democracy, foreign direct investment and natural resources', *Journal of International Economics* 84, 99–111.

Carkovic, M., and R. Levine, 2005. 'Does foreign direct investment accelerate economic growth?', in Theodore H. Moran, Edward M. Graham, and Magnus Blomstrom (eds), *Does Foreign Direct Investment Promote Development?* Washington, DC: Institute for International Economics Center for Global Development.

Easterly, William, 2009. 'Can the West save Africa?', *Journal of Economic Literature* 47.2, 373–447.

Harrison, Ann, 1996. 'Determinants and effects of direct foreign investment in Côte d'Ivoire, Morocco, and Venezuela', in Mark J. Roberts and James R. Tybout (eds), *Industrial Evolution in Developing Countries: Micro Patterns of Turnover, Productivity and Market Structure.* Washington, DC: World Bank.

Iyanda, Olukunle, 1999. 'The impact of multinational enterprises on employment, training and regional development in Namibia and Zimbabwe: a preliminary assessment', ILO Working Paper 84. Geneva.

Lipsey, Robert, 2004. 'Home and host country effects of foreign direct investment', in Robert E. Baldwin and L. Alan Winters (eds), *Challenges to Globalization: Analyzing the Economics.* Cambridge, Mass.: NBER.

Mazumdar, Dipak, and Ata Mazaherim, 2000. 'Wages and employment in Africa', Regional Program on Enterprise Development Paper 109, World Bank.

Ramachandran, Vijaya, and Manju Kedia Shah, 1998. 'Firm performance and foreign ownership in Africa: evidence from Zimbabwe, Ghana and Kenya', RPED paper 81, World Bank.

Sachs, Jeffrey D., and Andrew M. Warner, 1995. 'Natural resource abundance and economic growth', NBER Working Paper Series 5398, 1–47. Cambridge, Mass.

te Velde, Dirk Willem, and Oliver Morrissey, 2001. 'Foreign ownership and wages: evidence from five African countries', CREDIT discussion paper 01/19, Nottingham.

United Nations Conference on Trade and Development, 2002. *World Investment Report: Transnational Corporations and Export Competitiveness.* New York: UN.

——2007. *World Investment Report: Transnational Corporations, Extractive Industries and Development.* Geneva: UNCTAD.

——2009. *World Investment Prospect Survey.* Geneva: UNCTAD.

World Bank, 2009. *World Development Indicators.* CD-ROM. Washington, DC: World Bank.

Infrastructure

Andrew McKay

1. Introduction

After a long period in which the focus of much development strategy in Africa had been on the social sectors, the issue of infrastructure has once again become very important. The UN Secretary-General, Ban Ki-moon, argued at an African Union summit in February 2009 that poor infrastructure was a major constraint to economic and social progress in Africa. Infrastructure was a major issue stressed by the Africa Commission; the World Economic Forum 2007 strongly argued for its importance; and it is an important focus of Sachs's arguments for a 'big push' in Africa. UNCTAD in 2009 argued for the central role of infrastructure as part of an initiative to increase regional economic integration in Africa. While Western donors have remained reluctant to invest in infrastructure in Africa, China has been investing substantially in recent years.

In terms of the primary focus of this chapter, physical infrastructure (transport links, communications, power, markets, water, sanitation), Africa is particularly badly served in comparison to other regions of the world. The indicators compiled by Calderon and Serven (2008) show sub-Saharan Africa is usually at the bottom of all developing regions, especially when emphasis is placed on infrastructure quality. The relatively low population density in Africa and the high proportion of the population living in landlocked countries (40%, according to Ndulu 2006, counting DRC and Sudan as being landlocked) make infrastructure all the more important. Poor infrastructure adds to the geographical disadvantage Africa faces.

As highlighted by Ayogu (2007), infrastructure is important in two respects: it is part of the consumption bundle of households (or facilitates consumption), and it is an important input into production. Infrastructure is not necessarily a public good in the sense of being non-rival and non-excludable, and some aspects may be explicitly private or club goods.

The case for significantly expanding infrastructure is based on its potential impact on economic growth, trade, income distribution, and poverty. There is strong evidence, in Africa and internationally, of substantial benefits to infrastructure in terms of economic growth, trade, income distribution and poverty. We consider these in turn before discussing the challenges in effectively providing infrastructure.

2. Growth

In growth models, infrastructure can generate services which can be a complementary factor of production, or it can affect total factor productivity through a range of channels such as affecting labour productivity, reducing adjustment costs of private capital, or generating economies of scale or scope (Straub 2008). An early empirical study for the US (Aschauer 1989) found a substantial growth effect of infrastructure; and the majority of subsequent empirical studies (reviewed by e.g. Ayogu 2007), many now for developing countries, have found a significant positive impact of infrastructure on growth.

These macroeconometric studies do, though, face a number of challenges (Straub 2008; Calderon and Serven 2008), in particular identification (the expectation of two way causality between infrastructure and growth), measurement (often a choice between financial and—generally preferred—physical measures, and then there is the issue of which dimensions of infrastructure to consider), and heterogeneity (across countries, time periods, types of infrastructure). However, recent studies such as Calderon and Serven (2008), which try to deal with some of these aspects, still find positive impacts of both quantity and quality of infrastructure, for Africa and for developing countries as a whole. This is still not a fully resolved research issue though.

There is also evidence for positive impacts of infrastructure on sectoral output (e.g. agriculture, Ndulu 2006). And there is also evidence for adverse micro level effects of lack of infrastructure in Africa on manufacturing firms (Reinikka and Svensson 2002; Collier and Gunning 1999; Biggs and Srivastava 1996).

3. Trade

A major impact of infrastructure on growth is likely to operate via trade, and Ndulu (2006) highlights the importance of improved infrastructure and regional integration for increased growth in Africa. High transactions costs are a major problem, reflecting among other things high transport and communications costs, delays at roadblocks, and long customs/administrative procedures at ports and borders. These transactions costs create a serious competitive disadvantage, and infrastructure is clearly a key factor.

Limão and Venables (2001) estimate an elasticity of trade flows with respect to transport costs of around −3. Measuring transport costs as the ratio of CIF to FOB values, they find that this is substantially affected by infrastructure, and that this is especially severe in landlocked countries. They estimate that the median landlocked country has transport costs 55% higher than those of coastal countries. In a model for determinants of transport costs, they estimate that in coastal countries own infrastructure accounts for 40% of the predicted transport costs; in landlocked countries it accounts for 36% of the cost and transit infrastructure another 24%. Intra-African export costs are higher, and trade volumes lower, than predicted by standard gravity models, and much of this reflects poor infrastructure. Indeed they estimate that once infrastructure costs are allowed for, intra-sub-Saharan Africa trade is in fact at a level to be expected given the other economic variables.

Poor quality infrastructure has a substantial impact in deterring trade. Buys, Deichmann, and Wheeler (2008) estimate that the gains in trade volume from upgrading the continental road network could be around $250 billion, against costs of around $50 billion.

4. Income distribution, poverty, and micro outcomes

Calderon and Serven (2008) argue that improved infrastructure provision can have a disproportionate effect on the poor, increasing their asset values and lowering their transactions costs, if it is done in a way to expand access of the poor. They model determinants of inequality in cross-country regressions, including principal component-based measures of infrastructure quality and quantity, and find that improvements in these are indeed associated with lower inequality.

By definition, infrastructure provision has spatial dimensions. Taking a new economic geography perspective (Baldwin et al. 2003; Straub 2008) gives a somewhat different perspective, because it creates the likelihood of a trade-off between spatial inequality and growth. New economic geography models are concerned with the relative importance of dispersion and agglomeration forces, and reduced transport costs will increase agglomeration pressures. In many economic geography models, investment in infrastructure between regions will have a beneficial growth impact but will at the same time increase regional inequality. This might, though, be lessened or avoided if the infrastructure facilitates interregional technological diffusion. Investment in infrastructure in poorer regions will reduce regional inequality, but will at the same time lower the growth rate. In other words, investment in infrastructure creates a serious risk of increasing regional inequality, and perhaps overall inequality. That said, these conclusions do depend on the modelling assumptions underlying new economic geography models, some of which might be debatable.

At a more micro level, there is significant evidence of the benefits of proximity to roads for poverty (Dercon et al. 2006, for Ethiopia); of public investments as well as roads on income/poverty in Tanzania (Fan, Nyange, and Rao 2005); of roads in Morocco on primary school enrolment; of improved access to water/sanitation on reduced infant, child, and maternal mortality in the Central African Republic (Ndulu 2006); as well as many other examples of beneficial micro level impacts of infrastructure. Outside Africa, there is evidence of beneficial impacts of mobile telephony on welfare and market efficiency among fishing communities in South India (Jensen 2007); of improved water infrastructure on women's time allocation in Pakistan (Ilahi and Grimard 2000); of roads on poverty in Nepal and Papua New Guinea (Gibson and Rozelle 2003); and of electricity, water, and sanitation connections on child height in Brazil (Strauss and Thomas 1992).

In several of these cases, however, there are concerns in interpreting the results in terms of possible programme or household placement effects (Straub 2008). The evidence for the beneficial impact of infrastructure on poverty is nonetheless quite strong, although its impact on income distribution is much more ambivalent, almost certainly depending on the form of infrastructure, to whom it is provided, etc.

While the robustness of some empirical results are still open to debate, there does seem to be a very strong case for investment in infrastructure in Africa. But how can this be effectively delivered?

5. Issues in increasing infrastructure spending

Calderon and Serven (2008) estimate that halving the infrastructure gap between sub-Saharan Africa and other low income countries might cost around 15% of GDP, plus additional operational and maintenance spending. While the private sector is playing an increasing role in infrastructure provision, the burden of this falls on the public sector, and this is unlikely to be affordable in the absence of a substantial increase in aid flows. Even with substantial Chinese involvement in infrastructure provision, this scale of increase may be unlikely.

Historically, infrastructure investment has been associated with many 'white elephant' projects and with severely limited spending on maintenance. For twenty years or more, aid has prioritized the social sectors. In fact, as highlighted above, there is substantial complementarity between infrastructure and the social sectors, if the infrastructure can be effectively provided. Infrastructure spending, however, is strongly associated with corruption, a major issue in many African countries. Corruption inflates the cost of providing infrastructure and reduces the return to this spending, among other things because of neglect of maintenance. Collier (2006) argues that a big push in aid spending in Africa will not be effective without serious efforts to tackle the traps which many African countries are caught in: conflict, corruption, primary commodity dependence, and the fractionalized nature of their societies. He argues for four key policy measures: provision of a security guarantee; creation of a template of good government; temporary trade preferences; and conditioning aid on process of governance rather than policy.

Without these, he sees increased infrastructure spending as being doomed to be ineffective.

Ndulu (2006) recognizes an important role for the private sector in infrastructure provision (often through public–private partnerships) and argues that the involvement of the private sector has increased rates of return and enabled more effective financing of recurrent costs. To date, the private sector has been very active in telecommunications, but much less so in other sectors, though there is substantial scope in other areas such as road-building. The private sector can provide technical and managerial capacity for effective project implementation and sustained involvement in maintenance. It may have better access to finance. But the private sector remains reluctant, presumably in part due to high risk, reflecting such factors as governance problems, political interference, and policy inconsistency. Countries also need to develop appropriate regulatory policies.

There are almost certainly substantial returns to infrastructure investment in Africa, as long as it can be effectively delivered. Establishing a feasible action plan for infrastructure provision, covering construction, financing, and maintenance, remains a major challenge.

REFERENCES

Aschauer, David A., 1989. 'Is public expenditure productive?', *Journal of Monetary Economics* 23, 177–200.

Ayogu, M., 2007. 'Infrastructure and economic development in Africa: a review', *Journal of African Economies* 16 (AERC Supplement 1), 75–126.

Baldwin, R., R. Foslid, P. Martin, G. Ottaviano, and F. Robert-Nicoud, 2003. *Economic Geography and Public Policy*. Princeton, NJ: Princeton University Press.

Biggs, T., and P. Srivastava, 1996. 'Structural aspects of manufacturing in sub-Saharan Africa: finding from a seven country enterprise survey', Discussion Paper 346. Washington, DC: World Bank.

Buys, P., U. Deichmann, and D. Wheeler, 2008. 'Road network upgrading and overland trade expansion in sub-Saharan Africa', Policy Research Working Paper 4097. Washington, DC: World Bank.

Calderon, C., and L. Serven, 2008. 'Infrastructure and economic development in sub-Saharan Africa', Policy Research Working Paper 4712. Washington, DC: World Bank.

Collier, P., 2006. 'African growth: why a "big push"?', *Journal of African Economies* (AERC Supplement 2), 188–211.

——and J. W. Gunning, 1999. 'Explaining African economic performance', *Journal of Economic Literature* 37, 64–111.

Dercon, S., D. O. Gilligan, J. Hoddinott, and T. Woldehanna, 2006. 'The impact of roads and agricultural extension on consumption growth and poverty in fifteen Ethiopian villages', WPS/2007-01. Oxford: CSAE.

Fan, S., D. Nyange, and N. Rao, 2005. 'Public investment and poverty reduction in Tanzania: evidence from household survey data', Research Report 138. Washington, DC: IFPRI.

Gibson, J., and S. Rozelle, 2003. 'Poverty and access to roads in Papua New Guinea', *Economic Development and Cultural Change* 52, 159–85.

Ilahi, N., and F. Grimard, 2000. 'Public infrastructure and private costs: water supply and time allocation of women in rural Pakistan', *Economic Development and Cultural Change* 49, 45.

Jensen, R., 2007. 'The digital provide: information (technology), market performance and welfare in the South Indian fisheries sector', *Quarterly Journal of Economics* 122.3, 879–924.

Limão, N., and A. J. Venables, 2001. 'Infrastructure, geographical disadvantage, transport costs and trade', *World Bank Economic Review* 15, 451–79.

Ndulu, B. J., 2006. 'Infrastructure, regional integration and growth in sub-Saharan Africa: dealing with the disadvantages of geography and sovereign fragmentation', *Journal of African Economics* 15 (AERC Supplement 2), 212–44.

Reinikka, R., and J. Svensson, 2002. 'Coping with poor public capital', *Journal of Development Economics* 69.1, 51–69.

Straub, S., 2008. 'Infrastructure and growth in developing countries: recent advances and research challenges', Policy Research Working Paper 4460. Washington, DC: World Bank.

Thomas, Duncan, and John Strauss, 1992. 'Prices, infrastructure, household characteristics and child height', *Journal of Development Economics* 39.2, 301–32.

Thematic Perspectives
Macroeconomics and Finance

Fiscal Policy

David Bevan

1. Introduction

Some purists wish to restrict the term 'fiscal policy' to actions which affect the balance between government revenue and expenditure, i.e. the budget surplus or deficit, the evolution of this over time, and hence the evolution of its stock counterpart—government debt.[1] However, it is impossible to focus on these net effects or their consequences without paying some attention both to the scale of government activities and to their composition. A look at the recent behaviour of the main fiscal aggregates is followed by a discussion of financing, which leads naturally to the intertemporal budget constraint and issues of solvency and sustainability. There are then brief discussions of cyclicality, scale, expenditure composition, 'fiscal space', the costs and benefits of government actions, policy coordination, and the global crisis.

2. Trends in the main fiscal aggregates

Fiscal data for SSA tend to be unreliable and incomplete. The major source ought to be the IMF's annual compilation, *Government Finance Statistics*, but these data are not always compatible with those that the IMF itself uses in its operational mode, in its dialogue with partner governments. This disjuncture is very unsatisfactory and remains a major unresolved problem. Table 1 provides summary fiscal data for central government for a number of country groupings, averaged over two six-year periods.[2] They should be treated with considerable scepticism.

---

[1] There is also the issue of what public entity is to be analysed—central government, general government (which includes local government), or the public sector (which also includes the central bank and other public financial and nonfinancial enterprises). Data limitations in SSA usually restrict analysis to central government.

[2] These groupings are those adopted in IMF (2009). The oil-exporting countries are Angola, Cameroon, Chad, Republic of Congo, Equatorial Guinea, Gabon, and Nigeria. The middle-income countries are Botswana, Cape Verde, Lesotho, Mauritius, Namibia, Seychelles, South Africa, and Swaziland. The low-income countries are Benin, Burkina Faso, Ethiopia, Ghana, Kenya, Madagascar, Malawi, Mali, Mozambique, Niger, Rwanda, Senegal, Tanzania, Uganda, and Zambia. Fragile countries include Burundi, Central African Republic, Comoros, Democratic Republic of Congo, Côte d'Ivoire, Eritrea, The Gambia, Guinea, Guinea Bissau, Liberia, Sao Tome and Principe, Sierra Leone, and Togo. Not included are Djibouti, Mauritania, Somalia, Sudan, and Zimbabwe.

Table 1. Fiscal aggregates as per cent of GDP, averages 2003–2008 (1997–2002) for various SSA country groupings

	Revenue (ex grants)	Expenditure	Overall balance (ex grants)	Overall balance (inc grants)	Official external debt
Oil exporters[a]	33.2 (26.6)	26.3 (31.8)	6.9 (−5.2)	8.2 (−4.3)	28.1 (73.3)
Nigeria	20.2 (20.9)	16.1 (23.0)	4.1 (−2.1)	4.1 (−2.1)	17.8 (63.3)
Middle-income[b]	32.1 (34.7)	32.5 (37.2)	−0.4 (−2.5)	0.3 (−1.6)	11.1 (17.2)
South Africa	25.5 (23.5)	26.0 (25.7)	−0.6 (−2.2)	−0.6 (−2.2)	2.2 (3.6)
Low-income	16.4 (14.4)	24.2 (21.6)	−7.8 (−7.2)	−1.9 (−3.4)	39.9 (79.2)
Fragile states	15.7 (13.5)	20.4 (17.8)	−4.7 (−4.3)	−1.7 (−2.9)	84.8 (122.0)
SSA	23.4 (21.1)	23.7 (24.8)	−0.3 (−3.7)	1.3 (−2.6)	20.6 (45.3)

[a] Excluding Nigeria.
[b] Excluding South Africa.
Source: IMF (2009).

For SSA as a whole, revenue before grants and expenditure were roughly equal at a little under 24% of GDP, and the corresponding balance was in deficit by 0.3%. With grants running at 1.6%, the inclusive balance was in surplus by 1.3%, up by nearly four points from the earlier period.[3] Since grants rose by only half a point, the preponderance of this substantial fiscal tightening was domestic in origin, and notably reflects an increase in revenue.

This overall picture conceals wide variations between the groupings. For example, low-income countries (LICs) raise only around 16% in revenue, about half what is raised by middle-income countries. However, their expenditure is around three quarters (24% against 32%), assisted by around 6% in grants.

The very substantial reductions in external indebtedness overwhelmingly reflect the various instruments for debt relief that have been prominent in recent years; the role of improved fiscal balances and increased growth has been secondary.

3. Financing

Budget deficits must be financed by some combination of four financing instruments: grants, money financing, domestic borrowing, and external borrowing. There is some debate as to whether deficits should be measured before or after grants, which are important in SSA, as is apparent in Table 1. Grants impose no obligation to repay, and do not raise indebtedness. On the other hand, it may be dangerous to become dependent

---

[3] All unqualified references to percentages are relative to GDP; a reference to points means a change in the percentage share in GDP.

on them, since they are not under the control of the recipient government. If substantial grants are withdrawn, an intolerable fiscal adjustment may be required. However, in assessing the financing implications of any given budget, it is the balance after grants that matters.

A limited amount of money financing (seigniorage) is feasible, and indeed desirable, without inducing unacceptably high inflation. Empirical evidence suggests that in developing countries the growth-maximizing rate of inflation might be in the range 5–8% per annum. Attempts to finance spending by driving inflation above this level will eventually be at the expense not only of higher inflation but of slower growth and reduced seigniorage. On a sustained basis, seigniorage is unlikely to generate more than 0.5–0.75% of GDP, and for dollarized economies, much less than that.

Domestic borrowing has the advantage of being repayable in domestic currency, without foreign exchange risk.[4] On the other hand, it risks driving up domestic interest rates and crowding out private investment. When, as in much of SSA, the domestic financial markets are thin, interest rates may also be extremely volatile. It has been argued that domestic debt in excess of 15–20% of GDP is imprudent in LICs. Since far more attention has been devoted to the risks of external borrowing, the data for domestic debt in SSA have remained very poor.

External borrowing may be at market rates or, for LICs, on concessional terms. In the former case, the nominal value of an increment to debt is a fair summary of the costs of servicing it. In the latter case, these costs are reduced by the extent of the concessionality—the 'grant element'. It is now routine to calculate the net present value of concessional debt by discounting these costs at a market interest rate. The flow analogue to this stock treatment would be to split the borrowing between a market element, taken 'below the line' as part of deficit financing, and a grant element, taken 'above the line' along with outright grants and revenue. This proposal is controversial, and the IMF has not (except fleetingly) adopted it. Hence the 'inclusive' deficit in Table 1 may exaggerate the increase in government indebtedness.

4. The intertemporal budget constraint (IBC)

The overall balance considered so far includes interest payments on government debt as expenditures. The 'primary' balance is constructed by excluding these payments. (Notice that where government interest payments are significant, it is quite possible for a substantial overall deficit to be associated with a primary surplus.) The IBC is an accounting constraint which states that the present discounted value of primary

---

[4] Recent innovations have been eroding this feature, however.

surpluses must be no less than the initial value of the debt. It is helpful to inspect a simple equation derived on the implausible assumptions that the rate of interest (r) and the rate of growth (g) are both constant, as is the ratio of the primary surplus to GDP (s). Then if the initial ratio of debt to GDP is d, the IBC states:

$$s = (r - g)d^5 \tag{1}$$

If the government wished to freeze the initial debt to GDP ratio, and do so by a fiscal strategy which also maintained the primary surplus ratio constant, then equation (1) shows what that ratio has to be. The required surplus ratio is equal to the debt ratio multiplied by the excess of the interest rate over the growth rate. It will have to be higher if initial debt is higher, if the interest rate is higher, or if the growth rate is lower.[6] Use is sometimes made of the intertemporal fiscal balance—the gap between the actual primary surplus (preferably cyclically adjusted) and that derived in the equation.

5. Solvency and sustainability

A government is solvent when the IBC is satisfied. Clearly, for any projections of the future pattern of growth and interest rates, there is an infinite variety of paths for expenditure and revenue that will satisfy the constraint. In a sense, the IBC simply underlines the commonplace notion that current irresponsibility will have to be paid for later. There may, however, be levels of indebtedness where a government chooses to default because the pain of servicing the debt is deemed greater than the opprobrium (and sanctions) following default. This might happen even if the government was *technically* solvent, in that it would have been feasible to raise revenues or lower spending sufficiently to achieve the necessary flow of primary surpluses.

Fiscal policy is *sustainable* when, if it were to continue along the same lines in future, the solvency condition would be satisfied. How the 'same lines' are to be derived is open; this may be from simple historical averaging, or from a formal econometric exercise. Debt sustainability analyses with accompanying 'stress tests' are now routine in the dialogue between SSA governments and the international institutions.

However, the implication of the simple formula given above carries over to these more realistic exercises. Whether the current fiscal stance implies sustainability depends on the

---

[5] Note that if the rate of interest is below the growth rate (as it may be when a fast-growing country is offered concessional loans), maintenance of a constant debt ratio can be achieved with a primary *deficit*. The inference, drawn by some, that the government should increase its borrowing without limit in this case flies in the face of the fact that concessional finance is rationed in the present and will cease to be available to a growing economy at some date in the future.

[6] These insights carry over to the realistic case where constancy of the components is not imposed.

future evolution of growth and interest rates. Similarly, whether a particular fiscal history led to trouble depended not only on the original fiscal stance but on how growth and interest rates evolved. One analyst argues that what led to some LICs becoming HIPCs (highly indebted poor countries) was not because they ran larger primary deficits than the non-HIPCs but because they suffered a severe growth slow-down while the non-HIPCs did not.[7]

6. Cyclicality

The conventional assumption for advanced economies is that fiscal policy is and should be counter-cyclical, either automatically via built-in stabilizers or, more controversially, via discretionary interventions. For developing countries, the evidence suggests that it is pro-cyclical instead.[8] There are a number of explanations as to why this may be so, ranging from the role of credit constraints to that of political economy. There are even circumstances where pro-cyclicality may be optimal, but the converse seems more likely.

7. Scale of government activities over time

While there appear to be marked regional differences in the typical size of government relative to the economy, there is also a systematic relation with per capita income, with richer countries having relatively larger public sectors. This is demonstrated in Table 1 by the comparison between low- and middle-income countries. Two arguments as to why this may be so are: first, that public goods are income elastic, so that expenditure should shift to the public sector as incomes grow; second, that more efficient tax systems become available, so that the deadweight burden of taxation falls with income. The first argument suggests rising expenditure, the second rising revenue as income rises. Both support a relative expansion of the public sector, but it is unclear which would dominate; debt would be front-loaded in the former case, the reverse in the latter.

This is further complicated in the case of LICs by two factors; the availability of concessional finance, and the possibility of future debt relief to countries which do not succeed in reasonably rapid transition to middle-income status. These factors tend to tilt the balance towards front-loading of debt.

---

[7] Easterly (2001).   [8] See e.g. Ilzetzki and Végh (2008).

8. Composition

SSA has a very substantial infrastructure deficit. This partly reflects the fact that during earlier imperatives for fiscal tightening, there was a tendency to cut the capital budget because that was easier, even though it compromised long-run growth. Many SSA governments are keen not to repeat that mistake. Now consider a reduction in the primary deficit that, because it involves reduced infrastructure spending, reduces the growth rate. Equation (1) suggests that this may actually worsen the sustainability of fiscal policy.[9]

9. Fiscal space

Recently, the concept of 'fiscal space' has become much discussed. This has been defined as 'room in a government's budget that allows it to provide resources for a desired purpose without jeopardizing the sustainability of its financial position or the stability of the economy'.[10] There is an issue as to whether this new phrase adds to the discussion or simply confuses it.[11] The main extension from the perspectives already covered is the distinction between the 'fiduciary' and the 'development' payback to public investment. In one sense, this distinction simply rehearses the familiar point that the government may only appropriate a part of the returns to its investment. However, it remains the case that non-appropriable returns, however high, still require that the investment be financed.

10. Costs and benefits

Government expenditures, particularly on capital formation, are hard to assess. Their efficient selection is easily deflected by interest groups or by corrupt political processes. The tradition of cost–benefit analysis, which was strong in developing countries in the 1970s, has withered except for occasional stand-outs such as Chile. It will be difficult, but important, to resurrect this appraisal system to ensure that increased capital budgets do produce increased public capital stocks.

---

[9] This issue is explored in Easterly, Irwin, and Servén (2008).
[10] Heller (2005).
[11] As to the former, see Roy and Heuty (2009); as to the latter, see Perotti (2007).

11. Coordination with other macroeconomic policies

Fiscal policy needs to be integrated with monetary and exchange rate policy. There is no space to rehearse these issues here, except to note that the celebrated independence of central banks may be helpful when the fiscal authorities are irresponsible, but less so when they are not. In particular, there is a possibility that aid may be 'spent' (the fiscal authorities spend the additional resources by allowing the fiscal deficit to widen), but not 'absorbed' (the monetary authorities do not permit the additional resources to be available to the country, because they do not allow the current account deficit to widen).[12]

12. The global crisis

The initial impact of the crisis has been more focused on the advanced economies, but it is clear that second round effects will impact on SSA. The overall impact depends on how resilient to these challenges China and India prove to be. In SSA, revenues will fall sharply, and there will be pressures to maintain or increase expenditures. Whether this type of fiscal expansionary response is practical will depend on country-specific circumstances, such as the initial debt position, the way in which the global crisis impacts on the economy, and the government's response package.[13] In the short run, it is clear that fiscal balances will deteriorate, and that their sustainability will depend on the future patterns of aid flows, remittances, and FDI, as well as on growth prospects and domestic fiscal choices. There may also be scope for innovative financing, such as 'diaspora bonds' targeted at a country's own expatriate nationals.[14]

REFERENCES

Berg, A., et al., 2009. 'Fiscal policy in Sub-Saharan Africa in response to the impact of the global crisis', IMF Staff Position Note SPN/09/10, Washington, DC.
—— S. Aijar, and M. Hussain, 2007. 'The macroeconomics of scaling up aid: lessons from recent experience', IMF Occasional Paper 253, Washington, DC.
Easterly, W. R., 2001. 'Growth implosions and debt explosions: do growth slowdowns cause public debt crises?', *Contributions to Macroeconomics* 1.1, 1–24.

[12] See Berg, Aijar, and Hussain (2007).
[13] See Berg et al. (2009).
[14] See Ketkar and Ratha (2009).

—— T. Irwin, and L. Servén, 2008. 'Walking up the down escalator: public investment and fiscal stability', *World Bank Research Observer* 23.1.

Heller, P., 2005. 'Fiscal space: what it is and how to get it', *Finance and Development* 42.2.

Ilzetzki, E., and C. A. Végh, 2008. 'Procyclical fiscal policy in developing countries: truth or fiction?', NBER Working Paper 14191, Cambridge, Mass.

International Monetary Fund, 2009. *Regional Economic Outlook: Sub-Saharan Africa*. Washington, DC: IMF.

Ketkar, S., and D. Ratha, 2009. 'New paths to funding', *Finance and Development* (June), 43–5.

Perotti, R., 2007. 'Fiscal policy in developing countries', World Bank PRWP 4365, Washington, DC.

Roy, R., and A. Heuty (eds), 2009. *Fiscal Space*. Oxford: Earthscan.

Exchange Rate Policy

Christopher Adam

1. Introduction

Exchange rate policy in Africa has undergone a radical change in the last decade. The widespread foreign exchange controls and heavy management of exchange rates that typified countries outside the CFA Franc zone and the Rand Monetary Area in the 1980s, and which placed the exchange rate at the heart of the politics of economic policy-making, have been progressively dismantled. In their place have emerged regimes built around floating exchange rates with money as the preferred anchor for inflation. From a textbook perspective, this shift away from heavily managed exchange rates is surprising. Conventional wisdom, to the extent that it exists, tends to suggest that for low-income and small open economies, especially those at relatively early stages of financial development, fixed or relatively rigid exchange rate regimes offer more attractive inflation stabilization properties without compromising growth objectives, and only as these economies mature are the gains from exchange rate flexibility likely to be exploited.[1]

A central question in understanding the evolution in exchange rate policy in Africa is whether the shift from relatively fixed to relatively flexible exchange rate regimes reflects an efficient response to, or component of underlying processes of, development. Or whether instead it reflects an altogether more constrained choice, a recognition that structural weaknesses prevent the operation of an otherwise desirable fixed exchange rate regime. And what implications the shift towards greater exchange rate flexibility has for the conduct of macroeconomic management.

2. Policy choices: theory and evidence

The exchange rate is a key relative price in all open economies, shaping incentives for both producers and consumers, in the short and the long run; it represents one of the principal channels of transmission of macroeconomic shocks and volatility to the domestic economy; and changes in exchange rates have powerful distributional effects. More precisely, what matters fundamentally for long-run growth is the *real* exchange

---

[1] See Rogoff et al. (2003).

rate. If there were no money illusion, so that resource allocation decisions were unaffected by the level or growth in average prices, the choice of nominal anchor, and hence the exchange rate regime, would be irrelevant. But we know this neutrality does not prevail in practice, except perhaps in the very long run: over any meaningful horizon, the level and volatility of inflation matters enormously, which in turn means that policy towards the nominal exchange rate lies at the heart of the macroeconomic policy-making, either explicitly or by default. By determining the form of the nominal anchor for domestic prices, it determines the scope and independence of monetary policy,[2] and by determining the rate of inflation, decisions over the nominal anchor also shape the feasible fiscal stance.[3]

Exchange rate policy operates at two levels. The first is in shaping the overall exchange rate *regime* (the basic rules by which a central bank intervenes in the foreign exchange market to influence the external price of the domestic currency); the second is concerned with discretionary choices over the path of the nominal exchange rate, given the regime. Two non-discretionary cases define the range of possible regimes. At one extreme, a pure float (or a regime of strict non-intervention) passes responsibility for anchoring inflation to a domestic variable such as the money supply, nominal income, or, under inflation targeting regimes, inflation expectations themselves. At the other extreme, the authorities' intervention in the foreign exchange market is entirely focused on hitting a specific target level (or rate of crawl) for the exchange rate which itself becomes the nominal anchor, tying domestic inflation rate to that of the anchor currency or currencies (and domestic monetary policy to that of the anchor country depending on the operations of the capital account). Under a fixed exchange rate, macroeconomic compatibility requires monetary policy to be subordinated to the objective of hitting the exchange rate target, at least in the long run.[4]

In these polar cases there is, in effect, no exchange rate policy to speak of beyond the commitments entailed by the regime. In reality, with the exceptions in Africa of the CFA

---

[2] A nominal anchor is required to eliminate the indeterminacy of the price level. General equilibrium forces determine relative prices and real resource allocations, but to anchor the average price level, the authorities must fix one price (or the value of one quantity) in terms of the domestic unit of account. All other prices are then valued in terms of the anchor. In the long run, all nominal prices will grow at the same rate of growth as the nominal anchor.

[3] The intertemporal budget constraint of government requires that the fiscal accounts are consistent with the long-run inflation rate. Given revenue and expenditure and the long-run growth rate of the economy, for example, this defines the sustainable level of public debt.

[4] In the limit, the discipline of the fixed exchange rate leads to a currency board—in which the credibility of the exchange rate peg is enforced by curtailing central bank discretion altogether, through statute or practice—or full-blown monetary union, where the domestic currency itself is abandoned in favour of the external anchor currency or a supranational currency. In these cases, the institutional arrangements seek to offer protection against policy errors arising from discretionary or otherwise time-inconsistent behaviour, but at the cost of a complete lack of policy flexibility to protect the economy against short-run volatility in the face of shocks.

Franc Zone and the Rand Monetary Area, institutionally hard pegs are uncommon, while few, if any, countries have the institutional mechanisms to commit to a pure float. Rather, for the vast majority of countries, the domain of exchange rate policy is more extensive and is essentially concerned about where to locate on the continuum between full flexibility and a hard peg. This, in turn, entails navigating the constraint of the 'impossible trinity'. In an open economy, policymakers face three desirable yet incompatible objectives: to target the exchange rate so as to stabilize the external value of the currency and hence stabilize relative prices; to engage in activist monetary policy with a view to stabilizing domestic output in the face of shocks; and to allow for the free flow of capital across international borders, in pursuit of efficiency in resource allocation. Beyond the short run, however, it is not possible to simultaneously satisfy all three. Policy-makers must choose which objective to abandon. Experience suggests it is hard to limit cross-border private capital flows: the resolution of the impossible trinity therefore boils down to the strength of policy-makers' commitment to a pure float.

In striking this balance, policy-makers must evaluate four broad characteristics: the extent to which the regime offers a credible anchor for inflation; how well it insulates the domestic economy from potentially destabilizing balance of payments shocks; its ability to lower transactions costs and foster international trade and investment; and finally, its credibility in disciplining policy-makers and protecting the economy against time-inconsistent behaviour. The problem is that these objectives are often in conflict. Thus for a small open economy with a large traded goods share in expenditure, an exchange rate peg is likely to anchor domestic prices to world inflation more robustly than a floating rate with a domestic anchor. However, a floating rate may be better suited to ensuring the efficient adjustment of the real economy to external shocks arising from commodity price movements or shocks to global inflation, thereby avoiding prolonged, growth-retarding real exchange rate misalignment. Similarly, while fixed exchange rates may help reduce transactions costs in international trade, obviating the need for expensive hedging of exchange risks when domestic markets are thin or absent, flexible regimes may better foster financial market development. Different regimes may again have different properties when it comes to fostering discipline and policy credibility.

There is a vast literature on these questions assessing the properties of alternative exchange rate regimes, spanning the entire waterfront from the effects of exchange rate regimes on inflation and inflation volatility, through their impact on output stabilization, trade flows, financial sector development, fiscal performance, and credibility.[5] It would be nice if this literature could be summarized in the form of a simple checklist relating

---

[5] See e.g. Corden (2002), Ghosh, Gulde and Wolfe (2003), Rogoff et al. (2003), and Masson and Pattillo (2005) for general surveys; Frankel and Rose (2002) and Adam and Cobham (2007) on exchange rates and trade; Adam, Bevan, and Chambas (2001) on exchange rates and fiscal performance; and Tornell and Lane (1995) and Sun (2003) on fiscal discipline.

structural characteristics to the optimal choice of regime. But in reality this is impossible: despite the vastness of the research programme, the literature is surprisingly short of robust, unambiguous results. This reflects a range of difficulties, from problems in accurately measuring exchange rate regimes—the distinction in the jargon between a *de jure* classification based on countries' self-reported regimes and a *de facto* classification reflecting an assessment of how countries actually do—through to problems of identifying causality as opposed to statistical correlation. It is difficult, for example, to determine whether fixed exchange rate regimes promote lower inflation and greater fiscal discipline, or whether countries with strong institutions capable of delivering fiscal discipline also choose to adopt fixed exchange rates. What this means is that consideration of the 'optimal' exchange rate is highly country- and context-specific. But, as noted earlier, one strong message that does emerge from the sea of evidence, and which is highly relevant to contemporary Africa, comes from the work of Rogoff et al. (2003), suggesting that for countries at relatively early stages of financial development, fixed or relatively rigid exchange rate regimes appear to offer a degree of anti-inflation credibility (internal stability) without compromising growth objectives. However, as such economies mature and develop, not only are the gains from exchange rate flexibility greater but this flexibility in turn appears to promote more rapid financial sector development, which in turn further strengthens gains to exchange rate flexibility.

3. Exchange rate choices in Africa

At independence, many African countries inherited formal currency board arrangements from the colonial powers. Whilst this legacy has persisted with the CFA Franc Zone arrangements,[6] for most countries the notion that full sovereignty required monetary autonomy saw them move away from these arrangements—initially only symbolically by issuing their own currency but retaining the peg, but eventually by switching pegs and abandoning altogether the fiscal discipline of the currency board. The exchange rate quickly came to be seen as an additional policy instrument, so that by the late 1970s and throughout the 1980s exchange rate policy had moved centre stage. Unfortunately, this was also a time when, as Honohan and O'Connell (2008) argue, the prevailing economic orthodoxy on the continent asked both monetary and exchange rate policy to

---

[6] The CFA zone is partly a monetary union and partly a hybrid currency board. Monetary union prevails within the zone, but the two central banks lend to member governments and non-governments so that the money base is not fully backed. But because both can access overdraft facilities at the French Treasury, the external value of the CFA Franc is guaranteed. This has conferred huge advantages on the zone—most notably in anchoring inflation—but has come at the price of a chronic lack of real exchange rate flexibility, with the result that growth rates have been significantly below potential.

do 'too much', at least viewed from the perspective of today. Much of the incoherence in macroeconomic policy through this period can be traced back to attempts to defy the logic of the impossible trinity. Countries sought to manage their exchange rates, but with weak fiscal institutions that meant monetary policy was dominated by deficit-financing pressures so that compatibility with the exchange rate target was impossible without recourse to progressively more distortionary trade and exchange controls. By the late 1980s, most countries outside the CFA and Rand areas operated under heavily managed, highly distorted and fundamentally non-credible exchange rate regimes. Growth and macroeconomic stability duly suffered.

A turning point was reached in the mid-1990s when, with significant external assistance, many countries began to roll back the chronic fiscal dominance of the previous decade, dismantle the web of exchange controls, and move away from pegged or heavily managed regimes to intermediate and floating regimes.[7] Most African countries formally adopted Article VIII of the IMF's Articles of Agreement, obliging them to remove restrictions on current account transactions, and many moved to liberalize controls on the capital account. As a result, black markets in foreign exchange all but disappeared. Today, three-quarters of African countries outside the CFA zone operate under a monetary anchor or with some form of inflation targeting regime, supported by a *de jure* freely floating exchange rate.

4. Emerging challenges

The shift towards greater exchange rate flexibility raises two related challenges. The first concerns capital flows and the second the conduct of monetary policy. Even though many countries had liberalized their capital accounts *de jure*, private capital flows to Africa were small through much of the 1990s and early 2000s. As long as African countries remained off the radar of portfolio investors, the authorities could dodge the bullet of the impossible trinity for extended periods and enjoy many of the benefits of (heavily) managed exchange rates without losing control of monetary policy as a result of interest rate differentials triggering destabilizing private portfolio flows. The excess savings glut of the early 21st century, which presaged the financial crisis of 2008, put an end to this: global risk premia were compressed, investors sought ever more exotic investment opportunities, and by the mid-2000s, private short-term capital flows to Africa have become more responsive to arbitrage opportunities between world and

---

[7] Morris (1995) and Henstridge and Kasekende (2001) describe Uganda's pioneering moves to legalize the foreign exchange black market and unify it with the official rate, through progressive devaluation of the latter, and show how unification underpinned the successful fiscal and inflation stabilization of the early 1990s.

African bond markets. In many countries, surging private capital flows exposed weaknesses in small domestic financial markets and triggered sharply increased exchange rate and interest rate volatility, forcing central banks to recognize that the impossible trinity now constrained their actions more tightly than before. As a result, *de facto* policy shifted away from a *de jure* commitment to full exchange rate flexibility and towards the emergence of a generalized 'fear of floating'. Countries have shown a greater willingness to intervene to target the nominal exchange rate and, at the same time, the debate on the merits or otherwise of the taxation of short-run capital flows has resurfaced. And in the background, countries across the continent are re-engaging in discussions about monetary union, at the regional level (e.g. in the East Africa Community) and even at the pan-African level (e.g. the African Union's commitment to a single African currency by 2023).

This partial retreat from full flexibility exposes a second challenge for exchange rate policy. A number of countries in Africa have adopted, or are considering adopting, formal inflation targeting (IT) as their monetary framework. This immediately raises questions about the degree to which exchange rate objectives can be accommodated in the conduct of macroeconomic policy. Conventional IT regimes require exchange rate objectives to be fully subordinated to the inflation objective. Whether this is required in practice amongst African countries depends, first, on whether despite the *de facto* capital account integration of recent years capital markets is sufficiently imperfect that there is scope to intervene in the foreign exchange market in the short run, and second, on whether there exists sufficient institutional capacity such that the limits to exchange rate intervention can credibly be signalled to the private sector. Private agents need to know that if exchange rate and inflation objectives are in potential conflict, the latter will take precedence, so that expectations can credibly be formed on the basis of the authorities' pursuit of their inflation target.

REFERENCES

Adam, C., D. Bevan, and G. Chambas, 2001. 'Exchange rate regimes and revenue performance in Sub-Saharan Africa', *Journal of Development Economics* 64, 173–213.

—— and D. Cobham, 2007. 'Exchange rate regimes and trade', *Manchester School* 75.1, 44–6.

Corden, W. M., 2002. *Too Sensational: On the Choice of Exchange Rate Regimes*. Cambridge, Mass.: MIT Press.

Frankel, J., and A. Rose, 2002. 'An estimate of the effect of common currencies on trade and income', *Quarterly Journal of Economics* 117, 437–66.

Ghosh, A., A. Gulde, and H. Wolf, 2003. *Exchange Rate Regimes: Choices and Consequences*. Cambridge, Mass.: MIT Press.

Henstridge, M., and L. Kasekende, 2001. 'Exchange reforms, stabilization and fiscal management', in P. Collier and R. Reinikka (eds), *Uganda's Recovery: The Role of Farms, Firms and Government*. Washington, DC: World Bank.

Honohan, P., and S. O'Connell, 2008. 'Contrasting monetary regimes in sub-Saharan Africa', in M. Ncube (ed.), *Financial Systems and Monetary Policy in Africa*. Nairobi: AERC.

Masson, P., and C. Pattillo, 2005. *The Monetary Geography of Africa*. Washington, DC: Brookings Institution.

Morris, S., 1995. 'Inflation dynamics and the parallel market for foreign exchange', *Journal of Development Economics* 46, 295–316.

Rogoff, K., A. Husain, A. Mody, R. Brooks, and N. Oomes, 2003. 'Evolution and performance of exchange rate regimes', IMF Working Paper 03/243, Washington, DC.

Sun, Y., 2003. 'Do fixed exchange rates induce more fiscal discipline?', IMF Working Paper 03/078, Washington, DC.

Tornell, A., and P. Lane, 1995. 'Fiscal discipline and the choice of exchange rate regime', *European Economic Review* 39, 759–70.

Inflation Targeting in Africa

Stephen A. O'Connell

1. Introduction

In an inflation targeting (IT) framework, the central bank commits to a publicly announced numerical range for inflation, subordinates other intermediate targets, and institutionalizes its commitment through a set of mechanisms that emphasize transparency and accountability for outcomes. Between 1989 and 2008, the number of central banks practising full-fledged IT (FFIT) rose from zero to 27.[1] South Africa became SSA's first adopter in 2000, and in 2007 Ghana was the first low-income country in the world to adopt the framework. Many other countries adopted elements of IT while retaining a policy role for exchange rate or monetary targets; in SSA this list includes the region's two highest-performing economies, Botswana and Mauritius.

Ghana's decision was consistent with a global pattern that has encouraged adoption of FFIT at lower and lower levels of development. Durability has undoubtedly contributed: as of 2009 no country had abandoned IT, despite the fact that very few adopters satisfied all the preconditions emphasized in the early literature. But empirical studies also give the framework high marks. On balance, the evidence suggests that inflation targeters achieve more stable and somewhat lower inflation rates than non-targeters, with little or no sacrifice in terms of employment and output; and that external shocks are somewhat less likely to destabilize expectations (Mishkin and Schmidt-Hebbel 2007). The policy literature has accommodated this ever more impressive track record by gradually softening its concern for preconditions.[2]

In this chapter I review the logic of IT and examine its relevance for SSA. Issues like fiscal dominance, supply shocks, and institutional development loom large in SSA, relative to the constraints imposed—at least for now—by high capital mobility. Moreover Africa's central banks have already substantially increased the attention given to inflation in the conduct of monetary policy, and with considerable success. The appeal of FFIT may—ironically—be strongest in the CFA zone, where it would replace the most successful inflation anchor the continent has ever known.

---

[1] I use the IMF's online listing of *de facto* monetary policy anchors in April 2008. The total is 28 if the European Central Bank (which has officially resisted being characterized as an inflation targeter) is included.

[2] Freedman, Laxton, and Otker-Robe (forthcoming) review IT in theory and practice.

2. The global emergence of inflation targeting

The Great Inflation in the USA[3]—with its global impact and long aftermath among the emerging-market economies—created a revolution in the design and conduct of monetary policy. By the late 1990s, economists and central bankers worldwide were in agreement that good policy consisted in the exercise of 'constrained discretion' (Bernanke and Mishkin 1997). The intellectual underpinnings of this consensus are well covered elsewhere (Woodford 2003). In practical terms, the Volcker disinflation of 1979–84 was a watershed. Technically the Fed did not become an inflation targeter in 1979. But the Fed publicly took on the inflation rate as the unambiguous responsibility of monetary policy; it placed disinflation above other objectives; and it disinflated without regard to the exchange rate. These themes were taken up worldwide over the following two decades.

Attitudes towards the exchange rate evolved gradually, but by the late 1980s financial liberalization among the industrial countries had unleashed short-term capital movements on a global basis. Facing ever sharper dangers of speculative attacks and wishing to liberalize their own financial controls, central banks began to move away from fixed-but-adjustable pegs. Some adopted harder pegs, but the majority retained an active role for monetary policy by choosing greater exchange rate flexibility.

FFIT therefore emerged in a context of global disinflation and amid a shift away from exchange rate anchors. As nominal anchors, money growth targets were the obvious alternative and were widely employed starting in the 1970s. But they were less transparent than exchange rates, and outside SSA they became associated with policy instability under conditions of financial innovation. All anchors, moreover, were subject to credibility problems. In 1989, the Government of New Zealand cut through these concerns institutionally. Under the Reserve Bank of New Zealand Act, the central bank would be legally bound to achieving a tight numerical range for inflation.[4]

The spread of FFIT after 1990 was influenced both by the success of adopters and by a further development within academe. Taylor (1993) observed that Fed policy after 1980 was well approximated by a reaction function relating the policy interest rate to the deviations of inflation from a target and output from its natural rate. The Taylor rule gave operational content to constrained discretion, by reconciling a counter-cyclical role for policy (discretion) with an aggressive response to inflation (constraint). By the late 1990s it was clear that in models with forward-looking expectations and price rigidities, Taylor-type rules not only anchored expectations but also generated highly favourable combinations of volatility in inflation and output. The rule-based approach to

---

[3] Roughly 1965–84; see Meltzer (2005).
[4] Subsequent FFIT systems have been less draconian, but all constrain central banks to pursue numerical targets for inflation.

monetary policy evaluation bore more directly on constrained discretion than on FFIT *per se*, but acquired an important role in the internal discourse of inflation-targeting central banks (Berg, Karam, and Laxton 2006).

3. The African context

FFIT combines a novel choice of nominal anchor with a set of institutional commitments designed to enhance the credibility and predictability of policy. How relevant are these innovations for African countries?

The first of two dominant themes in Africa's inflation history is the effectiveness of monetary unions at maintaining hard exchange rate pegs and thereby anchoring the inflation rates of member countries to those of the pivot currency (Masson and Pattillo 2005). The institutions of the CFA zone overcame fiscal dominance—a situation in which public sector solvency has to be maintained through monetary finance, rather than through adjustments in spending or taxes—by locating monetary policy at the supranational level, where no single member government could dictate its terms. In the institutional dimension, therefore, it is not clear that FFIT offers important advantages for the fourteen CFA countries: the arrangements of the zone have been credible and predictable.[5] A hard peg, however, leaves very little room for discretion. If capital mobility is high, it effectively gives up monetary policy altogether. This rigidity produced a long and costly economic contraction in the zone when adverse shocks called for a real depreciation in the 1980s and early 1990s and the relative price adjustment had to be accomplished through deflation. A switch to inflation targeting, by allowing zone-wide exchange rate flexibility, might produce a superior balance of constraint and discretion.

There is also a deeper institutional question about the appropriate locus of accountability. The convertibility guarantee from France and the EU underpins the viability of the peg. While this form of dependence is almost certainly desirable relative to a unilateral zone-wide peg, it may have long-run costs in terms of institutional development, relative to a regime that can be managed autonomously by its own members.

The second dominant theme is that most of Africa did experience—and defeat—a 'great inflation' of its own. The phenomenon was restricted to the continent's national currencies, including the South African rand.[6] In contrast to the supranational institutions of the CFA zone, national central banks lacked the legal or *de facto* autonomy to resist fiscal pressures. By the early 1980s exchange rate anchors had been discredited—

---

[5] Mali (rejoining in 1984), Equatorial Guinea (1985), and Guinea Bissau (1997) were willing to give up their own currencies to join the zone.

[6] The rand is the pivot of the Common Monetary Area, but Lesotho, Namibia, and Swaziland have no influence over South Africa's monetary policy.

and marginalized—through a proliferation of distorting exchange controls and black markets. The structural adjustment era swept away these controls, so that by the early 1990s central banks were committed to fostering macroeconomic stability indirectly, through market-determined prices for foreign exchange and credit. Disinflation was by no means immediate; letting exchange rates go unleashed inflation, particularly where market-based reforms were undertaken before establishing fiscal discipline. The number of countries with annual inflation above 40% peaked at eleven in 1995. But by the late 1990s, central banks across the continent had successfully employed money-based disinflation programmes to bring inflation down into single or low double digits.

Tight fiscal rules (e.g. cash budgets) played a key role in overcoming fiscal dominance during the 1990s. The majority of non-CFA central banks now operate reserve-money frameworks that are the direct descendants of IMF conditionality programmes and retain severe limits on central bank finance to government. These frameworks target inflation in the well-defined sense that benchmarks for reserve-money growth are derived from projections of inflation-consistent growth in money demand; in most cases the central bank announces a desired range for inflation. Many countries now also boast new legislative charters that clarify the central bank's mandate and shelter it from short-term political pressures.

4. Why add binding numerical targets?

Existing frameworks have performed well over the past decade, and have incorporated many of the features of FFIT without committing to numerical targets. Outside the CFA zone, most central banks are practising versions of what Stone (2003) calls 'inflation targeting lite' (ITL), focusing seriously on inflation but also giving systematic attention to exchange rate targets.[7] Why go further? I offer observations rather than answers.

First, FFIT may ironically make more sense for African monetary unions than for national currencies. For the CFA zone, FFIT combines a better choice of nominal anchor with a transition path away from dependence on the exchange rate guarantee. A similar argument holds for planned monetary unions elsewhere in Africa, where exchange rate guarantees are not in prospect and the political instability of the major players—Nigeria in West Africa and Kenya in East Africa—strengthens the case for union-wide restraints.

Second, FFIT may—ironically again—be a more constructive choice for African countries still struggling with fiscal dominance than it is for those who have overcome it by other means. In contrast to the industrial-country situation, there is no empirical

---

[7] On the prevalence of exchange rate objectives in SSA, see IMF (2008: Table 2.1).

consensus in favour of very low inflation in low-income countries.[8] This gives the welfare logic of FFIT a distinctly second-best flavour in SSA: if credibility can be obtained through other means, keeping inflation low and stable may not be the best way to use it. However, where existing frameworks cannot be relied on to keep expected inflation below (say) 15%, FFIT has a reasonable chance of targeting the policy distortion at its source. The framework requires an explicit endorsement from the government, and it directly educates the public that monetary policy cannot create high public-sector wages, a competitive real exchange rate, or even cheap credit on a sustainable basis. This may be the right path to credibility when external props are absent. South Africa provides an example: without FFIT the Reserve Bank would undoubtedly be under even greater pressure than it already is, following the populist transition within the ANC, to accommodate the food and fuel price shocks of 2007–8.[9]

Third, since FFIT was never designed for low-income countries, their economic structure raises unresolved questions. Does it make sense to target inflation when exchange rates, food prices, and public-sector prices (utilities, fuel, and public-sector wages) are more prominent—and verifiable—in the public eye? Can the framework be deployed successfully when supply shocks are dominant and the GDP gap is difficult to measure? Is there a role for exchange rate targets, given imperfect capital mobility and the importance of export promotion? What operational policy rules can be used when there is not a strong transmission from policy interest rates to aggregate demand, and where (as in almost all African cases) central banks use balance sheet instruments rather than interest rates? Ghana faces all of these questions (Sowa and Abradu-Otoo 2009). As of late 2009 the Bank of Ghana had yet to achieve a target range that was already higher and wider than that of any other targeter. Its struggles with transparency are palpable; in some quarters the Bank describes itself as practising ITL rather than FFIT (IMF 2008: 5). It remains to be seen whether the distortions implied by committing to a target that is rarely met, of unclear salience, and difficult to forecast are fundamentally damaging to economic stability—or are more than compensated by committing the fiscal authorities to self-restraint and forcing the pace of institutional maturation within the central bank.

Finally, recent events are testing inflation targeting in new ways. A confluence of food and fuel price shocks in 2007 and 2008 pushed virtually all targeters above their ranges in 2008—the first time a miss of this scope had occurred. The global financial crisis sharply reversed this impetus, confronting industrial-country targeters with risks of deflation, and generating massive rescue operations with uncertain implications for future price stability. These developments have dampened the short-run enthusiasm for FFIT in

---

[8] Modest inflation allows large relative price changes to occur without outright deflation. The CFA experience of 1980–94 suggests, surprisingly, that deflation is damaging to growth even in low-income economies with small formal sectors.

[9] Frankel, Smit, and Sturzenegger (2007) discuss macroeconomic management in South Africa.

Africa—fortuitously in my view, given the viability of existing ITL systems and the scope for further improvements—while generating sharp reminders of the necessary regulatory complements to any successful monetary policy framework.

REFERENCES

Berg, Andrew, Philippe Karam, and Douglas Laxton, 2006. 'A practical model-based approach to monetary policy: overview', IMF Working Paper 06/80, Washington, DC.

Bernanke, Ben S., and Frederic S. Mishkin, 1997. 'Inflation targeting: a new framework for monetary policy?', *Journal of Economic Perspectives* 11.2, 97–116.

Frankel, Jeffrey, Ben Smit, and Federico Sturzenegger, 2007. 'South Africa: macroeconomic challenges after a decade of success', RWP 07-121, John F. Kennedy School of Government, Harvard University.

Freedman, Charles, Douglas Laxton, and Inci Otker-Robe, forthcoming. *On Developing a Full-Fledged Inflation Targeting Regime: Doing What You Say and Saying What You Do*. Carleton University and IMF.

International Monetary Fund, 2008. *Ghana: Selected Issues*. Country Report No. 08/332. Washington, DC.

Masson, Paul, and Catherine Pattillo, 2005. *The Monetary Geography of Africa*. Washington, DC: Brookings Institution.

Meltzer, Allan, 2005. 'Origins of the Great Inflation', Federal Reserve Bank of St. Louis, *Review* 87.2, part 2, 145–75.

Mishkin, Frederic S., and Klaus Schmidt-Hebbel, 2007. 'Does inflation targeting make a difference?', NBER Working Paper No. 12876, Cambridge, Mass.

Sowa, Nii Kwaku, and Philip Abradu-Otoo, 2009. 'Inflation management and monetary policy formation in Ghana', in Gill Hammond, Ravi Kanbur, and Eswar Prasad (eds), *Monetary Policy Frameworks for Emerging Markets*. Cheltenham: Edward Elgar.

Stone, Mark R., 2003. 'Inflation targeting lite', IMF Working Paper 03/12, Washington, DC.

Taylor, John B., 1993. 'Discretion versus policy rules in practice', *Carnegie-Rochester Conference Series in Public Policy* 39, 195–214.

Woodford, Michael, 2003. *Interest and Prices: Foundations of a Theory of Monetary Policy*. Princeton, NJ: Princeton University Press.

African Financial Systems

Lemma W. Senbet

1. Why finance for Africa?

There is an accumulating scholarly evidence which supports a strong linkage between financial sector development and economic development (e.g. Levine 1997). The evidence for the positive impact of financial-sector development on economic performance is supported by data from Africa itself, although the results are not as strong mainly due to the quality of available data (Senbet and Otchere 2008). Most African countries, particularly those in sub-Saharan Africa, went through extensive financial-sector reforms from the 1980s into the early 1990s. The reforms included removal of credit ceilings, liberalization of interest rates, restructuring and privatization of state-owned banks, and introduction of a variety of measures to promote the development of private banking systems and financial markets. Accompanying these measures were bank supervisory and regulatory schemes.

The central question for sub-Saharan Africa is then how to develop a well-functioning financial sector and build its capacity so as to exploit its potential contribution to economic development.

2. Payoffs to financial-sector reforms

At a broader level, there is no doubt that a more liberalized financial environment has emerged as a result of the financial-sector reforms in Africa. These reforms have also been stimulated by rapid improvements in global conditions and global technology connecting Africa with the outside world. It is not accidental, therefore, that Africa began to experience good performance both in the real and financial sectors.

2.1. ECONOMIC PERFORMANCE

Before the global crisis hit, in the aggregate, Africa began rising in the wake of the 21st century and experiencing something like a growth renaissance. According to the ADB data, the GDP growth for the five year period (2002–7) averaged over 5.2, outpacing population growth. Simultaneously, there was improvement in fiscal discipline, and inflation was brought under control. In addition, African countries experienced declining debt burden and increasing capacity for debt service, while enjoying increasing foreign investment and remittance flows.

2.2. PERFORMANCE FROM BANK PRIVATIZATIONS

An important outcome of financial sector reforms has been a sharp decline in the state ownership of banks in Africa. However, the payoffs to bank privatizations have been discouraging (Senbet and Otchere 2006). In general, privatized banks in Africa experienced deterioration in asset quality, credit quality, and profitability. The evidence on the performance effects of bank privatization in Africa appears inconsistent with the overall evidence for other regions which experienced positive outcomes (Clarke, Cull, and Shirley 2004). The evidence outside Africa also suggests that privatization gains are limited when governments held minority stake. Therefore, the likely explanation for poor post-privatization performance of banks may be due to the prevalence of partial privatizations of banks in Africa. Under partial bank privatization, the 'privatized' banks are still vulnerable to government intervention.

2.3. STOCK MARKET PERFORMANCE

During the pre-crisis period, African stock markets performed surprisingly well both in terms of absolute stock return and on a risk-adjusted basis (Senbet and Otchere 2008), despite the challenges they had faced in terms of low capitalization and liquidity. The standard Sharpe ratio, which scales an average excess stock return by the standard deviation, was used as a risk-adjusted metric. In absolute terms, the average annual return was 38.5% for the period 1990–2006. The Sharpe ratio was 0.54. To appreciate this a little better, these performance measures were benchmarked to Malaysia and Mexico (one country each from Asia and Latin America), and the stock returns in Africa compared favourably with these two countries: Malaysia (9.32%) and Mexico (31.5%), respectively. Of course, the global crisis hit these markets, and they experienced sharp decline in the face of the crisis. The 2008 market declines for selected markets were as follows: Nigeria 59%, Egypt 55%, Mauritius 49%, South Africa 33%, and Kenya 31%. Interestingly, the crisis did not change the pre-crisis positioning of African stock market performance relative to the two countries we benchmarked. In fact, on average they fared better than Mexico and Malaysia both in absolute terms and on a risk-adjusted basis.

2.4. FINANCIAL GLOBALIZATION

Sub-Saharan Africa was bypassed by the massive flow of private international capital to developing countries resulting from the opening up of the world economy in the 1980s. In aggregate, the private flows to developing countries have been rapidly exceeding official development assistance flows since the 1980s, except for sub-Saharan Africa. However, encouraging forces are now in place for the prospect of sub-Saharan Africa to integrate into the global financial economy and join the other developing countries in terms of increased private flows. First, there is growing integration of world capital markets, with increasing capital mobility. Barriers to international capital flows have been reduced. Second, there are rapid advances in information technology connecting Africa with the outside world, with the potential to facilitate capital flows. Thus, outside investors seeking the benefits of global diversification will be better able to access African financial systems. As Africa moves toward integration into the global economy, the development of the financial sector is crucial for accessing the benefits of financial globalization. With increasing financial sector reforms, Africa is bound to participate in the growing allocation of global investments to emerging markets.

3. Challenges

There are still many challenges, though. The African financial development gap remains enormously high. Based on development metrics, the financial sectors of most African countries remain quite underdeveloped even by the standards of other developing countries. In 2007, the liquid liabilities of financial sectors averaged about 30% of GDP for sub-Saharan Africa. Looking at the other developing regions, the financial development indicator approached or exceeded 50% in East Asia, Latin America, South Asia, and the Middle East and North Africa. On the metric for private credit provision, the financial development for sub-Saharan Africa is even more discouraging. The average level of credit extended to the private sector was 16.6% of GDP in 2007, whereas for the other developing countries, the financial development indicator ranged from 32.5 to 43.9% (Allen et al. 2009).

Moreover, African stock markets are characterized by low provision of liquidity based on standard indicators of trading activity: the value of shares traded scaled by GDP and/or market capitalization. Table 1 presents data for selected indicators relevant for financial development, including those for stock markets for the pre-crisis period. For Africa, the average stock turnover ratio is 6.5%, versus 34.1% for the rest of the world. Thus, the average liquidity of African stock markets is roughly five times below the average for the rest of the world.

Table 1. Financial development and selected determinants, 1995–2007 (averages)

	World	Africa
Liquid liabilities/GDP	64.2%	27.5%
Private credit/GDP	57.7%	17.6%
Stock market capitalization/GDP	52.1%	25.6%
Stock market value traded/GDP	34.1%	6.5%
Ln (population density)	0.44	0.09
Inflation rate	5.2%	9.3%
KKM index (Institutional Quality)	0.33	−0.54
Bank concentration	0.65	0.81
Foreign ownership share	27.1%	44.4%
Secondary/primary school enrolment	0.81	0.33
Roads/area	1.07	0.21
Geographical branch penetration	29.76	7.97
Demographic branch penetration	16.51	2.86

Source: Allen et al. (2009).

Several institutional factors contribute to the financial development gap. First, while there have been serious efforts to improve banking regulation in many African countries, it remains grossly inadequate. The quality of financial intermediation is either reflective of excessively high risk (leading to bank distress) or excessively conservative (leading to dearth of credit to the private sector). Second, the bank industrial organization is characterized by oligopoly and the dominance of state-owned enterprises. The highly concentrated banking structure observed in sub-Saharan Africa allows only for very limited deposit and lending competition. This leads to reinforcement of high lending and deposit spread environment.

Third, there are risk factors to worry about. High macro-economic and political instabilities, which are prevalent in Africa, lead to high volatility in the financial systems. The prevailing evidence is that stability, such as low and predictable rates of inflation, contributes to financial-sector development. Moreover, sub-Saharan Africa continues to conjure up images of war, massive corruption, grossly undisciplined governance, and gross violations of human rights in international news headlines. This perception is not in accord with the fundamentals, and contributes to untenable investment risks as perceived by outside investors. This is, in part, captured by low ratings for creditworthiness of sub-Saharan African countries relative to other regions (see Figure 1).

4. Policies

We catalogue below key policy measures that mitigate the challenges discussed above and help build capacity of African financial systems.

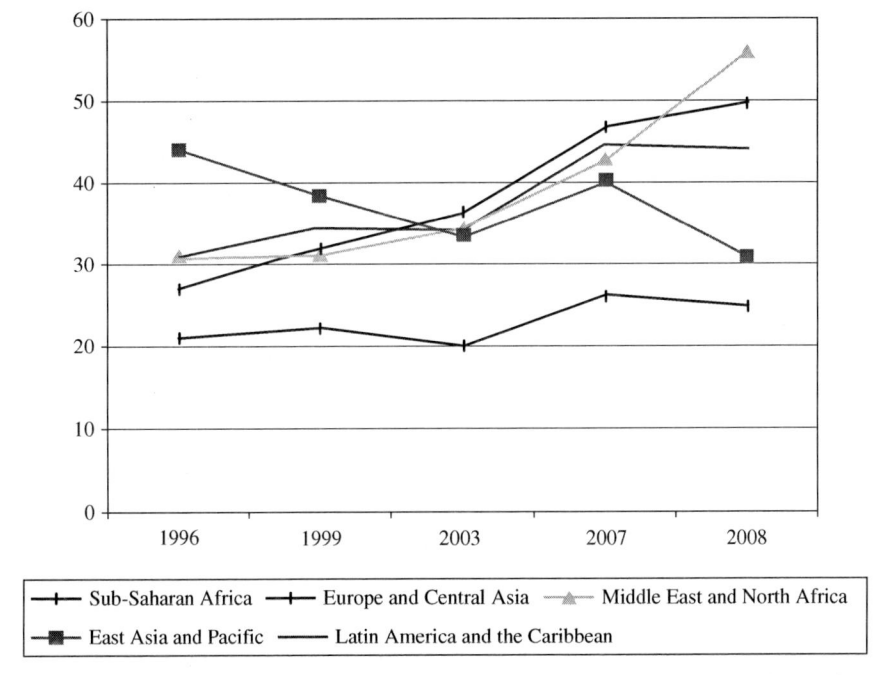

Figure 1. Institutional investor credit ratings (source: Senbet 2009, based on data from *Institutional Investor*)

4.1. REFORMING CAPITAL REGULATION

The global crisis has revealed severe regulatory gaps in the banking and the overall financial system, which are getting a great deal of global attention. African countries should consider this as an opportune time to think again about banking regulation so as to reduce the frequency and severity of future crises. Banking regulation should have appropriate capital standards to reduce excessive risk taking by banks. Moreover, apart from capital standards, there should be supervision and monitoring of bank liquidity position. One glaring feature of the current crisis was a drying up of liquidity which led to a shutdown of the credit markets.

4.2. REGULATING SHADOW BANKING

Traditional banks basically accept deposits and transform them into lending for longer-term assets. As financial systems develop, shadow banks emerge with functions similar to what banks do, and they include such institutions as investment banks, money market funds, and hedge funds. However, these shadow banks typically operate outside the banking regulatory regime. 'Shadow' banks are likely to emerge in Africa as financial systems develop, and this is an opportune time to think about the disciplinary mechanisms in a proactive fashion. Related to shadow banking is an emergence of systemically critical or interconnected institutions which can hold hostage the entire financial system. African economies, which are specialized in very few sectors, are particularly vulnerable to systemic failures when such institutions fail. The lesson here is that systemically critical institutions and shadow banks should be brought under the same regulatory umbrella and be subject to even higher capital and liquidity standards than 'plain vanilla' banks.

4.3. BUILDING CAPACITY FOR OVERSIGHT OF RISK AND RISK MANAGEMENT

Risk is endemic to a dynamic financial system. More broadly, finance and financial innovation have become increasingly complex and dynamic. African countries are increasingly committed to well-functioning financial systems, and increasingly integrated into global financial systems. There should be a commensurate commitment to the development of talented financial manpower with sufficient capacity to manage and control risk. Unfortunately, the African financial systems face severe shortages of well-trained manpower capable of performing modern risk management. Likewise, financial regulators need to understand how banks and financial institutions take and manage risk. Therefore, literacy in financial regulation requires sufficient understanding of how the regulated should manage risk to avert mismanagement that is destabilizing to the financial system. This is an opportune time for financial regulatory institutions, as well as financial institutions, to partner with higher education programmes to develop specialized training programmes to produce financial manpower and regulatory force that matches increasingly innovative and complex financial systems.

4.4. FOSTERING BEST GOVERNANCE PRACTICES

Around the world there is a growing recognition that financial systems cannot function properly without quality governance. The extensive privatization programmes in Africa bring companies and institutions under the disciplinary force of the market system, but management and corporate insiders may still engage in activities that are not aligned with long-term value maximization. There are certain features of good governance, and among them are a well-functioning corporate board and a well-designed compensation structure that provides proper incentives for executives in financial systems. Around the globe, there is a growing movement for board independence, a literate audit committee, a compensation committee composed of independent directors, and a compensation structure with incentives for undertaking appropriate risks. Thus, African countries should strengthen institutions for corporate governance and adopt best international practices to foster a financial system that is dynamic and stable.

4.5. FOSTERING MARKET DEPTH AND FUNCTIONALITY

Except for South Africa, financial systems in sub-Saharan Africa are still thin and illiquid. This is quite evident among the fledgling stock markets. Certain institutional factors impede the liquidity of these markets. Institutional investors, as well as governments which maintain minority stockholdings, are not active traders in the secondary market. Moreover, markets tend to be dominated by a few large companies (e.g. Ashanti Goldfields). Fortunately, though, these markets have been experiencing improvement both in capitalization and in liquidity. One important way to accelerate the improving trend is consolidation of regional markets through regional cooperative initiatives. There is a growing recognition of this, and some initiatives are already in place, such as that pioneered by the Abidjan-based *Bourse régionale des valeurs mobilières* (BVRM). The added advantage of market consolidation is that it will fuel the momentum of African integration into the global financial economy.

4.6. RESOLVING INFORMATION GAP AND BUILDING FINANCIAL MARKET DATABASE

In international headlines, the extensive economic and financial-sector reforms that have taken place in Africa are rarely mentioned, or, when they are mentioned, crowded out by the negatives. This perception, stemming from a severe information gap, is costly, and penalizes an entire region by lumping the genuinely reforming countries together with those which are not. The cost manifests in several forms, but in the area of finance it adversely affects the ability of the countries to access external finance and raise debt at terms which reflect economic fundamentals. As African countries become committed to the development of well-functioning financial systems, they should also recognize a vital need for the development of research and information capacity to provide more extensive, detailed, and reliable data capturing the financial characteristics of banks and other financial institutions. The timeliness and reliability of data allow investors to make accurate estimates of investment risks in Africa, and help mitigate the costly information distortion in international news headlines. Therefore, policy-makers in the African financial sectors should include the development of a financial system database and financial research on the financial development agenda.

4.7. PROMOTING MARKET-BASED PRIVATIZATIONS

An encouraging recent development is that a growing number of African state-owned enterprises (e.g. Kenya Airways) have used the stock markets as a vehicle for privatization (Senbet and Otchere 2008). This should be welcome, since large-scale privatizations through the markets contribute directly to market depth through supply of listed companies. Moreover, the stock market vehicle is a means of depoliticizing privatization programmes, since it allows for price discovery in a fair and transparent manner. It is worth mentioning additional but less obvious benefits. Privatized enterprises are brought to the discipline of the stock markets, potentially leading to improved investment efficiency and performance. Moreover, market-based privatization programmes with wider shareholdings can lead to diversity of ownership of the economy's resources and help alleviate public concerns that financial systems serve just the few elite in society.

4.8. PROMOTING INTEGRATION OF THE INFORMAL AND FORMAL FINANCE

The focus in this chapter has been on formal finance, inclusive of both banking and non-banking sectors due to space limitation. In closing, a mention of informal/micro finance is warranted. In view of the inadequate performance outcomes of the formal financial-sector reforms in Africa, there is a prevalence of informal and micro finance responding to financing gaps faced by small borrowers both in the rural and urban sectors. However, the informal sector faces challenges, among them lack of transparency in the lending and deposit relationships, and the price at which credit is available. Moreover, there is very limited integration between the informal and formal sectors. A linkage with the formal sector would be one way to get the savings mobilization into the open at an integrated market price. Introduction of appropriate legal and regulatory regimes to promote financial integration should be high on the policy agenda.

4.9. CONTROLLING THE PENDULUM

African countries may be rethinking about financial globalization in view of the collateral damage that they experienced from the global crisis through no fault of their own. In fact, the damage has been considerable, with adverse impact on trade, investment, and remittances, and consequent negative impact on economic performance. The threat is that the impressive gains achieved by two decades of genuine economic and financial-sector reforms may be derailed. Like it or not, though, financial globalization is here to stay. In fact, the current global crisis has brought home the fact that even those African countries which are weakly integrated, or shun financial globalization altogether, have not been immune, since the crisis was transmitted to those countries through the real sectors. Thus, this is not the time to reverse course toward the old but disastrous command financial systems. This is the time to strengthen policies and reforms, to return to a path of growth momentum, and to continue integration into the global financial economy.

REFERENCES

Allen, F., E. Carletti, R. Cull, J. Q. Qian, and L.W. Senbet, 2009. 'The African financial development gap', working paper, available at: http://fic.wharton.upenn.edu/fic/papers/10/10-18.pdf.

Aryeetey, E., and L. W. Senbet, 1999. 'Essential financial market reforms in Africa', paper presented at the 21st Century African World Bank project, Abidjan.

Clarke, G., R. Cull, and M. Shirley, 2004. 'Empirical studies of bank privatization: some lessons', mimeo, World Bank, Washington, DC.

Cull, R., L. Senbet, and M. Sorge, 2005. 'Deposit insurance and financial development', *Journal of Money, Credit, and Banking* 37, 43–82.

John, K., A. Saunders, and L. Senbet, 2000. 'A theory of bank regulation and management compensation', *Review of Financial Studies* 13.1, 95–126.

—— and L. W. Senbet, 1998. 'Corporate governance and board effectiveness', *Journal of Banking and Finance* 22, 371–403.

Kane, E. and R. Rice, 2001. 'Bank runs and banking policies: lessons for African policymakers', *Journal of African Economies* 10, 36–71.

Levine, R., 1997. 'Financial development and economic growth: views and agenda', *Journal of Economic Literature* 35, 688–726.

Otchere, I., 2005. 'Do privatised banks in middle and low-income countries perform better than rival banks? An intra-industry analysis of bank privatisation', *Journal of Banking and Finance* 29, 2067–93.

Senbet, L.W., 2009. 'Financial sector policy reforms in the post-financial crisis era: Africa focus', working paper 100, African Development Bank Group.

—— and I. Otchere, 2007. 'Financial sector reforms in Africa: perspectives on issues and policies', in F. Bourguignon and B. Pleskovic (eds), *Rethinking Infrastructure for Development*. Washington, DC: World Bank.

—— —— 2008. 'African stock markets', in Marc Quintyn and Genevieve Verdier (eds), *African Finance in the 21st Century*. Basingstoke: Palgrave Macmillan.

Banks and Credit Markets

Victor Murinde

1. Introduction

Arguably, banks and credit markets in Africa have evolved through three overlapping phases. The first was the colonial, pre-1960s phase. Colonies were served by currency boards, rather than central banks; for instance, the East African Currency Board (1919–66) and West African Currency Board (1912–68). Commercial banks were predominantly foreign-owned, and credit criteria were stringent for local entrepreneurs (Murinde and Tefula 2003). The entrepreneurs, according to Hyuha and Ddumba (1992, citing Uganda), were presumed to lack adequate business acumen and credit history, did not possess acceptable collateral, or fronted unconventional, high-risk projects. Hence, the banks were characterized by market failure.

The second phase, the post-independence 1960–80 era, saw the introduction of central banks, specialized banks, and state-owned commercial banks. Central banks replaced currency boards and issued national currencies; also, they initiated monetary policy and bank regulation. In order to address market failure, state-owned banks (notably, agricultural development banks, industrial development banks, and cooperative banks) were set up to finance specific sectors. The African Development Bank was established in 1964 to finance long-term developmental projects. Further, in the 1970s, some countries (e.g. Uganda and Tanzania) nationalized foreign banks. Governments used the state-owned banks to direct credit to local entrepreneurs (Brownbridge and Harvey 1998). However, the banks gradually experienced principal–agent problems: managers were political protégés, and credit was allocated through political peddling. Consequently, the banks suffered bad loans. Corruption and fraud contributed to banks' impaired loan portfolios (Maimbo 1999).

In the third phase, from 1980 to the present, the pendulum has swung back to private, mainly foreign-owned banks. Gradually, regulation has been revamped to allow foreign bank entry, and state-owned commercial banks have been privatized (Kasekende et al. 2009). Some countries (e.g. Nigeria, Kenya, and Uganda) have witnessed successful initiatives to start local private banks or to foster bank consolidation through mergers and acquisitions.

This chapter highlights the landmarks in the evolution of banks and credit markets in Africa, in terms of bank ownership, banking innovations, reform of credit markets, and the current status of bank competitiveness.

2. Foreign bank ownership: a mixed blessing for Africa?

In the third phase of bank evolution in Africa, foreign bank presence has increased from less than 10% to more than 50%, and stands at 100% in Botswana, Gambia, Lesotho, and Swaziland (Kirkpatrick, Murinde, and Tefula 2008). Some of the foreign banks are intra-African: South African, Nigerian, Kenyan, and Libyan banks have spread across the continent.

There is concern among researchers and policy-makers on whether increased foreign bank entry is a mixed blessing for Africa. Perhaps. Foreign banks tend to 'cherry-pick' lucrative business in the domestic market, by directing their loans to multinationals and the most creditworthy clients. Brownbridge and Harvey (1998) cite Kenya and Uganda, where some foreign banks reduced their branch network to concentrate on urban areas and multinationals. The lending strategy marginalizes local banks by pushing them to more risky businesses, especially small enterprises, which are prone to information asymmetry. Moreover, many African countries may lack the capacity to effectively supervise foreign banks across the range of financial services (e.g. derivatives trading). Also, regulatory complications may arise if foreign banks follow both domestic and foreign rules; early warning indicators of bank failure may elude domestic supervisors until the bank has actually failed, as was the case with the Bank of Credit and Commerce International (BCCI).

Perhaps not. Foreign banks may facilitate financial architecture in host economies, including the essential supportive systems (such as accounting and transparency), innovations (such as activating an inter-bank market and use of electronic banking), and the transfer of cutting-edge technologies for bank supervision and risk management (Murinde, Miroux, and Lim 2008). This factor is critical, because the global financial crisis has undermined bank regulatory models, and African regulators who have been transitioning from Basel I to Basel II are now at a crossroads (Murinde 2010). Also, foreign banks may engender bank consolidation and competition, which may generate spillover effects such as improving the overall quality and pricing of financial services (Murinde and Ryan 2003). Further, with an increase in foreign bank presence, domestic bank managers may be forced to give up their sheltered 'quiet life' and pursue cost efficiency.

Overall, although foreign bank ownership remains controversial, especially for some African countries with fragile banks, the preponderance of evidence is in favour of 'free entry and exit' (Murinde and Ryan 2003). An important policy implication is that, in order to reap the benefits of foreign bank presence, bank regulators must be selective in favour of high-quality and reputable international banks, or permit the immigration of skilled banking personnel who transmit new technology and specialized skills.

3. Banking innovations

Singular among the innovations in African banking is the introduction of Islamic banks. The first modern experiment with Islamic banking was undertaken in Egypt in 1963, and by 1967 the number of banks had increased to nine. Today, Islamic banks operate in 38 out of 53 African countries and the banking system is Islamized in the Sudan.

The innovation is that, unlike conventional banks, which rely on the interest rate metric, Islamic banks use novel financial instruments. The instruments used in Africa include *mudarabah* (profit sharing), *murabahah* (cost plus), *ijarah* (hire purchase), *musharakah* (joint venture), *sukuk* (Islamic bonds), and *takaful* (Islamic insurance). The banks are regulated partly by Islamic Law (*Shariah*) boards.

Egyptian and Libyan banks use these financial instruments to play a risk management role. For example, the *mudarabah* instrument provides a contract between the bank and an entrepreneur, whereby the former mobilizes the capital and the latter provides the management. There is dual incentive compatibility: both parties must succeed because, in case of loss, the bank loses the capital, while the entrepreneur loses his provision of management (Khalil, Rickwood, and Murinde 2002).

Other innovations include microfinance banking. Microfinance savings and lending in Africa is being scaled up from just over 1 million customers in 2010 to 30 million by 2015. Outreach is close to 1 million clients in Rwanda, Kenya, South Africa, Uganda, Ethiopia, Burkina Faso, and Morocco. The innovation includes access to finance by households and firms that suffer 'financial exclusion' from commercial banks.

But, one snag persists: central banks in Africa have yet to build capacity to regulate Islamic banks and microfinance banking, although the relevant laws have been enacted.

4. Credit markets and imperfect information

Africa credit markets are underdeveloped, with the lowest levels of credit penetration; for example, estimates by IFC suggest that Angola, Mozambique, and Tanzania have each 1–8% of the population served by the banking system (Mylenko 2007). Most financial institutions tend to focus on off-balance sheet activities (such as foreign exchange trading, bond trading, international trade financing, and remittances) rather than credit.

Also, segments of the credit market are poorly linked, with high interest rate differentials, mainly due to information imperfections. Beyond the segmentation identified by Nissanke and Aryeetey (1998) during the initial stages of financial reforms, the spotlight today is on credit markets, which are segmented in terms of the main types of banks. Foreign banks concentrate on loans to large rather than small enterprises, such that the banks have a higher average loan per borrower compared to domestic banks (Murinde and Tefula 2003). Because they have limited sources of funding, private domestic banks tend to serve small companies. State-owned commercial banks tend to finance government projects according to policy objectives directed by government. National developments banks, too, aim to finance government projects, which are aligned to national developmental goals.

However, there are positive developments to address credit market imperfections. Since 2000, private credit bureaus have been established in many African countries, including Angola, Ghana, Kenya, Madagascar, Mauritius, Mozambique, Nigeria, Tanzania, Uganda, and Zambia. The bureaus are essential for a well-functioning credit market; they help to reduce asymmetric information, moral hazard, and adverse selection problems between borrowers and lenders, thereby reducing credit risk, supporting access to credit, and improving credit repayments.

Nevertheless, some problems remain. Many countries are still characterized by weak creditor rights and poor enforcement of loan contracts, sometimes exacerbated by corruption among law enforcement agencies. Also, accurate identification and evaluation of collateral for credit tend to be protracted.

5. Bank competitiveness

Finance engenders economic opportunity and growth (Levine and Dermigüç-Kunt 2009). The vision for Africa is to evolve competitive banks and credit markets. The experience of bank restructuring and related reforms in Africa reflects contrasting approaches: South Africa, Algeria, Nigeria, and Egypt. South Africa represents a case of gradual restructuring of the banking sector, such that the banks have spawned the financial services sector in the rest of Africa. Nigeria has bravely designed and implemented a shock-treatment type of bank restructuring, which amounts to a 'big bang'. The banking-sector reforms in Egypt give mixed signals in terms of effort and success. Algeria is characterized as a slow reformer, which has yet to embrace full financial restructuring.

Evidence by Kasekende et al. (2009) suggests that the South African banking market faced intense competition during the reform period. Commercial banks were increasingly facing competition from the capital market and micro finance institutions. The overall competitiveness conditions in the lending market in Algeria are characterized by a higher level of oligopoly; the change in the degree of competition appears to decrease over time. Evidence for Nigeria suggests that competition improved after 1994 and ended up with 'super competition'; 'big bang' worked and the degree of competition improved. Evidence for Egypt suggests improvement in the degree of competition during 1993–2007 overall, although some years experienced weak competitive conditions.

Overall, the banking sector reforms in South Africa were not only comprehensive but were also carefully structured over a long period of time. Strong banks have emerged, and which have gone global. This gradualism approach offers important lessons for the rest of the continent. But it is also interesting that the 'big bang' approach adopted by Nigeria initially worked but has been derailed by the global financial crisis; this suggests the need for caution with 'shock treatment' type of bank reforms. The reforms in Algeria and Egypt continue.

6. Conclusion

At least two main conclusions should be highlighted. First, notwithstanding financial reforms during the last two decades, banks and credit markets in Africa face many challenges. Impaired loan portfolios are still high (in Côte d'Ivoire, Kenya, Mozambique, Senegal, Swaziland, and Tanzania); bank regulation and supervision is still weak (especially on-site and off-site surveillance); and corporate governance and internal controls are not well established. Second, the persistent areas of weakness have serious implications for Africa's recovery out of the global financial crisis. One lesson from the OECD for Africa was that it was not that banks did not have cash to lend; it was a crisis of confidence in bank solvency. So, central banks in Africa must continue to instil confidence in the fragile credit markets as the global economy rebounds.

REFERENCES

Brownbridge, M., and C. Harvey, 1998. *Banking in Africa: The Impact of Financial Sector Reform since Independence*. Oxford: James Currey.

Hyuha, M., and J. S. Ddumba, 1992. 'Financial decline in Uganda', paper presented to the Uganda Economics Society, November.

Kasekende, L., K. Mlambo, V. Murinde, and T. Zhao, 2009. 'Restructuring for competitiveness: the financial services sector in Africa's largest economies', in World Economic Forum (ed.), *Africa Competitiveness Report 2009*. Washington, DC: World Bank, 49–81.

Khalil, A., C. Rickwood, and V. Murinde, 2002. 'Agency contractual problems in profit-sharing (*mudarabah*) financing practices by Islamic banks', in M. Iqbal and D. Llewellyn (eds), *Islamic*

Banking and Finance: New Perspectives on Profit-Sharing and Risk. Cheltenham: Edward Elgar, 60–85.

Kirkpatrick, C. H., V. Murinde, and M. Tefula, 2008. 'The measurement and determinants of X-inefficiency in commercial banks in sub-Saharan Africa', *European Journal of Finance* 14.7, 625–39.

Levine, R., and A. Demirgüç-Kunt, 2009. 'Finance and economic opportunity', in *Proceedings of the Annual World Bank Conference on Development Economics*. Washington, DC: World Bank.

Maimbo, S., 1999. 'Bank failures in Tanzania, Uganda and Zambia', paper presented to Finance and Development Research Workshop, University of Manchester, 9–10 July.

Murinde, V., 2010. 'Bank regulation in Africa: from Basel I to Basel II, and now at a cross-roads', paper presented at African Economic Research Policy Seminars, Mombasa, March.

—— A. Miroux, and M. Lim, 2008. 'The impact of foreign banks in developing and transition economies', *International Journal of Financial Services Management* 3.2, 136–47.

—— and C. Ryan, 2003. 'The implications of WTO and GATS for the banking sector in Africa', *World Economy* 26.2, 181–207.

——and Moses Tefula, 2003. 'The participation of foreign-owned banks in the domestic banking sector of African economies. Mimeo, University of Birmingham.

Mylenko, N., 2007. 'Developing credit reporting in Africa: opportunities and challenges', *Access Finance* 19 (September).

Nissanke, M., and E. Aryeetey, 1998. *Financial Integration and Development: Liberalization and Reform in Sub-Saharan Africa*. London: Routledge.

Microfinance in Africa

William Steel and Jennifer Isern

1. Introduction

'Microfinance' refers to methodologies that enable low-income people to access basic financial services such as loans, savings, money transfers, and micro insurance. Like everyone else, people living in poverty need a diverse range of financial services to run their businesses, build assets, smooth consumption, and manage risks. Commercial banks have typically not considered small transactions with low-income people who have little collateral to be a viable market. Hence the poor have long managed their household finances through various informal financial relationships, including informal moneylenders and savings and credit associations.

Starting in the 1970s, new financial methodologies emerged worldwide to serve this market. Microfinance institutions (MFIs) can include non-government organizations (NGOs), financial cooperatives, community-based development institutions, commercial and state banks, and specialized financial institutions. This diversity of MFIs, and the resulting competition for different market segments, is an important strength for extending the reach of financial services in African countries, where commercial banks rarely serve more than 5% of the population. In some countries, microfinance has more than doubled that outreach.

2. Microfinance trends in Africa

MFIs in Africa have proven quite successful in mobilizing deposits, which are a stable source of funding for future growth. In a number of countries, central banks or ministries of finance have created favourable regulatory frameworks for deposit-mobilizing MFIs such as financial cooperatives, rural banks, and microfinance deposit-taking institutions (e.g. Ethiopia, Ghana, Kenya, Nigeria, Tanzania, Uganda, and countries in the CEMAC and WAEMU regions).[1]

---

[1] CEMAC = Cameroon, Central African Republic, Chad, Congo, Gabon, and Equatorial Guinea; WAEMU = Benin, Burkina Faso, Côte d'Ivoire, Guinea Bissau, Mali, Niger, Senegal, and Togo. Both monetary and economic zones have regional central banks.

Table 1. Microfinance data: Africa and other regions, 2007 (per MFI)

	Africa	Asia	LAC[a]	ECA[b]
No. of MFIs reporting	159	244	283	158
Outreach: breadth				
No. of voluntary depositors	4,720	568	0	0
No. of active borrowers	9,800	18,117	11,682	4,465
Voluntary deposits (US$ million)	0.47	0.05	0.0	0.0
Gross loan portfolio (UA$ million)	2.6	3.6	6.6	6.2
Outreach: depth				
Average outstanding balance/GNI	67.9	18.6	26.9	72.3
% women borrowers	60.0	97.7	63.1	45.8
Financing				
Assets (US$ million)	5.1	5.4	8.3	7.3
Deposits to loans (%)	24.8	2.1	0.0	0.0
Debt to equity	2.7	4.9	2.7	3.2
Costs/efficiency				
Operating expenses/loan portfolio (%)	31.7	16.0	19.5	15.4
Borrowers per staff member	125	129	120	66
Revenues/profitability				
Yield on gross portfolio (real; %)	23.4	18.1	26.2	19.7
Profit margin (%)	−5.0	2.6	8.1	7.2
Return on assets (%)	−1.1	0.2	1.7	0.8
Financial self-sufficiency[c]	95	103	109	108
Macroeconomic indicators (%)				
GDP growth rate	6.3	7.3	4.8	7.8
Financial depth	29.4	62.0	30.7	37.9
Inflation rate	8.2	6.4	4.0	9.0
Deposit rate	6.0	6.0	4.8	5.3

[a] Latin America and Caribbean.
[b] Eastern Europe and Central Asia.
[c] Implies ability to cover all financial and operational costs without subsidies if > 100.
Source: Microfinance Information Exchange (2008).

Nevertheless, Africa is only beginning to catch up with the success of other developing regions in lending to millions of poor clients through sustainable MFIs such as those in Bangladesh, Bolivia, and Indonesia. Particular challenges for Africa include shallow financial systems, low population density, higher operating costs, and government-subsidized credit schemes that inhibit emergence of commercially oriented private institutions.

The deposit-driven growth of many African MFIs demonstrates client demand for secure deposit services and their capacity to save. The first lesson of the 'microfinance revolution' in the 1980s was that low-income people can repay loans reliably if institutions use appropriate lending approaches. The more recent lesson is that these clients seek opportunities to save in financial form (instead of traditional forms such as animals and jewellery) if services are convenient, accessible, and affordable.

Access to finance is measured by breadth (number of clients) and depth (income level of clients) of outreach. Across Africa, MFIs reach 2–9% of the population with deposit and/or lending services and serve more than 300,000 depositors in Burkina Faso, Ethiopia, Ghana, Kenya, Mali, Nigeria, Senegal, South Africa, Togo, and Uganda.[2] Recent trends are encouraging: many African MFIs are growing, achieving economies of scale, and reaching profitability that allows them to expand outreach. From 2005 to 2007, the MFIs reporting to the MIX database increased their deposits and loan portfolios by 40% and 36%, respectively. Nevertheless, using average loan balance relative to gross national income (GNI) as an indicator of depth of outreach, the leading African MFIs do not reach as low as those in Asia and LAC, though comparable to ECA (Table 1). Women constitute 60% of clients, higher than in ECA but well below Asia. The implication is that African MFIs have further to go to achieve their potential for reaching low-income clients.

While Africa leads other regions in terms of deposit mobilization, African MFIs have the highest operating costs of all regions (Table 1). Consequently, profitability and returns on assets (and equity) are lower, and African MFIs are more likely to depend on grants to sustain their operations and portfolios—though trends in recent years are positive.

3. Current issues

The global challenge in access to finance is how to reach increasing numbers of low-income clients through viable financial service providers—including banks applying new techniques, specialized MFIs, and other emerging models. While increasing scale can lead to greater efficiency and lower unit costs, some in the industry are concerned about 'mission drift' toward larger transactions with less poor clients. Management capacity remains a challenge for African MFIs, especially given increasingly complex financial services, financing options, and scale of operations. The role of donor and government funding is changing from subsidizing start-up costs or loan portfolios to supporting innovations that reach poorer clients. Finally, the perception that microfinance is a panacea for poverty often leads to excessive, possibly counterproductive government intervention.

3.1. ADDRESSING THE COSTS OF REACHING POORER CLIENTS

The high operating costs of African MFIs relative to other regions are *not* because African MFIs reach poorer clients with smaller loans—on the contrary, they have significantly higher average outstanding balance compared to GNI (67.9). Higher costs

---

[2] Figures are based on MFIs that report to the MIX global database.

are driven by low population density, especially in underserved rural areas; poor road, electrical, and telecommunications infrastructure; and relatively high wage structures in sub-Saharan Africa. High costs imply relatively higher interest rates to achieve profitability, although interest rates in Africa are lower than in Latin America (Table 1, yield). New MFIs, banks entering the market, and new technologies (see below) have stimulated greater competition for services, and this has helped reduce interest rates in most countries over the past five years. Institutions are also competing on quality and services, going beyond basic deposit accounts and loans to adapt services to cash flows of clients and their households.

Village savings and loan associations represent a community-managed approach that systematizes informal and group-based microfinance methodologies (such as rotating savings and credit associations) to reach relatively poorer clients in ways that can be replicated and scaled up. This model can serve as a step toward more formal savings and credit cooperatives (or credit unions), especially where the regulatory environment is conducive to informal–formal linkages. Financial cooperatives play a key role in West and Central Africa, although some countries, especially in east and southern Africa, have yet to overcome legacies of excessive government intervention in promoting cooperatives to successfully integrate financial cooperatives into mainstream financial systems.

The immediate challenge is to raise efficiency and scale and to develop more cost-effective methods for reaching clients, especially low-income rural clients. Services need to evolve beyond short-term, frequent-repayment micro credit methodologies to match the realities of rural/agricultural finance. Developing and scaling up well-adapted financial products will require significant investments in capacity building of staff, system upgrades, improved governance structures, and financial awareness raising for clients.

3.2. EMERGING MODELS

National and international commercial banks are showing increasing interest in reaching the market niches served by MFIs, for example through lending to MFIs, launching subsidiaries, forming business alliances with microfinance agents, and establishing special windows or programs for micro/small enterprises. African banks with early success in microfinance are expanding across borders, such as Equity Bank's expansion from Kenya to Uganda and regional strategies by Ecobank (Togo) and United Bank of Africa (Nigeria).

'Branchless banking' using mobile phone and other communications technology and outsourced service agents offers potential to expand financial services to large numbers of clients. Through pioneers such as Safaricom's M-Pesa in Kenya and Wizzit in South Africa, the region is driving global innovation in using mobile phones, outsourced service representatives, ATMs, and point-of-sale devices as cost-effective approaches to make financial services available to lower-income clients, especially in rural areas with few MFI or bank branches. The challenge is to expand beyond basic payment and remittance transactions to a broader set of financial services across more countries.

3.3. ROLE OF GOVERNMENT

African governments have supported microfinance in many countries through policy frameworks and capacity-building projects. Most countries now have specific micro finance legislation and regulation or provisions within general banking laws, and are improving financial infrastructure (payment systems, credit bureaus). Nevertheless, government intervention has been counterproductive in a number of countries. A few countries still impose restrictions on interest rates that make it difficult to cover high operating costs. More pervasive and damaging are government-promoted lending schemes at subsidized rates that undercut commercially oriented MFIs and foster a politically oriented culture of entitlement that undermines general willingness to repay. Governments with supportive regulatory and policy frameworks such as Cameroon, Ghana, Kenya, Nigeria, Rwanda, and Senegal that encourage innovation and good institutional practices have seen impressive growth in access to finance. Consumer protection and awareness raising campaigns have been piloted in only a few African countries; national authorities and industry associations should coordinate approaches.

3.4. SOURCES OF FUNDING

Past support for MFIs in Africa has relied heavily on donor and government grants and technical assistance. CGAP's annual survey of donors and investors in Africa estimated $1.8 billion in funding for access to finance in 2007. Many African MFIs are fuelling their growth through impressive deposit mobilization. Diversification of funding sources is essential for sustained growth, and the trend is positive for debt and equity financing from national and international commercial (including 'socially responsible') sources. Increasingly hospitable legal/regulatory frameworks and low leverage of many African MFIs in Africa leave substantial room to expand debt financing (Table 1).

Nevertheless, much of the effort to reach lower-income and remote clients in Africa is through NGOs, financial cooperatives, and other community-based MFIs, whose legal structures constrain them from accepting external equity investments and mobilizing commercial debt. Some cooperative networks have created legal structures to receive debt and equity financing (which nevertheless increases management risk). Overall, tapping into international funds interested in Africa will require national political and economic stability plus measures for MFIs and banks to manage both foreign exchange and investment risks.

4. Conclusion

Microfinance represents the frontier of financial innovation by expanding access to secure deposit services, reliable money transfers, and convenient loans and other financial services to millions of clients in Africa. Worldwide experience indicates that current positive trends in Africa could be accelerated by reducing costs, targeting underserved rural market niches, building capacity to raise productivity and management ability, and applying available technologies to expand access to financial services. Governments can play a supporting role by adapting legal/regulatory frameworks that accommodate commercial MFIs and make financial infrastructure available to established institutions— and avoiding direct interventions such as interest rate ceilings and politically motivated, subsidized credit schemes. Building on Africa's success in expanding access to finance will require managed growth from financial institutions, continued deposit mobilization, and professionalization to attract private debt and equity.

REFERENCES

Isern, J., E. Lahaye, and A. Linthorst, 2008. *Africa Microfinance Analysis and Benchmarking Report 2008*. Washington, DC: CGAP and MIX.

Microfinance Information Exchange, 2008. *MicroBanking Bulletin 17*. Washington, DC: MIX.

Thematic Perspectives
Natural Resources

Managing Natural Resource Booms

Anthony J. Venables

1. Introduction

Endowments of non-renewable natural resources are unevenly scattered across Africa.[1] Thirteen African economies are classified as 'resource-rich';[2] in eight of these, natural resources revenues account for more than 80% of export earnings, and in seven, more than 50% of government revenue.[3] African oil exports were worth approximately $50 billion per annum between 2000 and 2005, a similar magnitude to aid flows, although virtually all these earnings accrued to countries with population totalling 250 million, less than one third of Africa's total. Amongst the resource-rich are one of the world's best-performing economies (Botswana) and several of its worst-performing (Sierra Leone, Nigeria). Econometric studies suggest that, on average, resource booms are short-lived with negative long-run effects (Collier and Goderis 2008). They establish that the effects of resources depend critically on the quality of governance, having a negative impact on countries with governance indicators at levels commonly found in Africa. The quality of governance itself can be eroded by resource wealth, creating vicious circles of mismanagement and, in the worst cases, conflict. There is a large and well-surveyed literature on the resource curse (for a survey see van der Ploeg 2008), and this chapter focuses on discussing three aspects of Africa's experience with resource revenues, and three policy implications for future resource management.

2. Lost opportunities

The record of Africa's management of its natural resource endowment has, by and large, been one of lost opportunities.

---

[1] 'Africa' means sub-Saharan Africa throughout.
[2] I focus on non-renewable natural resources, i.e. hydrocarbons and minerals.
[3] IMF (2007).

2.1. UNDER-EXPLOITED

Africa's natural resource endowment is less thoroughly prospected and exploited than that of other regions. The stock of undiscovered resources is, necessarily, unknown, but pointers indicate that most of Africa's natural resources are yet to be developed. Estimates based on World Bank (2006) suggest that subsoil assets per square kilometre in Africa are just 20% of those remaining in OECD countries—this most likely reflecting a failure of discovery rather than geological bad luck. The rate of discoveries points to the same conclusion; proven oil reserves worldwide increased by 87% between 1980 and 2008, while in Africa they increased by 225%; for natural gas, corresponding figures are 125% and 333% (BP 2009). The rate of discovery in Africa is accelerating, with recent hydrocarbon discoveries in Uganda and off the coast of West Africa. These figures indicate past failure to attract exploration and development, and point to the likelihood that natural resources will be of increasing importance to Africa in coming decades.

2.2. RENT CAPTURE AND RENT SEEKING

Throughout Africa, subsoil assets are the property of the state, whose responsibility it is to design and implement fiscal regimes which capture a substantial fraction of resource rents for public use. The design of such regimes is complex, since they have the dual objectives of collecting rent and creating incentives for prospecting and development. They have to be implemented in environments in which the state typically has little information about the resource, and in which potential investors are exposed to risk from future changes in government policy and regime change.

How successful have African governments been in capturing the rent? There are notorious cases where contract terms have not been advantageous (e.g. the 0.8% copper royalty on Zambian copper: see Adam and Simpasa 2011). Hydrocarbon contracts have generally been better, and average effective tax rates are high (Angola 95%, Nigeria 72%: see Daniels 2009). The Botswana government is estimated to take about 75% of diamond mining profits (IMF 2007).

The main way in which rents have been diverted away from government and citizens has been through corruption, theft, and dissipation on rent-seeking activities. Estimates for Nigeria suggest that direct theft of oil ('bunkering') is running at several billion dollars per year, and cumulative historical theft of resource revenues is many times this. A recent study of Cameroon 1977–2000 (Gauthier and Zeufack 2011) finds that, while a sizeable portion of oil rent (67%) was captured by the state, only 39% of government oil revenues were transferred to the budget. The remaining 61% are unaccounted for.

Rent-seeking activity has proliferated, ranging from the wasteful (diversion of entrepreneurial skills into rent seeking activities) to the damaging (undermining governance) and the dangerous. There is evidence that corruption is positively associated with resource rents (Bhattacharyya and Hodler 2009). Both the probability of civil conflict and the duration of conflict are positively linked to resource booms (Besley and Persson 2008; Collier, Hoeffler, and Rohner 2009). Resource wealth creates both the incentive to try and take over the state and, in some cases, the means to finance insurgency.

2.3. SAVING AND INVESTING

Revenue from depletable natural resources is inherently time-limited and is volatile, varying with commodity prices. A substantial fraction of resource rents should therefore be saved and invested. The record has generally been poor. Overall savings rates in resource-rich African economies have been low, and *genuine* savings (savings adjusted for depletion of resources and other changes in natural wealth) have frequently been negative, for Nigeria estimated at *minus* 34% of GNI (World Bank 2006). Similarly, for domestic investment; African resource producers have generally not had higher rates of capital formation than other countries, with the exception of Botswana (averaging 33% of GDP since 1990) and Equatorial Guinea, where rates of over 50% reflect oil sector investments in an otherwise tiny economy.

Further evidence comes from studies of the response of government spending to oil revenues received. The correlation between government expenditure and the world oil price (1970–2008) is more than 80% for eight African countries studied by York and Zhan (2009). In the recent boom (2006–8), five of these countries saw larger proportionate increases in current government spending than in oil revenues. In five of the countries, the non-oil fiscal balance deteriorated as oil revenues surged, but in only three did the growth of government capital spending exceed the growth in oil revenues.

3. Managing natural resource booms

The lessons of the past point to three policy recommendations for future booms.

3.1. TRANSPARENCY AND GOVERNANCE

The root cause of many of the lost opportunities is poor governance. Problems are deep-seated, but several measures can be taken to improve governance failures in the resource sector. The first is to improve transparency, making the sector more open to public and parliamentary scrutiny. For example, competitive auctions to award exploration and production contracts are more transparent than are negotiated deals, and can also improve the contract terms the government gets. Greater transparency makes participation more attractive to investors, increasing the rate of prospecting and development. The flow of funds between producers and government should be subject to the principles of the Extractive Industries Transparency Initiative, which commit signatories to publish audited accounts of resource revenues paid by companies and received by government. The regulatory structure for the resource sector needs to follow international best practice, with a clear assignment of responsibilities. This applies to national oil companies, many of which have operated without proper scrutiny, have engaged in wasteful quasi-fiscal activities, and have been vulnerable to theft and corruption.

3.2. SAVING AND INVESTING

The objective is to use resource revenues to achieve a sustained increase in incomes and consumption in society. To achieve this, society has to choose how much to save or consume, and how to allocate savings between domestic investment and foreign asset accumulation (or debt reduction).[4]

Past saving from resource revenues has been much lower than is needed to meet the objective of sustained increases in incomes. Savings need to be increased, while at the same time recognizing that taking some current consumption from resource revenues is appropriate in a low-income society in which there are urgent needs for poverty reduction. Future generations will be richer than the current generation, so arguing that savings should rise to the level where all generations benefit equally (the permanent-income hypothesis) is inappropriate. Furthermore, some expenditures that are classified as current—health and education—raise human capital and should be classified as investment for these purposes.

What assets should be purchased with revenue that is saved? Low-income societies are capital-scarce, so the priority should be to build domestic capital stock rather than accumulate foreign assets. The argument is reinforced by the presence of unemployed labour and the need to turn resource wealth into income from employment rather than rent on foreign assets. This suggests that long-term foreign asset accumulation in sovereign wealth funds should not be a priority for low income countries. However, use of overseas funds (or accumulation of foreign exchange reserves) as a temporary cushion is desirable in two sorts of circumstances. One is to smooth the volatility of revenues associates with price instability. The other is during an adjustment period

---

[4] See Collier, van der Ploeg, Spence, and Venables (2010).

when attempts to scale up investment are hampered by absorption problems. While absorption problems are addressed, some funds should be 'parked' abroad until they can be best used.

3.3. DIVERSIFICATION AND ECONOMIC GROWTH

While government controls some investment choices, the ultimate investment response needs to come from the private sector. Resource revenues provide a way to stimulate private investment, although government control is generally indirect, through spending, tax, and debt/asset management choices.

The first channel of influence is through public investments that are complementary with (raise the productivity of) private investments. Africa's shortage of infrastructure is well documented, and resource revenues provide an opportunity to overcome this. The second channel is through increasing the availability of funds for private investment. Lower government domestic debt can spur commercial banks to lend to the private sector (rather than just to government). Government can lend directly, although the historical record of development banks is poor. Or government can make tax reductions or 'citizen dividend' payments to citizens, although there is no guarantee that these funds will be invested rather than consumed. A further route is for government to pursue an active investment policy targeting industrial or agricultural sectors. This often appears attractive, particularly in resource-related activities. In upstream sectors there are likely to be prospects for increasing local participation. Downstream processing offers fewer possibilities, since the technology of processing industries—such as petrochemicals—are out of line with the comparative advantage of African countries. The over-arching criterion that must apply to such targeted policies is that activities must be credibly expected to attain commercial viability, without which they are a continuing drain on public funds and can be a source of value reduction, not value added.

REFERENCES

Adam, C., and S. Simpasa, 2011. 'Copper Mining in Zambia; from collapse to recovery', in P. Collier and A. J. Venables (eds), *Plundered Nations; successes and failures in natural resource extraction*. London: Palgrave Macmillan.

Besley, T., and T. Persson, 2008. 'The incidence of civil war: theory and evidence', NBER Working Paper 14585, Cambridge, Mass.

Bhattacharyya, S., and R. Hodler, 2009. 'Natural resources, democracy and corruption', Research Paper 2009-20, Oxford Centre for the Analysis of Resource Rich Economies, University of Oxford.

BP, 2009. *Annual Statistical Review*. London: BP.

Collier, P., and B. Goderis, 2008. 'Commodity prices, growth and the natural resource curse: reconciling a conundrum', mimeo, CSAE, Oxford.

—— A. Hoeffler, and D. Rohner, 2009. 'Beyond greed and grievance: feasibility and civil war', *Oxford Economic Papers* 61, 1–27.

—— F. van der Ploeg, A. M. Spence, and A. J. Venables, 2010. 'Managing resource revenues in developing economies', *IMF Staff Papers* 57, 84–118.

Daniels, P., 2009. 'Opportunities for country revenue through taxing national resources', IMF, Washington, DC.

Gauthier, B., and A. Zeufack, 2011. 'Governance and oil revenues in Cameroon', in P. Collier and A. J. Venables (eds), *Plundered Nations; successes and failures in natural resource extraction*. London: Palgrave Macmillan.

IMF, 2007. *Guide on Resource Revenue Transparency*. Washington, DC: IMF.

van der Ploeg, F., 2011. 'Natural Resources; curse or blessing', *Journal of Economic Literature* 49, 366–420.

World Bank, 2006. *Where is the Wealth of Nations? Measuring Capital for the 21st Century*. Washington, DC: World Bank.

York, R., and Z. Zhan, 2009. 'Fiscal vulnerability and sustainability in oil-producing sub-Saharan African countries', IMF WP/09/174, Washington, DC.

Natural Resource Exports and African Development

Alan Gelb

1. Introduction

Unlike rapidly developing regions, sub-Saharan Africa (Africa) has not diversified out of resource-based products into manufacturing industry. Why has diversification been so slow? Is a strong resource base a developmental benefit or a development trap? What special problems are faced by countries heavily dependent on natural resources, in particular in Africa? This chapter considers these questions.[1]

2. Africa's resource-dependence

Africa's exports have grown slowly and have also continued to be dominated by resource-intensive products. In 1970 the region's share of global trade (imports and exports) was almost 5%; by the mid- 2000s it had fallen to barely 2%. In 1990 Africa's exports represented over 10% of total exports from developing countries; despite a recovery in oil and other commodity prices, they had fallen to 6% by 2006—this from a region with many small economies and with 12% of the developing world's population. Several factors have contributed to this dismal record, including a long record of anti-export-biased policies and high transport costs.

As well as losing ground in many primary sectors, Africa has failed to move into the most rapidly expanding segments of international trade, including higher-technology products. Export patterns have shifted radically for other developing regions, from 80% primary-based in the 1960s to 80% manufactures, and rapidly growing countries have moved up the industrial value chain towards more sophisticated products. But Africa's export structure has been relatively stable over long periods. Table 1 shows the picture over 1985–2005. Fuels are the only major product where Africa's global share has risen; they now represent about half of all merchandise exports. Spurred by new investors like

---

[1] This chapter represents the views of the author, not necessarily those of the World Bank, its Executive Directors, or the countries they represent.

Table 1. Composition of exports, 1985 and 2005

	1985	2005
Food and beverage	18.3	9.1
Raw materials	12.3	7.9
Fuels	50.0	54.9
Manufactures and chemicals	18.6	26.4

Source: IMF (2007); data from UN Comtrade.

Table 2. Major manufacturing exports, 2005

Industry (three-digit SITC)	Value ($ m.)	Main supplier	Second supplier	Main market	Second market
Veneers, plywood boards, other wood	791.1	South Africa	Ghana	EU15	Ind. Asia
Pearls, precious stones	9,174.5	Botswana	South Africa	EU15	USA
Raw forms of iron	3,031.2	South Africa	Zimbabwe	EU15	Ind. Asia
Iron ingots	645.3	South Africa	n.a.	EU15	Dev. Asia
Sheet iron	940.9	South Africa	n.a.	EU15	China
Silver, platinum group	5,518.6	South Africa	n.a.	Ind. Asia	USA
Copper	890.6	Zambia	South Africa	China	Dev. Asia
Aluminium	2,632.0	Mozambique	South Africa	EU15	Ind. Asia
Non-electrical machinery, appliances	1,542.7	South Africa	n.a.	EU15	USA
Road motor vehicles	2,358.5	South Africa	n.a.	Ind. Asia	EU15
Clothing (except fur)	2,401.4	Mauritius	Madagascar	USA	EU15

Source: IMF (2007), UN Comtrade.

China and the drive to diversify supply outside the Middle East, fuel exports promise to grow as new fields are explored and developed, although some producers such as Gabon face declining reserves. Africa's nine oil-exporting countries now account for close to one third of its total population and land area, and several new producers, including Ghana and Uganda, are coming on stream.

Foodstuffs and raw materials account for much of the remaining exports. These categories have diversified to include non-traditional products such as horticulture, floriculture, and fish fillets. Entrepreneurs are increasingly seeking out the many climatic niches capable of producing exotic products, such as ultra-long-stemmed roses. However, with rapid population growth, loss of soil fertility (some 25% since the end of the Second World War), and climate change, Africa's agricultural resource base is under threat.

Manufactures and chemicals formally represent about a quarter of exports, but this category includes many processed raw materials, some little transformed from their primary state. A few major industries account for over 75% of manufacturing exports, but only three of them, equipment (5%), motor vehicles (10%), and clothing (8%), are not closely linked to the processing of resources (Table 2). These industries have also benefited from special incentives and preferences. Motor vehicle exports from South Africa are supported by costly and complex incentives. While their merit is debated, they have underpinned the only major manufacturing complex in Africa which is fully integrated into a global production chain. Clothing exports have benefited especially from the provisions of the African Growth and Opportunities Act (AGOA), and also from the desire of some Far Eastern producers to diversify output. Most countries have domestic import-competing manufacturing sectors, partly informal and often providing lower-quality goods for sale on local or regional markets. Major clients such as mines can also stimulate local manufacturing capacity. However, some countries such as Zambia have de-industrialized, and have less manufacturing industry than they had prior to the liberalization programmes of the 1990s.

Africa's diversified resource base is also reflected in its service exports. With increasing interest in wildlife, better infrastructure for mass beach tourism, growing interest in cultural tourism, and the opening of air transport routes, African tourism arrivals have grown faster than the world average. Tourism receipts have risen from 2% of total exports of goods and services in 1980 to about 12% by 2003.

In broad terms, Africa's revealed comparative advantage in 'footloose manufactures' (those not closely associated with a natural resource base) is therefore close to zero. While some countries are conspicuously resource-rich, all are resource dependent relative to developing countries as a whole. However, there are important differences between countries, such as Tanzania or Kenya, that are dependent on a broad and diversified resource base and those such as Nigeria, Equatorial Guinea, Gabon, or Botswana, that are heavily specialized in 'point-source' mineral exports such as oil and hard minerals. Resource taxes and fiscal linkages are often more important for mineral countries than direct linkages with other sectors. The quality of public budget and financial management and governance more generally is therefore even more important.

Africa's resource dependence is also reflected in its sectoral structure. 'Normal' patterns of development involve a shift out of agriculture, first towards industry and later towards services. Table 3 compares average sectoral growth elasticities over

Table 3. Growth elasticities: African countries, Asian comparators, and norms

	Eleven high-growth African countries	Selected Asian comparators	Chenery–Syrquin norm
Agriculture	0.29	0.25	0.48
Industry	0.76	2.09	1.36
Services	1.43	0.91	1.13
Overall growth GDP/head growth	21.6	35.2	n/a

Source: Gelb, Ramachandran, and Turner (2007).

1995–2006 for a number of well-performing low-income African countries that are not oil exporters with those for selected Asian comparators and with norms estimated for low-income countries by Chenery and Syrquin (1975). Both sets of countries moved away from agriculture at comparable speed, but the Asian countries shifted towards industry whereas the African countries transited mainly towards services, despite continuing rapid urbanization.

3. Why has Africa remained resource-dependent?

Three main factors perpetuate Africa's resource dependence: relative factor endowments, high transactions costs associated with poor governance, and the implications of its distinctive geography for dynamic economies of scale. Wood and Mayer (2001) find that Africa is more land- (resource-) intensive and less skill-intensive than other regions. The composition of exports is highly correlated with relative endowments; regions higher up the skills/land spectrum export more manufactures relative to primary and processed primary goods and also a larger proportion of higher-technology manufactures. Export structure evolves over time in line with trends in the skills/land ratio. These results argue that Africa's scant human capital and rich natural-resource bases ensure that manufactured exports that do not involve resource processing will be unprofitable. The emergence of India and China, two enormous resource-poor and increasingly high-skilled countries, into the world economy suggests that it is now more difficult for Africa to compete in manufacturing since it is relatively even more resource-abundant than before.

Factor proportions do not, however, fully account for Africa's low income level despite its resource abundance; neither do they explain the enormous flight of financial and human capital out of Africa which causes the region to appear more resource-rich than it otherwise would have been. The second set of factors stresses the business environment, the nexus of governance, policies, physical infrastructure, and other factors that influence the efficiency with which firms and industries can operate. A poor environment impacts more heavily on manufacturing and high-value services than on extractive sectors because the former require more 'inputs' of logistics and regulation (Collier and Gunning 1999). Macroeconomic instability, poor security, a weak and politicized financial system, shoddy road and power networks, and predatory officials will little affect offshore oil industries but will be devastating for manufacturing. Even firms able to transform inputs into outputs with high efficiency and low 'factory floor' costs can be driven out of business by a poor business environment.

A third factor is geography. Countries often specialize in narrow industrial lines because of dynamic economies of scale generated by learning processes, dense production networks, and industry-specific spillovers. As emphasized in the work of Krugman (e.g. Helpman and Krugman 1987), these partly shape the structure of production. Africa's economic sparseness emerges as a key factor. Fifteen countries are landlocked; excluding South Africa, GDP density is only one-tenth the level in Latin America and one-twentieth that in India. The location of new industries such as Kenya's horticulture–floriculture complex and the garment sectors of Madagascar and Lesotho also confirms the importance of industrial clustering. Moreover, the GDP of the median African country is barely $3 billion, suggesting that effort to overcome high regulatory costs will not be rewarded by large market potential.

Where does this leave us? Factor endowments are indeed a powerful influence on Africa's trade patterns, but they do not tell the whole story. Endowments evolve over time, and can be shaped by many influences, including the quality of governance and whether policies are put in place to encourage investment and technology upgrading to enable countries to move away from resource-based dependence. Meanwhile, Africa remains a high-cost region with 2005 PPP price levels higher than those in Asia, despite Africa being poorer. There is some evidence that the productivity of African manufacturing firms is related to exports, both as a cause and as a consequence, but in the face of high costs most African firms simply are not productive enough to export manufactures.

4. Development boon or development trap?

Is Africa stuck in a 'resource trap?' In theory, a strong resource base offers ways to surmount three traditional constraints to development: exports, savings, and fiscal revenues. Rich countries such as Australia and Norway and a number of developing countries such as Thailand, Chile, and Indonesia have built successfully on their resource endowments to create productive economies, but all too often resource exporters perform poorly, and prolonged resource dependence is not associated with economic success. Lederman and Maloney (2007) note that GDP per capita grew at only 0.6% in net natural resource exporters between 1980 and 2005, relative to 2.2% in net resource importers. The impact of resource abundance on development outcomes is estimated to be favourable. But measures of both resource dependence and resource abundance are endogenous; poor governance increases resource dependence by stifling other activities, and resource bases appear stronger for OECD countries because there has been more exploration and development in these countries.

Studies of the 'resource curse' suggest that two initial conditions are complementary to resources in shaping a favourable outcome. The first is human capital. Bravo-Ortega and de Gregorio (2007) find that it is not resource abundance *per se* that determines a country's growth opportunities but the human capital stock present in a resource-abundant country.

The larger the country's human capital stock, the more positive is the marginal effect of natural resource abundance on growth. Second is governance capital; differences in the quality of institutions between successful and less successful resource rich countries are at the root of their diverging growth paths. Mehlum, Moene, and Torvik (2006) find that the quality of institutions is critical in determining whether countries avoid the resource curse—resources are only found to have a negative impact on growth performance among countries with inferior institutions. Countries embarking on resource exploitation with strong initial conditions are likely to benefit; those less fortunate may find themselves in a long-term downward spiral of deteriorating governance and social and economic performance, as natural rent further reduces the need for governments to be accountable to their citizens.

What kinds of institutions are important? Collier (2007) suggests that the issue is not simply whether countries are democratic. Without effective checks and balances, competition for natural resource rents can make democracies malfunction. Unlike normal taxes, they do not invite public scrutiny and political accountability. Especially in factional settings, they encourage the emergence of patronage politics rather than effective state-building. In extreme cases, contests for natural resource rents can combine with grievances to fan civil conflict; its likelihood is far higher in highly resource-dependent countries than in others.

African countries span a range of governance. Considering Botswana, one of the outstanding successes in managing mineral resources, Acemoglu, Johnson, and Robinson (2003) stress the importance of good initial conditions, including conservative, continuous, and accountable institutions and the early decision to vest ownership of diamond reserves in the nation rather than in tribal hands. Most African resource exporters are not so fortunate, however; the nine oil exporters rank at or close to the lowest global decile in Worldwide Governance Indicators such as Voice and Accountability, Government Effectiveness, and Control of Corruption (Gelb and Turner 2007), although some, like Nigeria, have embarked on reforms (Okonjo-Iweala and Osafo-Kwaako 2007). Not surprisingly, the developmental impact of oil in Africa is often adverse (Karl 2003). Equatorial Guinea may be an extreme case where oil rents sustain a pathology of authoritarian rule, instability, and underdevelopment from which it is difficult to exit (McSharry 2006).

5. Special challenges of resource-exporting countries

Depending on the nature of their endowments, resource-dependent countries face special challenges. The first is how to manage the volatility of commodity prices. Nigeria bases its budget on a reference oil price which adjusts more slowly to market prices;

Botswana saved part of its diamond boom abroad in the Pula fund. All too often, however, resource exporters alternate between boom and bust, with adverse effects on long-run diversification and growth.

The second challenge is to maximize the developmental value chain, from resource taxation to public budget and financial management and then to procurement and public spending. Governments have sometimes lacked capacity to negotiate with producing companies. Corrupt officials may collude with mining companies against the interests of the citizen 'owners' of the resources, leading to calls for increased transparency. But often problems lie further down the chain, as struggles over rent erode transparency and accountability. Direct conditionality from external agencies is not likely to be effective; it is weakest when most needed, when resource prices are highest (Gould and Winters 2007). The Extractive Industries Transparency Initiative (EITI) aims to encourage voluntary compliance with disclosure standards, but is no substitute for stronger pressures for accountability that need to come from Africa itself.

A third challenge is economic diversification—how to use resource income to reduce domestic costs and raise the productivity of other tradeable sectors. Globally, only a few mineral exporters have managed to diversify; they include Malaysia, Indonesia, and Chile. Sometimes geography makes diversification difficult; despite good management, sparse, landlocked Botswana has yet to progress towards a competitive industrial sector.

6. Conclusion

For African countries rich in mineral wealth, the immediate challenge is to make better use of their own resources. More generally, countries need to encourage economic diversification and technological upgrading, to harness their rapidly growing young populations for growth. But diversification does not necessarily mean a major shift towards 'footloose manufactures'. Africa's economies will remain heavily dependent on natural resources for many years into the future.

■ REFERENCES

Acemoglu, Daron, Simon Johnson, and James A. Robinson, 2003. 'An African success story: Botswana', in Dani Rodrik (ed.), *In Search of Prosperity: Analytical Narratives on Economic Growth*. Princeton, NJ: Princeton University Press.

Bravo-Ortega, Claudi, and Jose de Gregorio, 2007. 'The relative richness of the poor? Natural resources, human capital, and economic growth', in Lederman and Maloney (2007).

Chenery, Hollis, and Moishe Syrquin, 1975. *Patterns of Development 1950–1970*. Oxford: Oxford University Press.

Collier, Paul, 2007. *The Bottom Billion: Why the Poorest Countries Are Failing and What Can Be Done About It.* Oxford: Oxford University Press.

—— and Jan Gunning, 1999. 'Why has Africa grown so slowly?', *Journal of Economic Perspectives* 13.3.

Gelb, Alan, and Sina Grasmann, 2009 'Oil rents: how to use them well?', paper for GDN Conference, Kuwait, February.

—— Vijaya Ramachandran, and Ginger Turner, 2007. 'Stimulating growth in Africa: from macro to micro reforms', *African Development Review* (April).

—— and Ginger Turner, 2007. 'Confronting the resource curse: lessons of experience for African oil producers', in Desker Barry, Jeffrey Herbst, and Michael Spicer (eds), *Globalization and Economic Success: Policy Lessons for Developing Countries.* Johannesburg: Brenthurst Foundation.

Gould, John, and Matthew Winters, 2007. 'An obsolescing bargain in Chad: shifts in the leverage between the government and the World Bank', *Business and Politics* 9.2.

Helpman, Elhanan, and Paul Krugman, 1987. *Market Structure and Foreign Trade: Increasing Returns, Imperfect Competition and the International Economy.* Cambridge, Mass.: MIT Press.

International Monetary Fund, 2007. *African Economic Outlook.* Washington, DC: IMF.

Karl, Terry L., 2003. *Bottom of the Barrel: Africa's Oil Boom and the Poor.* Baltimore, Md.: Catholic Relief Services.

Lederman, Daniel, and William Maloney (eds), 2007. *Natural Resources: Neither Curse nor Destiny.* Stanford, Calif.: Stanford University Press.

McSharry, Brandon, 2006. 'The political economy of oil in Equatorial Guinea', *African Studies Quarterly* 8.23.

Mehlum, Halvor, Karl O. Moene, and Ragnar Torvik, 2006. 'Institutions and the resource curse', *Economic Journal* 116.508, 1–20.

Okonjo-Iweala, Ngozi, and Philip Osafo-Kwaako, 2007. 'Nigeria's economic reforms: progresses and challenges', Washington, DC: Brookings Institution.

Wood, Adrian, and Jörg Mayer, 2001. 'African development in a comparative perspective', *Cambridge Journal of Economics* 25.

Managing Forest Commons in Africa

Lauren Persha, Ashwini Chhatre, Arun Agrawal, and Elinor Ostrom

1. Introduction

The commons feature prominently in Africa by any measure. Land used in common occupies an estimated 25% of the continent's total land area (Wily 2008). Water and rangelands are used and managed through community institutions in many parts of the continent (Pretty and Ward 2001). Commonly managed fisheries provide livelihoods to millions of Africans along its coastline (Bene et al. 2009). But forest commons are particularly significant, providing livelihoods, sequestering carbon, and supporting biodiversity across the continent as a whole. More than 70% of sub-Saharan Africa's 800 million people depend on forests for their subsistence and incomes (World Bank 2004).

However, the widespread existence of forests used in common by local communities in Africa has only recently begun to gain formal recognition, in conjunction with a renewed pan-African focus on governance issues that has extended to communally held and managed natural resources. This trend varies across countries, and formally recognized communal ownership or management of forestlands currently accounts for less than 3% of total forest area in Africa (Barrow et al. 2009). But this has grown over the past decade from less than 1% to more than 12% of forest area in countries at more advanced stages of decentralization reforms, such as Tanzania. If uninterrupted by major external shocks, the upward trend could continue in coming years, supported by new legal frameworks recognizing communal forest tenure rights now under implementation by 35 of 51 countries in sub-Saharan Africa (with most others in the process of designing similar legislation).

We preface our discussion of African forest commons with a clarification in usage of two related terms: forests as common-pool resources and forest commons. Common-pool resources encompass as ostensibly incongruous examples as oil fields and the atmosphere, but all share two basic defining characteristics. All common-pool resources are subtractable (one person's use of the resource limits the amount available for another's use), and it is costly to exclude potential users from using the resource. These characteristics of common-pool resources present a particularly difficult set of challenges for those who undertake to manage them, because they have to define authorized users as well as rules regarding how the resource is used.

All forests can be viewed as common-pool resources, but not all forests are forest commons. We define forest commons as forests with clearly defined physical boundaries and legally enforceable property rights, which provide resources to a variety of social groups. The nature of formal property rights in a forest commons may vary (e.g. public, private, co-managed, or communal), but rural households typically make some formal or informal claim to forest use. They may also be formally involved in forest management, typically via communal ownership or collaborative management arrangements between community-based and government institutions.

This chapter highlights some of the basic features of forest commons and their governance in Africa, examines important emerging issues, and draws key lessons from existing research on the governance of forest commons in the continent.

2. Important aspects of Africa's forest commons

2.1. ECOSYSTEM SERVICES

Forests commons are an especially important resource in Africa because of the diverse and sometimes competing benefits they provide to local, national, and international communities. Forest commons serve as a significant source of subsistence livelihoods for rural households and particularly for the rural poor. They provide fuelwood, building materials, fodder for livestock, non-timber forest products such as twine, medicines, and thatching materials, and food. They may hold cultural value as sacred areas, offer refuge during times of conflict, or provide vital alternative food sources to sustain families during times of hunger. They generate cash income for many people, for instance through the sale of timber and bushmeat. Timber and other high-value products from forest commons also contribute directly and indirectly to national revenues in many African countries, even as this has at times driven conflicts over management rights to the land and pitted local and national interests against each other. At national and global levels, forests are now well recognized not only for their provisioning services but also for the crucial ecosystem services they provide beyond their physical locales, namely as centres of biodiversity, water regulation, and carbon sequestration that accrue to populations much further afield. These global interests in ecosystem-regulating services increasingly drive new opportunities and challenges to forests commons use and management at local scales as well.

2.2. LAND TENURE

Trajectories of forest commons management in Africa over the past century are also centrally entwined with waves of contestation surrounding tenure rights over land in general. This contestation has been relentlessly shaped by Africa's history of extensive colonization and its enduring inheritances, which continue to impact contemporary land issues across Africa today. The colonial era largely revoked customary tenure rights to forest resources that were widespread among communities prior to colonization, by appropriating forest land for colonial administrations and alienating local communities from settlement within or access to forest resources (Wily 2001). Colonial administrations claimed large areas of productive forest land for revenue generation while typically allocating less productive forest lands to locally established authorities for their regulation and administration as sources of subsistence livelihoods products for local communities.

Virtually all newly independent African governments upheld this centralizing trend in forest governance and further eroded communal land holding practices as they emerged from colonization in the 1950s and 1960s. Post-independence constitutions in many countries designated most (if not all) categories of land to be held in trust for citizens by the central state, extending only occupancy rights to citizens, and provisions for communal land ownership were rarely recognized by new land laws (Wily 2001). Forests reserved under colonial administrations were maintained as part of national estates, and colonial approaches to their management were usually adopted such that local communities remained excluded from forest resources. Newly independent governments tended to view forests foremost as critical resources to help drive national development and replenish national treasuries, through production forestry and international timber markets, and secondarily as sources of subsistence resources for poor rural populations. In some instances, such as the Forest Reserves established in the West Mengo region of Uganda (Vogt et al. 2006) and the Eastern Arc Mountains of Tanzania (Burgess et al. 2007), residents surrounding government reserves were assigned rights to non-timber forest products and were regularly coopted by Forest Departments into reserve boundary maintenance activities, leading to high physical stability of the reserves over ensuing decades (though not necessarily high stability of forest quality), even as the area of non-reserved forest lands drastically declined.

New policy developments in many countries have, however, started to introduce more attractive incentives and an accompanying legal structure for local citizens to steward off-reserve forest land, which in many cases has been initiated with stronger tenure security over land and forest resources by local citizens. Since the late 1990s nearly all countries in sub-Saharan Africa have undertaken sweeping land reforms to establish formalized legal processes by which land may be held in common by communities or groups of individuals. In many of these countries, revised land policies have been enacted sequentially or in tandem with revised forest policies, and specify new provisions for legal recognition and titling of communally owned and managed forest land.

An example from Tanzania—widely considered to have forged one of the stronger policy frameworks for establishing formally recognized customary tenure and legal support for forest commons through its revised Land (1999), Village Land (1999), and Forest (2002) Acts—demonstrates the extent of these reforms. Under Tanzania's revised legal instruments, villagers who traditionally used in common a forest on village land may now obtain legal recognition of their customary land rights and register the land as common property. Furthermore, they may also take steps to declare and manage their forest as a community forest reserve, a newly created legal status.

3. Major policy shifts related to the governance of forest commons in Africa

3.1. DECENTRALIZATION

Transfer of forest related powers and responsibilities to lower-level territorial and decision-making bodies has been a prominent development in most sub-Saharan countries since the early 1990s—albeit with substantial variation across and within countries. National governments, under pressure from a variety of sources—external donors, smaller budgets, and citizen demands—have often used legislative acts and executive orders to provide more resources, decision-making powers, and responsibilities to district and local communities in an attempt to increase their choices over actions in forests. The range of policy changes varies enormously across different countries and communities in Africa, but one common criticism of the ongoing decentralization policy shifts has been the limited depth of decentralization beyond government agencies. In practice, the implementation of many decentralization reforms has resulted in a significant transfer of authority from central government to a lower-level government agency, such as a district or village government. It has not, however, fostered significant participation by local forest users within villages, despite this emphasis in written policies. In other cases, central governments appear reluctant to devolve full authority to lower levels of government in accordance with the policies they devise, or to back their decentralization efforts with adequate funding, institutional structures, or other necessary resources at local levels. This translates to negative results for forest resources and prospects for their management by local forest users (Ribot et al. 2006). For example, a recent study of decentralization and subsequent recentralization efforts in Uganda found that uncertainty among local users and forest officials about these policies precipitated substantial deforestation in the same long-stable West Mengo Forest Reserves mentioned above (Namubiru-Mwaura 2008).

3.2. REDUCING EMISSIONS FROM DEFORESTATION AND FOREST DEGRADATION (REDD)

A second major forest governance shift that is in process in much of Africa, and which is likely to have a significant impact on African forest commons, is the international REDD effort. REDD is a proposed performance-based mechanism under negotiation through the United Nations Framework Convention on Climate Change (UNFCCC), in which developed country donors, corporations, non-governmental organizations, and individuals will compensate developing countries for forest emissions reductions, including through market mechanisms. Payments will require demonstrated emissions reductions through improved forest protection, sustainable forest management, and/or enhancement of carbon stocks (now known as REDD+). REDD+ will be a key emissions mitigation strategy, as evidenced by extensive donor investments to prepare developing countries to implement REDD+ (e.g. $4.5B from six developed countries by 2012: Phelps, Webb, and Agrawal 2010).

Although substantial sums of money are already being targeted toward REDD, only limited attention has been paid to the design and institutional aspects of REDD implementation. Without more careful and systematic thought into how benefits from REDD can be structured toward those contributing to forest carbon storage, there is a real danger that forest commons management in Africa will be taken over by central governments as they seek to secure higher levels of REDD payments from the international community for their own treasury. Institutional safeguards and encouragement to local participation in REDD programmes and projects are critically necessary to ensure that the benefits of REDD are not captured by a few, and that REDD projects do not reverse ongoing efforts toward decentralization.

4. Research contributions to understanding sustainable governance of forest commons

The use and management of African commons continues to evolve, serving as a natural laboratory for many successes and failures alike to engender more effective forest governance, and a more refined understanding of the nature of complexities associated with sustaining multiple benefit streams from forest resources to meet diverse interests. In this context, some of the most salient drivers of contemporary change appear to derive from global rather than local influences and motivations. Perhaps most notable of these are global priorities related to biodiversity conservation and climate change mitigation, which have increased the focus on market-based mechanisms for non-extractive forest-based income in an attempt to offset the opportunity costs local households must shoulder when they curtail harvesting activities or wholesale conversion of forest land for more immediately lucrative land uses. However, these processes also raise concerns over the extent to which global agendas impinge on the dynamics of forest use and autonomous management on the part of local communities.

Recent advances in research on forest commons have shed some light on these processes, focusing particularly on the role of institutions in mediating complex interactions between and within tightly-coupled social and ecological systems (Wollenberg et al. 2007). This is reflected in greater attention to three issues relevant to the management of forest commons: (1) the role of contextual factors in driving local social-ecological dynamics; (2) the importance of cross-scale relationships, particularly between local institutions and larger policy environment; and (3) synergies and trade-offs among the multiple outcomes from forest commons.

4.1. CONTEXTUAL FACTORS

The last decade witnessed the gradual consolidation of public policies aimed at reducing forest loss and improving forest cover across the developing world. These included various decentralization initiatives that constituted community-level institutions for the management of forest commons through transfer of ownership to communities or co-management arrangements, as well as simply shifting authority from a central office to a regional office of a national agency. This transformation in forest governance and policy has at times been problematic in its conception or implementation, as noted above. Commons scholars have been at the forefront of contributing to a better appreciation of institutional design features in enabling positive outcomes in several countries across Asia, Africa, and Latin America. Though it has not always been incorporated into policy, commons scholarship has repeatedly pointed to the necessity of autonomy from external interference in local rule-making by forest users (Chhatre and Agrawal 2009), and also to the positive role of civil society in facilitating sustainable forest governance, especially in the context of perverse incentives that favoured deforestation.

4.2. CROSS-SCALE RELATIONSHIPS

Actors and processes at multiple social, institutional, and ecological levels interact with each other to generate outcomes relevant to forest governance. Significant progress on the issue has been made possible in recent years by gradual development of new theoretical approaches, drawing especially on insights from complexity theory. Empirical analysis of commons has matured, with greater frequency of comparative analysis of large multi-country samples, taking advantage of existing data at multiple levels to explore cross-scale relationships as they impinge upon forest commons outcomes. Of particular interest have been studies of the impact of decentralization policies in several domains across the developing world, such as communal forests in Tanzania, group ranches in Kenya, extractive reserves in Brazil, forest co-management in India and Nepal, and indigenous territories in several tropical countries. Scholars of commons, as a result of these advances, have been able to develop a better understanding of the conditions under which macro-level processes structure local outcomes and, conversely, when local processes and outcomes overwhelm the structuring role of more macro-level processes.

4.3. TRADE-OFFS AND SYNERGIES

Current research on forest commons has also substantially advanced our ability to distinguish clearly among the major outcomes from forest commons. Researchers are now beginning to outline outcomes along multiple dimensions—equity in allocation of benefits across different social groups and over time, management efficiency, resilience of resource systems, or conservation effectiveness. These were previously often merged together in empirical analysis because the theoretical literature itself did not carefully distinguish among these multiple outcome dimensions. In an abstract sense it is easy to recognize that these different outcomes may either be associated positively or negatively, depending on the context, and range of focus. In some situations, a focus on enhancing institutional or resource system resilience may be feasible, and go together well with improvements in equitable allocation of benefits from the commons. But where the social context itself is extremely inequitable, a focus on improving equity may undermine institutional resilience. Similarly, an exclusive focus on maximizing equity may undermine not only performance along the dimension of resilience, but also other performance dimensions. New research on forest commons is beginning to identify the combination of factors and causal pathways which may lead alternately to synergies or trade-offs among different outcomes desired from forest commons.

REFERENCES

Barrow, E., K. Ruhombe, I. Nhantumbo, R. Oyono, and M. Savadogo, 2009. 'Customary practices and forest tenure reforms in Africa: status, issues and lessons'. Washington, DC: Rights and Resources Initiative.

Bene, C., E. Belal, M. O. Baba, S. Ovie, A. Raji, I. Malasha, F. Njaya, M. N. Andi, A. Russell, and A. Neiland, 2009. 'Power struggle, dispute and alliance over local resources: analyzing "democratic" decentralization of natural resources through the lenses of Africa inland fisheries', *World Development* 37.12, 1935–50.

Burgess, N. D., et al., 2007. 'The biological importance of the Eastern Arc Mountains of Tanzania and Kenya', *Biological Conservation* 134.2, 209–31.

Chhatre, A., and A. Agrawal, 2009. 'Trade-offs and synergies between carbon storage and livelihood benefits from forest commons', *Proceedings of the National Academy of Sciences* 106.42, 17667–70.

Mwangi, Esther, and Elinor Ostrom, 2009. 'Top-down solutions: looking up from East Africa's rangelands', *Environment: Science and Policy for Sustainable Development* 51.1, 34–44.

Namubiru-Mwaura, E., 2008. 'Adaptive governance: coping with macro institutional changes in forestry', PhD dissertation, Indiana University, School of Public and Environmental Affairs.

Phelps J., E. L. Webb, and A. Agrawal, 2010. 'Does REDD+ threaten to recentralize forest governance?', *Science* 328, 312–13.

Pretty, J., and H. Ward, 2001. 'Social capital and the environment', *World Development* 29.2, 209–27.

Ribot, J. C., A. Agrawal, and A. M. Larson, 2006. 'Recentralizing while decentralizing: how national governments re-appropriate forest resources', *World Development* 34.11, 1864–86.

Vogt, N. D., A. Y. Banana, W. Gombya-Ssembajjwe, and J. Bahati, 2006. 'Understanding the stability of forest reserve boundaries in the West Mengo region of Uganda', *Ecology and Society* 11.1, 38.

Wily, L. A., 2001. 'Reconstructing the African commons', *Africa Today* 48, 77–99.

—— 2008. 'Custom and commonage in Africa: rethinking the orthodoxies', *Land Use Policy* 25, 43–52.

Wollenberg, E., L. Merino, A. Agrawal, and E. Ostrom, 2007. 'Fourteen years of monitoring community-managed forests: learning from IFRI's experience', *International Forestry Review* 9.2, 670–84.

World Bank, 2004. *Sustaining Forests: A Development Strategy*. Washington, DC.

Land Tenure

Christopher Udry

Farming in sub-Saharan Africa outside South Africa typically takes place on small plots cultivated by individuals. The land tenure system is often described as 'communal', meaning that land is owned by a kin-based or political group and that individuals obtain the right to cultivate through their membership in that group. If a generalization is possible about the process through which people obtain land for farming in such a broad and diverse region, the consensus would be that land tenure in Africa is characterized by flexibility, complexity, and negotiability (Shipton and Goheen 1992; Amanor and Moyo 2008). Claims to land and land resources commonly depend on membership in broader social groupings: extended families or lineages, villages, or other social networks. Land tenure rights in this broad region are often multi-layered, with differentiated rights over standing crops, crop stubble, fallowed fields, 'wild' foods, minerals, water access, or trees and forests. These multiple layers of rights over land and its produce can be associated with rich and flexible land use by multiple parties, as when grazing on crop stubble complements cultivation in many areas of the Sahel. They can also be associated with multidimensional conflict, as between timber extraction, cultivation, and wild food gathering in many forest areas. Layered on top of this customary tenure system is a growing share of land obtained by commercial transactions via sharecropping, rental, or outright purchase.

The flexibility and complexity of land tenure systems in sub-Saharan Africa is often associated with conflict: the fact that many individuals may have claims to the same piece of land, and to different dimensions of use of that land may imply that each one of those individual's claims are not fully secure. This apparent insecurity, and the hypothesized associated losses in productivity and incentives to invest, attracted for decades much of the attention of policymakers with respect to land rights.

There are a number of economic mechanisms through which one would expect insecure property rights to reduce investment and productivity on farms (Besley 1995). The most direct is the fact that there is some probability that the farmer will be unable to reap the full reward of any investment. A farmer considering an investment balances its cost against the expected future benefits generated by the investment; otherwise worthwhile investments will therefore not be made if those expected benefits fall. This mechanism has received a great deal of attention from scholars and policymakers concerned with land in Africa, and there is mixed evidence regarding its importance in various regions.

Less direct connections between secure property rights and increased investment and farm productivity run through credit markets (secure land could be used as collateral); gains from trade (farmers able to freely sell or rent out their land are more likely to make investments); or complementary factors of production (tenure security permits farmers to economize on guard labour). There is no evidence, however, that any of these indirect mechanisms has any quantitatively important impact on productivity or investment.

From the colonial period until the present day, there have been recurring worries that the insecurity of land tenure in Africa has inhibited productivity-increasing investments in agriculture. These worries have been founded primarily on the simple economic reasoning that insecure land tenure would reduce investment and lower agricultural productivity. Quantitative evidence that such a link exists, however, was always weak and partial. Partly, this weakness reflects the fundamental difficulty of measuring such an effect: it is difficult to quantify 'insecurity' of land. Formal laws regarding land tenure may have only a tenuous relationship to farmer behaviour or to the expectations people have regarding their ability to use or maintain control over their land (Pande and Udry 2006). Even when it is possible to measure tenure security and thus construct a correlation between this and agricultural productivity, it remains a challenge to understand the causal chain that might link land tenure regimes to investment and productivity. Causality could run in both directions: certain investments might themselves change the rights of a cultivator over her land, thus inducing a correlation between tenure security and investment or productivity. More importantly, there are surely many 'third factors' that might drive any observed correlation between land tenure regimes and agricultural productivity. An obvious example is the existence of an effective local government authority, which might reduce conflicts over land and at the same time provide infrastructural support that would increase agricultural productivity.

As late as the mid-1970s, the strength of the a priori theoretical arguments that there would be a strong effect of land tenure security and agricultural productivity was sufficiently persuasive that the dominant theme of land policy in international organizations and in many countries was focused on the desirability of providing secure, individual title to smallholder farmers (World Bank 1975). However, the weak empirical foundation of this point of view was apparent, and scholars from a wide variety of disciplines provided many examples of land tenure arrangements in Africa that were flexible, negotiable, complex, and that seemed compatible with a great deal of investment and agricultural intensification (Peters 2004 has a useful summary of some of the best of this research). Empirical research by economists found little evidence for a strong causal link from tenure security (via either formal titling programmes or variations in informal tenure security) to investment or agricultural productivity (a very useful brief review of this literature can be found in Brasselle, Gaspart, and Platteau 2002). By 1991, World Bank researchers were arguing that African 'indigenous land tenure systems appear to be adapting efficiently to changes in relative factor scarcities', that their quantitative evidence found no relationship between variations and land rights and variations in productivity, and that this evidence 'undermines the conventional view that land rights are a constraint on productivity' (Migot-Adholla et al. 1991: 171, 172). The conventional wisdom had been transformed from 'seeing customary land tenure in Africa as inhibiting agricultural modernization to lauding its adaptive and flexible character that, over time, allows "evolution" towards more efficient forms of landholding' (Peters 2004: 270). As a consequence, the primary focus of policy advice on land tenure has shifted from direct provision of individual title to support for better integration of customary tenure with the formal legal system.

However, it is clear that at least under some conditions the complexity, flexibility, and negotiability of land tenure arrangements in Africa can be associated with a high degree of insecurity and can inhibit investment and reduce agricultural productivity. Goldstein and Udry (2008) show that in the Akwapim area of southern Ghana, there is a high degree of tenure insecurity, particularly during periods when land is left fallow for weed control and fertility regeneration. Individuals in this region primarily obtain land for cultivation by virtue of their membership in a matrilineage. While 'in principle, any individual is entitled to use some portion of his or her family's land,... people's abilities to exercise such claims vary a good deal in practice' and depend in particular on their social and political status (Berry 2001: 145). Goldstein and Udry find that individuals who are not central to the networks of local political power through which land is allocated are very likely to have their land expropriated if it is fallowed. Women who do not hold a political office have more than a 40% chance of losing that plot in any year that it is fallow. The uncertainty associated with maintaining control over plots while they are fallow is pervasive in the area: even politically powerful men face a 20% chance of losing a plot in any year in which it is fallow. As a consequence, individuals fallow their land for much shorter durations than is technically optimal. As a consequence, farm profitability is correspondingly reduced: a quarter to a half of farm profits are lost as a consequence of the short fallows chosen because of the likelihood that land will be lost while it is fallowed.

These large effects of land tenure insecurity on investment and productivity stand in contrast to the substantial literature which tends to find no or only subtle impacts of insecure property rights on investment behaviour. It is also puzzling that these large effects of tenure insecurity on investment are found in Akwapim, the epicentre of the 20th-century cocoa boom which serves as perhaps the most important single example of massive investment and agricultural transformation under customary land tenure in Africa (Hill 1963; Austin 2004). How could the same land tenure system accommodate the large-scale transition from food crops into cocoa at the opening of the 20th century and so dramatically inhibit investment in land productivity in the same area at the opening of the 21st?

The resolution of this puzzle offers important lessons about the need for caution in generalizing about the economics of land tenure in Africa. In the case of southern Ghana, while rights over land itself are quite uncertain, cultivators almost never lose control over their growing crops.[1] This particular form of tenure insecurity has substantial negative consequences for investments in fallow in a food-crop farming system, but was irrelevant for long-term investments in a tree crop like cocoa. The congruence between a farming system centred on a long-lived tree crop and a customary land tenure system that provided secure rights over growing crops facilitated the meteoric growth of cocoa cultivation at the turn of the 20th century. The interactions between the rules of a particular land tenure system and incentives to invest in agriculture can be subtle; thus it is no surprise that the empirical evidence relating investment, productivity, and land tenure systems varies across Africa and over time. At the same time, these tenure systems play a crucial and flexible role in redistributing resources in the face of unpredictable variations in need. As a consequence, most of Africa is distinguished by the almost complete absence of a rural landless class. This system may provide important insurance in times of need, and a remarkable degree of social stability due to the redistribution of land within rural communities.

The dominant land policy recommendation has historically been to formalize property rights through land titling and registration. But, in many contexts, customary land systems are compatible with investment in agricultural intensification. Moreover, there are important transaction costs associated with any titling programme, and the cost of titling land seems to be much larger than the benefit for most small-scale producers. So only a few (typically elite) farmers and urban landowners go through the process of obtaining title when it is provided at cost. In addition, programmes of land registration and titling are often associated with exacerbated conflict over land (Shipton and Goheen 1992). The ambiguous social benefits of formalizing property rights, in turn, provide little reason for substantial subsidies from the state to support a large-scale titling or registration process.

A process of harmonizing formal legal land tenure with customary rights offers a potential opportunity to move away from state-run land surveys and formal titling of individuals to some form of community management and registration of customary rights. This prescription might relieve some of the burden from the state by offering an opportunity for civil society to play a major role in land administration. However, customary tenure systems are socially differentiated. Formal recognition of the authority of local authorities and 'civil society' to administer land rights may permit these local authorities to redefine their power in such a way as to appropriate additional value from

---

[1] The views expressed in this chapter are those of the author. They do not necessarily represent the views of the African Development Bank, its Board of Directors or the countries they represent.

these land resources.[2] In many contexts, better integration of formal legal land tenure with customary land systems will be an important step towards improving tenure security and promoting rural development. But it is important that the political and social ramifications of such policies be investigated in particular settings.

Land banks have been proposed to provide a decentralized, flexible, and context-specific mechanism for privately providing secure property rights in land (Aryeetey and Udry 2010). Land banks would be formal institutions which would take 'deposits' of land from landowners. In turn, land banks would lease out land to commercial farmers and developers. The shareholders of the land banks would be individuals from the community (including chiefs) and elsewhere, and local government. Land banks would serve as aggregators of land to resolve conflicts over ownership, separate property use from ownership rights, and reduce the transaction costs of transferring use right. The relatively large size and long-term perspective of land banks would permit them to capture a portion of gains from providing relatively low-transaction-cost, secure property rights to those seeking land, and they would have an incentive to operate precisely in those regions and farming systems in which the provision of secure land tenure is particularly valuable.

■ REFERENCES

Amanor, Kojo, and Sam Moyo (eds), 2008. *Land and Sustainable Development in Africa*. New York: Zed.

Aryeetey, Ernest, and Christopher Udry, 2010. 'Creating property rights: land banks in Ghana', *American Economic Review* 100.2, 130–34.

Austin, Gareth, 2004. *Labour, Land, and Capital in Ghana: From Slavery to Free Labour in Asante, 1807–1956*. Rochester, NY: University of Rochester Press.

Berry, Sara, 2001. *Chiefs Know Their Boundaries: Essays on Property, Power and the Past in Asante, 1896–1996*. London: Heinemann.

Besley, Timothy, 1995. 'Property rights and investment incentives: theory and evidence from Ghana', *Journal of Political Economy* 103.5, 903–37.

Brasselle, Anne-Sophie, Frederic Gaspart, and Jean-Philippe Platteau, 2002. 'Land tenure security and investment incentives: puzzling evidence from Burkina Faso', *Journal of Development Economics* 67.2, 373–418.

Goldstein, Markus, and Christopher Udry, 2008. 'The profits of power: land rights and agricultural investment in Ghana', *Journal of Political Economy* 116.6, 981–1022.

Hill, Polly, 1963. *The Migrant Cocoa-Farmers of Southern Ghana: A Study in Rural Capitalism*. Cambridge: Cambridge University Press.

---

[2] There is a rich literature describing these processes; see Onoma (2010) for a vivid recent account.

Migot-Adholla, Shem, Peter Hazell, Benoît Blarel, and Frank Place, 1991. 'Indigenous land rights systems in sub-Saharan Africa: a constraint on productivity?', *World Bank Economic Review* 5.1, 155–75.

Onoma, Ato Kwamena, 2010. *The Politics of Property Rights Institutions in Africa*: Cambridge University Press.

Pande, Rohini, and Christopher Udry, 2006. 'Institutions and development: a view from below', in Richard Blundell, Whitney Newey, and Torsten Persson (eds), *Advances in Economics and Econometrics: Theory and Applications*. Cambridge: Cambridge University Press.

Peters, Pauline, 2004. 'Inequality and social conflict over land in Africa', *Journal of Agrarian Change* 4.3, 269–314.

Shipton, Parker, and Mitzi Goheen, 1992. 'Understanding African land-holding: power, wealth and meaning', *Africa* 62.3, 307–25.

Wilks, Ivor, 1993. *Forests of Gold: Essays on the Akan and the Kingdom of Asante*. Athens: Ohio University Press.

World Bank, 1975. 'Land reform', sector policy paper. Washington, DC: World Bank.

Can Water Undermine Africa's Growth in the 21st Century? Issues and Options[1]

Abdul B. Kamara

1. Introduction

Water has always been central to economic activity, serving mankind as a critical anchor of farming, domestic, and commercial activities. For Africa, growth and development are intricately linked with water, given the continent's strong dependence on the primary sector—particularly on agriculture, which is the largest consumer of water. With increasing water scarcity, the need to balance water allocation among various sectors has gained importance in Africa (Rosegrant, Cai, and Cline 2003).

By 2025 Africa's population will have reached 1.3 billion, an increase of 32% over the 2008 level (UNFPA 2008). This increase will exert further pressure on the continent's water resources available for food production and domestic and industrial uses. In these sectors, water remains crucial for revitalizing and sustaining economic growth. As water-related tensions increase in the region, evident in key basins such as the Nile, Africa faces more challenges in balancing water allocation among competing sectors, both from the efficiency perspective and in terms of ensuring access of vulnerable social groups. The objective of this chapter is to review current water uses in Africa's key sectors and assess their implications for the continent's growth.

2. Water resource development, uses, and implications

With about 15% of the world's population, Africa has only about 9% of the world's internally renewable water resources (IRWR) (Food and Agriculture Organization 2006). This translates to only about 4,600 m^3 of water per capita per annum, compared to about 26,700 m^3 in Latin America or 9,100 m^3 in Europe (FAO 2006), underscoring

---

[1] The views expressed in this chapter are those of the author. They do not necessarily represent the views of the African Development Bank, its Board of Directors or the countries they represent.

the relevance of improved water resource management. The uneven spatial distribution of the continent's water resources renders its west and central regions relatively water-abundant, while the north and parts of the south are water-scarce. Irrigation thus becomes imperative for reliable crop production in these regions. Even more challenging is the temporal distribution, which subjects the continent to periods of extreme floods and droughts, with associated catastrophes (FAO 2003). The massive social and economic costs of such shocks make water resource development crucial.

To date, however, this challenge remains daunting: Africa is the least water-developed region, with only 6% withdrawal rate of its IRWR, compared to 21% in Asia. So far, only about 63% of the continent's population has access to improved water sources for basic needs, compared to 91% and 87% for Latin America and East Asia and Pacific, respectively (FAO 2006).

With the exception of northern and parts of southern Africa, lack of access to water is largely due to *economic scarcity*—the need for improved management and investments to capture, store, and deliver water when needed. In contrast, *physical scarcity* is a scenario of having developed most or all the water resources through the construction of dams, diversion, and delivery structures (Seckler et al. 1998; Kamara and Sally 2004). Economic water scarcity has implications for planning and prioritizing water-related investments in various sectors, and for improving management to increase temporal availability and minimize shocks.

2.1. CURRENT WATER USES

2.1.1. Water for food

Agriculture being a consumer of over 86% of exploited water in sub-Saharan Africa (SSA) (Fig. 1), food security in the 21st century will be closely linked to water security. This is because the weak fiscal policy positions of many African countries would not allow them to sustain food import bills over time.

Indeed, the recent escalation of food prices in 2007/2008 was a litmus test for the continent's high vulnerability to food-related shocks (Kamara et al. 2009). While Africa has massive unutilized agricultural potential, realizing it through new irrigation development or rehabilitation of existing schemes remains a daunting challenge (Lankford 2009). Today, only 3.7% of arable land in SSA is irrigated, compared to 40%, 29%, and 41% in North Africa, East Asia, and Southeast Asia respectively. It is therefore not surprising that 90% of rural cultivators in Africa currently depend on rainfed agriculture, which accounts for 30–40% of agricultural GDP (Rockström, Barron, and Fox 2003). With Africa's current emphasis on economic diversification to reduce vulnerability, investment in agriculture and water-related technologies remains key for producing

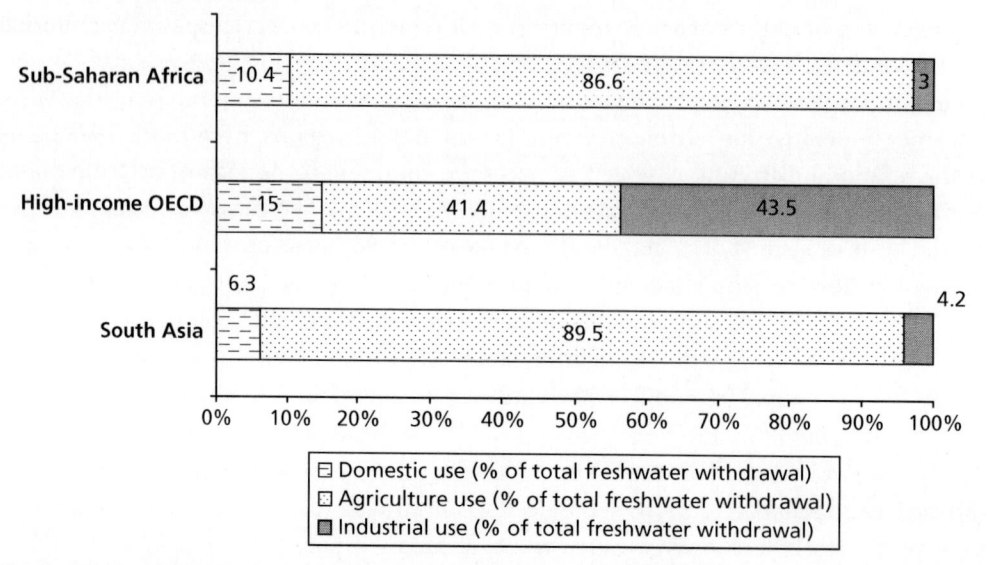

Figure 1. Annual freshwater withdrawals 2002 (source: FAO 2006)

Sub-Saharan Africa: Domestic 10.4, Agriculture 86.6, Industrial 3
High-income OECD: Domestic 15, Agriculture 41.4, Industrial 43.5
South Asia: Domestic 6.3, Agriculture 89.5, Industrial 4.2

food on a scale that would allow agro-industrial development as a vital component of the manufacturing industry.

The absence of such investments will reduce Africa's ability to achieve and sustain long-term food security, increase in productivity, and competitiveness. But getting the right investment in agricultural water use will also mean providing inputs and market support systems, targeted subsidies, and incentives for collecting water service fees to ensure cost recovery and sustainability. While the issue of water-user fees remains contentious, it needs to be critically examined in various settings and administered along with support services that raise farm productivity and incomes. In particular, assisting small-scale farmers to gain better access to low-cost technologies can make a large contribution to food security and economic growth in many parts of Africa (Merrey and Sally 2008). In doing so, a balance between public investment and encouraging private investment in low-cost productivity-enhancing technologies is needed.

2.1.2. Water for livelihoods

Improving access to safe drinking water and basic sanitation is a key target among the Millennium Development Goals (MDGs). Achieving this goal is crucial in Africa today, given that about 43% of African people live on less than a dollar a day and lack access to these basic services (African Development Bank 2009). With high rates of poverty, increasing access to domestic water and basic sanitation becomes a prerequisite for progress on other MDGs, such as reducing child mortality (MDG4), improving maternal health (MDG5), and combating diseases (MDG6).

Because of these linkages, the cost of lack of access to domestic water and sanitation is alarmingly high, not only in terms of escalated health cost, but also in terms of massive loss of human capital, a weaker labour force, and ultimately low productivity and competitiveness. All these factors impede economic growth. The current 10.4% water use for domestic purposes in SSA needs to be scaled up significantly if the continent is to increase its water use of 47 litres per person per day, compared to the recommended minimum usage of 50–100 litres for healthy living (Johns Hopkins School of Public Health 2009).

2.1.3. Water for industry

Industrial water use is crucial for Africa's economic growth from three perspectives: mining, which contributes about 20% of the continent's GDP; manufacturing, which is important for value addition, diversification, and increased trade; and hydropower generation, which is a key challenge for generating electricity on which mining, manufacturing, and domestic power supply crucially depend. Although industry accounts for only a small proportion of Africa's water use, the sector gives the highest return per unit of water. However, hard questions remain about the distribution of benefits from the industry.

In spite of high water use efficiency and sometimes major local benefits, national-level impacts of mining in SSA are limited only to isolated examples (e.g. Botswana), due to transparency challenges and high technological investments costs—usually affordable only for foreign companies, which unfortunately take the lion's share of the benefits. Also, negative externalities associated with mining raise questions about water use in the sector—especially health issues and destruction of ecosystems, including agricultural land.

2.2. IMPLICATIONS FOR AFRICA'S GROWTH AND DEVELOPMENT

Achieving economic growth on a significant scale requires harnessing opportunities especially in the agricultural and industrial sectors, both of which call for more water resources development. While water resources are fairly abundant, economic water scarcity leaves the continent with the world's lowest water withdrawal rates at a time of crucial need. Climate change also threatens to exacerbate the vulnerability of valuable ecosystems, including wetlands and agro-ecologies, with negative implications for food security. Since improved food security has positive effects on health-related MDGs, investment in agriculture will raise life expectancy, labour quality, and economic productivity over the longer term. For Africa to sustain economic growth, it must have a potential to reduce poverty on a scale that will raise aggregate demand and enhance savings. This will require minimizing the impact of climate change and associated shocks, which aggravate poverty with high social costs (World Bank 2006).

Given the relatively weak external and fiscal positions of several African countries, the issue of cost recovery in providing water and related services must be emphasized. This is also true from a sustainability perspective, given that water is a private good. For poor and vulnerable populations, however, some forms of cross-subsidy remain inevitable. In the domestic sector, sustainability can be sought through public–private partnerships (PPP), with donor involvement to enhance cost recovery and improve water use efficiency.

The challenges of water use in the industrial sector call for stronger regulation and improved government capacity to implement existing frameworks and regulations. Cross-border externalities related to water quality and use rights require greater regional cooperation in integrated water resource management (IWRM). This will not only improve water use efficiency but also serve as a spring board for dialogue in shared basins for greater cooperation, regional integration, and expansion of regional economies.

3. Going forward

Governments, donors, and the development community need to scale up investment to utilize Africa's water resource potential. Governments and regional organizations have exerted commendable efforts in developing frameworks, regulations, and action plans, but weak enforcement capacity and uncoordinated implementation deter progress. With initiatives such as the African Water Facility (AWF), the water-related pillar of the Comprehensive African Agriculture Development Program (CAADP), and the growing operations of development partners, water resource investment has received more attention recently. However, the investments fall far short of the $12 billion per annum required over the next twenty years for Africa to meet drinking water and sanitation targets, excluding investments for food and energy infrastructure, and adaptation to climate change (World Water Forum 2009).

■ REFERENCES

African Development Bank, 2009. 'Development aid and access to water and sanitation in sub-Saharan Africa', Development Research Brief 7, ADB, Tunis.

Food and Agriculture Organization, 2003. 'A perspective on water control in southern Africa: support to regional investment initiatives', Land and Water Discussion Paper 1, FAO, Rome.
—— 2006. Aquastat: http://www.fao.org/nr/water/aquastat/data/query/index.html.
Johns Hopkins School of Public Health, 2009. 'Population information program', Center for Communication Programs: http://www.infoforhealth.org.
Kamara, A. B., A. Mafusire, V. Castel, M. Kurzweil, D. Vencatachellum, and L. Pla, 2009. 'Update on the soaring food prices: Africa's vulnerability and responses', WPS 97, African Development Bank.
—— and H. Sally, 2004. 'Water management options for food security in South Africa', *Development Southern Africa* 21.2.
Lankford, B., 2009. 'The right irrigation?', University of East Anglia: www.uea.ac.uk/dev/lankford
Merrey, D., and H. Sally, 2008. 'Micro-agricultural water management technologies for food security in southern Africa: part of the solution or red herring?', *Water Policy* 10, 515–30.
Rockström, J., J. Barron, and P. Fox, 2003. 'Water productivity in rainfed agriculture: challenges and opportunities for smallholder farmers in drought-prone tropical ecosystems', in *Water Productivity in Agriculture: Limits and Opportunities for Improvements*. CABI, UK; Colombo: IWMI.
Rosegrant, M. W., X. Cai, and S. Cline, 2003. *World Water and Food to 2025: Dealing with Scarcity*. Washington, DC: International Food Policy Research Institute; Colombo: IWMI.
Seckler, D., U. Amarasinghe, D. Molden, R. de Silva, and R. Barker, 1998. *World Water Demand and Supply, 1990 to 2025: Scenarios and Issues*. Colombo: IWMI.
United Nations Population Fund, 2008. *UNFPA State of the World Population in 2008—Reaching Common Ground: Culture, Gender and Human Rights*. New York: UNFPA.
World Bank, 2006. 'Can water undermine growth? Evidence from Ethiopia', *Agriculture and Rural Development Notes* 18.
World Water Forum, 2009. 5th World Water Forum Report: http://www.preventionweb.net/english/professional/publications/v.php?id=11456.

Country Perspectives

Algeria Development Opportunities and Challenges

Ali Hemal

Algeria is a North African country and a member of OPEC and the Euro-Med Free Trade Association. The country is rich in natural resources and labour-abundant. Still in its early stage of transition from an administrative economy to a market-driven economy, Algeria has achieved a remarkable turnaround since 1999, thanks mainly to favourable external factors. Between 1999 and 2008, Algeria benefited from a continuous oil boom that allowed the country to accumulate international reserves of more than $135 billion and to generate unprecedented revenues for the state (World Bank 2009a: 1). The period was also one of relatively high growth, lower inflation, and decreasing rate of unemployment.

Although the global financial crisis has so far had limited adverse effect on the Algerian economy, mainly due to the limited integration of its financial system into the international one, the Algerian economy is bound to suffer from the continued global recession as a result of the reduction in remittances and the slowdown in global energy demand. However, this limited link to the global financial system may prevent the country from circumventing some of the vulnerability arising from the global recession in the event that it lasts beyond 2011. This is so for the following reasons: first, Algeria is highly integrated into the global economy through commodity trade and migration. Algeria's trade-to-GDP ratio is well above world average (World Bank 2009a: 58). Moreover, Algeria's lack of export diversification and its heavy reliance on food imports exposes the country heavily to commodity price shocks. As a result, Algeria (like most other MENA economies) leads the world in its exposure to commodity price shocks (Hirata et al. 2005). Algeria is also strongly integrated into the global economy through migration; the country has over 2 million emigrants abroad, representing about 7% of its total population. This ratio is well above the average of about 4.5% for the whole MENA region (Docquier and Marchiori 2009). In addition to remittances, migration has also provided a substantial outlet for local labour market imbalances in the face of domestic and external shocks.

Despite this overall improvement, compared to the 1990s, Algeria continues to face the following key development challenges.

The first challenge is the efficient use of hydrocarbon reserves for the long-term benefit of the Algerian population through investment in the non-oil economy. This will create permanent jobs, thus reducing social tensions provoked by unemployment, modernize the economy, and improve its global competitiveness. This requires management of hydrocarbon revenues with a long-term perspective, aimed at reducing the country's vulnerability to world oil and gas prices. Being relatively undiversified and dependent on exports of oil and gas, Algeria's economy is in urgent need of efficient use of hydrocarbon funds in a way that both helps manage the unpredictable and volatile oil prices and saves for the coming generations. In 2001 Algeria, like many other oil-exporting countries, created a stabilization fund for two purposes: first, to finance any fiscal deficit arising from an oil price that falls below the budget law reference price; second, to make advance payments on external debt principal. As a result of the external debt repayments, Algeria has been since 2008 a net creditor nation to the rest of the world, with an external debt-to-GDP ratio at less than 3% in 2008. The effectiveness of such funds requires that objectives, rules, and management are transparent and apolitical. In the Algerian case, there are no mechanisms in place so far that prevent misuse of these funds.

Another challenge is to speed up Algeria's structural reforms. The country has, by and large, not kept pace with worldwide and regional progress in this field; but trade reforms stand out as an area in which it has exhibited remarkable progress. This was mainly motivated by Algeria's bid to join the WTO, and regional and bilateral agreements. In other areas of reform, Algeria ranks in the bottom third of the world in terms of improvement across politically sensitive areas such as reform of the judiciary, business, and financial environment (World Bank 2007b; World Economic Forum 2009). Of greater concern is the lack of progress, and even regression, in the field of governance. Although it has many facets, governance comprises mainly two areas: the quality of public services and accountability.

The first area consists of the rule of law, protection of property rights including privacy, the control of corruption, efficiency of the bureaucracy, and quality of regulations. Algeria's ranking in *Doing Business 2008* (IFC/World Bank) provides a clear evidence of the regime's lack of will to create an environment that is conducive to investment, both local and international (World Bank 2007b). Various studies on corruption also suggest that Algeria has not made any significant progress in fighting corruption over the last decade.

All experts and papers consulted within the framework of this query agree that the [MENA] region is characterized by the paucity of accessible empirical data on corruption related issues, possibly due to a general lack of will for such scrutiny. However, there is a general consensus that both petty and grand corruption are widespread in the region and deeply rooted in the political infrastructure of the state... and relatively little opportunities for public participation. (U4 Anti-Corruption Resource Centre 2007)

The second area includes public access to information and citizens' ability to hold political leaders accountable. Algeria, like most Middle East and North African (MENA) countries, has recently showed a marked deterioration relative to the progress occurring elsewhere. This is especially true with regard to public sector accountability. Although each area of reform is important in its own right, the lack of progress, and even deterioration, in governance reform is of great concern because of its multi-facet implications for the success of other reforms. International experience shows that where social and political stability has improved and structural reforms have been successful, there have been strong social and political movements for change. The ability of such movements for change depends essentially on access to information, and on freedom to mobilize and to contest government policies. So far Algeria lags far behind in this area of reform. This in turn has resulted in social and political instability, increasing corruption, and inefficiency.

The third challenge is to diversify the economy and exports. 'Algeria has one of the least diversified economies among middle income and oil-producer countries' (World Bank 2007a: 13). Concentration and diversification indices of export products in 2007 show that Algeria's indices were much higher than the average for the Maghreb region as well as for middle-income oil-exporting countries (World Bank 2010). Hydrocarbon exports make up almost all of merchandise exports—98%, extremely high by international standards. Algeria's heavy reliance on hydrocarbon exports has led to both higher volatility and lower growth. The international evidence on trade shows that the level of export diversification raises productivity, allowing for greater innovation and knowledge spillover to the rest of the economy, while highly concentrated exports are negatively associated with lower growth (Naude and Roussouw 2008). As a result, Algeria's lack of export diversification means not only that its exposure to terms of trade deterioration is greater, but that the expected gains from external trade are lower. Heavy reliance on any one single export commodity leads to vulnerability to changes in international demand for it, with detrimental effects on local economy.

Historical evidence shows that only a handful of hydrocarbon-dependent economies have achieved some success in diversifying their economies and export bases out of hydrocarbon (e.g. Mexico, Bahrain, and Indonesia). Within the MENA region, some oil-dependent countries have managed to substantially diversify their exports. For example, Saudi Arabia has been developing its petrochemical industry and other hydrocarbon-related goods, thus allowing its economy to diversify exports within fuels and to move up the value-added chain. Other Gulf Cooperation Council (GCC) countries have opted to convert their oil revenues collected through sovereign wealth funds into longer-term revenue streams mainly in the developed countries. However, recently most GCC countries have been investing their oil revenues locally with the aim of developing new revenue sources, including financial and trade services and tourism.

With a tradition of high savings, average educational attainment, abundant natural resources, and a very strategically favourable geographical location, Algeria has an important potential for rapid and sustainable growth. To achieve this aim, it needs to create a business environment conducive to the development of the emerging private sector, and good governance to encourage the inflow of FDI particularly to the non-oil economy. The process also requires a continuous effort in restructuring the economy by ending recent practices. The present global economic downturn underscores the importance of developing an economic environment that is based on competitiveness and productivity enhancements to enable Algeria's economy to weather shocks. Yet the most recent report on competitiveness in Africa places Algeria 99th worldwide and last in the North African region. Worse, the country's ranking in 2007 was much better than that of 2008 (World Economic Forum 2009: 9).

Another challenge is food security. Algeria's reliance on food imports is rapidly increasing, despite massive investment in the agricultural and irrigation sectors during the last decade. The ratio of food imports to total household consumption expenditure in 2007 exceeded 12%, and the country is ranked fourth in the MENA region (World Bank 2009b: 71). For a number of reasons, it is unlikely that such high degree of dependence on food imports will decrease over time. First, scarce water supplies are increasingly strained. Second, the country's population is growing relatively fast, though less than in previous decades. Third, the impact of climate change can be seen in increasing water scarcity, desertification, deforestation, increasing soil salinity, and rising rural exodus, especially to coastal areas. Fourth, another source of frequent shocks to Algeria's economy and society is frequent droughts.

Another challenge is reducing unemployment. In common with the rest of the African continent, Algeria suffers from high unemployment. Although very recent official unemployment figures confirm a declining trend, the unemployed population in January 2009 stood at over 1.2 million—i.e. an unemployment rate of over 11% in December 2008. The 2007 rate was 13.8%, well below that of June 2008 at 12.3% and far below that of 1997 at around 27% (World Bank 2009a: 2; Conseil National Économique et Social, CNES: 2003). Much of this reduction is due to very high public spending rates from the 2001–4 Economic Recovery Programme and the ongoing 2005–9 Complementary Recovery Programme, and regional development programmes. The main feature of most jobs created through these programmes is their temporary nature, as most investment is carried out in socioeconomic infrastructure and agriculture. Furthermore, unemployment is very widespread among young people. Seventy per cent of the unemployed are younger than 30. The informal economy also provides employment to a substantial share of the labour force. The Algerian National Economic and Social Council estimated in 2003 that informal jobs represent over 17% of total employment (CNES 2003). Despite massive public investment over the last decade, recent ONS survey of employment and jobless in Algeria confirms CNES findings (Office National des Statistiques 2011).

The final main challenge is improving education. The main weaknesses of this sector have become evident as demand has drastically increased in recent years. Public resources allocated to the sector are inefficiently allocated. The priority in resource allocation is given to social services and infrastructure, at the expense of other areas which are essential for education quality. 'Algeria spends relatively more on higher education than many comparator countries; but this is mainly because of high social, not instructional, expenditures' (World Bank 2007a: 129). Almost 90% of higher education students benefit from scholarship, 50% are entitled to a subsidized university residence and board, and all are entitled to subsidized lunch. In sum, social expenditures accounted on average for nearly 50% of recurrent expenditure over the period 2002–7 (MESRS, various years). Another feature of Algeria's higher education is that it has a high proportion of administrative staff compared to teaching staff (1:1). Salaries of university teaching staff are extremely low compared to countries of similar per capita incomes, and even to neighbouring countries where per capita income is much lower. As a result, there is a continuous and increasing brain drain. In contrast to social expenditures, spending on non-salary materials is extremely low in Algeria's higher education by international standards. For example, in the 2005 budget, the average spending per student in instructional materials for both postgraduate and undergraduate levels was about $95. Furthermore, there is persistent regional gender and social inequality in terms of access and outcomes.

To meet its pressing development challenges of creating sufficient employment opportunities and improving living conditions of its population, Algeria will require still higher growth, which depends on implementing broadly based structural reforms and improving governance in order to sustain growth opportunities outside the hydrocarbon sector. Yet transition to a market economy in Algeria has been proceeding slowly since 1998, and since 2008 has been altogether shelved. 'Reforms to improve the business environment and expand privatization have been deferred' (World Bank 2010: 12).

REFERENCES

Conseil National Economique et Social (CNES), 2003. *Rapport sur l'Evaluation des Dispositifs d'Emploi*. Algiers: CNES.

Docquier, Frederic, and Luca Marchiori, 2009. 'MENA-to-EU migration and labor market imbalances', background paper for EC-funded World Bank Program of International Migration from Middle East and North Africa and Poverty Reduction Strategies.

Hirata, Hideaki, et al., 2005. 'Sources of fluctuations: the case of MENA', available at: http://ssrn.com/abstract=812386

International Finance Corporation/World Bank (various years and regions). *Doing Business*.

Ministère de l'Enseignement Supérieur et de la Recherche Scientifique (MESRS). *Annuaires universitaires*, various years

Naude, W., and R. Rossouw, 2008. 'Export diversification and specialization in South Africa: extent and impact', WIDER Research Paper RP2008/93. Helsinki: UNU-WIDER.

Office National des Statistiques (ONS), 2011. 'Emploi et chômage au 4ème trimestre 2010: http://www.ons.dz/-donnees statistiques.html

U4 Anti-Corruption Resource Centre, 2007. Overview of Corruption in MENA countries' (7 November). Bergen.

World Bank, 2007a. *People's Democratic Republic of Algeria. A Public Expenditure Review: Assuring High Quality Public Investment*, vol. 1. Washington, DC.

—— 2007b. 'Worldwide governance indicators: gains in sub-Saharan Africa', available at: http://web.worldbank.org/WEBSITE/EXTERNAL/NEWS/0, print

—— 2009a. *Country Brief, Middle East and North Africa Region (MENA): Algeria*. Washington, DC.

—— 2009b. 'Global economic prospects 2009: Middle East and North Africa: regional outlook:', available at: http://web.worldbank.org/WEBSITE/EXTERNAL/COUNTRIES/MENAEXT/0, print.

—— 2010 (Oct.). *Economic Integration in the Maghreb*. Washington, DC.

World Economic Forum, 2009. *The Africa Competitiveness Report 2009*. Geneva.

Algeria, Egypt, Morocco, and Tunisia Development Prospects for North Africa

Ahmed Galal and Khalid Sekkat

1. Introduction

The development performance of the North Africa (NA) region over the past two decades is puzzling. On the one hand, per capita GDP and per capita growth (in PPP terms) during this period were higher than the corresponding averages for sub-Saharan Africa (SSA) but much lower than the averages for East Asia (EAP) and to a lesser extent Latin America and the Caribbean (LAC). On the other hand, the NA region fares much better than the other three regions with respect to the level of poverty. This puzzle has been noted earlier by Murshed (2008) and Robinson (2009), and our focus here is on why and whether this outcome is sustainable in the long run.

We argue that past achievements, especially in terms of low poverty rates despite modest economic growth, are primarily the result of social policies, enhanced and/or motivated by cultural factors and political considerations. In the future, further reductions in poverty are unlikely to occur without higher and more sustainable economic growth and more efficient social policies. For growth to be pro-poor and for social policies to be more equitable, however, a more inclusive governance structure is essential.

Due to data availability, we limit our analysis to Morocco, Algeria, Tunisia, and Egypt, leaving out Libya. Further, we do not discuss inequality due to measurement and comparability problems (see Bibi and Nabli forthcoming). Finally, we focus on the period from 1985 onward, as this period is characterized by the initiation or acceleration of ambitious reform programmes to accelerate economic development.

2. Past performance

On average (calculated from the information provided in Table 1), the four countries in our sample grew, in terms of per capita PPP, at 1.41% between 1985 and 2005. This rate is higher only than the average for SSA (0.21%), and, while comparable to the average for LAC (1.06%), falls far below the average for EAP (6.95%). Yet the average percentage of the poor in the population of the NA region over the period 1985–2005, measured by the ratio of headcount at $1.25 a day (PPP), was in the neighbourhood of 5% during this period, compared to 11%, 42%, and 56% in LAC, EAP, and SSA, respectively.

These averages conceal notable variations among the four countries, but do not change the overall standing of NA relative to other regions. In terms of population in 2005, Egypt is by far the largest in size (above 70 million) and Tunisia the smallest (10 million). While the same classification holds in terms of GDP, the pattern is reversed regarding per capita GDP (see Table 1). With respect to poverty, Egypt exhibits the lowest ratio (2.7% during 1985–2005). Algeria exhibits the highest ratio (6.7%), with Morocco and Tunisia falling closer to Algeria than to Egypt.

Since the mid-1980s, all four countries have for the most part experienced steady per capita growth rates, although Algeria and Tunisia did better than Egypt and Morocco. However, the growth rates were more volatile in Algeria and Morocco than in Egypt and Tunisia, largely because Algeria is highly dependent on fuel exports (36% of GDP and 97% of merchandise exports) and Morocco is highly vulnerable to fluctuations in agriculture output due to weather conditions (Sekkat 2004). Poverty declined over time in Tunisia, Morocco, and Egypt while remaining essentially unchanged in Algeria (although data are old in the latter case).

3. How did the NA region reduce poverty despite unimpressive economic growth?

Given that growth rates in the region have not been as impressive as those in East Asia, what might explain the low levels of poverty? Available evidence suggests that social policies, cultural factors, and political considerations lie behind observed low levels of poverty.

With respect to social policies, a first approximation can be gathered from the share of government expenditure in percentage of GDP. By this measure, the NA region spent 15.6% over the period 2000–2005, which is slightly lower than the corresponding average of 16.8% for SSA but higher than the averages for EAP (13.8%) and LA (14.9). More important perhaps is that NA countries have sustained a variety of pro poor social policies for decades. For example, education has been provided free despite the shift since the mid-1980s from a state-led development strategy to a market- and private sector-based strategy. In the majority

Table 1. Growth and poverty in North Africa compared with other developing regions, 1985–2005

GDP per capita, PPP (constant 2000 international $)

	1985	1990	1995	2000	2005
Algeria	5,983	5,430	4,920	5,327	6,283
Egypt	2,554	2,799	3,003	3,526	3,858
Morocco	2,984	3,338	3,180	3,578	4,052
Tunisia	4,502	4,633	5,098	6,276	7,447
North Africa	3,541	3,634	3,625	4,137	4,685
Latin America & Caribbean		6,035	6,591	7,102	7,482
Sub-Saharan Africa		1,678	1,551	1,611	1,774
East Asia & Pacific		1,857	2,854	3,747	5,384

Average growth of GDP per capita, PPP (constant 2000 international $)

	1985–2005	1985–1990	1990–1995	1995–2000	2000–2005
Algeria	0.24	−1.92	−1.95	1.60	3.36
Egypt	2.08	1.84	1.42	3.26	1.82
Morocco	1.54	2.27	−0.97	2.39	2.52
Tunisia	2.55	0.58	1.93	4.25	3.48
North Africa	1.41	0.52	−0.05	2.68	2.52
Latin America & Caribbean	1.06	−0.06	1.78	1.50	1.05
Sub-Saharan Africa	0.21	−0.28	−1.56	0.76	1.94
East Asia & Pacific	6.95	5.76	8.97	5.59	7.52

Poverty headcount ratio at $1.25 a day (PPP) (% of population)

	1985	1990	1995	2000	2005
Algeria		6.61	6.79		
Egypt		4.46	2.46	1.81	1.99
Morocco	8.42	2.45	6.76	6.25	2.50
Tunisia	8.65	5.87	6.48	2.55	
North Africa	8.48	4.62	4.64	3.06	2.14
Latin America & Caribbean	15.25	11.32	10.94	10.89	8.22
Sub-Saharan Africa	55.84	57.58	58.78	58.37	50.91
East Asia & Pacific	65.50	54.72	36.00	35.51	16.78

Source: World Development Indicators (WDI) and http://iresearch.worldbank.org/PovcalNet/povcalSvy.html

of cases, free access at all levels is guaranteed by virtue of the constitutions. In recent years, private provision of education has been allowed in some countries (e.g. Egypt) but the earlier commitment remained (World Bank 2008). Similar policies have been put into effect with respect to health and infrastructure services. And NA countries have had multiple safety net programmes, especially for those who cannot earn an income for reasons of age, handicap, etc. In some cases, commodity subsidies are used heavily (e.g. in Egypt and Morocco).

Turning to cultural and religious factors, a number of studies pointed out that the region is more amenable to sharing of wealth than other regions. For example, Gradstein, Milanovic, and Ying (2001) suggested that across the diverse cultural/religious types in the world, built-in inequality aversion is strongest in Muslim-majority countries. The Islamic charitable practices of *zakat* and *sada'qa* seem to enhance private social responsibility, and to have a poverty-reducing impact (Sala-i-Martín and Artadi 2002).[1]

On the political front, Desai, Olofsgård, and Yousef (2007) suggested that observed redistributive policies in the region can be traced to politics. Focusing on non-democratic regimes in general, the authors sought to explain how such regimes stay in power. Considering that repression—the classic answer—is not the best strategy, they suggest that some redistribution to citizens might be necessary to secure and maintain citizen loyalty. Following this approach, NA regimes would prefer welfare spending to circumvent pressures rather than to liberalize politically. The authors' empirical tests support the validity of this thesis.

4. The prospects of growth and poverty reduction in NA

The preceding section suggested that the NA countries' track record in terms of poverty reduction owes less to growth *per se* and more to social policies as well as to cultural and political economy considerations. It is not apparent that past strategies will work well in the future.

Social policies cannot be sustained without strong economic growth: sooner or later, countries will be forced to comply with the 'law of macroeconomic equilibria' (budget and external balances). Moreover, these policies can be reversed suddenly depending on the whims of the rulers. Remittances, especially those coming from the Arabian Gulf countries, are too volatile to be relied on as the main instrument for poverty reduction. The experience of the early 1980s and the Gulf war in 1991 validates this point. While social solidarity (taking the form of *zakat* and *sada'qa*) is likely to remain a feature of the region into the foreseeable future, it is difficult to ascertain how many transfers will take place and whether the allocation of these transfers is optimal nationwide. Finally, with political liberalization the world over, following the collapse of socialism and the spread of democracy in Latin America and Asia, it is difficult to sustain less than inclusive political systems.

It follows that more rapid growth is probably the most reliable mechanism to prosperity. For growth to be pro-poor, however, it has to be sufficiently high to permit the continuation of smarter social policies. And none of the above will be possible without three things: (i) further economic reforms, (ii) more efficient social policies, and (iii) more inclusive governance structure.

---

[1] Note that *zakat* is not insignificant, as it amounts to 2.5% of a person's wealth and assets, owned for a full lunar year, including money, crops, harvests, herds, gold and silver, and merchandise excluding dwelling and items of personal use.

4.1. GROWTH

Taking *The Growth Report* (Commission on Growth and Development 2008) as a reference point, three fundamental policy and institutional preconditions seem to make a big difference for factor accumulation (human and physical capital) and for total factor productivity (TFP) growth: competition (internal and external), macroeconomic stability, and sound institutional framework and good governance.

Over the past two decades, progress has been made. However, the pro-growth reform agenda remains unfinished (for elaboration, see Easterly 2002; Makdissi, Fattah, and Limam 2006; Sekkat 2004; 2008).

- In term of competition, openness to trade ratio[2] rose markedly in NA (18 percentage points) between 1985 and 2005. However, the performance of individual countries is uneven, showing improvements in Tunisia and Morocco, stagnation in Algeria, and deterioration in Egypt. Turning to domestic competition, the Egyptian, Moroccan, and Tunisian[3] industries exhibit, in general, high mark-ups and high concentration ratios (Sekkat 2008). These ratios are higher than those in comparable countries (e.g. Turkey).

- With respect to macroeconomic stability and exchange rate regimes, inflation has been modest in the region and on the decline since 1985. In 2005, maximum inflation was 2.6% except in Algeria (5%). Regarding exchange rate management, Nouira, Plane, and Sekkat (2009), focusing on the period 1990–2005, found very high overvaluation of the pound (Egypt) but almost no misalignment of the dirham (Morocco) and the dinar (Tunisia).

- Finally, with respect to institutions, the World Bank's indicators of governance do not favour the region. On a scale ranging between −2.5 and +2.5 (higher values signal better governance), the region scores −0.35 on average over 1994–2005 compared with −0.12 for LAC, −0.39 for EAP, and −0.63 in SSA. Again, there are marked differences among the four countries (from a score of 0.10 in Tunisia to −1.08 in Algeria).

4.2. SOCIAL POLICIES

Clearly, sustained economic growth will help NA countries in affording to continue past social policies by relaxing private and public budget constraints.[4] However, there might be a need to rethink the kind of policies to adopt more emphasis on their outcome and effectiveness. There is ample evidence showing that the outcomes of past policies

---

[2] We use the ratio of imports plus exports (excluding oil) divided by GDP.

[3] The study covers the period 1980–2003. Due to lack of data availability, Algeria was not covered in this study.

[4] Note also that some growth-promoting policies might hurt the poor and should, therefore, be accompanied by redistributive policies to avoid their marginalization.

have been largely inefficient and even inequitable. For example, Galal (2006) shows that social expenditure in Egypt was poorly targeted, inefficient, and involved high transaction costs. El-Araby (2009) finds that spending on basic education in the region tends to favour the poorest households, but spending on universities and vocational training strongly favours the rich. Moreover, the distribution of schooling years was found to be biased against the poor, women, and rural people in Egypt (Datt, Jolliffe, and Sharma 1998) and Morocco (Abdelkhalek 2005). Regarding food subsidies, targeting errors, leakage, and undercoverage seem to be widespread. Cornia and Stewart (1995) find that, while in Egypt and Tunisia food subsidies show very low exclusion rates, leakage rates are large. They suggested that leakages could be significantly reduced, while maintaining negligible undercoverage, by concentrating the subsidy on a specific good (i.e. hard wheat). Laraki (1989), examining the welfare impact of various consumption subsidies reforms in Morocco, concluded that the country should move toward the removal of current subsidies and development of low-priced 'inferior' goods. The latter would decrease the cost of subsidies without hurting the poor.

In recognition of the above problems, tighter budget constraints, and the drying up of resources, policymakers in the region are increasingly concerned with reforming their social policies. Reform initiatives are under way in several countries, but the pace of these reforms is slow and fear of change is proving problematic. Their success depends not only on the willingness of governments to achieve equitable development but also on their ability to counter the opposition of potentially powerful groups. This, in turn, depends on building a more inclusive governance structure in these countries.

4.3. GOVERNANCE STRUCTURE

Olson (2000) argued that there is no way of understanding the extreme poverty of many nations without taking account of the extent to which they are misgoverned. Accordingly, good governance depends on the extent to which the ruling authority is inclusive. Dictatorship is superior to anarchy because the dictator has some encompassing interests in the society he/she rules. Democracy is superior to dictatorship because democratic majorities are more encompassing than the interest of the dictator. And, apart from any moral considerations, the above assertion is validated by empirical evidence. For example, Gradstein et al. (2001) suggest that democratization tends to reduce inequality through redistribution when the poor outvote the rich.

The problem in the region is that governance structure is too exclusive. According to the Freedom House Index, which combines the degrees of political rights and civil liberties, the NA region is classified as partially free, with an average score of 5.4

(a country is classified as not free if the index is between 5.5 and 7). In fact, only Morocco is considered as partially free, while the other three countries are classified as not free. Since 1972, the date of the publication of the first index, the score for the region has remained unchanged.

Some progress is being made with respect to political openness, although it is still not showing up in international indices. In Egypt and Morocco, for example, multi-party systems have been introduced, independent media are emerging, and non-governmental organizations are more active than before. However, the peaceful transfer of power remains problematic, full representation is questionable, and term limits are being relaxed to accommodate incumbent leaders. In short, democratization is in the making, but the road ahead may be long.

5. Concluding remarks

In this short chapter, we have sought to explain why the NA region has been successful in reducing poverty despite modest economic growth, and have attempted to speculate about whether past strategies are sustainable in the future. We have provided some evidence in support of the notion that low poverty in the region can be traced to social policies, cultural characteristics, and the nature of political regimes. Furthermore, we have argued that this favourable outcome is not likely to be sustainable in the future without higher economic growth, improvements of social policies, and more inclusive governance structures.

■ REFERENCES

Abdelkhalek, T., 2005. *La Pauvreté au Maroc. Rapport du Cinquantenaire sur 50 ans de développement humain au Maroc*: http://www.rdh50.ma/fr/pdf/contributions/GT7-1.pdf.

Bibi, S., and M. Nabli, forthcoming. 'Equity and inequality in the Arab region', Policy Research Report 33. Cairo: Economic Research Forum.

Commission on Growth and Development, 2008. *The Growth Report*. Washington, DC: World Bank.

Cornia, G. A., and F. Stewart, 1995. 'Two errors of targeting', in D. Van de Walle and K. Nead (eds), *Public Spending and the Poor: Theory and Evidence*. Baltimore, Md.: Johns Hopkins University Press, 350–86.

Datt, G., D. Jolliffe, and M. Sharma, 1998. 'A profile of poverty in Egypt, 1997', FCND Discussion Paper 49. Washington, DC: International Food Policy Research Institute.

Desai, R. M., A. Olofsgård, and T. M. Yousef, 2007. 'The logic of authoritarian bargains: a test of a structural model', Global Economy and Development Working Paper 3. Washington, DC: Brookings Institution.

Easterly, W., 2002. *The Elusive Quest for Growth: Economists' Adventures and Misadventures in the Tropics*. Cambridge, Mass.: MIT Press.

El-Araby, A., 2009. 'Access and equity in higher education: a comparative assessment of financing policies in six Arab countries', paper presented at the ERF Regional Conference on Financing Higher Education, 17–18 June, Amman.

Galal A., 2006. 'Social expenditures and the poor in Egypt', in Ahmed Galal and Nadeem Ul Haque (eds), *Fiscal Sustainability in Emerging Markets*. Cairo: American University Press.

Gradstein, M., B. Milanovic, and Y. Ying, 2001. 'Democracy and income inequality: an empirical analysis', Policy Research Paper 2561. Washington, DC: World Bank.

Laraki, K., 1989. 'Food subsidies: a case study of price reform in Morocco', LSMS Working Paper 50, Washington, DC: World Bank.

Makdissi S., Z. Fattah, and I. Limam, 2006. 'Determinants of growth in the MENA countries', in Jeff Nugent and Hashem Pesaran (eds), *Explaining Growth in the MENA Region*. Amsterdam: North-Holland.

Murshed, S. M., 2008. 'Development despite modest growth in the Middle East', *Review of Middle East Economics and Finance* 4.

Nouira, R., P. Plane, and Kh. Sekkat, 2009. 'Exchange rate undervaluation and export diversification: a deliberate strategy?', mimeo, University of Brussels.

Olson M., 2000. *Power and Prosperity: Outgrowing Communist and Capitalist Dictators*. New York: Basic Books.

Robinson, J., 2009. 'The political economy of inequality', Working Paper 493. Cairo: Economic Research Forum.

Sala-i-Martín, X., and E. V Artadi, 2002. 'Economic growth and investment in the Arab world', Columbia University Department of Economics Discussion Paper 0203–0208.

Sekkat, Kh., 2004. 'Sources of growth in Morocco: an empirical analysis in a regional perspective', *Review of Middle East Economics and Finance* 2, 1–17.

—— (ed.), 2008. *Competition and Efficiency in the Arab World*. Basingstoke: Palgrave Macmillan.

World Bank, 2008. *The Road Not Traveled: Education Reform in the MENA Region*. Washington, DC: World Bank.

Angola
China-Led Reconstruction

Ana Santana

1. Introduction

Situated in Southern Africa, Angola is the seventh largest country in the continent, with 335 miles of coastline on the Atlantic Ocean and borders with the Democratic Republic of the Congo, Zambia, and Namibia. It has a total population estimated at 15 million people, about a third of whom live in the capital city, Luanda. The country's official language is Portuguese.

After gaining independence from Portugal in 1975, Angola was immersed in a civil war for the next three decades, during which most of the country's infrastructure was destroyed, an estimated one million people died, and about one third of the population fled to neighbouring countries or were internally displaced. Sustained peace was only attained in 2002, and the country has since been registering notable improvements in its reconstruction and economic performance, although still presenting poor social development indicators.

2. Economic structure

Angola's economy is dominated by the oil sector. With an output of two million barrels of crude per day, oil production accounts for about 93.4% of total exports, 77.2% of government revenue, and 62.0% of GDP. Angola's GDP, averaging a real growth rate of around 18.5% in the last four years, has doubled every third year, from $19.8 billion in 2004 to $60.4 billion in 2007. In 2007, that rate peaked at 22.3%, reflecting a real growth of 20.4% in the oil sector and 25.7% in the non-oil sectors, including growth of 37% in construction, 32.6% in manufacturing, and 27.4% in agriculture.

Apart from oil, other minerals exploited in the country include diamonds, iron ore, phosphate, copper, gold, and bauxite. There is also a growing manufacturing sector with light industries. The agricultural sector employs most of the population but accounts for just 9.6% of GDP.

3. Policy issues

As a result of its GDP growth rates in recent years, Angola has now one of the highest levels of income per capita in sub-Saharan Africa, having progressively risen from $959 in 2003 to $3,595 in 2007, and reached $5,632 in 2010.

Nevertheless, the country still exhibits high poverty levels: UNDP data shows that it has a human development index ranked at 162 among 177 countries, an infant mortality rate of 154 per 1,000 live births, a probability of not surviving till the age of 40 of 46.7%, an adult illiteracy rate of 32.6%, while 47% of the population does not have access to an improved water source and overall unemployment rates affect about 40% of the active workforce.

Arguably, these indicators are symptomatic of the syndrome in the Angolan economy, common to many oil exporters, whereby the oil sector does not have significant multiplier effects in the rest of the economy, particularly in terms of employment generation and improvement of the majority of the population's living conditions.

In Angola, the situation is largely explained by the observed deficient levels of transparency and accountability of government's revenue management and distribution, within an institutional framework slowly evolving from a centrally controlled economic structure to a market-based one, in a country with a precarious democratic system where institutions are generally weak and general elections have taken place on only two occasions since independence—in 1992 and 2008.

Reflecting that reality, Transparency International ranks Angola 147 out of 179 countries in its Corruption Perception Index; the Bertelsmann Transformation Index—which measures economic and political development towards democracy and free markets—rates it 104 among 119 countries surveyed in 2006; and the World Bank places the country in the lower decile in terms of regulatory quality, rule of law, and control of corruption.

In terms of financial indicators, while in the process of opening its first stock exchange, Angola was ranked 79 among 141 countries in the UNCTAD Inward Potential Performance Index for 2003–5, placed at 114 among 122 countries in the Milken Institute Capital Access Index, and rated 2.4/10.0 in the 2005 Index for Banking Efficiency by the World Bank, which also ranked the country 167 out of 178 in its Ease of Doing Business Index. These indicators are also associated with the observed institutional weaknesses and low levels of transparency and accountability prevailing in the country.

4. Major developments

It is against this backdrop that a major development has been taking place in Angola over the last five years: China's growing involvement in the country's economy.

Economic relations between the two parties are shaped around a series of bilateral agreements, involving successive credit lines extended by China to Angola since 2004, currently amounting to an estimated $9 billion, mainly to finance reconstruction projects included in Angola's public investments programme (PIP) in exchange for oil and other mineral exports, and requiring that 70% of all inputs to be used in the projects under these credit lines are sourced from China, in what has become known in some quarters as the 'Angolan Model'.

The intensification of economic relations between the two countries to their current level came after the unsuccessful attempt by the Angolan government to convene an international donors' conference to source financing for the country's reconstruction in the aftermath of its protracted civil war. That setback was attributable to a failure by the Angolan government to reach an agreement with the IMF on such politically sensitive issues as transparency, good governance, and respect for human rights, imposed by that international financial institution (IFI) and by Angola's Western partners generally, as a precondition to the concession of any further loans to the country.

More recently, however, Angola's political and economic relations with its Western partners and the IFIs have registered significant improvement, as evidenced by a number of official visits to the country by Western dignitanies such as US Secretary of State Hillary Clinton, German Chancellor Angela Merkel and French President Nicolas Sarkozy, during which agreements spanning a number of economic and social sectors have been signed.

In conclusion, it is expected that, given some political, institutional, and social conditions yet to be fully met, and with its international partners' technical and financial cooperation, the Angolan economy can look forward to a promising future.

Benin
When Poor Economic Diversification is an Impediment to Poverty Alleviation

Yazid Dissou

1. Introduction[1]

From a historical perspective, the growth performance of Benin's economy has been remarkable during the last twenty years, 4.4% on average between 1988 and 2008. It has experienced a relatively strong growth rate since 1990, which marks the end of the militaro-marxist regime that lasted for 17 years and the beginning of the democratic era in Benin.

This growth performance is encouraging since it can now be likened to those achieved by other non-African developing countries. Nevertheless, this performance did not translate into a significant reduction of poverty in Benin, as the number of poor remains high. Insufficient diversification of the economy, high dependence on a single export crop, and the atrophy of the manufacturing sector constitute the main impediments to the achievement of high growth rates that are required for a significant reduction in poverty. This note reviews Benin's recent experience in economic growth and in poverty alleviation. It also discusses the main obstacles experienced so far and the challenges lying ahead in reducing poverty in Benin.

2. Snapshot of Benin's economy

Benin is a small country in West Africa, with a population of 7.6 million in mid-2006. It is a low-income country with a GDP per capita $US828 (2008). Composition of Benin's GDP is marked by the predominance of the service sector, which contributes 48% of the country's GDP, followed by the agricultural sector, accounting for 38%, and a weak

---

[1] I would like to thank Selma Djidic for her research assistance.

industrial sector contributing only 14% of GDP. Although Benin is well positioned geographically, as it serves its neighbouring landlocked countries through its deep-water port, the country is yet to exploit its full potential in that sector. The weak inter-industrial links within the economy are reflected in the high proportion of imports of intermediate inputs used by the manufacturing sector. Agriculture accounts for the majority of export earnings and employment. Benin's export earnings are dominated by a single crop—cotton—which represents on average 60% of its overall export proceeds.

The economy of Benin is characterized by the predominance of the re-exports sector to Nigeria and the other neighbouring landlocked countries, such as Niger and Burkina Faso, where business people take advantage of differences in regulations and trade policies between Benin and its neighbours. Unofficial estimates suggest that re-export activities represent more than 5% of Benin GDP, and constitute a significant source of trade taxes that account for more than 40% of government's trade revenue.

3. Snapshot of economic growth in Benin

Average economic growth in Benin declined from 4.5% between 1991 and 2000 to 4.0% between 2000 and 2006. This performance is mainly due to the economic liberalization performed in the early 1990s and devaluation of the CFA franc relative to the French franc in 1994. Overall, Benin's economic growth was not uniform during the whole period beginning in 1990. A relatively high growth rate was recorded between 1990 and 2001, peaking at 6.1% in 2001. Growth in this period was fuelled by a strong growth in agricultural production (cotton) and in services sector (transit activities, i.e., re-exports to Nigeria). The subsequent decline in economic growth was caused by several factors including a negative terms-of-trade shock, reduced demand for re-exports by Nigeria, and a fall in cotton production due to climatic perturbations.

4. Recent experience in poverty reduction and associated economic challenges

Despite improvements in the macroeconomic conditions in Benin, there has not been much progress in poverty alleviation. Poverty is still mostly prevalent in the rural areas, where it has increased, while registering slight decreases across the urban areas. Abstracting from the obstacles posed in translating economic growth into poverty alleviation in Benin, the growth performance in recent history is not sufficient to reduce poverty significantly. According to the IMF, an annual growth in GDP of at least 7% is required to achieve a sustainable reduction in Benin's poverty rate.

The average growth rate achieved by Benin between 1991 and 2006 was 4.2%. While the *macroeconomic* environment has improved in the country since the early in 1990s, the insufficient growth recorded in Benin could partly be attributed to the poor *microeconomic* environment of the country. A World Bank's analysis[2] suggests that labour productivity in Benin is very low in comparison to other countries in the region like Mali. Benin's low labour productivity is related inter alia, to its poor educational system, and the inadequacy between supply and demand for labour.

The most important obstacles to higher growth in Benin are threefold—insufficient diversification of the economy, Benin's high vulnerability to external shocks, and the atrophy of the manufacturing sector. The last obstacle, in particular, is partly related to Benin's inability to take full advantage of its giant neighbour (Nigeria) and to solve the challenges that are related to proximity. Nigeria is an unexploited large market for exports of manufactured goods produced in Benin, but currently the latter country only takes advantage of the transit activities to the former. Yet re-export activities toward that country constitute a challenge for the development of a viable domestic manufacturing sector in Benin because of two main reasons.

First, the development of re-export activities draws resources (financial and qualified workers) from other sectors, mainly the manufacturing sector. Second, and more importantly, the depreciation of Nigerian currency (the Naira) boosts the imports of Nigerian manufacturing goods in Benin. This is because re-exports activities between Benin and Nigeria occur in an informal market, using currencies that are traded in a parallel market. An increase in the demand by Nigeria for Benin's re-exports is matched by an increase in the supply of their currency in the parallel foreign exchange market. The latter puts downward pressure on its value and leads to a depreciation of the Nigerian currency. In return, the depreciation of Naira increases the imports of Nigerian manufactured goods, and eventually hurts the development of a viable manufacturing sector.

Removing these obstacles is a prerequisite for achieving a steady economic growth rate that would have a significant impact on poverty alleviation.

---

[2] Banque Mondiale (2005), 'Benin: Une évaluation du climat des investissements', Programme régional sur le développement des entreprises, Washington, DC.

Botswana
Diamonds, Relative Prices, and Growth Experience

Ita Mannathoko

1. Introduction

The growth story emerging from Botswana's short economic history is instructive. The real exchange rate and its effect on the relative productivity of different sectors have played a central role in explaining growth episodes (alongside prudent mineral resource management).

2. Central role of the real exchange rate

The real exchange rate is a pervasive relative price[1] that mirrors the relative productivity of different sectors. In Botswana's economy, characterized by double-digit unemployment and by market and institutional imperfections, non-mining sector growth is influenced by the speed with which policymakers shift underemployed labour out of subsistence and informal activities—both of which are of low productivity—into higher-productivity activities. Botswana's real exchange rate has played a central role in this process. When devalued, it compensated for market and institutional failures that rendered the economy uncompetitive. It stimulated growth and job creation by correcting relative prices.

Botswana's experience corroborates Dani Rodrik's evidence that in developing economies, while overvaluation of the real exchange rate hurts growth, undervaluation stimulates it (Rodrik 2008).[2] Rodrik found close relationships between undervaluation and rapid growth in China, India, Asian tigers such as South Korea, Taiwan, and various African countries. Conversely, growth slowdowns were accompanied either by increasing overvaluation or by reduced undervaluation. Causality ran from undervaluation to growth.

In Botswana, non-mining, non-government real GDP growth has mirrored appreciation and depreciation of the *real* effective exchange rate to an uncanny degree (Table 1).

---

[1] Relationship established empirically for Botswana: see Mannathoko, Atta, and Jefferis (1996).
[2] This relationship, however, disappears when Rodrik limits his sample to developed countries.

Table 1. The real exchange rate, productivity, and growth

Period	Real exchange rate chronology	Non-mining non-government GDP growth and productivity
1983–8	Steep depreciation of the pula real effective exchange rate	Growth recovery; very rapid growth from −7% to over 20%.
1988–93	Real pula appreciation, abolition of exchange controls	Growth reversal; growth dropping to −5% in 1993
1993–8	Real pula depreciation	Growth recovery; productivity increased.
1998–2004	Sharp real pula appreciation, by over 20%	Growth reversal; productivity decreased.
2004–08	Real pula depreciation from 2004	Growth recovery; productivity increased.
	Was real devaluation effective?	*Was prior inflation trend supportive?*
1983–8	May 1982 – Yes. Real devaluation sustained to end 1983.	Yes – Imported South African inflation was on a downward trend from early 1982 through end 1983.
	July 1984 – No. Reversed by inflation, real appreciation in the first half of 1985.	No – Imported South African inflation was on a sharp upward trend from the start of 1984 through end of 1985.
	Early 1985 – Yes. After initial marginal reversal, sustained from end 1985.	Yes – From end 1985, imported South African inflation declined from end 1985, reversing upward trend in 1985.
	January 1986 – Yes. Real devaluation sustained through 1988.	Yes – Imported South African inflation was on a downward trend from early 1986 through mid-1988.
1988–93	August 1990 – Yes. Real devaluation initially sustained.	Yes – Imported South African inflation remained relatively flat from end 1989 and to end 1990.
	August 1991 – No. Devaluation was inflationary. Real devaluation reversed by real appreciation.	No – Domestic inflation surged upward from early 1991 to early 1992, overshadowing downward trend for imported South African inflation from end 1991 through 1993.
1993–98	1994 real devaluation sustained.	Yes – Downward trend in imported South African inflation
1998–04	Change in policy stance, via much wider exchange rate band, allowed substantial appreciation/revaluation.	Despite sizeable pula revaluation annual average inflation rose from 6.4% in 1998 to over 11% in 2002 as government, consumer and retail sectors overheated
2004–08	2004 and 2005 – Real devaluations partially sustained up until global food and oil price shocks escalated.	Yes – Imported inflation on a downward trend. However, non-tradables inflation's downward trend not sustained. Global oil and food price shocks inflationary in 2008.

3. Relative productivity of sectors

The outcomes of exchange rate policies adopted in National Development Plan 7 (NDP7) and NDP8 differ distinctly. In NDP7 (1993/4–1998/9), productivity rose across the board,[3] especially in non-mining sectors including finance and business—consistent

---

[3] See Botswana National Productivity Centre (2007).

with the real pula depreciation. Advances were made in diversification. Rapid growth in the non-mining private sector led to a sustained decline in the share of mining in GDP. Shares of commerce, finance and business, health and education, rose noticeably. Manufacturing maintained a stable share in GDP, despite problems in significant industry sections due to challenges with trade agreements and the ending of some investor subsidies.

By contrast, in NDP8 sharp real pula appreciation stifled productivity in non-mining sectors. Sectoral productivity trends and progress in diversification were reversed. Mining's share in GDP rose back to pre-NDP7 levels with a sizable expansion in diamond production, even as the change in relative prices lowered the profitability of other tradable goods and service sectors. This adverse trend for non-mining sector profitability continued until the 2004/5 real pula devaluations, two years into NDP9.

4. Transitioning out of diamond dependency

Botswana is transitioning out of diamond dependency at a relatively high per capita income, with a wage that is high relative to the skills and productivity of many workers. The experience of economies that have successfully diversified on the back of primary product exports suggests deliberate measures are necessary to raise productivity, improve competitiveness, and encourage linkages beyond the mining economy. Mineral processing and utilization, alongside exploitation, characterized Industrial Revolution Lancashire and thereafter the Ruhr and the industrial Midwest of the USA (Greasley and Madsen 2008). Relative price effects, therefore, are important. In addition to the right real exchange rate, therefore, linkages that encourage cross-fertilization between industries, ensuring that the knowledge, research, and skill stock interacts with the mineral endowment, will enhance the size of the multiplier for output in total factor productivity (Romer 1987).

Botswana will need to build such linkages, engaging young talent in innovative, knowledge and technology based activities that employ the country's emerging demographic dividend (dominant youth population).

Looking forward:

- Relative prices have a key role in development planning for transition out of diamond dependence.
- Real pula depreciation is necessary to compensate for market imperfections and increase the relative profitability of investment in non-traditional tradable goods and services.
- Productivity is as important to growth as the quantity of labour and capital used, making technology, skills, education quality, and their interaction with mineral endowment especially important.

REFERENCES

Botswana National Productivity Centre, 2007. Botswana Productivity Statistics Update.

Greasley, D., and J. B. Madsen, 2010. 'Curse and boon: natural resources and long run growth in currently rich economies', *Economic Record* 86.274, 311–28.

Mannathoko, I., J. K. Atta, and K. R. Jefferis, 1996. 'Small country experiences with exchange rates and inflation: the case of Botswana', *Oxford Journal of African Economies* 5.2, 293–326.

Rodrik, Dani, 2008. 'The real exchange rate and economic growth', *Brookings Papers on Economic Activity* (Fall).

Romer, P., 1987. 'Crazy explanations for the productivity slowdown', in *NBER Macroeconomic Annual*. Cambridge, Mass.: MIT Press, 163–202.

Burkina Faso Economic and Growth Perspectives

Amadou Sidibé and Yamssekre Tiendrébeogo

1. Introduction

As in most African countries, growth of GDP in Burkina Faso has been robust over the last twenty years. However, trend breaks have been observed, mainly because of adverse exogenous factors like the strong appreciation/depreciation of the dollar, rising oil prices, heavy rains and floods, the falling world price of cotton, subregional political instability, inflation of food prices on the international market, and, more recently, the international fincancial and economic crisis. Their effects on the socioeconomic situation in Burkina were relatively moderate over the period 2001–2007.

2. Overview of economic statistics during the period 2001–2007

The average annual growth rate reached 5.8% over 2001–2007, and resulted in an increase in real income per capita of around 2.7% per year. This growth was driven by all sectors, especially the service sector, whose contribution to the growth rate of GDP was 2.8 percentage points during the review period. This dynamism of the service sector is mainly the result of an expansion of commercial activities—those relating to telecommunication as well as to transport. The industry/manufacturing sector, whose contribution to the real growth of GDP was on average 1.5 percentage points per year during the period, was mainly driven by the mining industries, drinks, and tobacco. The agriculture sector, 65% of which is driven by livestock farming, contributed up to 1.2 percentage points to this growth.

This economic performance took place in a context of relative price stability, which rose less than 3%, essentially due to government measures and good performance in agricultural production. At the same time the public financial situation has worsened, because of the rise of public expenditure in order to support the implementation of the strategic framework designed to reduce poverty and limit the effects of global shocks on the macroeconomic performance of the country. As for the balance of payments, it is marked by a strong influence of external impacts. Despite the rise in the export value of gold, the current account deficit of the balance of payments has increased on average by 6.3% during the period 2001–2007 because of the strong rise in oil imports and the drop in the world price of cotton.

3. Impact of the economic and financial crisis

Since 2007, unfavourable exogenous factors have multiplied or been exacerbated, with the food crises, the rise in the oil price, and the global financial crisis affecting the socioeconomic performance of Burkina Faso. This global crisis affected the Burkinabe economy in several ways. The latest economic statistics shows a trend break in 2009 (3.1%) of the growth of the GDP, while 2008 was marked by demonstrations against 'the expensive life' (inflation rate of 10.7%) challenging the achievements of macroeconomic stability in Burkina. The recent economic performance in Burkina and the short-term perspectives suffer from the effect of the financial crisis. It has led to a decrease in the economic growth rate in 2008 and a stagnation in real income per capita.

The increase of oil and food prices led to inflation in 2008 and a loss in competitiveness for several companies in 2009. The deficit of the current account balance relative to GDP was estimated at 12.7% in 2009, an increase of 4.8 points compared to 2008. The budgetary measures taken by the government to deal with the effect of the international financial crisis on vulnerable populations translated into an increase in total public expenditure that recovery efforts were not able to balance in 2009. As to the external balance during 2008 and 2009, one notes a contraction of export revenues of 18% compared to 2007 and a contraction of private transfers of 1.9% in 2009. In the same way, the financial sector showed a decrease of 2.8% in credits to the economy, thus damaging appropriate financing of the private sector in Burkina.

Consequently, there was a deterioration of living conditions for households, and a questioning of the achievements of the fight against poverty. Based on macroeconomic estimations, the percentage of population living below the poverty line in 2008 increased to 42.8%, the highest since 2003–4. The increase in the poverty rate in 2007–8 was followed by an increase in depth and severity of poverty, so that the challenge of reducing poverty appears to be more difficult.

4. Prospects for economic growth

The impact of the crisis may be more persistent on the economy of Burkina Faso, but due to good rainfall and farming conditions as well as a continuing structural reforms in the agricultural sector, GDP growth is expected to rise to 5.2% in 2010.

The economic performance before the financial crisis for a relatively long period shows that, without the heavy adverse exogenous shocks, economic growth would have been robust and sustainable. In light of these considerations, the country has undertaken a project to review in depth its growth strategy, on the basis of the strategic framework to fight poverty (CSLP). This new strategy will consolidate the lessons learned from the earlier CSLP while focusing on accelerating and sustainable economic growth. The strategy aims to reduce the vulnerability of the Burkinabe economy through better rainfall risk control, and hence to bring about an increase of agricultural production, improvement of human capital, diversification of exports, reduction of factor costs, support for small and medium enterprises, and effective social protection. This programme, which extends over the 2011–2015 period, will allow double-digit economic growth from 2012. However, as noted earlier, this economic growth may still be affected by a number of risks related to the international and regional environments.

Burundi
Challenges and Opportunities for Post-conflict Reconstruction

Léonce Ndikumana

1. Introduction

Located at the heart of Africa, Burundi is one of the smallest and most populated nations on the continent,[1] and one of the poorest in the world (per capita income of $140: see Table 1).[2] From its independence in 1961,[3] the country was ruled by military regimes up to the transition to democracy starting with the elections in 1993 which were followed by a long civil war.[4,5] The negotiations to end the war yielded the Arusha Peace and Reconciliation Agreement, establishing a coalition government in 2000 and leading to democratic elections in 2005. The country faces development challenges including unfavourable geography (small, landlocked, limited natural resources), poor infrastructure,[6] a conflict-prone neighbourhood, and the legacy of ethnic conflict. Burundi is nonetheless a rare African case of successful transition from civil war.

---

[1] Burundi is the home of 8.5 million people on a territory of 27,800 km². It shares borders with Tanzania in the east, Rwanda in the north, and the Democratic Republic of Congo in the west.

[2] Burundi ranked number 174 out of 179 countries on the UNDP Human Development Index scale in 2007.

[3] Burundi was colonized by Belgium. However, unlike other countries, the Burundian nation is not a creation of colonization. It existed as a monarchy headed by a dynasty of kings or *Abami* (singular *Umwami*) until 1966.

[4] Burundi was ruled by the following military regimes: 28 Nov. 1966–1 Nov. 1976 (Michel Micombero); 2 Nov. 1976–3 Sept. 1987 (Jean Baptiste Bagaza); 4 Nov. 1987–9 July 1993 (Pierre Buyoya); 25 July 1996–29 Apr. 2003 (Pierre Buyoya).

[5] A new constitution establishing a multiparty system was adopted in March 1992.

[6] The stock of infrastructure is both inadequate and of poor quality. In particular, transport costs are very high, representing 35% of import prices and 40% of export prices of agricultural commodities (AfDB 2009).

Table 1. Burundi: social and economic development indicators

Indicator	Burundi	Year	Africa
Population (million)	8.1	2008	986
Size	27,800 km²	–	30,323 km²
Density	314	2008	32.6
Per capita GDP (constant 2000 US$)	111	2008	–
GNI per capita (Atlas method, current US$)	140	2008	1,428
Life expectancy (years)	48.9	2006	54.5
HDI rank	174/179	2007	–
Gender-related development index	147/175	2006	–
Poverty: % below $1.25/day	81.3	2000–06	34
Poverty: % below national poverty line	68	2000–07	–
Underweight children (% of under-5s)	68	2005	25
Adult literacy rate (%)			
Female	52.2	2000	47 (2005)
Male	67.3		29 (2005)
Total	59.3		38 (2005)

Sources: UNDP, *Human Development Report* 2008; FAO, FAOSTAT (online); World Bank, World Development Indicators; World Bank, African Development Bank database.

2. Political instability: making a historical turn from ethnic conflicts

The early postcolonial period in Burundi was marked by intense elite competition and political tensions along ethnic (Hutu elite vs. Tutsi elite) and regional lines (Muramvya vs. Bururi).[7] Tensions also arose within the royal family between the proponents of independence, led by Prince Louis Rwagasore, and those who advocated the status quo. In the meantime, the king failed to mediate elite disputes, which further eroded social cohesion and fuelled tensions between the Tutsi and Hutu elites, sowing the seeds for the ethnic conflicts that would eventually erupt in 1965, 1972, 1988, and 1993.

Several explanations have been given for conflicts in Burundi. These range from the extreme view of conflicts as emanating from alleged age-old animosities between the Hutu and the Tutsi to balanced and evidence-based political economy analyses emphasizing institutional failure (Ndikumana 1998), distributional conflicts, and inequality (Ndikumana 2005; Nkurunziza and Ngaruko 2000; 2005; 2008). Detailed historical accounts of conflicts are provided in Ntibazonkiza (1993) and Lemarchand (1995).

Civil war has dealt a heavy blow to the Burundian economy through the disruption of agricultural production, the decay of infrastructure, and the deterioration of institutions. In particular, the recent conflict has taken a heavy human toll and caused prolonged

---

[7] The population of Burundi comprises three ethnic groups: the Hutu (majority), the Tutsi (minority), and the Twa (less than 1% of the population).

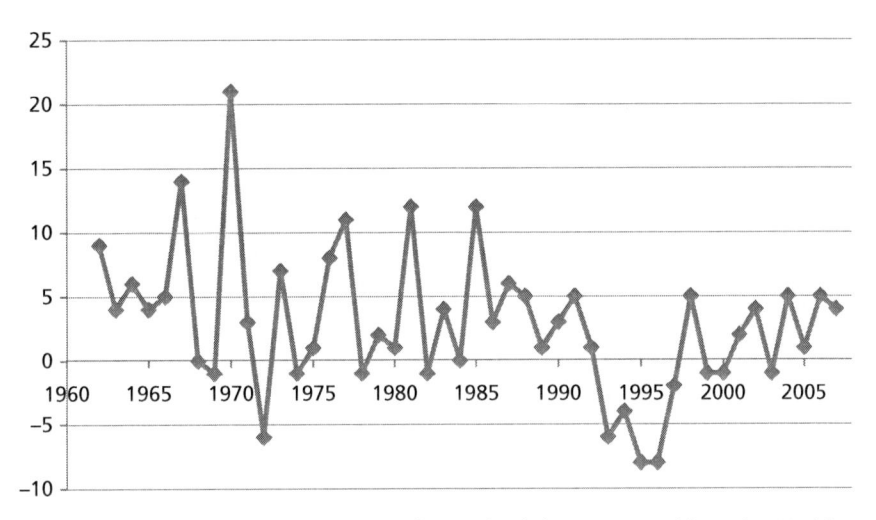

Figure 1. Burundi: GDP growth 1962–2007 (annual %) (source: World Bank, World Development Indicators)

economic contraction (Fig. 1). Nonetheless, despite its serious development challenges, Burundi has a unique chance to turn the page from the era of ethnic conflict.

The Burundian case has demonstrated that what is often depicted as ethnic conflict is not a result of inherent animosities between rival ethnic groups but rather the outcome of the manipulation of the political system by political elites claiming to represent the interests of particular groups. State institutions were privatized and used as a vehicle for the monopolization of economic and political power by the elites (Nkurunziza and Ngaruko 2005; 2008; Ndikumana 2005). However, it eventually became clear to the Burundian people that ethnicity was indeed a convenient natural factor exploited by political elites to perpetuate their hold on power. The case of Burundi offers valuable lessons for other countries experiencing similar challenges of overcoming civil conflicts.

3. Growth and development: challenges and opportunities

Growth in Burundi has been volatile, mainly as a result of the fluctuations in agricultural production due to weather shocks and shocks to export prices of agricultural commodities. The economy suffered large growth collapses during the episodes of ethnic conflict: a short-lived contraction in 1972 and a more prolonged recession during the conflict that followed the assassination of the democratically elected president in October 1993 (Fig. 1).

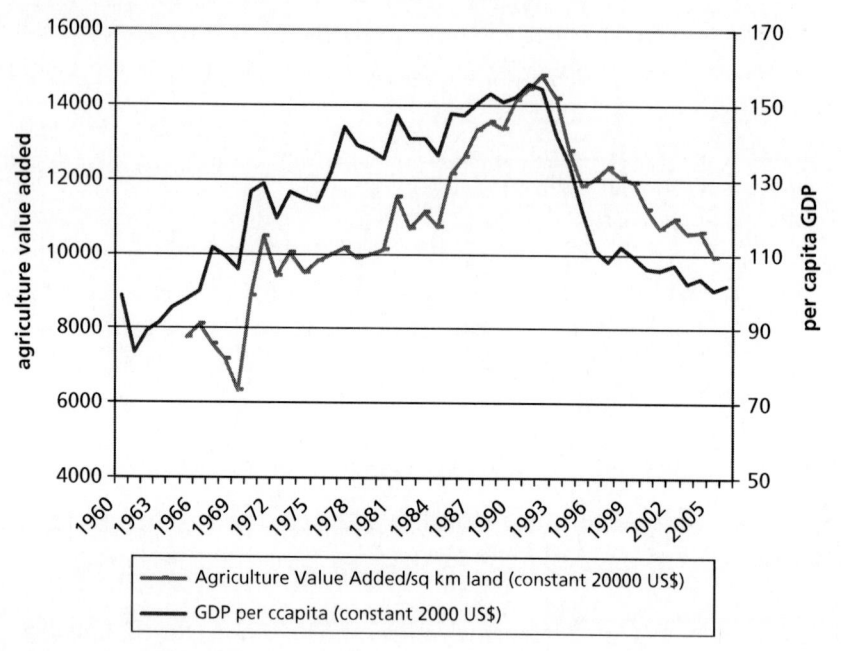

Figure 2. Burundi: agricultural productivity and per capita income (source: World Bank, World Development Indicators)

The country's inability to reach and sustain high growth is partly due to lack of economic transformation and heavy reliance on agriculture. With a high population growth (3% per year) and lack of innovation in agricultural technology, productivity has steadily declined. Net per capita agricultural production in 2007 ($78 per km^2 of land) was half the level achieved 30 years earlier ($153 in 1976) (Fig. 2).

In the context of ethnic-based politics and conflict, the motivation of policymaking under past regimes has been the control of the state as the main source of economic and political power rather than broad-based economic development. Thus economic policy promoted the development of the public sector at the detriment of modern private enterprise. At the same time the rural sector remained marginalized, with little investment in agricultural infrastructure and technological innovation. The establishment of state-owned enterprises as a vehicle of production and trade (import and export) served as a basis for rent extraction for the elite in power.

The lack of productivity improvements combined with rising demographic pressure on land constitutes a major threat to rural livelihoods, and can even exacerbate the risk of social tensions.[8] Indeed, during the recent conflict, the presence of a large unemployed

---

[8] Indeed, some have argued that pressure on land may have contributed to ethnic tensions and conflict in Rwanda (Uvin 1998).

rural youth served as a convenient recruitment base for the rebellion. Hence, it may be argued that strategies for expansion and diversification of rural sources of employment and livelihoods constitute a key element of the national agenda of peace consolidation and conflict prevention.

In this respect the integration into the East African Community (EAC) offers important promises to Burundi, not only as a potential growth driver but also as a means of diffusing potential social tensions, as opportunities for economic advancement begin to transcend national boundaries. Burundians will then begin to envision competition, not solely as against fellow Burundians of different ethnic or regional origins, but on the basis of individual ingenuity and capabilities within a broader regional context. At the regional level, political leadership will play a key role in peace building and democratic consolidation in Burundi, as was demonstrated in the mediation of the recent conflict. Thus regional integration may prove to be a critical factor for political stability, which in turn is a key condition for long-term growth in Burundi.

5. Conclusion

In addition to physical constraints to growth such as being small, landlocked, and resource-scarce, Burundi also faces the legacy of social tension and political instability. Today, it nonetheless has the unique chance of emerging as a rare African case of successful transition from conflict under the new constitutional power-sharing arrangements. However, achieving sustainable long-term growth is also dependent on successful transition from dependence on the primary sector and on promotion of private-sector development, especially to allow the country to take advantage of regional integration opportunities. But by and large, the consolidation of peace and political stability is the penultimate prerequisite for Burundi's economic performance in the medium to long term.

REFERENCES

African Development Bank, 2009. *An Infrastructure Action Plan for Burundi: Accelerating Regional Integration*. Tunis: AfDB.
Food and Agriculture Organization, various years. FAOSTAT statistical database (online).
Lemarchand, R., 1995. *Burundi: Ethnic Conflict and Genocide*. Cambridge: Cambridge University Press.
Ndikumana, L., 1998. 'Institutional failure and ethnic conflicts in Burundi', *African Studies Review* 41.1, 29–47.
—— 2000. 'Towards a solution to violence in Burundi: a case for political and economic liberalization', *Journal of Modern African Studies* 38.3, 431–59.

Ndikumana, L., 2005. 'Distributional conflict, the state and peace building in Burundi', *Round Table* 94.381, 413–27.

Nkurunziza, J. D., and F. Ngaruko, 2000. 'An economic interpretation of conflict in Burundi', *Journal of African Economies* 9.3, 370–409.

—— —— 2005. 'War and its duration in Burundi', in N. Sambanis and P. Collier (eds), *Understanding Civil War: Evidence and Analysis*, vol. 1. Washington, DC: World Bank.

—— —— 2008. 'Why has Burundi grown so slowly? The political economy of redistribution', in B. Ndulu et al. (eds), *The Political Economy of Economic Growth in Africa, 1960–2000*, vol. 2. Cambridge: Cambridge University Press.

Ntibazonkiza, R., 1993. *Au Royaume des Seigneurs de la Lance: une approche historique de la question ethnique au Burundi*, vol. 2. Brussels: Bruxelles-Droits de L'Homme.

United Nations Development Programme, 2008. *Human Development Report* 2008. New York: UNDP.

Uvin, P., 1998. *Aiding Violence: The Development Enterprise in Rwanda*. West Hartford, Conn.: Kumarian.

World Bank, 2009. World Development Indicators (online).

Cameroon
A Pragmatic Approach to Policy for Sustainable Growth

Séraphin Magloire Fouda

In recent years, Cameroon's growth rate has fluctuated between 3% and 3.5%. Such a growth rate could not enable the country to reach the poverty reduction target set by the government within the framework of the Growth and Employment Strategy Paper (GESP), to significantly reduce unemployment, and, much less, to achieve the Millennium Development Goals. In particular, the goal to halve extreme poverty by 2015 is based on an assumption of a minimum real growth rate of 7%. Accordingly, the issue of designing an economic policy that ensures sustainable economic growth is yet to be resolved.

In the 1990s, based on the development of models of endogenous growth, most empirical works were more interested in the search for factors of economic growth. It thus emerged that the promotion of sustainable growth should be based on investment in human capital, innovation, research and development, health, infrastructure, financial development, democracy, good governance, openness to trade, etc. At the same time, little attention seems to have been paid to the sectoral analysis of economic growth. More consideration of the contribution of various sectors to economic growth could be useful in understanding where money should be directed in order to stimulate growth.

In 2009, the real growth rate of the Cameroonian economy was estimated at 1.8%. The contribution of each sector to economic growth was as follows:

- primary sector (agriculture, fisheries, livestock, forestry, oil): 0.6%
- secondary sector (industries, civil engineering and public works, water, energy): –0.5%
- tertiary sector (services, banks, insurance, transport, communications, trade): 1.6%

The following are the main findings (Table 1):

(i) The cumulative contributions of the primary and secondary sectors (0.1%) to economic growth are lower than those of the tertiary sector alone (1.6%), even though the two sectors occupy the largest portion of the active population.
(ii) The tertiary sector is the engine of economic growth.
(iii) This situation is not specific to the year 2009. It constitutes a major trend of the development of economic activity since the end of the 1980s.

Table 1. Contribution to economic growth by sector (%)

Sector	2005	2006	2007	2008
Primary	0.5	0.6	1.2	1.1
Secondary	−0.3	0.5	−0.4	0.2
Tertiary	1.3	1.6	2.2	1.2

Source: Ministry of Economy, Planning and Regional Development (Department of Analysis and Economic Policies)

Two trends emerge from these developments: the primary and secondary sectors must be reactivated, and the tertiary sector must be consolidated.

It is important to note that the GESP is based on an assumption of a primary and secondary sector growth rate of more than 5% in order to achieve a real growth rate of 7% by 2020. There is therefore a need to develop agricultural and industrial policies that allow each of these two sectors to reach the targeted growth rate. Yet the growth of the primary and secondary sectors remained below the set objectives. The two sectors recorded growth rates estimated at 2.7% and −2.1% respectively.

A more detailed analysis of the contribution of the various sectors could give some indication of the possible guidelines on the economic policies to be implemented. In 2009, the performance of the main components of each sector was as follows:

Primary sector
- food crop production   0.9%
- cash crop production   0.1%
- livestock production   0.1%
- fisheries   0.0%
- forestry   −0.5%

Secondary sector
- extractive industries   −0.8%
- agri-food industries   0.3%
- other manufacturing industries   −0.3%
- electricity, gas, and water 0.0%
- civil engineering and public works   0.2%

Tertiary sector
- trade, restaurants, hotels   0.4%
- transport, warehouses, communications   0.3%
- banks and other financial institutions   0.0%
- other trading services   0.3%
- assessed indirect intermediation services   0.0%
- non-trading public administration services   0.4%
- other non-trading services   0.1%

Some policy recommendations could be drawn from the above figures:

1. In the primary sector, specific attention should be paid to cash crop production, livestock production, fisheries, and forestry. Food crop production must be intensified, as imports of foodstuffs continue to weigh heavily on the country's trade balance. In the last few years, the government has invested nearly US$1 billion in the development of agriculture, livestock production, and fisheries. However, this remains far below the objective of 10% of annual GDP recommended at the Maputo Conference. Challenges in the agricultural sector call for greater donor commitment. The President of the World Bank recently stated that, within the framework of a 'new deal in favour of food policy', the World Bank should devote US$800 million to revamp agriculture in sub-Saharan African countries in the coming years.

2. The contribution of the secondary sector to economic growth remains very weak, due to poor performance of extractive industries, other manufacturing industries, and electricity, gas, and water. Investments in electrical energy and water production are a matter of priority, as energy and water shortages discourage foreign investment and stifle local businesses. About US$3 billion needs to be invested in the construction of electrical energy-generating infrastructure in the coming years.

3. In the tertiary sector, the performance of banks and other institutions is a matter of concern, while the performance of the other components should be improved. In fact, the financial system is dominated by over-liquid banks, a narrow financial market, and fragile microfinance businesses. Incentives should be designed to encourage the system's involvement in the development, as the economy is faced with the nagging problem of financing.

The sectoral approach to economic growth gives room for the design of pragmatic and more relevant economic policies. Moreover, such an approach could serve as a guide for a more efficient allocation of funding by governments and donors in an international context marked by the scarcity of financial resources and the stagnation of aid. Cameroon's challenge is to raise the investment rate from the current 19% to 38% by 2020.

Chad
Recent Economic Growth

Nadjiounoum Djimtoïngar

A small, landlocked, and partially desert country of approximately 11 million inhabitants in 2009, Chad has long been economically dependent on two products for export—cotton and farming—both of which are highly exposed to climatic variations, but also to the impact of international environment for the former.

The history of economic growth in Chad has been in the recent past dominated by the cotton sector and internal rivalries amid political and economic failures whose consequences on society have been enormous. From independence to the end of the 1980s, growth was driven by climate and political shocks, but the general trend was downward, leading the country to adopt structural adjustment policies (PAS) in 1987, reinforced by the 1994 devaluation, which led to a boom in cotton exports, helping the economy grow during the period 1994–2000 (Azam and Djimtoïngar 2004). Membership in the CEMAC zone also has had a positive effect on growth thanks to the relative macroeconomic stability it provides under the multilateral surveillance mechanism adopted in 2001 to ensure the coordination of economic policies of member states, and consistent implementation of national budgetary policies with the common monetary policy.

But the decisive factor in the recovery was the start of oil production. Oil investments increased from 2.6% of GDP in 2000 to 26.9% in 2001, 83.6% in 2002, and 33.6% in 2003 (BAfD/OECD 2007). Oil exports began in mid-2003, and benefited from increased oil prices on the international market since that time until the third quarter of 2008. This was only possible thanks to the introduction from 1990 of a relatively stable political climate, giving confidence to investors in the exploitation of oil. Reforms in the area of decentralization, civil service, justice, and capacity building have contributed to these results.

From experience, growth driven by the exploitation of raw materials is potentially risky and therefore not sustainable, not only because the resource is non-renewable and sometimes unstable but also because of the associated risks of bad governance. Chad is thought to have learned from the experiences of other oil countries by establishing a mechanism for oil revenue management (Act No. 001/PR/99 of January 11, 1999, amended in 2000 and in 2006; Ministère du Pétrole 1999). This law identified public health and social affairs, education, infrastructure, rural development, environment and water resources as priority sectors that should receive oil resources directly. It created a fund for future generations which received 10% of direct oil resources. But reality was different. Oil has intensified rural–urban migration and highlighted the performance of the fiscal authorities: eligible for HIPC debt relief in mid-2001 and having reached the decision point in 2003, Chad has not yet reached the completion point. The resurgence of conflict in the east, seen as a result of oil exploitation, has contributed to the opacity of oil revenue management. The future generations fund was abolished in 2006 to broaden the scope of the priority sectors to include security. Although since the outbreak of the first rebellion in 1966 Chad has never had a period of calm, the conflict in the east is different in nature and magnitude. Indeed, beginning as more or less an ethno-religious rivalry, the Chadian conflict today has penetrated within regions or clans (Djimtoïngar and Avocksouma 2003). In every case, this is a problem of sharing resources The prospect of oil resources in an environment lacking political change could explain the simultaneity between the start of oil production and the resurgence of troubles in the country. Oil revenues also have an impact on the scale of fighting and the duration of the conflict, in that they allowed the government to strengthen its fiscal resources.

The favourable results achieved in macroeconomic balances and growth have not resulted in a significant improvement in the population's living standards. According to household survey data from 2003–4, poverty in Chad is mainly a problem in rural areas, where 87% of the poor live (Ministère du Plan et de la Coopération 2008). Strong growth of exports of oil—a sector that is not labour-intensive—has very little impact on poverty and the standard of living as a whole. Chad's growth reflects mainly the accumulation of factors of production and very little improvement in their productivity.

Nevertheless, the increase in export earnings has resulted in a substantial increase in spending in priority areas. But the quality of infrastructure is bad, and the less-than-transparent conditions of public procurement promote corruption and do not penalize poor work and unmet specifications. This raises the question of sharing the fruits of growth and efficiency of expenditure, when, following the negative shock of the fourth quarter of 2008, 2009 shows a loss of budgetary revenue from oil of 88%, a deterioration of the budget deficit (−14.4 % of GDP), and a collapse of the current account (−40.7 % of GDP) (Commission de la CEMAC 2009).

To achieve satisfactory and shared growth, therefore, the Chadian authorities must restore peace and security in the territory, ensure respect for institutions, and fight against corruption in particular to ensure the physical, legal, and judicial safety of economic activity. The goal is to create conditions for better governance, particularly in revenue management for optimal use of oil revenues to diversify the economy. For this purpose, special emphasis must be placed on the development of economic infrastructure (energy, transport and telecommunications, rural infrastructure), agriculture, promotion of investment through the mobilization of resources, and access to financial services. Improving the quality of public spending, including taking into account the gender aspect, will maximize the impact of this spending on poverty. Chad must also develop its technical expertise and human capital. The practice currently under way in many services, particularly in the financial authorities and ministry of finance, is the abandonment of experienced managers in favour of a younger workforce. Effective ways must be found to guard against lower-level false diplomas.

Finally, Chad must strengthen regional and international cooperation to promote an environment of peace and security, the implementation of common sectoral policies, convergence of macroeconomic policies, and the building of a common market.

REFERENCES

Azam, Jean-Paul, and Nadjiounoum Djimtoïngar, 2004. *Cotton, War and Growth in Chad (1960–2000)*. Nairobi: AERC (August).

Banque Africaine de Développement/Organization for Economic Cooperation and Development, 2007. *Perspectives économiques en Afrique*.

Commission de la Communauté Économique et Monétaire de l'Afrique Centrale, 2009. *Rapport du Comité de veille pour le suivi des effets de la crise financière* (June).

Djimtoïngar, Nadjiounoum, and Djona Atchénémou Avocksouma, 2003. *Économie des conflits en Afrique: cas du Tchad*. Nairobi: AERC (May).

Ministère du Pétrole (Tchad), 1999. *Loi n°001/PR/99 sur la gestion des revenus pétroliers* (January).

Ministère du Plan et de la Coopération (Tchad), 2008. *Document de stratégie de croissance et de réduction de la pauvreté*.

Congo, Democratic Republic of (DRC) Unlocking the Political Economy Constraints to Development

Johannes Herderschee[1]

DRC's development has not lived up to expectations, although its record has improved since 2001. Since President Kabila took office in 2001, growth has picked up and averaged some 6%, thanks in part to favourable prices for mining products on international markets and improved security after the end of the war. While respectable, the modest post-conflict boost has not yet lifted incomes above 1985 levels. Furthermore, growth remains narrowly based on mining and some services, such as telecommunications; agricultural growth rates exceed population growth but there is almost no job creation in the formal sector. Poverty remains widespread, affecting some 70% of the population. Maternal mortality rates are close to 1% of live births and only 6% of the population has access to electricity (Democratic Republic of Congo 2010a).

DRC's development is constrained by weak institutions. During 2002–10, DRC remained close to the bottom of the Doing Business Indicators. Governance indicators bottomed out as the conflict drew to a close in 2002 but remain low, and the weak business and governance environment constrains economic activity. Any support to DRC needs to take into account the reasons for the weak institutional environment.

Elite fragmentation is the main underlying cause for weak institutions in the DRC. President Mobutu (1965–97) systematically undermined horizontal networks that could challenge his authority. During the conflict (1997–2001), ethnic appeal fragmentation was used to fuel conflict at the local level. Keefer and Wolters (2011) documents the fragmentation of the elite in the run up to the 2006 election and since then. The 2006

---

[1] The findings, interpretations, and conclusions in this note are entirely those of the author and should not be attributed in any manner to the World Bank, to its affiliated organizations, or to members of its Board of Executive Directors or the countries they represent. The note draws on some of the issues presented in a country economic memorandum that is being prepared at the World Bank. I am grateful for comments by Eric Bell, Eustacius Betubiza, Phil Keefer, Shiho Nagaki, and Jan Walliser. All remaining errors are of course mine.

Constitution paved the way for the first democratic elections in forty years, but was not rooted in national political economy realities. Despite the strengthening of provinces in the Constitution, the Presidency remains the predominant power, even in provinces that did not support the incumbent in the last elections National and Provincial Assemblies have little contact with their constituents. State institutions are not strong enough to protect the population from violence, and the world's largest UN forces are unable to do it on behalf of the government.

Elite fragmentation affects economic performance directly and indirectly. The lack of commonly agreed and transparently enforced rules raises risk levels for all economic agents, leading to myopic policymaking and a focus on short-term investment. The absence of a single generally accepted operator to enforce all rules and regulations allows a multitude of agencies to request private payments (Democratic Republic of Congo 2010b). The indirect economic effect of fragmented elites is a defensive posture to reduce contestation of ideas. Social accountability organizations, which could direct policy towards more long-term development objectives, are weak and unable to challenge the authorities.

Elite fragmentation can be overcome with the right incentives. Even during the war in the Great Lakes region, warring parties could reach a consensus on issues of common concern. Telecom towers survived the war largely unscathed, as all parties relied on mobile phones: armed groups that might have destroyed a mobile telephone tower would have disconnected their own telephone. There was an implicit consensus that such installations would not be damaged because all stakeholders received *continual* benefits.

Some agreements among elites materialize thanks to powerful backing. DRC succeeded in implementing improved fiscal policies recently, despite political opposition from certain groups whose interests were under threat. This policy was implemented with political backing at the highest level. However, such compromises may not always benefit long-term objectives—for example, in the current situation in DRC the fiscal tightening largely relies on reducing transfers to provinces that are meant to build up provincial services.

Agreements that require high-level support are becoming more widespread, but the full and permanent benefits require broader support and transparency. Examples are resources-for-infrastructure agreements and the Rwanda peace agreement. Resources-for-infrastructure deals allow the construction of debt-financed infrastructure, while revenues from specific mines guarantee debt service payments. In some of the large-scale Chinese projects, mining revenues are scheduled to be directly transferred to the creditor, limiting the involvement of DRC government officials. These agreements have accelerated infrastructure construction, addressing a key constraint to growth. Project selection and maintenance, however, is fully a Congolese responsibility. This is challenging, as demonstrated by the administrative difficulties to establish a fund to maintain established roads. Similarly, high-level policymakers decided on the Rwanda peace agreement, which has benefited the border provinces. Extending and broadening the benefits from this agreement requires institutional follow-up, notably close cooperation between Rwandan and DRC national and provincial authorities. Cooperation takes trust and therefore time and transparency, but it is emerging, as evidenced by cooperation among customs officials from both countries.

Regional or multilateral frameworks of accountability may play a role in dispute settlement among DRC elites. Foreign investors always had the option to include arbitration clauses in their contracts, and international arbitration has also been used by the DRC authorities for sovereign disputes. The DRC authorities may go further by adopting the OHADA treaty that revamps the legal framework. OHADA provides DRC companies the option to appeal for arbitration to the Common Court in Abidjan. At the same time, macroeconomic policies are supported by an IMF programme, providing an external anchor including policy indicators that have been successfully observed since the programme started in mid-2009. The DRC authorities may wish to strengthen their participation in regional institutions such as EAC, SADC, CEMAC, and COMESA, anchoring their own institutions and policy frameworks.

REFERENCES

Democratic Republic of Congo, 2010a. *Report on Implementation of the Growth and Poverty Reduction Strategy*. Kinshasa: published as part of World Bank Report No. 54742-ZR.

—— 2010b. *Diagnostic Trade Integration Study Enhanced Integration Framework Program (EIF)*. Kinshasa: Ministry of Trade, Small and Medium-Sized Enterprises.

Keefer, Phil, and Stephanie Wolters, 2011. 'Governance and political economy for growth in DRC' Washington, DC: World Bank.

Congo, Republic of Entrepreneurship Promotion Policies and Development

Jean Christophe Boungou Bazika

1. Introduction

Entrepreneurship constitutes a critical element for economic and social development in the wake of public-sector failure in the Republic of Congo. The public sector is responsible for 80% of employment in the modern sector. Beside a dominant oil sector, there is a non-oil sector with many small and micro enterprises, most of which are in the informal sector and in commercial activities. Economic and social development in Congo therefore strongly needs to include the enhancement of production capacities of these enterprises and diversification of the non-oil sector (Boungou Bazika 2007).

2. Priorities in promotion of entrepreneurship

One of the key priorities is to improve the investment climate. According to World Bank (2008), the business environment in Congo is poor. Complex administrative procedures and corruption prevent entrepreneurs from easily doing business. Administrative procedures must be improved, and another priority is to provide better public services, such as the supply of water and electricity. Interruptions in the supply of electricity and water lead to high transaction costs for small and medium enterprises (SMEs), which do not have access to alternative sources like generators or wells. Another priority is to create a guarantee fund to ensure security of credit offered to small entrepreneurs who are refused bank loans due to their high risks. It is necessary that the government provide resources to the microfinance institutions, mainly those which have demonstrated their sustainability. International financial institutions such as the World Bank and African Development Bank could develop special programmes that support microfinance; otherwise microfinance institutions will not be able to overcome constraints associated with training and logistics.

3. Necessary institutional reforms

At the institutional level, some reforms are necessary to ensure that the process of social and economic development is a reality. In Congo, civil servants do not believe that small enterprises can create employment and constitute a foundation for development. Therefore, the government must carry out a broad campaign aimed at educating civil servants to work in partnership with entrepreneurs. An innovation could be achieved in constituting committees in which civil servants and representatives of the private sector can work together to solve problems and improve administrative procedures. The creation of professional organizations that can represent and defend the interests of small enterprises is a necessity. The lack of such organizations makes it difficult for managers in the different sectors to defend their corporate interest. The professional organizations that exist are very weak and have no capacity to mobilize the majority of small and micro entrepreneurs. By contrast, transport managers, who belong to a strong organization, were able to achieve a reduction of police abuse on the roads.

4. Women's entrepreneurship

Feminine entrepreneurship is an important issue that must be addressed because of the critical role played by women in economic activities. Most of the managers and producers in agriculture and trade are women. Some of them created some years ago several women's mutual benefit funds. From 1991 until today, some of these microfinance institutions have been running very well. An example is the evangelicals' mutual and benefit fund, which had 100 members at its creation in 1991, and now has 1,600. For the last three years, this institution has been autonomous and is operating without any grant.

Women entrepreneurs face constraints of credit restrictions and high costs of transport and taxation. They have developed a strategy to buy stocks in centralized fashion (import network) and to use *tontines* for funding. Several authors recognize the role of female entrepreneurship in reducing poverty through investment in family welfare. It would be interesting to establish special programmes to support women's entrepreneurship.

5. Competitiveness once again

Entrepreneurs need to compete in the context of globalization and regional trade arrangements. From 1960 to 1970, Congo was the main exporter of manufactured goods in the Custom and Economic Union of Central Africa. Now it has become a net importer from Cameroon. This reverse trend is explained by the fall of its competitiveness due to political instability. In addition, the proximity of the Democratic Republic of Congo provides opportunities to export goods to the biggest market in the Central Africa. For a small country like Congo, exports are vital for growth and development. Several authors argue for the promotion of an outward-oriented policy through export diversification (Banque Africaine de Développement 2009; Stiglitz 1999). Competitiveness must be analysed from two perspectives: internal and external. At the internal level, skills development needs to be improved in order to enhance labour skills. Training is the means to reach this objective. At the external level, infrastructure, public services, and administrative procedures need to be improved. Public policies will play a key role here.

6. Entrepreneurship and public policies

Policies that affect small and medium enterprises (SME), agriculture, trade, infrastructure, education, etc. have multiple implications for entrepreneurship. In the same way, fiscal policy may be utilized to improve the performance of enterprises. One important consideration is the need to harmonize all these policies.

There is a need for public policies that are conducive to a favourable investment climate and that provide incentives to stimulate the creation and strengthening of business. If there is such massive public-sector failure in Congo, why would we expect the government to undertake all these business-promoting policies? First, experiences carried out in other developing countries show that government plays a key role in promoting entrepreneurship. The case of Southeast Asia is relevant (Yergin and Stanislaw 2000). Second, the government is engaged in the diversification policy. Third, several programmes aiming to support the private sector will be implemented soon with the aid of the World Bank and the European Union.

7. Conclusion

Entrepreneurship is a major factor in promoting sustainable growth and development in Congo. A broad plan is necessary for defining clear objectives and providing resources to reach them. Government and international partners have to focus on policies that allow the promotion of SMEs. The approach to address all these complex issues must be a participative one, as was the case in Kenya in 1986, in order that the strategy of poverty alleviation may provide better results.

REFERENCES

Banque Africaine de Développement, 2009. *Impact de la crise sur les économies africaines –maintenir la croissance et poursuivre la réduction de la pauvreté: perspectives et recommandations de l'Afrique au G20*. Un rapport du Comité des Ministres des Finances Africains et des Gouverneurs des Banques Centrales établi pour le suivi de la crise, 21 March, Tunis.

Boungou Bazika, J. C. (ed.), 2007. *L'entrepreneuriat et l'innovation au Congo Brazzaville*. Paris: L'Harmattan.

Programme des Nations Unies pour le Développement, 2005. *Rapport sur le développement humain*. Paris: Economica.

Stiglitz, J., 1999. *Principes de l'économie moderne*. Brussels: De Boeck.

Yergin, D., and J. Stanislaw, 2000. *La Grande Bataille: les marchés à l'assaut du pouvoir*. Paris: Odile Jacob.

World Bank, 2008. *Doing Business*. Washington, DC.

World Economic Forum, World Bank, and African Development Bank, 2009. *Africa Competitiveness Report*. Geneva.

Côte d'Ivoire Economic Reversibility

Tchétché N'guessan

1. Introduction

At independence, Africans staked their hopes on rapid and sustainable development. Between 1965 and 1973, the average annual GDP growth rate was 5.9%. These fairly satisfactory economic results created an illusion of an Africa anxious to close its development gap. Unfortunately, that initial period of fairly rapid economic growth only lasted a decade in many African countries. From the mid-1970s, the economic performance indicators began to deteriorate. In many African countries, per capita GDP was even lower than before independence. What have we learned about this reversibility?

Today, despite the international financial and economic crisis, the predicted economic growth of African countries is on average 5%. This level of growth is almost the same as after independence, which did not give the expected results in terms of welfare; therefore it is important to take stock of African countries' economic growth reversibility. This chapter discusses the structural problems that are at the root of this reversibility, with a focus on the specific case of Côte d'Ivoire.

2. The trend of the Ivorian economy

For a long time, Côte d'Ivoire was presented as an example of economic success; but this image has since deteriorated as the country lost the momentum of the economic model and socio-political system established from 1960 to 1980, exhibited an unsatisfactory response to the new economic and social demands, and failed to adapt its political practices to the standards of democratic governance.

2.1. FROM GROWTH TO ECONOMIC CRISIS

During the first two decades after independence, the Ivorian government adopted a proactive policy that boosted economic growth driven primarily by agriculture. The plan obtained outstanding results by using different types of public incentives, producer supervision, and agricultural diversification. For instance, from the 1980s through to the present, it has ranked among the top world and African producers of coffee and cocoa.

Côte d'Ivoire's outward-looking policy fostered massive capital inflow, and the central government took advantage of this to guide and carry out the financing of industry and development of infrastructure. From 1965 to 1980, public investments in terms of direct action on production and infrastructure represented over 60% of national investment. Commercial activities flourished as a result of infrastructural investments. All of this generated excellent economic results, as seen by the 7% average growth rate in real terms from 1965 to 1978, and provided substantial resources for Côte d'Ivoire's central government, which was able to meet collective requirements, safeguard employment, create social transfers, and oversee redistribution of the fruits of growth in hopes of narrowing social and regional disparities.

However, the economic system and political regime revealed their respective limitations from the late 1970s through to the 1990s. The average annual GDP growth rate dropped, and eventually became negative (World Bank 1989). This deterioration was the result of the combined effect of rapid population growth and weaknesses in the Ivorian economy—namely, its overdependence on external financing and the shortcomings of its internal management. In addition, it experienced three shocks from 1978 to 1980: the sharp turnaround in the markets for primary commodities, the prices of which slumped by over 35% from 1978 to 1979; the oil shock, which made imports more expensive; and the drying up of the capital markets as a result of the upward trend in international interest rates and the appreciation of the dollar.

On the domestic front, there were obvious economic management weaknesses. The strong dependence of agriculture on the vagaries of the weather, and the patrimonial and clientelist management of public affairs associated with a one-party system, exacerbated the economic crisis. Laxity was the rule in public administration, state-owned companies, and national public establishments. For example, one third of the public debt was attributable to borrowings by parastatals guaranteed by the state. The public deficit widened from 2.2% of GDP in 1975 to 12% in 1980. By limiting the opportunities for party–state intervention, the economic slump constituted the first major crack in the sociopolitical system established in 1960.

To address the economic and financial crisis, a harbinger of subsequent sociopolitical tensions, the Ivorian authorities turned to structural adjustment programmes (SAPs) from 1981. The SAPs had mixed economic and financial results. The external balance was achieved, and measures targeting inflation and reform of the financial sector also attained their objectives until 2007. The public financial balance, however, was far from achieved. The average economic growth rate has been zero since 1981, despite a transient rise from 1994 to 1998 following devaluation of the CFA franc.

The intrinsic limitations of the SAPs are that, on the demand side, the contraction of public expenditure tended to be more to the detriment of public investment, which has organic links to private investment and economic growth in Côte d'Ivoire. On the supply side, price liberalization did nothing to remove distortions or foster competition. The highly anticipated technical innovation, competition, and job creation did not materialize. By targeting price stability as a virtually exclusive priority, the restrictive policies inspired by the SAPs penalized growth by widening the economic financing gap.

2.2. CONSTRAINTS ON ECONOMIC RECOVERY

The difficulties of economic recovery and maintenance of sustainable growth and development have been largely due to institutional, behavioural, technological, economic, and financial constraints. (Stiglitz 2002; Koffi 2002; Severino and Ray 2010). The state has also established an incoherent and often contradictory incentive system, in which it has shown entrepreneurial spirit and has strongly encouraged initiative and risk-taking, as well as horizontal social mobility through spatial migration, but has also implemented a political and administrative management system that has considerably dampened this entrepreneurial spirit among representatives of the state bourgeoisie and in private-sector opportunism.

From a behavioural standpoint, Ivorian society has probably not yet begun to make the decisive shift towards ownership of the credible source of continuing material enrichment. Côte d'Ivoire has not yet reached the threshold that will trigger the process of productive capital formation.

The virtual absence of technological innovation has impeded industrial development regarding value-added processing of raw materials and employment, both of which are low. It maintains high factor costs in the face of international competition, in particular from emerging countries, highlighting the critical problem of competitiveness.

There are many other economic constraints, including the absence of a framework law on small and medium enterprise businesses, and weak institutional support structures for private-sector development and promotion. Also, investment in Côte d'Ivoire remains structurally weak due to a combination of four factors: a dramatic reduction in public investment since 1999; continually unsatisfactory levels of private investment and declining foreign direct investment; the unstable political and institutional environment that coincided with this period; and the financing problem.

3. How to emerge from the crisis

In order to reverse this economic trend, Côte d'Ivoire needs a pro-poor growth policy. Only such a strategy, in keeping with ethics and logic, will loosen the grip of poverty, the rate of which was 48.9% in 2008.

Theoretically, growth should be driven by exports and by increased public and private investment, which themselves should be fuelled by the growth of the global economy (Venables 2009; Easterly et al. 1993) Public authorities will therefore have to redouble their efforts to create conducive conditions for private investment and, especially, provide investors with reasons to believe that the direction of macroeconomic policy is appropriate and viable.

The inadequacy and deterioration of infrastructure needs to be prioritized, in particular in sectors such as communications, electric power generation, and water production, which inhibit private investments by raising their cost.

The reform and enhancement of institutional effectiveness is also necessary to create an enabling environment for investment and growth. Indeed, confidence in institutions can encourage individuals to engage in economic activities, invest in human and physical capital, and carry out research and development and other work. The inadequacy of the judicial and legal systems, for example, constitutes a problem. It will be necessary to create and maintain a transparent, impartial, and efficient regulatory apparatus which is capable of protecting the rights of ownership, ensuring compliance with contracts, and fostering healthy competition and, generally speaking, the sound management of public affairs. General progress has been made at the regional level as a result of the work of the Organization for the Harmonization of Business Law in Africa; however, much remains to be done to encourage investors.

Lastly, such reforms will only lead to sustainable growth if political stability is maintained. Peace is often fragile in a post-conflict country (Collier 2000), and if peace is not consolidated, sustainable development has little chance of materializing. For that reason, the Ivorian authorities and the international community must strive to create stability and lasting peace after the crisis to ensure the achievement of economic growth.

REFERENCES

Collier, P., 2000. *Economic Causes of Civil Conflict and their Implications for Policy*. Washington, DC: World Bank.
Easterly, W., M. Kremer, L. Pritchett, and L. H. Summers, 1993. 'Good policy or good luck? Country growth performance and temporary shocks', *Journal of Monetary Economics* 32.3.
Koffi, P. K., 2008. *Le Défi du développement en Côte d'Ivoire*. Paris: L'Harmattan.
Severino, J. M., and O. Ray, 2010. *Le Temps de l'Afrique*. Paris: Odile Jacob.

Stiglitz, J. E., 2002. *Globalization and Its Discontents*. New York: Norton.

Venables, A. J., 2009. 'Rethinking growth in a globalizing world: an economic geography lens', *African Development Review* 21.2, 331–51.

World Bank, 1989. *Sub-Saharan Africa: From Crisis to Sustainable Growth. A Long-Term Perspective Study.* Washington, DC.

—— 1994. *Adjustment in Africa: Reforms, Results and the Way Ahead.* Washington, DC: World Bank.

Egypt
The Changing Role of the State

Heba Handoussa

1. Egypt's demographic profile

'Egypt is the gift of the Nile,' as Herodotus once said, and it has never been truer than today, where only 4% of the country's massive land area of 1 million km^2 is inhabited and only 3% is cultivated. The shortage of Nile waters has become the leading constraint on ensuring food security and maintaining the legendary high yields and productivity of Egypt's fertile Nile Valley and Delta. With a population of 75.5 million, Egypt is the second largest country in Africa. The country is still undergoing its demographic transition, with a youth bulge of more than 1 million new entrants to the labour force annually. Although fertility declined from 4.1 to 3.1 between 1991 and 2005, it has since plateaued, with serious implications in terms of growing imbalances between land, water, and population. Turning Egypt's demographic transition into a window of opportunity is therefore the most difficult challenge in the coming decade.

2. The changing role of the state

One of the salient features of Egypt's economy has been the centralized role of the state since the time of the pharaohs. One reason has been the total dependence on controlling the waters of the Nile and annual flood, which has required enormous investments in irrigation and drainage as well as fair regulation and allocation of water to Egypt's farmers. In addition to its 'hydraulic state' function, government has had to adapt to more recent historical political shifts, first towards socialism after the 1952 revolution and then reverting to capitalism with the 'open door policy' in 1973. It can be claimed that reinstating the private sector in Egypt has taken longer than for any transition economy in Eastern Europe. For example, although agricultural land was never state-owned or state-managed, it has taken over twenty years to dismantle the price controls on the operation of the market for inputs and output in the agricultural sector. With manufacturing and services, the process of privatization is still ongoing, with significant numbers of state-owned enterprises in industry, finance, tourism and even retail trade still operating.

3. Employment generating growth

Along with other countries in the Middle East, Egypt has suffered from a problem of structural unemployment since the 1970s. Three reasons can be identified: a major bias in government expenditure towards tertiary (university) education at the expense of raising access to and quality of secondary and technical vocational training; a populous public sector and civil service employment regime which has extended since the Nasser years and until recently; and the closed economy model and very limited trade integration (except for petroleum), neither of which generate jobs. The results of these policies have been great expectations for white-collar jobs among Egypt's youth that have gone largely unfulfilled. Over the last decade, the mismatch between education and labour market demand has been exacerbated, leading to the jump in unemployment of university graduates to nearly 45% for females and 25% for males, and causing a trend for educated youth to seek employment opportunities abroad (Wolfensohn Center for Development 2008).

4. Key challenges over the coming decade

Five challenges loom large for Egypt's policymakers: climate change, water scarcity, population growth, poverty, and economic growth. While the number of Egyptians living on less than $1 per day is only 3.4%, the number living on less than $2 per day is 42.8% (Ministry of Economic Development 2008). The reason poverty has continued to plague society is that periods of growth over the past three decades have been sporadic, and growth has not translated into significant poverty reduction. In spite of generous public expenditure on subsidies on all basic food products and energy, the system has lacked any effective targeting of the bottom income classes. The subsidy package is now under review by the government, with such alternative programmes as conditional cash transfers being piloted for scaling-up.

The problems of climate change and water scarcity are mostly exogenous, but Egypt is forecasted to be a major victim of global warming. It is also expected that the Mediterranean coastline will recede by several metres and a major part of the fertile Delta will become submerged by the sea. The issue of Egypt's share of Nile waters is under difficult negotiations, and the per capita availability of water plummeted from 1,893m^3 in 1959 to 934m^3 in 2000, which is below the recommended world standard of 1,000m^3 per person per year (United Nations 2001). The option of charging farmers for water usage has been consistently avoided for sociopolitical reasons. The implications for policymaking are the urgent need to conserve water and reduce cultivation of such crops as rice and sugarcane (UNDP and Institute of National Planning 2008).

On the macro-policy front, three sets of directions have proved successful over the present cabinet's five-year life. The first has been a major overhaul of the investment regulatory framework. This resulted in a tremendous increase in foreign direct investment (FDI), from $6.1 billion to $11.1 billion between 2006 and 2007, making Egypt the top FDI recipient in Africa and the second largest of the twenty-two Arab countries (OECD 2008). Institutional reforms have also been accompanied by trade liberalization and an incentive and technical assistance scheme for exporters, which raised the value of manufactured exports to $3.2 billion. The third area of reform has involved renewed concern for poverty reduction and the necessary interventions in geographical targeting of budget expenditure on infrastructure in the south (Upper Egypt), where 30% of the population lives. In addition to revising the allocation of investment resources in favour of poor communities, the government has introduced the achievement of the Millennium Development Goals (MDGs) as a key pillar to the current Five-Year Plan (2007–12) (Ministry of Planning 2007). The president's election programme of 2005 in fact promoted the delivery of a number of innovative and ambitious pro-poor development projects such as credit and technical assistance for small and medium enterprises (SMEs), housing schemes for the poor, conditional cash transfers, and universal health insurance.

A number of weaknesses are still impeding Egypt from taking off on a high and consistent growth trajectory. The first is the country's debt exposure, at 10% of GDP, and the continued crowding out of the private sector because of the overwhelming share of government bank borrowing. Egypt's financial sector is well regulated, and has been totally resilient to the global recession that started in 2008, but it continues to favour large business and the trade sector. Access to credit for manufacturing is difficult to obtain in a market where more than 90% of firms have fewer than 50 employees. Poor trade performance is another area of weakness which can be traced to the inability of private-sector exporters to establish long-term links with their buyers.

5. A vision for progress

According to the 2005 Egypt Human Development Report (EHDR; UNDP and Institute of National Planning 2005), which was well received by government, Egypt can count on six employment-generating engines of growth, most of which will help Egypt catch up on its export performance and trade liberalization. The first and most promising sector is labour-intensive and export-oriented manufacturing, particularly in the textile and food sectors, where the percentage of export to production is still relatively low. Another sector that can contribute to growth is the SME sector, which represents a great way to provide a large number of jobs at a low capital cost per job. Moreover, SMEs have a broad range of activities that spread across trade, service, and manufacturing. The vision for Egypt is such that SMEs play a more positive role in generating income, employment, and exports (UNDP and Institute of National Planning 2005). Agriculture is also part of the vision, with the introduction of rapid mechanization and expanded exports of high-value crops. Service sectors are also expected to continue to grow fast, especially tourism, which creates significant new jobs both directly and indirectly. Additionally, the ICT sector is providing export revenues as well as employment opportunities, while improving access to information, knowledge, and education (UNDP and Institute of National Planning 2005). Finally, the housing and construction sector has acted and will continue to act as an engine for economic growth and employment, as the need for housing units undoubtedly grows in proportion with rising incomes of a relatively young and growing population.

On the social front, a vision of Egypt was developed for the 2005 EHDR, in which the disadvantaged are seen not only as MDG targets or recipients of aid, but as major players in a new social contract between the state and its citizens (UNDP and Institute of National Planning 2005). Optimally, the state will reduce its central control in favour of political, social, and economic participation from civil society and the private sector, and cultural and behavioural changes will lead to prevailing values of participation, entrepreneurship, innovation, and transparency.

REFERENCES

Ministry of Economic Development (formerly Ministry of Planning), 2008. *Egypt: Achieving the Millennium Development Goals—A Midpoint Assessment.* Cairo.

Ministry of Planning, Arab Republic of Egypt, 2007. *The Sixth Five-Year Plan for Socio-Economic Development* (2007–12). Cairo.

Organization for Economic Cooperation and Development, 2008. *African Economic Outlook.* Paris: OECD.

United Nations, 2001. *Common Country Assessment.* Cairo, Egypt.

United Nations Development Programme and Institute of National Planning, 2005. *Egypt Human Development Report 2005. Choosing our Future: Towards a New Social Contract.* Cairo.

—— 2008. *Egypt Human Development Report 2008. Egypt's Social Contract: The Role of Civil Society.* Cairo.

Wolfensohn Center for Development at Brookings, 2008. *Missed by the Boom, Hurt by the Bust: Making Markets Work for Young People in the Middle East.* Washington, DC: Brookings Institution.

Equatorial Guinea
Oil and Other Resources, But Slow Growth

Damian Ondo Mane

1. Introduction

Equatorial Guinea became independent from Spain in 1968. In the run-up to independence, the economy expanded significantly, driven by agriculture and forestry sectors following a labour agreement between the colonial administration and Nigeria, and the gradual easing of sanctions against Spain by the international community.

After independence, Francisco Macias was democratically elected president in a multi-party contest. The economy collapsed because of the cessation of the labour agreement with Nigeria, the expansionary fiscal stance, and the financial crisis, which arose due to the withdrawal of two Spanish banks as part of the Spanish economic blockade.

2. Towards the change of the economic structure

In these circumstances, in 1979 a new government was installed under the leadership of President Obiang Nguema, which changed the course of economic development. The government initiated reforms to create a competitive environment for private sector development and facilitate foreign capital inflows. Major reforms included the returning of abandoned properties to their former owners and offering financial incentives to run the returned properties. In addition, a Recovery and Economic Development Program 1982–5 was adopted, and in 1982 the first donors' conference was held, to finance projects amounting to US$145 million.

Nonetheless, economic growth based on agriculture and forestry was insufficient to reduce poverty, due to the drop in productivity in both sectors. Inflation spiked and the exchange rate was overvalued. In order to tackle this situation, the Obiang government changed the centralized economy toward a market-oriented economy. In addition, several devaluations and other economic and monetary adjustments were implemented. Equatorial Guinea joined the Franc Zone and adopted the CFA franc in January 1985 as its legal tender. However, structural problems and the banking crises of the 1980s led to liquidity problems and the liquidation of two banks. In this context, the Second Development Strategy 1988–91 was adopted.

3. The oil era and the development of infrastructure

Despite the implementation of the Second Development Strategy, real economic growth was negative between 1989 and 1991. The oil era began with 3,000 barrels per day in 1992 and reached 350,000 b.p.d. in 2008. Consequently, real GDP grew 33% between 1992 and 2007 and GDP per capita increased from $218 in 1980–91 to $2,559 in 1992–2007 (Fig. 1). Public finances and the external sector strengthened. The first National Economic Conference was held in 1997 to design the mid-term development strategy 1997–2001.

The implementations of the 1977–2001 strategy led to significant changes in the economic structure. The agriculture and forestry sector fell from 25% in 1997 to 4% of GDP in 2007. While oil fell from 58% to 48%, the relative share of oil derivatives increased from 13% in 2002 to 27% in 2007. As a result, the hydrocarbon sector maintained its share at 70% in the period 2002–7. Construction's contribution to GDP rose from 2% in 1997 to 12% in 2007.

Oil revenue growth led to a significant increase of public investment and a strengthened fiscal position. Public indebtedness declined, accounting for only 1% of GDP in 2007. Exports jumped from $37 million in 1991 to $13,524 million in 2008. Similarly, current account surpluses improved and international reserves climbed from $8 million to $4,350 million between 1999 and 2008.

The banking system expanded due to the growth of financial assets and the installation of new commercial banks. However, progress in financial intermediation has proved elusive.

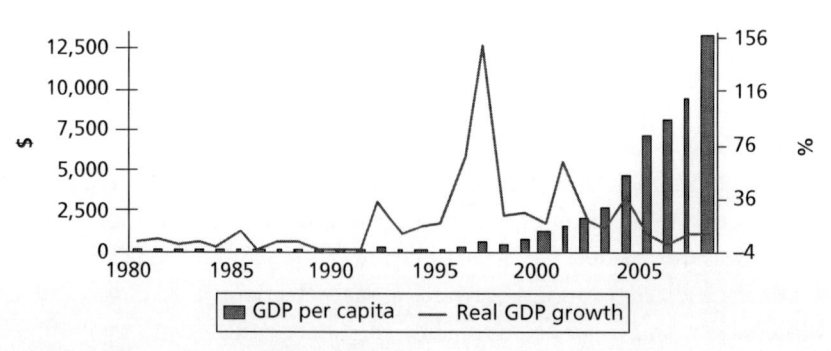

Figure 1. Real GDP growth and GDP per capita

Social indicators improved, albeit at a slower pace than economic growth. In fact the country ranked 118th out of 182 in the UNDP's Human Development Index of 2007. Despite the government's efforts, growth did not spread to poor people, due to the lack of qualified workers and the low participation of the population in the economy. To address this imbalance, the government created a fund for social development to improve social conditions and provide assistance to vulnerable households.

In addition, the government undertook a review of its medium-term strategy to lessen the dependence of the economy on oil revenues. The Second National Economic Conference was held in 2007 to establish a long-term strategy for 2007–20. This new strategy aims to achieve sustainable economic development through economic diversification and increased competitiveness based on four pillars: better infrastructure, better human capital, increased welfare, and better governance. In this order, the government is taking crucial steps. Most of the basic infrastructure will be built by 2012, so more resources will be released to improve human capital. At present the government is executing significant projects in water, sewage, and sanitation to improve people's quality of life. As part of governance enhancement, the government has joined the Extractive Industries Transparency Initiative (EITI), with important progress so far, and has participated in the publication of the IMF Article IV Consultation over the last ten years.

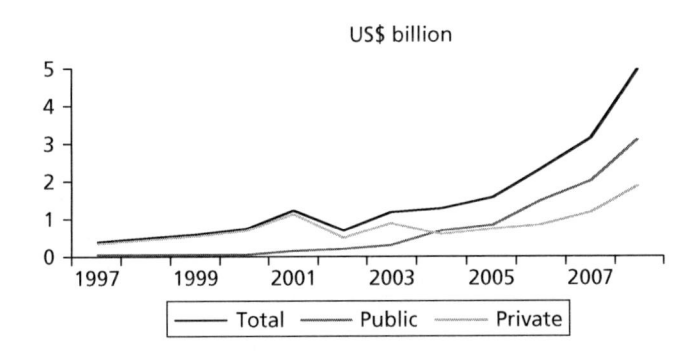

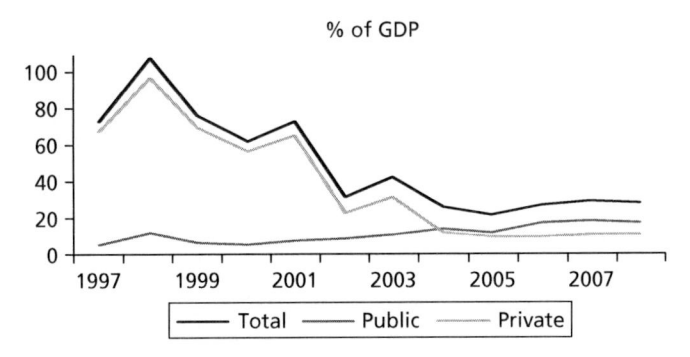

Figure 2. Gross investment (US$ billion)

4. Investment opportunities

Private investment growth is strongly associated with increasing foreign direct investment (FDI), which rose from $0.1 billion to $1.3 billion between 1979 and 2008 (Fig. 3). Oil companies expanded their exploration and production of oil and gas to produce butane, propane, methanol, LPG, and LNG. Since 2004 the boom in construction has opened new opportunities for private capital inflows and diversification.

Public investment increased from 1997, to represent 18% of GDP and 79% of expenditures in 2008. The public investment programme is supporting the strategy of economic diversification, increased competitiveness, and social development (Fig. 2). Between 2004 and 2008, 43% of capital spending was directed to infrastructure, 27% to government, 18% to the productive sector, and 12% to the social sector.

According to the 2020 Horizon Development Strategy, the public investment programme over the medium term (2008–12) proposes to allocate 5.531 million CFA francs to improve infrastructure (40%), to productive sectors including electricity and communication services (30%), to the social sector in the area of education, health, water supply, and sanitation (20%), and to state administration (10%). This programme opens up opportunities for private investments in sectors other than hydrocarbon.

To expand FDI beyond the oil sector in the form of joint ventures with domestic partners, the investment law, framed in line with international standards, does not differentiate between domestic and foreign investors. In addition it allows investors to repatriate dividends, redeploy liquidation or sale of investments, and pay debts abroad. The government is also making efforts to improve human capital.

Finally, the continued economic and social development of the country—supported by a stable macroeconomic framework, a sound diversification strategy, competitiveness improvements, financial viability, more human capital (more than 1,000 university graduates in 18 years of oil production), and a stable fiscal stance based on the permanent income hypothesis—provides ground for optimism concerning the prospects of Equatorial Guinea to achieve sustainable economic growth and meet the standards of an emerging economy by 2020.

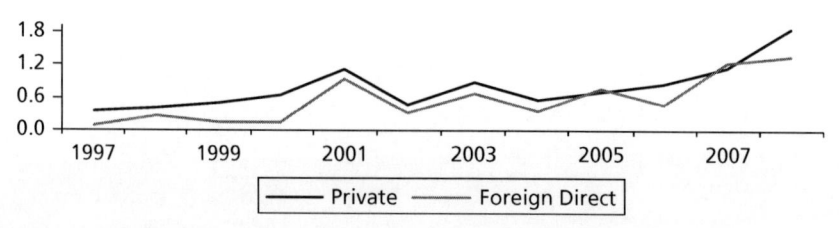

Figure 3. Private investment and foreign direct investment (US$ billion)

REFERENCES

Mane, Damian Ondo, 1975. 'Financiamiento del desarrollo en África y el sistema bancario de Guinea Ecuatorial'. Budapest Economic University.

—— 2007. 'Oil and the emergence of the Gulf of Guinea'. infinity publishing.com.

Ministry of Planification, Economic Development and Public Investment, 2007. Estrategia economica horizonte 2020. Malabo.

International Monetary Fund (various years). Article 4, consultation with Equatorial Guinea, 2007, 2008, 2009, 2010.

Eritrea
Economic Performance, Potential, and Constraints

Asmerom Kidane

1. Introduction

Eritrea is a country located in Northeast Africa along the eastern shores of the Red Sea. The country has an area of 125,000 km² and an estimated population of about 3.5 million. It gained independence in 1991. Before this period the country was in a state of war, with no meaningful economic activity—despite the fact that the country has been a nation of skilled and entrepreneurial people. During the 1930s, when the country was under Italian administration, Eritrea was exporting primary goods. As a result of thirty years of liberation struggle (1961–1991), the economy was in a steady decline, the limited infrastructure had been severely damaged, and some of it was beyond repair. After independence a new macroeconomic policy was formulated and became operational in 1994. Among other points, the policy adopted national macroeconomic objectives that highlighted the development of capital, and of knowledge-intensive and export-oriented industries and services.

2. Macroeconomic performance

Between 1992 and 1998, GDP at factor cost and at market prices grew by an impressive 9.0% and 16.0% respectively. Income per capita increased from 818 nakfa (US$117) in 1992 to 1,199 nakfa (US$171) in 1998—an annual increase of 6.3%. Sectoral distribution of GDP showed a shift from agricultural to other sectors—an indicator of diversification. While agriculture grew by 4%, industry grew by 14% and within-industry construction grew by 32% per year, reflecting significant postwar reconstruction activities.

Since independence there has been significant progress in enhancement of human resources, particularly in education and health. Female enrolment constitutes 45% of the total. Expenditure on education as a percentage of GDP shows an average of 7.4%, which is close to the average for sub-Saharan Africa. Eritrea's health indicators are about equal to the sub-Saharan averages. Clinics, health centres, and hospitals have been built in most parts of the country. For the first time in independent Eritrea, a public-sector pension scheme was promulgated and launched in 2003.

In 1998 a border war broke between Eritrea and Ethiopia. This had a major negative effect on the growth and structure of the economy, as the government was forced to reallocate a major portion of its limited resources to defence. The border issue has been referred to an international court, and is now officially delimited and demarcated. In spite of this, Ethiopia continues to occupy sovereign Eritrean territory, and the impasse continues to impact the country's macroeconomic performance.

3. Investment potential

Under the 'no war no peace' scenario, the country continues to be engaged in the development of physical and social infrastructure that is prerequisite for a takeoff to a higher macroeconomic performance. Some of the physical and social infrastructure includes the building of new asphalted and all-weather roads as well as the rehabilitation of the existing ones. Before 1991 the country had about 500 km of asphalted roads that needed considerable repair. Since 1991 these roads have been repaired; in addition, more than 800 km of new asphalted roads and more than 600 km of all-weather roads have been constructed. Despite its small size, the country possesses three international airports—one in the capital, Asmara, and one in each of the two major seaports, Massawa and Assab. The above activities were undertaken despite the fact that the country ranks as one of the lowest per capita recipients of foreign loans and grants. In the port city of Massawa a duty-free zone was established, enabling potential investors to conduct all transactions free from taxes and excessive government regulations.

Eritrea continues to be identified as a country which is relatively free from corruption. A study by Court, Kristen, and Weder (1999) established that Eritrea ranked alongside with Botswana, Mauritius, and Namibia as the least corrupted countries in Africa.

The country's major potential lies in irrigated crop production, where there is a relatively large area of under-utilized fertile land with micro dams nearby. The country has more than 1000 kms of coastline with a high potential for fisheries, related marine products, and recreational activities for incoming tourists. Eritrea is also believed to possess a significant amount of mineral wealth, including gold, silver and copper. Efforts are under way to exploit these resources.

4. Constraints

Eritrea depends on domestic resources, with little external resource for development; the country is not yet integrated into the global trading environment, and earning from abroad is still minimal. As a result, the country continues to face acute shortage of foreign exchange—reflected by the ever-widening gap between the official and parallel market exchange rates. During the early years of independence, the parallel market premium was almost nonexistent. By the year 2000, the ratio of parallel to official exchange rate was 1:3; in 2005 the premium increased to 1:5, and in 2009 it appeared to have reached 2.5. This widening premium is an indicator of disequilibrium in foreign exchange markets and trade regimes, and is inconsistent with the declared macroeconomic policy of the government. A wider parallel market premium may lead to capital flight; remittances from abroad may be channelled through informal markets, and thus deny policymakers the ability to monitor economic activities.

Currently public expenditure constitutes more than 60% of GDP; most basic necessities such as food and fuel are heavily subsidized; tertiary education is free; health services are either free or at nominal prices. Basic necessities are one of the most subsidized factors in sub-Saharan Africa; households appear to depend on the state for their day-to day-needs. A way forward is to reverse the scenario, and create an atmosphere where the role of the private sector is enhanced and the tax base is enlarged, thereby enabling the government to perform its traditional duties efficiently.

■ REFERENCES

Court, J., P. Kristen, and B. Weder, 1999. 'Bureaucratic structure and performance: first Africa survey results'. Tokyo: United Nations University.

Degefa, D., 2001. 'The parallel foreign exchange market and macroeconomic performance in Ethiopia', Research Paper 107. Nairobi: AERC.

Kidane, A., 2001. 'Eritrean macroeconomic performance (1992–2000)', paper presented at the International Conference on Eritrean studies, Asmara.

State of Eritrea, 1994. 'Macro policy'. MS, Asmara.

Ethiopia Perspectives Beyond Growth and Poverty

Abbi Kedir

1. Introduction

Documenting key aspects of the Ethiopian economy consists of occasional flickers of hope and abundant tales of tribulation. After ousting the military government in 1991, the current regime in Ethiopia introduced a number of economic reforms aimed at restructuring the economy and macroeconomic stabilization. In the last five years, the GDP growth rates have been encouraging, even if the current estimate of double-digit growth is unrealistically optimistic. Since the 1990s there have been encouraging developments in poverty reduction at the household level in some but not all rural regions of the country (Dercon 2006). However, there are parallel alarming poverty increases in urban areas (Gebremedhin and Whelan 2008; Kedir and McKay 2005). There is an expanding private sector which suffers from lack of foreign exchange. Most of the poor in Ethiopia and the largest proportion of the urban labour force are supported by the credit-starved and impoverished informal sector. One can clearly see improvements in Ethiopian roads, given the continued intensified support of the World Bank.

The fundamental problems of the Ethiopian economy include high levels of urban as well as rural poverty driven by population pressure (Kedir, Aassve, and Gabriel 2008), inflation, environmental degradation, diseases, illiteracy, power shortages, and erratic rainfall patterns. In this essay, I venture beyond the growth–poverty link.

The above brief narrative highlights some developments in Ethiopia as well as the scepticism needed to put the much-heralded positive growth in some perspective. I discuss the key analytical and policy issues in relation to growth. I also discuss issues related to long-term development challenges peculiar to Ethiopia.

2. Analytical issues

Primarily, we start our discussion with a number of analytical issues which are not necessarily restricted to the Ethiopian case. First, there is an enormous difficulty in understanding the micro-level impact of macroeconomic changes such as trade liberalization (Winters, McCulloch, and McKay 2004). To some extent, general equilibrium analysis can be helpful. Most existing works of growth and poverty are based on partial equilibrium analysis (Dercon 2006; Geda, Shimeles, and Weeks 2009). Therefore, more intellectual effort needs to be channelled to uncover the transmission mechanisms of macro changes and their micro-level impacts. The debate about whether growth leads to poverty reduction should be understood in this context.

Second, understandably, there is more focus on rural than urban poverty even if the chronic poverty rates in the latter are as high (if not higher in some locations) than the former. Redressing the balance of analytical studies focusing on both poverties is necessary for a better-informed debate on the extent of poverty in Ethiopia. Third, the reliability of the government's macro model in forecasting the GDP growth rates is questionable, as there are conflicting growth figures depending on the source one consults. This makes claims of improved living standards based on reported GDP figures unreliable.

Fourth, the power of growth to reduce poverty is severely limited if it perpetuates existing income inequality (Geda et al. 2009). The collapse of the whole rural economy of Ethiopia following the 1976 land reform is a case in point (Collier and Dercon 2006). Ill-conceived reforms still are leading to similar economic disasters in other parts of Africa (e.g. Zimbabwe). However, one should also note that reducing inequality is not costless.

Fifth, improvements in other living standard indicators such as life expectancy, gender equality, and better health are the ultimate goals of development. Therefore, policymakers should ensure equality of opportunity which, in turn, leads to equality of other welfare indicators. In the spirit of Sen's seminal work on social justice and deprivation, tackling poverty in Ethiopia means addressing deprivation of basic capabilities and freedom.

Sixth, interdisciplinary perspectives (especially with demographers, epidemiologists, anthropologists) offer much promise in efforts to understand determinants of poverty and to address key policy issues. For instance, culture has a role to play in determining work ethic. Finally, disaggregated welfare analysis shows a different picture relative to aggregate studies. Even if poverty dynamics show a decline of poverty at the household level, putting one's trust in such a finding can be misleading. Studies that focused on individuals within households (e.g. child malnutrition) indicate an increase in extreme poverty in recent years (Kedir 2009). Analysis of intra-household resource allocation and welfare gives valuable insight about poverty of individuals (e.g. women) within a given household (Kebede 2008).

3. Policy issues

Theoretically speaking, a number of policy instruments can help to facilitate growth and poverty reduction. But often the practical application is limited, mainly due to the controversial nature of the proposed policy instruments. First, transforming Ethiopian agriculture is fundamental. Leaving production for exports aside, feeding the expanding Ethiopian population is still an enormous challenge. The green revolution escaped the whole of the African continent despite its enormous potential. For some change to occur, smallholders should be able to access crucial inputs such as land, fertilizer, technology (e.g. GM crops), and credit. Carefully piloted redistribution policies, non-partisan government budget allocations, and targeted aid to farmers are urgently needed. It is not sufficient to introduce these policies; it is equally important to gauge their effectiveness transparently, in line with the spirit of recent efforts to track the destination of macro-level expenditures.

Second, the government has to address the intolerable food, fuel, and other price rises which erode the returns on household endowments (e.g. education and health). High prices are easily felt and are detrimental to survival because they exacerbate long-term chronic problems such as malnutrition. One may argue that prices are important only in urban areas in agrarian economies. In Ethiopia, however, chronic consumption poverty in rural areas in the 1990s persisted mainly due to price changes (Dercon 2006).

Third, growth can be sustained if investment in human capital is sustained; if population policy leads to effective birth control; if infrastructure is provided for exporting firms; if inequality in political power and the problem of partisanship are addressed. Matters which require urgent attention in Ethiopia are the energy crisis as well as the large-scale environmental degradation. Handling the population issue as a priority objective helps to address the problem of rural community conflicts over land distribution, and to ease the pressure on available food supply, the environment, urban centres, and the social services.

4. Conclusion

I have argued that the debate about economic performance and welfare in Ethiopia should not be preoccupied with growth alone but development. What matters is not only an increase in income but also an enhanced opportunity to get access to food, shelter, schools, hospitals, roads, jobs, cleaner environment, freedom, and security. The development objectives should aim at addressing the needs of a majority of neglected but vulnerable groups in society: the homeless, widows, the elderly, the disabled, women, and abandoned children in the streets and some regional hospitals. In addition to the technical problems surrounding targeted transfers, limited and biased social safety-net handouts to compensate for the failure of donor and poor government policies cannot ensure long-term improvement in living standards. In all this the state has a crucial role to play, supporting those who eke out survival from the informal sector in the current climate of global economic downturn (Kanbur 2009).

Effective, transparent, systematic, sustained, and coordinated policy efforts are necessary to save the Ethiopian economy from the brink of collapse. Reporting double-digit GDP growth figures without lifting the majority of Ethiopians from the clutches of inflation, hunger, diseases, drought, and conflict may amount to gross failure and cynicism.

REFERENCES

Collier, P., and S. Dercon, 2006. 'The complementarities of poverty reduction, equity, and growth: a perspective on the *World Development Report 2006*', *Economic Development and Cultural Change* 55, 223–6.

Dercon, S., 2006. 'Economic reform, growth and the poor: evidence from rural Ethiopia', *Journal of Development Economics* 81, 1–24.

Gebremedhin, T., and S. Whelan, 2008. 'Prices and urban poverty in Ethiopia', *Journal of African Economies* 17.1, 1–33.

Geda, A., A. Shimeles, and J. Weeks, 2009. 'Growth, poverty and inequality in Ethiopia: which way for pro-poor growth?', *Journal of International Development* 27.

Kanbur, R., 2009. 'What determines poverty reduction?', Foreword to David Hulme, David Lawson, Imran Matin, and Karen Moore (eds), *What Works for the Poorest? Poverty Reduction Programmes for the World's Extreme Poor*. Rugby: Practical Action.

Kebede, B., 2008. 'Intra-household allocations in rural Ethiopia: a demand systems approach', *Review of Income and Wealth* 54.1, 1–26.

Kedir, A., 2009. 'Health and productivity: panel evidence from Ethiopia', *African Development Review* 21.1, 59–72.

—— A. Aassve, and H. W. Gabriel, 2008. 'Simultaneous random effect models of poverty and childbearing in Ethiopia', *Ethiopian Journal of Economics* 14.2, 1–32.

—— and A. McKay, 2005. 'Chronic poverty in urban Ethiopia: panel data evidence', *International Planning Studies* 10.1, 49–67.

Winters, A., N. McCulloch, and A. McKay, 2004. 'Trade liberalization and poverty: the evidence so far', *Journal of Economic Literature* 42.1, 72–115.

Gambia, The Macroeconomic Management and Development Challenges

Serign Cham

1. Introduction[1]

The Gambia, with an area of 11,285 km^2 and a population of 1.7 million, is one of the smallest countries in Africa. With a narrow resource base and a small domestic market, it exemplifies inherent challenges faced by small open economies. It depends heavily on external trade, aid, and foreign investment to overcome its scale and resource constraints.

Re-exports, remittances, and tourism are the most dynamic sectors earning foreign exchange, but these have been adversely affected by the recent global economic slowdown. Despite bumper crop harvests and good performance by electricity, telecom, and financial sectors, the real GDP growth decelerated marginally from 6.1% in 2007 to 5.9% in 2008. With ongoing governance reforms and donors' commitment, the Gambia can strengthen and diversify its domestic production.

2. Economic reforms

Following independence in 1965, the Gambia maintained stable macroeconomic conditions with modest rates of economic growth. Economic performance deteriorated after 1983 due to adverse terms of trade, unsustainable budget deficits, and government intervention in private-sector development. To address these problems, the government embarked on an Economic Reform Programme in 1985 and the Programme for Sustained Development in 1990.

Reforms were disrupted by a change of government in July 1994, leading to the withdrawal of donors' assistance. Presidential and parliamentary elections, held in 1996 and 1997 respectively, led to the resumption of donor support and economic

---

[1] The author would like to thank the editors for constructive comments on an earlier draft.

reforms. In June 1998 the government entered into a three-year arrangement under the IMF Enhanced Structural Adjustment Facility—renamed in November 1999 as the Poverty Reduction and Growth Facility (PRGF) with redefined purposes.

The Gambia was one of the initial countries to prepare a detailed Poverty Reduction Strategy Paper (PRSP), also called the Strategy for Poverty Alleviation (SPA), which replaced the prescriptive, mainly donor-driven structural adjustment programmes of the 1970s and 1980s. The first SPA was formulated in 1992 and considered by donors in 1994, with a view to reducing the incidence of poverty, measured at 58% at the time.

The SPA was supplemented in 1996 by the preparation of Vision 20/20 'to transform the Gambia into a financial centre, a tourist paradise, an export-oriented nation, with free markets and vibrant private sector'. The second SPA, which was the country's first PRSP, was implemented during 2003–5.The second PRSP, for 2007–11, prepared in November 2006, incorporated programmes focused on achieving the Millennium Development Goals with macroeconomic stability.

A new PRGF was approved by the IMF in February 2007. Successive reviews by the IMF have concluded that performance has been satisfactory.

3. Economic stability and poverty reduction

The Gambia has attained significant economic stability over the years. During the period 2000–2008 it achieved average real GDP growth rate of 4%, supported by an average growth of 6.6% in agriculture, 5.4% in industry, and 3% in services, mainly driven by trade, financial services, transport, and communications. Average inflation was contained at 7%; the average fiscal deficit was 4% of GDP; and the average current account deficit was 5% of GDP.

Satisfactory performance under the PRGF-supported programme helped the country reach the HIPC completion point in December 2007 and thus benefit from substantial debt relief. At present, total public debt stands at 57% of GDP, comprising domestic debt at 26% of GDP and external debt at 31% of GDP, and is manageable. External debt service at 6.2% of gross exports of goods and services is comfortable.

Despite this progress, achievement of the MDGs has been mixed. The Gambia has made significant progress on gender equality, primary school education, and primary and secondary healthcare. But the country remains significantly off-track with respect to the reduction of poverty, hunger, malnutrition, maternal mortality, incidence of malaria and tuberculosis, and access to safe drinking water. This implies that the so-called trickle down effects of growth have been delayed, and there is slow and uneven development in the Gambia.

4. Development challenges and issues

Weak productivity performance and the low quality of employment help explain the poverty record. On the macroeconomic side, an excessive reliance on monetary policy instruments and poor development of capital and labour markets created a high-interest rate regime, discouraging investment and employment creation.

These trends have led to various development challenges, such as how to sustain high growth with fiscal prudence, how to eradicate poverty and disease at a faster speed, and how to create an enabling environment for public–private partnership for delivery of basic public goods and services. The country needs to adopt a more pro-poor growth strategy, whatever the definition of pro-poor growth. It needs to continue with the focus on agriculture development and other employment-generating programmes, along with governance reforms for capacity-building and development of social and physical infrastructure. If these reforms and poverty reduction strategy are carried to their logical ends, the Gambia will emerge in the medium term as one of the dynamic economies in Africa.

5. Conclusion

The Gambia is a small, open, and vulnerable economy, which relies heavily on trade, agriculture, tourism, and services. For the past five years, growth rates have averaged 5.5%, while inflation has remained in single digits. Foreign exchange reserves stand at five months of imports. Key enablers of growth include energy and roads infrastructure. However, poverty still remains a major problem and the majority of the poor live in rural areas.

The Gambia's economic management experience has shown that economic growth is a necessary but not sufficient condition for meaningful economic development and poverty reduction. Economic reform programmes by the IMF have largely been successful, but have limited the state's desire to invest in critical infrastructure necessary to generate a 'big push' and put the country on a sustainable and desired growth path, thus making the case for the fiscal space argument.

■ REFERENCES

African Development Bank and World Bank, 2008. *The Gambia: Joint AfDB and World Bank Assistance Strategy 2008–2011*, pp. 1–86, 10 March.
International Monetary Fund, 2009. *The Gambia: Fourth Review under the Three-Year Arrangement under the Poverty Reduction and Growth Facility*, pp. 1–82. Washington, DC.

Ghana
The Development Record and the Washington Consensus

Augustin Kwasi Fosu

1. Introduction[1]

Less than a decade following Ghana's independence from colonial rule on 6 March 1957, the country had begun experiencing substantial declines in economic growth. By the early 1980s, per capita income was less than its value at the time of independence.[2] Much of this poor economic performance has been attributed to the 'hard control' that thwarted the functioning of markets (Aryeetey and Fosu 2008).

Beginning in 1983, Ghana resorted to a new development strategy of economic liberalization, dubbed the 'Washington Consensus': fiscal discipline; trade liberalization; liberalization of (inward) foreign direct investment; privatization; strong protection of property rights; reordering of public expenditure priorities toward public goods (e.g., health and education); liberalized interest rates; tax reform involving broad tax base and moderate marginal rates; and deregulation to ease barriers for firms' entry and exit of sectors (Williamson 1990).[3] Economic growth both improved and stabilized markedly.

2. What went wrong?

Ghana embarked on a government-led development strategy following independence, involving state controls as a rationing mechanism. Unfortunately, such a system represented a major anti-growth 'syndrome' (Fosu and O'Connell 2007). The country's per capita income fell by one-third during 1974–83 alone. From near-parity in 1960, the country's GDP per capita was about one-half (0.55) of the median sub-Saharan Africa (SSA) value by 1983.

---

[1] No institution of affiliation is responsible for views expressed herein.
[2] Unless otherwise indicated, all statistics cited herein are derived from World Bank and other sources and are as reported in Fosu (2009b).
[3] There have been subsequent revisions, but this version constitutes Williamson's original formulation.

Government dominance in resource allocation led to urban-bias policies that reduced growth (Bates 1981). It also resulted in rent-seeking and elite political instability (EPI) in the form of *coups d'état*; Ghana had the dubious distinction of being a leader in EPI (McGowan 2003), with adverse growth implications (Fosu 1992).

Accompanying the considerable decline in per capita income was substantial deterioration in other macroeconomic variables. Gross capital formation as a percentage of GDP had fallen from nearly 25.0% in 1965 to 6.2% by 1982, and inflation reached a zenith of 123% in 1983, compared with near-zero in 1960. Ironically, despite the centrality of industrialization and government in the strategy, the share of industry declined from nearly 20.0% in 1965 to a mere 6.2% by 1982, while the share of government expenditure in GDP dropped from 17.1% in 1965 to 3.3% by 1982. Similarly, the government's tax base was particularly hard-hit, with the central government revenues falling from 20.0% of GDP in 1970 to a mere 5.0% of a smaller GDP[4] (Aryeetey and Fosu 2008).

Meanwhile, appeals to Ghana's socialist allies, particularly the Soviet Union, in the early 1980s resulted in little support. With limited alternatives, accepting a capitalist-based reform in exchange for assistance was imperative (Aryeetey and Cox 1997).

3. The new development strategy

Crafted in conjunction with the Bretton Woods Institutions, the economic reform was intended to minimize the role of government in the Ghanaian economy and to allow markets to work—the Washington Consensus. The Economic Recovery Programme, instituted in April 1983, was designed first to first stabilize the economy. It liberalized the foreign-exchange and other markets in order to halt the downward economic spiral that saw a reduction in per capita income of 10% in 1982 alone (Aryeetey and Fosu 2008). The second phase began in 1986 with the adoption of the Structural Adjustment Programme, which was geared toward correcting structural imbalances.

For the first time since independence, there was a functioning floating-exchange rate system, import licenses were abolished, import tariff schedules dramatically reduced, and restrictions on foreign exchange outflow substantially relaxed. In addition, fiscal and monetary policies were rationalized, and a programme of privatization embarked on.

---

[4] In fairness, Ghana's extreme economic difficulties were precipitated not only by the cumulative effects of bad policies but also by adverse shocks such as the substantially higher prices of imported petroleum in the 1970s due to OPEC action. The country also experienced in the early 1980s a severe drought, accompanied by a massive emigration from the rural sector as more than 2 million Ghanaians migrated to Nigeria in response to that country's oil boom.

4. Responsiveness to the reform

That Ghana's economic direction has changed positively since the reform is incontrovertible. Most macroeconomic and development indicators have substantially improved. Per capita income has risen steadily, from as low as $1,387 dollars (PPP-adjusted 2000 international dollars) in 1983 to $2,300 in 2006. This performance has outstripped that of SSA generally, which in 2006 registered a median income of $1,327, even though its (median) income was slightly higher than Ghana's in 1983.

The country's human development index (HDI) has also risen from 0.47 in 1980 to 0.55 in 2005, ranking Ghana in the 'medium human development' category and among the top SSA performers. The country has, furthermore, reduced its $1-standard poverty rate from 51.1% in 1992 to 30.0% in 2006.[5]

Meanwhile, both total factor productivity and gross capital formation have increased substantially since the reform, the latter from the nadir of 3.4% of GDP in 1982 to 32.4% in 2006, including a rise in the private portion as well, from 6.9% in 1990 to 17.0% in 2006. From over 100% in 1983 to less than 20% by 2006, the inflation rate has also fallen considerably. The share of industry has risen, from 6.2% of GDP in 1982 to 25.4% in 2006, while the manufacturing share of GDP has increased from 3.6% in 1982 to 8.5% by 2006. Exports have increased from about 5.0% of GDP in 1983 to nearly 40% in 2006, with positive implications for growth (Fosu 1990a). Perhaps more importantly, the share of manufacturing in exports has risen to 30.9% in 2006, following its dismal value of less than 1.0% in 1982.[6]

The political economy has improved considerably as well. Incidence of rampant coups during the post-independence era has now given way to a stable multiparty democracy. Such maturity is exemplified by the peaceful transfer of political leadership twice from one civilian government to the opposition.[7] Indeed, Ghana's measure of electoral competitiveness has improved from 1.5 in 1975–9 to the maximum possible score of 7.0 in 2000–2004. This represents an important transformation, for the country has reached the growth-enhancing democratization regime (Fosu 2008).[8]

---

[5] Technically, this is the $1.25 level. This poverty-reduction performance outstrips e.g. that of India, whose poverty rate at the same standard fell from 49.4% in 1994 to 41.6% in 2005.

[6] The manufacturing share of exports is a particularly potent ingredient in growth due to its measure of relative competitiveness (Fosu 1990b).

[7] Most recently in 2009, Ghana transitioned from the incumbent to the opposition despite the latter's extremely marginal lead, 50.23% versus 49.77%, in the run-off presidential election.

[8] Fosu (2008) finds that democratization tends to be growth-inhibiting until a threshold of about 4.4 of either the index of legislative or executive electoral competitiveness.

5. Conclusion

Ghana's economic fortunes have substantially improved since the liberal economic reforms of the early to mid-1980s. Economic growth has risen substantially, and so has income, supported by strong productivity growth and capital formation. The poverty rate has fallen, and HDI has increased to rank Ghana among medium human-development countries. Many of the other macroeconomic and democratic indicators have also improved markedly, which augers well for further growth and development. Ghana's current Achilles' heel, though, seems to be the external and fiscal deficits that appear to plague the country, currently running at more than 10% of GDP each. External aid has strongly supported the reforms by funding such deficits, with ODA rising from near-zero in the early 1980s to over 10% of GDP since the mid-1980s.

Despite the risk of 'post hoc ergo propter hoc', it seems reasonable to conclude that market liberalization based on the Washington Consensus, supported by external assistance and deepened democratization, has been effective in resuscitating Ghana's heretofore moribund economy. Further progress will, however, depend crucially on the country's ability to resolve its current fiscal and external deficit difficulties as well as improving its productive infrastructure. Above all, Ghana must maintain its political stability.

REFERENCES

Aryeetey, E., and A. Cox, 1997. 'Aid effectiveness in Ghana', in J. Carlsson, G. Somolekae, and N. van de Walle (eds), *Foreign Aid in Africa: Learning from Country Experiences*. Uppsala: Nordic Africa Institute.

—— and A. K. Fosu, 2008. 'Economic growth in Ghana, 1960–2000', in B. J. Ndulu, S. A. O'Connell, J.-P. Azam, R. H. Bates, A. K. Fosu, J. W. Gunning, and D. Njinkeu (eds), *The Political Economy of Economic Growth in Africa, 1960–2000*, vol. 2: *Country Case Studies*. Cambridge: Cambridge University Press, 289–324.

Bates, Robert H., 1981. *Markets and States in Tropical Africa*. Berkeley: University of California Press.

Fosu, A. K., 1990a. 'Exports and economic growth: the African case', *World Development* 18.6, 831–5.

—— 1990b. 'Export composition and the impact of exports on economic growth of developing economies', *Economics Letters* 34.1, 67–71.

—— 1992. 'Political instability and economic growth: evidence from sub-Saharan Africa', *Economic Development and Cultural Change* 40.4, 829–41.

—— 2008. 'Democracy and growth in Africa: implications of increasing electoral competitiveness', *Economics Letters* 100, 442–4.

Fosu, A. K., 2009a. 'Inequality and the impact of growth on poverty: comparative evidence for sub-Saharan Africa', *Journal of Development Studies* 45.5, 726–45.

—— 2009b. 'Country role models for development success: the case of Ghana', UNU-WIDER Research Paper No. 2009/42. Helsinki.

—— and S. A. O'Connell, 2007. 'Explaining African economic growth: the role of anti-growth syndromes', in F. Bourguignon and B. Pleskovič (eds), *Annual Bank Conference on Development Economics (ABCDE)*. Washington, DC: World Bank, 31–66.

McGowan, P., 2003. 'African military coups d'état, 1956–2001: frequency, trends and distribution', *Journal of Modern African Studies* (Apr.).

Williamson, J., 1990. 'What Washington means by policy reform', in J. Williamson (ed.), *Latin American Adjustment: How Much Has Happened?* Washington, DC: Institute for International Economics.

Guinea
Poverty, Governance, and Growth

Kerfalla Yansane

1. Introduction[1]

Despite a rich endowment of natural resources, Guinea remains one of the poorest countries in the world. The growth rate of the GDP per capita has been on a downwards trend in recent years, averaging only 0.5% since 2000, resulting in a significant decline of per capita GDP from US$379 in 2002 to US$332 in 2006 (IMF 2009). On the other hand, year-on-year inflation has risen steadily, from 5.4% in 2002 to 17.5% in 2004, and to a record 39.1% in 2006.

This fragile economic environment, characterized by low economic growth and high inflation, inevitably led to the deterioration of the living conditions of the population. According to the second PRSP report by the Government of Guinea (Ministry of Economy and Finance 2006), the incidence of poverty increased from 49.2% in 2002 to 53.6% in 2005, with 19.1% of these people living in extreme poverty. It is then not a surprise that Guinea still ranks amongst the fifteen countries lowest in the ranking based on the Human Development Index.[2]

The poor economic and social performances of Guinea may be explained by a variety of factors, including persistent insecurity in the subregion and the sizeable influx of refugees from neighbouring countries (estimated at its peak at between 5% and 10% of the Guinean population), increased defence spending in response to security concerns along Guinea's borders, higher oil prices, and a sharp decline in external assistance (Ministry of Economy and Finance 2006). However, the various progress reports of the PRSP I by the Government of Guinea also acknowledge that governance has constituted the weakest link in implementing the PRSP, and that corruption is one of the principal factors behind the poor performance in the handling of public affairs (Ministry of

---

[1] The author is grateful to Sékou Falilou Doumbouya, Groupe de Recherche et d'Appui au Développement Economique et Social (Economic and Social Research Network) for helpful assistance in data collection and for comment.
[2] Guinea ranks 167 out of 179 countries (UNDP 2008).

Economy and Finance 2006). This view is confirmed by a number of national and international reports.

The Ibrahim Index of African Governance is a comprehensive ranking of African countries according to governance quality. According to this Index, in 2009 Guinea ranks 44th out of 53 countries (Mo Ibrahim Foundation 2009). And Guinea seems to be stuck amongst the 10 countries at the bottom, with no improvement over time. The Worldwide Governance Indicators (WGI) 2009 reports six governance indicators for more than 200 countries on six dimensions of governance. Governance Matters 2009 (Kaufmann 2009) shows that the percentile ranking of Guinea has significantly deteriorated between 1996 and 2008 for Regulatory Quality, and Control of Corruption, from above 50 out of 100 to nearly 10.

The Doing Business reports present quantitative indicators of a set of regulations affecting 10 stages of a company business's life. The Doing Business report for 2010 (World Bank 2010) covers 183 economies, including 46 countries in sub-Saharan Africa. In this report, Guinea is ranked 173 out of 183 economies for the overall ease of doing business, far behind neighbouring countries such as Burkina Faso, Mali, and Senegal.

According to the National Report on Corruption and Governance in Guinea initiated by the Government with the technical support of the World Bank Institute (National Committee Against Corruption 2005), corruption affects almost every citizen. Half of the households interviewed in the surveys report that bribes are always requested when dealing with the public administration to obtain various public services. The prevalence of corruption in Guinea is estimated by surveys at 36 on a scale of 100, below 32 for Sierra Leone and 28 for Zambia. These figures are consistent with the rankings and scores of the Corruption Perceptions Index (CPI) of Transparency International (TI). In the 2006 CPI report, Guinea was ranked 160 out of 163 countries. In the 2010 CPI report, the corruption perception of Guinea has further deteriorated, as it is now ranked 173 out of 180 countries. Overall, corruption is considered as one of the top three problems for Guinea, jointly with the high cost of living and unemployment (National Committee Against Corruption 2005).

One of the lessons from the foregoing review is the strong correlation between corruption and poverty. The other lesson is that institutions are significant as far as the rate and quality of economic growth are concerned. Strong institutions, which embody and protect social and moral values, and ensure adequate laws and regulations in a stable framework, have positive influence on both political governance and economic governance (Pei 1999). In sum, the decrepitude of national institutions of Guinea in recent years may be considered as the root cause of bad governance in the country.

REFERENCES

Kaufmann, Daniel, 2009. Governance Matters, Worldwide Governance Indicators 1996–2008, Country Profile, Guinea.

International Monetary Fund, 2008, 2009. 'Joint Staff Advisory Note on the first and second Poverty Reduction Strategy Paper'. Washington, DC.

Ministry of Economy and Finance, 2006, 2007. 'Second and Third Progress Reports of the Poverty Reduction Strategy (PRS), Permanent Secretariat of the Poverty Reduction Strategy'. Conakry.

Mo Ibrahim Foundation, 2009. *Ibrahim Index*. London.

National Committee Against Corruption, 2005. *National Report on Corruption and Governance in Guinea*. Conakry.

Pei, M., 1999. 'Economic institutions, democracy and development', paper presented at the Carnegie World Bank Conference on Democracy, Market Economy, and Development (Feb.).

Rivera-Batiz, F., 1999. *Democracy, Governance, and Economic Growth: Theory and Evidence*. New York: Columbia University Press.

United Nations Development Programme, 2008. 'Human Development Indices: a statistical update'.

World Bank, 2006. *Global Monitoring Report*. Washington, DC.

—— 2010. *Doing Business 2010: Guinea*. Washington, DC.

Guinea Bissau Primary Commodity Vulnerability

Steven Kyle

1. Introduction

Guinea Bissau is a relatively small (37,000 km^2) country, comprising mainly coastal lowlands and marshes and dry savannah in the interior. No point in the country is above 300m of elevation, and its topography is dominated by estuaries formed by its major rivers.

Guinea Bissau is by almost any measure one of the poorest countries in the world. It is ranked in the bottom 10 by all available comparisons (IMF, World Bank, and CIA), and more than two thirds of the population lives below the poverty line. Average per capita income is about $300 per year, though it is extremely unequally shared across the population of about 1.6 million.

2. Macroeconomy

The economy of Guinea Bissau is much influenced by four important facts.

- Guinea Bissau has an extremely high level of dependence on a single export—cashew—which is grown by the vast majority of peasant farmers in the country, covers close to 5% of the total land area, and accounts for 98% of export revenue as well as 17% of government revenue.
- Guinea Bissau suffers from an extremely degraded infrastructural base. Very little has been done to maintain roads or ports since independence in the 1970s. Indeed, recent reports in 2009 emphasize that the country is in imminent danger of losing its direct access to seaborne trade through the degradation of the physical condition of its port in Bissau. Lack of electricity is another area of extreme concern.
- Guinea Bissau is heavily dependent on imports of its most important staple food, rice.
- Fish exports are a major source of government revenues, through licensing of foreign flagged vessels fishing in Guinea Bissau waters but landing their catch elsewhere.

It is important to note that trade policy itself is not the most important of the obstacles confronting Guinea Bissau at this time. While there are certainly areas where some useful changes could be made, Guinea Bissau's accession to the West African Economic and Monetary Union (WAEMU) and the Banque Centrale des États de l'Afrique de l'Ouest (BCEAO) has brought its overall policies regarding external trade and financial arrangements in line with those of its neighbours, and have made them broadly conducive to progress in international trade relations.

A major obstacle to progress is the extreme instability of government officials in any given post, leading to exceedingly short-term planning horizons and an almost total absence of long-run vision in policy formulation and implementation. Government ministers and lower-level bureaucrats change on an annual or even more frequent basis. Political power is often viewed simply as a means to accumulate wealth, rather than as something which imposes responsibilities as well as offering opportunities.

Guinea Bissau scores very low on internationally recognized measures of bureaucratic burdens, being the lowest of any country in West Africa and third from the bottom in the world overall in the World Bank's annual Ease of Doing Business Survey. It is indicative of the problems faced by potential entrepreneurs in Guinea Bissau that just opening a business takes an average of 233 days and more than 250% of the per capita GDP in costs. Many observers describe the situation using terms such as 'strangulation'. Given the numerous potential locations for international businesses in West Africa and beyond, Guinea Bissau's problem is primarily in making the country one which businesses will want to operate in—a tall order, given its relative standings vis-à-vis its neighbours in the various aspects of business environment.

3. Agriculture

Agriculture is by far the most important occupation, with more than three-quarters of the population engaged in it. Rice is the traditional staple crop, but in recent years production has fallen, with an increasing emphasis on cashew grown for cash and export. Indeed, the degree of export dependence on this crop exceeds even the export dependence of most members of OPEC on oil exports. The resulting shortfall in staple grain has been made up by a combination of rice imports and cassava cultivation.

In the near term, improvement in cashew production and marketing are a prerequisite for improvement in the lot of the majority of small farmers as well as the macro balances of the country in general. Simple arithmetic underscores this observation—with 98% of export earnings and 17% of fiscal revenue derived from this crop, even unprecedented success with other products can yield only a marginal increase in the total. However, much more than arithmetic dictates that a primary goal of any trade effort be directed toward the cashew sector:

- First, it is abundantly clear that Guinea Bissau possesses near-optimal conditions for cashew production. Indeed, not only is cashew produced virtually without purchased inputs in most cases, but the quality of the nuts is superior to those from many other exporters and so is capable of commanding a premium on the international market.
- Second, the great bulk of the cashew crop is produced by small farmers. In many areas it is hard to find small farmers who do not grow at least some cashew. This is extremely important, in that it means that alterations in the farm gate price of cashews have a greater impact on the incomes of the poorest than any other variable in the economy.

4. Mining

Historically, the mining and petroleum sectors of Guinea Bissau have been nonexistent except for quarrying and a small amount of artisanal mining. While it has been known since the 1970s that there are potentially significant deposits of bauxite and phosphates, due to quality and infrastructure concerns, low international prices, and political instability, these were never fully explored. However, in recent years both the bauxite (2007) and phosphate (1997) areas have entered long-term exploration leases. There also have been several offshore discoveries of heavy oil deposits. Although an economically exploitable deposit has yet to be found, several companies are currently active in the field. If any of the above opportunities are realized, it would have a profound impact on national income, fiscal revenues, and foreign exchange earnings for Guinea Bissau.

5. Fisheries

The coastal area of Guinea Bissau has waters with some of the highest primary productivity in the world. Industrial and artisanal fishing fleets intensively exploit a significant part of these resources. However, the fishery management systems of the countries of the region are, in general, ineffective, particularly with regard to controlling the movements of fishing fleets that share among themselves most of the resources. Due to the predominance of an agricultural tradition in Guinea Bissau, foreign artisanal and industrial fishermen catch most of the fishing produce in the country's coastal waters, part of which is undertaken outside the control of the fisheries administration.

Kenya
A Structural Transformation Paradox and Challenges for the Current Decade

Jane Kiringai

1. Introduction

Before the economic and political shocks of the late 2000s, economic growth in Kenya averaged 4% during the decade, peaking at 7% in 2007, and the medium-term prospects looked rosy. The results of fiscal consolidation and strong revenue mobilization started paying off, and Kenya substantially weaned herself off dependence on donor aid, unlike most countries in sub-Saharan Africa (SSA). At 40% of GDP, debt had been reduced to sustainable limits, creating fiscal space to increase spending on infrastructure and social sectors, diagnosed as the binding constraints to growth. Inflation was low, averaging 4%, and foreign exchange reserves were at an all-time high, at 4.2 months of import cover. Political risk was moderate, and Kenya was ready to venture into the international credit market to issue a euro bond to finance an ambitious infrastructure programme. Through a macro lens, Kenya's economy was ready for takeoff, and the aspiration to become a middle-income country by 2030 seemed feasible, albeit ambitious.

However, although incomes per capita increased during the decade, the benefits were not broadly shared, and spatial and vertical inequality also increased. Incomes per capita increased from US$ 400 to about $700 and poverty declined from 56% in 2000 to 47% by 2005/6. But inequality increased: in urban Kenya the richest households (top 10%) spent 22 times more than the poorest households, and in rural Kenya the richest households spent 12 times more than the poor (World Bank 2009c). Spatially, the wealthiest province (Nairobi) had a headcount index of 22 while the poorest (North Eastern Province) had a head count index of 74 (Kenya National Bureau of Statistics 2007). Certainly, some of these indicators have deteriorated after the four negative shocks and especially the drought in 2009. The challenge in Kenya is that economic geography closely mimics ethnic boundaries and, for a democracy at the teething stage, the socioeconomic profile creates a volatile disequilibrium which became the platform for political contest. The bubble burst into the political crisis in 2008. Thus, through a micro lens, the political violence demonstrated that Kenya straddles a dangerous precipice, with the potential to become a middle-income country or, like her neighbours, degenerate into a fragile state.

These two possibilities point to the long-term development challenges and nuance the importance of shared growth. At the same time, the economy is undergoing a structural transformation in which underlying incentives inadvertently create winners in the nontradable sectors of the economy and which casts doubt on the long-term sustainability of high growth rates.

2. Composition of final demand

In Kenya, final demand has shifted towards consumption. Comparing averages over two decades—the 'lost decade', 1990–2000, and the 'growth decade', 2000–2008—consumption as a share of GDP increased by 6 percentage points and, as would be expected, savings contracted . The reverse happened in SSA: consumption contracted and savings increased. In the external account, the share of exports in GDP contracted by 2.3 and imports increased by 3.0. In SSA the growth in imports was closely matched by growth in exports (see Fig. 1). Thus although the decade of growth in SSA has been attributed to a favourable external environment, Kenya seems to have missed the boat, and domestic consumption

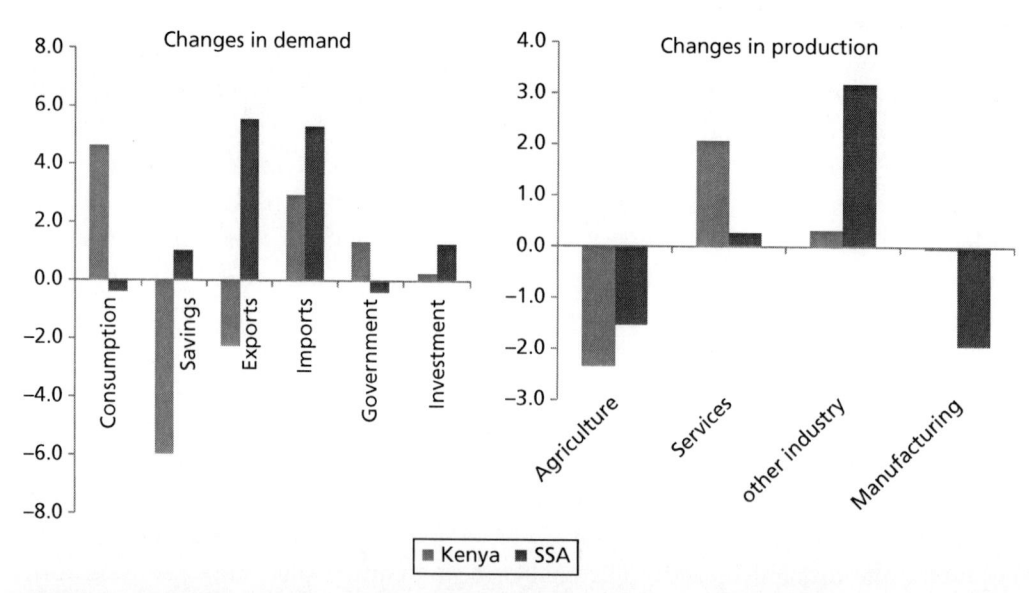

Figure 1. Changes in supply and demand, 1990–2000 and 2000–2008 (% GDP) (source; author's computation)

provided the growth stimulus. But even as consumption drives growth, incomes per capita remain relatively low (about US$700), and a population of 38 million people is not sufficient to provide a meaningful push in production capacity to sustain growth.

The current structure of demand signals the need for expenditure-switching incentives to increase savings and investment, and production for the export market rather than production for the domestic market. In this regard, exploiting the EAC common market and the larger COMESA is a useful starting point for Kenya.

3. Can Kenya leverage the strong services sector to balance and sustain growth over the next decade?

On the supply side, structural transformation in Kenya has differed from the broader SSA. As the share of agriculture in the economy contracted, Kenya witnessed a rapid expansion in services, but for the rest of SSA other industries (except manufacturing) expanded faster than services. With the exception of tourism (transport and travel), services are largely not traded. Therefore this pattern of transformation with the prospects of contracting industry is likely to constrain the pace of outward orientation, and will remain a key policy challenge for the next decade.

The good news is that between 1995 and 2007 Kenya's ICT exports increased from 1 to 2% share in total exports. Although the services sector has been driving growth, it contributes only about a third of total exports, and the share declined from 39% in 1995 to 35% in 2007. Furthermore, Kenya's share in Africa's trade in services declined from 10% in 1995 to 6% in 2007—which means that, although Kenya's services sector has been driving growth, the tradable share of services has declined and is dominated by transport (over 90%), out of sync with trends in emerging markets. In India, for instance, service exports as a share of the total exports increased from 18% to 38%, mainly driven by ICT subsector, whose share in total exports increased from 6% to 28% during the last decade. With an average growth of 22% over the last decade, Kenya is going through an ICT revolution; but it is not yet evident that it can ride the ICT revolution to increase exports and become a middle-income country by 2030.

Thus as structural change in production continues, the composition of exports remains broadly unchanged. Agriculture exports account for more than 50% merchandise exports and about 30% of total exports. Besides cut flowers, export diversification has been limited, with a high share of primary commodities with inelastic demand and declining global prices. It is therefore not surprising that Kenya's terms of trade declined from 100 in year 2000 to 83 in 2007, compared to 104 for Uganda and 109 for Tanzania. Kenya is a more diversified economy, with a geographical advantage over her EAC trading partners, but the trend in external trade and recent growth performance does not reflect this reality and is a paradox.

4. Geography and trade

Empirical evidence suggests that, as a coastal country with a port, Kenya should have 1.5 growth advantage over her landlocked neighbours (Collier and O'Connell 2007). Estimates from Doing Business indicators 2009 (World Bank 2009a) show that in Kenya, it takes double the time and costs three times more to export compared to Egypt, one of the key competitors in the regional COMESA market. Furthermore, the inefficiencies at the port escalate all the way along the northern corridor to the hinterland, where fixed operating costs in Kenya are double the costs in West Africa. At 29 days, the time taken to export is broadly comparable to other countries in SSA, but the cost to export a container is relatively high in Kenya, and comparable to the costs in landlocked economies. For instance, it costs US$2,055 to export a container in Kenya, US$2,012 in Mali (38 days), and only half that amount in Ghana at US$1,003 (19 days), US$737 in Egypt (14 days), and a quarter of the cost in Malaysia at US $450 (18 days) (World Bank 2009a). Inefficiency and high transaction costs negate Kenya's geographical advantage.

5. Conclusion

I highlight three closely related policy challenges for the current decade. First, the Kenyan economy requires a radical shift and expenditure-switching policies to reverse the declining share of exports in final demand; growth driven by private consumption cannot be sustainable in the medium to long term. Second, if Kenya is to leverage growth on services and especially ICT, then the export share of the sector has to increase significantly. Notably, service exports are not constrained by inefficiencies at the port and the northern corridor. The third policy challenge concerns the stifled growth of Kenya's manufacturing sector and its ability to lead growth through exports in the regional market.

REFERENCES

Collier, Paul, and Stephen O'Connell, 2007. 'Opportunities and choices', in Benno J. Ndulu, Stephen A. O'Connell, Robert H. Bates, Paul Collier, and Charles C. Soludo (eds), *The Political Economy of Economic Growth in Africa, 1960–2000*, vol. 1. Cambridge: Cambridge University Press.

Kenya National Bureau of Statistics, 2007. *Basic Report on Well Being in Kenya*. Nairobi: Kenya National Bureau of Statistics, Ministry of Planning and National Development.

World Bank, 2008. *Kenya: Accelerating and Sustaining Growth*. Washington, DC: World Bank Africa Region.

—— 2009a. *Doing Business 2009*. Washington, DC: World Bank.

—— 2009b. *World Development Indicators 2009*. Washington, DC: World Bank.

—— 2009c. *Kenya Poverty and Inequality Assessment: Executive Summary and Synthesis Report*. Washington, DC: World Bank Africa Region.

Lesotho Experiences and Challenges from the Textiles Manufacturing Sector

Adelaide R. Matlanyane

1. Introduction

The manufacturing sector has been the pillar of the Lesotho economy in the last twenty years, with the country being the largest and most successful exporter of textiles under the Africa Growth Opportunity Act (AGOA) in sub-Saharan Africa. The development of the manufacturing sector, and prolonged droughts that reduced agricultural output, transformed the structure of the economy. The manufacturing sector has grown significantly to outperform the agricultural sector, which was in the lead, and to become the largest employer and the driver of growth. It currently contributes 18% to GDP and is dominated by the textiles and clothing subsector, which contributes 29.8% to total manufacturing and accounts for about 61% of total exports. The growth of exports of goods and services averaged 9.2% during 1980–2004, reaching a peak of 32.6% in 2001. As a ratio of GDP, exports of goods and services rose from 17.3% in 1980 to a remarkable 41.6% in 2004, reaching a peak of 55.2% in 2002.

2. Background and policy environment

The economy of Lesotho experienced high growth rates in the 1990s resulting from two key sources; the construction related to the Lesotho Highlands Water Project (LHWP) and the rapid development of the textiles and garment manufacturing subsector. The growth of Lesotho's manufacturing sector accelerated following efforts to attract foreign direct investment, and remained the key anchor of the economy following the completion of the LHWP in 1998/99. The subsector is dominated by Asian companies that produce for the export market. Many of the companies established in Lesotho mainly to take advantage of the relatively cheap labour and access to the United States and other markets under facilities such as the Generalised System of Preferences (GSP), the Multi-Fibre Agreement (MFA), and AGOA of 2000.

Part of the strategy to attract foreign investment entailed provision of basic infrastructure to ease entry. Through the Lesotho National Development Corporation (LNDC), government provided financial assistance in the form of soft loans and infrastructure in the form of factory shells, access roads, and utilities, which lowered entry costs. Over the years, basic legal and regulatory reforms were instituted to improve the ease of doing business. Key among these were tax holidays to complement hard infrustructure.

In comparison with other efficient producers such as China, India, and Vietnam, Lesotho ranks low in terms of competitiveness, relating to labour efficiencyand transportation costs, leaving access to the US market through AGOA as one of the few advantages, if not the only one, it has over its rivals. In 2005, following the expiration of the Multifibre Agreement, the government further instituted exemptions from taxation on profits for exports outside the Southern African Customs Union (SACU) area, with a view to retain firms, to encourage new entrants and promote exports to markets outside SACU.

3. Structure of Lesotho's textiles manufacturing sector and its challenges

With the exclusion of diamonds, about 59.5% of Lesotho's exports are destined for the US market, while 40.1% go to South Africa, rendering Lesotho's exposure to these markets excessive. Access to the South African market is driven to a large extent by close proximity and resulting strong trade relations between Lesotho and South Africa, and by Lesotho's membership in SACU, which allows free movement of goods and services among member countries.[1] On the other hand, access to the US market is facilitated by the concessions under AGOA. Although it has not taken much advantage of other existing arrangements, Lesotho also has preferential access to the Canadian market and a GSP (Generalized System of Preferences) access to the Japanese and Nordic markets. It is also a member of the Southern African Development Community (SADC), and therefore, the SADC free trade area (FTA) established in 2008 and part of the SADC economic partnership agreements (EPAs) negotiations.

Despite the success achieved in the manufacturing of textiles, major challenges face Lesotho in relation to innovation of strategies to enhance its competitiveness and hence

---

[1] Members of SACU are Lesotho, South Africa, Botswana, Swaziland, and Namibia. The SACU–EFTA FTA was effected in 2008 together with a trade, investment, and development cooperation agreement (TIDCA) with the US. SACU concluded negotiations with MERCOSUR for a preferential trade agreement (PTA) that was due for signing in 2009.

retain the existing, and expand the investor base. The sector's dependence on AGOA renders its roots in Lesotho shallow and hardly sufficient to guarantee long-term sustainable growth. A related challenge is to diversify its products and markets beyond the USA, and beyond the anchor provided by AGOA to minimize exposure to market- and country-specific shocks.

With exports of textiles in the lead, economic growth derives from a narrow, difficult, and expensive base to sustain, rendering the economy fragile and susceptible to shocks. After twenty year of operating in Lesotho, Lesotho National Development Corporation-assisted companies in the categories of knitted and woven garments and fabric and yarn are still 100% foreign-owned and mostly Asian, showing that the industry has not diversified ownership or attracted local ownership. Estimates show that equity and non-equity liabilities of Lesotho are concentrated in a few Asian countries, primarily China and Taiwan. Furthermore, 57.1% of these companies are in knitted garments, employing 49% of the total labour force in manufacturing, while 17.9% are in woven garments, employing 26.8% of labour, and 16.1% are in fabrics and yarns, screen printing, packaging and home textiles. Only 8.9% of the firms produce footwear.

There is evidence of marginal degree of vertical integration in the sector as larger companies occasionally subcontract work to smaller companies, although still of foreign origin. Although this is seen as a positive development, there are risks of contagion. Integration to sectors such as transportation, construction, and other service sectors in which local ownership is strong is limited. From 2003 to 2007, credit to the manufacturing sector averaged 11.6% of total credit, amounting to M40 million compared with the estimated size of the sector of M1.6 billion in 2006, confirming that the sector's integration with the Lesotho banking services is shallow, as textile manufacturing companies continued to source financing from Asian banks despite the conditions of excessive liquidity in the Lesotho banking sector. The Lesotho financial sector provides services limited to attestation for exported goods, receipt of foreign currency proceeds related to operating costs, and management of foreign currency accounts and payrolls. With financing sourced from Asian financial institutions, and parent companies based in Asia, profits are remitted to Asia and only amounts relating to coverage of operating costs actually reach Lesotho. This arrangement has tended to limit the sector's value added and increase the risk of exposure to international financial markets and development—as experienced during the recent global trade credit squeeze, when the manufacturing companies could not access credit from the Asian banks, and turned to local banks for financing.

Excessive exposure to the US market also proved detrimental when demand in the US fell as the recent economic crisis took a toll on the US economy. A few small companies shut down, and many of the textile companies' orders were either cancelled or reduced considerably, leaving them on the margins of survival.

Although recorded proceeds have boosted Lesotho's external position considerably, with the institution of tax exemptions on profits of exports outside SACU, the government has given up a direct source of revenue with the anticipation that value added tax (VAT) collections, through employment creation, will make up for the lost revenue from profit tax.

The sector's weak integration with the domestic economy seriously undermines the potential gains that could be derived from possible multiplier effects. Likewise, its limited access to markets and concentration in a few markets and products are potential risks to its sustainability. Although the sector survived the expiration of the MFA and continues to be competitive in international markets, the risk of FDI relocating to more efficient countries remains—especially post-2012, when AGOA's new rules of origin come into effect.

4. Conclusions

Lesotho's success with textile manufacturing under AGOA has not been without practical challenges. While the sector contributes significantly to output and employment, it remains weakly integrated with the domestic economy and renders the economic base narrow and exposed. Ownership is highly concentrated, with negligible linkages with the local economy and weak integration to external markets. In addition, the sector is concentrated in a few product lines and its survival is strongly anchored in preferential trade arrangements, in particular AGOA, without which it faces much more competitive rivals in other potential source markets. This points to a fragile foundation for the sector and a weak and unsustainable basis for growth for the economy of Lesotho. If this situation persists, the cost of exceptions to attract FDI into the sector may soon outweigh the benefits derived from it. In light of the renewed vigour of the Asian investments in Africa, careful analysis of benefits and costs is of utmost importance to guide initiatives that will secure sustained growth, diversify the economic base and markets, and promote skills transfer and development of indigenous entrepreneurship in Lesotho.

■ REFERENCES

African Development Bank, 2009. *African Economic Outlook*. Tunis.
Central Bank of Lesotho, various years. *Annual Report*. Maseru.
―― 2006. *Private Capital Flows Survey 2006*. Maseru.
Masenyetse, R., 2006. 'Testing the export-led growth hypothesis: the case of Lesotho', MSc dissertation, Dept. of Economics, National University of Lesotho, Roma.
World Economic Forum, 2009. *African Competitiveness Report*. Davos.

Liberia
Debt Relief

Benjamin Leo

1. Introduction

In July 2010, the Liberian government secured comprehensive debt relief under the Heavily Indebted Poor Country (HIPC) Initiative and Multilateral Debt Relief Initiative. In roughly two and a half years, the Liberian government cleared its arrears to the international financial institutions (IFIs), secured comprehensive debt relief from bilateral and multilateral creditors, and concluded a landmark commercial debt buyback deal. These achievements are particularly noteworthy given the nearly wholesale destruction of the country's economic, institutional, and social infrastructure following over twenty years of political instability.

2. Liberia's re-engagement challenges

Liberia's long period of political instability started in 1980 when Samuel Doe seized power from President William Tolbert in a coup. Following the fraudulent elections of 1985, the former Commanding General of the Liberian Armed Forces attempted unsuccessfully to overthrow President Samuel Doe. Government crackdowns ensued against several ethnicities. In 1989, outright conflict began—with widespread destruction continuing until 2003. The First Liberian Civil War (1989-96) and the Second Liberian Civil War (1999-2003) resulted in the deaths of over 250,000 Liberian citizens and nearly wholesale destruction of the country's economic, institutional and social infrastructure. Moreover, the majority of educated Liberians—including civil servants—fled the country.

2.1. ACCUMULATION OF LOAN ARREARS AND UNSUSTAINABLE EXTERNAL DEBT

Beginning in 1980, the Liberian government started to accumulate arrears to external creditors (Fig. 1). In December 1984, it fell into arrears to the International Monetary

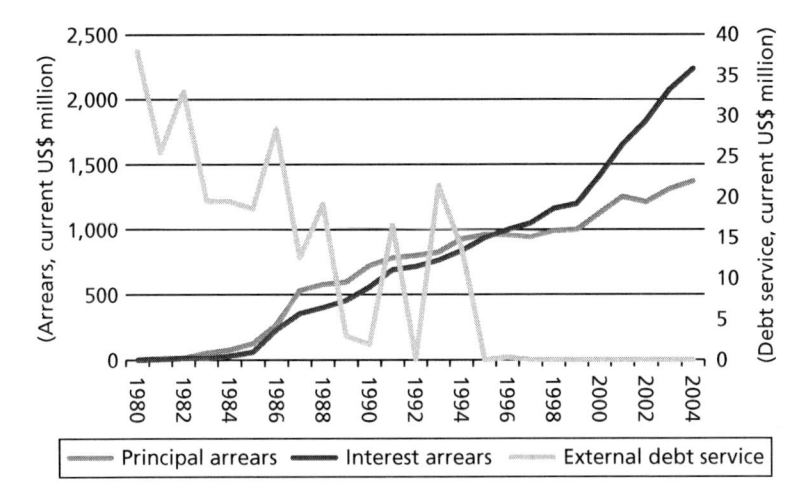

Figure 1. External debt service and arrears, 1980–2004 (source: World Bank)

Fund, and to the World Bank the following year (IMF 2002). By the end of 2007, Liberia's external debt obligations had grown to almost $4.7 billion in net present value terms—of which roughly 96% was in arrears (IMF 2008). Liberia's external debt totalled nearly 1,600% of annual exports (IMF 2008). Every Liberian owed approximately $1,290—or six times more than average per capita income. Before Liberia could re-engage with the international financial community—particularly the IFIs—it first needed to clear its massive loan arrears.

2.2. INSTITUTIONAL CAPACITY

The lack of human capacity and high corruption levels presented monumental challenges for the Liberian government's re-engagement efforts. Twenty years of political instability had a dramatic effect on the quality of Liberian government institutions. Based on World Bank Country Policy and Institutional Assessment (CPIA) levels, Liberia scored above the low-income country median in 1980. By 1985, it was tied for the worst country. It remained at or near the bottom until the Sirleaf administration assumed office in 2006.[1]

3. Key factors in Liberia's re-engagement efforts

Despite its significant challenges and capacity constraints, the Liberian government successfully completed its re-engagement with the international financial community

---

[1] The World Bank did not prepare CPIA ratings for Liberia between 2003 and 2008.

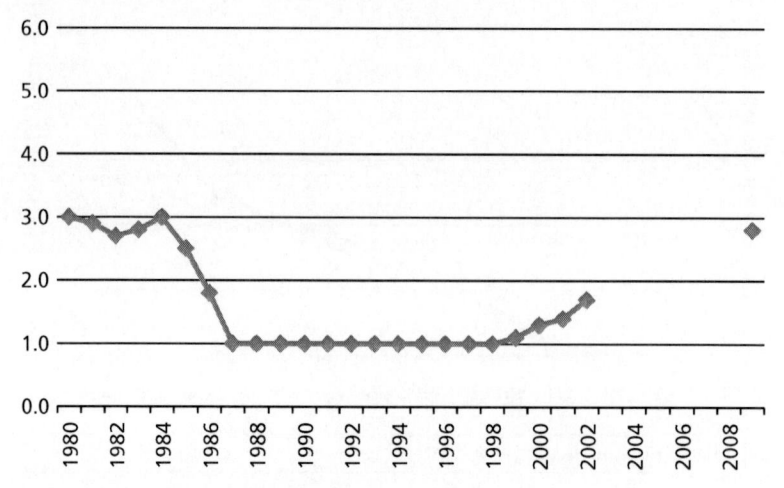

Figure 2. World Bank CPIA scores, 1980–2009

in near record time. On average, low-income countries have taken nearly five years to complete the HIPC process—roughly double the time required for Liberia (IMF 2009). How did Liberia complete the financial re-engagement process so quickly? Three factors played a critical role.

3.1. STRONG, UNIFYING POLITICAL LEADERSHIP

Countries emerging from conflict or prolonged periods of political instability typically have fractious populations, which pose a significant challenge to securing public buy-in for reform agendas. Liberia's experience demonstrates the importance of strong, unifying political leadership for overcoming these challenges.

The Sirleaf administration successfully implemented a series of controversial government reforms—such as establishing a new Anti-Corruption Commission and eliminating 2,100 ghost workers at the Ministry of Education—required under the HIPC Initiative (IMF 2010). It did so even though President Sirleaf's Unity Party held only 12% of the seats in the Liberian House of Representatives and 10% of Senate seats. To achieve this, the administration largely pursued a three-track approach.[2] First, it communicated directly to the Liberian public about the government reforms, including how they would benefit from them. Second, it largely refrained from framing the reform agenda in terms of political parties. Lastly, it utilized third parties to pressure specific actors in the event of political impasse.

---

[2] See http://www.cgdev.org/content/calendar/detail/1424252/.

3.2. A CREDIBLE PLAN AND VISION

Clearing external debt arrears and providing comprehensive debt relief can entail significant costs for donor governments and multilateral aid agencies. Given this, donor governments first require that the recipient government outline a credible plan and vision both for the financial re-engagement process and for long-term development programmes.

The Sirleaf administration outlined a 150-day action plan almost immediately after assuming office. By May 2008 it had presented a complete poverty reduction strategy to the donor community. According to the IMF and the World Bank, the Liberian government completed 'unprecedented consultations' at the district and national level with communities, civil society, the private sector, the legislature, and international partners (IMF 2010). The Liberian government was also candid about its assessment of the strategy's implementation. Following slow progress initially, the government reported openly about delays (World Bank 2010). It then instituted results-based management approaches and established a series of 90-day action plans—which in a short time raised implementation rates from 19% to 90% (World Bank 2010).

3.3. MOBILIZING CAPACITY—BOTH INTERNALLY AND EXTERNALLY

When the Sirleaf administration assumed office in January 2006, Liberian government institutions were nearly nonexistent. Most government ministries lacked qualified, experienced staff as well as desks, chairs, computers, and functional bathroom facilities.

To address this, the Liberian government implemented a multi-pronged capacity mobilization strategy. First, President Sirleaf recruited officials with extensive knowledge of and work experience at the IFIs. For example, former finance minister Antoinette Sayeh had previously served in a variety of management positions at the World Bank. Second, the administration recruited a small cadre of professionals with education and/or work experience in the United States and other countries to serve in senior advisory positions. Lastly, the government mobilized significant external advisory capacity through think tanks, law firms, and civil society organizations. While capacity remained very constrained throughout the financial re-engagement process, the Liberian government assembled a core team that executed reforms and negotiations.

REFERENCES

International Monetary Fund, 2002. *Liberia: 2001 Article IV Consultation—Staff Report*, IMF Country Report No. 02/147. Washington, DC.

International Monetary Fund, 2008. *Liberia: Enhanced Initiative for Heavily Indebted Poor Countries—Decision Point Document*, IMF Country Report No. 08/106, page 39. Washington, DC.

—— 2009. *Heavily Indebted Poor Countries (HIPC) Initiative—Status of Implementation*. Washington, DC.

—— 2010. *Liberia: Enhanced Initiative for Heavily Indebted Poor Countries—Completion Point Document and Multilateral Debt Relief Initiative*, IMF Country Report No. 10/113. Washington, DC.

World Bank, 2010. *Republic of Liberia, Joint IDA-IMF Staff Advisory Note on the Poverty Reduction Strategy Paper, First Annual Progress Report.*

Libya
Post-war Challenges and Opportunities

Jacob Kolster and Paula Ximena Mejia

1. Introduction

Endowed with the largest proven oil reserves in Africa, Libya was the wealthiest country of the continent prior to the 2011 civil war.[1] Since discovering oil in the 1950s, Libya has achieved some of the highest living standards in the region, with gross per capita income above US$14,000 in 2008, a literacy rate of 80%, and life expectancy at birth of 74 years.

Libya's economic performance was equally unique for the region's standards, with average real GDP growth of more than 5% during the previous decade, fiscal surpluses of more than 25%, and external current account surpluses above 40% of GDP in recent years. Its limited integration in the global financial system, and the cushion provided by sizeable net foreign assets, allowed Libya to weather the recent financial crisis with limited adverse effects.

As the wave of uprisings brought political change to neighbouring Tunisia and Egypt, Libyans felt empowered to confront the grievances that affected the majority of the population, in spite of the country's strong economic performance. Rising inflation, high unemployment (especially amongst the youth), and the country's opaque governance structures left much to be desired. In 2009 Libya ranked in the 5th and 12th percentile for voice and accountability,[2] and government effectiveness,[3] respectively, according to the Kaufmann index.[4]

---

[1] With almost 75% of its territory unexplored, Libya's proven reserves are currently at more than 40 billion barrels, which at current production levels would take nearly 70 years to exhaust. Libya comes fourth in Africa in terms of natural gas production and reserves (equivalent to about 0.25 million barrels per day and 9 billion barrels of oil, respectively).

[2] This indicator accounts for the perceptions of freedom of expression, association, and speech in comparison to other countries. A 5th percentile rank shows that 95% of the other countries measured performed better than Libya.

[3] Government effectiveness is defined as the quality of public services, and the degree of its independence from political pressures, the quality of policy formulation and implementation, and the credibility of the government's commitment to such policies. Libya's percentile rank shows that 88% of the other countries measured performed better than Libya.

[4] World Bank data 'World Wide Governance Indicators', http://info.worldbank.org/governance/wgi/index.asp.

The contrasts between the country's economic wealth, and the extent to which the average Libyan benefited from this, pointed to the inefficiencies created by Libya's 'clientalist'[5] structure. Patronage, however, proved untenable and it was the combination of economic and political disenfranchizement that led to regime change.

Libya's transition is an opportunity for the country to undo the negative political, social, and economic legacies of the past. Beyond the obvious need for reconciliation, re-ignition of financial circuits and payment systems, and reconstruction of economic infrastructure, the silver lining in the policy challenges that lie ahead relate to Libya's ability to implement efficient, transparent, and fair governance structures—at the macroeconomic level as well as at industry and individual levels—and to commit to economic reforms, effective provisions of basic public services, and full valorization of its human resources.

2. Creating Governance and Accountability Mechanisms

Libya's 'clientalist' state structure, which centralized economic power in the hands of the state, created an environment in which individual interests both outweighed, and were in conflict with, the interests for the common good.[6] In the aftermath of the war, Libya will need to take measures to prevent fighting between competing interest groups.

Improved governance has the capacity to undo the 'clientalist' system, and emphasize the importance of the public good. By bolstering transparency and participatory mechanisms, a new social contract could be created in which the government is accountable for the delivery of public services and the equitable redistribution of the country's wealth.

The deep-rooted nature of Libya's patronage structure, however, is grounded in the institutionless nature of the Jamahiriya, or 'rule by the masses'. Effective governance reforms therefore imply the creation of institutions capable of ensuring accountability and transparency, while balancing the power of elected officials. This could be achieved through the establishment of independent executive, legislative, and judiciary branches of government.

Additionally, the participatory rights of civilians should be strengthened by allowing civil society to evaluate public services. These measures have the capacity to engage

---

[5] A clientalist state structure depends upon an asymmetrical relationship between a small group of patrons with access to political and economic wealth, and their clients. The relationship between the two is characterized by the doling out of favours on the part of patrons in exchange for political support from clients. These systems, though facilitated by natural resource wealth, as was the case in Libya, are difficult to maintain because they depend on patrons' consistent access to wealth. Once patrons fail to deliver on their promise, the system is at risk of collapsing.

[6] D. Vanderwalle, 'Post War Challenges in Libya', The African Development Bank, September 2011.

citizens as actors within Libya's political system rather than strictly as clients that expect favours from the state in exchange for political support.

3. Committing to Economic Reform

Despite a series of economic reforms pursued during the previous decade, Libya was never successful in altering the dynamics of its economy. The 'clientalist' state had given a group of individuals the greater part of the country's economic and political wealth, making them reluctant to support reforms that would chip away at their power. However, if it was necessary to reform Libya's economy in the past, the impact of the war has intensified the need to do so even more.

Prior to the conflict, the Libyan economy was virtually undiversified and entirely dominated by the hydrocarbon sector, which generated nearly 75% of GDP, more than 90% of government revenues, and 95% of export earnings.[7] The very limited backwards and forwards integration of the industry confined the wealth generated from oil riches to export and fiscal revenues, while it generated less than 5% of employment in Libya.

Following 5-6 months of virtual inactivity and war-inflicted damages to infrastructure, Libya will face the challenge of bringing oil production back to former levels—something that could take at least another year.

This challenge, however, also presents an opportunity for Libya to finally diversify its economy. Diversification will help compensate for the decline in oil revenues while reducing the economy's vulnerability to the exogenous shocks of the oil market.

There are a number of sectors with potential for growth including construction, agriculture, banking and financial services, as well as upstream and downstream hydrocarbon activities. Small and medium enterprises are equally promising. Although their contribution to growth has been low in the past, this can be attributed in part to the previous regime's reluctance to create incentives for entrepreneurship by limiting access to finance.

Diversification also has the potential to address Libya's pressing issue of youth unemployment, while at the same time reducing the burden on the public sector, which represents approximately 75% of formal employment despite its low contribution to growth.

Increased opportunities for employment would not only provide necessary financial benefits to the youth, but could also facilitate the demobilization of those Libyans who took active part in the armed struggle in 2011.

---

[7] IMF Country Report No. 08/301, September 2008.

4. Developing an Efficient Public Sector and Human Capital

Setting the stage for economic reform and a more diversified economy requires a public sector that efficiently provides both core public services and a conducive environment for private entrepreneurs. As such, the tax system should be simplified by creating an efficient taxpayer entity, adopting lower rates, and eliminating tax exemptions. Similarly, public finance should be consolidated and centralized under the responsibility of a ministry of finance, which should also strengthen budgetary procedures, develop medium-term expenditure frameworks including sound preparation and efficient monitoring of public investment programmes, and finally, implement much-needed civil service reforms.

The new government should recognize not only the immediate importance of addressing human needs in the wake of war but also the need to build and 'valorize' the country's human capital. Comprehensive social-sector reform programmes are long overdue to strengthen the quality and accessibility of the education sector and the efficiency of the healthcare system. As it stands the Libyan social security system, as a major component of social safety, needs to be restructured and strengthened to effectively respond to the needs of a transitioning economy.

Despite achieving high rates of access to education, Libya was not able to improve the quality of education, nor was it successful in linking the national curricula to the labour market demands. As a result, the country suffered from a mismatch between skills available and skills in demand in the private sector, contributing significantly to the country's estimated 25% unemployment rate[8] prior to the conflict. In order to address the economic challenges the country faces in the aftermath of the conflict, the new government must promote education reform and address this mismatch of skills.

Finally, Libya has relied heavily on the foreign workers to sustain its fast-growing oil economy—a phenomenon that is likely to persist if not increase during post-war reconstruction.[9] It is therefore important to ensure the reintegration of, and where needed, reconciliation, with these groups.

5. Concluding Remarks

The economic, social, and political challenges facing Libya in the aftermath of its civil war are enormous. The reconciliation and reconstruction of economic infrastructure destroyed by the conflict are immediate and daunting tasks in their own right.

---

[8] IMF Country Report No. 08/301, Sept. 2008.
[9] It is estimated that prior to the 2011 conflict Libya was the home to approximately 2.5 million foreign workers.

However, the transition underway presents Libya with a significant opportunity to start afresh by decisively undoing the negative socio-political and economic legacies of the past. With its enormous natural wealth and sizeable foreign assets, Libya is in a unique position to undertake critical and well-sequenced reforms to diversify its economy, ensure a public sector that delivers much-needed services to its people, and strengthen its human capital.

For the first time in nearly half a century Libya has within its reach the option of launching the country onto a path of strong and inclusive growth towards prosperity for all Libyans.

REFERENCES

World Bank data 'World Wide Governance Indicators', http://info.worldbank.org/governance/wgi/index.asp.
Vanderwalle, D., 2011. 'Post War Challenges in Libya', (September) The African Development Bank.
IMF Country Report No. 08/301, September 2008. Washington, DC.

Madagascar Poverty and Economic Growth

Jean Razafindravonona

1. Introduction

Although Madagascar has huge natural resources, poverty rates are still very high. Madagascar has followed various different economic policies: pegging to the CFA zone franc, massive investment, a Structural Adjustment Programme (SAP) from 1985 to 1999 (STA 1996), and two Poverty Reduction Strategy Papers, interim (PRSP-I) from 2000 to 2001 (STA 2003) and final (PRSP-II), from 2003 to 2005. These policies often generated uneven economic growth. Most Malagasy people question whether these uneven levels of economic growth improve the overall wellbeing of the entire country in the form of reducing poverty rates. Answers to these questions will be analysed in this article, starting with observing and analysing the evolution of poverty rates over time. Particular emphasis will be put on the analysis of the link between poverty and economic growth.

2. The origin of poverty

After Madagascar's independence in 1960, the poverty rate in 1962 was 42.9% (B. Essama-Nssah 1997). A first update of these statistics was done in 1993 (World Bank 1996), which documented that Malagasy poverty is predominately rural poverty (Paternostro, Razafindravonona, and Stifel 2001). At least 75% of the population of Madagascar live in rural areas (INSTAT 2001).

Analysis of the urban/rural composition of poverty rates (Ravallion and Huppi 1991) and their influence on the overall trend indicates poverty has essentially been driven by urban rates, except from 2002 to 2004 (see Table 1).

Table 1. Origin of changes in poverty

Years	P_0 : poverty ratio (%)	Changes: ΔP_0 in points	Origin (%)
1993–1997	70–73.3	+ 3.3	Urban (72)
1997–1999	73.3–71.3	−2	Urban (85)
1999–2001	71.3–69.6	−1.7	Urban (100)
2001–2002	69.6–80.7	+ 11.1	Urban-rural (59)
2002–2004	80.7–72.7	−8	Rural (88)

Source: Author calculation

3. Measuring the impact of growth on poverty

In order to analyse the nature of poverty rate changes, a model is used which decomposes changes in poverty into changes in growth and in distribution (Datt and Ravallion 1992). This model tries to find the empirical link between growth and poverty. This model has already been applied by the team of the World Bank to the case of the Côte d'Ivoire (Demery and Squire 1996).

Table 2. Contribution of growth and distributional changes to changes in poverty at national level

	1993	1997	1999	2001	2002	2004
Poverty ratio	70.0	73.3	71.3	69.6	80.7	72.1
		1993–1997	1997–1999	1999–2001	2001–2002	2002–2004
Changes P_0		3.2	−2.1	−1.7	11.1	−8.6
Growth component		1.9	−1.3	−2.6	7.7	−3.7
Distribution component		−4.1	−0.6	7.0	4.1	−8.5
Residual		5.5	−0.1	−6.1	−0.7	3.7

Source: Author calculation

3.1. DEVELOPING RATE OF GROWTH BUT UNCHANGED DISTRIBUTION OF REVENUE: THE IMPACT ON POVERTY

In the two periods 1997–1999 and 1999–2001, economic growth stemming from continuity of economic policy contributed to decreasing the poverty rate by 1.3 points in the first period and 2.6 points in the second). The contribution in 1997–1999 and in 1999–2001 is in part the result of the SAP, of Madagascar's hosting of the Indian Ocean Games in 1999, of PRSP-I in the context of HIPC, of AGOA, and of the development of the tourist industry. Likewise, the economic recovery after the crisis of 2002 contributed strongly to the decrease of the poverty ratio; this contribution is estimated to be 3.7 points.

However, the situation for 1993–1997 and 2001–2002 seems to indicate that economic growth is not sufficient to reduce poverty.

3.2. VARIABLE DISTRIBUTION OF INCOME BUT STATIC RATE OF GROWTH: THE IMPACT ON POVERTY

The 4effect of distribution on changes in the poverty rate differs according to the political situation. During the periods of continuity and stability, 1993–1997 and 1997–1999 (SAP), the effect on the increase of the poverty rate is estimated at −4.1 and −0.6 points respectively. These reductions are explained by at least 28% and 85% respectively in the urban area. During the period of recovery in 2002–2004, on the other hand, the distribution had an effect of −8.5 points. This decrease came from the effect of increases in agricultural prices and the effect of policy connected to infrastructure. From 1999 to 2001 (PRSP-I), the contribution of distribution to the decrease in the poverty ratio just from the urban area was very high, at 7.0 points.

Whereas growth had an overall effect on poverty rates, distributional changes affected poverty primarily in urban areas.

REFERENCES

Datt, G., and M. Ravallion, 1992. 'Growth and distribution components of changes in poverty measures: a decomposition with application to Brazil and India in the 1980s', *Journal of Development* 38, 275–95.

Demery, L., and L. Squire, 1996. 'Macroeconomic adjustment and poverty in Africa: an emerging picture', *World Bank Research Observer* 11.1.

Essama-Nssah, B., 1997. 'The impact of growth and distribution in Madagascar', *Review of Income and Wealth* 43.2.

INSTAT (Institut National de la Statistique), 1997. *Récensement Général de la Population et de l'Habitat*. Antananarivo.

—— INSTAT (Institut National de la Statistique), 2001. *Rapport Principal de l'Enquête Permanente des Ménages*. Antananarivo.

Paternostro, S., J. Razafindravonona, and D. Stifel, 2001. 'Changes in poverty in Madagascar: 1993–1999', Africa Region Working Paper Series 19. Washington, DC: World Bank.

Ravallion, M., and M. Huppi, 1991. 'Measuring changes in poverty: a methodological case study of Indonesia during an adjustment period', *World Bank Economic Review* 5.1, 57–82.

STA (Secrétariat Technique à l'Ajustement), 1996. *Document Cadre de Politique Économique (DCPE)*. Antananarivo.

—— 2003. *Rapport Annuel d'Évaluation du Document de Stratégie pour la Réduction de la Pauvreté*. Antananarivo.

World Bank, 1996. *Poverty Assessment in Madagascar*. Washington, DC.

Malawi
Psychological and Political Economy of Exchange Rate Policy

Khwima Nthara

1. Introduction

A weak currency is generally preferred to a strong one in most developed economies. Such economies are predominantly export-oriented, and products for export are priced in local currency. As a result, depreciation of the local currency is usually a positive development, and is viewed as such because it makes export products more competitive on the international market. On the other hand, appreciation of the local currency tends to dampen foreign demand for export commodities by making them more expensive to foreign buyers at the same local currency price.

In contrast, devaluation or depreciation in Malawi carries a very negative connotation. Most ordinary Malawians perceive it either as a regrettable consequence of bad economic management or as a policy imposed on the government by the international financial institutions. It is construed as a sign that those entrusted with the management of the economy have lost control of the situation. People wonder why the currency should 'lose' value if the Malawi economy is doing well. Such is the effect that devaluation has had on the public's psyche that policymakers try to avoid it to every extent possible.

2. Background and Issues

The public's negative attitude towards devaluation can be traced back to the late 1970s, when Malawi started implementing stabilization and structural adjustment programmes supported by the International Monetary Fund and the World Bank. Among a number of macroeconomic policy reforms implemented was devaluation of the Malawi kwacha. The rationale given at the time was that devaluation was necessary to solve balance of payments problems that had become unsustainable. Subsequently, it became a trend that devaluations happened whenever the government signed a new programme with the IMF or World Bank. It is against this background that devaluation has been perceived either as a symptom of an economy in trouble or as a price the country has to pay in return for financial assistance from the World Bank and the IMF.

Because of sensitivities surrounding exchange rate devaluation, politicians and civil society in Malawi often emphasize the possible negative impacts of devaluation, and downplay its possible positive effects. In particular, it is the impact that devaluation has on inflation that is highlighted as the main reason for the government's opposition to devaluation (*The Nation* 2009). A strong association between devaluation and inflation seems to have been indelibly marked in people's minds following the flotation of the Malawi kwacha in 1994. Soon after the floatation, the kwacha depreciated by 243% against the US dollar between February and December 1994 (Reserve Bank of Malawi 2003). During the same period, inflation more than tripled, rising from 20% to 66%, reaching a record high of 95% in August 1995. Since then, whenever there is devaluation or depreciation, retailers of goods and services hike up prices, citing as the reason an increase in the cost of imported inputs due to devaluation.

Unfortunately, there does not seem to have been a period in Malawi's economic history when devaluation had a spectacular positive effect. It is for this reason that the policy has become difficult to sell. Politicians and civil society have always found reasons why devaluation would not have a positive effect in Malawi. First, while development partners have argued that devaluation would be beneficial to Malawi's economy through improved export competitiveness, the counterargument has been that this would not be significant because prices of the main export crop, tobacco, are quoted in foreign currency. As a result, devaluation would not have any dampening effect on prices of tobacco facing foreign buyers. Instead, they say, a potential benefit could have been that for every dollar Malawian tobacco farmers earn, devaluation should translate it into more in the local currency equivalent—but unfortunately the inflationary effect of devaluation tends to wipe this out.

Second, development partners have also argued that devaluation would help improve the country's balance of payments position through its expenditure-switching effect by reducing import demand in favour of domestically produced goods. The counterargument from politicians and civil society in Malawi has been that this impact is unlikely to be significant because the bulk of Malawi's imports—including fuel, fertilizer, and drugs—are price-inelastic and do not have domestic substitutes.

Debate on the role of devaluation in helping solve balance of payments problems has been heightened in times when foreign exchange reserves have been low. During such periods, there has been increased pressure, particularly from development partners, for government to devalue the local currency. But government has not accepted arguments that the scarcity of foreign exchange in the market is due to the overvaluation of the local currency. Instead, blame has been placed on the World Bank and the IMF for advising countries to embrace liberal market policies (AFP 2009). The government has argued that such liberal policies, and not overvaluation, are responsible for foreign exchange bureaus externalizing and hoarding foreign exchange—hence the acute shortages. Consequently, the government has moved to close some of the bureaus (*Africa News* 2009).

More recently, the Government has also attributed the shortage of foreign exchange in the country to the IMF's advice against a policy where it was mandatory for major exporters, including tobacco farmers, to sell their foreign exchange to the Central Bank of Malawi. The Government has argued that with exporters now free to keep their foreign exchange with commercial banks, it has not been able to exercise control over the availability of foreign exchange (*World Post News* 2011).

3. Way Forward

Short of coercion, if one is to effectively advocate a more flexible exchange rate in Malawi, it is imperative to employ a comprehensive strategy that can effectively deal with these psychological and political economy issues. In particular, such a strategy needs to deal with the fear amongst Malawian policymakers and civil society that devaluation will lead to high inflation. At the same time, the strategy must also deal with the strong scepticism amongst Malawians in relation to the possible positive impact of devaluation. For instance, clear examples, if any, may need to be provided of how countries in the region with similar characteristics to Malawi have benefited from a flexible exchange rate policy.

REFERENCES

Agence France-Press, 2009. 'Malawi leader blames World Bank, IMF for forex shortages' (26 Nov.).
Africa News, 2009. 'Malawi: Forex bureaus closed down' (5 Aug.).
Reserve Bank of Malawi, 2003. 'Evolution of exchange rate determination in Malawi: past and present'. Lilongwe.
The Nation, 2009. 'No kwacha devaluation, says [President] Bingu' (10 June).
World Post News, 2011. '[President] Bingu government blames World Bank, IMF for economic woes' (29 Aug.).

Mali
Fragile Economic Dynamics

Massa Coulibaly

1. Introduction

To briefly describe the dynamism of the Malian economy and to show the fragility of that dynamism, this chapter examines successively the macroeconomic growth and its principal explanatory factors, the sectoral decomposition of the growth, and the trade performance of the country.

2. Macroeconomic dynamics

Over the period 1990–2008, real GDP has increased to 4.9% per year, a growth rate less than the objective rate of 7% of the CSCRP (Cadre stratégique pour la croissance et la réduction de la pauvreté). This growth rate of 4.9% followed the lowest rate over the first five years of the period (1990–95), only 2.5%; the decline started in 2005, and was no doubt worsened by the energy and food crisis of 2008 and also by the financial crisis that followed. Expressed in US dollars, GDP per capita has only increased by 3.2% over the period, with declines of –2.6% from 1990 to 1995 and a virtually stagnation from 1995 to 2000 (0.3%).

Over the period 1990–2008, the labour productivity or real GDP per capita grew annually by 7.9%, mainly due to the growth of technical capital (8.1%), human capital (3.6%), and only 1% of overall productivity. The expected positive impact of investment on growth can be constrained by the overall productivity of factors, as has been noticed since 2005 and as has been the case during the period 1995–2000. The magnitude of the impact is related to the structure of the physical capital installed, whether or not it is very productive or whether it is mainly in one sector or another.

3. Sectoral dynamics

Structurally, the Malian economy is primary because it is mainly dominated by agriculture and mining (only gold so far, although other mining operations, including oil, are imminent). These two subsectors account for between 44% and 53% of the nominal GDP. While the share of agricultural activities in the Malian economy is declining (−1.3%), mining has increased (by 8.2% per year). The decline in the importance of agriculture in GDP is observed for all major activities—with the notable exception of rice, whose contribution increased by 3.3% per year, indeed by 10.8% from 2005; this trend will continue under the influence of agricultural policies initiated in recent years by the government in response to the food crisis (e.g. the Rice Initiative).

The increasing importance of the extractive industries (eight extraction sites in 2008 for more than 50 tonnes of gold exported per year) has allowed the secondary sector to increase its contribution to GDP of 2% per year, while those of manufacturing industry fell by −1.2% per year over the same period, with a significant decline since 2005 (−10.4%). The dynamism of this sector is somewhat more fragile—a fragility which has resulted from the structural adjustment policies of the early 1990s, and which has worsened since the recent privatization followed by the reduction of the scale of production or even repeated stopping of production in many cases, as in the oilseed industry.

Over the long term, the annual growth of 4.9% of GDP is dependent on the secondary sector, mainly because of mining and the public building works programme (BTP). While the service sector accounts for the growth in the actual sub-period, we are witnessing a decline in the secondary sector, including the mining industry—unlike the previous period, where it combined with the secondary sector to produce an average annual growth of 6.8%. On the whole, the growth of the service sector is driven by telecommunications (especially mobile) and by tourism. This is a cultural tourism, favouring sites like the old mosques of Djenné and Timbuktu, the tombs of the Askia (kings of the Songhai empire), the Dogon plateau, and the prehistoric sites of the Sahara desert. Tourism revenues now represent over 3% of GDP or 13% of total exports of the country, almost as much as cotton and more than animal breeding. The annual growth of those revenues over the period 2001–7 exceeds the growth of total exports, 9% against 7%.

One of the characteristics of the economic dynamics of Mali is the weak contribution of the agricultural sector to economic growth—0.3% annual growth from 1990 to 1995 and 0.7% per year since 2005. This adds to the fragility of the Malian economy, whose growth will falter with the depletion of gold reserves and the saturation of the single market for mobile telephony without any investment in other areas of new information technologies and communication.

4. Commercial performance

During the period 1990–2002, the foreign trade of Mali grew at about an average of 10% per year, for both exports and imports. Its key feature is the lack of diversification of export products facing a greater variety of imports. Today, gold alone accounts for over

Table 1. Dynamics of the Malian economy (FCFA billions and %)

	1990	1995	2000	2005	2006	2007	2008	Average annual growth				
								1990–95	1995–2000	2000–2005	2005–8	1990–2008
1. Baseline data												
Nominal GDP	673	1,187	1,742	3,114	3,490	3,757	4,305	12.0%	8.0%	12.3%	11.4%	10.9%
Real GDP (base year 1987)	661	747	965	1,340	1,410	1,472	1,559	2.5%	5.3%	6.8%	5.2%	4.9%
Official exchange rate (FCFA/$)	275	499	650	530	522	480	448	12.7%	5.4%	–4.0%	–5.5%	2.7%
Population (000)	8,130	9,013	10,017	11,732	12,051	12,377	12,712	2.1%	2.1%	3.2%	2.7%	2.5%
Working population (000)	3,391	3,890	4,395	5,064	5,202	5,342	5,487	2.8%	2.5%	2.9%	2.7%	2.7%
2. Strength of the economy												
GDP per capita (US$)	301	264	268	501	555	633	756	–2.6%	0.3%	13.3%	14.7%	5.2%
Gross domestic investissement (% nominal GDP)	19%	25%	20%	14%	15%	18%	16%	5.6%	–4.4%	–6.9%	4.6%	–1.0%
Informal economy (% real GDP)	68%	72%	64%	60%	60%	60%	61%	1.0%	–2.1%	–1.5%	1.0%	–0.6%
3. Economic outlook												
Real GDP growth		2.5%	5.3%	6.8%	5.3%	4.4%	5.9%					
Gross domestic investment growth (% GDP)		5.6%	–4.4%	–6.9%	7.1%	20.0%	–11.1%					
4. Source of added value activity (% real GDP)												
Primary sector	49%	49%	47%	37%	36%	36%	38%	0.3%	–1.0%	–4.5%	0.7%	–1.3%
Cereals excluding rice	19%	18%	16%	13%	13%	14%	15%	–0.5%	–3.0%	–3.6%	4.1%	–1.3%
Rice	3%	4%	5%	4%	4%	4%	6%	4.1%	5.8%	–4.0%	10.8%	3.3%
Cotton	5%	5%	6%	3%	2%	1%	1%	–0.7%	4.8%	–14.8%	–32.7%	–9.5%
Animal breeding	13%	13%	12%	11%	10%	10%	10%	0.5%	–2.0%	–2.8%	–1.6%	–1.5%
Horticulture	5%	6%	5%	4%	4%	4%	4%	1.4%	–2.4%	–3.1%	–1.2%	–1.4%
Secondary sector (% of real GDP)	15%	16%	19%	24%	24%	22%	21%	2.0%	3.3%	4.4%	–3.9%	2.0%
Mining	2%	2%	6%	9%	9%	8%	7%	3.9%	23.9%	6.7%	–5.3%	8.2%
Manufacturing	7%	7%	6%	8%	8%	7%	6%	–0.4%	–3.3%	6.3%	–10.4%	–1.2%
Construction industry	4%	5%	5%	5%	4%	5%	5%	4.5%	–1.4%	–1.4%	0.5%	0.5%

Tertiary sector (% of real GDP)	36%	35%	34%	39%	40%	42%	41%	-0.7%	2.8%	2.1%	0.8%
Trade	17%	15%	15%	14%	15%	16%	16%	0.7%	-1.2%	3.9%	-0.2%
Transport and telecommunications	5%	5%	6%	6%	7%	8%	8%	1.8%	1.7%	8.8%	3.1%
5. Internal market dynamics											
Final consumption (% GDP)	101%	104%	97%	80%	76%	75%	74%	-1.4%	-3.8%	-2.6%	-1.7%
Growth of final consumption		0.6%	-1.4%	-3.8%	-5.0%	-1.3%	-1.3%				
Real inflation rate	1.6%	12.4%	-0.7%	6.4%	1.5%	1.4%	9.2%	2.0%	-2.4%	1.4%	0.4%
6. State participation											
Total tax revenue (% GDP)	10%	11%	13%	14%	14%	13%	12%	3.2%	2.0%	-5.5%	1.2%
Direct tax (% GDP)	3%	2%	2%	3%	3%	4%	3%	2.0%	4.2%	5.7%	1.6%
Indirect tax (% GDP)	7%	9%	11%	12%	11%	9%	9%	3.4%	1.5%	-8.8%	1.0%
Domestic indirect tax (% GDP)	6%	6%	9%			9%	8%	7.9%			1.5%
Tax on imports (% GDP)	1%	3%	2%			2%	1%	-6.5%			0.4%

Source: DNSI, Economic Accounts, Bamako, and author's calculations.

half of export earnings; imports range from food to machinery, equipment, petroleum products and other manufactured goods. The share of cotton has decreased from 36% in 1999 to only 6% in 2008, and animal breeding from 8% to 3%.

The vulnerability of the country's exports is coupled with that of its market structure—another reason for calling for major efforts to diversify export (for industrial processing of primary products) and its sources of supply.

Mauritania
Sustaining Growth with Equity

Zeine Ould Zeidane

1. Introduction[1]

Mauritania has significant growth potential based on its natural resources and strategic location, but it is unlikely to achieve the Millennium Development Goals. Poverty has slightly decreased, but is still lagging far behind the MDG target of 28.3%. The unemployment rate climbed to 32.5% in 2004, severely affecting youth and women. Considering that the government is committed to achieving sustainable growth while reducing poverty, the main objective of this paper is to discuss recent trends and analysis, and also make recommendations in that regard.

2. Past trends, policies, and challenges

In recent years, real growth has been positive but insufficient to achieve poverty reduction objectives. Between 1980 and 2007, growth averaged 3.2% per year and only 0.7% per capita, far below the 3.7% needed to achieve the MDG1. The analysis of contributing sources to growth shows that it has been mainly driven by the service sector and by government spending in public works and administration (26%).

2.1. MACROECONOMIC POLICIES

Fiscal policy has been unsustainable and inconsistent with macroeconomic stability objectives. In addition, the external situation has been vulnerable. Trade balances have more or less remained negative, resulting from an exports decline that was mainly due to the poor performance of iron ore and fishing activities, and an imports increase fuelled by domestic absorption and world prices. The overall current account balance was

---

[1] I would like to thank Maria Do Valle Ribeiro, UNDP Resident Representative in Mauritania, for her useful comments.

negative between 1992 and 2005 and only partially financed by foreign direct investment (FDI) and overseas development assistance (ODA). International reserves have declined to their second-lowest level in two decades, putting a high strain on the exchange market and economic activity.

Government debt has also been an issue in the last decade. In 2003, the government's debt to the Central Bank was six times higher than in the previous decade—in fact, the financial debt of the economy has gone from 20% of GDP in 1992 to more than 30% since 2003. Long-term misreporting practices led to an irrelevant and incoherent monetary policy. Inflation was high, averaging 6.6% a year between 1992 and 2007. However, the end of misreporting practices in 2004 brought more relevant monetary policy through raising the interest and mandatory reserves rates, which in turn helped contain inflation and reduce the disequilibrium of the foreign exchange market.

2.2. BROADER GAINS AND CHALLENGES

Many reforms have been implemented to enhance the business environment in the country, but results are disappointing. FDI is still insufficient to accelerate growth, and the business environment is cumbersome. Mauritania is ranked 160 out of 181 countries in the World Bank Doing Business 2009 ranking.

In addition, while the country has made gains toward a knowledge-based economy and education has experienced positive developments in terms of access and gender parity, it still suffers from high dropout rates and low quality, and does not meet the needs of the labour markets. The country is also hindered by its low international connectivity.

There have also been lost opportunities to take advantage of potential growth of some promising sectors. Looking at the agricultural sector, only 10% of the irrigated land is cultivated, whereas rain-fed agriculture suffers from very low yields. Livestock comprises an estimated 20 million heads, and has contributed to more than 10% of total growth and to a small share of exports, but it is still under-exploited. Fishing activity contracted by more than 13% a year from the first full year of the agreement with the EU, but considering the huge catch potential the trend can easily be reversed. Proven and probable crude oil reserves amount to more than 300 million barrels; there are also substantial gas reserves and promising exploration prospects, but the exploitation is still limited to one field. Successful reforms in the mining sector have attracted foreign investment, stepped up exploration, and brought into production two mines of copper and gold, but SNIM (Société Nationale Industrielle et Minière) still has not reached its potential. Urban development, especially real estate, has a significant potential for growth due to the strong demand and interest from FDI.

Lastly, poor governance is hindering growth and equity. The lack of a shared vision, operational strategies, and a culture of results-based management has wasted a large part of past efforts.

3. Recommendations

Mauritania has to accelerate growth and reduce inequality by pursuing better policies. As aforementioned, addressing the issue of poor governance will be important for growth. Policies to stimulate growth in promising sectors are also needed, specifically agriculture, livestock, fisheries, oil and gas, mining, and real estate. In addition, the government needs to pursue policies such as:

- effectively accumulating physical assets that attract more private investors, especially FDI;
- reducing external vulnerability and maintaining the actual exchange rate policies; and
- improving public expenditures management to help reap benefits from domestic resources and international aid.

Major financial reform must be implemented to increase access to credit, strengthen competition, and prepare the in-depth development of financial markets. In addition, a major and coherent tax reform would be useful to reduce the burden on the private sector while maintaining actual returns and reducing its regressive pattern.

Education policy should focus on quality and retention, and be more efficient in terms of completion rates and effective in meeting the needs of the labour market. Innovation should be encouraged through a more structured research capacity and a more open society. Labour market reform which increases flexibility, and proactive employment policies to step up labour force participation and job creation, especially for women and youth, are the top priorities. The country also needs to focus on achieving a better and more sustainable use of natural resources, while developing policies that take account of climate change and the environment.

All these recommendations should be taken into account while keeping in mind that poor people must be supported to contribute more and more to the production of wealth, and that the state, through budget and regulation, must ensure an effective redistribution of wealth, which is necessary to reduce inequality.

Mauritius
A Small Open Economy Fully Integrated into World Markets

Désiré Vencatachellum

1. Introduction

Located off the coast of the African continent in the southwest Indian Ocean, Mauritius is a small island of 720 square miles which was uninhabited until the Dutch first settled there in 1638. The French, who took control of the island from 1715, were defeated by the British in 1815. At the time of independence, on 12 March 1968, the country, exclusively reliant on sugar exports, was poor and vulnerable to tropical cyclones that could destroy the total harvest in a short space of time. Further, due to its geographical location, the nation is far away from its main export markets, therefore increasing transportation costs.

As a legacy of its colonial history, Mauritius has a diverse social demographic with an evident plurality of ethnic and religious groups. Most of the population are of Indian descent, and were brought onto the island to replace African slaves on sugarcane fields when the British abolished slavery in 1835. However, Indians do not constitute a homogenous group, as there are different castes and religions (namely Hindus and Muslims) within the group. Additionally, there are the Franco-Mauritians—who are a minority in numbers but who controlled a large proportion of assets and resources—creoles who are descendants of African slaves or of mixed heritage. The literature Nobel prizewinner V. S. Naipaul famously described Mauritius as 'an overcrowded barracoon overpopulated with a starving people, idled by unemployment and plagued by despair'.

Given the factors and constraints discussed above, there would be no surprise in suspecting that the nation should fall into the club of fragile states.

After more than forty years of independence, Mauritius has proven the pundits wrong. The nation has achieved among the highest standards of living in Africa, and is classified as a middle-income country. It has made major progress in promoting social equity and reducing poverty. In 2009 the average fertility rate was 1.6 per woman, while in 2007 the crude birth rate was 13.2 per thousand compared to a rate of 17.4 in 1997. Life expectancy at birth was estimated to be 69.1 for males and 75.9 for females, compared to 66.4 and 74.3 respectively in 1997. The infant mortality rate was estimated at 15.3 per thousand live births in Mauritius (African Economic Outlook 2009). Further, the 2005 Human Development Index has ranked the nation 65th in the world and second in Africa (after the Seychelles).

With reference to the economy, sustained growth of more than 6% was seen in the 1990s and the first half of the 21st century, and growth stood at 5.3% in 2008. Mauritius is known for its business-friendly environment and was ranked 17th worldwide and 1st in Africa in the 2009 World Bank Cost of Doing Business survey. However, the financial and economic crisis witnessed in 2008 and 2009 has taken its toll on the economy, and growth is expected to be around 2.5% in 2009. The main drivers of Mauritius' good economic performance have been textiles and sugar exports, and tourism, as explained below. A skilled population and strong institutions, which have led to good policy decisions and opened up preferential access to the European Union, have been some of the key factors behind the good performance of those sectors.

2. Engines of economic growth

Mauritius still maintains high levels of sugar exports, mainly through the benefits offered by the EU Sugar Protocol, which provides preferential prices to African, Caribbean, and Pacific (ACP) countries. Exports to the EU account for more than 90% of the sugarcane production of Mauritius. However, following a WTO ruling, the EU had to reduce the ACP's guaranteed sugar price, which has resulted in a decline of 36% in the price between 2006 and 2009.

Mauritius saw the need to diversify out of sugar exports because of its restricted capacity. This was achieved by attracting investors, mainly interested in textiles, in the Export Processing Zone (EPZ), created in 1971. Incentives in the form of tax holidays and exemptions from import duties and from some aspects of the regulatory regime, as well as preferential credit, were provided to foreign and domestic investors who would concentrate on the export market. EPZ activity expanded very fast, benefiting from high profits recycled from the sugar industry and from trading arrangements and the protectionist policies of the EU and the US. In testament to the success of EPZ, in 1985 textile exports overtook sugar exports, providing much-needed foreign exchange earnings and employment.

The coastline, beautiful beaches, and tropical conditions of the island nation, as well as increased security, has meant that the government of Mauritius was able to earn revenue from tourism by promoting as an exclusive location. Tourist arrivals grew by 3.1% between 2005 and 2006, increasing receipts from tourism by 23% in the period. Current projects include green tourism and the Integrated Resorts Scheme (IRS), the latter introduced in 2002 with the hope of boosting foreign direct investment in the tourism sector.

3. Institutions

Mauritius is a multi-party democracy characterized by strong social, political, and institutional stability. The judiciary is viewed as being able to function independently from political pressures. In 2008, Mauritius topped the Ibrahim Index of African Governance for the second year running, with a score of 85.1 out of 100, retaining the highest score out of 48 sub-Saharan countries. The independence of the judicial system in Mauritius was reaffirmed in 2008 when the election of a parliamentarian was invalidated and rendered null and void. The death penalty has been abolished, but abortion and same-sex marriages remain illegal.

4. Outlook and challenges

As a small open economy that is fully integrated into world markets, Mauritius is vulnerable to external shocks. The ability of the nation to react to these shocks depends on the capacity of the government to pursue reforms to modernize the economy, the capacity of the private sector to improve its competitiveness, and the efficacy of the government's stimulus package. Recently, Mauritius has diversified into financial services and information and computer technologies (ICT). In the coming years, the main challenges will be for authorities to sustain non-inflationary growth, and to react to growing labour and infrastructural bottlenecks whilst promoting and implementing its diversification policy. Whatever agenda is pursued, it must take into consideration the ethnic fragmentation of the nation so as not to cause marginalization and risk conflict.

Morocco
Positive Reforms

Mina Baliamoune-Lutz

1. Introduction

Morocco, the fifth largest economy in Africa, is a middle-income country with a relatively open and diversified economy. Morocco's export sector constituted about 34% of GDP in 2002–5. The country relies considerably on tourism, which reached $7.2 billion in 2007 (about 10% of GDP) and workers' remittances (9.5% of GDP in 2006). Morocco is one of the top five tourist destinations (arrivals and receipts) in Africa.

Morocco's economy is based on the market system, but growth in the 1970s was led mainly by the state. In the early 1980s the country experienced a serious economic crisis (which almost emptied currency reserves) due to rising import costs, falling phosphate prices (after having quadrupled during the 1970s), a significant food deficit, and the cost of the Western Sahara conflict. In return for facilities from the Paris Club, the IMF, and the World Bank, Morocco agreed to a major structural adjustment which included devaluing the dirham, liberalizing trade and investment, reducing inflation through high interest rates, privatizing state-owned enterprises, and curbing government subsidies (Nsouli et al. 1995). Morocco was able to successfully manage the period of liberalization and did not suffer from the fiscal deficits that often result from the elimination of trade restrictions. In 2005, its real GDP per capita was almost double the level in 1975. The country's annual real GDP growth averaged 3.4% in the 1990s and exceeded 5% in the 2000s. Agriculture (mainly rain-dependent) constitutes about 14% of GDP but employs close to 45% of the population. Morocco has ratified several free trade agreements, notably the Euro-Mediterranean free trade area agreement with the European Union (aimed at integrating the European Free Trade Association in 2012), and the Free Trade Agreement with the United States, which took effect in January 2006. Two major developments have marked Morocco's economy in the last twenty-five years: financial reforms and trade liberalization. It is generally agreed that the policy reforms pursued by Morocco in the mid-1980s and early 1990s were instrumental in the country's recent growth performance and the diversification of its production and exports.

2. Financial reform

Real interest rates were negative during the decades of financial repression in the 1970s and early 1980s. Soon after the early reforms took effect, real interest rates became positive and high, reaching 5.80% in 1987 and 6.14% in 1988 (Baliamoune-Lutz 2008; Baliamoune and Chowdhury 2003). Prior to the mid-1980s, monetary policy was implemented mainly through direct allocation of credit and refinancing while interest rates were set administratively. The reforms aimed at improving the capacity of financial institutions to mobilize domestic savings, allocating financial resources based on market demand, curbing direct government intervention, and increasing competition in the banking sector. In 1985 the monetary authorities liberalized interest rates on above-one-year deposits. In 1989–90, the six-month and three-month deposit rates were liberalized. Over the period 1986–91, a minimum interest rate replaced the fixed rate, which was in place for all other deposits that were still subject to regulation. Interest rates on all time deposits were liberalized in 1992, and in February 1996 lending rates in Morocco were effectively liberalized.

The financial reform programme was accompanied by the repeal in September 1993 of the 'Moroccanization' law of 1973 which limited foreign ownership of businesses to 49%. In addition, tax reforms that included changes in the corporate profit tax in 1984 and the introduction of the value added tax (VAT) in 1986 ensured simplification, neutrality, and more transparency of the tax system. Important privatization initiatives took place in the early 1990s, including in the banking sector. The Casablanca stock exchange (CSE) was privatized in 1993; its turnover increased from 672 million dirhams in 1989 to around 24 billion dirhams in 1995, and market capitalization rose from 5 to 39 billion dirhams over this period. There is empirical evidence (Baliamoune and Chowdhury 2003) that financial reforms boosted domestic savings in Morocco.

3. Trade sector reform

Significant trade liberalization began in the mid-1980s. For non-agricultural products, the maximum custom tariff has been reduced from over 70% in the mid-1980s to 50% in 2001, and most quantitative restrictions were removed or converted into tariff equivalents. From 1993 to 2000, tariffs fell from 72% to 52% on food imports, from 99% to 50% on clothing, from 92% to 38% on textiles, and from 65% to 17% on electrical machinery.

Trade diversification and volume have improved over the past two decades. The growth of merchandise exports was –2.6%, 8.7%, and 9.4% in 1980–85, 1990–95, and 2001–3, respectively. In 1980, the top three exports in Morocco (based on data from UN Comtrade) were crude fertilizers and crude minerals (32.4%), vegetables and fruit (20.7%), and inorganic chemicals (8.3%). In 2007, the top three exports were articles of apparel and clothing accessories (24%), electric machinery, apparatus and appliances (13.9%) and fish, crustaceans, and molluscs and preparations thereof (9.1%). Thus, there was a significant increase in the share of manufactures in exports. Trade liberalization was greatly enhanced by the introduction of current account convertibility in 1993, which allowed banks to accept deposits from exporters and importers in foreign currencies.

REFERENCES

Baliamoune, M. N., and A. R. Chowdhury, 2003. 'The long-run behavior and short-run dynamics of private savings in Morocco', *Savings and Development* 27.2, 135–60.

Baliamoune-Lutz, M., 2008. 'Financial reform and the mobilization of domestic savings: the experience of Morocco', in George Mavrotas (ed.), *Domestic Resource Mobilization and Financial Development*. Basingstoke: Palgrave Macmillan, ch. 6.

Clerides, S., S. Lach, and J. Tybout, 1998. 'Is learning-by-exporting important? Micro-dynamic evidence from Colombia, Mexico, and Morocco', *Quarterly Journal of Economics* 113.3, 903–47.

Currie, J., and A. E. Harrison, 1997. 'Sharing the costs: the impact of trade reform on capital and labor in Morocco', *Journal of Labor Economics* 15.3, S44–71.

Fafchamps, M., S. El Hamine, and A. Zeufack, 2008. 'Learning to export: evidence from Moroccan manufacturing', *Journal of African Economies* 17.2, 305–55.

Nsouli, S. M., S. Eken, K. Enders, V.-C. Thai, J. Decressin, and F. Cartigila, 1995. 'Resilience and growth through sustained adjustment: the Moroccan experience', IMF Occasional Paper 117. Washington, DC.

Mozambique
The Promise...

Channing Arndt

1. Introduction

This chapter considers the economic contours of Mozambique's development. Space considerations preclude discussion of the political contours, which are equally important. I begin with Mozambique's development trajectory, focusing on the post-independence period. I then evaluate the ascent from the nadir in 1992, when Mozambique was labelled 'the poorest country in the world'. Finally, I offer some suggestions on new policy directions.

2. Development trajectory

To understand the development trajectory of a country, historical context is required. This is particularly true of Mozambique, where a phenomenal volume of history has been crammed into less than four decades. In 1973 Mozambique was a Portuguese colony, and home to more than 200,000 Portuguese citizens. By 1975, due to a *coup d'état* in Portugal and the hard-line policies of Mozambican leaders, Mozambique was an independent socialist state and the large majority of Portuguese residents had left the country. The Portuguese left Mozambique with a particularly poor legacy of educational attainment even by African standards. While the new government managed to arrest the freefall in GDP induced by the exodus of human capital embodied in the Portuguese, growth remained elusive and crisis management remained the order of the day.

By the early 1980s, the idealistic optimism that characterized the immediate post-independence period had given way to frank recognition of distressing economic trends. However, before reforms could be implemented, the combination of discontent from failed economic policies and finance and military assistance from the white regimes in Rhodesia and South Africa plunged Mozambique into a devastating civil war. More than one million Mozambicans died and approximately one third of the population of about 15 million was displaced. Rural infrastructure was decimated. Coincident with the release of Nelson Mandela from prison in 1990, negotiations between the warring sides began in earnest. A peace accord was signed in 1992 and elections were held in 1994; however, the era of peace in Mozambique began with the unwanted label 'poorest country in the world'.

Since the early 1990s, trends have been decidedly more positive. Mozambique has grown rapidly. The World Bank, in the 2007 edition of *African Development Indicators* (ADI), listed Mozambique as the fastest-growing diversified African economy with growth averaging about 8% per year between 1996 and 2008. Capital intensive investments, the so-called mega-projects, contributed to measured growth in GDP over the period. However, a careful look at national accounts reveals that these activities directly contributed about one percentage point to growth over the period. So, even with the direct contributions of the mega-projects removed, GDP growth in Mozambique has been rapid. Improved economic conditions have been felt by nearly all segments of the Mozambican population, though not in equal measure. Headline statistics include the poverty headcount, which fell from 69% of the population in 1997 to 54% in 2003, and infant mortality rates, which dropped from 149 in 1996 to 101 in 2003.

Economic growth and substantial aid volumes also made possible rapid expansion in public services. For example, access to education was severely circumscribed in the aftermath of the civil war, with only a little more than one million students enrolled. By 2007, enrolments had increased to more than five million students. This increment of about four million student enrolments amounts to about 20% of the current total population. Despite these gains, education levels are one of the Millennium Development Goals (MDGs) that Mozambique is unlikely to achieve, principally because universal access to primary school is an absolute goal with no reference to initial conditions. Mozambique does, however, have the possibility of achieving a number of MDGs, and of registering significant progress towards the achievement of the remainder.

3. Evaluating the recent ascent

Five factors have combined to bring about the rapid improvements in social and economic conditions since the early 1990s. First comes the establishment of peace. Second, the low economic and social conditions that prevailed at the nadir in 1992 clearly played a role. It is not hard to imagine that conditions could improve from those levels. Even so, dismissing the achievements of recent years as 'bounce-back' fails to capture the story. Policy is a third factor. The policy agenda included achieving and maintaining macroeconomic stability, investment in human capital and basic economic infrastructure, openness to trade and investment, principal reliance on markets and the private sector as a source of growth, and the creation/nurturing of institutions necessary to support a market-based economy, including government institutions for the provision of public goods. Mozambican policymakers can point to a long list of achievements under each of these agenda items. Fourth, foreign assistance greatly expanded the scope to undertake the physical and institutional investments required.

Finally, Mozambique's numerous assets have played a role. The country is blessed with large quantities of arable land, reasonable rainfall particularly in the north and centre, numerous rivers, a long coastline, rich fisheries, natural harbours, and substantial mineral resources. In addition, the rise of the new South Africa in 1994 opened up links with the largest and most sophisticated economy in Africa, located on Mozambique's doorstep. In sum, the combination of peace, a low starting point, high potential, substantial foreign assistance, and reasonable policy has combined to produce growth and poverty reduction to date.

While real achievements have been registered, huge and fundamental development challenges remain. It is a long way up from poorest country in the world. The example of education illustrates the point. As indicated, expansion of education access is a recognized achievement; yet in 2007 the level of the Human Development Index for education in Mozambique remained below the average for the least developed countries and for sub-Saharan Africa. So, even in an area posting large gains, there remains some way to go to achieve even the average for sub-Saharan Africa.

Finally, not all trends are positive. While recent data remains to be analysed, few would be surprised to find an increase in measured inequality. Within urban zones, poverty prevalence is lower than in rural zones but the depth of poverty is often more profound. Recent qualitative work echoes these findings, and serious urban rioting following transport fare price increases in early 2008 underscores the point. In rural areas, half or more of the population remains trapped in very low-productivity subsistence agriculture.

4. Looking forward

While the fundamental policy building blocks mentioned above should remain, there is ample need and scope to adjust policies and priorities to meet new challenges. I finish with five policy priorities. I list these because they represent a fairly decisive break from the past.

4.1. EMPLOYMENT

To date, Mozambique has been unsuccessful in establishing labour-intensive manufactured exports. Scepticism over the likelihood of success was part of the problem. That scepticism, perhaps appropriate until recently, should be rethought. While the current global recession has cooled wage growth, it remains the case that the stock of unskilled labour is relatively stagnant or actually declining in East Asia, particularly China. Over the next decade, Mozambique may well be in a favourable position to compete for the footloose capital that underpins large-scale employment of low-skilled labour. It should start competing now.

4.2. PUBLIC ECONOMIC INFRASTRUCTURE

The rebuilding of Mozambique's economic infrastructure essentially reflects a 'rebuild what was there before' strategy. Certainly, since peace in 1992, there has not been a comprehensive infrastructure development plan that proposes a coherent package of long-run investments, consistent with a well-articulated development strategy, along with appropriate financing plans. The time has come to develop the plan that will produce the infrastructure backbone for the 21st century.

4.3. POPULATION

Recent census data places the population growth rate at about 2.4% per annum. This is fast, especially in the context of a severe and mature HIV/AIDS pandemic. There is ample evidence that bringing population growth rates down can provide substantial economic benefits over time, especially when complemented by policies that facilitate the reaping of benefits from a demographic transition. More serious policies aimed at lowering population growth rates are required.

4.4. AGRICULTURE

In terms of rhetoric, agriculture has been a priority for decades. Nevertheless, a perplexing lack of attention to priority areas such as research, extension, and land cadastre has remained characteristic since the onset of peace. The ministry of agriculture should focus on provision of public goods and addressing selected market failures. This focus is too often absent.

4.5. DATA

Data collection, analysis, and dissemination efforts in Mozambique are good by African standards. Even so, there are powerful arguments for enhanced efforts to produce timely and relevant economic data. Today, on the cusp of elections and the elaboration of a new five-year development plan, the most recent national level data on poverty and wellbeing are from 2003. Agricultural statistics are a recognized disaster. Despite a series of efforts, there is no coherent enterprise monitoring programme. National accounts suffer directly from these shortcomings. Our current ignorance is costly, and there is much to gain from enhanced attention to data systems.

Namibia
History, Politics, and Unequal Growth

Robin Sherbourne

1. Introduction

Namibia attained Independence on 21 March 1990 after more than a century of colonial rule, first by imperial Germany (until 1915) and then by South Africa, under a League of Nations mandate from 1920. Moves towards Namibian independence gathered pace in the 1950s and the 1960s, with the South West Africa Peoples' Organization (SWAPO) declaring armed struggle in 1966. Diplomatic efforts focused on the United Nations, which in 1973 anointed SWAPO 'the sole and authentic voice of the Namibian people' after the International Court of Justice declared South Africa's occupation of Namibia illegal. As apartheid South Africa fought a bush war against SWAPO centred mainly on the northern Namibian border, SWAPO found military support from eastern bloc countries: Cuba, China, and North Korea. The military stalemate of the 1980s that ensued was finally brought to an end by UN-brokered peace negotiations and elections which saw SWAPO win a majority and form Namibia's first independent government.

This pre-independence history is critical in understanding post-independence economic policies. SWAPO, which with each of the four subsequent elections has entrenched its position as the dominant party, has pursued economic policies which can be characterized as mildly nationalistic, pan-Africanist, and statist, while remaining generally market-friendly and open towards foreign investment.

Two of the most important macroeconomic policy decisions were made soon after independence. Despite the immediate establishment of its own central bank and the introduction of the Namibia dollar in 1993, monetary policy has remained closely tied to that of South Africa. Within the Common Monetary Area (CMA), the Namibia dollar has stayed pegged one-to-one to the South African Rand which remains legal tender. Under this arrangement and with a relatively unrestricted flow of capital, interest rates have closely followed those in South Africa. The benefits of inflation targeting, introduced in South Africa in 2000, have been transmitted to Namibia so that inflation in the second decade of independence has been substantially lower than in the first decade.

Namibia's decision to formalize its *de facto* membership of the Southern African Customs Union (SACU) meant that trade policy remained largely outside the hands of Namibian policymakers. Changes in tariffs and non-tariff barriers continued to be driven by South Africa's commitments to the WTO. Namibia's trading arrangements were complicated by parallel membership in the Southern African Development Community and, from 1993, in the Common Market of Eastern and Southern Africa (COMESA—which Namibia ended up leaving in 2003) as well as South Africa's own Trade and Development Cooperation Agreement (TDCA) with the EU. The muddled nature of trading relationships has been exposed by the advent of economic partnership agreements (EPAs) and has resulted in a two-year impasse.

Having effectively tied its own hands on monetary and trade policy, the country's attention naturally centred on fiscal policy. In the period following independence, Namibia found generous support for its development programmes from a wide range of donors. In 1997 South Africa formally wrote off pre-independence debts, leaving the government virtually debt-free. Furthermore, the establishment of a domestic debt market allowed government to start tapping the significant amounts of contractual savings that had historically found a home in South Africa. One consequence of the policy of national reconciliation was that large numbers of new black civil servants joined the existing administration to create an extraordinarily large public service, a trend that grew through the creation of a host of state-owned enterprises (SOEs) and agencies.

The size of government and the stock of public debt expanded steadily in the course of the 1990s thanks to heavy spending on public administration, education, health, and Namibia's system of welfare cash transfers. As the ratio of public debt to GDP surpassed the government's self-imposed limit of 25%, Namibia's first female minister of finance, Saara Kuugongelwa-Amadhila, started to bring public debt back under control. By the time the global economic crisis broke, the government was in a position to actively use public spending as a way of countering the downturn in demand for Namibia's exports.

Namibia's success in maintaining macroeconomic stability has yielded twenty years of virtually uninterrupted economic growth, growth that accelerated from a modest 3% a year in the 1990s to a healthier 4.5% in the second decade of independence. However, the increase was largely a consequence of the international minerals boom. Namibia is a world-class producer of gem diamonds and uranium oxide, and exports a variety of other minerals. Entering its third decade of nationhood, Namibia looks set to become more dependent on the minerals sector than ever. Uranium is likely to take the place of diamonds as the mainstay of the mining economy just as the country's onshore diamond resource is beginning to dwindle.

Foreign investment has flowed into a variety of sectors—agriculture, fishing, mining, manufacturing, construction, trade, tourism, transport, telecoms, and financial services—from a wide range of countries including Spain, France, India, Australia, Canada, the UK, Holland, Germany, China, Portugal, and Egypt. Namibia's economy has become truly globalized rather than just being South Africa's back yard.

Economic policy has had a good deal more success in achieving macroeconomic stability than in achieving productivity growth, innovation, and export competitiveness. Education policies have fallen short in developing the skills and attitudes of the labour force. Labour market policies have generally served to help those already in work while creating additional rigidities which discourage the use of labour. As a result, formal employment has stagnated.

Namibia has achieved two decades of economic growth. However, this growth has benefited the urban (and especially white) middle classes. It has not translated into rapid employment growth, so that levels of poverty and inequality remain high. There appears little sign of organized disquiet on a scale that could force the government's hand. But the danger is that policymakers might conclude that past policies have failed, and turn to more nationalistic, authoritarian and less market-oriented approaches. The fact that the nettle of racial disparities in the economy has yet to be adequately grasped only adds to the danger that Namibia's pragmatic if unspectacular progress may yet be derailed.

Niger
The Importance of National Consensus for Effective Social and Economic Reform

Amadou Ibrahim

1. Social and political context

The country's political situation has been relatively stable since it gained independence in August 1960. Niger enjoyed peaceful social and political environment up to the early 1990s, notwithstanding the three military coups in 1974, 1996, and 1999 and a decade of instability, marked by recurrent union strikes in the 1990s, in the aftermath of the Sovereign National Conference. The first transparent and fair general elections were held in 1993. However following a political deadlock between the President and the Prime Minister in 1995, the military took over in January 1996 and held contested presidential elections and, later, legislative elections boycotted by main opposition parties. In 1999, the general who took over in 1996 was removed from office by his chief security officer, who organized transparent and fair elections in late 1999 under pressure from the international community.

2. Recent political developments

The last decade has been marked by the building of democratic institutions and active civil society network. The newly elected government resumed dialogue and reached consensus with unions on key economic reforms[1] in earlier 2000. Civil society organizations flourish, and play a key role in the scrutiny of public actions regarding basic service deliveries (especially in the education and health sectors). There have been workers' strikes since 1999 and political turmoil up to 2007. The country enjoyed social and

---

[1] This includes the control of the wage bill, a new civil service status, and settlement of internal arrears plan.

political stability under the leadership of the incumbent President, who was elected in 1999 and re-elected in 2004. Also Niger's first local elections were successfully completed on 24 July 2004, as part of a programme of political decentralization. Meanwhile, the country has faced resurgent rebellion in the northern region since early 2007. The roots of this armed insurgency lie in concerns over the equitable share of mineral revenues. The government initiated ongoing direct peace talks with the three rebel groups in 2008.

In 2004, the majority and opposition parties created a framework for resolving political issues. With the goal of enhancing democratic roots, political leaders decided to establish a National Council for Political Dialogue (CNDP), chaired by the Prime Minister and the opposition leader. The CNDP contributed to settling most political disputes regarding the electoral code and to reaching consensus on key economic and social reforms (population policy).

3. Historical economic growth trends

Niger's economic growth over the past five decades has been very volatile and low on average. From 1960 to 1974, before the uranium boom in the mid-1970s, the economy was essentially dominated by rain-fed agriculture, and GDP growth averaged 1.4%. Following a fivefold increase in uranium prices during the international oil crises, real GDP growth rose to 3.3% from 1975 to 1983. Through a negative combination of declining uranium prices due to the stabilization of oil prices, a succession of droughts, and political upheavals in the 1990s, real economic growth decelerated to 2.2%.

4. A more resilient economy in the last decade

Economic growth has revived since 2000, averaging 4.8% compared to a sustained slowdown in the 1990s, averaging about 2.2%. Political stability and national consensus on key economic reforms resulted in steady growth. GDP growth averaged 5.5% from 2000 to 2008, which was 2.4% above the population growth rate. In 2008 real GDP reached 9.5% due to exceptional increase in the agricultural-sector output, estimated at 25.0%, and also by increased investment, amounting to 26.4% of GDP. Private investment, for drilling and building a new oil refinery and in the uranium sector, was notable. These variations underscore the country's vulnerability to droughts and its undiversified and small private-sector base in sectors other than natural resources. Niger's growth potential is essentially derived from the oil and mining sectors, which are expected to contribute substantially to economic growth around 2012 when the new larger uranium mine and a refinery will come on stream.

Donor assistance has increased steadily since 2000. In the 1990s, foreign aid granted to Niger slumped due to recurrent social and political turmoil and poor macroeconomic management. The stable political situation favoured the gradual resumption of international aid, and Niger benefited from all debt relief programmes. Net ODA flows increased from US$211 million in 2000 to US$443 million in 2007. Niger's budget is largely financed by donors (45% on average). This has helped massive investment in the social and rural sectors which has resulted in tangible improvements of social indicators and strong real growth in the agriculture sector of about 6% since 2000.

5. A new episode of political turmoil and uncertainty

Niger's political stance has deteriorated since earlier 2009, when the incumbent President expressed officially his willingness to stay in power against constitutional provision. The President dissolved key democratic institutions, opposed to his move to stay in power after his second term, supposedly in order to protect vested interests in the oil and mining sectors. He held a controversial referendum in August 2009, which granted him a three-year 'bonus' period in office and no limit terms thereafter. The social context has also deteriorated regarding freedom of expression and liberty of the press. Without a consensual resolution of the political crisis, Niger will probably lose some of its hard-won progress in building strong democracy institutions and attracting substantial aid from the international community. This will also impede effective implementation of key economic reforms and may hamper economic growth.

6. Lessons learned from the last decade in Niger

- Building effective democratic institutions is key for reaching national consensus on social and economic reforms.
- A good understanding of the political economy in the extractive industry is important for mitigating risks of political and social turmoil.
- A strong civil society and freedom of the press are important for promoting economic governance by providing 'checks and balance' to executive power together with the opposition parties.
- The international community should anticipate possible political instability in election years, and support fragile developing countries in holding regular, transparent, and free elections.

Nigeria
Managing Volatility and Fighting Corruption

Ngozi Okonjo-Iweala

1. Introduction[1]

Actions speak louder than adjectives like 'incorrigible', and Nigeria has proved by what it has done in recent years that it *can* manage volatility and fight corruption, its persistent development foes. Notwithstanding $300 billion from oil between 1970 and 2001, Nigeria's per capita GDP actually fell from $264 to $256 in constant 1995 US dollars over 1970–2001. Infrastructure deteriorated because of the cutback in public investments. In 2001, per capita electric power consumption was only 82 kW compared to the low-income country (LIC) average of 317 kW and a huge 3,800 kW in South Africa. Its citizens had suffered notwithstanding the oil bonanza: in 2003, the infant mortality rate was 101 per 1,000 live births compared to 79 in LICs and 54 in South Africa.[2]

By 2000, it was evident that the only way out was a multi-pronged strategy with reducing macroeconomic volatility and fighting corruption as prime goals. Building on the political stability nurtured during its first tenure, the second Obasanjo administration (2003–7) launched a comprehensive economic and governance reform programme. Tangible progress was made but much is left unfinished. This chapter was written while the global economic and financial crisis of 2008–9, christened the Great Recession by the IMF, was unfolding. Lessons learned during this crisis only reinforce the need for Nigeria to manage oil price volatility, fight corruption, and seize the opportunities which have eluded it for so long by improving basic service delivery and eliminating infrastructure bottlenecks.

---

[1] The findings, interpretations, and conclusions expressed here are entirely those of the author. They do not necessarily represent the views of the International Bank for Reconstruction and Development/World Bank and its affiliated organizations, or those of the Executive Directors of the World Bank or the governments they represent.

[2] Okonjo-Iweala and Osafo-Kwaako (2007).

2. **History matters**

In 1970, oil was 60% of exports. By 1982, it was close to 99% because agricultural exports had been decimated. This was hardly an inevitable consequence of Dutch Disease.

2.1. FISCAL AND DEBT POLICY

Even though oil revenues more than tripled to 20% of GDP after the OPEC-led 1973–4 oil price hike, large fiscal deficits were racked up, approaching 7% of GDP. The fiscal deficit rose again after the second oil price shock of 1979–80, averaging over 8% of GDP for the period 1981–4.[3] The sizeable deficits meant fiscal policy was procyclical, actually amplifying oil price volatility! Besides, the composition of public spending did little to support long-run growth and diversification. External debt rose in order to help finance the rising fiscal and current account deficits, from less than a billion dollars in 1970 to $19 billion in 1985, at which point Nigeria was having difficulty rescheduling a relatively paltry $2 billion in insured trade credits in spite of its considerable oil wealth. Nigeria had developed an external debt overhang.

2.2. AGRICULTURAL POLICY

Between 1970 and 1982, the production of Nigeria's major cash crops—cocoa, rubber, cotton and groundnuts—fell 43, 29, 65, and 64% respectively. By the mid-1980s, cocoa was virtually all that was left of agricultural exports, but its share in world trade had halved. Not only did the government-run commodity boards not link their procurement prices to international prices, they retained a significant part of producer prices. By 1985, the real producer prices (nominal commodity board price deflated by the rural CPI) for cocoa, cotton, and palm oil were less than 50% of their levels in 1975; and for rubber, groundnuts and soyabeans, less than 70%.[4] This added insult to the injury caused by a public expenditure composition that did little to serve agriculture in terms of better rural infrastructure and improved R&D. But the fall in oil prices in the early 1980s could have paved the way for at least some recovery had the naira been allowed to depreciate.

---

[3] Numbers based on Pinto (1987: table 4).
[4] Based on Pinto (1987: table 6).

2.3. EXCHANGE RATE POLICY

Nigeria's real exchange rate (dollars per local currency) appreciated by almost 200% over 1974 and 1984, by which time an oil glut had set in. Indonesia had similar initial conditions; its experience suggests that this scale of appreciation was far from inevitable. The key difference: Indonesia was quick to let the rupiah depreciate whenever oil prices fell so that its real exchange rate *depreciated* by 22% over 1974–84. Instead of letting the naira depreciate, Nigeria rationed foreign exchange through a strict import-licensing system. As a result, the black market premium over the official exchange rate went from 65% in 1980 to 320% in 1984 and by 1985, the 'lucky ones' getting import licenses received rents of between 8.5% and 13% of GDP! This meant a costly hidden subsidy from the public exchequer. Besides, with commodity boards setting cash crop prices with reference to the official exchange rate, it is little wonder that agriculture was devastated.

3. Breaking away from the past

Nigeria proved by its actions during the second Obasanjo administration that it had learnt from its past mistakes. Volatility had interacted with weak governance and corruption during the oil boom of the 1970s and the subsequent bust to produce an external debt overhang and a costly black market premium on foreign exchange.[5] These then amplified the effects of oil price volatility: the inability to borrow externally because of the debt overhang meant draconian cuts in public expenditure when oil prices fell; and the devastation of agriculture as a result of the exchange rate and pricing policies heightened oil dependence. In addition, the government failed to improve basic service delivery and infrastructure. Not surprisingly, the priorities during the second Obasanjo administration were to strengthen governance, lower macroeconomic volatility, and eliminate the debt overhang.

But how? Reducing public debt, which stood at 72% of GDP at the end of 2004 (50 percentage points external, 22 domestic) to sustainable levels would require an agreement with the Paris Club, which accounted for the lion's share of external debt. For this, Nigeria would need resources to first clear its arrears to the PC. Fortunately, the resolve to break from the past coincided with a big run-up in oil prices. But Nigeria also needed substantial resources for the social sectors and infrastructure to stand any chance of meeting the Millennium Development Goals as well as for a reserves cushion against oil price volatility. Simulations showed that even though oil prices had risen to $50 a

---

[5] An analysis of volatility and the debt overhang is contained in Budina, Pang, and van Wijnbergen (2007).

barrel from just $10 a few years earlier, it would be impossible for Nigeria to reduce debt to sustainable debt levels while also meeting the MDGs and building up a reserves cushion: debt relief was unavoidable.[6] But why would donors long sceptical of Nigeria's governance record agree to debt relief?

Anticipating this, the Obasanjo administration had formulated a comprehensive National Economic Empowerment and Development Strategy focusing not just on macroeconomic stabilization but also fighting corruption, making oil operations more transparent, and implementing a wide range of structural reforms in the energy, telecoms, banking, and other sectors. The most visible sign of its break from the past was Nigeria's adoption of an oil price-based fiscal rule (OPFR) in 2004 coupled with the monthly transparent publication in national newspapers of revenues accruing to each tier of government: the budget would be based on a conservative reference price for oil, with any savings transferred to the 'Excess Crude Account' to serve as a rainy-day fund. This would also dampen the transmission of oil price volatility to the non-oil economy by breaking the link between government spending and current oil prices. Nigeria also became one of the first countries to sign on to the Extractive Industries Transparency Initiative (EITI). The Economic and Financial Crimes Commission and the Independent Corrupt Practices and other Related Offences Commission were established, and successfully prosecuted several high-profile political and other appointees as part of fighting corruption.

Based on its strong start to governance reform, the transparency engendered by its adoption of the OPFR and EITI and with World Bank and IMF support, Nigeria finally concluded an agreement with the Paris Club in October 2005, wiping out the $30 billion it owed by paying off its arrears and buying back the remainder at a significant discount, and securing an $18 billion write-off. As a result, Nigeria obtained a BB– sovereign credit rating for the first time in its history. And economic growth picked up, from a little over 2% over the decade ending in 2002 to over 6% overall and eventually to above 9% for the non-oil economy.

4. Looking ahead

The global financial and economic crisis of 2008–9 was the ultimate stress test for Nigeria's reforms. The country entered this crisis with $60 billion in reserves (of which ECA amounted to $17 billion) as of September 2008, low public and external debt, and resilient banks as a result of the consolidation exercise of the past few years. The non-oil economy had benefited substantially from the better management of volatility

---

[6] World Bank (2005).

associated with the adoption of OPFR and the elimination of the debt overhang. And no doubt helped by market-oriented prices in contrast to the previous oil boom, agriculture had become the main driver of non-oil growth.

True to form, oil prices went from $115 per barrel in the first quarter of 2008 to over $150 in early July, then dropped to less than $40 by the end of 2008—below the $45 reference price for the 2009 budget. Oil prices at the time of writing were in the $70 range, but unrest in the Niger Delta led to a drop in production well below budgetary assumptions, leading to drawdowns from the ECA. These fiscal and current account balances deteriorated significantly in 2009 relative to 2008. And cracks appeared in the banking system, with concerns about the accuracy of the commercial banks' financial reporting, their true level of capitalization, and their exposure to the stock market on account of margin lending for buying stocks. Fortunately, the central bank, CBN, acted decisively to avert a systemic failure. An estimated $4–6 billion was spent by CBN to recapitalize several banks, and the CEOs of some banks were sacked and investigated. At the same time, the basic infrastructure for accounting, financial reporting, regulation, collateral registration, and credit rating are in considerable need of upgrading—transparency and confidence being the cornerstones of finance.

But reminiscent of the early 1980s, CBN was slow to let the naira depreciate when oil prices fell sharply after July 2008, resulting in a reserve loss of $10 billion. In January 2009, it effectively shut down the interbank foreign exchange market, fuelling a significant parallel market premium on foreign exchange. Owing to the reluctance to let the official exchange rate depreciate, another $7 billion of reserves was used up. However, exchange restrictions were subsequently phased out with the parallel market premium all but vanishing.

Let me conclude by highlighting a few of the challenges going forward.

First, managing volatility in all its facets remains a top priority. With oil continuing to account for over 95% of exports and some 80% of government revenues, Nigeria cannot afford to make matters worse by amplifying oil price volatility with domestic policy, governance, and corruption shocks, which were particularly severe during the Abacha years. Otherwise, discontinuities of governments and governance will impede steady growth and development and interact with oil price volatility to erode the gains of the past few years. Thus, governance and corruption remain the binding constraint to faster growth and poverty reduction. The government must create an environment with the regulation, property rights, infrastructure, taxation, and financial-sector development which will channel the energy and the talents of a small, corrupt elite away from raiding the public exchequer towards creating businesses which will provide jobs to young Nigerians graduating from universities. For example, of the 900,000 students completing secondary school in Anambra state, only 10% go on to university. If the rest are not gainfully employed, they will tend to get sucked into criminal activity, including kidnapping and extortion.

Second, diversification away from oil is badly needed. Notwithstanding its strong growth performance over the past few years, agricultural exports have almost vanished and low productivity is a concern. What should be done, in addition to managing volatility? Public expenditure composition is a major factor, in that targeted investments to alleviate infrastructure bottlenecks could help the labour-intensive agricultural and manufacturing sectors while also providing jobs for Nigeria's youth. The role of state governments is vitally important in strengthening the investment climate. For example, Bayelsa, Enugu, Delta, Kwara, and Lagos states are pursuing various projects with potential domestic and foreign direct investors to generate jobs and diversify their economies.

Third, the poor performance on HD indicators must be reversed. Even though Nigeria's poverty rate fell from 66% in 1996 to 55% in 2004, this was still very high, and new surveys will hopefully show further improvement given strong non-oil growth. The Gini coefficient came down from 0.47 in 1996 to 0.43 in 2004 and is by no means an outlier. But Nigeria lags far behind on its human development indicators. Even though infant mortality has been declining, it was still above the LIC average in 2006. While immunization against measles (percentage of children aged 12–23 months) has picked up substantially since 2000, at 62% in 2006 it was well below the LIC average of 75%. And in 2006, electric power consumption per capita was not even half that of the LIC average. The only area in which Nigeria is doing better than the LIC average is on primary school enrolment. Better-targeted programmes to increase the efficiency and effectiveness of social spending programmes would help and needs to be made a priority.

Fourth, fiscal sustainability must be preserved. Adhering to the oil price-based fiscal rule, passing and implementing fiscal responsibility laws by all the states, a framework for governing public borrowing at all tiers of government, and adhering transparently to the rules set up for drawing from the ECA are all essential ingredients. While the Great Recession was an appropriate time to be using ECA funds to compensate for the decline in aggregate demand and shortfall in oil revenues, the keys going forward are transparency and aiming towards removing bottlenecks for the private sector, such as with the $5.3 billion investment envisaged in the Nigerian Integrated Power Project. If the money is well spent and actually goes into the designated activity, not only will there be a fiscal stimulus, but long-run solvency will be helped through faster non-oil growth and tax revenues.

Nigeria thus has a lot going for it. It has demonstrated it can rise to the challenges of managing volatility and fighting corruption which only a decade ago appeared insuperable. I look to a bright future when Nigeria will unlock the talents and opportunities of all its citizens, and its leaders accept that they have a responsibility to the rest of Africa for good governance and good economic performance.

REFERENCES

Budina, Nina, Gaobo Pang, and Sweder van Wijnbergen, 2007. 'Nigeria's growth record: Dutch Disease or debt overhang?', World Bank Policy Research Working Paper 4256, Washington, DC.

Okonjo-Iweala, Ngozi, 2008. 'Nigeria's fight for debt relief: tracing the path', in Lael Brainard and Derek Chollet (eds), *Global Development 2.0: Can Philanthropists, the Public, and the Poor Make Poverty History?* Washington, DC: Brookings Institution Press, 101–19.

—— and Philip Osafo-Kwaako, 2007. 'Nigeria's economic reforms: progress and challenges', Global Economy and Development Working Paper 6, Washington, DC: Brookings Institution.

Pinto, Brian, 1987. 'Nigeria during and after the oil boom: a policy comparison with Indonesia', *World Bank Economic Review* 1.3, 419–45.

World Bank, 2005. 'Nigeria's opportunity of a generation: meeting the MDGs, reducing indebtedness', report prepared by the PREM Anchor for the Africa region.

Rwanda
Leadership for Economic Growth and Development

Thomas Kigabo Rusuhuzwa

1. Introduction

It is agreed that good leadership is a key factor for economic growth, since growth requires committed, credible, and capable governments and high-growth economies typically built their prosperity on sturdy political foundations. Indeed, sustained growth does not just happen; it must be consciously chosen as an objective by the country's leadership and as an organizing principle of the country's politics. It has to be planned for the long term and guided by a vision for the future direction of the economy (Commission on Growth and Development 2008). The objective of this chapter is to show how this factor, leadership, has contributed to current economic development in Rwanda.

Sixteen years ago, Rwanda was considered as a dead country, whose future was simply unclear following the 1994 genocide. The whole system was destroyed, from the economy to security to justice and infrastructure. However, important socioeconomic gains have been achieved in Rwanda after the genocide, and in some respects the country can constitute a model of development in Africa (De Lorenzo 2008). Although Rwanda still has challenges in its economic development due essentially to structural problems, the country has achieved very good results and has built a solid foundation for its development in the long term. These achievements during the last sixteen years are the result of good leadership, committed to finding durable solutions for the Rwandan people despite significant challenges. Consequently, the country today is safe and stable, with little corruption and a clear anti-corruption policy.

Rwandan economic growth has been strong, reaching 11.2% in 2008, 7.9% in 2007, with an average of 8% between 2004 and 2008. Indeed, the Government of Rwanda has planned to implement the Economic Development and Poverty Reduction Strategy (EDPRS), where the overall agricultural-sector goal is to achieve sustainable economic growth and social development, leading to the increase and diversification of household incomes and ensuring food supply and food security for the entire population. To

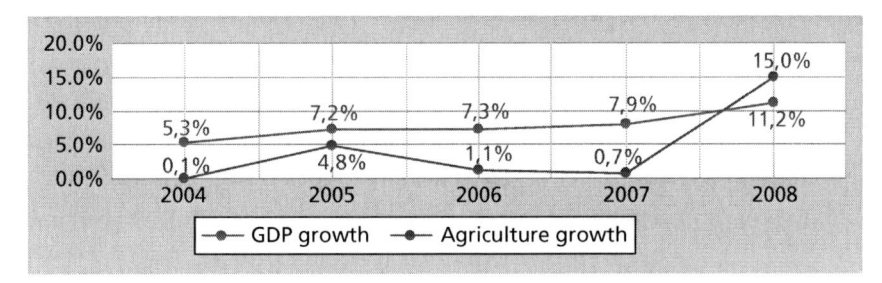

Figure 1. Real economic growth and agricultural-sector performance

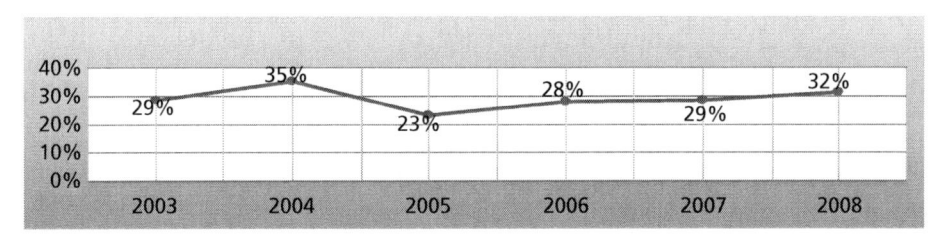

Figure 2. Rwanda–EAC trade evolution

address the falling trend in productivity of crops and the minimal use and low availability of fertilizer, the government embarked on a plan to improve productivity and increase fertilizer availability, accessibility, and affordability through the crop intensification programme. As result, the agriculture sector has significantly contributed to economic performance since 2008, with agricultural-sector production increasing by 15% and 10.4% in 2008 and 2009 respectively.

Rwanda is a landlocked and resource-scarce country, with a relatively small market. Rwandans are among the so-called 'bottom billion' which have been prevented from growing and developing in poor countries in Africa (Collier 2007). In its 'Vision 2020' (2000), the Government of Rwanda clearly showed that regional integration will be one of the responses to these problems. The accession of Rwanda to the East African Community (EAC) on 1 July 2007 was in this direction, and was aimed to contribute to the economic development of the country by placing it in a regional market with 113 million people. Kenya and Uganda are two principal trading partners of Rwanda, and the total trade in EAC has been increasing significantly, from 29% in 2003 to 32% in 2008 as percentage of Rwandan total trade.

The accession of Rwanda to the EAC will increase economic activities in the country and around the region through the benefits of economies of scale and attracting foreign investment. In the medium and long term, this process of liberalization and integration should contribute to reducing dependence on foreign aid, which Rwanda is committed to. Rwanda is also engaged in progressively replacing donor conditionality with internal

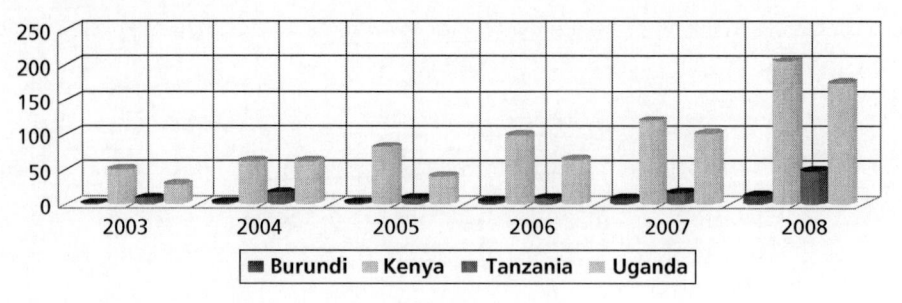

Figure 3. Rwanda trade with EAC country members

policy clarity, by creating its own policy space: good policy never comes from donor conditionality or pressure, it must come locally (De Lorenzo 2008).

As result of good leadership with clear policies, Rwanda has achieved success in different sectors, and its experience may contribute toward regional development. Indeed, Rwanda has invested much in good governance, through the creation of structures, mechanisms, and practices that guarantee participation of all and transparency in public-affairs management.

Gender equity, a cross-cutting aspect of good governance, is a component of socio-economic development and empowerment, as are a clear vision to improve education for all and the eradication of discrimination across all levels of society. Rwanda is recognized as having the highest percentage of women in parliament in the world (56%).

Innovations in Rwanda's health system, including country-wide community health insurance and the introduction of a performance-based pay initiative, should also be a good model in the EAC region to increase access to health services, especially for the poor. Rwanda has also made enormous efforts in fighting corruption by introducing a zero tolerance policy against corruption. This has made Rwanda the least corrupt country in EAC (Worldwide Governance Indicators, 1996–2006).

REFERENCES

Collier, P., 2007. *The Bottom Billion: Why the Poorest Countries Are Failing and What Can Be Done About It.* Oxford: Oxford University Press.
—— 2008. 'Growth strategies for Africa', Working Paper 9, Commission on Growth and Development, Washington, DC.
Commission on Growth and Development, 2008. *The Growth Report: Strategies for Sustained Growth and Inclusive Development.* Washington, DC: World Bank.
De Lorenzo, M., 2008. *The Rwandan Paradox: Is Rwanda a Model for Africa Beyond Aid?* Washington, DC: American Enterprise Institute for Public Policy Research.
Government of Rwanda, 2000. 'Rwanda vision 2020'.

Mkapa, Benjamin William, 2008. 'Leadership for growth, development, and poverty reduction: an African viewpoint and experience', Working Paper 8, Commission on Growth and Development, Washington, DC.

Rusuhuzwa, Thomas Kigabo, 2008. 'Leadership, policy making, quality of economic policies and their inclusiveness: the case of Rwanda', Working Paper 20, Commission on Growth and Development, Washington, DC. Development.

Senegal
After Devaluation, Improving Signals

Ahmadou Aly Mbaye

1. Introduction

Since the 1994 devaluation, Senegal's growth performance has become much better. While GDP annual growth rates used to be stagnant, or even sometimes declining, they have averaged 4.9% in the 1996–2007 period (Fig. 1). In recent years, these growth performances have turned out to be fragile, because the economy has shown very high vulnerability to exogenous shocks. Inappropriate policy response to shocks, coupled with very poor policy-targeting capabilities, are identified as being the major explanations of recent deterioration in growth as well as living standards performances.

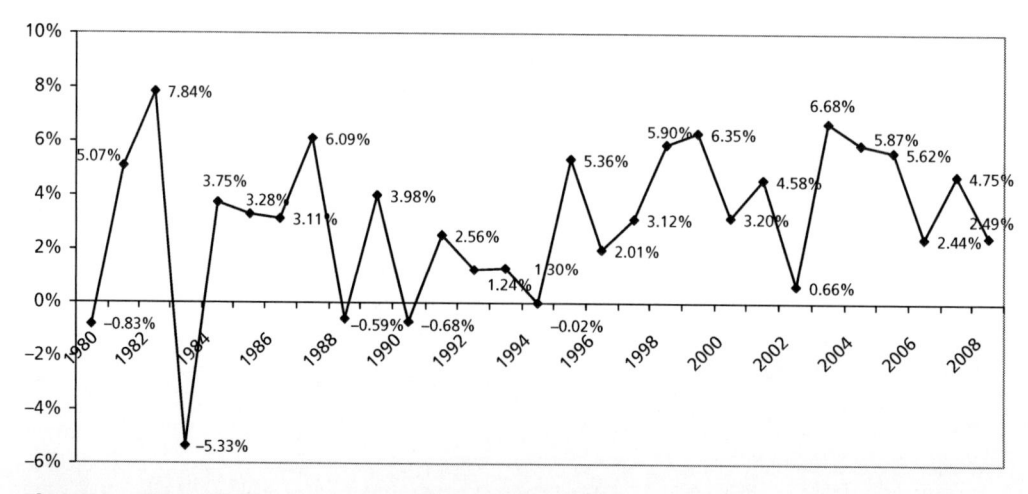

Figure 1. GDP growth rate, 1980–2008 (source: IMF 2009)

2. Impressive growth accomplishments supported by a few sectors

A detailed analysis of growth decomposition reveals very high levels of concentration of production and exports, due to the small number of productive sectors that are supporting them. Worth noting is the quite small contribution of agriculture to growth, contrasting with its share in the labour force. In effect, despite employing more than 60% of total labour force, agriculture's contribution to GDP is weak at 7%, while this sector also encompasses fisheries, vegetable production, and livestock. Most of these subsectors are characterized by contraction. With regard to agriculture, a number of factors account for its dismal performance, including reduction in cultivated areas, dramatic reduction in yields, low and declining soil fertility, weak water availability, low use of equipment, and erratic government interventions. These are compounded by exogenous factors such as frequent declines in international prices for cotton and groundnuts (the major Senegalese output and sources of exports). From 1967 to 2006, this sector experienced a decline in growth averaging 0.8% per annum.

Regarding the secondary sector, its contribution to GDP is much higher, averaging 21% per annum. The main subsectors in this sector are: mining, groundnut, cotton, and phosphates light transformation, as well as seafood processing, and building and public works. The share of manufacturing remains small. The big players are cement-producing companies (SOCOCIM and Cimenterie du Sahel) and ICS (Industries Chimiques du Sénégal), which is a joint venture including shares from Indian sources, as well as the governments of Nigeria and other developing countries. While cement production is thriving, due to expansion in demand supported by important buildings and public work programmes, both in Senegal and in neighbouring countries, ICS has undergone serious tensions in cash balance and a sharp decline in production that almost jeopardized its existence.

Several public-work programmes are under way in the subregion. This is mainly justified by West African governments' willingness to catch up with other developing countries in terms of infrastructure, and donors' acceptance of this trend. Plus, remittances from immigrants based in Europe or the US are mainly destined to support local families and to build houses. As a result, cement production, which is the major input used in these activities, is experiencing high increase in demand, while the main exporting companies are based in Senegal. Hence this sector is one among the few that have withstood the adverse effects of global recession.

The ICS used to be one of the biggest firms in the country, contributing to GDP by 2.42% in 2004, and to exports by 8.90% in 2004. It specializes in fertilizer production as well as phosphoric acid, with almost all its production absorbed by Indian and Nigerian markets. At the beginning of the 2000s, due to a combination of several factors, including mismanagement as well as an international downturn for ICS main exports, the company experienced serious difficulties, culminating in cessation of activities in 2006. It then benefited from a restructuring programme that ended up increasing the Indian group (IFFCO) share in ICS equity to 85%. Thanks to this restructuring plan, growth in activity is resuming.

Another big contributor to GDP is the telecommunication sector. Recent growth in telecoms is strongly supported by the meteoric rise in the use of the mobile phone. The number of mobile lines increased from 390,000 in 2000 to 1.7 million in 2005, and 3.3 million in 2007. Therefore, growth rate in telecoms was as high as 18% in 2007, contrasting with only 7.2% for overall GDP growth rate.

One important feature of the productive landscape of West African economies, and particularly of Senegal, is the significance of the informal sector in the economy. This sector makes up more than 60% of total value added and 80% in total labour force. Some sectors are almost totally controlled by informal actors. Hence an important share of growth performances referred to in previous paragraphs are outcomes of the informal sector. Besides, this sector is playing a critical role as a safety net for pervasive unemployment and high poverty incidence, mainly in urban areas. For Senegal, Benjamin and Mbaye (forthcoming) report a 57% contribution of the informal to total non-farm value added, and 3% contribution to government revenue. Trade across borders is one of the areas where the dynamism of the informal sector can be fully appreciated. Golub and Mbaye (2009) document important trade flows between Senegal and The Gambia—flows which remain largely invisible to the official statistics on trade flows. Benefiting from a quite large differential in the tariff and the porosity of the frontiers between African states, the actors in the informal sector engage in significant trade that remains unregistered.

3. Weak policy response to exogenous shocks

Recently, the Senegalese economy has been subject to serious exogenous shocks, such as dramatic oil price increases and huge variations in the prices of major imported food items. These have triggered an important safety net programme from the government to mitigate their potential social effects and avert any social unrest, mainly from urban citizens. As a result, the government has had to divert resources from budgeted payments to service private-sector debt to the unprogrammed expenditures. Even then, the fiscal deficit to GDP has widened, and a number of private firms affected by the government action face financial difficulties.

The case of the SAR[1] is worth singling out. SAR is the biggest firm that imports crude oil, refines it, and supplies it to domestic gas stations. In addition, SAR is also the main fuel supplier to SENELEC, the major electricity production and distribution monopoly.

---

[1] Société Africaine de Raffinage, a company in charge of importing and refining crude oil, which is the major supplier to oil companies and to SENELEC, the electricity production and distribution monopoly.

SAR suffered considerably from the government default in payments: it was even compelled to stop operations in 2006, and needed a significant bail-out programme, in terms of government increasing its share in equity (to 65%) and guaranteeing important consortium bank loans. Therefore, SAR experienced serious problems in supplying gasoline to gas stations, and fuel to SENELEC. This eventually led to huge shortages in gas and several power outages. The economic and social consequences of the subsidy programme were so high that the government eventually announced its cancellation in 2008.

While the important subsidy plan, huge and very poorly targeted, has been the main factors explaining huge fiscal deficits and increased payments arrears to private firms (subsidies to energy and necessities amounted to 7% of GDP in 2006–8), it is not the only factor. Parallel to this, the government put in place an important investment programme, with very weak control over funding sources. The total amount of money the government owes to private firms is as high as CFA 225 billion, which makes up 3% of GDP, while fiscal deficit is set at more than 4% of GDP—far beyond the ceiling of WAEMU convergence criteria for this indicator.

An area in which the government has made a substantial improvement is the increase in fiscal revenue collection. Since 2000, we have experienced very important accomplishments in terms of fiscal revenue collection. Several factors contribute in explaining this. First and foremost, the implementation of the VAT tax at a unique rate of 18% has been central; second, an incentive programme has targeted tax collecting services; last, in the mid-2000s the government significantly benefited from an increase in oil prices by levying taxes on oil-based products.

Regarding private-sector development, Senegal still lags behind in international rankings, at 100th position out of 131 countries in the World Economic Forum ranking, and in 162nd position of 168 in the World Bank Costs of Doing Business (CDB) ranking. However, important signals have been sent to private businesses by the government, expressing willingness to improve the business environment. Corporate tax has been reduced from 35% to 25%, and several measures have been taken to shorten the length of procedures involved in setting up a business. Senegal is quoted by the CDB as being among the three biggest reformers in Africa.

REFERENCES

Benjamin, N., and A. A. Mbaye, forthcoming. 'Informality, productivity and enforcement in West Africa: a firm-level analysis', *Review of Development Economics*.

Golub S., and A. A. Mbaye, 2009. 'National trade policies and smuggling in Africa: the case of The Gambia and Senegal', *World Development* 37.3, 595–606.

International Monetary Fund, 2009. *World Economic Outlook Database*. Washington, DC.

Sierra Leone Economic Governance, Agriculture, and Rural Development

Victor Davies

1. Introduction

Sierra Leone appears to be a success story of political transition from civil war in Africa. It emerged from the 1991–2001 civil war as a budding democracy, with the opposition winning the second of two peaceful post-war elections. However, the overarching development challenge has always been to manage a vast natural resource wealth—diamonds, marine resources, arable land, and a long coastline—to alleviate widespread poverty: over 70% of the population subsists on less than US$1 a day. The civil war has added a peace building dimension to this challenge. Economic governance and agricultural and rural development are critical issues in addressing this challenge.

2. Economic governance

Sound economic governance, aiming for pro-poor economic growth with job creation, is essential. Employment creation would consolidate the peace by absorbing abundant unemployed labour, including ex-combatants. It would address youth alienation, which, in a context of economic mismanagement and corruption, characterized the patrimonial system of governance blamed for inducing state collapse, culminating in civil war (Peters 2006; Abdullah 1998).

Progress has been realized. Markets have been liberalized, eliminating rents and their use as instruments of corruption and patronage. Public management institutions have been reformed towards a degree of transparency and accountability. An Anti-Corruption Commission has been set up. President Koroma, elected in 2007, has declared his assets, requiring all public officials to follow suit. Tracking surveys occasionally monitor government expenditures from Freetown, the national capital, to the intended beneficiaries.

However, Sierra Leone's ranking on Transparency International's Corruption Perception Index, and many other accounts, suggest that corruption remains widespread. Why is this so? My opinion is that the incentive to tackle corruption remains weak. Patronage networks, and entrenched interests which benefit from corruption, dominate the polity. The country still lacks a critical mass of informed, independent citizens to hold the government to account. Anti-corruption reforms have been instituted principally to satisfy donors whose requirements are mainly input-driven—set up institutions—rather than outcome-driven—increase your score on the Corruption Perception Index.

Postwar per capita GDP growth averaged 7.6% in 2002–6. However, per capita income remained low at US$228 dollars in 2006, compared with US$290 dollars in the early 1980s.

It is imperative to increase the very low public revenues from the present 14% of GDP, compared with 25% in neighbouring postwar Liberia. Reforms, such as consolidating revenue collection in a National Revenue Authority, set up in 2003, have had limited impact. This may be due to corruption; a weak institutional and policing mechanism for generating revenues from natural resources like fisheries; and possible complacency and reliance on the easier alternative, aid. Aid dependency is high: donors finance nearly 50% of the budget. Unsurprisingly, economic governance is strongly donor-driven. A clear development strategy is yet to emerge. Aid is sometimes costly: delays and shortfalls in donor funding sometimes force domestic borrowing, raising interest rates and domestic debt, and inducing banks to hold government debt at the expense of more socially productive investment.

There is a need for sound natural resource management. Alluvial diamonds helped sustain the rebellion. Before the war the diamonds were mostly smuggled abroad, generating virtually no government revenues while fostering black market activity (Davies 2007). The Kimberley certification scheme may have helped to increase official exports. However, fiscal revenues remain low—below $7 million dollars a year—due to the ease of diamond smuggling and the difficulty of policing activity. Alluvial diamonds offer little scope for government revenues, unlike Kimberlite diamonds, a 'point' resource that can be policed, exploited since 2003. The global economic meltdown has taken its toll in Sierra Leone, forcing the cessation of bauxite mining. A key issue is to ensure that the country gets a fair deal with companies exploiting iron ore, bauxite, rutile, and other resources.

3. Agriculture and rural development

Agriculture employed some 70% of the prewar population and now accounts for some 60% of GDP. However, agricultural activity is largely smallholder and rudimentary. Key issues include the land tenure system, which critics argue impede rural investment by precluding freehold. Young rural men who formed the bulk of the rebel movement cited an unjust rural land tenure system as a motivation for war enlistment (Peters 2006). The government appears to have shied away from tackling this sensitive issue.

Attention needs to focus on reducing large post-harvest losses of over 30% of output. Public policy has emphasized smallholder agriculture. But the potential here is limited, suggesting that the emphasis must change to encourage plantation agriculture which is beginning to emerge with foreign investment, somewhat analogous to land deals in Ethiopia, Sudan, and elsewhere. Assuming the government and host community get a fair deal, the injection of foreign capital and expertise offers scope for raising production, creating jobs, and decongesting urban areas.

A decentralization programme was launched in 2004. Decentralization offers both risks and opportunities. While it could increase rural participation in governance, and fiscal efficiency with the direct involvement of the intended beneficiaries, there is scope for corruption at the local level which might be subject to less focus.

4. Conclusion

Sierra Leone has come a long way from the prewar years characterized by widespread black markets and rent-seeking, and collapsed basic services. However, the country still has a long way to go to alleviate widespread poverty. Strong leadership, commitment to fighting corruption, and a clear development vision are essential. The civil war may be over, but some underlying risk factors—youth unemployment, widespread poverty and corruption, and alluvial diamonds—endure. Despite a seemingly successful political transition, changes in underlying behaviour and institutions will take much longer.

REFERENCES

Abdullah, I., 1998. 'Bush path to destruction: the origin and character of the Revolutionary United Front', *Africa Development* 23.3, 45–76.

Davies, V. A. B., 2007. 'Sierra Leone's economic growth performance, 1961–2000', in B. Ndulu et al. (eds), *The Political Economy of Africa: Country Case Studies*. Cambridge: Cambridge University Press.

Peters, K., 2006. 'Footpaths to reintegration: armed conflict, youth and the rural crisis in Sierra Leone', PhD thesis, Wageningen University.

Somalia
Sustaining an Economy Without Central Authority

Ali Issa Abdi

Since 1991, Somalia has been marked by conflict that continues to simmer and by the implosion of the central state institutions. The generalized insecurity, lack of appropriate domestic policies, and external shocks further impoverished the most vulnerable segments of the population. In view of the absence of an effective central authority and protracted instability, the country achieved the status of the pre-eminent example of a failed state.

The absence of a central state authority and almost two decades of civil conflict left key economic and social institutions inoperative and the management of economic and social policies nonexistent. Local administrations in the northern half of the country (Somaliland since 1991, and Puntland since 1998) have maintained weak governance and relative stability. The rest of the country has not been governed, or governed only intermittently by nominal transitional governments. Reconciliation efforts culminated in mid-2004 in the establishment of a transitional federal government, which was broadened to include some opposition elements in January 2009. The latest incarnation of a federal transitional administration in central/southern Somalia has been confronted with insecurity and has not been able to take control of and build governance institutions in any part of the country.

Somalia's economic institutions, including the ministry of finance and central bank, ceased to function, and the country's meagre professional and skilled personnel were displaced and depleted. As a consequence, the management of public finances and other central state responsibilities has remained undelivered—there has been no national government budget for eighteen years, and revenue collection has been usurped by 'warlords' or assumed by ineffective local administrations. As revenue collection also suffers from low administrative capacity and substantial growth of illicit transactions, the revenue-to-GDP ratio, estimated at 2%, provides very limited resources for running a modern government, while priority expenditures dominated by security needs remain unmet.

The lack of a functional central bank and commercial banks left a monetary control vacuum and destroyed the payments system. Without a central monetary authority, the Somali shilling has been printed by regional governments and independent private agents, and the ensuing liquidity expansion led to significant currency substitution, high inflation, and depreciation of the national currency, which increased poverty throughout the country. The collapse of the formal financial sector and associated disruption of the payments system had substantial adverse impact on trade and overall economic growth.

In many ways the economy of Somalia has been in unmitigated free fall, as the country has experienced major decline in crop production, in the small industrial output, and especially of tradable goods, and the degraded economic and social infrastructure requires massive resources to rebuild. The most evident results of the protracted conflict include the very limited provision of public goods and absolute lack of safety net and social welfare programmes. These developments are evidenced by pervasive food insecurity and mass migration by any available means, and offer testimony to the importance of a central authority to provide not only security but also basic services and an enabling environment for economic agents to invest and produce.

In other remarkable ways, available indicators suggest that the Somali economy has remained resilient. Reliable data on macroeconomic developments since 1991 are sketchy; nevertheless there has been significant private sector-driven expansion in domestic commerce, transportation, and telecommunications that has benefited the segment of the population that has had regular sources of income. The sustaining private sector developments took place in the context of an overarching policy vacuum, absence of a central authority, and generalized insecurity (World Bank 2006a).

The major force driving economic expansion in the conflict-dominated macroeconomic situation has been the large inflow of remittances and the extensive payments and telecommunications network that it has spawned (World Bank 2006b). Though limited in scope and constrained by external regulatory systems, remittance companies have provided a secure and efficient money transfer system for domestic and foreign transactions at an affordable cost and with minimal documentary requirements. The more successful Somali money transfer companies (Hawalas) have global reach, extensively cover the East Africa subregion, and are evolving into traditional banking business and other financial services in the subregion.

The vibrancy of the private sector extends to the provision of education and health services and basic utilities. Whereas the traditional public institutions of economic and social development collapsed or withered during the prolonged state of instability, private domestic investors have proved more adaptable and resilient, and in many instances have prospered once the public sector controls and interventions were lifted. The performance of Somalia's private sector was constrained and crowded out for many years by expansive and inefficient government structures. The country was poorly managed for decades by a succession of civilian and military governments that did not effectively utilize domestic resources and international assistance. These governments were characterized by heavy engagement in most economic activities, which they mismanaged through inefficient public agencies and enterprises.

The 'experiment' of Somalia during the last two decades shows that a 'minimalist state' with limited reach in the economy has certain advantages in developing economies. The recent developments under the limited state capacity attest to the need for government interventions in the economic realm to be conditioned on what services the state can deliver better than the private sector, including maintaining adequate security, providing for laws and regulations, and properly managing the economic and social policy framework. Accordingly, to tackle the fundamental issues related to the country's economic and social recovery, Somalia needs to rebuild effective institutional capacity to deliver critical public goods, without over-extending the reach of the state, and to leverage the vibrant and resilient private sector to provide for investment, efficient production, and sustainable high growth. Also, international support for Somalia's reconstruction should be committed to and targeted at rebuilding effective focused public institutions and providing space for private-sector operations.

REFERENCES

World Bank, 2006a. 'Somalia: from resilience towards recovery and development', Country Economic Memorandum for Somalia. Washington, DC.
—— 2006b. 'Remittances and economic development in Somalia: an overview', Social Development Paper 38. Washington, DC.

South Africa
An Emerging Market in an Emerging Continent

Haroon Bhorat

1. Introduction

As part of an ongoing tour through the African continent, it was Harold Macmillan, then the British prime minister, who noted, in a now-famous speech made to the Parliament of South Africa in Cape Town on 3 February 1960:

It is...a special privilege for me to be here in 1960 when you are celebrating what I might call the golden wedding of the Union. In the fifty years of their nationhood the people of South Africa have built a strong economy founded upon a healthy agriculture and thriving and resilient industries...The wind of change is blowing through this continent, and whether we like it or not, this growth of national consciousness is a political fact. We must all accept it as a fact, and our national policies must take account of it.

Little did Macmillan, nor indeed the rest of the world, realize that this breeze of democracy would only reach the borders of South Africa in the early 1990s, and be formalized in April 1994—some 34 years after the famous 'wind of change' speech. It would be a long and arduous struggle to free the country from the shackles of institutionalized prejudice, which found expression in its various forms as the infamous system of apartheid. Indeed, as I demonstrate below, South Africa remains a country of exceptions and contrasts—which often define its character, nature, and status in the developing world in general and Africa in particular.

I attempt in what follows below to provide an overview of the South African economy in its post-apartheid manifestation relative to other developing countries, and within the African context. After providing a basic economic overview of the country in Section 2, Section 3, as one entry point to understanding this economy, reflects on the shifts in poverty and inequality since democracy in South Africa. Section 4 then considers whether South Africa has been able to translate its positive post-apartheid GDP performance into significant gains for the poor. Section 5 concludes.

2. South Africa in Africa: stylized facts

The first, perhaps most infamous attribute is of course the country's history of pursuing a system of racial exclusivity which permeated every facet of everyday lives of South Africans for a period going as far back as the 1600s. In doing so, this system of apartheid created a society and economy which, as indicated in detail below, continues to be segmented very widely and deeply along racial lines.

The more subtle but equally powerful exceptions regarding South Africa are apparent in the standard economic and socioeconomic data. Firstly, the country remains a behemoth on the African continent. South Africa's Gross National Income stands at $5,410 per capita at current prices—over 600 times the average for sub-Saharan Africa (SSA) as a whole. Its GNI of $252 billion constitutes 35% of all output in Africa. Export volumes over the 2000–2006 period averaged about $50 billion, which was a third of all exports from SSA. Various infrastructure and technology indicators also manifest this gap: South Africa possesses some 365,000 km of a paved road network, whilst its nearest competitor (Nigeria) has only half of this road transport network. For SSA as whole, there are 17.5 mobile phone users per 100 individuals. The estimate for South Africa is 83.7. Perhaps one of the most powerful representations of the fact that South Africa (with a few other notable economies) is an exceptional case within the continent is that its market capitalization of listed companies in 2006 stood at 280.4% of GDP. The average for SSA was 22.1%. Ultimately, any economic analysis of the continent and any appreciation of the drivers of economic growth and development in Africa cannot and should not overlook the centrality and importance of this economy. It remains at the heart of the continent's current and future prosperity.

South Africa, though, also reflects very similar socioeconomic challenges to those found in other developing countries. Life expectancy in 2006, at 57, was not significantly different from the African average; HIV prevalence, at 18.1 in 2007, was one of the highest in SSA and well above the average of 5.5; and education enrolment figures, whilst good, belie its poor quality, as evidenced by internationally comparable test score results (Bhorat and Oosthuizen 2009). Finally, possibly the most stark indicator of the country's socioeconomic challenge is an unemployment rate of 22.4% in 2007, which by all accounts has consistently remained, for over a decade and a half, the highest in the world.

3. Post-apartheid growth challenges

The above represents a society in its rawest and perhaps most simplistic form, with a sketch of the empirical coordinates of its characteristics and indeed the scale of the

Table 1. Estimates of poverty and inequality, by race, 1995–2005

Race of household head	1995	2005
Headcount index		
African	0.38	0.27
Coloured	0.15	0.12
Asian	0.01	0.02
White	0.00	0.00
Total	0.31	0.23
Poverty gap ratio		
African	0.15	0.09
Coloured	0.04	0.04
Asian	0.00	0.01
White	0.00	0.00
Total	0.12	0.07
Gini coefficient		
African	0.55	0.56
Coloured	0.49	0.58
Asian	0.45	0.53
White	0.39	0.45
Total	0.64	0.69

Notes:
1. Poverty Line in 2000 prices and set at R174 per month.
2. All changes in the values of the headcount rates and poverty gap between 1995 and 2005 are statistically significant at the 95% level.
3. The changes in the values of the Gini coefficients between 1995 and 2005 are statistically significant at the 95% level, with the exception of Africans.
4. The population in 1995 has been weighted by population weights according to the 1996 Census. The 2005 weights are based on the 2001 Census.

Sources: Statistics South Africa (1995, 2005), own calculations.

challenges faced. I attempt below a more nuanced assessment of South Africa's growth path and trajectory in the post-1994 era, with a focus on two key areas. South Africa's welfare challenges are possibly most cogently captured by estimates of poverty and inequality in the post-1994 period. I present a set of these estimates for the 1995–2005 period. I then examine the growth path experienced by the economy since the demise of apartheid, explicitly focusing on whether the consistently positive economic growth recorded since 1994 (until the economic crisis struck at the end of 2008) has benefited all citizens equally.

Table 1 presents the changes in the headcount index, the poverty gap ratio, and the Gini coefficient between 1995 and 2005, both nationally and by race of household head. All these poverty measures have been calculated using individual per capita household expenditure, and the indicators are based on the standard class of poverty measures, first defined by Foster, Greer, and Thorbecke (1984).[1]

The headline result, as it were, and possibly the most important in policy terms, is that in the ten-year period from 1995 to 2005, household poverty, as measured by the headcount rate at an in-country poverty line of R174 a month in 2000 prices,[2] declined by 8 percentage points from 31% in 1995 to 23% in 2005. The measure of relative poverty—the poverty gap—indicates a similar national trend. It is clear that over the 1995–2005 period, the poverty gap index declined significantly. For example, at the poverty line utilized here, while the average poor household lived about 12% below the poverty line, a decade later the household was 7% below the poverty line. Ultimately however, the key result here is that both absolute and relative poverty have declined significantly in the first decade of democracy in South Africa.

The data by race indicate that while African-headed households did experience the largest relative declines in their headcount rates, their poverty levels as measured by the headcount rate still remain higher than the national estimates. In fact, in both years Africans accounted for a disproportionate share of poor individuals in the country. Hence, whilst Africans accounted for about 77% of the population in 1995, with their share increasing to 79% in 2005, in both years about 95% of the population who lived on less than R174 a month were African.

Whilst the first decade of democracy can point to a significant decline in national poverty levels in both absolute and relative terms, the trends in terms of income inequality are more worrying. Hence, on the basis of per capita expenditure, the data suggest that South Africa experienced a rise in income inequality over the period 1995–2005. Specifically, the economy's Gini coefficient increased from 0.64 in 1995 to 0.69 in 2005. This is a disturbing result for a number of reasons. First, measures of income inequality, by international experience, do not alter significantly over time in either direction. It takes large shifts in economic growth, for example, to change an economy's income distribution or a very particular pattern of growth (Kanbur 2005). Secondly, the trend is disturbing in the context of South Africa being historically ranked with Brazil as the most unequal society in the world. This new result would suggest that South Africa is now the most consistently unequal country in the world. Simply put,

---

[1] All poverty and inequality measures are individual measures, calculated using per capita total household expenditure. The 2005 total household expenditure variable was created by adding income tax payments and Unemployment Insurance Fund contributions to total household consumption. Per capita total household expenditure was created by dividing total household expenditure by the number of people in the household (household size). The population weight was estimated by multiplying the household weight (based on the 2001 Census) with the household size. We do not have information on the number of adults and children in the household, and therefore household expenditure cannot be adjusted using adult equivalent scales.

[2] The 2000 poverty lines were adjusted for the impact of inflation both in 1995 and 2005, and these adjusted poverty lines were used to calculate the poverty measures in the two years.

while the democratic period has delivered declining (albeit modest) poverty levels, it has also been marked by a significant rise in aggregate income inequality.

The data by race, however, are interesting. While all race groups apart from Asians experienced a decline in their poverty levels as measured by the headcount rate and the poverty gap ratio, the evidence suggests that all population groups except Africans experienced increases in inequality. While Africans were the only population group that did not experience any statistically significant change in inequality as measured by the Gini coefficient, African inequality remained high, at around 0.55 in both years.

4. The elusive pursuit of pro-poor growth

Whilst the above alludes to a government which has, at least in terms of the standard measures of income poverty, partially succeeded in reducing the incidence of poverty, it is not entirely evident whether South Africa's consistently positive growth rates have also, in and of themselves, managed to generate consistent returns to the poor. To be clear, the years since 1995 have witnessed one of the longest uninterrupted periods of positive economic growth for South Africa in the post-war era, with GDP growth averaging about 3% per annum over 1995–2007.

Technically, we are concerned with whether this growth in GDP since 1995 in South Africa has managed to afford rising returns to all individuals and households across the entire income distribution. To some extent we have the elements of our answer in the above discussion: we know that amidst an economic growth spurt in the post-1995 period household poverty levels declined, but simultaneously income inequality also increased. If we delve more deeply, there are a number of key additional results which arguably are crucial to understanding the nature of economic growth in the democratic era for South Africa.

4.1. WHO IS GETTING AHEAD?

Analysis of data for the 1995–2005 period asked the question: by how much did the expenditure of the poor grow relative to the rich in South Africa? A more refined version of this question is to examine the growth in expenditures of all households, across the entire income distribution from the poorest to the richest household. The data has three key results for the population as a whole. First, poor households did experience a rise in income levels: the data shows that over the 1995–2005 period, expenditure by poor households increased by approximately 9%. In absolute terms, therefore, poor households did witness a rise in income levels. Secondly, individuals in the middle of the income distribution—typically the working and middle classes—experienced the *lowest* growth in incomes, at around 6% over the decade. Thirdly, though, the same data shows that rich households—those in the top 10% of the distribution—enjoyed the highest average annual growth rates of all households in the society, just over 9% since 1995.

Taken together, these results point to the following distributional outcomes from South Africa's post-1995 economic growth experience: Firstly, poorer households did experience a gain in incomes, although the source of this income growth (discussed below) is important to note. Secondly, whilst rich households clearly gained from the growth process, it is those individuals in the middle of the distribution (the blue-collar and lower-end white-collar workers) who have been relatively excluded from the gains of economic growth. Put simply, South Africa's positive growth performance in the post-apartheid period has disproportionately benefited the rich and indirectly those households in deep poverty, whilst excluding many of those individuals and household who are located in the middle of the country's income distribution.

4.2. INEQUALITY SPOILS THE GROWTH PARTY

We saw above that South Africa's growth trajectory has delivered rising income inequality to such an extent that one of the world's most unequal societies has become possibly *the* most unequal. The importance of this fact is that inequality serves to dissolve the potential gains that growth can deliver to poverty reduction. If growth is spread to a declining share of the population, then it becomes harder to realize poverty reduction gains. This is precisely the scenario that has been played out in South Africa over the last decade or so. Our results illustrate that if inequality had stayed constant since 1995, then economic growth would have resulted in a 29% reduction in household poverty. Of course, though, the nature of the economic growth pattern—which accrued returns disproportionately to those at the top end—meant that income inequality did in fact rise. This, as noted above, erodes any poverty reduction gains. Put simply, the changing distribution of expenditure as a consequence of growth was not sufficiently large to offset the gains realized in terms of a reduction in poverty.

Inequality increases since 1995 have truly spoilt the post-apartheid economic growth party for this fledgling democracy at the southern tip of the continent. Indeed, this maldistribution of the gains from growth lies at the heart of the difficulty in achieving both pro-poor and shared economic growth in South Africa.

4.3. SOCIAL SECURITY: THE SAVIOUR?

One important facet of the above, somewhat turgid overview of trends and results is that poor households have seen an increase in their incomes since 1995. However, it is crucial to note that this was an *indirect* result of economic growth: these households were the beneficiaries of an ever-widening and deepening social security net. Recent data indicates that the share of government transfers grew from 2.5% of GDP in 1996/7 to just over 3% in 2005/6. Grant expenditure increased from R20,553 million in 2001/2 to R51,927 million in 2005/6, representing a 26.1% growth in social assistance expenditure by the state.

This increase in grant expenditure saw a significant rise in the number of beneficiaries from social grants. Specifically, the total number of grant beneficiaries grew from approximately 3 million in 1997 to 9.4 million in 2005—at an average annual rate of 15.3%. Whilst all types of grants experienced a surge in the number of beneficiaries, it was the Child Support Grant which fuelled this rise:[3] the number of CSG recipients rose from 975,000 in 2001 to 5.6 million in the space of four years.

In terms of the gains from growth, therefore, we have a storyline which runs along the following lines. Consistently positive levels of economic growth in the post-1994 period resulted in a healthy revenue base for government. Whilst holding firmly onto fiscal prudence and general macroeconomic stability, the state was able to utilize this revenue effectively to redistribute income to the poor. This came in the form of social security grants. Ultimately, whilst the poor have benefited through state redistribution via social grants, they were not direct but indirect beneficiaries of the process of economic growth in South Africa. It remains unclear, however, whether this cycle (from growth to redistributive revenues) is sustainable.

5. Conclusion

The above has suggested that in addition to the wretched system of apartheid unleashed onto its populace, South Africa is also distinguishable as an economic goliath within SSA. In turn, however, a series of socioeconomic challenges, many differentiated according to race, remain an ongoing policy focus for the democratic government and their attendant policymakers. The chapter makes it plain also that—despite some reductions in household poverty amidst a solid run of positive GDP growth estimates since democracy—the spectre of exorbitantly high and rising income inequality is deeply worrying. My analysis of the incidence of this positive economic growth suggests that, whilst the rich have gained from growth, those in the middle of the distribution have gained marginally, and those at the bottom are heavily reliant on state transfers. In an environment where South Africa was in mid-2009 in the midst of a global economic

---

[3] CSGs are offered to all persons responsible for looking after a child younger than 15 years old (the child's primary caregiver).

crisis, undergoing its first post-apartheid recession, this trajectory of economic growth is going to prove increasingly untenable and difficult to maintain.

REFERENCES

Bhorat, H., and M. Oosthuizen, 2009. 'Determinants of Grade 12 pass rates in the post-apartheid South African schooling system', *Journal of African Economies* 18.4, 634–66.

Foster, J., J. Greer, and E. Thorbecke, 1984. 'A class of decomposable poverty measures', *Econometrica* 52.3, 761–6.

Kanbur, R., 2005. 'Growth, inequality and poverty: some hard questions', *Journal of International Affairs* (Spring).

World Bank, 2009. *Africa Development Indicators*. Washington, DC.

South Africa Corporate Governance

Mthuli Ncube

1. Introduction

The importance of corporate governance has recently received much attention due to high-profile corporate collapses and scandals such as Enron, WorldCom, and Lehman Brothers. The enactment of the Sarbanes–Oxley Act of 2002 in the US, the most sweeping corporate governance regulation in the US in the last seventy years, has its roots in the collapse of corporate governance practices. Furthermore, Jensen (1986; 1993) has argued that the internal mechanisms of corporate governance in US corporations have not been effective. On the other hand, legal scholars, including Easterbrook and Fischel (1991) and Romano (1993), view the US mechanisms and the legal system in a favourable light. There is also an issue relating to the relative efficacy of the corporate governance systems in the US and UK, where shareholding is dispersed and the secondary market trading of shares is prominent, vs. the corporate governance systems in Japan and Germany, which are typified by more concentrated shareholdings and a prominent role for banking institutions. Several empirical studies have found that the quality of governance has an impact on the value of the firm as measured by such indicators as Tobin's Q (Gompers, Ishii, and Metrick 2003; Cremers and Nair 2005). The literature identifies key governance measures that underpin the link with firm value: board members being elected annually; a company either having no poison pill or one approved by shareholders; option repricing, average options granted recently as a percentage of basic shares outstanding not exceeding 3%; attendance by directors at least at 75% of board meetings or having a valid excuse for non-attendance; and directors' stock ownership being governed by clear guidelines. The first two factors represent external governance, while the remainder are internal governance factors.

The purpose of this chapter is to investigate the relationship between corporate governance, as it pertains to the board of directors, and the financial performance of companies in South Africa. Corporate governance covers a wide area, and this chapter only focuses on certain aspects of the board of directors such as the composition of the board, board size, and the separation of the duties of the CEO and chairman of the board.

The chapter tests whether these aspects are correlated with the financial performance of a company.

Why is corporate governance necessary? It exists as a mechanism for dealing with the separation of ownership and control, and the agency problems it creates (Jensen and Meckling 1976). The agency problems and conflicts of interest differ with different stakeholders in a company, and are closely defined by the capital contribution of and pay-off to each shareholder.

In a firm, corporate governance deals with mechanisms by which stakeholders of a corporation exercise control over corporate insiders and management such that their interests are protected. Stakeholders of a corporation include equity-holders, creditors, and other claimants who supply capital, as well as employees, consumers, suppliers, the government, and society at large. The professional managers, and other corporate insiders, control the key day-to-day decisions of the corporation. Given the separation of ownership and control, how stakeholders control management is the subject of corporate governance.

The monitoring role of the board of directors is an important component of corporate governance. Board effectiveness in its monitoring function is determined by its *independence*, *size*, and *composition*. The board of directors is presumed to carry out the monitoring function on behalf of shareholders, because the shareholders themselves would find it difficult to exercise control due to wide dispersion of ownership of common stock. This problem in monitoring is endemic to most large corporations with diffuse ownership, because an individual shareholder lacks a sufficient stake in the firm to justify spending resources to closely monitor managers. This leads to a free-rider problem, as shareholders, individually, attempt to free-ride on others to monitor managers.

The board of directors is fundamental to the implementation of sound corporate governance, profitability, long-term sustainability, and the protection of shareholders' interests of a company. South Africa has been at the forefront in developing corporate governance standards, through the King II Report (2002). This research explores the contributions made by the board in line with the requirements and recommendations of King II Code of Corporate Governance in South Africa to the financial performance of a company (see also King 2006). The factors examined include the composition of the board, the size of the board, and the separation of the functions of the chairman of the board and the CEO.

2. Methodology

This section presents the methodology utilized to measure the relationship between the board and the financial performance of a company. As a measure of profitability we use earnings per share (EPS). EPS is measured as net income divided by the average total fully diluted shares outstanding (Grant and Motara 2006). The use of this variable as a measure of company performance has some limitations as it may not reflect a firm's true underlying value of performance. Executives can manipulate indicators to make themselves look good (Gomez-Mejia, Tosi, and Hinkin 1987). Practices include manipulation of depreciation policy, inventory valuation procedures (FIFO vs. LIFO), using short-term non-capitalized leases to obtain productive equipment, and using window-dressing techniques such as holding borrowed money at year end to make the balance sheet look good (Gomez-Mejia et al. 1987).

We also make use of three other measures:

(i) The return on equity (ROE) as a measure of financial performance. Grant and Motara (2006) defines ROE as the net income divided by average majority equity The ROE has the advantage of being a ratio (Madura, Martin, and Jessel 1996).

(ii) The return on assets (ROA). Grant and Motara (2006) define ROA as net income divided by average total assets.

(iii) Tobin's Q as a measure of financial performance. Tobin's Q (q) is defined as the ratio of the market value of a firm to the replacement cost of its assets. Chung and Pruitt (1994) suggest the following formula in the computation of Tobin's Q:

$$\text{Tobin's } Q = (MVE+PS+DEBT)/TA \tag{1}$$

where MVE is the product of a firm's share price and the number of common stock shares outstanding, PS is liquidating value of the firm's outstanding preferred stock, DEBT is book value of the firm's debt, and TA is the book value of the total assets of the firm.

Having defined the variables for measuring financial performance, we now define more precisely the variables for board characteristics. The characteristics of the board that we utilize are:

- the number of board members;
- the percentage of independent directors as a percentage of the total number of directors;
- the number of board meetings held in the last financial year;
- the number of directors that missed over 25% of the meetings;
- the annual performance assessment of the board;
- whether or not the chairman is independent of the CEO.

In order to measure the degree of relationship between board characteristics and activities, we estimate regression equations. We estimate each of the financial indicators as a function of six board characteristics and activities:

$$\text{Tobin's } Q = \alpha + \beta_1 \text{TBM} + \beta_2 \text{IBM} + \beta_3 \text{TM} + \beta_4 \text{MM} + \beta_5 \text{IBC} + \beta_6 \text{APA} + e \tag{2}$$

$$\text{ROE} = \alpha + \beta_1 \text{TBM} + \beta_2 \text{IBM} + \beta_3 \text{TM} + \beta_4 \text{MM} + \beta_5 \text{IBC} + \beta_6 \text{APA} + e \qquad (3)$$

$$\text{EPS} = \alpha + \beta_1 \text{TBM} + \beta_2 \text{IBM} + \beta_3 \text{TM} + \beta_4 \text{MM} + \beta_5 \text{IBC} + \beta_6 \text{APA} + e \qquad (4)$$

$$\text{ROA} = \alpha + \beta_1 \text{TBM} + \beta_2 \text{IBM} + \beta_3 \text{TM} + \beta_4 \text{MM} + \beta_5 \text{IBC} + \beta_6 \text{APA} + e \qquad (5)$$

where ROE is return on equity, EPS is earnings per share, ROA is return on assets, TBM is total number of board members, IBM is number of independent board members as a percentage of total number of board members, TM is total number of meetings held in last financial year, MM is percentage number of directors who missed over 25% of meetings, IBC denotes separation of chairman from CEO, APA denotes annual performance assessment of directors, and e_i is an error term.

3. The data

A sample of 46 companies listed on the Johannesburg Securities Exchange was selected, covering those large companies by market capitalization where information on board characteristics and activities was available. The companies cover the industrial, resources, and financial sectors. The data were collected from the annual reports of companies and from data compiled by Grant and Motara (2006) of Deutsche Securities (Pty) Ltd. The summary statistics on the data are in Tables 1 and 2.

From Tables 1 and 2, we can see that for the 46 companies, the average number of board members is 14, with a minimum of 5 and a maximum of 24; the median is 13. The average composition of independent directors on the board is 35%, with some boards having no independent directors whilst others had a maximum of 62%.

The average number of board meetings held during the financial year is 6. All companies held a board meeting at least once every quarter, whilst some held a maximum of 10 meetings for the year. An average of 18% of directors missed at least 25% of the meetings held during the year. The minimum number of meetings missed is zero, whilst a maximum of 80% for non-attendance of 25% of meetings is observed.

Figure 1 shows the composition of the board in terms of the percentage composition of independent directors and the percentage composition of non-independent directors. Of the sample of 46 companies, the board included an average of 35% of independent directors. The balance of the board (65%) was made up of non-independent directors.

Figure 2 indicates that of the sample of 46 companies, 79% (37) companies carried out an annual performance assessment of the directors and 21% (9) companies did not. It would seem that the practice of performing annual assessments is being carried out by many companies as part of the monitoring and evaluation of director performance.

Table 1. Board characteristics and financial variables for JSE companies, 2006

Observation	Company	Tobin's Q	EPS	ROE	ROA	Total No. of Board Members	No. of Independent Board Members – % of Total	No. of Meetings in last Financial Year	No. of directors who missed 25% of meetings % of Total	Independent Chairman of Board: Yes =1, No=0	Annual Performance Assessment of Directors: Yes=1, No=0
1	Anglo American	1.54	4.01	27.00	17.20	15	60%	8	0%	1	1
2	African Bank	6.42	2.23	52.70	14.80	19	47%	6	17%	1	1
3	Aveng	4.26	1.45	18.30	6.30	11	45%	5	40%	1	1
4	Anglo Plat	7.63	45.42	46.70	30.80	19	21%	4	25%	0	1
5	Anglo Gold Ashanti Ltd	4.06	11.67	11.70	4.40	17	47%	6	17%	1	1
6	African Rainbow Minerals	1.52	3.61	7.20	4.40	17	41%	4	50%	0	0
7	ABSA	2.73	11.28	26.50	1.70	21	14%	9	33%	0	0
8	AVI	2.55	1.06	15.00	8.20	11	55%	4	25%	0	1
9	Brait	2.52	3.04	37.20	20.80	13	8%	4	0%	0	0
10	Barloworld	2.42	11.48	19.10	8.20	19	26%	6	0%	0	1
11	BHP Billiton	240.01	1.68	50.00	22.10	14	50%	7	0%	0	1
12	Bidvest	4.62	7.68	29.80	10.90	24	21%	4	0%	1	1
13	Coronation Fund Managers Ltd	11.92	0.55	87.90	0.00	5	40%	4	25%	0	0
14	Consol Limited	3.35	1.14	25.00	16.50	6	50%	5	0%	1	1
15	DRD Gold	5.03	-0.53	0.00	0.40	6	50%	5	0%	1	1
16	FirstRand	3.15	1.44	24.60	1.90	18	22%	5	20%	0	1
17	Gold Reef Casino	3.22	1.22	21.50	18.70	9	11%	6	33%	0	1
18	Goldfields	3.22	2.49	9.20	6.50	13	0%	10	10%	1	1
19	Group 5 Ltd	4.94	1.89	21.60	4.10	8	50%	4	25%	0	1
20	Harmony	2.03	-2.63	-3.90	-2.90	9	56%	4	0%	0	1
21	Impala Platinum	7.01	7.58	28.10	19.80	13	38%	5	0%	1	1
22	Investec Plc	4.03	0.42	32.70	0.00	17	35%	6	0%	0	1
23	Imperial Holdings Ltd	2.80	11.49	23.10	6.90	21	29%	5	0%	1	1
24	Lonmin Plc	433.01	2.88	32.50	17.30	9	56%	6	0%	1	1
25	Mittal Steel SA Ltd	1.65	10.54	21.80	16.70	10	40%	5	40%	0	0
26	MTN Group	3.44	6.30	42.30	17.80	12	50%	9	0%	1	1
27	Murray & Roberts Holdings Ltd	3.61	1.85	16.30	6.50	15	60%	5	20%	1	0

28	Mvelaphanda Resources Ltd	0.92	1.40	58.90	48.80	12	8%	5	80%	0	0
29	Nedbank Group Ltd	2.08	10.29	19.40	1.20	19	26%	8	25%	0	1
30	Northam	5.78	2.83	39.30	32.20	10	20%	5	80%	0	0
31	Nampak Ltd	2.33	1.47	16.00	8.10	13	15%	6	0%	0	1
32	Naspers	6.30	7.17	46.40	20.40	12	42%	5	20%	0	1
33	Pick'n Pay Stores	18.76	1.44	89.00	11.20	12	8%	4	0%	0	1
34	Pretoria Portland Cement co Ltd	9.47	22.57	58.20	35.60	12	17%	5	0%	0	1
35	Peermont Global Ltd	2.79	0.76	17.90	12.80	9	56%	6	17%	1	0
36	Remgro	3.61	10.18	41.60	34.30	14	21%	6	17%	0	1
37	SAB Miller	115.71	1.06	14.50	7.50	14	36%	7	14%	0	1
38	Sappi	14.95	−0.09	−1.10	−0.30	13	62%	5	20%	0	1
39	Standard Bank	2.62	7.87	23.40	1.90	18	28%	5	20%	0	1
40	Shoprite	4.86	1.45	33.80	10.70	13	23%	4	25%	0	1
41	Sasol	3.05	22.58	30.00	15.60	16	44%	4	25%	0	1
42	Spar Group Limited	8.60	2.31	49.50	13.10	7	57%	4	0%	1	1
43	Sun International Limited	4.27	5.39	19.30	8.00	15	33%	6	0%	0	1
44	Tiger Brands	1.44	11.76	11.10	8.30	16	44%	7	29%	0	1
45	Telkom	2.40	17.40	32.90	15.90	11	36%	6	33%	0	1
46	WBHO	5.97	3.16	33.00	8.00	5	20%	4	25%	0	1

Source: Annual Reports and 'Beyond the Numbers', Deutsche Securities (Pty) Ltd, JSE Limited

Table 2. Descriptive statistics for board activities

Variable	Mean	Median	Minimum	Maximum
TBM[1]	14	13	5	24
IBM[2]	35%	36%	0%	62%
TM[3]	6	5	4	10
MM[4]	18%	17%	0%	80%

[1] Total no. of board members.
[2] No. of independent directors as % of total board members.
[3] Total number of meetings held in last financial year.
[4] % of directors who missed over 25% of meetings.

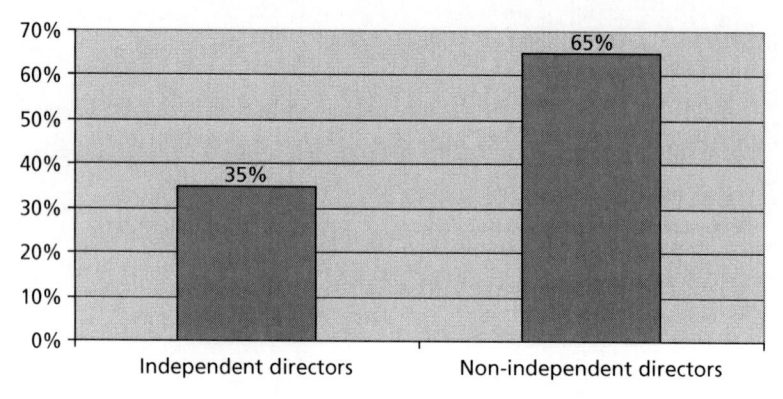

Figure 1. Board composition

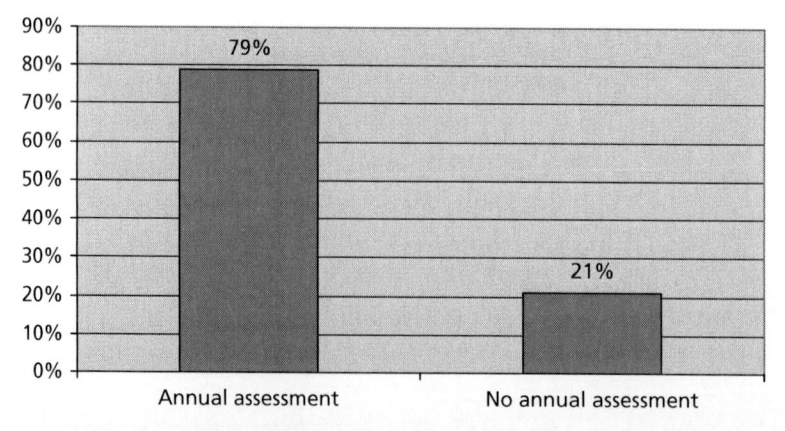

Figure 2. Percentage of companies that perform an annual performance assessment of directors

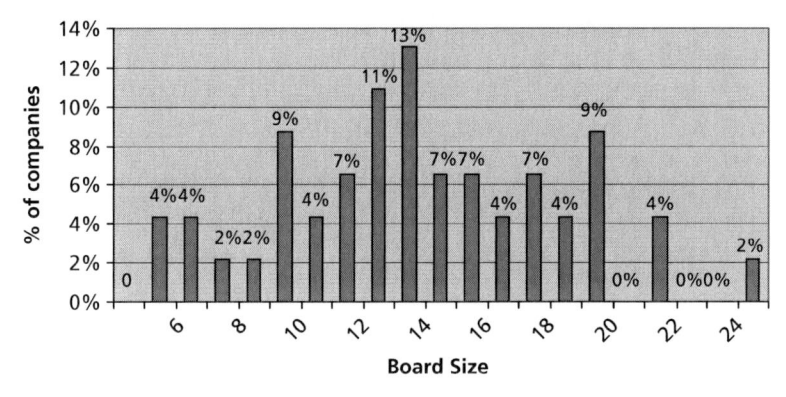

Figure 3. Board size per company (frequency table)

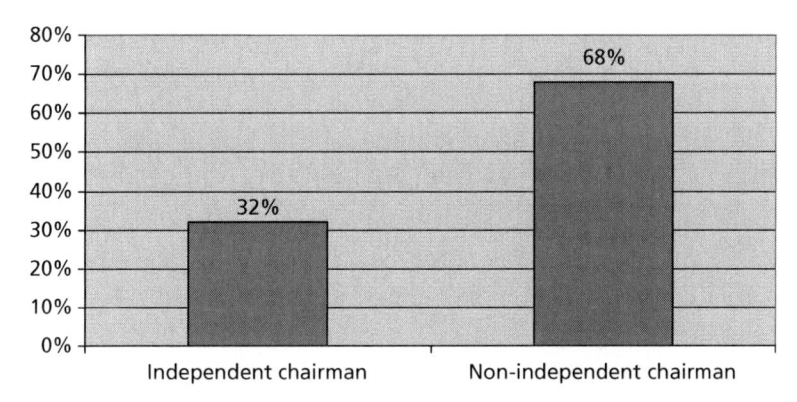

Figure 4. Percentage of companies that have an independent board chairman

Figure 3 represents the size of the board in relation to the percentage of companies sampled. 13% of the companies had a board size of 13 directors whilst 4% of the companies have a board size of 5 directors at a minimum. 2% of the companies operated with a board of 24 directors. The mean number of directors is 14, and 50% of companies operate with a board of between 11 and 13 directors.

Figure 4 reflects that 32% (15) of the companies had an independent board chairman as defined by the independence criteria and 68% (31) did not. It is important to note that in the sample of 46 companies, the positions of CEO and chairman of the board were held by separate people.

4. Results

In this section we present the regression results of the analysis (see Table 3).

Table 3. Regression results for the board of directors and financial performance and board

	Tobin's Q	EPS	ROA	ROE
Constant (a)	−17.5002	−1.8887	22.2178	74.33
	(−0.2519)	(−0.2563)	(2.2429)	(4.1115)
TBM	−2.0864	0.7206	−0.3566	−0.7099
	(−0.7964)	(2.5930)	(−0.9546)	(−1.0412)
IBM	85.7885	−4.2110	22.3367	−41.0583
	(1.1483)	(−0.5313)	(−2.0964)	(−2.1114)
TM	8.6222	−0.6373	−0.3424	−2.3491
	(1.0920)	(−0.7609)	(−0.3041)	(−1.1431)
MM	−60.1133	4.881	16.3263	−13.8313
	(−0.8357)	(0.6397)	(1.5916)	(−0.7388)
IBC	−9.7386	−1.3227	3.8821	−0.2412
	(−0.3566)	(−0.4566)	(0.9970)	(−0.0339)
APA	3.5983	3.7260	0.7385	−6.8437
	(0.1098)	(1.0722)	(0.1581)	(−0.8027)
R-Squared	0.1103	0.2176	0.1879	0.1677

Note: For abbreviations see Table 2.

We estimated the regression equation of Tobin's Q in relation to the variables; total number of board members, number of independent board members as a percentage of total board members, percentage of directors who missed over 25% of meetings, independent chairman of the board, chairman independent of CEO, and annual performance assessment of directors.

The percentage of independent board members as a percentage of total board members (IBM) has a t-value of 1.1482, which reflects the strongest significance in relation to Tobin's Q. Increasing the percentage of independent directors will increase Tobin's Q, hence enhancing financial performance.

The total number of meetings held in the financial year has a t-value of 1.092, which is the next significant relationship to Tobin's Q. It indicates that increasing the number of meetings during the year could have a positive impact on Tobin's Q. This should be viewed with caution: too many meetings during the year could have a negative impact on decision-making and increase the overhead costs in terms of directors' fees.

These results show that the percentage of independent directors and the number of meetings held in the financial year have the strongest significance in relation to Tobin's Q. The rest of the variables do not have as much of a significant relationship with Tobin's Q, as their t-values are less than 1. This indicates that the other variables have a weak relationship with Tobin's Q.

The findings confirm the view of Jensen (1993) that there is an implicit relationship between the board of directors and a firm's financial performance, as in the results above, the board has a positive influence over the financial performance of a company.

The findings by Firer and Swartz (2005) that if the board performs its duties effectively, the value of the firm is likely to increase and the wealth of the shareholders will therefore be enhanced is also supported by the results above.

Let us now turn to EPS results. The board size variable has a t-value of 2.5930, which indicates the strongest relationship to EPS. Increasing the total number of board members will have a positive impact on the EPS—i.e. EPS will increase. Conducting an annual performance assessment of directors has the next highest t-value of 1.0722, which implies the next significant relationship to EPS. An increase in the number of performance assessments conducted during the year could also have a positive impact on EPS. Although there is a significant relation of APA to EPS, it is not as strong as the relationship of the total board size to EPS.

The other variables have t-values less than 1, which indicates that these variables have a weak relationship to EPS and hence are not significant.

We estimated the regression equation of ROA in relation to the same variables. The presence of an independent board chairman, independent of the CEO, has a t-value of 1.0, which indicates that there is a significant relationship between the IBC and ROA. As there can only be only one chairman, ROA is not impacted by increasing IBC. The percentage of directors who missed 25% of the meetings has a t-value of 1.5916, which also indicates a strong relationship with ROA. It must be understood that missing a large number of meetings can contribute negatively to decision-making and to that director discharging his responsibilities as required. Although a strong relationship exists between MM and ROA, the significance of IBC to ROA is more important and significant.

We also estimated the regression equation of ROE in relation to the same variables. The t-values for the variables are all less than 1, which indicates that there is no significant relationship between the variables and ROE. It would seem that there are other variables that can be used to explain ROE.

An increase in IBM and TM will have a negative impact on ROE. ROE decreases as the number of independent board members increase or as board size increases. This perverse result implies that the board characteristics have no positive relationship with ROE.

5. Conclusion

Several empirical studies have been carried out internationally testing the relationship between corporate governance and financial performance. Not much extensive research has been carried in South Africa, as an emerging market. Nevertheless, South Africa has been at the forefront of developing corporate governance standards, and has subsequently implemented the King II Code of Corporate Governance. Therefore, this chapter set out to investigate the relationship between corporate governance, as it pertains to the board of directors, and the financial performance of companies in South Africa.

The corporate governance elements utilized are total number of board members, number of independent board members as a percentage of total board members, percentage of directors who missed over 25% of meetings, independence of chairman from CEO, and annual performance assessment of directors. We estimated regression equations of various financial indicators in relation to various elements of board characteristics and activities. The financial indicators we examined are Tobin's Q, EPS, ROA, and ROE.

It was found that the financial performance of companies as captured by Tobin's Q is strongly related to the composition of the board in terms of the number of independent directors as a percentage of the total board size. This finding concurs with international findings. The stringent definition of the independence of a director that was used in this research further lends weight to the proposition that independent directors positively affect financial performance in terms of Tobin's Q. The other measures of financial performance were not significantly related to the number of independent directors.

It was also found that the size of the board and the annual performance assessment of the board are critical in explaining EPS. Annual performance assessments seem to have a positive influence on the board members in discharging their duties as directors and enhancing shareholder wealth. An average board size of 14 has a positive impact on the financial performance of a company. It is clear that the board is pivotal in steering the company and supporting management. This is in line with international findings, as presented in the literature review. The other measures of financial performance were not significantly related to the size of the board.

Separating the role of chairman of the board from that of CEO was found to have a significant relationship with the financial performance of a company as measured by the ROA. This finding is consistent with international studies and the recommendations made by King II (2002) in separating the roles of the chairman and CEO. The other measures of financial performance were not significantly related to the separation of the roles of the chairman and CEO.

The results show that corporate governance factors pertaining to the board have no impact on ROE.

REFERENCES

Cadbury Committee, 1992. *Report on Financial Aspects of Corporate Governance*. London: Gee.
Chung, K. E., and S. W. Pruitt, 1994. 'A simple approximation of Tobin's Q', *Financial Management* 23.3, 70–74.

Cremers, K. J. M., and V. B. Nair, 2005. 'Governance mechanisms and equity prices', *Journal of Finance* 60, 2859–94.

Easterbrook, F., and D. Fischel, 1991. *The Economic Structure of Corporate Law*. Cambridge, Mass.: Harvard University Press.

Firer, S., and N. P. Swartz, 2005. 'Board structure and intellectual capital performance in South Africa', *Meditari Accountancy Research* 13.2, 146.

Gomez-Mejia, L. R., H. Tosi, and T. Hinkin, 1987. 'Managerial control, performance and executive compensation', *Academy of Management Journal* 30.1, 51–70.

Gompers, P., J. Ishii, and A. Metrick, 2003. 'Corporate governance and equity prices', *Quarterly Journal of Economics* 118, 107–55.

Grant, G., and A. Motara, 2006. *Beyond the Numbers*. Johannesburg: Deutsche Securities, 24–5.

Jensen, M. C., 1986. 'Agency cost of free cash flow, corporate finance, and takeovers', *American Economic Review* 76.2, 324–9.

—— 1993. 'The modern industrial revolution: exit and the failure of internal control systems', *Journal of Finance* 48, 831–80.

—— and W. Meckling, 1976. 'Theory of the firm: managerial behavior, agency costs and ownership structure', *Journal of Financial Economics* 48, 831–80.

King II (King Committee Report on Corporate Governance) 2002. *The King Report on Corporate Governance in South Africa*. Johannesburg: Institute of Directors in Southern Africa.

King, M., 2006. *Corporate Governance Citizen: Governance of All Entities*. Harmondsworth: Penguin.

Madura, J., A. D. Martin, and K. A. Jessel, 1996. 'Determinants of CEO compensation in small publicly-traded businesses', *American Business Review* 14, 80–88.

Romano, R., 1993. *The Genius of American Corporate Law*. Washington, DC: American Enterprise Institute Press.

Sudan
Unable to Accelerate and Sustain Growth

Adam B. Elhiraika

1. Introduction

Sudan provides perhaps the most pertinent example of the African countries where recent commodity-driven growth has had little impact on poverty and economic transformation. This chapter investigates the key drivers of growth performance in Sudan, discusses why the country remains unable to accelerate and sustain growth for poverty reduction, and presents policy recommendations as to how this could be achieved.

2. Growth trends and drivers

After decades of low growth and decline, Sudan has recorded high growth rates since the late 1990s, thanks mainly to the commercial exploitation of oil, the end of the civil war in South Sudan, increased private capital inflows, and high global commodity demand and prices. Sudan's real GDP growth rate fluctuated widely over the years, averaging about 4% between 1970 and 1999. Since then it has generally increased, averaging 7.2% between 2000 and 2008, the longest period of high positive growth and relative macroeconomic stability in Sudan during the last four decades (Fig. 1).

However, with a narrow production and export structure, and inadequate human capital development and job creation, poverty and inequality rates remained very high in Sudan despite notable increases in per capita income, from $394 in 2000 to $1,443 in 2007. Sudan's growth is also highly vulnerable to external shocks, especially changes in commodity demand and prices, weather, and political conflicts.

Numerous factors contribute to the inability of the country to accelerate and sustain growth for poverty reduction. In addition to failure to diversify production and exports, the key factors include poor political, economic, and corporate governance associated with inconsistent growth and development strategies and erratic implementation of development plans, frequent shifts in development ideology, inappropriate allocation

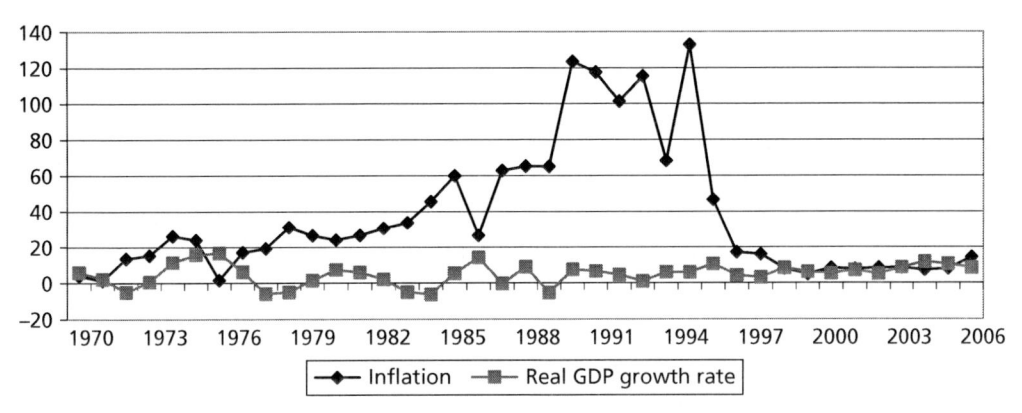

Figure 1. Inflation and real GDP growth rates, 1970–2008 (source: IMF, *World Economic Outlook*, April 2009 (1990 price))

of resources, civil wars and conflicts and a foreign policy marred by economic isolation, sanctions, and erratic aid flows.

From independence up to the present, Sudan has lacked the necessary institutions to design and implement consistent long-term development strategies to effectively mobilize domestic and external resources and allocate them according to development priorities and economic feasibility. Resource allocation often failed to promote equity across sectors and regions, resulting in political discontent and conflict as manifested in recent civil strives in the South, Darfur, the East, and the so-called marginalized areas in Southern Kordofan and the Blue Nile States. At the same time, development ideology has frequently shifted between capitalism, socialism, and Islamism. From independence until 1970, Sudan adopted a mainly market-oriented economic system that encouraged private investment and attracted substantial foreign assistance to build infrastructure. In the early 1970s, however, the country shifted to a central planning system and many financial and other private enterprises were nationalized.

Towards the end of the 1970s, a mixed system of private and public enterprise was adopted. While the lines of demarcation between different development orientations were often unclear, government used ideology to manipulate resources and institutions for political objectives, with adverse consequences on long-term economic and social development. The adoption of interest-free Islamic financial institutions has empowered certain religious parties to dominate both politics and the economy over the last two decades.

Besides inefficient allocation and management of resources, weak economic and corporate governance in Sudan has manifested itself in widespread corruption and an unattractive business and investment climate. Sudan ranked 173rd out of 180 countries in the Corruption Perceptions Index (CPI) in 2008. Public-sector management in the country is characterized by weak popular participation and by lack of transparency and accountability. Public accounts remain unaudited for several years. 'Corruption is considered as the key factor behind poor performance and weak compliance among government banks and has discouraged FDI as well as development partners from providing more resources' (*African Economic Outlook* 2009). At the same time, although Sudan has adopted an investment act intended to promote competition and has set up a one-stop business registration facility, it ranked 147th out of 181 countries in the 2009 World Bank Doing Business indicators. Investment risk is high due to corruption and inadequate enforcement of regulations.

Recently, macroeconomic policy reforms have been successful in reducing internal and external deficits, combating inflation, and reducing exchange rate instability. But they failed to promote productivity and investment outside the oil sector, despite increased public spending on infrastructure. Exchange rate overvaluation and the lack of a coherent industrial policy are two of the main policy constraints in this regard. Also, gross domestic savings and investment rates remained low, at 16.4% and 23.6% in 2008, respectively. Moreover, having failed to qualify for debt relief, Sudan is among the most highly indebted low-income countries, with its external debt estimated at $31.9 billion in 2008.

Geography, environment and climate change, inadequate human capital development, and a relatively low labour participation rate have also influenced growth in Sudan. With an area of about 1 million square miles and a sparsely distributed population of fewer than 40 million in 2008, Sudan is characterized by high transportation and energy costs that discourage private investment, especially in remote areas, and reduce its global competitiveness. Economic activity in Sudan has also suffered from the adverse consequences of climate change and rapid desertification that was partly blamed for conflicts in Darfur and other areas and led to rapid internal migration.

Sudan's labour force (11.6 million in 2008) is characterized by low skill level and participation rate (48% in 2008) and employment has been concentrated in agriculture (65% of total in 2008). The unemployment rate has increased from 18% in 2000 to 22% in 2008, reflecting the low rate of investment in the non-oil sector and a trend of jobless growth. Both labour participation and unemployment rates varied considerably across regions as a result of inequity in the distribution of public investment and services, among other factors.

3. Growth sustainability and poverty reduction major concerns

Progress in economic diversification in Sudan remains limited, and growth sustainability is a major concern. The country has only moved from excessive dependence on agriculture and natural resources to heavy dependence on oil from 1999 onwards. The share of agriculture in aggregate value added declined from 40% in 1970 to 33% in 2008, mainly due to increases in the shares of mining and services sectors. Meanwhile, the share of manufacturing declined from 9% to less than 7%.

The oil sector accounted for 17.2% of GDP and 65.3% of public revenue in 2008. This poses high risks to growth and fiscal sustainability in times of fluctuating oil demand and prices. Indeed, as a result of the global financial crisis and economic downturn, oil revenue is estimated to fall by 43.7% in 2009. In addition to fluctuations in its output, oil presents important policy challenges in terms of public-sector management and allocation of investment across sectors. With rising oil revenue and foreign reserves, Sudan allowed its currency to appreciate against the US dollar by 27.5% in real term between 2005 and mid-2008, significantly eroding the competitiveness of non-oil exports (*African Economic Outlook* 2009).

Despite notable progress in some areas of social development such as primary school enrolment (56% in 2008), poverty, income inequality, and access to social services remain serious issues in Sudan. Estimates indicate that the national poverty rate declined from 59% in 2000 to 42.7% in 2008 for urban areas and from 58.9 to 52.7% in rural areas (World Bank 2008). The reduction in poverty rates was mainly the result of peace and improving general economic conditions. Sudan has yet to implement a comprehensive poverty reduction strategy, and estimates of income inequality suggest that the Gini coefficient ranges between 0.5 and 0.74.

Progress in all areas of social development varied markedly across regions. For example, on average, net primary school attendance varied from 84% in the five highest-income states to 7% in the lowest five. This is largely a reflection of inequity in the allocation of public expenditure; over 80% of public investment in infrastructure in 2008 was concentrated in the five highest-income states. Meanwhile, fiscal decentralization is limited, and state governments and local authorities lack adequate political and administrative autonomy.

4. Policy recommendations

Sudan needs strong institutions and sound long-term development strategies to exploit its huge untapped economic potential. Improved governance, economic diversification and productivity improvement, human capital development, efficient allocation of resources, and increased equity in the distribution of public investment and services across sectors and regions are key to accelerating and sustaining growth for poverty reduction in the country.

The success of the democratization process is essential for Sudan to promote good governance. In addition to promoting macroeconomic stability, sound public-sector management, and competitive exchange rates, economic policy should focus on mobilizing domestic resources for strategic investments in infrastructure and pro-poor projects. Development strategies should incorporate effective industrial and sectoral policies to enhance productive capacity and investment in new and innovative areas, focusing on agro-processing and related industries.

■ REFERENCES

African Economic Outlook, 2009. Joint publication by the African Development Bank, OECD, and the United Nations Economic Commission for Africa.
World Bank, 2008. Country data (October).

Swaziland
Resilient Amidst Many Challenges

Phindile Ngwenya

1. Introduction

Swaziland is a middle-income country, with estimated GNI per capita of $2,500 in 2008. Average real economic growth fell just shy of 3% over the last five years, much lower than the targeted 5% set out in the 2006 Poverty Reduction Strategy and Action Plan (PRSAP) as required, in order to eradicate poverty. Investment reached 14.9% of GDP in 2008 and international reserves were reasonable, equivalent to 4.6 months of imports in 2008. The economy is reasonably diversified (Table 1), with the manufacturing sector contributing about 30% to GDP, followed by government (13%), agriculture (9%), transport (8%), retail trade (7%) and real estate (6.5%).

Table 1. GDP growth (%) by sector

	2002	2003	2004	2005	2006	2007	2008
Agriculture, hunting and forestry; fishing	5.3	4.9	−2.9	5.4	−2.4	2.6	−0.1
Mining and quarrying	11.2	−20.1	9.0	−21.5	15.8	−39.1	−16.0
Manufacturing	2.1	1.8	1.0	0.9	1.5	2.6	1.6
Electricity, gas and water supply	14.2	2.3	−2.5	3.8	5.1	4.8	2.4
Construction	−10.7	−9.9	17.3	5.6	3.5	−3.4	−3.0
Wholesale and retail trade	−8.3	−1.3	10.1	7.9	11.2	10.1	4.1
Hotels and restaurants	4.3	3.1	3.3	9.3	7.9	7.4	6.0
Transport, storage and communications	14.8	11.5	7.6	13.3	5.6	3.0	7.2
Financial intermediation	11.8	6.9	3.4	4.3	4.3	3.5	3.0
Real estate, renting and business activities	3.5	2.2	1.2	2.2	2.7	3.6	4.6
Public administration and defence; education; health and social care	1.2	2.8	3.3	−4.3	5.8	4.4	1.8
Other community, social and personal service activities	2.0	2.0	2.0	2.3	2.4	3.7	3.0
GDP at market prices	1.8	2.2	2.9	2.5	3.3	3.5	2.4

The infrastructure, including roads and telecommunications, is very good. Government aims to reduce poverty through ICT by enabling low-cost access to ICT by the poor. This would not only raise the low teledensity of about 4%, but would also facilitate competitiveness in the economy.

While the macroeconomic indicators are impressive, Swaziland's social indicators are poor. It has a poverty incidence of 69%, the unemployment rate is a high 28%; the HIV/AIDS incidence is 26% among the 15–49 age cohort—the most productive population group; population growth is near zero; life expectancy was 45 in 2008 and has been projected to decline to 33 by 2015; and the Gini coefficient of 0.6 places inequality in Swaziland among the highest in the region.

2. Policy challenges

The structure of the Swaziland economy is dualistic in nature, with a rural population of about 60%. The rural/urban composition of land has pre-colonial origins, which over time bred a dual system of administration and led to unequal economic growth. Enshrined in the Constitution of Swaziland is advancement towards a single system of local government, through which the rural/urban divide can be reduced.

Economic activity takes place in both the formal and informal market. The informal sector is dominant, and competition from the sector is rated as one of the highest challenges faced by large firms. Only an estimated 75% of small, medium, and large enterprises (SMLEs) are likely to report their registration with any government agency because of the high financial burden associated with registration.

The geographical challenges that Swaziland has are threefold: size—it is a small country, with 17,000 km^2 of land; it has low density, boasting a population of just 1 million; it is landlocked, with South Africa and Mozambique as its neighbours, and is one of forty-three countries of the world that have no access to the coast. The disadvantage of not having access to the coast is that global markets are much more distant; low population density means the advantages of economies of scale cannot be fully realized. Swaziland's economic activity is closely linked with that of South Africa; therefore many of the larger corporations that operate in Swaziland have their parent companies in South Africa.

Unlike other countries in the region, Swaziland is not highly endowed with natural resources. It boasts only coal, quarried stone, and forestry in its resource basket. The agriculture sector is responsible for about 9% of GDP. The rural population predominantly practises subsistence farming, mainly growing maize—the staple crop. In recent years, the contribution of agriculture to the economic performance of the country has declined, hampered by persistent drought conditions. Programmes such as the Comprehensive Agricultural Sector Policy (CASP) and National Programme for Food Security, which aim to improve production and competitiveness in the agriculture sector, have not delivered the desired goals. The country is a net importer of food.

In the manufacturing sector—the economy's engine of growth—total factor productivity is above the sub-Saharan region's average, labour productivity compares well with other middle income countries, unit labour costs are low, and a modest number of SMLEs export. While these variables seem reasonable when compared to other countries, improvement in these areas would increase the sector's competitiveness.

The financial sector is characterized by low credit uptake, thus high liquidity. There is thus room for micro lending institutions that would cater for a wider range of clientele, e.g. fashioned after the Grameen Bank. The capital market is small: the Swaziland Stock Exchange is new, having been established in 1999, and activity here is minimal. Increased competition from other countries in the region as their economic and political climates improve has made it difficult for Swaziland to attract new direct investment. Rather, a significant proportion of capital inflows can be attributed to transfers from parent companies abroad.

Swaziland's economic interlinkages with South Africa permeate its fiscal, monetary, trade, and regional integration policies. Through its Southern African Customs Union (SACU) membership, its revenue and therefore fiscal space are determined; the trading bloc also determines the country's trade policies. Swaziland is a relatively open economy with relatively low import tariff barriers. The Common Monetary Agreement with South Africa, by which the lilangeni is pegged at par with the South African rand, limits monetary policy manoeuvre.

There is broad-based lack of competition, ranging from agriculture goods to financial services. The structure of the economy is such that a few companies are dominant, stifling competition.

3. Conclusion

Swaziland has made significant progress in overcoming its geographical and historical challenges, but many policy challenges remain. Declining SACU revenues pose a serious challenge for fiscal policy. Lack of competition remains a significant challenge that hampers competitiveness across all sectors of the economy.

REFERENCES

African Development Bank, 2009. *African Economic Outlook*.
Lowsby, J., and D. De Groot, 2007. *A Brief History of Urban Development and Upgrading in Swaziland*. Mbabane: Government of Swaziland.

Organisation for Economic Co-operation and Development, 2009. *African Economic Outlook: 2009*. Paris.
Swaziland Tourism Authority, 2008. *Swaziland Review: An Overview of the Kingdom of Swaziland's Economy 2008*. Mbabane: Swazi Review of Commerce and Industry.
World Bank, 2007. *Swaziland: An Assessment of the Investment Climate*. Washington, DC.
World Bank, (2009). *World Development Report: Reshaping Economic Geography*. World Bank, Washington D.C.

Tanzania
Reflections on Economic Growth

William Lyakurwa and Jehovaness Aikaeli

1. Introduction

Tanzania is one of the five East African countries, with estimated population of 40.1 million people and per capita gross national income of US$400. The country's life expectancy is 52 years and literacy of the people aged 15 years and above is 69% (World Bank 2007). Tanzania is in the great lakes region, where there are political upheavals in some countries; nevertheless, Tanzania's peace and security remains firm, and macroeconomic performance is encouraging: in recent years the economy has registered high growth and stability.

This chapter presents a brief review of economic and social developments in Tanzania for the recent past, highlights sources of economic growth, and reviews future prospects. Whereas the next section describes economic development, section 3 summarizes the poverty situation. Section 4 underscores sources of growth, while section 5 discusses prospects for the future, and section 6 presents brief concluding remarks.

2. Economic development

2.1. NATIONAL OUTPUT AND PRICES PERFORMANCE

In recent years Tanzania has been among the better-performing economies in sub-Saharan Africa. As a result of sound macroeconomic policies and increased rate of investment following economic reforms, coupled with political stability and enhanced good governance, GDP growth rose to 7.4% in 2008 from 4.9% in 2000. The structure of the economy has undergone a remarkable change over the past decade. While agriculture contributed more than 30% of GDP before 2002, its share to GDP has been declining, reaching 24% in 2008. This transformation has given rise to displacement of agriculture by other sectors, notably services, manufacturing, and construction. During 2001–8, the fastest-growing sectors were mining and quarrying (13.6%), construction (10.7%), manufacturing (8.4%), and transport and communication (9.4%).

Prices have generally been stable over the past decade. Inflation declined from 34.9% in January 1995 to 13.5 % in December 2008. Inflation was in single digits from January 1999 to November 2008 before returning to double digits following upward pressure in prices due to the global economic crisis. On the monetary side, the margin between lending and deposit rates declined consistently, while overall, exchange rate depreciation was recorded over the past decade.

2.2. THE FINANCIAL SECTOR

Tanzania's financial sector is vibrant and has contributed well to the performance of the economy through inter alia provision of credit to the private sector which (as a percentage of GDP) rose to around 14% in 2008 from 5% in 2003. The financial sector has experienced commendable diversification, with the emergence of various institutions and products that were not available (or were government-monopolized) before financial service liberalization starting 1991. The number of commercial banks, insurance companies, and investment funds increased correspondingly, from 10, 9, and 1 in 1995 to 28, 18, and 4 in 2007. During the same period, savings and credit societies exploded from 450 to 3,469, and microfinance institutions from 1 to 57, while the number of pension funds rose from 4 to 6 and that of bureaux de change from 93 to 142. Diversification of financial sector is improving, with commercial banks' assets proportion falling from above 90% of the total national financial assets in 2003 to less than 75% in 2007, whereas, respective assets of pension funds, insurance companies and investment funds were more than doubled.

2.3. FISCAL PERFORMANCE

After a series of tax reforms, government revenue collection has been on the increase. Total revenue expanded from 11% of GDP in 2003 to 15.9% in 2008, while total expenditure expanded from 18.5% to 22.8%. External debt declined from 83.5% to 38% of GDP in the same period—mainly due to the industrialized countries' debt forgiveness through the Highly Indebted Poor Countries (HIPC) initiative. The trend of government domestic credit has been falling because of its abstinence from borrowing from banks, thereby creating a wider space for private investment financing.

2.4. EXTERNAL SECTOR DEVELOPMENTS

Subsequent to a slowdown in export growth together with a sharp increase in imports demand, Tanzania's current account deficit as a proportion of GDP widened from 5.1% in 2000 to 11.1% in 2008. Exports growth stalled as gold mining in the country approached its capacity, and also because primary commodity prices performed poorly in the world market. The increase in imports was triggered by a sustained high demand for capital and intermediate goods. Regarding sources of exports, the contribution of traditional (agricultural) products to total exports is diminishing. The share of traditional exports fell from 30.8% in 1998 to 15% in 2007/8, while that of non-traditional exports rose from 69.2% to 85%. Transport, manufacturing, and gold registered sizeable increases in exports, with respective growth rates of 8.9%, 8.3%, and 21.1% in 2007, up from 3.6%, 3.1%, and 0.3% in 1998. These developments marked some displacement of the contribution of tourism services, whose annual growth decreased to 27.8% from 34.5% over the same period.

3. Poverty and social development

According to household budget surveys (2001, 2007: National Bureau of Statistics 2002; 2007), between 2000 and 2007 poverty decreased, but at a slower pace in rural than in urban centres—thus indicating that, besides poverty being severer in the villages, the alleviation process is less favourable to the poor rural areas than to the relatively better urban centres. In terms of the head count index, during 2000–2007 the overall basic needs poverty incidence fell by 2.4 percentage points in mainland Tanzania, while in the rural areas it declined by 1.3 percentage points. Overall, there was a decrease in incidence of food poverty by 2.2 percentage points compared with 2.0 percentage points for the rural areas.

From the viewpoint of social development, between 2000 and 2007 there were substantial improvements in schooling and assets ownership. Expenditures per capita on education and consumer durables were more than doubled, while expenditure on health services grew by 56.5%. The household budget survey (2007) also shows some improvement in housing materials. There is a continuing shift from farming to other activities, in particular, the non-farm rural enterprises.

4. Sources of growth

The share of agriculture to GDP is dwindling, and this raises questions because more than 80% of the population lives in rural areas. The declining trend indicates some displacement of the share of agriculture in GDP by the other fast-growing sectors, including services, construction, manufacturing, mining, and quarrying. Contribution of agriculture to GDP in 2008 was 24%, having grown by 4.6%, which was less than the overall economic growth of 7.4%. Although agriculture is the largest source of income in Tanzania, it has on average been growing by less than 5% since 2000, implying that economic growth is constrained by a sluggish development of its major source of GDP. If agriculture were growing at relatively high rates, the trickle-down effects of growth on poverty reduction would be clear.

Trade and repairs is the second largest source of income, which contributed 14.1% of GDP in 2008, with average growth of 8.3% since 2001. Manufacturing registered a contribution of 9.4% in 2008 and average growth of 8.4% over the past eight years. Since high-value agricultural products (spices, fruits, vegetables, fish, and livestock products) require processing before reaching the market, this provides enormous opportunity for investment in food processing in Tanzania.

The real estate and business services sector is booming, with a total share of 10.2% in GDP for 2008, and average growth of 7% during 2001–8. In line with good performance in industry and services, construction is excelling, achieving 6.7% of GDP and the highest average growth rate, 11%, since 2001. Other sectors that are small in terms of their shares in GDP but growing fast include mining and quarrying, with a contribution of 2.6% of GDP in 2008, but growing on average by 14% from 2001. In recent years, the transport sector has boomed due to increased transit trade to the neighbouring landlocked countries (Democratic Republic of Congo, Burundi, Rwanda, Uganda, Zambia, and Malawi). Transport contributed 5.1% of GDP in 2008, and its average growth was 6.8% for the four years up 2008.

5. Future prospects

Based on Tanzania's Development Vision 2025, the National Strategy for Growth and Reduction of Poverty (NSGRP) was adopted in 2005 as a framework for putting the focus on poverty reduction by fast-tracking the targets of the Vision in the period of five years, 2006–10. The Vision 2025 focuses on high and shared growth, good-quality livelihood, peace, stability and unity, good governance, high-quality education, and international competitiveness, among others (United Republic of Tanzania 2005).

In the light of Vision 2025 and NSGRP, there are prospects of achieving high economic growth and social development. The government has declared a commitment to stay in the course of economic and social reforms to maintain improved macroeconomic stability. The areas given special importance and targets include the following.

5.1. GROWTH OF THE ECONOMY AND REDUCTION OF INCOME POVERTY

In NSGRP targets, it is expected that growth of 6–8% per annum will be attained by 2010. GDP growth was 7.4% in 2008, signalling a possibility for the economy to grow as targeted. However, the threat of the current global financial crisis may jeopardize prospects of attaining high growth. To ensure sound macroeconomic management, the inflation operational target was set to be no higher than 4% by 2010. But, following the current global economic crisis, inflation is likely to have remained in double digits during 2009/10. Unemployment is expected to decline to 7% by 2010 from 13% in 2000.

5.2. IMPROVEMENT OF QUALITY OF LIFE AND SOCIAL WELLBEING

The challenge is to translate growth into improved quality of life for the poorest and most vulnerable groups. Tanzania's priority is to ensure equitable access to quality primary and secondary education, universal literacy, and expansion of higher, technical, and vocational education. Operational targets include increasing gross and net enrolments at primary schools to 99% by 2010 from 90.5% in 2004. The NSGRP Review 2008 (United Republic of Tanzania 2008) indicates enrolment of 97.2% in 2008, showing a high likelihood of attaining the target. There is a commitment to achieving secondary school net enrolment of 25% by 2010; this reached 23.5% in 2008. In pursuit of improved survival, health, and wellbeing of children and women, especially those in vulnerable groups, the targets were to reduce infant mortality from 95 in 2002 to 50 (per 1,000 live births); and maternal mortality from 529 to 265 per 100,000 births by 2010. Developments show small likelihood of achievement of these targets, as the proportions of deaths remain high. There is also a target of reducing HIV prevalence among 15–24-year-old pregnant women from 11% in 2004 to 5% by 2010. Many efforts have been made in this area, but the extent to which the target is being achieved is not immediately clear.

5.3. GOVERNANCE AND ACCOUNTABILITY.

NSGRP aims at: achieving good governance and the rule of law; making leaders and public servants accountable; deepening democracy and political and social tolerance; attaining cultivated and sustained peace, political stability, national unity, and social cohesion. Among other measures, in 2007/8 the government updated and reviewed twelve laws in order to facilitate proper implementation of the framework for good governance. These developments indicate prospects of a positive movement towards the goals.

5. Concluding remarks

Tanzania has made commendable progress over the recent past, and there are prospects of growth despite the current effects of the global economic crisis. Nevertheless, emphasis should be placed on raising the level of national savings/investments, creation of requisite social capital, and addressing the challenges so as to facilitate harnessing available opportunities in a manner that is more effective in reducing poverty and enhancing growth.

REFERENCES

National Bureau of Statistics, 2002. *Tanzania Household Budget Survey 2000/01*.
—— 2007. *Tanzania Households Budget Survey 2006/07* (Preliminary Presentation).
Tanzania Development Vision 2025. http://www.tanzania.go.tz/pdf/theTanzaniadevelopmentvision.pdf
United Republic of Tanzania, 2005. *National Strategy for Growth and Reduction of Poverty* (NSGRP).
—— 2008. *MKUKUTA Annual Implementation Report 2007/08*.
World Bank, 2007. http://devdata.worldbank.org/AAG/tza_aag.pdf (downloaded 10 June 2009).

Togo
Diagnosis and Challenges in a Context of Crises

Kako Nubukpo

1. Introduction[1]

The economic situation in Togo has been characterized by long-term stagnation and decapitalization. For the past thirty years, the country has had very short periods of growth, alternating with very long stretches of stagnation and recession. Per capita GDP in real terms has fallen steadily at a rate of 1% per annum since 1990. This has led to severe poverty for the majority of the population, whose per capita income is estimated at $350 per year, compared to other low-income countries, which are at $650 per year, and to sub-Saharan Africa, which is estimated at $850 per year.

And yet this country, with its small size and limited resources, could still see considerable growth if its resources were well managed.

Since the end of the 1990s, Togo has entered into a cycle of regression characterized by economic stagnation as well as political and institutional difficulties. The periods of relative stability and political appeasement have coincided with phases of economic improvement, but until now solid and durable economic reform has not been established. Under these circumstances the country's resources have continued to deteriorate, from the overly exploited land with ill-equipped rural regions, to the lack of workers, and to the greatly diminished economic and social infrastructure.

With over 56,785 square kilometres (35,285 square miles), the population was estimated at 6.3 million in 2006, and showed a relatively high population growth rate of 2.4% per annum. Based on poverty thresholds, approximately 62% of the population were poor. This statistic can be broken down to 74% of the rural population and 37% of urban populations. According to the 2007 *Human Development Report* of the United Nations, Togo is 152nd on the list of 177 nations for poverty.

---

[1] The author wishes to thank Véronique Dossou and Jolivet Alagbo for their valuable contribution to the preparation of this document. He remains, however, solely responsible for the opinions expressed herein, as well as for any errors or omissions which might have been overlooked.

These data—resulting from the QUIBB (unified Questionnaire of the Indicators of Basic Needs) study done in 2006 under the aegis of the UNDP—do not truly reflect the current poverty situation because of the exogenous shocks the country has suffered, notably the huge increases in food prices in 2008 as well as the 2007 and 2008 floods. This situation has in all likelihood brought on an overall increase in income poverty. In fact, the sharp rise in prices—in 2008 it was over 8.4% on average—has certainly brought with it an increase in poverty levels in the whole country. Economic growth in Togo was not sufficiently strong in 2008 to engender an increase in household incomes capable of compensating for price increases. As a result, per capita GDP in Togo fell by 1.4% in 2007 and 0.8% in 2008, illustrating even further the degradation of the economic situation of households.

Moreover, because of budget restrictions, the public education and sanitation systems are in a state of extreme degradation. Public administration, which has suffered extensive losses (more than a third since 1999), has reduced capacity. Many professionals have opted to emigrate. The share of personnel expenses in the budget, regularly decreasing, has reached 5.5% of the GDP, the lowest in the West Africa region.

Emigration has reached very high levels, and includes not just unqualified labour but also highly qualified categories (e.g. executives, business owners, and technicians), a direct consequence of the country's political crisis. To be sure, remittances by the migrants significantly contribute to family incomes. An unprecedented and very sharp rise in transfers from emigrants from this region took the figures from 34 billion FCFA in 2001 to 68 billion FCFA in 2005, an increase of 6% of GDP. Even if the current figures on migrant transfers to Togo are not yet known, the economic situation of their destination countries leads us to forecast that these monetary transfers could be affected by the crisis.

2. The sectors' performance is below the country's growth potential

Togo draws the essential part of its income from three principal sources: mining (phosphate and clinker), agriculture (cotton, coffee, and cocoa), and revenues from the port of Lomé. The failures in management of the phosphate sector and the cotton industry have brought about a continuous decline in productivity followed by decapitalization of both sectors.

The deficiencies and dysfunctions in management of these sectors are among the many factors that have caused the country's public debt, notably the very large internal debt, to rise, which has in turn contributed to the degradation of the banking system. It is in these two sectors that we find two thirds of the banking system's unproductive loans, which in turn represent one third of the total portfolio of domestic loans.

3. The need for improved management of public finance

Budget balances will probably deteriorate considerably as fiscal yields, particularly those tied to raw materials, suffer in the current international circumstances, and the Togolese government will have to respond to a growing demand for social expenditures. In addition, the increases in the service cost of the debt, with increasing borrowing costs (reflecting high risk premiums) in regional and international financial markets, should not be overlooked.

That being said, Togo's public finances are plagued with structural weaknesses, which augment the vulnerability of its economy and could lead it to fall prey to numerous exogenous and endogenous shocks. In fact, Togo had the lowest ratio of public investment to GDP in the entire UEMOA (Union économique et monétaire ouest-africaine/West African Economic and Monetary Union) (2% of GDP and 10.4% of total public spending) for the period 2004–7. In addition, for this same period, the ratio of 'publicly financed investment from internal/fiscal resources' reached 7.6% of total investment in Togo, against an average of 21.6% for the other countries in the UEMOA and the 20% norm imposed by the UEMOA's convergence criteria (World Bank 2009). This highlights the necessity to drastically increase investment spending during the coming few years, notably in order to comply with the objectives of growth and poverty reduction established by the country's poverty reduction strategy.

4. Challenges

Today, Togo finds itself more than ever at a crossroads. In spite of its abundance of natural resources and its geo-economic advantages, the country suffers from increasing poverty accentuated by the increasingly visible effects of international crises. The correlation coefficient between worldwide growth and that of the Togolese economy is 0.55 (IMF 2009; Ocampos 2009). Hence, any shocks affecting the world economy also affect the Togolese economy. The recurring problem of floods in recent years may constrain rural–urban migration.

However, delays in the transmission of international shocks and the Togolese economy's means of responding to these shocks are relatively uncertain because of the lack of current data regarding the various price and revenues elasticities concerned. Among other numerous and urgent measures which the government must enact are promoting good management of public resources, a better distribution of growth, a revaluation of wages, and the facilitation of access to credit.

In addition, it will be important to have structural responses to recurring problems in the Togolese economy, specifically:

- the weakness of the internal market;
- poor governance, illustrated notably by corruption and the dubious orientation of public spending to the detriment of investment spending;
- the very high emigration of the elite in response to deep ethnic cleavages;
- the pronounced defiance of the population vis-à-vis elected government officials.

A return of confidence in its leaders and confidence in the capacity of its economy to rebound appears to be today the prerequisite for making Togo's economy one of progress.

REFERENCES

Ocampos, Lorraine, 2009. Presentation during the FMI Mission in Togo on 18 February.
World Bank, 2009. 'Togo: review of public spending and financial responsibility of the state', vol.1, *Principal Report* (March), 22.

Tunisia
Top Performance in Africa and the Middle East (But Less than Stellar Globally)

Mustapha K. Nabli

1. Introduction

Assessed on the basis of most social and economic development indicators, Tunisia has performed near the top of African and Middle East and North Africa (MENA) countries. But on most counts it has lagged the successful East Asian countries. The level of life expectancy at birth of 73 achieved by 2004 and the increase, of 24 years since 1960, are comparable to or higher than those achieved by the most successful oil-rich MENA countries as well as the East Asian countries. Similar success is shown for the reduction of child mortality under 5 from 254 per 1,000 to 25, and of illiteracy rates, from 55% in 1960 to 25.7% in 2003. Poverty rates as recently measured in the international standards of $2 per day declined dramatically from 27% in 1981 to 7.3% in 2005. Tunisia's success is in many ways comparable to the most successful East Asian countries.

While some other MENA countries also achieved average growth rates of GDP of around 5% over the last five decades, in terms of per capita GDP growth Tunisia shows the strongest performance after Oman and Egypt. But Tunisia's growth performance was much weaker than that of the most successful East Asian countries.

2. Why has Tunisia performed better than most African and MENA countries?

Among the possible explanations for Tunisia's comparative success are several that would have to be considered as extremely favourable initial conditions. First, a long history of independent and stable states goes back to the Hafside dynasty over more than three and a half centuries (1228–1574) and the Husseinite dynasty for two and a half centuries (1710–1957). The colonial experience (1881–1956) had its costs, but it also brought a more efficient state, and the building of a more modern educational system. Second, relative to many of its neighbours in Africa and the Middle East, Tunisia enjoyed much greater homogeneity in its population. Third, Tunisia's location close to the heart of Western Europe was certainly a major advantage. Fourth, there is the fortuitous emergence of Habib Bourguiba, the country's first president after independence, as a strong leader who undertook a number of major reforms during the honeymoon period of the new regime that proved irreversible: the focus on building a strong national state capacity, a modern educational system with wide coverage, and active population control policies and emancipation and equal rights for women.

While the favourable initial conditions undoubtedly played a role, the evidence suggests that neither individually nor even collectively could they constitute the primary explanation. Tunisia's development strategy shares a number of the ingredients which have been found to be common to the highly successful growth experiences identified by the Commission on Growth and Development (2008).

The first factor was the political leadership's choice of a development strategy that remained remarkably and consistently focused on the goal of social progress, modernization, and industrialization. Tunisia's strong state capacity and a strong bureaucracy allowed it to pursue consistently and effectively this vision by (1) ensuring domestic peace, stability, and security of property, (2) successfully coordinating the various components of economic policy design and implementation, and (3) recognizing and implementing the needed for policy changes in the face of problems and changing circumstances.

This has supported significant structural transformations. For instance, industrial development has been a basic objective of Tunisian policymakers, and while in terms of share of manufacturing in GDP Tunisia was only in the middle of MENA countries in 1975, by 2005 it was among the highest, achieving the largest increase of almost 8 percentage points.

Second, Tunisia, like most MENA and East Asian countries, has maintained a relatively stable macroeconomic environment throughout the decades. The relative autonomy—if not full independence in the modern sense—of the Central Bank contributed to this outcome, as well as the generally prudent fiscal policies. Tunisia never defaulted on its debt during the post-independence period.

Third, this strategy has been buttressed by the heavy emphasis on building human capital, with strong expansion of secular public education, provision of health services, access to other public services, and the liberation of women. The gender parity index for gross enrolment in primary education reached 0.66 in 1970, higher than the average for MENA countries, and 100% by 2003. Similar progress, although with some lag, was achieved for secondary and tertiary education. Women were able to enter the labour market in large numbers. Active population policies, together with an emphasis on girls' education, led to a dramatic decline in total fertility rates from 7.2 in 1962 to 2.0 in 2003.

Fourth, Tunisia has continuously relied on leveraging the global markets, particularly European, to benefit from access to FDI, ideas, technology, and potential economies of scale. Non-oil merchandise exports as a ratio of GDP increased from about 11% in the 1970s to more than 30% during 2001–5. This performance is similar to that of East Asian countries. Even during the state-led import substitution period of the 1960s, the encouragement of tourism meant continued openness. Tunisia has achieved consistently high receipts from tourism, of around 10.5% of GDP.

Fifth, Tunisia has consistently made use of some rather pragmatic and heterodox policies to help achieve its industrialization and economic diversification goals. After an initial period of indiscriminate import substitution, the state has leveraged global markets by making use of various elements of the two-track strategies used in East Asia. It has used mechanisms to encourage offshore production and export of clothing with the extensive development of foreign-owned firms often located away from urban centres. The key to their success was offering complete tax holidays on corporate profits and allowing duty-free imports of inputs irrespective of the location of the activities. Other examples of heterodox policies include: the unusually generous system of providing long-term finance for hotels with credit guarantees which allowed international tourism to spread rapidly through the country; a special deal with European automakers that allows imports of cars into Tunisia on the condition that parts and components of an agreed-upon value would be purchased from Tunisia; the use of special financial facilities to support SMEs, technological upgrading, debt consolidation, and trade facilitation activities; and the signing of a number of preferential trade agreements (the most important of which is its Association Agreement with the European Union), but continuing to have high MFN tariffs.

3. Why has Tunisia not done as well in economic growth and economic development as the most successful East Asian countries?

One can argue that Tunisia's economic performance has been weaker than one would have expected given the advantages it had over other African and MENA countries, and perhaps even some Asian countries, in terms of human development, state capacity, homogeneity, and social stability. In a sense, therefore, the Tunisian paradox is not why it has been successful compared to other African and MENA countries, but why it has failed to achieve the same success as that of many East Asian countries.

3.1. LIMITED SUCCESS IN ACHIEVING HIGH RATES OF SAVINGS AND PHYSICAL CAPITAL ACCUMULATION

Tunisia has been successful in achieving relatively high and steady rates of national savings, of around 23%, and investment of about 25–7%, but since the 1980s it has not matched the achievements of savings and investment rates of 30–35% or more by most East Asian countries. In East Asia, and other cases of high growth episodes such as India since the 1990s, the main driver for the increase in savings and investment was the private sector. The investment of the private sector as a share of GDP reached high levels, of the order of 20–30% of GDP or more, while in the case of Tunisia it remained stubbornly at the level of 12–14%. The question is, then, why the private sector in Tunisia did not show the dynamism and growth which would have capitalized on the positive ingredients present in the country.

3.2. THE HEAVY HAND OF THE STATE, AND LIMITED SUCCESS IN MAKING THE PRIVATE SECTOR THE ENGINE FOR INVESTMENT AND PRODUCTIVITY GROWTH

In Tunisia the state continued throughout the decades, and despite the many changes and reforms, to intervene heavily in markets and the allocation of resources. Success in entrepreneurship continued to depend on closeness to the political regime and government. The state continued to have available to it a wide range of instruments, and enough discretion in the design and implementation of laws and regulations, to be able to affect in any desired direction the success of any private entrepreneur in any activity.

The pervasive interventions undermine the credibility of the many reforms which have aimed to improve the business environment and encourage the private sector to take the lead in wealth creation. The lack of credibility of commitment of government to reforms and markets may be due to the unwillingness of the incumbent authoritarian rulers to commit to a broad-based and strong private sector, which may become stronger and a threat to the regime itself if it does not respect its commitment to protect property rights (Nabli, Silva-Jauregui, and Aysan 2008).

3.3. INSUFFICIENT USE OF COMPETITION AND MARKETS TO ALLOCATE RESOURCES AND PERSISTENCE OF TOO MANY INEFFICIENCIES

In addition to the lower level of capital accumulation, Tunisia continued to have lower levels of efficiency than the successful East Asian countries. Total factor productivity (TFP) growth, though having recovered from the negative growth of the 1980s, has remained relatively low, at 1–1.5%, since the 1990s. There has been an inability to dismantle costly policies, and an approach to policy changes which proceeds very slowly, often trying to get around problems by creating new mechanisms such as the dual-track trade policy regimes. While this has had its benefits, it has also tended to perpetuate inefficient situations. This has meant that Tunisian growth has been more of the 'stop and go' type than in countries in East Asia. Surges in growth have been interrupted by crises like those during the late 1960s and mid-1980s.

The continued strong, heavy hand of the state is seen in the financial sector, where Tunisia has achieved a high level of financial development similar to many other MENA countries, but has been much below the financial depth of the most successful East Asian countries. A notable feature of the Tunisia experience has been the limited increase in credit to the private sector since the 1980s.

The cost of these inefficiencies is most dramatically reflected in the labour markets, with the persistence of high unemployment, particularly among the youth and women. The overall unemployment rate has remained around 14–16% over the last two decades. The rates of return to schooling were generally low both for males and females: they ranged from 2.7 to 5.5% in 2001 for primary and secondary education, below such rates for successful developing countries, which are in the range of 8–10%.

3.4. INSUFFICIENT USE OF GLOBAL MARKETS, LIMITED DIVERSIFICATION AND EXPLOITATION OF KNOWLEDGE AND TECHNOLOGY TRANSFER

Without facing the competition of world markets, Tunisia has generally been unable to take full advantage of the available global markets and integrate into the world economy to the same extent as Asian countries, where there has been a continuous upward movement in the technological and organizational sophistication of industry. Tunisia's industrial development has remained stuck for too long in the low-technology textiles and clothing sector, with limited integration into global supply chains. The diversification into more promising activities has been too slow.

East Asian countries have varied more than MENA countries in the timing of liberalization and integration into the global economy. This means that within the Asian region, there are greater differences in factor endowment and stages of development—and hence greater opportunities for developing intra-industry trade and trading networks—than in MENA. As a result, neighbourhood effects for Tunisia in MENA and the Mediterranean have been much less favourable than those enjoyed by many countries from the dynamic East Asia region.

REFERENCES

Commission on Growth and Development, 2008. *The Growth Report: Strategies for Sustained Growth and Inclusive Development*. Washington, DC: World Bank.

Nabli, Mustapha K., Carlos Silva-Jauregui, and Ahmet Faruk Aysan, 2008. 'Authoritarianism, credibility of reforms and private sector development in the Middle East and North Africa', in *Institutions and Economic Development: Selected Papers from the Economic Research Forum 14th Annual Conference*.

Uganda
Turning Sustained Growth into Structural Transformation for Human Development

Barbara Barungi

1. Background

Uganda's sustained growth for two decades, an African model, provides an insightful illustration of the challenges of translating growth into structural transformation for sustainable human development. Uganda has demonstrated a strong track record of continued growth, but poverty and inequality patterns have varied over time. Human development indicators remain low, and have not improved as significantly as would have been expected for a country experiencing a growth rate on average of above 5% since the mid 1990s.

Has continued fragility in northern Uganda undermined the gains of pro-poor growth in Uganda over the past twenty years? Or can it be argued that there has been a trade-off between maintaining macroeconomic fundamentals and ensuring broad structural transformation and human development? This chapter reviews the evidence and draws some policy conclusions. While Uganda experienced sustained positive growth rates over the period 1992–2006, with a GDP growth of over 5% on average, there were reversals in poverty and inequality trends. In the period 1992–9, poverty continuously declined; the period 1999–2003 was marked by an increasing trend in poverty estimates; and the period 2003–6 saw a reversal in this trend. Inequality measured by the Gini coefficient increased from 0.364 in 1992/3 to 0.395 in 1999/2000 and to 0.428 in 2002/3, but declined to 0.408 in 2005/6. Fast growth and poverty reduction during the 1990s were due to immediate benefits of recovery from civil war and from overcoming the economic mismanagement that prevailed during much of the 1980s. However the early 2000s seem to have been a period of *immiserizing* growth.

Despite growth contributing to a sharp decline in poverty from 55% of the population in 1992/3 to 31% in 2005/6, the economy remains dependent on subsistence agriculture, the majority of the population live in the largely underdeveloped rural areas, infrastructure services are poor, export competitiveness remains low, human development indicators are weak, and there has been no significant structural transformation. Several studies provide some useful analysis of the dimensions of poverty in Uganda.

2. A review of the poverty and inequality trends

Ssewanyana and Okidi (2007), based on analysis of the national household surveys, show the reversals in poverty and inequality trends, the persistence of poverty in northern Uganda, and the rural–urban differences. From their analysis of the 2005/6 survey, the north remains significantly poorer and poverty is still predominantly a rural phenomenon (Table 1). This poses a challenge in sustaining progress towards attainment of the Millennium Development Goals and the Poverty Eradication Action Plan (PEAP) targets despite the decline in poverty registered in 2005/6 as reflected in Table 1.

The largest reduction in the proportion of people in poverty has been found in the western region, where the headcount declined from 32.9% to 20.5%. The proportion of people in poverty in the eastern region declined from 46% to 35.9%. In the central region the decline was from 22.3% to 16.4%. Only the northern region experienced no change in headcount poverty, with an insignificant fall from 63% to 60.7%. However, some signs of improvement are beginning to be experienced in the north, with increased humanitarian assistance and the return of relative peace and security. But this does not guarantee the much-needed transformation to enable the population to rebuild their destroyed livelihoods.

Even without the conflict in northern Uganda, the human development indicators of the country as a whole are generally low. As reported in the UNDP 2007 Human Development Report on Uganda, despite the achievements in poverty reduction, the challenges linked to high infant and maternal mortality rates, the prevalence of HIV/AIDS, and continued decline in the state of environment and natural resources could undermine agricultural performance, social transformation, and ultimately human development. With respect to regional levels of human development, the central region

Table 1. Poverty and inequality in Uganda, 2005/6

Poverty measures[a]	National	Rural	Urban	Central	East	North	West
Headcount	28.9	32.2	10.6	16.4	35.9	56.8	19.7
Poverty gap	7.8	8.7	2.7	3.6	9.1	19.1	4.7
Severity of poverty	3.0	3.4	1.0	1.3	3.4	8.3	1.6
Gini coefficient	0.408	0.363	0.432	0.417	0.354	0.331	0.342

[a] Estimates exclude the districts of Bundibugyo, Kasese, Kitgum, and Gulu.
Source: Ssewanyana and Okidi (2007).

had the highest Human Development Index (HDI) both in 2003 (0.547) and 2005 (0.570), while the northern region had the lowest HDIs of 0.418 (2003) and 0.436 (2005). The western region came second with HDIs of 0.487 and 0.539 for 2003 and 2005 respectively. The eastern region was ranked third in 2003 with HDI of 0.459, showing a slight improvement in 2005 with its HDI standing at 0.532. The HDI was generally higher for urban areas than for rural areas.

3. The challenge of structural transformation

It can be argued that Uganda is a paradox of a success story that still faces the structural and political challenges of societal transformation and sustainable development. For the past twenty years two economies have coexisted—one developed and more successful, with functioning institutions and functioning markets, alongside the wrecked economy in the north due to a protracted conflict since 1986, poor governance, weak institutions, economic deterioration, and social decay.

To understand the reason for the absence of structural transformation would require a much deeper examination of the underlying political economy. In the immediate present this failure can be attributed to three main factors:

1. Fragile democracy and political instability: the prolonged conflict and resultant vulnerability of large segments of the population in northern Uganda is testimony to this fact.
2. Inability to make institutions work in a self-sustaining manner: the regulatory framework remains constrained by the weak enforcement of reforms to facilitate doing business, to strengthen property rights, and to improve commercial dispute resolution.
3. Policy reversals with far-reaching political and socioeconomic consequences: a glaring example of this is the amendment to the constitution which removes the limits on the tenure of office of the President.

It is recognized that Uganda's achievements over the last twenty years, against the backdrop of weak fundamentals and significant exogenous shocks, are remarkable; but nonetheless there is room for improvement. As emphasised by Selassie (2008), the weak point of Uganda's performance is the fact that economic transformation has been limited relative to the very high benchmarks set by the countries enjoying sustained growth (see Table 2). Uganda must invest more in human capital, infrastructure, quality of institutions, governance, and improving export competitiveness. By changing its policy focus primarily to these priorities, it should be able to reach and sustain medium human development status, passing the HDI threshold of 0.500. It can, however, be argued that Uganda faces constraints on such progress: its landlocked position curtails access to

Table 2. Indicators of fundamental country attributes

	Uganda	SSA	Sustained growth cases	Other LDCs
Geography				
Distance from coast line (km)	969	526	202	274
Disease burden	100	85	22	34
Ethnolinguistic fractionalization	0.90	0.66	0.34	0.32
Integration				
Export plus import to GDP (%)				
1990	26	69	100	84
2003	40	73	118	92
Institutions				
Heritage Foundation (low score better)				
1995	3.15	3.6	3.01	3.24
2005	2.95	3.4	2.97	3.07
Economic freedom of the world (aggregate index, high score better)				
1990	2.68	4.67	6.18	5.29
2004	6.35	5.59	6.66	6.44
World Bank Government Effectiveness Index (high score better)				
1996	0.39	−0.65	0.54	−0.15
2005	−0.48	−0.79	0.48	−0.08

Source: Selassie (2008); World Bank, World Development Indicators.

markets, it has a high disease burden, and a high level of ethnic fractionalization that points to high potential for conflict.

Granted, there are challenges, but Uganda is now well positioned to make more creative policy decisions that aim at consolidating the gains from growth and deepening the opportunities for societal transformation and human development. The state should be more visible and proactive in ensuring human development and a better life for all, as opposed to the traditional minimalist approach of providing an enabling environment.

3. **Bold policies for structural transformation**

Uganda is at a turning point where it must forge a developmental state that has an effective national government public service delivery apparatus while engaging more proactively in productive interaction with markets so as to improve the competitiveness of the Ugandan economy. Societal transformation can only be achieved through more creative and engaged state action that aims to jumpstart and guide local creativity, entrepreneurship, and development.

The basic objectives of a developmental state that promotes human development for its citizens while consolidating the gains from growth for a self-sustaining market-driven economy are the following:

1. establishing professional state security institutions as part of security sector reforms;
2. consolidating the institutional framework for 'human security' so that citizens enjoy individual rights and liberties to shape their livelihoods;
3. deepening institutions for market-led growth and for enhancing export competitiveness, widening the opportunities for all;
4. improving human development in all regions of the country, be it rural or urban, north, west, central, or east.

REFERENCES

Barungi, B., and E. Zepeda, 2005. 'The challenge of pro-poor growth in Uganda', *One Pager* 11, International Poverty Centre. New York: UNDP.

Selassie, A. A., 2008. 'Beyond macroeconomic stability: the quest for industrialisation in Uganda', Working Paper WP/08/231. Washington, DC: IMF.

Ssewanyana, S. N., and J. A. Okidi, 2007. 'Poverty estimates from Uganda National Household Survey III, 2005/2006', Occasional Paper 34, Economic Policy Research Center, Kampala.

United Nations Development Programme, 2007. *Uganda Human Development Report: Rediscovering Agriculture for Human Development*. Kampala: UNDP.

—— 2009. *Africa Human Development Report*. Draft, 22 October: *Building on Success: An Agenda for the Human Developmental State*. New York: UNDP.

Zambia
Bringing Back the Shine

Situmbeko Musokotwane and Vinayak Nagaraj

1. Looking back

Tracing the history of most modern African countries, the borders of which were decided by colonial masters many thousands of kilometres away, is at best a daunting task. Zambia is no exception to this, although what is known is that it has served as a melting pot of cultures over many centuries (Roberts 1976). The Bushmen, the Bantus, the great kingdoms of the Bemba, Lozi, Chewa, and Lunda all flourished on the vast and fertile land that Sir David Livingstone would later explore and fall in love with, and where Frederick Russell Burnham would, in 1895, alter the course of Zambia's economic history forever by announcing the find of rich copper deposits. It is a tragedy, then, that Zambia's modern economic history in its entirety could be summarized by the distressing comparison that every student of macroeconomics learns in her first class: that Zambia's per capita income at independence, in 1964, was three times higher than that of South Korea, and that by 2008, South Korea's per capita income was seventeen times higher (World Bank 2008a). Between 1945 and 1974, Zambia was one of the most successful global economic growth stories, between 1975 and 1991, the 'dark age' of Zambia's economic history, it was one of the worst (Hill and McPherson 2004).

This incredible erosion of wealth can be attributed to the failed social experiment of the then ruling United National Independence Party (UNIP). Beginning with a nationalization drive in 1968, followed by the single-party declaration of 1972, Zambia witnessed a steady decline of her productive assets and institutions. By 1975, when Kaunda delivered his famous 'watershed speech' abolishing freehold land, everything from cinemas to newspapers had been taken over by the Party (*Economist* 1975). Nor was Zambia's main export and source of economic prosperity, copper, spared. Copper mines were nationalized under the umbrella of Zambia Consolidated Copper Mines (ZCCM), and went into spiralling decay, with production falling from a peak of 720,000 metric tonnes in 1973 to a low of 226,000 by 2000 (according to data from the Ministry of Mines).

Over the next two decades, it is estimated that over US$12 billion of capital left the country, resulting in a catastrophic decline in economic activity (Hill and McPherson

2004). By 1991, when multi-party elections were restored and UNIP ousted, Zambia's economy was at its lowest point. The external debt stock was in excess of US$7 billion, 200% of the country's GDP and over three times its annual exports (IMF 1989). While formal poverty comparisons are unavailable, real per capita incomes in 1991 were about a third of 1975 levels, and over 60% of the population lived below the poverty line (IMF 1991; PIC 1991).

The new government that came to power in 1991 implemented painful but far-reaching structural reforms to eliminate economic distortions that included the elimination of maize subsidies, introduction of cash budgeting, establishment of a revenue authority, downsizing of the public service, and liberalization of trade and exchange rate restrictions (Hill and McPherson 2004). In 1996 the government began the process of privatizing copper mines, and by 2000 the sale of ZCCM was completed, paving the way for the revival of the industry. By 2001 there were clear signs of a copper revival, although there were initial hiccups as a result of low international copper prices. Alongside the copper revival, there was also an effort to improve economic governance. In parallel to the above reforms, the government implemented measures aimed at strengthening the public financial management system and conduct of monetary policy. The introduction of cash budgeting and commitment controls improved budget management, freeing up resources to support private-sector credit growth. Simultaneously, tax reforms that had started in the 1990s boosted revenue collection. These measures combined to rein in the budget deficit and support liquidity management. Annual inflation, which had reached 188% in 1993, was brought down to 19% by 2001. Real economic growth also improved substantially from an average of 0.72% in the period 1975–90 to an average of 4% in the period 1991–2010. With the improved macroeconomic environment, Zambia attained its HIPC completion point in 2005, and received MDRI assistance in 2006. As a result, the country's external debt stock, which had reached a high of 415% of GDP in 1986 and averaged 215% of GDP between 1990 and 2000, fell to 24% of GDP in 2006, offering the hope of fiscal space for the first time in three decades.

2. **Looking ahead**

For the first time, there is a genuine feeling of hope that Zambia's economic troubles are behind her. Over the last five years, Zambia's economy has experienced a transformation, with real GDP growth averaging close to 6%, and inflation falling to single-digit levels. Copper production has exceeded its historic peak of 720,000 tonnes per annum, and is on track to reach 1 million tonnes by 2015. Investments in other mineral exploration, such as nickel, manganese, gemstones, and uranium, have yielded positive results, and are expected to play a key role in Zambia's long-term growth prospects.

The government has embarked on efforts to diversify the economy away from copper dependence. Close to half of Zambia's land is arable, but only around 15% is under cultivation, and a much smaller fraction under irrigation (Bank of Zambia 2003). With improvements in plant and animal disease control, studies have shown that Zambia could emerge a regional leader in crop and livestock exports (World Bank 2011). Under the right conditions, beef could become Zambia's next copper. An abundance of hydroelectric potential is also expected to be a source of diversification. It is estimated that less than a third of Zambia's electricity potential has been tapped, despite having close to 40% of the region's water resources (World Bank 2008b). Tourism also holds great promise for a country that has abundant nature and wildlife.

While economic prospects look bright for Zambia, there remains a considerable challenge in translating these prospects into improvements in the livelihoods of ordinary citizens. Despite the impressive growth performance over the last decade, over 75% of Zambia's rural population still remain below the poverty line (Central Statistical Organization 2006), over 80% of the total population lives below the $2 a day threshold, and close to 90% of Zambia's labour force works in the informal sector.

Domestic revenues are well below potential, due to poorly negotiated mining development agreements. In 2010, the mining sector contributed roughly 2% of total domestic revenues (IMF 2010), disproportionately below its contribution to GDP (about 19%: Ministry of Finance and National Planning 2008), and far lower than the average in Zambia's peer group of natural-resource-rich countries. On the expenditure side, exponential real increases in annual wage awards have eroded the capacity of the budget to support much-needed capital expenditure. Without serious reform, these trends could wipe out the gains made over the last ten years and once again make Zambia a textbook example of poor economic management.

Overcoming these challenges should be the main focus of reform over the coming years for Zambia to attain its vision of 'becoming a prosperous middle-income country by 2030' (Ministry of Finance and National Planning 2007). This vision is by no means out of reach, but will require firm, reform-minded resolve from Zambians. The private sector in particular, which has for so long been a neglected participant in the economy, must lead the effort to translate macroeconomic prosperity into meaningful social benefit, as the public sector will never be able to play the transformational role that private enterprise and entrepreneurship can. For their part, successive governments must continue to realize that in a country of about 12 million people, Zambia's economic prosperity lies in its ability to look outwards and embrace investors and markets across the world, much as East Asia did in the latter part of the last century.

Zambia enjoys abundant natural resources that are, arguably, unrivalled in the region. Since independence she has been an oasis of peace and stability, and showed great economic promise for a fleeting moment in time. Many Zambians were lucky enough to witness that promise, while a great many others were born into an era of economic despair and extreme poverty. The time has come for us to bring back Zambia's shine.

REFERENCES

Bank of Zambia, 2003. Zambia Agricultural Investment Promotion Conference, Lusaka, 23–5 November.
Economist, 1975. 'The banks stay' (5 July).
Central Statistical Organization, Government of Zambia 2006. *Living Conditions Monitoring Survey* (revised). Lusaka.
Hill, Catharine B., and Malcom F. McPherson, 2004. *Promoting and Sustaining Economic Reform in Zambia*. Cambridge, Mass.: Harvard University Press.
International Monetary Fund, 1989. *International Financial Statistics*. Washington, DC.
—— 1991. *International Financial Statistics*. Washington, DC.
—— 2010. *Zambia: Fifth Review Under the Three-Year Arrangement Under the Extended Credit Facility. Staff Notes*. Washington, DC.
Ministry of Finance and National Planning, Republic of Zambia, 2007. *National Long Term Vision 2030* (*Vision 2030*). Lusaka.
—— 2008. 'Annual Business Survey First Phase'. Unpublished draft.
Prices and Incomes Commission, Government of Zambia, 1991. *Household Expenditure and Incomes Survey*. Lusaka.
Roberts, Andrew, 1976. *A History of Zambia*. London: Heinemann.
World Bank, 2008a. *World Development Indicators 2008*. Washington DC.
—— 2008b. 'Zambia Country Water Resources Assistance Strategy' Draft, Africa Region Water Resources Unit, Washington, DC.
—— 2011. 'Jobs and prosperity: building Zambia's competitiveness', World Bank Analytical Study. Washington, DC.

Zimbabwe
Returning from the Brink

Kupukile Mlambo

1. Introduction

Zimbabwe is close to emerging from a deep political and economic crisis which is the result of poor governance and an unstable political environment. The crisis saw prolonged hyperinflation, exchange rate collapse, shortages of essential goods and services, and a mass exodus of close to 3 million Zimbabweans, exacerbated by isolation from the international community. This is certainly different from the early post-independence years, when the country had one of the strongest and more diversified economies in sub-Saharan Africa. At independence in 1980, per capita GNP stood at US$930 (atlas method), manufacturing value added accounted for 23% of GDP, while agriculture produced a food surplus that made Zimbabwe a regional food basket.

A series of events, starting from 1997 with the 70% fall in the value of the Zimbabwean dollar, drove the economy to near collapse. During the ensuing ten years (1997–2007), Zimbabwe's real GDP fell by 40%, while per capita income fell from US$660 to US$340. By 2008, Zimbabwe had the highest inflation on record, which reached 231 million per cent in July of that year. By some accounts, many of the macro- and socioeconomic indicators resembled those of a country going through a war situation (Moss 2007).

2. The genesis of the crisis: a failed land reform programme

In explaining Zimbabwe's challenges, most analysts focus on immediate causes, including the unbudgeted payments to war veterans in 1997, the country's participation in the DRC conflict in 1998, the violent seizure of white farms from 2000 onwards, mismanagement of the national economy, including the quasi-fiscal expenditures by the Reserve Bank, and the intolerance of the incumbent regime to political opposition (Davies 2003).

However, deeper analysis suggests that the crisis has historical roots, and to a large extent reflects the shortcomings of the Lancaster House agreement, which failed to deal adequately with the issues of inequality, especially the racial distribution of land. At independence in 1980, some 4,500 white famers owned close to 45% of the country's arable land. For the first ten years of independence, the constitution prevented the government from forcibly acquiring white-owned land. Farms could only be acquired on a 'willing seller, willing buyer' basis under which government was able to acquire only 3.2 million hectares, and on which more than 50,000 families were resettled.

With the expiration of the Lancaster House agreement in 1990, the government amended the constitution and passed the 1992 Land Acquisition Act, which inter alia allowed the state to acquire land for resettlement without recourse to the market. Farmers whose lands were acquired were to be awarded a 'fair' price fixed by a committee of six, using guidelines that did not necessarily follow market principles. Curiously, government appeared less inclined to move faster on land reform, only resettling fewer than 20,000 families by 1997, against the target of 110,000 (see UNDP 2008). And by the mid-1990s, the programme was increasingly being criticized for its slowness and for benefiting mostly the political elite. Moreover, external funding for the programme dried up as the British government and other donors became increasingly reticent in providing more resources for a land resettlement programme that appeared to benefit only the political elites.[1]

The post-independence government also faced the dilemma of addressing the inherited inequalities that included not only land but access to jobs and social services without harming the main growth drivers in agriculture, manufacturing and mining (Mlambo and Kayizzi-Mugerwa 1991). After a decade of experimenting with socially oriented and inward-looking programmes that included the Growth with Equity Strategy and the Transitional National Development Plan, in 1991 the authorities finally adopted the Economic Structural Adjustment Programme (ESAP), which was underwritten by international financial institutions. While improving macroeconomic stability, and resulting in modest economic growth, its social impacts were controversial. In the labour market, the introduction of ESAP led to wholesale restructuring as wage and employment protection regulations were removed, leading to labour retrenchment in both the private and public sectors (Ncube 2000). At the same time, the economy was not growing fast enough to absorb the 300,000 or so school leavers joining the job market every year.

The shortcomings of the land reform programme and the failure of the economy to provide jobs against the backdrop of policies and practices that stifled the growth of the informal sector led to growing urban discontent in the 1990s. Urban unemployment was rising, wages were falling at a time of rising food prices, and the state was becoming increasingly intolerant and heavy-handed in dealing with dissent. In the midst of this, the Fast Track Resettlement programme targeting white-owned farms by war veterans failed to

---

[1] In 1997 the UK Minister for International Development, Claire Short, wrote to the Government of Zimbabwe absolving Britain of any responsibility of meeting the cost of land purchase.

solve the land problem and the problem of food insecurity. Between 1998 and 2007, commercial production of food crops declined by 42% (UNDP 2008).

3. Emerging from the crisis

In September 2008 Zimbabwe's political parties reached an agreement followed by the establishment of a Unity Government in February 2009, which included the three main political parties.[2] The Unity Government has instituted a short-term emergency recovery programme (STERP), which places emphasis on ensuring political stability and good governance, social protection and promoting macroeconomic stability. However, STERP was premised on quick and substantial financial support from the international community, which did not materialize.

STERP has made progress in addressing some of the symptoms of the economic crisis, such as eliminating hyperinflation and improving the supply of goods in the market, but it remains essentially focused on dealing with short-term challenges. Policy should now focus on developing a more transformative medium- to long-term economic development strategy. One such strategy will be a mix of enhancing export competitiveness and promoting domestic demand-led growth in which the revival of agriculture will be critical.

3.1. MAKING ZIMBABWE MORE COMPETITIVE

Exports remain an important source of growth for Zimbabwe, given the small size of the domestic market. Exports are critical for the recovery of the manufacturing sector (Hawkins and Ndlela 2009). Monetary and exchange rate policies are key tools for economic management, especially where competitiveness is a major goal. In January 2009, the Zimbabwean economy became officially dollarized, with the US dollar and the South African Rand operating as de facto national currencies, to all intents and purposes replacing the collapsed Zimbabwean dollar. This served the function of stabilizing prices and eliminating hyperinflation. However, as Hawkins and Ndlela (2009) note, dollarization implies that the government does not have the luxury of manipulating the exchange rate to enhance competitiveness. Instead, government should focus on improving the investment climate through better infrastructure, improved access to finance, and a regulatory framework characterized by protection of property rights and respect for rule of law.

---

[2] The GPA allowed for the creation of the post of Prime Minister and two Deputy Prime Ministers. The leader of the Movement for Democratic Change (MDC), Morgan Tsvangirai, assumed the post of Prime Minister, while Robert Mugabe retained the post of President.

3.2. GENERATING DEMAND-LED GROWTH THROUGH REVIVAL OF AGRICULTURE

While export competitiveness remains critical for sustained economic growth, the need to stimulate domestic drivers of growth, such as boosting domestic demand, cannot be ignored. According to Palley (2002), demand-led growth rests on four pillars: income distribution; getting the macroeconomic environment right (especially financial stability); good governance; and adequate and fairly priced development finance. The policy enablers include a combination of strong institutions, labour market reforms, appropriate reform and regulation of the financial sector, and increased development assistance, including debt relief. Zimbabwe has problems of sluggish wage growth, low government revenues and levels of development assistance, and debt distress.

Over the medium to long term, government has to address these constraints in order to generate sustained economic growth. Agricultural revitalization and recovery will play a critical role in accelerating economic growth. By increasing incomes and assets for farmers, wages of farm workers, and generating non-agricultural employment through backward and forward linkages, reviving agriculture has the potential to boost domestic demand and become an engine of recovery and sustained growth.

Agricultural recovery requires the availability of critical inputs, increased efficiency and productivity, support to new farmers through access to credit and extension services, better marketing, and ownership. Land reform, including a land audit, will form an important part of the strategy to revive agricultural productivity. In addition, government will need to address a number of issues related to property rights and fair compensation for the previous owners, and incentives for new owners to use land productively and invest in land improvement.

4. Conclusion

Generating sustained economic growth in Zimbabwe will primarily depend on revitalizing the agricultural sector. Agriculture is critical for export growth and increasing household consumption. But reviving the country's agriculture crucially depends on finding a lasting resolution to the land ownership problem, which is at the heart of the chaos. Given the emotions that surround the issue, a mixture of fair compensation and restitution may offer a way out.

REFERENCES

Davies, R., 2003. Review of C. Jenkins and J. Knight, *The Economic Decline of Zimbabwe: Neither Growth nor Equity*, *Journal of Economic Literature* 41.3, 938–40.

Hawkins, T., and D. B. Ndlela, 2009. 'Foreign trade, competitiveness and the balance of payments', Comprehensive Economic Recovery in Zimbabwe, Working Paper 6. Harare: UNDP.

Mlambo, K., and S. Kayizzi-Mugerwa, 1991. 'The macroeconomics of transition: Zimbabwe in the 1980s', *African Development Review* 3.1, 47–67.

Moss, Todd, 2007. 'Zimbabwe's meltdown: anatomy of a peacetime economic collapse', *Fletcher Forum of World Affairs* 31.2, 133–48.

Ncube, M., 2000. 'Employment, unemployment and the evolution of labour policy in Zimbabwe', *Zambezia* 27.2, 161–94.

Palley, T., 2002. 'Domestic demand-led growth: a new paradigm for development', in D. Jacobs, J. Weaver and J. Baker (eds.), *After Neo-liberalism: Economic Policies That Work for the Poor in New Rules for Global Finance*, Washington, DC.

Palmer, R., 1990. 'Land reform In Zimbabwe, 1980–1990', *African Affairs* 89.355, 163–81.

United Nations Development Programme, 2008. 'Comprehensive economic recovery in Zimbabwe: a discussion document'. Harare.

INDEX

Aassve, A. 487
Abacha, President 559
Abdelkhalek, T. 435
Abdulai, A. 83
Abdullah, I. 570
Abradu-Otoo, P. 363
absorptive capacity 321, 324, 325
accountability 209, 211, 212, 221
   Algeria 425, 426
   Angola 429
   DRC 464, 465
   electoral 194, 195–6
   and inflation 359, 361
   political 228, 399–400
   public sector 426
   Sierra Leone 570
   Sudan 596
   Tanzania 609
   see also democracy; governance
Accra Agenda for Action 91
Acemoglu, D. 11, 201, 202, 205, 216, 217, 237, 253, 399
Acumen Fund 96
Adam, C. 354, 389
Adams, A. 202
Adedokun, O. A. 189
Adepoju, A. 187, 189
Africa Growth and Opportunity Act (AGOA) 62, 171, 396, 510, 512, 513
African Commission 35, 290, 337
African Development Bank (AfDB) 27, 49, 90–1, 259, 466
African Economic Research Consortium 7
African Union 54, 239, 259, 337
African Water Facility (AWF) 420
age dependency 161
Aghion, P. 236
Agrawal, A. 406, 407
agricultural productivity:
   Burundi 453–5
   and land security 410–13
   Rwanda 562–3
   of women 277
agriculture:
   Benin 442
   and climate change 148–50, 157
   collective farming 13

   Côte d'Ivoire 470–1
   and development 70–78
   Egypt 478
   employment 299, 571
   and environmental services 72, 74
   Equatorial Guinea 479
   Ethiopia 489
   green revolution 11, 35, 38, 39
   Guinea 479–80
   Guinea Bissau 503–4
   interest groups 227–8
   large farms 76, 189
   Mali 530–1
   Mauritania 536
   Mozambique 547
   need for strong state 72
   Nigeria 556
   outgrower-based production 219
   potential 240–2, 242
   private sector 312
   product demand 176–7
   productivity 35, 70, 74–5, 299
   rainfed 74, 417
   relative rates of assistance (RRA) 226
   resource saving 72, 74
   Rwanda 563
   Senegal 567
   smallholders 72, 75–7, 572
   subsistence farming 72
   Sudan 598–9
   Swaziland 602
   Tanzania 607–8
   taxation 225–6
   technology 291–2
   Togo 612
   transition out of 140
   value added 298–9
   workers' nutrition 255
   yields 76
   Zambia 628
   Zimbabwe 633
   see also food
Agriculture for Development Strategy Papers (ADSPs) 72
agro-processing 73, 163
Ahmed, A. 82

aid 190, 329
  allocation criteria 90-1
  budget support 92, 95
  business models 95-6
  conditionality 92
  criticized 87-8
  crowding-out effects 91-2
  and democracy 91-2
  dependency 571
  and development 86-93
  effectiveness 91, 96-7
  food 83-4
  impact analysis 87-8
  institutions for managing 120
  official 94, 97
  private 94-8
  quality of 35
  and shock-dampening 89-90
  tied 178-9
  volatility and unpredictability 89
    see also food aid; Official Development Assistance
aid-for-trade 55-7
Aijar, S. 350
Ajayi, S. I. 321, 323, 324
Akinboade, O. 324
Akresh, R. 125
Aksum 202
Al-Sanarri, S. 271
Alderman, H. 45, 247, 256
Alesina, A. 194, 195
Alfaro, L. 325
Algeria 424-8
  commodity price shocks 424
  competitiveness 427
  cultural factors 432-3
  development performance 430-6
  diversification 426
  Economic Recovery Programmes 427
  education 428, 431
  effect of global financial crisis 424
  external debt 425
  financial reform 377-8
  food security 427
  governance 425
  oil 424-5
  political reform 425-6
  poverty reduction 431-3
  social policies 431, 434-5
Ali, A. G. 264
Allen, F. 367, 368
Amanor, K. 410
Amprou, J. 90
Angola 80, 438-40
  and China 439-40
  financial indicators 439
  oil 333, 389, 438, 439
  population 438
  poverty 439
Annan, J. 125, 127
Annez, P. 19
anti-growth syndrome 236
antiretroviral therapies (ARTs) 258
antiretrovirals (ARVs) 261, 262
Appiah, E. N. 269, 270
Arbache, J. S. 305
Armendariz de Afhion, B. 46
Arndt, C. 254
Arnell, N. W. 149
Artadi, E. V. 169, 266, 270, 433
Aryeetey, E. 7, 11, 180, 377, 414, 494, 495
Asafu-Adjaye, J. 150
Asante, Y. 324
Aschauer, D. A. 338
Ashraf, N. 248, 290
Asian Drivers 174-80
  as competitors 175-6
  imports of primary commodities 176-7
Asiedu, E. 323, 330, 331
Atienza, J. 94
Atta, J. K. 444
Austen, R. A. 203
Austin, G. 412
authoritarianism 224-6
    see also governance
Avocksouma, D. A. 461
Aylmer, G. E. 202
Ayogu, M. 337, 338
Aysan, A. F. 618
Azam, J.-P. 16, 110, 111, 113, 230, 460
Azikiwe, Nnamdi, President 183

Bagaza, Jean Baptiste 451
Bagchi, A. K. 296
Baird, S. 289
Bakker, J. I. H. 202
balance of payments 10, 325, 354, 449
Baldwin, R. 339
Baliamoune, M. N. 542
Ban Ki-moon 337
Banerjee, A. 95
Bangladesh 38
Bank of Credit and Commerce (BCCI) 375
banks 143, 369-70, 374-8
  branchless 383-4
  colonial 374
  competitiveness 377-8
  concentrated structure 368
  foreign ownership 374, 375-6
  intra-African 375
  Islamic 376

and microfinance 383
privatization 366
regulation 368, 369, 375, 376
see also financial system
Banque Centrale des États de l'Afrique de l'Ouest (BCEAO) 503
Barker, D. J. P. 247
Barrett, C. B. 44, 79, 80, 83, 247
Barro, R. J. 182, 253, 266
Barron, J. 417
Barrow, E. 402
Barwa, S. D. 142
Bates, R. 66, 216, 225
Bates, R. H. 202, 495
Bates, R. J. 226, 228, 229, 230
Baum, M. 197
Bazika, B. 466
Beegle, K. 43, 44, 45
Bell, C. 254
Bellows, J. 125
Ben, Ali, President 196
Benabou, R. 194
Bene, C. 402
Benhabib, J. 181
Benin 190, 240, 441–3
Benjamin, N. 568
Bennell, P. 271
Berg, A. 350, 361
Berge, K. 168
Berhane, M. 183
Bernanke, B. S. 360
Berry, J. 248, 290
Berry, S. 412
Berthélemy, J.-C. 161, 271, 300
Besley, M. 194
Besley, T. 209, 390, 410
Bevan, D. 354
Bhargava, A. 182
Bhattacharya, R. 99
Bhattacharyya, S. 390
Bhorat, H. 577
Bibi, S. 430
Biggs, T. 318, 338
Bigsten, A. 166, 168, 171, 306, 309
Bill and Melinda Gates Foundation 96
Binningsbø, H. M. 118
biodiversity 149, 407
Björkman, M. 214, 247
Black Death 205
Blanchflower, D. 137
Blankespoor, B. 20
Blattman, C. 124, 125, 129
Bliss, C. 252
Block, S. A. 226
Bloom, D. E. 254, 285

board of directors 584
chairman 586, 591, 594
characteristics of 586
and company performance 585–7
composition 586, 587, 590, 592, 594
size 586, 587, 591, 593, 594
Bodea, C. 118
Booth, D. 216
Borenzstein, E. 324, 325
Bosnia Herzegovina 117
Bosworth, B. P. 160
Botswana 359, 375, 444–6
demography 284, 285
diamonds 218, 388, 389, 390, 400, 446
governance 202, 217, 240, 399
landlocked 59
real exchange rate 444–5
sectoral productivity 445–6
Bourguiba, Habib 616
Bourguignon, F. 235
Bourse régionale des valeurs mobilières (BVRM) 371
brain circulation 183–4, 184–5
brain drain 6, 181–5
see also human capital; migration
Brasselle, A.-S. 411
Bratton, M. 201
Bravo-Ortega, C. 398
Brazil 38, 39, 177, 196, 408
Brenner, R. 205
Brenton, P. 55
Brewer, J. 202
Britain *see* United Kingdom
Brown, D. 196
Brownbridge, M. 374, 375
Bruck, T. 125
Buckle, R. 19
budget 389
constraints 14, 113, 346–7, 353
deficits 345–6
household 260
and natural resources 396, 400
support 91–3, 95
transparency 195
see also fiscal policy
Budina, N. 557
Bundervoet, T. 125
Bundy, C. 205
Burgess, N. D. 404
Burgess, R. 168
Burkino Faso 43, 59, 83, 220, 448–50
Burnham, Frederick Russell 626
Burnside, C. 88, 90
Burundi 451–5
agricultural productivity 453–5
ethnic conflict 452–3, 454

Burundi (cont.)
  landlocked 59, 61, 64, 66, 242
  political stability 452-3
  unemployment 454-5
business environment 171, 397
  Algeria 427
  Côte d'Ivoire 473
  defined 166-7
  Mauritania 536
  Republic of Congo 466
  Senegal 569
Buyoya, Pierre 451
Buys, P. 339

Cadot, O. 305
Cai, X. 416
Caines, K. 11
Calderon, C. 337, 338, 339, 340
Caldwell, J. C. 282, 283, 284
Caldwell, P. 283, 284
Calvo, C. 45
Cameroon 80, 389, 457-9
  Growth and Employment Strategy Paper (GESP) 457-8
Campbell, A. 195
Campos, J. E. L. 219
Canada 511
Cape Verde 31, 83, 182, 242, 285
capital:
  costs 169
  deepening 167
  micro-economics of 125-9
  physical 125-6, 133
  social 129
  see also human capital
capital flows 6, 10, 324, 596
  and exchange rate policy 356-7
  private 367
Cardi, E. 236
Carey, K. 166
Carkovic, M. 334
Carrere, C. 305
Carrington, W. J. 182
cash transfer programmes 289-90
cashews 502-4
CEMAC 460, 465
cement 567
Central African Republic (CAR) 59, 66
CFA Franc zone 352-6, 359, 361, 362, 479, 524
Chad 460-2:
  governance 461-2
  landlocked 59, 60, 66
  leakage 210-12
  oil production 460-1
Chambas, G. 354
Chandra, V. 218

Chang, H.-J. 38
Charumilind, C. 236
Chaudhury, N. 212
Chauvet, L. 89
Chawdhury, A. R. 542
Chen, 235
Chen, M. 140, 142
Chen, S. 11
Chenery, H. 298, 397
Chhatre, A. 407
childbearing 253
children:
  malnutrition 44-45
  mortality levels 208, 244, 245, 284
  undernourishment 81-2
Chile 38, 218
China 26, 38, 164, 314, 397
  agricultural imports 176-7
  aid 174, 178, 178-9
  and Angola 439-40
  demand for primary products 163
  development model 115
  education 269, 291
  emigration 182
  Forum on China-Africa Cooperation (FOCAC) 177
  Going Global 177-9
  high-technology products 176
  investment in Africa 337
  a learning approach 218
  structural shift 50
  see also Asian Drivers
Chipeta, C. 64, 66
Christiaensen, L. 44, 45
Chung, K. E. 586
Cisco Networking Academy 96
citizen report cards (CRCs) 212
citizens, well-informed 29
civil servants 31, 112, 297, 467
civil wars *see* conflict; violence; wars
Clarke, G. 366
Clarke, G. R. G. 308
Clemens, M. 6, 182, 271
Clements, B. J. 99
clientalist state structure 520
climate change 26, 27, 146-53, 407
  adaptation to 151-2
  and agriculture 35, 148-50, 157
  consequences of 19-20, 21, 87
  discounting fallacy 155-6
  and future generations 155-7
  health effects 156
  mitigation 152, 155, 419
Cline, S. 416
Cline, W. 148, 150
Clinton, Hillary 440

clusters *see* industrial clusters
Cobham, D. 354
cocoa 412, 471
coffee 471
Cohen, J. 247, 290
Collier, P. 16, 17, 26, 27, 28, 29, 70, 92, 118, 120, 124, 169, 171, 216, 220, 224, 225, 230, 242, 305, 338, 340, 388, 390, 391, 397, 399, 473, 488, 508, 563
Collins, S. 160
colonial banks 374
colonial extractive industries 253
colonialism 616
   currency boards under 374
   elections under 224
   impact on institutions 205
   land tenure 404
   legacy 4, 51, 61, 270, 355, 544
Commission for Africa 35, 290, 337
Commission on Growth and Development 215–16
commodities:
   Asian imports 176–7
   global demand 161, 163
   prices 333, 399–400, 424
Common Market of Southern and Eastern Africa (COMESA) 54, 465, 507, 508, 550
Common Monetary Area (CMA) 549
Comoros 242
comparative advantages 48, 73, 163, 168–9
   described 166–7
   dynamic 167
   institutional 167
   policies to increase 170–1
   recycling 176
competitiveness:
   Algeria 427
   Lesotho 511
   Republic of Congo 467–8
   Tunisia 618–19
Comprehensive African Agriculture Development Programme (AWF) 420
conflict 16–17, 21, 87
   Chad 461
   and development 110–13
   ethnic 452–3, 454
   and famine 81
   and land tenure 410, 413
   postwar growth 17, 48
   resolution 194, 196–7
   Sudan 597
   see also violence; war
conflict-poverty trap 115
Congo, Democratic Republic of (DRC) 80, 242, 463–5
   Bushong and Lele 203–4
   OHADA treaty 465
   resources-for-infrastructure deals 464–5
   Rwanda peace agreement 464, 465
Congo, Republic of:
   civil servants 467
   competitiveness 467–8
   entrepreneurship 466–8
contagion 162
contraceptives 284
contracts 76
control regimes 224–5
convertability guarantee 361
Conway, G. 27
Cooper, F. 205
copper 389, 626, 627
Corbridge, S. 19
Corden, W. M. 354
Cornia, G. A. 435
Cornwall, A. 274, 275
corporate governance 584–94
corruption 37, 195, 196, 368, 389, 400, 425
   costs of 29, 31, 113, 340
   Eritrea 485
   and FDI 326
   Guinea 499–500
   landlocked countries 65
   Liberia 515
   Nigeria 555, 557, 558, 559
   Rwanda 562
   Sierra Leone 570–1
   Sudan 597–8
Corruption Perception Index (CPI) 500
costs:
   capital 169
   of corruption 29, 113, 340
   of doing business 308, 313–15
   transaction 169, 338, 397
Côte d'Ivoire 112, 255, 331, 470–3
Country Policy and Institutional Assessment (CPIA) 90
Court, J. 485
Cox, A. 495
credible commitment capacity 113
credit:
   access to 141, 143, 277–8, 316–18
   cost of 372
   markets 252, 376–7, 378
   microcredit 278, 279–80
   private provision 367
   see also banks; debt; microfinance
Cremers, K. J. M. 584
crime 42
crowding out 325
Cuddington, J. T. 263
Cull, R. 366
currency:
   devalued 527–8, 566–9
   overvalued 169

currency (*cont.*)
  substitution 574
  undervalued 115, 120–1
currency swap arrangements 164
Custom and Economic Union of Central Africa 467

Dakor-Ngor Declaration 284
Dambisa, M. 217
Daniels, P. 389
Dasgupta, P. 29, 82
Datt, G. 435, 525
Datta, B. 296
Davies, R. 630
Davies, V. A. B. 571
Ddumba, J. S. 374
de Gregorio, J. 398
De Lorenzo, M. 562
de Mello, L. R. Jr. 324
De Weerdt, J. 43, 45
de-industrialization 297–8, 306–7
Deaton, A. 43
debt:
  contributory factors 100
  domestic 105, 346
  external 99, 228, 497
    African levels of 10
    Algeria 425
    costs of 346
    Egypt 477
    Kenya 505
    Liberia 514–15
    Nigeria 556
    relief 99–107, 178, 345, 461, 517, 606
    Sudan 598
  long-term sustainability 107
  Mauritania 536
  overhang 106
  service 105
  see also Highly Indebted Poor Countries; Multilateral Debt Relief Initiative
debt distress indicators 101–2, 104
debt-to-export ratio 105
deficit financing 356
Deichmann, U. 339
demand:
  domestic 142
  final 506–7
Demery, L. 525
democracy 15, 115, 116–19, 194–7, 221, 399
  and aid 92
  and conflict resolution 196–7
  definition 194
  factional and consociational 118
  and growth 194–7

  instrumental value of 194
  Mauritius 540
democratic institutions 16
democratization 278–9
demographic dividend 254, 285
demographic transition 161, 282–6
demography 5, 87
  see also population
Deng Xiaoping 218
Dercon, S. 41–5, 339, 487, 488, 489
Dermigüc-Kunt, A. 377
Desai, R. 96
Desai, R. M. 433
Detragiache, E. 182
Devarajan, S. 254, 263
development:
  and aid 86–93
  assistance 6
  and conflict 110–13
  micro-economics 124–9
  policy-plus school 115, 116–19
  politics-plus school 115, 119–21
  post-conflict 115–22
  role of agriculture 70–78
  see also growth; human development
developmental value chain 400
diabetes 255
diamonds 218, 388, 389, 390, 400, 446, 550, 571
disease burden 5, 12
distribution 8–9
  income 254, 339–40
  intertemporal 242
diversification 301, 305
  Algeria 426
  challenge of 400
  economic 298, 299
  of exports 53
  in farming 42–3
  Libya 521
  Mauritius 540
  Morocco 542–3
Djankov, S. 61, 64, 65
Djimtoïnger, N. 460, 461
Djurfeldt, G. 11
Docquier, F. 182, 424
Dollar, D. 88, 90
Douglas, M. 204
Doyle, M. W. 116
Dreher, A. 96
drought 41, 44, 81, 553
Duflo, E. 212, 288
Dunning, J.H. 62
Dupas, P. 247, 290
Durevall, D. 168

earnings per share (EPS) 585–6, 594
East African Community (EAC) 54, 455, 465, 507, 559, 563
Easterbrook, F. 584
Easterlin, R. 283
Easterly, W. R. 86, 182, 184, 217, 230, 330, 348, 349, 434, 473
Economic Commission for Africa 259
economic management 8–10, 65
economic partnership agreements (EPAs) 54
economic sparseness 398
economic stability 216–18, 492, 555, 557
economic structure 396–7
Economic Vulnerability Index (EVI) 89
education 33, 51, 195, 208, 266–72
   Algeria 428
   attainment 267–8
   costs and benefits of 184
   delivery 210–11
   Egypt 435
   enrolment rate 12, 267, 276, 279
   Eritrea 484–5
   female 267
   and human development 270–1
   level of 16
   Mauritania 536, 537
   micro-economics of 126–7
   Mozambique 544, 545, 546
   Namibia 551
   primary 269, 276, 279
   production 268–70
   remedial programme 291
   South Africa 577
   stock and quality 267–9
   teachers 49, 269
   Uganda 270
   see also skills; social policies
efficiency wage hypothesis 252
Egypt 366
   agriculture 478
   banks 376, 377–8
   cultural factors 432–3
   development performance 430–6
   external debt 477
   FDI 322, 477
   poverty reduction 431–3
   social policies 431, 434–5
   state role 475–8
   trade liberalization 477
Egypt Human Development Report (EHDR) 477, 478
Eifert, B. 166, 169, 313, 315
El-Araby, A. 435
Elbadawi, I. A. 16, 99, 100, 118, 120
elections 224, 229
elite capture 195

elite fragmentation 463–4
Emery, J. 319
emigration *see* brain drain; migration
employment:
   in agriculture 299
   determinants of 134–5
   generation 477–8
   Libya 521
   meaning of 133
   with MNCs 51
   Mozambique 546–7
Emran, S. 38
enclave economy 325
Endeley, J. B. 274, 275
Englebert, P. 205
enterprises *see* firms; multinationals
entrepreneurship:
   indigenous 316–18
   polices for 468
   Republic of Congo 466–8
   women 467
environmental degradation 19–20
environmental services 72, 74
environmental sustainability 75
Enyimayew, K. A. 247
Equatorial Guinea 390, 479–82
   agriculture 479
   infrastructural development 480–1
   Recovery and Economic Development Program 479
   Second National Economic Conference 481
equity 48, 535–6, 564
   see also inequality
Eritrea 484–6
   war with Ethiopia 485
Espejo, A. 105
Essama-Nssah, B. 524
Ethiopia 218, 220, 487–90
   agriculture 76, 489
   food aid 83
   footwear 176
   income inequality 488
   landlocked 59, 62
   poverty rate 43–4
   price rises 489
   rural and urban poverty 487, 488
   unemployment 136
   war with Eritrea 485
Ethiopian Rural Household Survey 43
ethnic conflict 452–3, 454
ethnic diversity 230
ethnic minorities 319
ethno-linguistic fragmentation 237
Euro-Med Free Trade Association 424
Euro-Mediterranean free trade area 541
European Commission 92

European Union 361, 541
Ewald, J. 203
ex-combatants 129
exchange rate
    Botswana 444–5
    devaluation 14, 15
    flexibility 360
    floating 352, 354
    Nigeria 557
    nominal 353
    overvalued 314–15, 598
    real 352–3
    regime 353–4
    Zimbabwe 632
exchange rate policy 352–7
    and capital flows 356–7
    conflicting objectives 354
    inflation 354, 356
    and monetary policy 356–7
    theory and evidence 352–5
export processing zone (EPZ) 309–10, 539
exports 9, 309
    agricultural 73
    clothing 396
    diversified 53
    and foreign direct investment (FDI) 324
    natural resources 394–400
    non-transport costs 65
    re-exports 442, 443, 491
    structure 394–6, 397
    see also trade
external debt *see* debt
externalities 13, 39
Extractive Industries Transparency Initiative
    (EITI) 29, 301, 400, 481, 558

factor endowments 168, 398
Fafchamps, M. 61
Faini, R. 183
Falco, P. 133
famine 79, 81
Fan, S. 339
Fattah, Z. 434
Faye 64, 60
Fearon, J. D. 110, 113
Fenno, R. F. 195
Ferraz, C. 196
fertility:
    cultural aspects 283–4
    decline 282, 283, 284–5
Fields, G. 140
Fields, G. S. 135
Filmer, D. 208
Finan, F. 196
financial crisis 49–50, 162

financial market data 371
financial services 292
financial system 365–73
    access to 27, 382
    development 325, 367–8
    and economic performance 365–6
    globalization 367
    governance 370–1
    informal/formal integration 372
    liberalization 360
    regulation 370
    risk 370
    see also banks; microfinance
Findlay, R. 167
Fiorina, M. P. 195
Firer, S. 593
firms:
    size 133, 316
    start-ups 316
    see also multinationals
fiscal deficits 497
fiscal policy 344–50
    cyclical 348
    data 344–50
    Nigeria 556, 560
    and policy integration 350
    sustainability 347–8, 349
    see also budget
fiscal rule, oil price-base (OPFR) 558
fiscal space 349
Fischel, D. 584
fishing 179, 502, 504, 536
flying geese hypothesis 176
Fogel, R. W. 255
food:
    aid 83–4
    exports 395
    prices 73, 80–1, 363, 449
    security 72, 73–4, 79–82, 419, 427, 574
    see also agriculture
foreign direct investment (FDI) 190, 321–6,
    329–35
    absorptive capacity for 321,
    324, 325
    by sector 322–3
    challenges to 333–4
    determinants of 323–4
    Egypt 477
    and exports 324
    in extractive industries 332–4
    and growth 324–5
    Mauritania 536
    natural resources 330
    and poverty reduction 330
    spillover effects of 321

trends 321-3, 330
Tunisia 617
foreign direct investment (FDI) Equatorial
    Guinea 482
foreign exchange 333
    black market 356
    Eritrea 486
foreign trade *see* trade
forest common-pool resources 402-3
forest commons 402-8
    decentralization 405-6, 407-8
    definition 403
    ecosystem services from 403, 406-7
    land tenure in 404-5
Foster, J. 579
Fosu, A. K. 66, 236, 494, 495, 496
Fox, P. 417
fragile-and conflict-affected states (FACS) 17
France 323, 361
Frankel, J. 354, 363
Freedman, C. 359
Fremont-Smith, M. R. 97
Freund, N. 61, 64
Frolich, M. 260, 262

G8 72
G20 53
Gabon 105, 242
Gabriel, H. W. 487
Galal, A. 435
Gallup, J. L. 237, 254
Gambia 240, 375, 491-3, 568
Garcia-Penalosa, C. 236
gas 2, 301, 303, 389
    Algeria 425
    Cameroon 459
    Equatorial Guinea 482
    Libya 519
    Mauritania 536, 537
    Senegal 568, 569
    see also hydrocarbons
Gaspart, F. 411
Gauthier, B. 211, 389
Gebreeyesus, M. 306, 309
Gebremedhin, T. 487
Geda, A. 488
Gelb, A. 166, 313, 396, 399
gender:
    capital distribution 277-8
    definitions 274
    dimension 11
    equality 564
    and human development 274-80
    inequality 277

norms 277
    see also women
Generalised System of Preferences (GSP) 511
Genicot, G. 247
geography 34-5, 236, 237, 397-8, 508
Germany 323, 584
Gersbach, H. 254
Gersovitz, M. 300
Ghana 190, 220, 255, 494-7
    agriculture 76, 240
    Bank of 363
    colonial rule 202, 205
    deficits 497
    education 276
    emigration 182
    employment 136, 139-40, 142
    external debt 105
    food security 76, 80
    human development 496
    land tenure 412-13
    liberalization 494, 495
    vulnerable 190
Ghatak, M. 209
Ghazvinian, J. 113
Ghosh, A. 354
Gibson, J. 340
Glaeser, E. L. 306
Glewwe, P. 255, 269
Glick, P. 255, 262, 279
global developments 26-7
global economy 6-8, 20, 49
global financial crisis 26, 49, 190, 191, 350, 363, 372,
    449, 558
Global Health Partnerships 12
global interdependence 162-4
global policy environment 34
globalization 296, 367
Go, D. 35
Goderis, B. 118, 305
Goheen, M. 413
Gohen, M. 410
gold 531, 607
Goldstein, A. 177
Goldstein, M. 201, 246, 261, 277, 412
Gomanee, K. 88
Gomez-Mejia, L. R. 586
Gompers, P. 584
Google.org 96
Gould, J. 400
governance 34, 51, 500
    Algeria 425
    autocratic regimes 242
    capital 399
    Chad 461-2

governance (cont.)
　corporate 584–94
　DRC 463–5
　good 29, 340
　and growth 36–8
　natural resources 390–1
　no central authority 573–5
　quality 32, 237
　structure 435–6
　Tanzania 609
　　see also accountability; authoritarianism; institutions
government:
　agreements 28
　expenditure 349
　role 384
　　see also state
Gradstein, M. 266, 432, 435
Grant, G. 586, 587
grants 345–6
Greasley, D. 446
Great Zimbabwe 202
greenhouse gases (GHGs) 148
Greenwald, B. 36, 38
Greer, J. 579
Gregorie, J. de 324
Gregory, R. 53
Grimard, F. 340
Gromes, T. 117
Grossman, G. 167, 310
Grossman, M. 259
growth:
　accounting 125
　and democracy 194–7
　and equity 535–6
　exogenous and endogenous 34–5
　export-led 163
　and the financial system 365–6
　and foreign direct investment (FDI) 324–5
　and gender inequality 277
　and governance 36–38
　immiserizing 621
　and income 235–7
　and inequality 235–7
　and infrastructure 338
　long-term 160
　policies for 434
　political economy of 215–22
　pro-poor 433–4, 493, 580–2
　rate 1, 3, 9, 15, 146
　record 33–4, 300–1
　spillovers 55
　stable 90
　sustainable 8, 48–52
　　see also development

Guan Zhong 266
Guillaumont, P. 89, 90, 92
Guillaumont Jeanneney, S. 90, 92
Guinea 255, 316, 499–500
Guinea Bissau 240, 502–4
Gulde, A. 354
Gulf Cooperation Council (GCC) 426
Gunning, J. W. 61, 92, 230, 242, 338, 397
Gupta, S. 166
Gwatkin, D. R. 248
Gyimah-Brempong, K. 11, 266, 269, 270

Habyarimana, J. 263
Haddad, L. 246
Haddad, S. 275
Hall, R. J. 300
Hanna, R. 212
Hanushek, E. A. 266, 268
Harris, J. R. 135, 137, 140
Harrison, A. 332
Harrison, E. 274
Hart, K. 139
Harvey, C. 374, 375
Hausmann, R. 38, 170, 171, 218, 305, 307
Hawkins, T. 632
Hayami, Y. 318
He, R. 95
Headrick, D. 203
health 33–4, 208, 252–6
　and behaviour 246–7
　challenges 244–9
　and climate change 156
　de-worming 270, 290
　delivery 210–11
　disease burden 5, 12
　Eritrea 484–5
　experimental studies 255
　and gender 248
　impact on schooling 255–6
　and income 11
　international comparisons 244–6
　macroeconomic evidence 254–5
　mental 127–8
　microeconomic evidence 124, 255
　of mothers 247
　physical 127
　and productivity 11, 252
　Rwanda 564
　treatment costs 255
　user fees 290–1
　vaccinations 246
　and women 252–3
　　see also HIV/AIDS
health production function 246–7

health services:
  demand for 247–8
  inequalities in 248–9
  user fees 247
Heckman, J. J. 136
Heintz, J. 140
Heller, P. 349
Helpman, E. 167, 398
Henderson, J. V. 306
Henstridge, M. 356
Hermias, J. 95
Herodotus 475
Heuty, A. 349
Highly Indebted Poor Countries (HIPC) 99–107, 461, 606
Hill, C. B. 626, 627
Hill, P. 205, 412
Hinkin, T. 586
Hirata, H. 424
HIV/AIDS 5, 11, 246, 258–64
  access to treatment 258
  and behavioural change 262–3
  challenges from 258–9
  cost of treatment 261–2
  death toll 258
  demand for treatment 261–2
  and economic growth 254–5, 263
  global response 264
  Mozambique 547
  orphans 259
  prevention 292
  transmission 259, 263
  Uganda 622
  women with 253
  see also health
Hoddinott, J. 41, 45, 82, 83, 137, 256
Hodler, R. 390
Hoeffler, A. 16, 118, 124, 390
Hoekman, B. 56
Hoff, K. 38
Hoffman, V. 247, 290
Holla, A. 248, 269
Honohan, P. 355
Hopkins, A. G. 203
Houphouët-Boigny, Felix, President 13, 14, 112, 113
household welfare determination model 259–61
households:
  cash transfer 259
  consumption 337
Howe, R. S. 262
Hsieh, C.-T. 309
Hulten, C. 298
human capital 133, 325, 616
  the evidence 126–7
  in household welfare determination 259–61
  investment in 489
  stock 398–9
  see also brain drain
human capital formation 308
human development 10–13, 20–1
  and education 266, 267, 270–1
  and gender 274–80
  Uganda 621–5
  see also development
human development indicators 1, 2
  see also United Nations
human welfare dimensions 72
Humphreys, M. 39, 125
Hunter, W. 196
Huntington, S. 194
Huppi, M. 524
Hussain, M. 350
Hwang, J. 305, 307
Hyuha, M. 374

Ibrahim Index of African Governance 500
ICS 567–8
Idson, T. L. 133
Ikiara, M. M. 323
Ilahi, N. 340
Imbs, J. 305
immigration *see* migration
imput costs 315
incentive system 472
inclusiveness 51
income:
  and growth 235–7
  and inequality 234, 235–7, 238, 488
  low 16
  productivity and health 11
  share 5
income distribution:
  and infrastructure 339–40
  world 254
  see also distribution; inequality
income-growth elasticity 236
India 38, 340, 408
  education 291
  emigration 182
  growth 174, 397
  interest in Africa 50, 177, 178
  life expectancy 5
  manufactures 163
  see also Asian Drivers
Indonesia 37, 557
industrial clusters 30, 304, 305–6, 309–10, 398
industrialization 296–7

industrialization (*cont.*)
  picking winners 297, 309
  policies for 307–10
  reasons for 304–6
industry, foreign ownership 512
inequality 11, 234–42
  data on 234
  and growth 235–7
  in health 248–9
  and income 234, 235–7, 238
  Kenya 505
  power 278
  South Africa 578–80, 581
  see also equity; income distribution
infant industry argument 13, 57, 170
inflation 9, 161, 217
  and exchange rate policy 353, 354, 356, 528
  trends 361–2
inflation targeting (IT) 357, 359–64
  fully fledged (FFIT) 359–64
  lite (ITL) 362
informal sector 10, 135–6
  links with formal sector 141–2
  productivity 141–3
  self-employed 139–43
  Senegal 568
  Zambia 628
information 26, 212
  asymmetries 256
  gap 371
information technologies enabled services (ITES) 56
information technology 163, 219
  see also technology
infrastructure 337–41, 473
  budgetary deficit 349
  Côte d'Ivoire 473
  Equatorial Guinea 480–1
  Eritrea 485
  and growth 338
  and household consumption 337
  inadequate 61, 308, 392, 473
  and income distribution 339–40
  for manufacturing 170
  micro outcomes 339–40
  need for 320, 326
  private sector provision 341
  and production inputs 337
  social dimensions 339
  spending on 340–1
  and trade 338
innovation 128–9, 298
instability *see* stability
institutions 201–5
  democratic 16
  effects of war on 128–9

  impact of colonialism 4, 205
  for managing aid 120
  multinational 49
  political 65–6
  quality of 65, 208–14
  regional 465
  responsive 21
  transformative 37
  see also governance
insurance 43, 44, 46, 126, 151, 252, 255
  agriculture 82, 413
  aid 90
  companies 606
  health 477, 564
  self- 161, 164
  see also microfinance
integrated water resource management (IWRM) 420
InterAction 94
interest groups 227–8
International Conference on Population and
    Development 284
International Monetary Fund (IMF) 344, 440, 493,
    517, 527, 528, 558
  Articles of Agreement 356
  conditionality programmes 362
  Enhanced Structural Adjustment Facility 492
  Poverty Reduction and Growth Facility
    (PRGF) 103, 492
investment 16, 354
  climate for 307–8, 326
  Eritrea 485
  external 50
  foreign 10
  infrastructure 49
  postwar 48
  private 482
  and property rights 410–11
  public 49, 392, 482
  rates 161
  regional 319
  see also foreign direct investment
Investment Climate Facility for Africa 320
irrigation 416
Irwin, T. 348
Isaksson, A. 298
Ishii, J. 584
Isinika, A. 11
Itzetzki, E. 348
Iyanda, O. 331

Jackman, R. W. 324
Jacoby, H. 255
Jamison, E. A. 266
Jamison, T. J. 266
Japan 38, 176, 511, 584

Jayne, T. 81
Jefferis, K. R. 444
Jensen, M. C. 584, 585, 592
Jensen, R. 340
Jessel, K. A. 586
Johnson, S. 201, 202, 205, 217, 237, 253, 399
Jolliffe, D. 435
Jones, R. 300
Jones, G. 19
Jordan, K. 308
Just, D. R. 247
Justino, P. 124
Justman, M. 266

Kabila, President 463
Kalarickal, J. 19
Kaldor, N. 236
Kaltani, L. 120
Kamara, A. B. 417
Kambou, G. 263
Kamgnia, B. 237
Kanbur, R. 91, 490, 579
Kaplinsky, R. 175, 176
Karam, P. 361
Karl, T. L. 399
Kasekende, L. 356, 377
Kassimir, R. 183
Katseli, L. T. 188
Kauda, President 626
Kaufman, R. R. 196
Kaufmann, D. 500
Kayizzi-Mugerwa, S. 631
Kazianga, H. 43
Kebede, B. 488
Kedir, A. 487, 488
Keefer, P. 197, 463
Kenya 220, 408, 505–8
   agriculture 45, 277
   business in 314, 316
   debt 505
   demography 284
   education 291
   Equity Bank 383
   factor endowments 168
   final demand 506–7
   health 247, 255
   inequality 505
   migration 182, 190
   randomized evaluations 287
   Safaricom 383
   self-employment 139–40, 143
   service sector 507–8
   stock market 366
   trade 508, 562
Keohane, R. 94

Ketkar, S. 350
Keynes, J. M. 1
Khalil, A. 376
Khan, M. 37
Khan, S. 324
Kharas, H. 95, 96
Killick, T. 6
Kim, J.-O. 195
Kimberly Process 29
Kimenyi, M. S. 283
King, M. 585
Kingdom, G. 136, 137
Kinsey, B. 256
Kinsey, W. 45
Kirk, D. 283
Kirkpatrick, C. H. 375
Klassen, S. 277
Klenow, P. 309
Knight, J. 137
Koch, D.-J. 94, 96
Koffi, P. K. 472
Kongo 203–4
Korea 37
Koroma, President 570
Kosaras, A. 97
Kremer, M. 247, 248, 255, 269, 270, 290
Krishnan, P. 43
Kristen, P. 485
Krugman, P. 62, 167, 398
Kuugongelwa-Amadhilla, Saara 550
Kuznets, S. 296

labour:
   incomes 133–4
   price of 132–7
      see also employment; self-employment
labour market 76
   effects of military service 124
   segmentation 51, 136–7
Lake, D. A. 197
Lal, D. 227
Lamanna, F. 277
land:
   banks 414
   distribution 236, 237
   pressure on 18
   property rights 76
   quality 236, 237
   reform programme 630–2
   titling 413
land tenure 410–14
   and agricultural productivity 410–13
   colonial times 404
   communal 410
   in forest commons 404–5

land tenure (*cont.*)
    insecure 410
    Sierra Leone 571–2
landlocked countries 398
    attracting investment 62
    and growth 34, 59–67, 161, 236
    neighbours 59–60, 61, 64
    resource-rich 220
    resource-scarce 30–1, 163, 241
    trading cost indicators 60–1
    transit countries 64
Lane, P. 354
Lankford, B. 417
Laraki, K. 435
Lavy, V. 255
Law, R. C. 203
Lawrence, S. 94
Laxton, D. 359, 361
Le Manchec, M.-H. 105
leadership 216, 219, 220, 222
    Liberia 516
    Rwanda 562–4
leakage 210–11
Leamer, E. 167
learning industrial and technology (LIT) policies 38–9
learning-by-doing 175
Leblang, D. A. 197
Lederman, D. 398
Lee, J.-W. 182, 324
Lee, R. D. 254
Leibenstein, H. A. 252
Leke, A. 300
Lemarchand, R. 452
Lesotho 240, 510–13
    financial sector 512
    foreign banks in 375
    Highlands Water Project (LHWP) 510
    landlocked 59, 60, 62
    textiles 175, 511–13
Levchenko, A. A. 167
Levine, R. 230, 334, 365, 377
Lewis, W. A. 51
Lewis, J. D. 254
Lewis, W. A. 134
Li, H. 195
liberal capitalism 220–1
    partial 220–1
liberalization 326, 360, 494, 495, 542–3
Liberia 196, 514–17
Libya 376, 519–23
life expectancy 3, 5, 244–6, 253, 577
Lim, M. 375
Limam, I. 434
Limaõ, N. 61, 338
Limau, N. 169

Limongi, F. 194
Lin, J. Y. 297, 301
Linnemayr, S. 247
Lipsey, R. 331
liquidity 371
literacy 3, 268
Little. M. D. 227
Livingstone, Sir David 626
Lopamudra, C. 160, 161, 163
Lovejoy, P. E. 204
Low, P.S. 19
Lucas, R. E. 137, 188, 266
Lundberg, M. 277
Luque 268
Lyakurwa, W. 7
Lybbert, J. 45

McCormick, D. 306
McCulloch, N. 488
McDonald, S. 263
McGowan, P. 495
Macias, Francisco, President 479
McIntosh, S. K. 202, 289
McKay, A. 487, 488
McMahon, W. 270
Macmillan, Harold 576
McPherson, M. F. 626, 627
macroeconomics 8–10
    impact at micro level 488
    policies 31
McSharry, B. 399
Madagascar 140, 143, 175, 242, 524–6
Madani, D. 310
Madsen, J. B. 446
Madura, J. 586
Magnac, T. 137
Mahal, A. S. 254
Maimbo, S. 189, 374
Major, S. 96
Makdissi, S. 434
malaria 5
Malawi 59, 60, 76, 271, 289–90,
    527–9
Malaysia 28, 37, 174, 177, 366
Mali 59, 202, 242, 530–4
malnutrition 44–5
Maloney, W. 398
Mamdani, M. 205
Mandela, Nelson 544
Manin, B. 195
Mankiw, N. G. 266
Mannathoko, I. 444
manufacturing 36
    cheap 175
    costs 29–30

exports 395, 396
  informal 140
  labour-intensive 175
  productivity 141
Marchiori, L. 424
Marfouk, A. 182
market:
  capitalization 577
  failures 13, 39, 77, 252
  incentives 48
  size 314, 334
  subregional 54
market-friendly policies 216, 217, 218
Martin, A. D. 586
Martin, C. 197
Maskin, E. 195
Masson, P. 354, 361
Masten, A. S. 127
Masud, N. 96
Mattes, R. 197
Mauritania 242, 535–7
Mauritius 168, 322, 359, 366, 538–40
Maxwell, D. 83
Mayer, J. 168, 397
Mayoux, L. 274
Mbakile, B. 263
Mbaye, A. A. 568
Mehlum, H. 399
Meckling, W. 585
Mellinger, A. D. 254
Mengiste, T. 309
Merrey, D. 418
Messner, D. 175
Metrick, A. 584
Metzler, A. 360
Mexico 366
Meyer, J. 175
Meyerhoefer, C. 244
Michaelowa, K. 269
Micombero, Michel 451
microeconomics:
  and macroeconomics 488
  policies 31
  of post-conflict period 124–9
microfinance 96, 143, 380–5
  and the formal sector 372, 383–4
  funding sources 384–5
  government role 384
  microcredit 278, 279–80
  mission drift 382
  operating costs 382–3
  record of 46, 376, 380–2
  regulation 380
  trends 380–2
Migot-Adholla, S. 412

migration 6, 187–91, 574, 612
  benefits of 187
  causes 187, 189–90
  from Kenya 182
  immigration rules 189
  incentive effect 184–5
  internal and intra-regional 189–90
  mass 181
  return 183–4, 190
  rural to urban 140, 189, 461
  skilled 181–5
  theory 188
  and training costs 191
Miguel, E. 124, 125, 247, 255, 270, 290
Milanovic, B. 432
military coups 14, 230
military service 124
Millenium Development Villages 75
Millennium Ecosystem Assessment 147
Mills, G. 322
Mincer, J. 132
mining 28, 28–9, 253, 332–4, 389, 504
Miroux, A. 375
Mishkin, F. S. 359, 360
Mitiku, W. 266
Mkandawire, M. 64, 66
Mkandawire, T. 37
Mlambo, K. 631
Mobuto, President 463
Moene, K. O. 399
Mölders, F. 96
monetary autonomy 354
monetary policy 353, 356–7, 361
monetary union 357
Monga, C. 297, 300, 301
Monitor group 96
Morduch, J. 41, 46
Morocco 322, 331, 430–6, 541–3
Morris, M. 175
Morris, S. 356
mortality rates:
  adults 41, 43
  declining 283
  infant 208, 244, 245, 253, 284, 622
  maternal 244, 622
  and war 126–7
Mortensen, D.T. 132
Motara, A. 586, 587
Mozambique 80, 240, 544–8
  colonial legacy 544
  conflict 196, 544
  data 547–8
  education 545, 546
  employment 546–7
  HIV/AIDS 547

Mozambique (*cont.*)
  political economy 217, 220
Mugabe, Robert, President 632
Multi Fibre Arrangement (MFA) 175, 511
Multilateral Debt Relief Initiative (MDRI) 10, 99, 103
multinationals 49, 162
  employment 51, 331, 334
  wages 331–2
Murinde, V. 374, 375, 376, 377
Murshed, S. M. 430
Mwabu, G. M. 246, 247
Mwega, F. 324
Mylenko, N. 376
Myrdal, G. 33

Nabli, M. 430
Nabli, M. K. 618
Naipaul, V. S. 538
Nair, V. B. 584
Namibia 196, 331, 549–51
  South West Africa People's Organization (SWAPO) 549
Namubiru-Mwaura, E. 406
Nasser, President 476
Natural Resource Charter 29, 51
natural resources 2, 5, 39
  booms 388–92
  and conflict 16
  Equatorial Guinea 479–82
  exploration and exploitation 28, 389
  exports 394–400
  management of 48, 390–1
  and regime type 230
  rent capture 242, 389
  and rent-seeking 390
  sub-soil assets 28, 389
  transparency 390–1
  use of revenues 390, 391–2
    see also copper; diamonds; gold; hydrocarbons; mining; oil
Naude, W. 426
Nayyer, D. 174
Ncube, M. 631
Ndikumana, L. 452–3
Ndlela, D. B. 632
Ndulu, B. 3, 66, 99, 160, 161, 163, 216, 224–6, 229, 236, 237, 240, 241, 299, 300, 338, 339, 341
Ndung'u, N. S. 99
Nelson, M. A. 197
neo-patrimonialism 216
Nepal 340, 408
networks 318
New Partnership for Africa's Development (NEPAD) 329–30
New Zealand 360

Ngaruko, F. 61, 66, 452–3
NGOs 94, 95, 97
Nguema, Obiang, President 479
Nguyen, T. 99
Nie, N. 195
Niger 59, 83, 242, 552–4
Nigeria 190, 366, 390, 555–60
  agriculture 76, 80, 556
  banks 377–8, 559
  corruption 555, 557, 558, 559
  Economic and Financial Crimes Commission 558
  economic volatility 555, 557
  FDI 322
  fiscal policy 556, 560
  Igbo 203
  insurance 43
  migration 184
  oil 242, 389, 559
  United Bank of Africa 383
  war 111–12
Nigria, Independent Corrupt Practices and other Related Offences Commission 558
Nikiema, B. 275
Nissanke, M. 176, 177, 180, 377
Njinkeu, D. 55, 56
Nkrumah, Kwame, President 13, 14, 183, 304
Nkurunziza, J. 16, 61, 66, 452–3
Noman, A. 33, 35, 37
Northup, D. 203
Nsouli, S. M. 541
Ntibazonkiza, R. 452
Nunnenkamp, P. 96
Nyange, D. 339
Nyarko, Y. 182, 184
Nye, J. S. 94

Obasanjo, President 111, 555, 557, 558
Obura, D. 149
Obwona, M. 324, 325
Ocampos, L. 613
O'Connell, S. A. 3, 28, 160, 225, 230, 355, 494, 508
Oduro, A. D. 274, 279
OECD 83
  Development Assistance Committee (DAC) 178
Official Development Assistance (ODA) 10, 188–9, 330, 554
  see also aid
Ogunkola, E. 324
Oi, W. Y. 133
oil 9, 19–20, 36, 113, 301, 332, 390, 397, 499
  Algeria 424–5
  Angola 438, 439
  Burkino Faso 449
  Chad 460–1
  exports 110–11, 177, 321, 344, 388, 399

Libya 519
Niger 553
Nigeria 242, 389, 559
   prices 1, 14, 33, 161–2, 163, 300
   sub-soil assets 28, 389
   Sudan 596–8, 599
   and war 110–11, 113, 120
oil price-based fiscal rule (OPFR) 558
Okidi, J. A. 622
Okonjo-Iweala, N. 300, 301, 399, 555
Olofsgård, A. 433
Olson, M. 194, 195, 435
Omidyar Network 96
Oostendorp, R. 61
Oosthuizen, M. 577
OPEC 424, 503
openness 48, 49, 216, 217, 218, 320
Oppenheimer, J. 322
Organization for the Harmonization of Business Law 473
Orubuloye, I. O. 283
Osafo-Kwaako, P. 399, 555
Oswald, A. 137
Otchere, I. 365, 366, 372
Otker-Robe, I. 359
Over, M. 255, 261, 262, 263
overseas development aid (ODA) 88, 161, 188–9, 330, 536, 554
Owens, T. 168
Oyejide, T. A. 7, 168
Ozler, B. 289

Pack, H. 297
Paddison, O. 266
Page, J. 35, 187, 305, 306, 307
Pakistan 38, 340
Palella, F. 262
Palley, 633
Palmer, R. 205
Pande, R. 411
Pang, G. 557
Papua New Guinea 340
Paris Club 557, 558
Paris Declaration 91
Parsons, Q. N. 205
participation:
   local 212, 292
   political 195
Patel, A. C. 127
Paternostro, S. 524
patrimonialism 201–3, 205, 216
patronage politics 216, 219
Pattillo, C. 166, 309, 354, 361
Paxson, C. 300
Payet, S. 149

peace:
   nation-building first 117–18
   political economy of 111–12
   and redistribution 112–13
   social cost of 111
   theory 110–11
   see also post-conflict
Pei, M. 500
performance-based allocation (PBA) 90–1
Perotti, R. 194, 195, 348
Persson, T. 197, 277, 390
Peters, P. 411, 412
Peters, K. 570, 572
Petersen, G. 6
Pettersson, G. 182
Phelps, J. 406
Pham, C. 61, 64
Pincus, S. C. A. 202
Pinovskiy, M. 300
Pinto, B. 556
Pipa, T. 97
Pires, M. 183
Pissarides, C. 271
Platteau, J.-P. 318, 411
Plaza, S. 187
Pliny 1
Plumper, T. 197
Polaski, S. 35
political economy 215–22, 224–30
political institutions 65–6
political management 8–10
political participation 195
political parties 224, 229
political reform 425–6
political stability 326, 368, 452–3, 552–4
polity scale 116
Pollitt, E. 255
polygamy 275
Pop-Eleches, C. 263
population 416, 438
   density 4
   growth 5, 18
   see also demography
Porter, C. 45
Portugal 544
post-conflict:
   development 115–22
   growth 48, 119–21, 124–9
   reconstruction 17
   recovery 106
   see also conflict; peace; war
Potvin, L. 275
Poullier, J. P. 11
poverty 1–3
   Angola 439

poverty (cont.)
  Chad 461
  and costs of war 111–12
  data 234
  and food insecurity 81–2
  and growth 535–6
  and human development 10–13
  indicators 146
  and inequality 234–42
  rural and urban 487, 488
  South Africa 578–80
  trends 234–5
  vulnerability to 45, 46
Poverty Eradication Action Plan (PEAP) 622
poverty reduction 431–3, 442–3
  and economic stability 492
  and foreign direct investment (FDI) 330
  from agriculture 73
  from growth 20–1
  and remittances 188–9
Poverty Reduction Strategy Papers (PRSPs) 72
Powell, G. B. Jr. 195
power:
  centralization 202–3
  relations 275, 278
  unequal 278
power supply 314
Prahalad, C. K. 96
Prat, A. 194
Preston, S. H. 244
Pretty, J. 402
prices 489
  commodities 333, 399–400, 424
  food 73, 80–1, 363, 449
  shocks 14, 42, 80–1, 363
    see also exogenous shocks
Pritchett, L. H. 208
private sector 312–20, 569, 618
  agriculture 312
  infrastructure 341
  policies for 318–20
  Tunisia 618
privatization 366, 372, 475
product concentration 5
production:
  fragmented 169
  inputs 337
  trade in tasks 30
production-consumption integration 164
productivity:
  agriculture 35
  growth 160–1
  and health 11, 252
  and income 11
  informal self-employed 141–3

  labour 332
  low 10, 169
  sectoral 445–6
  total factor 309
programmes:
  attribution problem 288–9
  rigorous impact evaluation 287–92
property rights 76, 197, 326, 425
  see also land tenure
Pruitt, S. W. 586
Przeworski, A. 194, 195, 196
public administration 31
public expenditure 348, 486
public sector 10, 31, 34, 522
  accountability 426
  investment in 52, 340
  management 65
  size of 348
  wages 218–19, 363
public service delivery 196, 208–14
  institutional arrangements for 209–14
  public and private provision 209–10
public service provision 195
public works 567
Puga, D. 167

Quartey, P. 189

rainforests 147
  see also forest commons
Raleigh, C. 118
Ramachandran, N. 308
Ramachandran, V. 166, 313, 332, 396
Ramaswamy, R. 297
Rand Monetary Area 352, 354, 356
Randriamamonjy, J. 262
Rao, N. 339
Ratha, D. 350
Ravallion, M. 11, 235, 524, 525
Ray, O. 472
Razafindravonona, J. 524
re-exports 442, 443, 491
redistribution 236, 239, 249
  constraints on 112–13
  intertemporal 241, 242
  land 42, 413
  and peace 110–11, 113
reducing emissions from deforestation and forest
    degradation (REDD) 406
refugees 499
regional cooperation 74, 334, 371
regional economic communities (RECs) 54, 55
regional fragmentation 161
regional institutions 465
regional integration 49, 308, 338, 563

regional trade agreement (RTA) 54
Reid, A. 202
Reinikka, R. 208, 210, 212, 269, 338
relative factor endowment 397
remittances 27, 162, 187, 612
    Gambia 491
    level of 6, 183
    and poverty reduction 188–9
    as return to education 184
    Somalia 574
    sustainability 190, 191, 433
Remmer, K. 230
rent capture 242, 389
rent seeking 39, 390
Renz, L. 94
reserve-money frameworks 362
reserves 161, 164
resource dependence 397–8
resource endowment 236, 237
resource rents 242
resource trap 398
resource-rich economies 28–9, 241–2
resource-scarce economies 29–30, 30–1
Ribot, J. C. 405
Ricardo, D. 166
Rickwood, C. 376
risk:
    consequences of 42–5
    coping strategies 42, 46
    financial 370
    long-run cost of 44–45
    management mechanisms 42, 82
    measure of 41
    nature of 41–42
    reduction 42
    see also insurance
Roberts, A. 626
Roberts, J. 263
Robinson, J. A. 201, 202, 205, 216, 217, 237, 399, 430
Rocha, L. A. 149
Rocha, N. 61
Rockström, J. 417
Rodrik, D. 38, 119, 120, 169, 170, 171, 216, 218, 305, 307, 309, 444
Rogers, M. 271
Rogoff, K. 352, 354, 355
Rohner, D. 118, 390
Roland, G. 125
Romano, R. 584
Romer, D. 266
Romer, P. 446
Root, H. L. 219
Rose, A. 354
Rosegrant, M. W. 416
Rosenzweig, M. R. 259

Rossi-Hansberg, E. 310
Rothgeb, J. 324
Roussouw, R. 426
Rowthorn, R. 297
Roy, A. D. 136
Roy, R. 349
Rozelle, S. 340
Russia 177
Rwagasore, Prince Louis 452
Rwanda 217, 220, 562–4
    Economic Development and Poverty Reduction Strategy (EDPRS) 562
    landlocked 30, 59, 66
Ryan, C. 375, 376
Ryan, S. 212

Sabel, C. P. 170
Sachs, J. D. 39, 86, 237, 254, 333, 337
Saggi, K. 297
Sahn, D. E. 244, 247, 248, 255, 262
Sala-i-Martin, X. 169, 266, 270, 300, 433
Sally, H. 417, 418
Sambanis, N. 16, 116
Sandefur, J. 136
Sander, C. 188
sanitation 208
SAR 568–9
Saudi Arabia 426
Sauve, P. 57
Save the Children UK 290
savings
    domestic 164, 167
    national 161, 216, 217
    private 142–3
Sayeh, Antoinette 517
Schapera, I. 205
Schmidt-Hebbel, K. 120, 359
Schultz, T. P. 255
Schultz, T. W. 259, 260
Scitovsky, T. 227
Scott, M. 227
Seckler, D. 417
security guarantees 340
Segura-Ubiergo, A. 196
seigniorage 346
Sekkat, Kh. 431, 434
Selassie, A. A. 623, 624
self-employed:
    informal sector 139–43
    productivity 141–3
self-insurance 164
self-provisioning 252
Sen, A. 37, 194, 266, 488
Sen, A. K. 133, 134
Senbet, L. W. 365, 366, 372

Senegal 220, 240, 566–9
  agriculture 30, 242, 567
SENELEC 568–9
Serven, L. 337, 338, 339, 340, 349
service guarantees 320
service sector 56, 140, 175, 218, 323, 507–8
services, trade in 56
Severino, J. M. 472
sexual violence 253
Shah, M. K. 308, 318, 332
Shapiro, J. M. 248, 290
shareholders 584, 585
Sharma, M. 435
Shemyakina, O. 125
Shimeles, A. 488
Shipton, P. 410, 413
Shirley, M. 366
shocks 162–4
  and aid 89–90
  covariate and idiosyncratic 42, 43
  exogenous 566, 568–9, 596, 612
  from commodity prices 333, 399–400, 424
  fuel price 363
  policy response 46
  reaction to 204–5
  see also food; oil; prices
Shughart, W. F. 283
Siegfried, W. R. 147
Sierra Leone 388, 570–2
Silva-Jauregui, C. 618
Simmons, E. 83
Simpasa, A. 389
Singh, R. D. 197
Siphambe, H. 324
Sirleaf, President 515, 516, 517
skills 184, 308
    see also education; human capital
Skinner, C. 142
slavery 203–4
smallholders 72, 75–7, 572
Smit, B. 363
Smith, A. 252
soccer players 185
social policies 12
  Algeria 431, 434–5
  Egypt 431, 434–5
  Morocco 431, 434–5
  Tunisia 431, 434–5
  see also education; health
social security 581–2
socialist models 225
Soderberg, M. 177
Söderbom, M. 118, 133, 169, 171, 306, 309, 314
Söderling, L. 161, 300
Somalia 573–5

Songhay 202
sophistication 305, 306–7
South Africa 61, 576–83
  apartheid 576, 577
  banks 359, 377–8
  corporate governance 584–94
  education 577
  employment 141–2
  inequality 578–80, 581
  King II 585, 593, 594
  life expectation 577
  macroeconomy 577
  poverty 578–80
  Rand 549
  Reserve Bank 363
  social security 581–2
  stock market 366
  and Swaziland 602, 603
  unemployment 136, 577
  Wizzit 383
South African Customs Union (SACU) 239–40, 511, 513, 550, 603
South African Development Community (SADC) 465, 550
South Korea 174, 177, 269, 626
South-South cooperation 174, 177–9
Sovereign Wealth Funds 27
Soviet Union 117, 495
Sowa, N. K. 363
Spain 205
Spence, A. M. 391
Spence, M. 215–16, 217
Spiegel, M. 181
Spilimbergo, A. 266
spillovers 321, 331
Squire, L. 195, 277, 525
Srivastava, P. 338
Ssewanyana, S. N. 622
stability
  economic 216–18, 492, 555, 557
  political 326, 368, 452–3, 552–4
Stark, O. 184
Stasavage, D. 195
state:
  failed 239
  role 475–8, 490;
  in agriculture 72, 75, 77
  see also government
state-business relations 37
Steele, w. 143
Stern, N. 252
Stewart, F. 435
Stifef, D. 524
Stiglitz, J. E. 35, 36, 37, 38, 39, 134, 468, 472
stock markets 366, 367, 371

Stokes, S. 195
Stone, M. R. 362
Straub, S. 338, 339
Strauss, J. 44, 244, 245, 247, 255, 340
Strauss-Kahn, V. 305
structural adjustment programmes (SAPs) 471
structural adjustment reforms 14
structural change 167, 296–301, 304–5
Sturzenegger, F. 363
Subbarao, K. 45
subsidies 171
subsistence farming 76–7
Sudan 596–600
   Comprehensive Peace Agreement (CPA) 117
sugar 539
Sun, X. 325
Sun, Y. 354
super-commodity price cycle 177
Svensson, J. 208, 210, 212, 214, 247, 269, 338
Swallow, B. M. 44
Swartz, N. P. 593
Swaziland 175, 375, 601–3
   agriculture 602
   health services 247
   landlocked 59, 61, 240
   oil production 333
   rural/urban divide 602
   and South Africa 602, 603
Switzerland 60
syndrome free policies 229
Syrquin, M. 397

Tabellini, G. 197, 277
Taiwan 37, 38, 512
Takane, T. 274
Tangri, R. 319
Tansel, A. 255
Tanzania 220, 408, 605–10
   agriculture 44, 607–8
   brain circulation 184
   business 314, 316
   debt 105
   Eastern Arc Mountains 404–5
   education 271
   gold 607
   health 247
   unemployment 136
tariff protection 170
taxation 42, 225–6, 400
   on agriculture 225–6
   arbitrary 42
   on capital flows 357
   Congo 467
   deadweight burden 348
   from natural resources 28
   Lesotho 511
   Nigeria 559
Taylor, J. B. 360
te Velde, D. W. 37
teachers 49, 269
Teal, F. 133, 134, 136, 169, 309, 314
technology 96
   adoption 203–4
   agriculture 291–2
   upgrading 298
   see also information technology
technology transfer 88, 324, 325, 331, 332, 334
Tefula, M. 374, 375, 377
terms of trade 34, 35, 161, 177
textiles 511–13, 539
Thailand 37
Thirumurthy, H. 246, 261, 262, 263
Thomas, D. 44, 244, 245, 247, 255, 340
Thorbecke, E. 11, 176, 236, 237, 239, 264, 579
Thornton, J. 203
threshold problem 30
Tirole, J. 195
Todaro, M. P. 135, 137, 140
Togo 240, 611–14
   Ecobank 383
Tolbert, Willam, President 514
Tollison, R. D. 283
Tornell, A. 354
Torvik, R. 399
Tosi, H. 586
tourism 396, 491, 531, 539, 628
Townsend, R. M. 41
trade 354, 531, 534, 568
   facilitation 57
   and geography 508
   and infrastructure 338
   intraregional 6, 8, 53–8
   liberalization 7–8, 15, 477
   pattern 167, 168–9
   preferences 171, 340
   preferential treatment 55
   reciprocity 55
   restrictions 53
   in services 56
   tariff protection 170
   in tasks 310
   see also exports
trading cost indicators 60–1
transaction costs 169, 338, 397
transparency 65, 212, 390–1
   see also Extractive Industries Transparency Initiative
Transparency International (TI) 500

trust 129
Tsvangirai, Morgan 632
Tunisia 430–6, 615–19
Turner, G. 396, 399

Udry, C. 43, 201, 277, 411, 412, 414
Uganda 220, 405–6, 621–5
   black market 356
   education 270, 271
   Equity Bank 383
   FDI 325
   Forest Reserves 404
   health 247
   landlocked 59, 62, 65, 66
   leakage 212
   migration 184
   trade 562
   unemployment 136
underemployment 11
undernourishment 80, 81–2
unemployment 11, 136, 577, 619
   Burundi 454–5
   graduates 271
   skilled labour 184
   structural 476
   Sudan 598
Unigovskaya, A. 105
United Kingdom 202, 205, 323, 584
   Department for International Development (DFID) 290
United Nations 549
   Human Development Index (HDI) 3, 146, 188, 496, 499, 560, 623
   Millennium Development Goals (MDGs) 11, 99, 106, 146, 162, 208, 278, 329, 418, 457, 477, 492, 535, 545, 557, 622
   Millennium Project 290
United States 83, 94, 323, 511
   African Growth and Opportunities Act (AGOA) 175
   Export-Import Bank 178
   Free Trade Agreement 541
   Great Inflation 360
   Sarbanes-Oxley Act 584
uranium 550, 553
urbanization 18–19
Uvin, P. 454

vaccinations 246
Valodia, I. 141
value added 314, 315
value-chain approach 56–7
van der Ploeg, F. 388, 391
van der Walle, N. 201, 319
van Wijnbergen, S. 557

Vansina, J. 202, 204
Varoudakis, A. 271
Vazquez-Alvarez, R. 260, 262
Végh, C. A. 348
Venables, A. 167, 168, 169, 171
Venables, A. J. 61, 338, 391, 473
Venables, T. 27, 29
Verba, S. 195
Verwimp, P. 125
Vietnam 38, 175
violence:
   political 229–30
   sexual 253
   see also conflict; war
Vogt, N. D. 404
Volcker, P. 360
vulnerability 45, 46, 89, 91, 163, 190

Wacziarg, R. 305
Waddington, C. J. 247
wages 133–4
Wambugu, A. 133
Wane, W. 211
Wantchekon, L. 196
war 368
   costs of 111–12
   deterrence 100, 111
   and oil production 113
   political economy of 111–12
   regional dimension 118
   theory 110–11
   see also conflict; violence
Ward, H. 402
Warner, A. M. 333
Warnholz, J.-L. 26
Washington Consensus (WC) 34, 35–6
water 416–20
   cost of providing 420
   drinking 291
   for food 417–18
   increasing pressure on 149, 157
   for industry 419, 420
   for personal use 208, 418–19
   scarcity 417, 419, 427
   spatial distribution 416
   temporal distribution 417
   user fees 418
Webb, E. L. 406
Weber, M. 201, 202
Weder, B. 485
Weeks, J. 488
Weil, D. N. 254, 266
Weinstein, J. M. 125
West African Economic and Monetary Union (WAEMU)/(UEMOA) 503, 613

West African Wager 13–15
Wheeler, D. 339
Whelan, S. 487
Whitehead, A. 274
Wilks, I. 413
Williams, O. 324
Williams, S. 324
Williamson, G. J. 285
Wilson, M. 266
Wily, L. A. 402, 404
Winters, M. 400
Winters, A. 488
Winters, L. 175
Woldehanna, T. 41
Wolfe, H. 354
Wolgemuth, J. C. 255
Wollenberg, E. 407
women 246
   agricultural productivity 277
   entrepreneurship 467
   and health 252–3
   heterogeneity 274–5
   in the labour force 139–40
   Tunisia 616–17
   see also gender
Wood, A. 18, 168, 175, 308, 397
Woodford, M. 360
World Bank 89, 466, 517, 527, 528, 558
   International Development Agency (IDA) 103
World Economic Forum 337
World Trade Organization (WTO) 7, 29, 53, 55, 57, 425, 550
   Doha round 35
Worldwide Governance Indicators (WGI) 500
Woronoff, J. 13
Worthington, S. 97

Xenogiani, T. 188
Xu, B. 325

Ying, Y. 432
Yoder, R. 247
Yontcheva, B. 96
York, R. 390
Young, A. 254, 300
Younger, S. D. 247, 248
Yousef, T. M. 433
Yusof, S. 175

Zambia 190, 220, 626–9
   agriculture 76, 628
   copper 389, 626, 627
   de-industrialization 396
   landlocked 59
   productivity 314
   United National Independence Party (UBIP) 626
Zeufack, A. 389
Zhan, Z. 390
Zhang, F. 62
Zimbabwe 45, 630–3
   Economic Structural Adjustment Programme (ESAP) 631
   education 271
   exports 632
   fertility transition 284
   food insecurity 80
   health 256
   landlocked 59, 61
   Unity Government 632
Zivin, J. G. 246, 261
Zoellick, President 27
Zou, H. 195